Sport Finance

Fourth Edition

Gil Fried, JD
University of New Haven

Timothy D. DeSchriver, EdD
University of Delaware

Michael Mondello, PhD
University of South Florida

HUMAN KINETICS

Library of Congress Cataloging-in-Publication Data

Names: Fried, Gil, 1965- author. | DeSchriver, Timothy D., 1968- author. | Mondello, Michael, 1968- author.
Title: Sport finance / Gil Fried, Timothy D. DeSchriver, Michael Mondello.
Description: Fourth edition. | Champaign, IL : Human Kinetics, [2020] | Includes bibliographical references and index.
Identifiers: LCCN 2018036026 (print) | LCCN 2018052038 (ebook) | ISBN 9781492588771 (epub) | ISBN 9781492559740 (PDF) | ISBN 9781492559733 (print)
Subjects: LCSH: Sports--Finance. | Sports administration.
Classification: LCC GV716 (ebook) | LCC GV716 .F75 2020 (print) | DDC 796.0681--dc23
LC record available at https://lccn.loc.gov/2018036026

ISBN: 978-1-4925-5973-3 (print)

The web addresses cited in this text were current as of November 2018 unless otherwise noted.

Acquisitions Editor: Andrew L. Tyler
Senior Developmental Editor: Melissa Feld
Managing Editor: Anna Lan Seaman
Copyeditor: Janet Kiefer
Indexer: Dan Connolly
Permissions Manager: Dalene Reeder
Graphic Designer: Dawn Sills
Cover Designer: Keri Evans
Cover Design Associate: Susan Rothermel Allen
Photographs (interior): © Human Kinetics, unless otherwise noted
Photographs (cover): Jared Silber/NHLI via Getty Images, SAM YEH/AFP/Getty Images, franckreporter/iStock/Getty Images, dlewis33/iStock/Getty Images
Photo Asset Manager: Laura Fitch
Photo Production Manager: Jason Allen
Senior Art Manager: Kelly Hendren
Illustrations: © Human Kinetics, unless otherwise noted
Printer: Sheridan Books

Printed in the United States of America   10 9 8 7 6 5 4 3

The paper in this book is certified under a sustainable forestry program.

Human Kinetics
1607 N. Market Street
Champaign, IL 61820
USA

United States and International
Website: **US.HumanKinetics.com**
Email: info@hkusa.com
Phone: 1-800-747-4457

Canada
Website: **Canada.HumanKinetics.com**
Email: info@hkcanada.com

E7202

Tell us what you think!
Human Kinetics would love to hear what we can do to improve the customer experience. Use this QR code to take our brief survey.

Contents

Preface

We'll be blunt. Many people are scared of finance, particularly sport finance.

This is nothing personal. As the joke goes, some of my best friends are financial folks. All kidding aside, although finance classes have a very negative image, and finance texts are likewise often despised, sport finance can be one of the most exciting courses you might take in any sport management degree program. While so many folks focus on the formulas, industry ratios, complex financial statement analysis, time value of money, and related issues, sport finance is so much more. Sport finance focuses on not just the numbers but on the story behind them, what the numbers mean, and, most importantly, what to do with the numbers. That is where the fourth edition of this text has really evolved. We do not just cover the numbers; we do a deep dive into what the numbers mean and how they can help serve as the backdrop for making sound financial decisions for any sports organization.

The importance of understanding finance can be seen in the growth of open book management. The theory is that managers can better motivate employees if they involve them in the financial decision-making process. Some managers feel that if they tell employees they are in financial trouble and show them some books and statements, that is enough to motivate them to work more or reduce expenses. That is actually a horrible practice. It is akin to telling employees that the number one cause of deaths in the sport workplace is automobile accidents (which is true) and then telling employees to drive safely. However, if some employees do not know how to drive, cannot drive certain vehicles, or have a suspended license, then the nugget of knowledge management just shared with them really has little value. Just as a better approach for these employees would be a driving course, a better financial approach starts with teaching employees about basic financial terms and issues. It is important to cover some basic terms and ideas, not 20 or more ratios. It is hard enough for finance students to understand and remember so many ratios; it's even tougher for an employee who might not have graduated from high school. Thus, managers should not focus just on ratios or statements and formulas but on helping employees see how their actions can affect all these numbers. If the sports organization has multiple key performance indicators (such as selling 1,000 tickets for each game or selling concessions of at least $9 per fan), employees need to know how their actions affect the key performance indicators and what specific steps they can take to help the organization reach or exceed those indicators. This basic concept is at the heart of this text. Yes, we will cover a lot of material in the text. Yes, there will be a lot of formulas, ratios, and statements. However, the goal is not to help you memorize something you might not use in the future. The goal is to help you apply those numbers in a strategic manner. Knowing how numbers help a sports organization succeed, knowing what steps you can take to manipulate the numbers, and knowing how to evaluate your success will give you an advantage in this and any other industry.

Understanding the broader context of sport finance will help you become a better employee and speed your journey to the managerial level. All managers are judged on whether they can meet their numbers, so if you want to be a sport manager, then you have to understand sport finance.

This text is designed to provide the basic financial literacy a sports executive needs to operate effectively. Students and seasoned executives alike need to have enough financial literacy to make solid decisions. Instead of focusing on strict financial concepts, we have realized that many students do not have some of the underlying accounting basics that help lead to more effective financial strategies. That is why this text walks the readers through the basics of some financial concepts to allow them to reach the end of the text, which focuses on strategy and what specific financially related steps can be taken to help a sports organization become more successful.

The fourth edition of *Sport Finance* is significantly revised to reflect the evolving needs of instructors and students entering careers in the sport industry. Like previous editions, this edition continues to ground students in foundational financial principles and concepts and demonstrates how they are applied in real-world sport management settings. This edition takes practical applications a step further to encourage students to take a strategic organizational perspective to understanding sport finance. Each one of the authors has taught sport finance for years. Based on how we teach and what students need to know when they enter the workforce, we felt we needed to radically change the text. Thus, certain chapters, such as those discussing the time value of money or production analysis—while important—were not as critical for future sport managers as some other areas and were therefore reduced or eliminated. Based on these changes, readers will not only understand the *what* and *how* of sport finance but also the *why*, creating a more valuable and accessible learning experience and achieving better preparation for future careers.

The revamped structure includes the following changes:

- A new chapter covering assets such as players, facilities, and goodwill; and liabilities such as player salaries and long-term debt
- Greatly expanded coverage of revenue and expenses, including an example from a real athletic department, strategies to reduce expenses and increase revenue, and an examination of nonprofit organizations and how they raise funds
- More discussion on financial statements and how and why they are used in financial analysis
- New chapters covering financial planning, financial strategy, and using strategy when deciding to create, expand, or exit a sport business or organization
- Several real-world case studies covering a variety of sectors, sports, and countries replacing the single final-chapter fictional case from the previous edition and offering readers an enhanced opportunity to understand each part of the text
- Industry spotlights in which an industry executive explains why each part of the text is relevant for real-world application

In addition, the entire format of the text has been changed, and the five parts we developed will hopefully help move the reader through the key concepts in a more strategic manner that will help them move from financial basics to executing financial plans. **Part I** is a basic introduction so students can appreciate the terminology, issues, and opportunities so they can understand issues from the very beginning. One new element to this introductory section is a greater coverage of assets and liabilities so readers appreciate how these affect a sport institution. **Part II** examines revenues and expenses—the heart of any sports organization. Besides identifying various elements of revenue and expenses across a wide variety of sports organizations, this section proposes strategies to help increase revenue or decrease expenses, which results in greater profitability for a sports organization. **Part III** is one of the more applied sections and examines how to develop, track, and determine compliance with a budget. A budget is a road map; it can take an organization in the right direction, or it can steer the organization to doom. **Part IV** explores the world of cash and how to meet the cash needs of a sports organization. Although some sports organizations are flush with cash, most are not, and there is always a very delicate balancing act to determine how, where, and when to search for cash to keep the organization running. **Part V** starts by examining the principal financial statements (income statement, balance sheet, and cash flow statement) and how they help a sports organization identify its strengths, weaknesses, opportunities, and threats. The section then tries to integrate all the prior elements into execution. Using financial information, how do sports organizations make decisions that take into consideration various financial issues? The part starts with how to plan, moves to how to execute, and then concludes with what happens at the end.

The key for this edition is the evolution from just identifying financial issues and providing students with a great vocabulary and understanding to the applied components of sport finance. It is not enough to know the sport finance language and formulas. Readers need to be able to apply sport finance concepts to decisions that can guide a sport business. Similar to learning terms about sport marketing and then actually having to develop a sport marketing plan, this edition similarly focuses on the applied approach to understanding how financial concepts intersect throughout a sport business and how every decision has financial implications. The industry spotlights in each part of the text help highlight how individuals working in sport finance utilize the concepts in that part to do their jobs. Furthermore, the case studies associated with each part provide an in-depth analysis of how the topics are playing out in real life with examples from the industry. These two parts will help a reader apply the concepts within, see how they relate to their current or future career, and examine how sports organizations are dealing with those issues today. Similar to our prior editions, we have chapter objectives to help highlight what each chapter will try to convey to the reader, discussion topics at the end of each chapter, various sidebars, an extensive glossary, an appendix with time value of money charts, and an appendix summarizing key financial ratios.

Sport Finance, Fourth Edition, offers a web resource with a new Excel-based simulation activity for students to complete individually or in groups throughout a semester. The "$2 Team" gets students involved in various finance topics such as assets and liabilities, revenue and expenses, budgeting, cash management, and borrowing so that so they understand how various finance issues affect financial strategy. The instructor resources also include Excel-based activities, a major case study from the golf industry, and case study discussion topics that can be assigned to assess student understanding and progress. The instructions for accessing the web resource are at the front of the book and accessible at **www.HumanKinetics.com/SportFinance**.

Acknowledgments

I could not have asked for two better coauthors. They diligently wrote their chapters and assisted with the instructor guide, making this one of the best texts I have had the pleasure to work on. Tim was helpful throughout the entire process, and Mike, who really understands sport finance, was a significant boost to the project. My two coauthors went beyond the call for this text, and I thank them for their efforts. Each coauthor brought significant value and helped shape the text into one of the strongest in the sport management area.

I would like to extend a special thanks to my colleagues Dr. Kimberly Mahoney and Dr. Ceyda Mumcu and to the entire College of Business faculty and staff at the University of New Haven for all their assistance. They have recognized the value of sport finance and have helped me launch various online sport finance and sport analytics certificates and classes. I would also like to thank my graduate research assistants, especially Mitch Fliss and Lauren Doyle, for their help in researching changes for this revised edition.

A special thanks also goes out to my wife and children (Gavriella, Arieh, and Rebecca) for their patience during the writing and revising of this text. It was a time-consuming process that took a significant amount of their understanding.

The folks at Human Kinetics (HK) were wonderful in helping us make this fourth edition that much stronger. Subsequent editions of texts from other publishers often contain only minor updates. However, the gang at HK—including Andrew L. Tyler, Melissa Feld, and many others—challenged us to make the book revolutionary and fresh.

Gil Fried

I would like to extend a special thanks to my two coauthors. Gil Fried has been the driving force behind this project since its inception. His guidance and persistence were critical for ensuring the successful completion of this book. Mike Mondello's contributions have been invaluable, and he has been a pleasure to work with. I would also like to thank all of the Human Kinetics staff members who we have worked with over the years. Their efforts on each edition have been greatly appreciated.

I would also like to thank my colleagues in the sport management field whom I have worked with over the past years. Their encouragement and kind words have not gone unnoticed. People such as Dave Stotlar, Bill Sutton, Jay Gladden, Dan Mahony, Dennis Howard, Dan Rascher, Lisa Masteralexis, Brianna Newland, and Edgar Johnson (just to name a few) make me proud to be an academician in sport management. I would like to thank my parents, Richard and Jean DeSchriver, for loving and supporting me for all these years. They instilled within me a passion for education and teaching that will last forever. I dedicate this book to the memory of my late father, Dr. Richard L. DeSchriver. He was a truly amazing mentor, educator, coach, and parent, and I miss him dearly every day. Last and most important, I would like to thank my wife, Kerry, for her patience and encouragement during the publication process.

Tim DeSchriver

I would like to thank both Gil Fried and Tim DeSchriver for having the confidence in me to extend an invitation to collaborate with them. As someone who has admired their work, I was excited to work with these scholars. My initial involvement allowed me to gain a greater appreciation for the significant roles that my colleagues fulfilled and the overall time commitment that a project of this magnitude requires. Gil and Tim both provided timely mentoring with questions and suggestions. Also, the Vinik Sport and Entertainment Management Program at the University of South Florida provided me with the necessary resources and time to complete the project. In addition, I would like to acknowledge the professional approach that HK's staff brought to the team. Finally, a special thanks goes to my family, whose support has always remained unwavering, regardless of my limitations.

Mike Mondello

©Will Cashman

Will Cashman

E-Commerce Buyer and Planner at Reebok

I graduated from Miami University in Ohio in 2000 with a bachelor of science degree in business and a major in finance. My first job out of school was working as a fund administration analyst at JP Morgan Chase, and while I enjoyed the planning and numbers side of corporate finance, my interests always lay in the sports arena. After obtaining my masters in sport management at the University of New Haven, I decided the best way to combine my love for sport and finance would be to ultimately work for a sports apparel company.

I got my first job after obtaining my master's degree at the TJX companies and completed their merchandising development program. This program provided a solid foundation and understanding of the retail industry. I gained experience in the allocation of product from distribution centers to stores based on analysis and inventory management, financial planning, and how it relates to sales targets as well as buying strategy based on trends and forecasting. What I loved most about working in merchandising at TJX was the role I played in owning a business category and the continuous performance data reviewed in weekly sales reports that demonstrated our progress throughout the season. My first business category as an allocation analyst was in men's outerwear, and every Monday I would get excited to come in to work to review my jacket sales from the prior week. Seeing these numbers each week felt akin to receiving a report card with incentive to continually adjust plans to optimize category forecasts. I discovered I enjoyed working closely with tangible products, which solidified my career direction in merchandising. After developing as a planner, I jumped on the opportunity to work at Reebok to combine my passion for finance, merchandising, and sport.

Reebok is named after the grey rhebok, a very fast African mammal similar to an antelope—a fitting name for a company with a long history in athletic footwear where speed is valued. The founder, Joseph William Foster, was one of the first designers of the spiked running shoe in 1895. Building brand equity with consumers is instrumental for any profitable organization, and Reebok's rich history in footwear and apparel made it one of the biggest names in sport. Athletes like Shaquille O'Neal, Allen Iverson, and Sidney Crosby are a few names that helped shape the Reebok brand. Today, Reebok has rebranded the company and strives to become the leader in fitness, running, and CrossFit apparel and footwear.

As an associate buyer of men's apparel, it is my responsibility to manage inventory and cost for all men's clothing that best fits the needs of the U.S. customer for three direct-to-consumer channels. These omnichannels are broken down among factory outlets, full price stores, and our e-commerce business; and I need to ensure that the right product is in the right stores at the correct time. Buyers work in conjunction with allocation, planning, purchasing, marketing, branding, and product development to help manage this process to drive sales.

That process starts with a sales and receipt plan (where we analyze all sales and order receipts) passed down by the finance team, which follows the company's overall fiscal plan for the year. Each year is divided into two selling seasons—spring and fall—with new global assortments created for both by the product development teams. Once these assortments are passed off to merchandising, we work to identify the products that best suit the needs of the U.S. consumer. Once our seasonal assortment has been determined, we then work closely with the planning team to forecast sales and receipts. There are several planning tools and key performance indicators that are used when forecasting sales for a season.

The first planning matrix utilized to forecast sales is sell-through. Sell-through is the rate at which a product will sell compared to the amount of total product that is bought. For example, if I buy 1,000 units of receipts in a men's short but I only plan on selling 800, my sell-through rate would be planned at 80%. Both my sales of 800 units and my receipts of 1,000 units need to be accounted for in the financial plan. Another important planning matrix used is rate of sale, which is defined by the number of units you plan on selling per store per week. This analysis is pulled from sales history of the prior year or season from similar styles based on the total stores and the number of weeks on the sales floor. If we have sold 800 units of a men's short after 10 weeks across 50 total stores, the rate of sale would be 1.6 units per week.

Inventory management is the practice of overseeing and controlling the ordering, storage, and use of components that a company uses in the production of the items it sells. From a buying perspective, it is my responsibility to purchase the appropriate amount of product to achieve the overall sales plan without creating an excess of goods. Overbuying product creates a financial liability for the company by exceeding capacity at the distribution centers, which prohibits their ability to process and ship goods in a timely fashion, which can negatively affect sales. An abundance of excess inventory decreases the freshness and turn of the product as well as forcing the liquidation of stock by promotions and discounts, which reduces the gross margin.

Companies evaluate their overall effectiveness by the inventory turnover ratio. This is defined by the number of times a company's inventory is sold and replaced in a year's time. At Reebok, our inventory turnover ratio is planned at four times per year, meaning we want to sell and have brand new assortments per quarter. There are a few factors that are used to help achieve inventory turn. The first matrix used is length of life (LOL), or the number of weeks planned for a product. Retail is a seasonal business, and certain products need to be planned accordingly. For example, I buy more layering products (fleece, jackets, sweatpants) in the fall with an October introduction date and a planned LOL of 13 weeks for the fourth quarter. After the allotted period of time, promotions will be applied to accelerate sell-through and liquidate inventory. As a result of these discounts, we also need to factor in a point of sale rate. This is the planned discount rate applied to the total retail price. For example, a men's jogger is priced at $70, and it sells at full price for 13 weeks (planned LOL) and then is marked down 40% ($42) until the product is liquidated. Therefore, my planned point of sale rate for the season needs to account for both full price and markdown sales for that jogger.

Discounts and promotions need to be accounted for when managing costs as well as pricing goods at the correct value to sell. Cost management is an essential component of profitability for any company and something that I'm held accountable for as a buyer. Cost starts at the product level where sourcing works closely with the product teams on cost of goods based on materials. Factory location and the transportation of product from overseas including taxes and tariffs all need to be factored into the total cost of a product. This requires a close working relationship with the product teams to ensure that they are optimizing costs that fit into my pricing strategy. Initial markup (IMU) and the overall gross margin are two financial matrices that need to be accounted for when pricing goods to fit into the value strategy. IMU is based on the starting prices of the product, and the planned gross margin is the overall profitability of selling merchandise. An IMU of at least 70 basis points is the starting target retail price at Reebok. This means that the initial retail value needs to be 70% greater than the cost of the product. While the IMU is the starting target, the gross margin reflects the actual profits gained by a company after sell-through, LOL, and point-of-sale rates. I need to ensure my seasonal forecasts are meeting the margin requirements set by finance to optimize returns.

Merchandising has been referred to as more of an art than a science. All companies are affected by external factors such as natural disasters, social and economic influences, and an ever-changing retail landscape with a constant influx of innovation, products, and trend. Buying the correct assortment of product at the optimal stock quantities will always be like aiming at a moving target, which is why financial strategy and the planning tools utilized by historical data and research are imperative to the overall profitability of any business.

Basics of Sport Finance

The first part of this text offers a basic introduction so students can understand sport finance terms and issues from the very beginning. The part starts with an industry spotlight featuring Hugo C. Chávez Barroso, a soccer entrepreneur and digital analyst for Major League Soccer. He discusses how he had to increase his finance knowledge and how this education helps him in his position in international soccer.

Chapter 1 is designed to provide a basic overview of the finance field and how it applies to sport management. For those who have never been formally introduced to the finance field, the will explain some basic concepts. The chapter examines real-world issues and, using The Sports Authority as an example, how financial hardship can destroy a company.

The sport sector is composed of a number of industry segments. Many people think of the sport sector only in relation to college athletics and professional sports, but there are a lot more areas where sport and finance overlap. Chapter 2 examines some of these industry segments and explores trends and current issues found in these sectors. Special attention is given to the amateur and participatory sport sector and subareas such as extreme sports, fitness facilities, and e-sports. The chapter then examines some of the issues affecting college athletics and professional sport.

Chapter 3 explores some of the basic finance concepts that will appear throughout the text. Although financial statements will be reviewed in greater detail in chapter 11, it is important to know the basics of income statements, balance sheets, and cash flow statements, so these financial statements are introduced in this chapter. This chapter also covers audits, financial ratios, the time value of money, and the differences between sport finance and economics.

The final part of part I is chapter 4, which focuses on assets and liabilities. This is a new chapter—one we feel is critical, because it is impossible to generate revenue without assets (whether physical assets or intellectual property), and the purchase of assets is often done with borrowing, which creates a liability. This chapter provides an in-depth exploration of topics such as players, facilities, goodwill, salaries, and long-term debt.

Part I ends with a case study focused on the World Cup and various financial issues the sport of soccer has faced over the past several years.

Hugo C. Chávez Barroso

Digital Content Producer and Editor at Major League Soccer (MLS); Owner and Chief Executive Officer, Quetzalli Sports Group

I'm a professional in the sport industry—specialized in soccer.

I graduated with a bachelor of arts in communications degree with a specialization in public relations from Missouri Southern State University.

It wasn't playing soccer that forged my professional future, but rather the business side of the sport. This is my story.

In my last year at Missouri Southern, two business partners and I started a new soccer league in rural Midwest America. We took advantage of all the resources available to us through professors, friends, local business owners, city officials, and the soccer community in the area to help get the league started. We took care of every aspect of the business from press conferences to marketing campaigns to sponsor deals, even painting the lines on the field, carrying the goals, and setting up banners.

In our first year of business, we received an incredible response and had a much more successful year than we expected. We weren't prepared to take care of one aspect of the business that grew with our success: finance. The business had grown past the basics and required professional help. We had to bring in a fourth partner to handle the accounting, budgeting, taxes, insurance policies, and finances.

When I moved home to Mexico, I adapted and evolved the soccer league concept. My new associates and I built soccer fields, locker rooms, stands, a full bar, a beach volleyball court, and soccer tennis courts. The business was no longer just a soccer league. We had different sports leagues, women's leagues, an affiliate academy of a respected first-division Mexican club, and a sports bar. We had created an entire sports complex.

The infrastructure we created wasn't enough to compete. We were no longer in Joplin, Missouri; in Torreon, Mexico, there were other strong competitors. We managed to gain a considerable amount of the market through a strategic business plan, well-orchestrated events, and the sponsorship of a world-renowned Mexican beer brand. The complex offered an experience far beyond playing in a typical Sunday league.

However, once again, there was a major challenge in this entrepreneurial venture: finance. I found it especially challenging because I was a board member and had to come to agreement with my business partners who each have different perspectives and business goals. Most of the issues were directly related to financing: how money was being spent, how the budget was distributed, profits, assets, and liabilities.

My experience in the sport business until then had mainly been on the amateur side. But my interest grew on breaking through to the professional ranks. The two questions that emerged were *how far can I get?* and *how do I get there?*

It was then that I made one of the most important decisions in my life, a game changer that gave me the opportunity to work at the highest levels of the business. I decided to go to grad school.

I invested in my future by attending the University of New Haven to obtain my master of science in sport management degree. It was not only the highly rated program that attracted me but also the location—close enough New York City—a pro sport hub.

I learned quite a bit in my classes at the University of New Haven and was making my best grades since elementary school. I was very interested in classes that focused on sport, but I found the business classes almost as appealing—probably because I wish I knew more about business before I started my ventures. Those challenges gave me an appreciation for accounting, macroeconomics, and sport finance classes.

I was taking advantage of everything I could, including getting myself involved in the athletics department and the school soccer program.

The academic program required me to do an internship, which I knew beforehand and was gambling on getting in the door of a well-respected professional sports league, club, or organization. I never anticipated what was to come.

I had three consecutive internships with prestigious institutions in which I worked with some of the most respected executives in the industry. In the process, I had to turn down an offer from an MLS club and a yearlong internship in Florida at Disney's Wide World of Sports.

I still remember going to my advisor with my "problem" of having to choose. He said something among the lines of, "You don't have a problem. There are students that struggle to get just one internship. You just have to pick."

And so I did.

Through a mentor introduced by my advisor, I started out at the New York Red Bulls. Ten days after the Red Bulls, I was at the venerated ESPN campus in Bristol, Connecticut. And a week after ESPN, I was at the Major League Soccer headquarters in New York City.

In more than one way, it seemed like I was very lucky. And maybe I was, but I was the one who put myself in the right situation for things to happen, and once something happened, I made sure to make the most of it.

Since then, I have been working for MLS.

However, in order to keep my sports entrepreneurial ventures going and give birth to my newest one, I made my move back to Mexico and managed a deal to keep working for MLS. Thus, I currently have two roles: digital content producer and editor at MLS and owner and CEO of Quetzalli Sports Group.

Through the years, I've also taken full advantage of the network I've immersed myself in within the professional soccer world. That's how I got to collaborate seasonally with U.S. Soccer and different digital outlets such as the Bleacher Report, Soccerly, Prost Amerika, and Pared Virtual.

That's also how I've been recommended and had the privilege to work directly in international tournaments with the respected Uruguay national team and the world-class Futbol Club Barcelona, both of which feature some of the most influential executives and best players of our time.

My current sport company, Quetzalli Sports Group, is divided into three main areas, covering both aspects of the spectrum—amateur and professional.

On the amateur side we manage sport complexes, run leagues, and administer a soccer complex to raise money and donate directly to an educational foundation that supports a high-level bilingual education program for low-income children. Each deal was completed based on financial considerations and benchmarks.

We provide career management and consulting for athletes, opening doors according to their goals, ranging from college scholarships to trying out for academy teams to playing in the pros. Networking is key in this area, but knowing how to manage a budget is crucial. If a scholarship will not cover the entire cost of educa-tion, where would the student obtain the necessary funds and at what cost?

And finally, my company is involved in advising, consulting, and management of professional sport institutions.

The only area that I haven't talked about in my life revolving around sport is my preparation as a soccer coach, holding credentials from both the Mexican and the U.S. federations. Although it has little to do with the business side directly, it helps to keep the perspective of the actual game at its roots. In return, if you pay attention closely, it also provides you with insight and market research—from youngster players, parents, and clubs. Such background research is critical for making sound business decisions.

Through my experience as an intern, small business owner, larger business owner, consultant, and employee of a professional league, I've come to the realization that making savvy business decisions, at any level, requires financial literacy. I've learned to apply my financial knowledge to effectively administer budgets, allocate resources, have the adequate financial platform that better fits my interest, and structure business models that are profitable in the sport industry. Derived from such learning, from an entrepreneurial stand point, I've been able to know when, where and how to reinvest, which has increased our return on investment.

I certainly wish I would had given more importance to finance on my early ventures. That would have helped me avoid many financial issues with the board, and I would have set quantitative goals based on return on investment, financial analysis, and research, instead of primarily relying on just subjective opinions.

Finance is essential to understand and perform at the highest levels in this industry. As you advance in your career, no matter if you're an intern, low-level employee, manager, or a business owner, you need to appreciate, understand, and execute financial plans and strategies.

Sport finance is a powerful tool to add to your skill set regardless of the area you want to focus on. If you want to be the one running the show at any given level, you've got to be prepared to deal with finance. It's the foundation for a profitable business and a great career in any industry.

Introduction to Sport Finance

Chapter Objectives

After studying this chapter, you should be able to do the following:

- Examine your own financial circumstances more critically.
- Identify the basic elements of sport finance.
- Describe the scope of the current financial problems facing sporting goods retailers.
- Interpret how financial issues flow throughout a sports organization.

Often when someone learns about a new topic, they try to connect it to something they already know. Likewise, when teaching sport marketing, a teacher might give examples of a Super Bowl advertisement that the students might have seen. When teaching sports facility management, a teacher might give examples of a well-known sports facility. Likewise, when examining sport finance, it is helpful to examine what students have done in the past with their own finances. This could include examining bank accounts, discussing whether students have ever created a budget, and exploring how often students pay credit card bills in full versus only making minimum payments. These issues also apply to various sports organizations, and this chapter will explore some of the basic financial issues faced by everyone. The chapter then moves on to explore financial issues facing the sporting goods industry as an example of how financial problems can destroy a business. Lastly, the chapter will explore how financial issues flow throughout an entire sports organization. The purpose of this chapter is to help the reader get their feet wet and appreciate how broad and exciting sport finance really is.

PERSONAL FINANCE BASICS

How financially astute are you? Do you pay off your credit card bill every month? Should you take out a student loan to pursue a new degree? Should you change your cell phone plan? Should you buy or lease a vehicle? Should you buy a used vehicle that might require some repairs or a new vehicle that hopefully would not require any immediate repairs? What is the harm of not having a credit card? These are just some of the questions that require a financial analysis.

Questions about credit cards are only the beginning. Another major question is, *what assets do you have?* Your education is an asset. Your vehicle is an asset. Your network of contacts in the industry is an asset, even though it is hard to place a monetary value on it. In contrast, not having an appropriate education, not having a vehicle, and not having contacts can all be potential liabilities.

How many times have you tried to buy something, only to find you did not have enough money to complete the transaction? Was your credit card maxed out? Were you expecting money to be deposited that wasn't? Were you not aware of how much cash you had in your wallet or pocketbook? These are all issues that deal with **budgeting** and **cash management**.

Have you thought about your financial future? When should you start saving for retirement? How much would you need to retire in a financially sound manner? Have you thought about whether you would be able to afford major expenses you might face, such as surgery from an accident or expenses you would incur if you want to travel abroad? These are long-term decisions, which require planning now to be ready for the future. Many people put money aside (often called a sinking fund) to make major purchases in the future.

These are just a sampling of financial issues and concerns that affect everyone. These same financial concerns affect every business. That means every sport business needs to understand these exact same issues. Without knowing the numbers, it is impossible for a sports organization to appropriately plan for the future. That is where this book comes into play. It will help cover various fundamental skills and issues and then put them into the context of how to plan for both the **short term** and **long term**. So what basic skills are needed by everyone and every sports organization? That is how this book is laid out.

Every individual, as well as every sports organization, is different. It is very difficult to compare one year to the next or one company to another. However, like every game, keeping score matters. You might know that your **income** increased $2,000 from last year when you get your W-2 or other tax forms. You also might be able to track your financial condition through examining bank statements or your retirement account and track them year to year or even day to day. Similarly, you might be able to compare yourself to your friends. If one of your friends makes more money than you, you might aim to earn more than them in the future. Sports organizations engage in the same activities. They check their bank accounts on a regular basis, they calculate their inventory over various periods, and they compare their tax and other government filings from quarter to quarter or year to year. Sports organizations can also compare themselves to their competition. This can often be seen by teams looking at their players' **payroll** expense, win–loss record, or average number of fans. Other sport entities might be publicly traded, and then their financial statements can be compared to see how they are doing compared to similar companies. Using this perspective, it would not be wise to compare yourself to a billionaire such as Warren Buffet or Bill Gates. Sports organizations also have to be realistic, and it would not be appropriate to compare two soccer teams and feel they should be in about the same financial position when one team is a youth soccer club in a small town being compared with Manchester United. Finance requires perspective. Financial decisions are also not made in a vacuum. Each decision will be affected by various considerations such as your age, income level, family situation, other expenses, credit history, risk tolerance, economic outlook, and other issues. Sports organizations are affected by many issues outside of their control, such as economic conditions, political changes, wars, **interest (*i*)** rates, sponsors' budgets, technological changes, and numerous other issues that need to be taken into consideration.

Just as you might not know what will happen in the future due to numerous variables, a sports organization has the same exact concerns. That might be why you try to save some money in case of an emergency. Well, organizations need to do the exact same thing.

These examples are designed to show you that you should not be scared of finance or think it is just a topic you will never deal with in the future. You are dealing with finance every day whether you like it or not. The most successful people master this skill. A famous book called *The Millionaire Next Door,* by Thomas J. Stanley and William D. Danko, examined how everyday people have acquired and maintained their millions by paying close attention to finance-related topics. These individuals often own businesses, but, most importantly, they have a great perspective of the value of money. They do not buy all the fanciest gadgets, they drive older cars, they do not eat out all the time, they save, and they invest. These are all things anyone can do. They are also steps that every sports organization has to do. That is why financial literacy is so important. You want to protect what you have worked so hard for, and everyone wants to create financial stability.

One thing everyone should understand is that there are various efforts to generate more revenue or take away money from people. An example is upselling at a fast food restaurant

MAKING AND KEEPING THE MONEY

There are several important strategies every person and sports organization needs to follow to be successful such as:

- *Know your numbers.* You need to have confidence that the numbers you are using to make decisions are accurate and that employees know and understand the numbers.

- *Measure twice . . . cut once.* While this is a common phrase for carpenters, it is similar with any financial decisions. Before undertaking any decision, make sure the numbers are correct.

- *Plan, plan, and plan.* You need to know where you want to go in the future, and the only way to effectively go there and make sure you can continue in a proper direction is through having a written plan, making sure the plan is followed, and tweaking the plan when necessary.

- *Always be prepared.* You never know what will happen in the future, and you need to prepare for financial issues that might arise.

- *Honesty counts.* Whether dealing with friends, colleagues, employees, the government, suppliers, or others, it is imperative that you are honest and maintain your honesty, as numbers leave a trail and financial fraud is one of the most damaging crimes for individuals and sports organizations.

or a concessions stand at a stadium or arena. For an additional $1 you might be able to purchase a large soda to go with the other food you were purchasing. You think it is a deal and buy the package, but is it really a deal? Computers (including cash registers) can now process the cost and profit points for each item, and the "deal" is actually a deal for the concessionaire—a way to maximize their own revenue and sell you something you otherwise might not have purchased. Being smart with your money is important, but there are times when both the seller and buyer can both benefit and not feel bad after a deal is completed. An example is selling furniture on Craigslist. The seller gets something when otherwise they might have donated the item or just thrown it away. The buyer gets a piece of furniture at a good price. This is an example of a win–win deal, and such deals normally make both parties to the transaction happy.

Similarly, there can be more sophisticated or nefarious means to separate someone from their money. This can be seen in terms of financial fraud. There are numerous scams online, counterfeit tickets being sold, unlicensed products sold as official merchandise, and other crimes. All these efforts can cause financial harm not just to consumers but to businesses as well. The most common scam according to government research entails pressure to pay an alleged tax liability or face arrest. Such a scam was forced on almost two million people, and as many as 200 people a week fell for the scam in 2016. Besides the Internal Revenue Service (IRS) scam (which received over 100 times as many complaints as the next highest concern), other major scams—which primarily took money from seniors—included fake sweepstakes, money transfer scams, and counterfeit bank website scams. In total, these various financial scams costs seniors at least $2.9 billion in 2010 (McCoy, 2017b). Customers and the general public need to cautiously guard their hard-earned income, similar to how businesses have to take steps to protect their assets and their integrity.

This section has tried to show that every reader is already using their existing financial background and understanding to make a multitude of decisions. These skills can be used to help make you—or save you—money if used correctly. Similarly, these same skills can be applied to any sports organizations to help address their financial issues.

WHAT IS SPORT FINANCE?

Sport **finance** can be viewed from numerous perspectives and can overlap with **economic** and accounting issues. For example, the concept of moving a team from one city to another is based on financial projections for the team and possible attendance and media rights deals. Through **accounting**, a team can determine how much money it has available and how to **budget** current and future funds. From an economic perspective, the team and local government agencies will examine the potential for economic issues that affect the area, the potential future interest rates that might affect bond interest rates, and other similar local, national, and international issues. When the Oakland Raiders decided to move to Las Vegas, staff examined a variety of financial, economic, and accounting-based data. Municipalities are willing to invest in order to hopefully generate additional future income streams. That is why the city of Las Vegas was willing to invest $750 million for a stadium (Schrotenboer, 2017b). While making money is important, that is not always the end result. Many stadium projects for teams, Olympics, or the World Cup have not produced the intended economic benefits promised to citizens. Before the Los Angeles Rams moved back to Los Angeles from St. Louis, the city of St. Louis offered to spend $400 million in public funds to help build a $1.1 billion stadium. The team turned down the offer and bolted. The citizens of St. Louis are still paying for the Rams' old domed stadium. Similarly, with the Oakland Raiders planning to move to Las Vegas, the city of Oakland still owes $95 million for a 1995 bond issue to renovate the old Oakland-Alameda Coliseum (Schrotenboer, 2017b). These two examples show that the investment to make money might generate a local economic benefit from the team, but in financial terms, the experiment with helping to pay for the honor of hosting a professional sports team might not generate a net economic gain.

This is not meant to say that a team or stadium cannot make a profit. In fact, the most successful teams in professional sports are often those teams that have financed and owned their own facility and all possibly affiliated revenue streams. In one interview, New England Patriots owner Robert Kraft examined how he got into the professional sports team ownership business, and he said his first stop was owning a professional team tennis franchise (the Boston Lobsters). He realized that in order to make money he needed more than just ticket revenue, and his team was not receiving the parking and concession revenue. His opportunity to own the facility came when Foxboro Stadium's owners, the Sullivan family, loaded the $6 million stadium (when it was initially built) with $48 million of **debt** after losing money on the 1988 Michael Jackson Victory Tour. When it became clear that Foxboro Stadium was going to be sold in bankruptcy, Kraft bought the stadium for $25 million. He then controlled all **revenue** except for ticket sales, which another tenant, the Patriots, received. The Patriots owners at that time were threatening to move the team to St. Louis unless they were able to get a better deal. Kraft, though, had the team under a long-term lease, which the team was obligated to complete or face significant penalties. The team offered him $75 million to buy the stadium. Kraft refused and then bought the team in 1994 for $175 million. That was the highest price at that time for any professional franchise, and the team was a franchise that had never had a sellout in 34 prior years. The day after he bought the team, 6,000 fans descended on Foxboro to buy tickets (Murphy, 2017). The prospect of a new owner willing to spend money and invest in a team, with the goal to win championships, was very attractive to fans. The team has not looked back since then. Besides their on-the-field success, the stadium was replaced with Patriot Place and Gillette Stadium. Patriot Place (www.patriot-place.com) became a destination location where fans and nonfans can spend a day eating out, going to movies, bowling, attending a comedy club, visiting a hall of fame, getting out of an escape room, and numerous other attractions—all benefiting Kraft's growing family fortune.

Kraft realized he needed to control all revenue. If a stadium is built with public funds, there might be restrictions on how much could be spent and what occurs with surrounding land, for example. Kraft, Dallas Cowboys owner, Jerry Jones, and Los Angeles Rams owner, Stan Kroenke, are examples of owners who have built or are building their own privately financed entertainment complexes to leverage as much money as possible from their investment while exerting complete control of decisions. Some professional team owners understand that they can make more money if they control more revenue but do not want to invest close to a billion dollars for a stadium, so they get others to pay for building the stadium or arena. That is why teams can spend a significant sum to get public support for a publicly funded stadium. One such example is the Texas Rangers' stadium scheduled to be completed in 2020 at a cost of around $1 billion. Those opposing public funds going to the project raised $7,000 in their Save Our Stadium campaign. In contrast, stadium advocates (primarily the team) spent $1.78 million, which included 7,000-8,000 lawn signs, 300 billboards, a door-to-door campaign that hit 75,000 homes, 300 volunteers, and 150 presentations in the six-month Vote Yes to Keep the Rangers campaign ("To build a ballpark," 2017).

These examples start to show how, with the right accounting and economic information, a team can start making sound financial decisions. Finance focuses on the science or art of managing funds. The authors have not found one best definition of finance—especially in the sport finance context. However, the following elements come to bear in understanding what sport finance entails:

- How to determine the value of various decisions
- How to appropriately allocate resources to meet organizational demands or goals
- How to effectively manage resources, whether buying, retaining, or selling them
- How to invest any additional resources
- How to leverage the relationship between time, money, and risk
- How to leverage cash and credit-related opportunities and constraints
- How a sports organization can make sound decisions for the present or future that aim to (1) not cause harm to the organization and its stakeholders and (2) generate a profit to help the organization grow, whether it is a nonprofit or a for-profit organization

Going back to the example of a team moving or building a stadium, the financial part of the equation explores what risks might exist and the potential for financial gains for a team. Owning a facility is important, but if it is in the wrong market, it can actually harm a team's ability to generate revenue. For sports teams, location is the key to revenue growth. Take, for example, the parity in the National Football League (NFL). Many observers would feel that owning an NFL team is tantamount to owning a printing press to print dollar bills, but that is not necessarily true. Let's explore this in greater detail. In 2011, the NFL's salary cap was $120 million per team. By 2015, that had grown to $155 million and then grew again in 2016 to $167 million (Schrotenboer, 2017a). Each team was supposed to spend around this amount on player salaries. Yes, there was a major national broadcast contract bringing in millions (the league distributes around $225 million annually to each team from broadcasting, licensing, and similar league-wide revenue streams), but every market was different in terms of its ability to generate revenue. A small-market team such as the Oakland Raiders had a revenue gap of $300 million, while a major-market team such as the Dallas Cowboys had a $700 million gap. Revenue streams are affected by market size and opportunity (economic implications). A large-market team might be able to sell 250 luxury suites for $200,000 each a year. A small-market team might only be able to sell 100 such suites at $100,000 each. This would create a discrepancy of $40 million a year between the teams. This would mean that small-market teams might be spending 60% of their revenue on player payroll, while major-market teams might only spend 40% of their revenue on player payroll. To compound the pressures associated with expenses, the expenses are based on league-wide totals divided by the number of teams in the league. The collective bargaining agreement (CBA) guarantees players 47% of NFL revenue, including league-wide and local revenues. Thus, as revenue increases for major market teams, small-market teams are forced to increase how much they spend on payroll, even if their own local revenue is flat or even declining. It should be noted that the salary cap just applies to salary and does not apply to benefits. Benefits such as players' pensions, insurance premiums, and disability insurance typically cost an NFL team around $37 million a year (Schrotenboer, 2017a). These examples help show how sport finance has so many different tentacles. It might encompass some economic issues, such as the lack of large businesses in some small markets.

It might examine revenue and expenses and their budgetary implications. Sport finance will examine how a team budgets and prioritizes for the future or what strategy it might take (such as moving to a different city) to address any specific revenue or expense-related issues it might have. These numbers are all calculated using accounting basics, and the resulting decisions are based on hopefully sound financial analysis.

CURRENT FINANCIAL PROBLEMS FACING SPORTING GOODS RETAILERS AND OTHER RETAILERS

One of the biggest sport finance stories in the past couple of decades is the bankruptcy of The Sports Authority (TSA) in 2016. TSA was owned by Leonard Green & Partners, which purchased the company in a leveraged buyout in 2006 for $1.3 billion (Xu Klein, Church, and Coleman-Lochner, 2016). A **leveraged buyout** occurs when a suitor buys a company primarily with debt and using the newly acquired company's assets as collateral for the debt, rather than buying the company with cash or possibly an exchange of stocks. At the time of the bankruptcy filing, TSA owed creditors $1.1 billion (Peltz, 2016). The situation for the United States' fourth largest sports retailer (behind Dick's Sporting Goods, Academy Sports, and Bass Pro Shops) started to unravel when it was not able to make a $21 million interest payment, which would have resulted in a default on its $343 million of subordinated debt. Several factors led to the bankruptcy filing. One was the heavy debt burdening the stores from when the company was purchased in 2006. Other factors included

♦ TSA's deep discounting of merchandise, to clear inventory from stock, which cut into **profit margins**;
♦ growing e-commerce sales that actually backfired by raising shipping and fulfillment costs; and
♦ go-dark lease clause provisions that would leave TSA on the hook for rent even after the underperforming stores were closed for good—unless TSA filed for bankruptcy (Wallace, 2016b).

Landlords are considered unsecured **creditors**, so if a company goes bankrupt and wants to cancel a lease, the bankruptcy court will normally allow the lease to be cancelled without significant compensation to the landlord. If a store voluntarily closes, the company would otherwise be obligated to keep paying the rent until another tenant can be found. This could mean that if TSA did not go bankrupt, it could have been on the hook for rent at around 450 stores for years to come.

While TSA was unraveling, a battle ensued from various parties trying to acquire some or all of TSA's assets during the bankruptcy process. One such suitor was Modell's Sporting Goods. However, the primary creditors—who owned a combined $300 million in term loans due by November 2017—felt that Modell's offer was too low (Xu Klein, Church, and Coleman-Lochner, 2016). Another suitor was Dick's Sporting Goods (DSG), which was exploring purchasing 80 to 180 of TSA's stores before backing out (Wallace, 2016a). In the end, DSG converted 22 TSA locations into DSG stores and purchased all of TSA's intellectual properties, including the website, which was redirected to DSG's website (Bomey,

2017c). This expansion increased DSG's size to 676 Dick's stores, 74 Golf Galaxy stores, and 27 Field & Stream stores (Bomey, 2017c).

TSA's primary brick-and-mortar competitor (other than Walmart, Target, and Costco) was DSG, which saw its stocks stumble in 2017 due to decreased apparel sales and an admitted computational blunder that resulted in overstating fourth quarter income by $23.4 million. The key metric for store sales is the sales at stores open for one year, and DSG only saw that number grow 2.4% compared with the projected increase of 3 to 4% (Bomey, 2017b). The decreased growth in sales was expected to increase inventory levels by 10%, which would result in less income and more carrying costs (Bomey, 2017b). Similar to TSA, DSG faced higher costs due to lease obligations and significant online competition, especially in the area of sport-related electronics—such as fitness trackers. Brick-and-mortar sales for the 2016 holiday season decreased 6.9% for sport- and entertainment-related businesses—while online sales for similar companies jumped 19% (Bomey, 2017d).

The TSA saga helps highlight how complex the financial system is. The financial system

A fancy display can help sell more sporting goods, but that would not have helped The Sports Authority and their significant financial challenges.

is composed of many different individuals and organizations, each with their own agendas and interests. Companies have their own rules and regulations, often contained in by-laws. Non-profit organizations might have specific dictates of their boards and government regulations they have to follow. Government entities are involved in everything from tax requirements to bankruptcy courts, setting interest rates, and federal reporting requirements. There are numerous banks and other lenders involved. There are **stock exchanges** listing publicly traded companies. There are professional accountants and lawyers who have to act according to specific regulations. Besides all the different parties, there are also numerous ethical constraints—published or implied, which should guide most or all financial decisions. Is it okay to hurt some people in order to make some money? Should a product that can generate revenue but exposes someone to risk be sold? Is it okay to lie to get a deal done? These are the types of issues that affect the sport finance industry as well. When a company such as TSA goes bankrupt, it sends a ripple effect through the entire field. Lenders, landlords, employees, manufacturers, banks, local cities, state government, and others will be affected. Furthermore, many ethical questions will be asked: Was it appropriate for the private equity firm to buy the company and saddle it with so much debt? Is it ethical to lay off so many dedicated workers? Should executives be held accountable when they make bad decisions?

TSA is not alone. Midwest-based MC Sports shuttered their 68 stores in 2017. The chain had $5.4 million in net losses on sales of $174.6 million. MDC's bankruptcy was just one of several in 2016 to 2017 including the golf equipment chain Golfsmith, the outdoor gear chain Eastern Outfitters, and the 50-store chain of Sport Chalet (Bomey, 2017a). Another major sport bankruptcy in 2016 was Performance Sports Group (PSG), the parent company for Bauer hockey gear and Easton baseball equipment. The factors contributing to the bankruptcy included accounting controversies (the group delayed filing its 10-K [government-required financial statements] and **annual report**), a **default** in loan repayment, the slump in bat sales, and TSA's issues. The company listed $594 million in assets and $608 million in debts. PSG was able to acquire access to $386 million in bankruptcy loans (called

debtor-in-possession financing) to keep going (Bomey, 2016) during bankruptcy, if it needed the funds. By October 31, 2016, the company had filed for Chapter 11 bankruptcy protection and then issued the following titled press release: *Performance Sports Group Enters Into "Stalking Horse" Asset Purchase Agreement With Investor Group Led by Sagard Capital and Fairfax Financial for U.S. $575 Million* (Jones, 2016). A stalking-horse bid is an initial bid on a bankrupt company's assets from a potential buyer that the bankrupt company chooses. This process requires the company to first go bankrupt and then accept the stalking-horse bid to set a bar so a suitor does not come in and try to lowball an offer to acquire the company. In essence, the stalking-horse bid sets the bar that any future offers have to be for more money. It should be noted that Sagard Capital and Fairfax Financial each had owned a significant percentage of PSG's shares that were traded on the New York Stock Exchange under the symbol PSG. After the acquisition, PSG was traded over the counter (OTC) as a wind-down entity (going out of business).

An example of the **ripple effect** of financial actions can be seen in the retail sector. The entire retail landscape has suffered through very challenging fiscal times. It was estimated in 2017 that between 20 and 25% of American Shopping malls might close by 2022 and that 8,600 malls would close in 2017 alone ("The bottom line," 2017). By the middle of May 2017, 2,770 national chain stores had closed. Many of the closures were due to inappropriate financial or marketing strategies. Some stores are nondescript—selling the exact same thing as everyone else. This has significantly affected stores such as Sears and Kmart, which are noted for being mall anchor tenants. Approximately 150 Sears and Kmart stores were scheduled to be closed in 2017, a trend across the country, where it is estimated that 25% of malls in the United States will lose their anchor tenant (Madhani, 2017). Why such retail carnage? Every situation is different, and many people like to claim that it is because the retailers (and other troubled businesses) have too much debt. Debt represents money the companies owe to others for everything such as leases or **mortgages**, to **bonds**, **inventory**, and even back-owed taxes.

One big issue faced by Sears, Kmart, and other retailers is the lack of cash. Thus, owing $1 million is not necessarily bad for a large company. Even owing $100 million is not necessarily bad, especially if the company has revenue that greatly exceeds those debt levels. In contrast, if you owe $100, but your revenue is only $50, you do not really have a debt issue but rather an income issue, and once you have more income, the debt level becomes insignificant. This explanation comes into play when looking at Sears and Kmart, where they have been losing sales and have fallen well below their rivals. This has occurred in part due to the Internet. Sears used to be the location to shop for almost everything, but now a customer can just as easily shop for everything online. In addition, the company has not kept up with changing customer trends and the 2004 merger of Sears and Kmart left the company with significant debt (Jones, 2017b). One of the biggest issues has been poor management decisions that have led Sears to shedding some lucrative businesses to earn some quick cash, such as selling its $30 billion credit portfolio to Citibank in 2003 and the 2016 proposed $900 million sale of Craftsman to Stanley Black & Decker (Jones, 2017a). Selling some assets might generate quick cash now, but it also eliminated an income source for the future. Quick cash now would result in decreased income for years to come. In 2017, Sears' liabilities exceeded assets by $4 billion. Sears had other financial and legal concerns. Due to lucrative contracts given to employees and past employees, Sears Holding Company owed retirees and employees a combined pension obligation of $5.2 billion, but the fair market value of the pension plan was only $3.6 billion—resulting in $1.6 billion pension shortfall (McCoy, 2017a). Sears had incurred and continues to have significant debt. To address all its debt obligations, it has resorted to cutting costs and selling business units. Such acts could serve as a Band-Aid, but were not enough to keep growing the business. Maybe borrowing enough money to expand in the right areas (whatever they might be) would have been a better business decision—but such Monday morning financial quarterbacking is often wrong. Executives are paid a significant amount to help make solid business decisions, but there is no guarantee that such decisions will actually work. Decisions can be affected by actions of various stakeholders from government agencies, competitors, foreign markets, and consumers.

Another issue is that consumers are fixated on discounts (Wahba, 2017). They use Amazon and their smartphones to look up what they want to buy and see where they can purchase an item for the least amount. Some small stores have reported that customers come in asking for advice, obtain advice from the proprietor, and then admit they will not purchase the item from that retailer but will instead search online for a better price. An example of customer search for the lowest price (whether online or in stores) can be found with Costco's Kirkland Signature golf balls, which sold out in 2016 and sell for $15 a dozen—compared with name brands sold for up to three times that cost. The cheaper balls affected other companies with, as an example, Titleist golf ball sales declining 3.6% in the first nine months of 2016 (Bomey, 2017e).

While some physical stores are closing, others are opening. Outdoor Voices, a female athletic apparel company, has been able to grow to four stores rather quickly through focusing on brand experiences (rather than just sales). For example, the stores offer community brunch parties, community yoga gatherings, and even yoga classes where people can bring their dogs (Griffith, 2017).

FINANCIAL SOLUTIONS

The problems faced by the sports retail business are not alone. Many sports organizations can face financial hardships. A European soccer team can face relegation. A star player can go bankrupt. A team can misread fan interest and overprice its tickets, resulting in a fan backlash. A company can launch a new sports product, and it can take off as planned or fail miserably. A 5K run for a charity can lose money. There is no one formula for what will result in sport financial success. Possibly the best formula would be to spend less than the endeavor costs. But there can be other formulas—for example, don't invest what you cannot afford to lose, don't take too much risk, or take a number of small risks with the hope that one will result in a big payday. Each formula is what is right for an organization at that time and under specific circumstances. Even when all the stars are aligned and it seems like a no-lose situation, fortunes can be lost. This is where strategy comes into play. The best strategies would grow revenue and minimize debt. Yes, debt should be kept in check, but revenue also needs to be examined. Increasing revenue is where sport marketing really comes into play. Unsold game tickets represent lost potential income that can never be recaptured. Marketers need to work with their financial colleagues to develop a marketing budget that reflects how much will be spent on marketing and the anticipated return on such an investment. Just spending in hopes of increasing sales is normally an invitation for a fiscal disaster. If a sport business is facing some fiscal-related challenges, it can take some steps such as the following:

- Prioritize debt by identifying amounts owed, repayment dates, what **interest rate** is charged, and similar critical information to help prioritize repayment.
- Increase sales by rewarding loyal customers, decreasing price to sell more items, or increasing sales numbers, such as volume-based discounts.
- Cut costs by shedding unneeded equipment, downsizing facilities, and **cost sharing** with others.
- **Refinance** debt with high interest rates to a lower rate.
- Ask buyers to pay more quickly. This can be accomplished by giving a small discount if customers pay sooner rather than later (Nicastro, 2017).

HOW SPORT FINANCE AFFECTS AN ENTIRE SPORTS ORGANIZATION OR INDUSTRY

The best way to help understand and appreciate the financial issues faced by a sports organization is to use an example. The example we will use is a professional soccer team. Assume the soccer team is owned by one owner who has the team classified as a **limited liability corporation (LLC)** as a way to minimize taxes and maximize liability protection. That owner has to pay all the expenses and will benefit if the team makes any money. If the team loses money, she has to suffer the loss. The team has some key assets, such as soccer equipment, ticketing machines, and front office equipment (computers, phones, photocopiers, etc.). The team plays at a local college, and the rent is $50,000 a year. Other liabilities include loan repayments for when the owner bought the team, league fees, and payroll taxes.

The owner created a budget at the start of every year. She lists all the expenses she anticipates, from player salaries to all other personnel costs, operating costs, administrative expenses, marketing, insurance, and professional fees. Some expenses are borne by the local college, which pays for all field maintenance, lights, security, and related expenses. The college also provides all concession items such as food, equipment, and personnel. In exchange, the college keeps 70% of all concession revenue at the soccer games and gives the team 30%. Revenue is derived from concessions, ticket sales, and sponsorship. To generate $10,000 in ticket sales, the team normally incurs around $7,000 in direct expenses (such as ticket sellers, players, and coaches) and $2,500 in administrative expenses. Thus, to generate $20,000 in profits from ticket sales, the team needs to sell $400,000 in tickets. With the average ticket costing $20, that means that the team needs to sell 20,000 tickets. The owner develops a **break-even budget** where she will know that she has made a profit from tickets once a certain number of tickets are sold. This is based on analyzing her **fixed costs** and then the **variable costs**. Since the fixed costs are incurred whether 100 or 10,000 fans attend the games, her focus is to cover the basic ticket expenses with all fixed expenses so that concession revenue and sponsorship revenue is icing on the cake. The total fixed expense is $950,000, which means that the team needs to sell 47,500 tickets to break even. If only 40,000 tickets are sold during the season, then the team would lose $150,000. In the best-case scenario, if the team sells 60,000 tickets, then the team will make a $250,000 profit just on tickets. Thus, break-even analysis is undertaken by every team, but it only serves as a starting point for the financial issues the team might face.

The financial issues start at the very beginning with whether the prospective owner should actually purchase the team and at what price. How should the prospective owner finance the purchase? Should the prospective owner use cash, borrow money, use her credit cards, and so on? Should she renegotiate the deal with the college? What could be the risks if the college asks for more money or refuses to renew the contract, thus leaving the team without a good facility to play at? How much should players be paid—and does the league have any regulations about salaries? Are the players unionized and, if so, what does that collective bargaining contract require for the owner to undertake financially? These are just some of the questions to ask before the owner should make an offer on the team Some of the other financial questions that will need to be asked include the following:

- What if interest rates drop and the owner needs to renegotiate the loan she used to purchase the team?
- What if the college raises the rent to $75,000 a year?
- What if two sponsors owe a combined $100,000 but are over 90 days past due when the payment needed to be made?
- What if the league increases the amount of money needed to be paid to officials?
- How can the team balance the slow months when the money is not coming in but bills still need to be paid?
- What if the team has an exceptionally good year and generates some extra money—what should be done with the money?
- Should the team consider building its own facility, and what factors need to be determined?
- Should the team consider moving to a different city?
- Should the team consider raising ticket prices?
- Would changing the marketing strategy and ticketing options help increase revenue or will it decrease revenue?
- Will switching from printed to e-tickets save money or make sense?
- Should the team take over concessions to be able to generate a greater share of such revenue even though it will cost more and open it up to more risks?

These are just some of the questions that need to be considered by not only this sample team but also every sport-related organization. This is where financial strategy comes into play. Is the organization maximizing its assets and revenue? Is the organization minimizing liabilities and reducing expenses strategically? Is there a budget that accurately reflects income and expense streams? Is cash flow monitored in real time? Are there options to obtain additional cash when needed? These are topics that every sports organization wrestles with on a daily basis. No decision can be made in a vacuum, and almost every decision has a financial ramification and impact. That is why it is so critical to take a big picture look at a sports organization, with a keen eye to financial considerations.

CONCLUSION

Everyone needs to appreciate how revenue and expenses flow through an organization. Whether there might be too much debt or too little revenue, the failure to appreciate financial issues can lead to financial disasters. Many executives are now pursuing open book management, where the numbers are shared throughout an organization so everyone understands the financial issues encountered in running the organization. If an employee knows that their work directly increases the organization's bottom line, they often are more engaged and take more pride in their work. Similarly, the more the reader knows about finance, the easier it is to make sound decisions. Thus, throughout this text we hope that you keep an open mind to sport finance and appreciate how even seemingly small details can lead to significant problems.

Class Discussion Topics

1. Identify a specific plan to change your own financial situation.

2. What does sport finance mean to you?

3. How comfortable do you feel making sport-finance-based decisions, and what information would you need to make such decisions?

4. What do you think The Sports Authority could have done to possibly stave off bankruptcy?

5. Examine the implications of TSA's bankruptcy and what impact it might have had on others in the sport industry. Take a close look at how TSA's bankruptcy specifically affected sports apparel companies such as Under Armour. Students should examine various online articles concerning TSA and Under Armour to learn more about the bankruptcy's impact. What should Under Armour have done to protect itself from financial circumstances out of its control?

6. Research a publicly traded sport business and examine what it has accomplished in the past year and what its future plans are based on online chatter by analysts. If you had $10,000 to invest in shares related to that company, would you buy? Why or why not? Use only the information you currently know about sport finance. At the end of the class, after you have acquired a stronger financial background, you can revisit your analysis to see if your decision has changed.

Sport Industry Financial Trends

Chapter Objectives

After studying this chapter, you should be able to do the following:

- Compare and contrast various segments within the sport industry and how they handle financial issues.
- Examine how sports facilities can become an economic engine for revenue generation.
- Forecast the future of the sport industry based on changes in the sports broadcasting field.

There are various trends in any industry. Sport finance is not immune to these trends. Some trends are long term while others are fads. Through examining various industry segments from a financial lens, we can determine how strong that segment might be or whether there are potential concerns—whether current, imminent, or far in the future and very remote. In Chapter 1 we discussed one specific topic associated with sporting goods retailers and how some companies were not able to coordinate their finances and strategy to avoid bankruptcy. Some companies and sports teams or organizations can effectively handle the financial bumps in the road, while others might implode from the financial strain. What causes one to succeed and the other to fail? Are there any specific factors or trends that can give guidance to where the sport industry might go in the future? What is the hot trend, or what might be a major disaster in the future? We will examine these trends in light of several select areas such as amateur participant sport, collegiate athletics, professional sport, e-sports, and sports broadcasting around the world.

TRENDS IN AMATEUR AND PARTICIPATORY SPORT

Amateur sport around the world can encompass a wide variety of issues. From fitness trends and extreme challenge events to youth sports and senior games, there are numerous possible financial concerns. While professional sports might have ticket revenue, broadcast revenue, licensing, and sponsorship as primary income streams, youth sports organizations often have to struggle. The primary expenses for professional teams include player salaries, administrative expenses, and **debt service** for building stadiums. The most common revenue sources for amateur sports are sponsorship, membership fees, registration fees, tax subsidies, national lotteries, fund-raising opportunities (such as raffles or 5K races), and social events. Expenses at the amateur youth sport level often go to field or facility expenses, as well as to uniform, equipment, travel, and related expenses. It would be impossible to explore every amateur sport, but we will explore fitness trends, travel teams, extreme competitions, and government funding of amateur sports as just some examples.

Fitness

Fitness facilities seem to open and close at a staggering rate. Several years ago, Curves was considered a very popular fitness chain. The chain started in 1992. The company began franchising in 1995. To acquire a franchise today, a franchisee needs an initial investment of around $40,000, a net worth of at least $75,000, and a liquid cash requirement of $50,000. The initial franchise fee is around $25,000, and franchises have to pay an ongoing royalty fee of around 6% of their revenue to the parent company (Entrepreneur, 2017). At its peak, Curves had over 10,000 franchises. In 2011 alone, 833 Curves franchises closed, representing 16% of all franchises at the time (Gibson, 2011). By 2014, there were 6,000 Curves clubs in 88 countries with 2,500 in North America (representing a 65% drop just in North America) (Strauss, 2014). If a club decides to close, it could still be on the hook for thousands of dollars owed to Curves International to cover lost future royalties. One element driving the lower number of franchises has been the resale value of clubs and whether an owner could get their original investment out if they had to sell their franchise.

Curves attempted to offer a one-size-fits-all experience to serve women with specific programs and hours. In contrast, other facilities utilize different approaches to generate revenue. Soul Cycle is an example of a relatively newer chain offering a high-end experience. Customized and high-end experiences are the in trend for fitness. With about one in five Americans paying for gym membership, some people are looking for a basic gym, while others are looking for the more high-end experience such as Equinox or specialty facilities focused just on kickboxing, spinning, or numerous other options. In contrast, the market might dictate having multiple activities or being open 24 hours. Each facility is trying to serve a specific market that management feels will generate the greatest return on investment.

The number of people working in the fitness industry is significant. There are an estimated 34,000 fitness facilities in the United States and over 180,000 throughout the world. It was estimated that over 500,000 people worked in the United States fitness field in 2014, and that number was supposed to increase by 8% by 2024 (Franchise Help, 2017). Many of these fitness employees and instructors need to be certified, and they need to be trained, purchase equipment, purchase clothing, recommend membership options, recommend food supplements, and engage in numerous other financial decisions or suggestions. Thus, within the fitness industry, there are numerous side industries that support them. These include equipment manufacturers, specialty software companies, specialty insurance carriers, direct marketing companies, and numerous other providers.

Travel Teams

Over the past 20 years the number of travel teams in the United States has skyrocketed. That has led the youth sport industry in the United States to generate over $15 billion annually. It is estimated that nearly 20% of U.S. families spent over $12,000 a year on youth sports per child. Of these dedicated parents, 67% hope that their investment will lead to a college scholarship, and 34% think their child athlete will make it to the Olympics or become a pro (Shell, 2017). Travel teams are youth teams where the athletes often train year-round in one specific sport. The travel team craze has created a culture of families spending sometimes over $10,000 a year on coaching and team-related activities. This is on top of the amount families spend traveling all over for tournaments. The travel team explosion has not been without victims. There have been a number of cases where people trying to make a quick buck defrauded parents who are so focused on their kids becoming the next star athlete that they fail to notice the signs of trouble. Some signs might include practices being cancelled, the promised uniforms do not arrive, maybe a trip is cancelled, or maybe the coach or administrator stops returning parents' phone calls. Whatever the signs, the end result from unscrupulous promoters can be financial carnage for parents.

Travel teams are also affecting high school sports. Some high schools have developed rules stating that if a student plays on a travel team, they cannot play on the high school's team. Furthermore, competition between travel teams can be cutthroat for the dollars. There are tournament sponsors, team sponsors, travel agents, sports facilities, and numerous others who want a piece of the action. This is similar to any other facet of the sport industry or any other industry. Money is tight, and there are always those interested in generating as much revenue as possible—sometimes at any expense. So how can travel team maximize their revenue? It all starts with a plan. The financial plan is outlined in a budget.

Due to all the money involved with travel teams, there needs to be an accountable person tasked with monitoring the money, rather than relying on one person to collect and spend the money without any accountability. Travel Team Treasurer's for the Arlington Soccer Association (ASA) in Texas is a job description that outlines **treasurers**' duties as:

> developing and implementing a budget for the team, managing the team's account and team fees budget, as well as collecting team funds, assisting in the collection of player club and team fees and handling reimbursements and payments for team expenses. (Arlington Soccer Association, 2012)

Costs to play travel soccer include items such as coaching salaries, field fees, state or league fees, referee expenses, club administration costs, team equipment (first aid kits, game balls, etc.), tournament fees, coach travel expenses, and uniforms. Other expenses such as those for extra uniforms or equipment, team social events, awards, unexpected field rental fees, player scholarships for poorer kids, a team website, and additional tournament fees and travel will arise. Revenue is derived from parents paying club and team fees. When establishing a budget, the team treasurer for any travel team should explore some basic budgeting strategies such as:

- creating a budget and adding enough of a buffer zone so parents would not need to be approached again during the year for more money;
- making sure the first payment is the higher amount if parents are expected to make two payments;
- verifying cash flow will be sufficient to cover all the team's obligations;
- always having a contingency fund; and
- keeping records of all deposits and outlays and making the budget available to all officials or parents to ensure transparency (Arlington Soccer Association, 2012).

BUDGET FOR A TRAVEL TEAM'S EXPENSES

How much does it cost to outfit and run a 12-player baseball team with a 65-game schedule? The breakdown that follows helps highlight the potential cost.

UNIFORMS			
Hats (2 colors)	24	$20	$480
Socks (2 pairs home and away)	48	$5	$240
Jerseys (home and away)	24	$50	$1,200
Jerseys (coaches)	6	$50	$300
Pullovers (players and coaches)	30	$30	$900
Pants (home and away)	24	$30	$720
Helmets (batting)	12	$30	$360
Helmets (pitching)	12	$30	$360
Equipment bags (regular)	10	$50	$500
Equipment bags (catchers)	2	$55	$110
Equipment bags (team)	2	$55	$110
Shipping expense			$225
Subtotal			$5,505
EQUIPMENT			
Game balls (dozen)	6	$50	$300
Practice balls (bucket)	1	$100	$100
Scorebooks	3	$10	$ 30
Medical bag	1	$200	$200
Other gear (L screen, etc.)	1	$500	$500
Subtotal			$1,130
FIELD AND FACILITY RENTALS			
Winter indoor	1	$1,500	$1,500
Home games*	15	$50	$750
Practice field	1	$500	$500
Subtotal			$2,750
UMPIRE FEES			
Assignment fee	1	$50	$50
Scheduling fee	1	$150	$150
Game fees	25	$75	$1,875
Subtotal			$2,075
TOURNAMENTS, LEAGUE, ADMINISTRATION			
Season tournaments	8	$600	$4,800
League tournament	1	$500	$500
State tournament	1	$1,000	$1,000
National tournament	1	$1,000	$ 1,000
Team sanction fee	1	$50	$50

Insurance	1	$200	$200
League fee	1	$500	$500
Miscellaneous (administration, party, etc.)	1	$1,000	$1,000
Subtotal			$9,050
Grand total			$20,510
Cost per player			$1,710 per player

*Assumes 15 home games—all other games are away or tournaments (StatsDad, 2011).

Extreme Competitions

Extreme competition started a number of years ago with triathlons and then advanced to ultramarathons. Over the past 10 years, it has morphed into CrossFit, Tough Mudder, Spartan, and American Ninja Warriors. There are numerous specialty events designed to push people to the extreme or to help people work as a team. They are also designed to generate revenue. The math is pretty simple. If Tough Mudder, as an example, runs an event with 10,000 participants paying $50 each, the revenue stream would be $500,000. This might seem like a lot, but then all the expenses need to be calculated. There is the cost of the race course, the administrative team, advertising, personnel, legal counsel, accounting, and numerous other expenses. That is why income can be misleading. Analyzing income without examining expenses will lead to failure. That is where the road map of a budget comes into play.

Numerous nonprofit organizations have been trying to run similar events over the years to generate revenue. Unfortunately, for many of these organizations, the result has been the opposite. They see the dollar signs but fail to properly calculate their expenses. It is not just extreme events, but even 5K runs have turned from strong money makers to losing propositions. This can be due to the fact that besides all the expenses, there are so many events competing for the same consumer dollars. This forces some nonprofit organizations to spend a significant sum to market their event, add the latest bells and whistles (which means more money), increase prizes, and incur other expenses. Some of these expenses are not as apparent. For example, while many executives understand the cost to add insurance coverage for an event, there is also a cost if someone is injured—in terms of legal fees, increased insurance premiums, and organizational resources spent on litigation rather than other activities. The more extreme the event, the more costs involved, the more possible revenue can be generated, but hidden costs also need to be considered in the equation.

Government Funding

Throughout the world, sport is often funded by the local or national government. Whether the sport is run by local parks, after school programs, high school sports, or elite athletic preparation programs, governments around the world are the largest funders of sport. With more pressure on governments to cut expenditures, there is a trend to cut such funds. Some physical education programs are being cut so kids are only having one hour of physical education a week. At the same time, there is an enhanced effort to reduce obesity, and sport can be a critical part of such health-related efforts. In the United States, there are some government funds that go to park and recreation departments, but most amateur and youth sports programs are funded by private citizens. While some nonprofit organizations might own their own fields or gyms, most are operating on small budgets and do not have the funds that government coffers can sustain. Thus, youth and amateur programs in various countries are often more robust than in others. For example, public-sector expenditure on recreational and sporting services in the United Kingdom declined from 4,388 million GBP (Great Britain pounds) in 2011 to 2012 to 3,119 million GBP (approximately US$4 billion) in 2016 to 2017 (Statista, 2017). The decline could be attributed to an overall governmental decrease in spending. This represented a robust 0.4% of the country's gross domestic product (GDP). This amount might be higher than many other countries spending on recreation and sport, but it fell below the 1.7% of GDP spent by Bulgaria and 1.5% of GDP spent on recreation and sport by Iceland (Eurostat, 2017). Every country is different, but in Australia, a family with an income of around $59,000 (Australian) would have paid approximately $10,000 in federal taxes in 2016, and of that amount, $78 would go to recreation, arts, and sport expenditures by the federal government. This is part of the $3.4 billion spent by the Australian federal government on recreation and sport, but this figure does not include even more money spent by the states and local government (Evershed, 2016).

Every government will spend differently on recreation and sport depending on its goals and objectives. Spending is based on the perceived value or political value associated with such expenditures. While some governments might fund sport as part of a broader recreation or tourism initiative, others might fund sport to help win medals (international acclaim) or to reduce obesity and address other health-related concerns. The purpose of the expenditure helps drive what money is needed and the political muscle that would be required. This goes to the question, *what is the plan for the money?* The plan varies by government and every local, state, and national government will have different ideas and strategies. Strategies help drive collegiate athletics as well, and spending on collegiate athletics is influenced in the United States by alumni, students, administrators, faculty, sponsors, broadcasters, and government officials.

TRENDS IN COLLEGE SPORT

Over the previous two decades, athletic expenses have outpaced athletic revenues in all National Collegiate Athletic Association (NCAA) divisions. Consequently, collegiate athletic programs are facing unprecedented financial challenges.

Although a myriad of factors are contributing to these challenges at all NCAA institutions, at the Division I level, coaching salaries, facility construction, and tuition increases appear to be the major items affecting collegiate budgets. Alabama's Nick Saban was the highest paid college football coach in 2017, earning over $11 million under his employment contract. The shouts to let athletes partake in some of the funds generated through college sport grew to screams with some when news broke during a 2017 pay-to-play Federal Bureau of Investigations investigation into college basketball practices. University of Louisville basketball coach Rick Pitino was eventually terminated as part of a scandal. Two months earlier, Adidas (also implicated in the scandal through the actions of several of its employees) renewed its 10-year $160 million apparel contract. Under the prior contract, while funds were meant to go to the athletic department, records indicated that 98% of cash provided by Adidas ($1.5 million) went just to the head coach, and only a small fraction went to the athletic department to benefit students ("Pitino pocketed," 2017). No wonder those challenging college athletics are claiming the system is broken.

One shining example of the problems with collegiate athletics is the University of Michigan. The storied athletic department was supposedly $240 million in debt due to significant facility construction and renovation related expenses (Dalgleish, 2017). This is only part of the athletic department's debt, which is expected to grow to $371 million by 2046. While that might be high, it is still lower than the University of California's $445 million debt (Dalgleish, 2017). However, the athletic department debt cannot be viewed in a vacuum as the entire university had debt of $2.1 billion.

The athletic department was banking on the Big Ten's new (2016) six-year media rights deal with ESPN, which, combined with FOX and CBS Sports contracts, would bring in $2.64 billion over a six-year period—approximately $188.6 million to each Big Ten member school during the contract. If such funds are insufficient, the school might have to raise ticket prices (Dalgleish, 2017). That was not a preferred option as ticket sales, especially for students, had declined

COLLEGE ATHLETIC EXPENSES

What has happened to college athletic expenses over the past couple of years? The following table highlights the amount spent on each category as a total of an athletic department's expenditures (for public Division I programs).

Category	2014-2015	2015-2016	Change
Athletics-related financial aid	4.9%	8.8%	3.9%
Coaching compensation	7.6%	5.0%	-2.6%
Administrative and support staff	6.7%	4.7%	-2.0%
Team travel	4.3%	1.0%	-3.3%
Equipment and uniform/supplies	8.4%	3.1%	,-5.3%
Game day operations	6.2%	3.1%	-3.1%

Source: Berkowitz and Myerberg (2017).

These numbers show that there is a significant amount of belt-tightening going on to reduce overall expenses associated with running an athletic department.

significantly (from nearly 19,000 students in 2013 to less than 12,000 in 2014) (Murphy, 2014). In 2014, the cost for a student season pass was $280, but due to weak demand, the athletic department dropped the price 37% to $175 for the 2015 season.

Besides highly paid coaches, athletic programs have been mandated to provide additional support for student athletes. The University of Arkansas absorbed a $1 million hit to help cover the full cost of attending college and paid $1.5 million to help feed student-athletes—all prohibited expenses until the NCAA changed its rules for 2014. Even with these added expenses, Arkansas was able to generate a $19.3 million profit in 2015 to 2016 (Berkowitz & Schnaars, 2017). The largest chunk of these increased expenditures to run athletic departments was financial aid for scholarships—covering tuition, fees, room and board, and the new category of incidental expenses.

In 2011, the University of Texas reached an agreement with ESPN to launch the Longhorn Network, a channel devoted exclusively to broadcasting and promoting both the university's athletic department and the university. As part of the agreement, UT was to receive payments totaling over $300 million distributed over 20 years. This money is in addition to the share of Big 12 revenues that the university already receives as a conference member. Although the University of Texas will certainly reap the financial benefit of having its own dedicated network, the biggest advantage for Texas may not be the financial payoff, because half of the money will initially go to academics but rather the biggest advantage could be the constant presence on television and other platforms. Potential high school recruits will see the Longhorn Network in their homes and on their tablets and smartphones. Potentially, the Longhorn Network became the nation's first regional college sports network focusing on one school with a limited high-profile inventory. Not every school can be similar to Texas. Notre Dame has had a major broadcast agreement with NBC since 1991 (and runs through 2025), but the value of that deal is relatively small (only $15 million a year) compared to the Texas deal, which spans more than just football. In 2014, the Southeastern Conference, famous for football powerhouses such as Alabama, Auburn, Florida, and Louisiana State University, created its own network (owned by ESPN through 2034 and similar to networks for the Big 10 and Pac-12 conferences). ESPN has made a significant investment in college

Beer and other concession items are a major revenue source at almost all levels of the sport industry.

athletics, but such an investment is not without risks as a number of the bowl games witnessed significant ratings declines. With as many as 40 bowl games, the broadcast rating (and attendance numbers) for many games dropped, on average 13% from 2015 to 2016. With 41 bowl games, the NCAA put a moratorium on new bowl games until 2019. It is hoped that such an effort will help stop the eroding ratings, which can entail significant risk—especially for Disney as it has invested $49 billion in broadcast rights fees through ESPN.

The NCAA has the most valuable properties in U.S. college athletics. It owns the NCAA basketball tournament popularly known as March Madness and helps administer the college football championship through the Bowl Champion-ship Series. The rights to broadcast the basketball tournament were locked up in 2010, when the NCAA and CBS and the Turner Broadcasting System agreed to a 14-year, $10.8 billion deal that will run through 2024. The parties were so happy with the deal that they negotiated an eight-year extension worth $8.8 billion in 2016 (Sherman, 2016). The Bowl Championship Series contract entailed a 12-year contract from 2014 through 2025, worth around $5.64 billion, or about $470 million annually. These numbers help show the value of marquee events and top-level teams.

While salaries are growing, based in part on higher broadcast revenues, programs are asking for more money from state legislatures when it comes to public universities. Private universities do not have the same funding options and often rely on donations or student fees to help cover the cost of running an athletic department. With student debt increasing to unsustainable levels, many are asking why students should be paying several thousand dollars a year to help support athletics when they are borrowing money to make these payments and it will burden them for years to come.

TRENDS IN PROFESSIONAL SPORT

The National Football league (NFL) is a behemoth of a league. It is considered the most profitable league in the United States. It has a short season, so its games are critical, and they occupy a space with minimal competition from other professional sport. This has helped drive up the league's revenue, yet it wants more. The NFL is interested in hitting the $25 billion mark by 2027. Is that number realistic? In 2014, the NFL generated revenue of $10 billion (Schrotenboer 2014). This would represent an annual revenue increase of 7% compounded annually, or around $1 billion increase in revenue annually. The 2014 revenue was estimated to have been broken down as follows:

- $5 billion from media and television rights for game broadcasts
- $1 billion to $2 billion in sponsorships, such as the league's long-term deal with PepsiCo, which is worth about $90 to $100 million per year
- $2 billion in ticket-related sales
- $1 billion in merchandise and licensing (Schrotenboer, 2014)

While the NFL has its sight set on growing revenue, the league faced significant issues and consumer backlash in 2016 and 2017. The backlash was attributed to player protests, election broadcasts, and people cutting cable cords. Viewership in 2016 and 2017 fell around 8% (Snider, 2017). Political wrangling between the league and Washington could possibly affect the tax benefit provided to bondholders for **municipal bonds** issued to help build stadiums or those in the surrounding area. Some financial dangers are endemic to the game itself. The concussion-related scare for current and future players could significantly affect the game, as many parents are discouraging their children from playing football, which could affect the pipeline for both future fans and future players.

The revenue from football (soccer) teams around the world has significantly increased over the past 10 years, and revenue can be closely tied to a star player (similar to Michael Jordan or LeBron James in basketball). Soccer star Neymar moved from FC Barcelona to Paris Saint-Germain FC in 2017, and his popularity sparked a frenzy for League One broadcast rights, which were expected to increase from around €750 million to €1.2 billion a season (Boksenbaum-Granier & Jefferson, 2017). The investment was one of a number of Middle Eastern investments in famous soccer teams in England and Europe over the past 15 years, which has sent player salaries soaring and increased the marketing and sales of soccer-related tickets, sponsorships, and broadcast rights. To help generate the revenue needed to pay for the added talent, teams are searching for new revenue sources. For example, some teams in Europe feel they have tapped out all their local revenue options and are looking for new markets such as the United States. FC Barcelona generated €655 million in 2017 and hopes to increase that mark by roughly 79% to €1 billion ($1.17 billion) by 2012 (Novy-Williams, 2017). In one 2017 trip to the United States, the team played against archrival Real Madrid in front of 66,000 fans, and 35,000 fans paid to watch the teams practice the night before.

The previous discussion is meant to show how much money is involved in professional sport around the world. Having significant revenue and **expenses** also generates significant issues. The NFL had to deal with a national anthem issue and the polarization of fans on the topic in 2017. There are other numerous topics that arise every day for professional teams. Although not exhaustive, this section focuses on various issues related to professional sport including stadium subsidies, franchise values, e-sports, and broadcasting issues.

Stadium Subsidies

One of the major concerns for professional teams is the ability to keep growing revenue. The average family of four cannot afford to go to a game for $1,000. The average fan might become extinct. Professional teams realize that to charge more they have to find a market segment that can afford to pay more, and that market includes business people and corporations. They have more funds, and teams realize that they represent the future financial lifeblood for sport. That is why corporate seating, such as luxury suites, is so critical. To build or renovate facilities to tap this market, teams are often going back to the average fan to pay for stadium and arena renovations. That is where subsidies by local taxpayers has become such an important issue. Between 1990 and 2010, the total luxury-suite inventory in the four major sports leagues in the United States (Major League Baseball, the NFL, the National Basketball Association, and the National Hockey League) grew 147% to more than 10,000 luxury suites. Similarly, club-seat inventory experienced explosive growth, increasing by a whopping 624% to reach an estimated 450,000 club seats (Rhoda, Wrigley, & Habermas, 2010). This was fueled by the demand from major sponsors and wealthy businesses wanting a place to entertain clients and employees. While luxury seating has become a major revenue source all over the world, arena and stadium construction efforts have faced some challenges, especially from alienated fans.

Professional sports franchises face several significant challenges when attempting to obtain a stadium subsidy. Among these is the opportunity cost of the project. Specifically, what good or service is being sacrificed for the stadium to be constructed? In addition, political issues are often present, including obtaining voter approval through a public referendum. In 2011, the New York Islanders were unsuccessful in convincing voters to approve a new arena, which meant the team would have to leave its old arena when the lease expired in 2015. The vote encouraged the team to move to Barclays Center in Brooklyn. Also in New York, the famous Madison Square Garden spent over a billion dollars on a major renovation between 2010 and 2013. It was anticipated that the newly refurbished arena would still be able to generate a good **rate of return** on the investment, even when it would lose its lease in 2023 so Penn Station under the

arena can undergo major renovations. The arena would have to find a potential home and hope voters approve the site and possibly some funds to help guarantee the facility would not move. As of this writing a new home has not yet been found, and a new lease has not been completed with MSG's landlord.

Cities are willing to help subsidize stadiums and arenas hoping to keep a team. While elected officials might want to build a facility to show they are doing something for the community, many voters are expressing their concern about spending money to help make a team owner wealthier. The promise from team owners and elected officials is normally that the city needs a big league team, and then there is a promise of job growth. Such promises have fallen on deaf ears around the globe. Besides possible Olympic bidders dropping out due to the high costs of building an Olympic village (see generally articles such as "Rome, Hamburg, and Budapest Dropping out of Bidding for the 2024 Olympics"), several elections in the United States resulted in "no" votes for using public funds to help build stadiums, with two recent and famous examples including San Diego and St. Louis, where both city's NFL teams relocated to a privately financed $2 billion stadium to be built in Los Angeles. The cost to build facilities has scared and will continue to scare voters and the public. To obtain voter support, team owners need to prove the business case for the voters. The voters will argue, if building a facility is such a great investment, why isn't the owner paying for the facility themselves? With that said, the most successful professional stadium projects have been destination locations built primarily with private funds from team owners, such as Patriots Place (Gillette Stadium) and AT&T Stadium in Dallas.

Franchise Values

One universal practice is for owners of professional sports teams to claim that they lose money operating their franchises. Consequently, they can justify raising tickets prices, charging premiums for concessions, and persuading the public to subsidize new stadiums. Because team owners are not required to disclose their financial statements publicly, the general population has to rely on anecdotal information about the financial solvency of professional teams or records produced during litigation. Yet despite the lack of publicly available financial information, one fact is not disputed—the value of these franchises increase, often at rates far exceeding those of other business entities. In other words, although owners may claim they do not make money running a team, they make a lot of money when they sell one. In 2011, Forbes compiled a list of the 50 most valuable sports organizations. For the seventh consecutive year, Manchester United topped the list with an estimated value of $1.86 billion. Although Man U and two other soccer clubs, Real Madrid at number 5 and Arsenal at number 7, were in the top 10, every one of the 32 NFL franchises was included in the top 50 most valuable franchises. By 2016, the Dallas Cowboys were ranked as the most valuable team ($4.8 billion), followed by Manchester United ($4.123 billion), Real Madrid ($4.09 billion), Barcelona ($4.064 billion), and the New York Yankees ($4 billion) (see figure 2.1) (Leader Board, 2017). The ranking showed that only 10 of the top 25 most valuable teams were NFL teams. The rankings are estimates of value and the true value of a franchise can be monitored by the value of their publicly traded shares (if they issue stock) or the price when a team is sold.

The success that Manchester United has enjoyed on the pitch, demonstrated by winning its record 20th league championship, is consistent with their lucrative sponsorship deals. In 2012, the team signed a new sponsorship agreement with Chevrolet. The seven-year deal was estimated to be worth £52 million annually. The team raked in £581.2 million in revenue during the 2016 to 2017 season, fueled in part by a 40% increase in broadcast revenue. That revenue mark resulted in a £80.8 million profit for the team. Just as important as the profit was that the team reduced its debt from £260.9 million in 2015 to £213.1 million in 2016 (90min, 2017).

E-Sports

Over the past several years, one of the trends in the sport industry has been the rapid growth of e-sports. This was an obscure activity played by some years ago, but there are now millions of players all over the world playing games such as League of Legends, Call of Duty, StarCraft and Counter Strike: Global Offensive. What is unique about e-sports is that games were developed by large computer gaming companies (many of them publicly traded corporations) as a way to sell products, and they have evolved into competitions with players from all over the world.

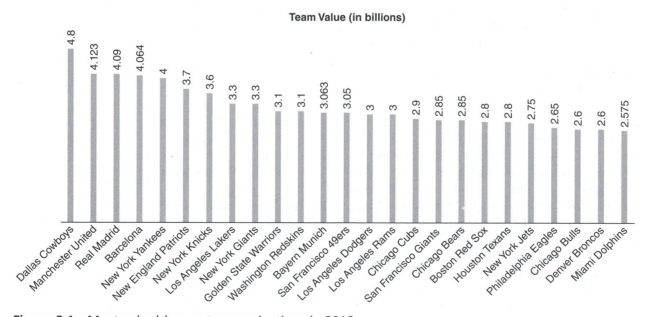

Figure 2.1 Most valuable sports organizations in 2016.

Matches are now regularly played in major arenas, selling out in a matter of minutes and making stars out of former nerds. The growth has been explosive and can be seen from the following facts just from the past several years:

- *Franchises.* Activision Blizzard's Overwatch League will have franchises in 28 international cities for $20 million each franchise. Similarly, Riot Games is planning on having 10 permanent franchises in its North American League of Legends Championship Series, costing $10 million for existing team owners and $13 million for new team owners (Badenhausen, 2017).

- *Broadcasting.* Riot Games struck a six-year, $300 million deal with Major League Baseball's BAMTech in 2016 to stream and distribute League of Legends content. Similarly, Activision Blizzard signed a two-year streaming deal with Amazon's Twitch (Badenhausen, 2017).

- *Microtransactions.* Riot Games is the king of microtransactions. It reportedly made $1.6 billion in 2015 by selling just cosmetic items for characters in League of Legends.

- *Professionalism.* Professional e-sports teams are popping up across the world with major sponsors (chasing the coveted 18- to 30-something males), competing in major tournaments, and having professional dieticians, trainers, coaches, and related personnel—similar to any major professional team.

Broadcasting

One of the recent developments in the sports broadcasting industry encompasses the world of new media. Some efforts have created major problems for sports promoters. For example, live streaming through platforms such as Periscope can significantly decrease the value and potential revenue for a pay-per-view fight if someone can stream the fight to others free, and millions of people could possibly view the fight without purchasing the rights through pay-per-view.

One of the major issues (and covered in a case study for part V) is the growing number of cord cutters. Cord cutters have cancelled their cable subscriptions to watch shows on Netflix, Amazon, Hulu, YouTube, and numerous other service providers. This has had a significant impact on the bottom line of ESPN and other sports channels. ESPN has lost an estimated 11 million subscribers in the United States alone from those who have canceled their cable subscriptions. This has resulted in significant losses from not only subscription fees but also lost revenue from advertisers, as there were not as many viewers, so advertising rates decreased. This revenue impact and the high price paid for broadcast rights were putting significant financial pressure on the cable sports giant.

While the United States broadcasting market might have been facing some hardships, the international broadcast market still seemed to be thriving. One example was Star India, which agreed to pay £1.97 billion ($2.6 billion) for the television and digital rights of the Indian Premier League (Cricket) for 2018 to 2022. Star group also owns broadcast rights for 18 International Cricket Council global events held during an eight-year cycle from 2015 and India's home international matches (Reuters, 2017).

CONCLUSION

Although anticipating future financial trends for amateur, college, and professional sport, as well as for e-sports and sports broadcasting will be difficult given their dynamic properties, it will be interesting to see how the issues discussed in this chapter evolve over the next decade. Clearly, several developments will affect the financial operations of sport, individual sports organizations, and overall league policies. For example, will the public continue to subsidize stadiums and arenas in times of scarce resources? Will broadcast rights fees keep growing? Will franchise values keep growing? Will high school athletic programs continue to be reduced or eliminated altogether in some circumstances? There are no clear answers to these and many other questions. However, through utilizing financial skills, sports executives can develop and implement appropriate plans to weather any potential financial storm or to, hopefully, financially thrive in the future. Some strategies will work while others will fail. Even the best planners might not see technological or other changes that can significantly affect the finances of a given industry, team, sport, or league.

Class Discussion Topics

1. Should local, state, or federal taxes be increased with the resulting funds used to provide more fitness and sport opportunities? What could be the ramifications?

2. Are travel teams hurting the youth sport industry?

3. Provide three specific examples of how stadium subsidies can positively influence a local community.

4. What variables will continue to drive up the market value of sports franchises?

5. What do you think the future of e-sports will be, and will they make it to the Olympics? If they become full Olympic sports (rather than exhibition sports), how would that affect the game publishers?

6. Will broadcast rights decrease at a certain time? What variables might affect the future direction of broadcast rights? What is the best e-sports game publisher? Use financial data to support your conclusion rather than just what game you personally like.

3

Basic Financial Concepts

Chapter Objectives

After studying this chapter, you should be able to do the following:

- Distinguish between revenue and expenses.
- Describe the differences among finance, economics, and accounting.
- Identify the elements of the three primary financial statements: balance sheets, income statements, and cash flow statements.
- Define common financial ratios used to assess an organization's liquidity, activity, and profitability.
- Understand the concept of time value of money.
- Understand the concept of future value, including its calculation for a single amount of cash received today.
- Understand the concepts of present and future value.
- Calculate the present value of annuities.

Chapter 3 deals with the keys to financial understanding—revenue and expenses. Some of the basic tools of financial management such as financial statements, financial ratios, and time value of money will also be addressed in this chapter. All businesses revolve around money. Money is needed to pay bills, pay employees, order items, sell items, pay taxes, or borrow money. Businesses need to address where the money comes from, where it goes, how to track it, and why the economy functions in a given manner. This chapter investigates these issues by first examining revenue and expenses for various sports organizations. The chapter then examines the role that accounting plays in identifying and tracking revenue and expenses.

REVENUES AND EXPENSES

We all have bills to pay. We also normally have a source of funds, whether from a job, loans, or family. This section highlights how we make and spend money in the sport business. Revenues represent money coming into a sport business. Revenue can come from ticket sales, broadcast contracts, concession sales, sponsorship agreements, and a host of other opportunities. The opposite of revenues is expenses. Expenses are costs that are incurred. Typical expenses for a professional team include player salaries, equipment, travel, executive salaries, rent, and insurance premiums. Each business has different revenues and expenses, and they are constantly changing. A health club might have revenues of $2 million one year, but if 250 members do not renew their memberships, the revenues can plunge. Similarly, if members owe the club money, the club has **credit** in money owed. On the flip side, if the club does not pay its employees, then it owes money, which is a debt. If you have ever spent more than you could afford on a credit card, your expenses might spiral out of control and create debt. Debt is money owed to others.

Revenues and expenses are numbers; they are not abstract ideas. To understand and use these numbers to make financial decisions, one must have a basic knowledge of accounting concepts and audited financial statements. The next two sections will cover these topics.

Art of Accounting

Many refer to accounting as an art rather than a science (Griffin, 1991). There are two primary forms of accounting: financial accounting and managerial accounting. Both are important for sports organizations, but each serves a different purpose. **Financial accounting** is the process of recording, summarizing, and reporting the financial transactions of an organization. The end result of this process is the creation of three primary **financial statements**: balance sheets, income statements, and cash flow statements. In comparison, **managerial accounting** is the use of these financial statements to make managerial decisions about the organization. Overall, managerial accounting is for internal use to make decisions about the organization while financial accounting is outward focused toward external stakeholders. An audited income statement can be used to help make internal decisions, but it is primarily used for **shareholders**, other investors, and government authorities—so it is considered a tool of financial accounting. Managerial accounting will produce an internal budget, as an example.

Although financial analysis cannot exist unless accounting systems have developed the appropriate numbers for analyzing past performance, there is never any guarantee that the numbers relied on are correct. Accounting produces financial statements consisting of numbers, but the numbers refer only to those components of a business that are quantifiable. Over the past several decades, a new approach to managerial accounting has been the **balanced scorecard** approach, which examines numerical and subjective criteria to understand how an organization is doing. The balanced scorecard is a performance evaluation tool used to evaluate all aspects of a company's operation in an integrated fashion. Through taking a cause-and-effect approach, the balanced scorecard can help a business understand that every action has an effect and that without proper planning and acting across a company, the company will have a hard time meeting financial and other objectives.

Accounting systems also use professional judgments and estimates when absolute objective evidence does not exist (Griffin, 1991). Although such judgments are typically accurate, anyone reading financial statements has to assume that the information may include inaccuracies. There is never a sure bet in finance, and the best you can hope for from financial statements is an accurate portrait of a business based on data analyzed by an accountant—a human being who can also make errors.

There is often confusion among the terms *accounting*, *finance*, and *economics*. As mentioned previously, accounting is a system of recording, summarizing, analyzing, verifying, and reporting business and financial transactions. Finance is the management, creation, and study of money, investments, and other financial instruments. In contrast, economics is a social science focused on the production, distribution and consumption of goods and services by people, companies, and nations. Economics studies how individuals, businesses, governments, and nations make choices on allocating scarce resources such as whether building a stadium will increase tax revenue for a community. Economics will not tell a sports executive the financial impact of a decision, but it can help identify needs or threats to consider when making a decision. For example, if a local economy is struggling, then economists might predict slower growth. This slower growth can affect the ability to sell tickets, which can result in lower ticket demands—which should be reflected in lower sales in a budget. Thus, finance, economics, and accounting all come to play when making sound fiscal decisions.

Audited Financial Statements

Financial statements are compiled from a firm's accounting records. These financial statements include the balance sheet, income statement, and statement of cash flows. Financial statements are intended to provide information about a business in a consistent manner as a result of efforts by accountants to follow **generally accepted accounting principles (GAAP)**.

Accountants can make errors, and some make outright falsehoods; an auditor is often the last person who can possibly discover any discrepancies. This concern was highlighted in the multiple accounting scandals at companies such as Enron,

WorldCom, Tyco, and Adelphia in the 1990s and early 2000s. The ease with which companies, executives, and accountants could manipulate company records encouraged Congress to pass the Sarbanes-Oxley Act of 2002, forcing executives of publicly traded companies to certify that all their financial data were accurate. Violators could face significant fines and even incarceration. Executives still need accountants to **audit** the numbers to ensure their accuracy. Most companies attempt to obtain an **independent audit** of the work performed by their accountants. Such an audit is often undertaken even if an external accounting firm was used to prepare the initial financial statements. An **auditor** uses the statements on auditing standards issued by the Auditing Standards Board of the American Institute of Certified Public Accountants. These standards were developed to help ensure that audits are conducted in a systematic manner. After thoroughly analyzing all the financial statements, the auditor prepares a report that includes the following statements (Griffin, 1991):

♦ The auditor is independent from the company's management.

♦ The financial statements were audited.

♦ The financial statements are management's responsibility, and the auditor's role is to express an opinion on the financial statements.

After the audit is completed, the auditor prepares an opinion that addresses the fairness of the financial statements, the degree to which the financial statements comply with generally accepted accounting principles, and any noticeable changes in accounting principles from industry norms (Griffin, 1991). The final opinion reached by the auditor can be

♦ an unqualified opinion that the statements are accurate,

♦ a qualified opinion,

♦ an adverse opinion indicating that the statements do not conform with required principles, or

♦ a **disclaimer** indicating that the auditor was unable to complete the report because the company failed to provide certain data.

A typical unqualified opinion might include a statement such as the following:

> In our opinion, the financial statements above present fairly, in all material respects, the financial position of the team as of June 31, 2018, and the results of its operations and its cash flows for the year then ended in conformity with generally accepted accounting principles.

The accounting system objectives discussed in this section relate to what has already happened. Accounting statements are reviewed to determine what occurred during the designated period. But accounting does not indicate what should occur in the future. Budgeting is the process that can indicate what steps should be taken in the future. The budget sets the company's road map for the future and is based on the company's goals and objectives. Budgeting, which is covered in chapter 7, is the first step in the financial process after the accountants analyze past performance.

TYPES OF FINANCIAL STATEMENTS

The balance sheet displays the financial condition of a business at a single point in time, offering information about assets, liabilities, and owners' equity. The income statement describes a business' profit or loss over a given length of time, such as a month, quarter, or year. It provides information about a business' operating performance over that period. The statement of cash flows indicates how the cash position of a business has changed over a given period. For example, the firm may see its cash position depleted through the purchase of machinery or supplies. The firm's cash position can also be diminished through the paying down of debt or the paying of dividends to shareholders. For example, the income statement may show that a business had a profitable year, yet the company's cash holdings can decline. The statement of cash flows can be used to determine what happened to the business' cash. When examining financial statements, note that some terms are interchangeable whereas others are not. For example, *sales* and *revenues* are interchangeable;

profits, *earnings*, and *income* are the same; but *costs* are different from *expenses*. Costs refer to money spent on manufacturing a product or service, whereas expenses refer to money spent on developing, producing, selling, and managing the product or service. Chapter 11 will go into greater detail on financial statements.

Balance Sheet

The balance sheet is used by accountants to give a picture of the business at a single point in time, as if the business were standing still. Here is the basic equation that all balance sheets follow:

$$assets = liabilities + owners'\ equity$$

Because this basic definition must always hold, **capital** provided by investors is always equal to the assets of the firm minus the liabilities of the firm. The left side of the balance sheet (debit side) is what a company owns; the right side (credit side) indicates how the assets were financed. Given the preceding equation, when any two variables of the equation are known, we can always solve for the third using basic math.

In the liabilities section of the balance sheet, liabilities are listed in the order in which they must be paid. Current liabilities consist of obligations that must be paid down in one year or less, and long-term liabilities consist of items that will not be paid for within one year. The liabilities and **stockholders' equity** (capital provided by investors) portions of the balance sheet typically reflect decisions about the sources of financing for the business.

Income Statement

The income statement measures a business' profitability over a specific period, such as a year or a quarter. Income is defined as follows:

$$income = revenue - expenses$$

Whereas the balance sheet provides us with a snapshot at a single point in time, the income statement can be viewed as a film portraying how the organization performed between the single snapshots depicted on two balance sheets.

The income statement typically consists of three sections. The first section includes the revenues and expenses from the company's

Selling concession items can generate significant revenue that will be reported on the income statement.

operations. Second, a nonoperating section of the income statement includes financing costs and any income earned by financial investments. For Under Armour, the interest expense represents financing costs. Typically, the nonoperating section of the income statement includes all taxes paid by the enterprise. The third section of the income statement is the net income of the business.

Statement of Cash Flows

From the perspective of financial analysis, the importance of financial statements lies in their ability to provide information about an organization's **cash flow.** Firms have value when they generate cash flow for investors. *Cash flow* refers to cash flowing both into and out of the business. Recall that income statements include noncash expenses such as depreciation. The amount of depreciation reported on a business' income statement has no effect whatsoever on the cash generated by the business. When the business reports depreciation, the dollar amount reported as depreciation is not directly paid to any vendors or employees, as would be the case with other operating expense categories. The statement of cash flows is a financial statement that reports changes in a company's cash holdings over a particular period.

FINANCIAL RATIOS

Now that we have a good understanding of financial statements, it is important to address the goal of financial ratios. Financial ratios aid in the evaluation of financial statements. Information from financial statements is used to compute financial ratios that provide insight into the condition of a business. Commonly used financial ratios focus on the following areas:

◆ Liquidity
◆ Activity
◆ Financial leverage
◆ Profitability
◆ Firm valuation

Liquidity focuses on the ability of an organization to meet its short-term financial obligations. Activity ratios measure how effectively a firm manages its assets, while **financial leverage ratios** provide information about the extent to which an organization relies on debt (loans) rather **equity** (stocks) for financing. When a firm relies on more debt than equity, its financial leverage ratio increases. Firms with a higher level of financial leverage may be more likely to face financial distress or bankruptcy.

The bottom line for for-profit companies is their ability to generate sufficient earnings to continue to grow and reward shareholders. The level of profits for a sports organization is measured through a series of profitability ratios such as the **net profit margin**, **gross profit margin**, **return on assets (ROA)**, and **return on equity (ROE)**. Finally, **firm valuation ratios** inform us on the value of sports organizations. In general, this is achieved through two methods: **market value** and **book value**.

Financial ratios are also important for companies because they serve as a barometer against three different benchmarks:

1. Previous company ratios
2. Competitors' ratios
3. Ratios of other firms of similar size and scope

Chapter 13 will go into greater detail on the specific ratios such as the current ratio, inventory turnover ratio, debt ratio, net profit margin, and price–earnings ratio. But it should be remembered that financial ratios are a key component in the analysis of financial statements. They are critical in the analysis of sports organizations, their competition, and the industry as a whole.

TIME VALUE OF MONEY

No discussion on financial analysis can be complete without examining the time value of money. It is impossible to examine a $1 investment today versus one from 15 years ago without realizing that $1 from 15 years ago might be worth $5 in today's dollars. This section highlights why money is sensitive to time and how to calculate changes in value based on time constraints.

A key issue in valuing these flows is their timing. A dollar received today is worth more than a dollar received in the future. **Time value of money** represents the concept that money in today's dollars decreases in value the further out into the future it is expected to be received because it could be invested over that time. With this concept in mind, any investor or business needs to examine the time in which investment decisions will be made and critically examine how that time frame will ultimately affect the invested amount and projected payout.

CONCEPTS INTO PRACTICE

Assume that Under Armour (UA) has a parcel of real estate that it wishes to sell and has lined up two prospective buyers. One buyer, SportsTech, is willing to enter into a contract to pay $1,000,000 immediately for the parcel of land. A second buyer, Sports Worldwide, has offered to pay $1,025,000 for the land but will make the actual payment in one year's time. At first glance, it may appear that UA should take the Sports Worldwide offer, because Sports Worldwide is willing to pay more for the land, but looks can be deceiving!

The way to evaluate which offer UA should accept is to note that if it accepted the offer from SportsTech, it could hypothetically deposit the funds in a one-year certificate of deposit (CD) that earns 5% interest per year. UA would start out with $1,000,000 in the bank (**principal**) and would earn interest equal to 0.05 multiplied by $1,000,000. As a result, UA would have the following on deposit in one year:

$$\$1,000,000 + (0.05 \times \$1,000,000) = \$1,050,000$$

or

$$\$1,000,000 \times 1.05 = \$1,050,000$$

In other words, UA would have on deposit its initial $1,000,000 principal plus $50,000 in interest, which equals $1,050,000. By contrast, if UA accepted the Sports Worldwide offer, it would have only $1,025,000 available in one year—$25,000 less than it would have if it had invested the initial $1,000,000 in the one-year CD. Clearly, UA is better off taking the offer from SportsTech.

In working through this example we made use of the concept of future value. **Future value (FV)** is the value of an initial lump sum of money after it is invested over one or more periods. The future value in one year's time of the $1,000,000 received from SportsTech is $1,050,000. Note that the future value of any given investment income reflects the interest earned on that investment.

Another way of looking at this example is to examine how much money UA must deposit in a CD that earns 5% to have $1,025,000 in one year. The amount of money that would yield $1,025,000 if invested today at a 5% interest rate is the **present value (PV)** of $1,025,000 received in one year. We can solve for PV as follows:

$$PV \times 1.05 = \$1,025,000$$

Solving for PV gives us the following:

$$PV = \$1,025,000 / 1.05 = \$976,190$$

So, if UA has $976,190 today, this lump sum can grow to $1,025,000 in one year as a result of earning interest.

In general, the formula for the present value can be written as follows:

$$PV = C_1 / (1 + r)$$

PV = present value

C_1 = cash flow received at the end of one year

r = appropriate interest rate

The variable r, the interest rate or percentage return that can be earned on an initial amount of money, is also known as the **discount rate**. In our example, the 5% annual return that UA earns on its financial investment (i.e., a one-year CD) is used as the discount rate to value the $1,025,000 received in one year.

Our analysis of present value indicates that a payment of $1,025,000 received in one year from Sports Worldwide has a present value of $976,190 today. In other words, at a 5% interest rate, UA would find receiving $976,190 today from Sports Worldwide or receiving $1,025,000 in one year equally acceptable alternatives. Given $976,190 today, the company can deposit the funds in a one-year CD that will allow it to receive $1,025,000 in one year.

Because SportsTech offered to pay $1,000,000 today, this offer has a present value of $1,000,000. Thus, our present value analysis suggests that UA should take the SportsTech offer.

Future Value More Than One Period Into the Future

So far, we have looked at the concept of present value and future value in the context of cash flows over a single period. We will now show how this can be generalized over more than one period. This process is critical because most business deals do not start and end in one year but rather last several years.

CONCEPTS INTO PRACTICE

Assume that Jane Smith owns shares of UA common stock, and the return on the stock is 6%. To keep things simple, let us also assume that Smith paid $1 per share for UA's common stock. If she sells her shares at the end of one year, she will have $1 plus the return on that dollar at r% for each share. Because r is 6%, she will have $1.06 at the end of one year.

$$\$1 + \$1r = \$1 \times (1 + r) = \$1 \times 1.06 = \$1.06$$

r = expected rate of return

At the end of the year, she has two choices. She can cash out her stock and take the $1.06 per share or hold the stock for a second year. The process of holding the stock and accruing a further return over the second year is referred to as **compounding**.

If Smith decides to hold the stock for another year, then at the end of two years she will have the following:

$$\$1 \times (1 + r) \times (1 + r)$$
$$= \$1 \times (1 + r)^2 = \$1 \times (\$1.06)^2 = \$1.1236$$

At the end of two years, she will have transformed $1.00 into $1.1236. Notice that at the end of two years, she will generate $0.1236 in **compound interest** or return. That is, each payment of interest or return that is reinvested earns a return also.

This process can be generalized over many periods of time (t) with the following formula for the future value (FV) of an investment:

$$FV = C_0 \times (1 + r)^t$$

FV = future value

C_0 = initial amount of cash that is invested today

r = interest rate or rate of return

t = number of years over which the cash is invested

We can do this calculation by hand or with the help of a table. Table B.1 presents future values of $1 at the end of t periods, a variable number of periods into the future over which the $1 is earning interest. Traditionally, t periods on a future value chart range from 1 year to 20 or 30 years. To use the table, locate the appropriate interest rate or return column and move down to the appropriate period row as indicated in the period column. For example, you could find that the future value of $1 that is received two years into the future is $1.1236. This figure is reached if you assume a 6% rate of return. If you started out with $500 and earned a 6% annual return over two years, then the future value at the end of two years would be $561.80.

$$FV = 500 \times 1.1236 = \$561.80$$

As another example, suppose that an investor buys a $1,000 bond issued by UA. The bond pays 10% interest and is redeemable in 20 years. Going to table B.1, you can find 20 years as the t period and then move across to the column labeled 10% interest. The number on the chart is 6.7275. Thus, FV = $1,000 multiplied by 6.7275, which yields a future value for the $1,000 investment after 20 years of $6,728. Through compounding interest, the bond increases more than sixfold if it is kept for the entire 20 years. This example highlights how the federal government can sell U.S. bonds for $50 now and guarantee payment of $100 in 10 years. Through compounding, the $50 investment can produce a four to five times greater return in 10 years, while still allowing the government to pay the investor double his or her money.

Present Value More Than One Period Into the Future

Assume that a professional athlete such as Mike Trout has signed a contract including $2 million in deferred compensation that will be paid at the end of two years. Assume that if he were to receive compensation today, he could invest that money in a financial vehicle (such as a CD) that earns a 4% annual return. We would like to know how much money received today would be worth $2 million after earning a 4% annual return for two years. This can be written as follows:

$$PV \times (1 + r)^t = FV$$

PV = present value

r = annual rate of return

t = number of years

FV = future value

$$PV \times (1.04)^2 = \$2,000,000$$

In this equation, PV is the amount of money that would need to be invested today to grow to $2 million in two years.

Solving for PV gives us the following:

$$PV = \$2,000,000 / (1.04)^2$$
$$= \$2,000,000 / 1.0816$$
$$= \$1,849,112$$

This equation indicates that if Mike Trout received $1,849,112 today, invested it, and earned a 4% annual return, he would have $2 million at the end of two years. This process of obtaining a present value is known as **discounting**. The $2 million is discounted by a **discount factor**, or **present value factor**, which equals 1 divided by $(1.04)^2$, or 0.9246, in this example. Using this discount factor, we can calculate the present value as $2,000,000 multiplied by 0.9246, or $1,849,112.

An alternative way to calculate the results obtained from this equation is to use table B.2 in appendix B to obtain a present value factor. This table shows the present value of $1 to be received after t periods. To use the table, locate the appropriate number of periods row and go across to the appropriate interest rate column. In our example, the number of periods is 2 and the interest rate is 4%. Thus, the present value factor is 0.9246. If we multiply $2 million by the present value factor, we find that the present value of $2 million received in two years is $1,849,112.

In general, the present value of a sum of money received t periods in the future can be written as follows:

$$PV = C_t / (1 + r)^t = C_t \times PVF_{r,t}$$

PV = present value

C_t = cash flow received at the end of t periods

r = annual return of interest

$PVF_{r,t}$ = the appropriate present value factor for $1 received t periods into the future

We can extend this example to finding the present value of multiple payments. Assume that Elena Delle Donne, a player in the Women's National Basketball Association, has signed a contract that will pay her $100,000 immediately, $110,000 at the end of one year, and $115,000 at the end of two years. Assume that she can earn a

Table 3.1 Present Value of Elena Delle Donne's Cash Flows Over Several Years

Year	Cash flow ($)	Present value factor	Present value ($)
0	100,000	1.0000	100,000
1	110,000	0.9615	105,765
2	115,000	0.9246	106,329
Total			312,094

4% annual return investing the money. The present value of the cash flows is shown in table 3.1.

The present value of the cash flows under this contract equals $312,094. In other words, the payment structure under this contract is equivalent to paying Donne $312,094 in one lump sum today.

Annuities

For certain types of finance problems, shortcuts can be used to calculate present values. In particular, we will discuss shortcut methods for annuities. An **annuity** is a constant stream of payments that is received for a fixed number of periods. Annuities are common in the real world. Home mortgages, leases, student loans, and pensions paid at retirement are all examples of annuities. When evaluating annuities, we use the following formula:

$$PV = C / (1 + r) + C / (1 + r)^2 + C / (1 + r)^3 + \ldots + C / (1 + r)^t$$

PV = present value

C = a constant cash flow per period

r = annual rate of return

t = number of periods during which the cash flow will be received

This equation is cumbersome, but fortunately it can be simplified to yield the following formula for an annuity that is paid over t periods (Brigham & Ehrhardt, 2014):

$$PV = C\{1 - [1 / (1 + r)^n]\} / r$$

PV = present value

C = a constant cash flow per period

r = annual rate of return

n = number of periods during which the cash flow will be received

CONCEPTS INTO PRACTICE

An example of an annuity is the compensation package received by Nick Saban, the head football coach at the University of Alabama. In May 2017, Saban signed a contract extension that would pay him approximately $7,000,000 in salary for eight years (Patterson, 2017). For our purposes, this is treated as an eight-year annuity, effective August 1, 2017. If the appropriate discount rate is 7%, then by plugging these values into the equation, we obtain the following:

$$PV = \$7,000,000 \times \{1 - [1 / (1.07)^8]\} / 0.07$$
$$= \text{periodic payment} \times \text{annuity factor}$$
$$= \$7,000,000 \times 5.9713$$
$$= \$41,799,100$$

The present value of Saban's contract, as of August 1, 2017, when he signed it (and assuming a 7% discount rate), equaled $41,799,100. The numbers in braces in the equation are the present value factor for an annuity. In this example involving the value of Saban's salary, the present value factor for the annuity equals 5.9713. Table B.3 assists in determining the present value of $1 per period for t periods. Again, interest rates are shown across the top row, and the number of periods is shown on each row in the far left column. Consulting the table, you will see that for an interest rate of 7% and an annuity that is received for 8 periods, the present value factor is 5.9713, which we obtained in the calculation.

ECONOMIC VERSUS FINANCIAL ANALYSIS

One final note of importance to those starting to analyze the foundation of sport finance is that, as with accounting and finance, there is significant difference between finance and economics.

Economics is the study of social, governmental, and numerous other factors that can influence the financial state of the sport industry, but economics is not sport finance. For example, economic analysis can highlight that the economy is in a tailspin or that that the oversupply of tickets will drive down the value of certain tickets. Such analysis would be important to help a sports organization make a financial decision if too many outstanding tickets exist.

One example of how economic analysis is critical for financial decision making is the concept of **elasticity of demand**, which measures the degree to which a change in pricing affects the unit sales of a product. Thus, if ticket prices were increased $10 for a previously $100 ticket, the demand would be inelastic if such a change would not affect demand. If 1,000 fans purchased a ticket at $100 the prior year and 1,000 will purchase the ticket at the new price, the demand is inelastic. But if 500 fans refuse to pay the increased price, the demand would be considered elastic.

Finally, **economic impact** is a key focus of sport economics. Many people disapprove of public funding to build sports facilities. The argument raised by these people is that a private owner is gaining a benefit when public funds are used to build these facilities. Supporters of such projects point to the increased economic activities associated with building a sports facility. Their claim is that the construction spurs economic activity and creates employment opportunities. Economic impact analysis is sometimes focused on financial analysis and the ability of a given public entity to afford to build a facility. This analysis would examine the cost for issuing debt and the source of the money to pay back the debt. Economists can track whether such deals are a value for a community. Sometimes a new stadium will produce a positive impact on a local community with new businesses opening around the stadium. At other times, the economic impact might be negative as local government might have provided the stadium developer significant tax incentives to build and that would pull away valuable tax dollars needed in a community. Needless to say, the process of determining the economic and financial costs and benefits of facility construction is quite complex.

CONCLUSION

This chapter provided an initial glimpse into the variety of revenues and expenses that sports organizations can encounter. The chapter then examined sport accounting as a means to determine where money is going or coming. By using standardized methods, all parties can hope to have accurate information on which to base financial decisions. Due to this, all sports organizations need to have timely and accurate financial statements in the form of a balance sheet, income statement, and cash flow statement. These financial tools are vital to a sports manager's knowledge of the financial situation of their organization.

Additionally, this chapter addressed ratio analysis. Ratios allow the sports manager to compare the financial performance of the organization to prior years, other organizations, and the industry as a whole. They are vital to understanding an organization's liquidity, profitability, and financial leverage.

Finally, this chapter covered the use of time value of money to place values on future expected cash flows. This concept is particularly important for sports organizations that must look at valuing a future stream of lease payments to make decisions about whether to own or lease an asset. As a result, understanding time value of money will be shown to be important in financial decision making throughout the rest of this book.

Class Discussion Topics

1. What is the difference between accounting and finance?

2. Why is understanding sport economics important for someone working in sport finance?

3. Briefly explain the differences among a balance sheet, a cash flow statement, and an income statement.

4. What happens to the present value of an annuity if the discount rate is increased? What happens to the future value if the discount rate is increased?

5. If we assume an interest rate of 5%, would you rather have $1,000 today or receive $1,120 in 3 years?

6. Assume that two athletes sign 10-year contracts that pay out a total of $100 million over the life of the contracts. One contract will pay the $100 million in equal installments over the 10 years. The other contract will pay the $100 million in installments, but the installments increase 5% per year. Which athlete received the better deal?

Assets and Liabilities

Chapter Objectives

After studying this chapter, you should be able to do the following:

- Classify assets and liabilities for a sports organization.
- Differentiate between different types of assets and liabilities.
- Identify strategies to reduce liabilities and increase assets.

The goal of this chapter is to provide an overview of assets and **liabilities**. Some people might confuse assets with revenue and liabilities with expenses. However, they are a lot more. As discussed in chapter 3, assets and liabilities are reflected on a balance sheet. Revenue and expenses are highlighted on an income statement. While this is one difference, the major difference is that it is usually impossible to generate revenue without having some valuable assets. The amount of expenses owed can be affected by liabilities but will extend beyond liabilities. If a team does not have any liabilities, there still could be numerous expenses.

The best way to look at this is a personal example. Assume you are looking for work because you do not have any income. Because you do not have any income, you have no revenue coming in. However, you own a car. The car is an asset. You can start a driving service or start working for Uber or Lyft and turn that asset, which had value but was not effectively utilized, into an asset that produced revenue. Assume you are leasing your car and pay $200 a month for the car. The **note (promissory)** associated with your lease is a liability that is due every month, and failure to pay it will result in default and losing the vehicle (i.e., losing the asset that can make you money). There are going to be expenses with the vehicle such as gas and maintenance. These expenses are not liabilities because they are associated with how much you utilize the asset. Furthermore, if you prepay your auto insurance then that is not only an expense but also an asset because you have several months of insurance to protect you and the asset. This simple example helps highlight why it is so important to understand assets and liabilities in contrast to just revenue and expenses. Revenue and expenses are covered in the next chapters, but many people think only about making and spending money while their foundation—assets and liabilities—are the underlying key elements.

This chapter will explore what assets and liabilities are and their intersection with revenue and expenses. The chapter also helps explain what issues can affect an asset, which can result in the asset losing its ability to generate revenue. Lastly, this chapter will help show how liabilities are not necessarily a bad thing and that companies will normally need liabilities in order to grow.

WHERE TO FIND ASSETS

As mentioned at the start of this chapter, assets help generate revenue or have the potential to generate revenue. According to accounting standards, an asset is something an organization owns that can provide future economic benefits. Examples include cash, inventory, accounts receivable, land, buildings, equipment, and intangible assets. We will discuss the various types of assets shortly. Current assets, inventory, fixed assets, and employees are some examples. It should be noted that assets can be found throughout a sports organization. There are various ways to categorize assets, but a good manager knows how to find the necessary assets and leverage them to help a sport business achieve its goals.

There are multiple types of assets that can be owned. They are often classified as tangible and intangible. **Tangible assets** can be touched. A car is a tangible asset. In contrast, **intangible assets** cannot be touched. Examples can be your love of a car or the joy it provides you. There is value, but that asset associated with the car cannot be touched. Even with intangible assets, there are those that have no real value (love of a car) and those that do, such as the copyright or trademark of the car, which has value and can be sold by the car manufacturer.

Current Assets

Current assets refer to anything on hand that can quickly—usually in less than one year—be turned into cash to help pay bills. Because current assets can be converted quickly to cash, they are often called cash equivalents. Of course, cash is already **liquid** (and sometimes called a **liquid asset**), so it is easy to see how it falls within the classification of current assets. Typical current assets include the following:

- *Cash.* This can be in bank accounts or even a petty cash drawer.
- *Bank deposits.* These can be **certificates of deposits (CDs)** or other investments that can be removed from the account at a set date or early.
- *Marketable securities.* These can be stocks or bonds owned in other companies that can be quickly sold on the open market (some **securities** are encumbered and more dif-

ficult to sell and as such would not be considered current assets).

♦ *Accounts receivables*. There are various accounts from customers owing you money to refunds that are owed. Not all receivables are current assets, as some debts might be hard or impossible to collect. An aged account is one that is older and might be hard to collect. For example, if you have not paid a bill in six months, the account has aged and might be considered uncollectable (don't think this means they will not have a bill collector chase you down or sue you). That is where aging of accounts receivables comes into play, and some debts that are owed will be written off if not paid in a certain time because they would either be uncollectable or litigation will be necessary to get any of that money back.

♦ **Prepaid expense**. This represents any prepaid amount for items that have yet to be consumed such as insurance, phone service, advertising, Internet service, and legal services.

Inventory

There is a debate by some as to whether inventory should be a current asset or a more long-term asset. Part of this debate is whether an inventory item can be sold quickly. Some raw materials can be sold quickly. Other raw materials might be too specialized to sell easily in their raw state. Similarly, there are some inventory items that might be partially completed and would be hard or impossible to sell. Furthermore, there are costs associated with maintaining inventory as an asset such as storage and moving costs. The various types of inventory include

♦ raw materials inventory,
♦ work-in-process inventory,
♦ finished goods inventory,
♦ merchandise inventory, and
♦ supplies.

Many teams have significant inventory that might be overlooked. For example, how many uniforms does a team have, and in what condition are the items? Imagine having to purchase 90 to 100 new football helmets every year. Even if new helmets are not purchased, the old helmets might need to be reconditioned. It should be noted that a football helmet would be more closely compared to supplies (such as paper clips and pens), which are needed by the business but have a much lower resale value as only fans or youth sports programs might purchase such helmets. They are a major asset, though, because it could cost thousands of dollars if a team would have to replace all of its helmets.

One of the key job responsibilities for someone responsible for ordering equipment and supplies is the cost to purchase, store, and dispose of inventory. There is a cost to order items used by a sports organization. For example, if a team is going to print some T-shirts to sell at a concession stand, there will be various costs associated with the purchase. Some of these costs will turn into assets. For example, the ordering time, time to pick colors, and copyrighting or trademarking the logo and design all take time and cost money, but not everything in the process is an asset. The design, logo, and color scheme all represent intangible assets. However, the screens to undertake the silk screening cost money and can be used again, so they are an asset. Then there are the T-shirts themselves, the cost to transport them, to store them, to sell them, and even to donate them. This example helps show how assets do not just sit around but have various expenses associated with them.

Fixed Assets

Fixed assets refer to assets that are more difficult to convert to cash and are often associated with a facility. Some people refer to the term **property, plant, and equipment (PPE)** to refer to fixed assets. For many sports organizations, a stadium or arena could be the largest fixed asset as it can be worth hundreds of millions of dollars. Even if a sports organization does not own its building, but leases it, it will still have many fixed assets such as treadmills, spinning bikes, and weights. While the most common type of fixed asset is a building and the land it is on, there can be other fixed assets such as

♦ computer equipment and software;
♦ furniture, fixtures, and office equipment;
♦ leasehold improvements (if the organization does not own the land or building);

- machinery such as production equipment; and
- vehicles from cars to forklifts and golf carts.

The assets highlighted are tangible assets that can be touched. Some fixed assets are classified as intangible and are recorded on the balance sheet within a separate line item. Not all intangible assets are fixed assets. This has been seen when some teams have moved and taken their name and intellectual property with them (such as the Baltimore Colts when they moved to Indianapolis). These intangible assets are either purchased or obtained as part of an acquisition. Examples of these intangible assets are

- brand names,
- broadcast licenses,
- copyrights,
- domain names,
- franchise agreements,

PROFESSIONAL TEAM BALANCE SHEET

It is hard to find balance sheet examples of major professional teams in the United States. Unlike many international professional soccer teams that are publicly traded, very few U.S.-based teams are publicly traded. Published financial reports can shed significant light on how a team operates. Due to a lawsuit involving the owner of the Carolina Jaguars, financial data from 2012 was published, analyzing the financials of the Richardson Sports Limited Partnership and subsidiaries (the parent company for the team). Table 4.1 is a snapshot with the rough numbers from the 2012 balance sheet as reported by the partnership's accountants, Deloitte Touche.

This example helps show how player contracts represent both a noncurrent asset and a liability. As highlighted in some of the categories, areas that might be thought of as revenue are actually liabilities. For example, deferred revenue can come from season ticket sales. Revenue is received, but it is a liability since the team then has to play the games, and that is a liability.

Table 4.1 Balance Sheet

ASSETS		LIABILITIES AND PARTNERS' CAPITAL	
CURRENT ASSETS (IN MILLIONS 2012)		**CURRENT LIABILITIES**	
Cash and cash equivalents	$38	Accounts payable	$14
Restricted cash and investments	$0.25	Deferred revenue—current	$22
Accounts receivables	$4.3	Player contract liabilities—current	$53
Prepaid expenses	$23	Accrued interest	$1.8
Total current assets	$66	Total current liabilities	$91
NONCURRENT ASSETS		Notes payable to bank	$45
Investment in NFL franchise	$47.7	Customer deposits	$10
Player contracts (net)	$141.4	Fair value of interest rate swaps	$3.5
Fixed assets (net)	$36.6	Player contract liabilities	$33
Cash reserves held by the NFL	$0	Permanent seat license revenue sharing	$1.8
Stadium related intangible assets	$5	Deferred revenue	$11.7
Other assets	$16.5	Other noncurrent liabilities	$16
Total noncurrent assets	$247	Total liabilities	$214
Total	$313	Partners' capital	$99
		Total	$313

♦ goodwill,

♦ licenses,

♦ patents,

♦ permits, and

♦ trademarks.

Other items that are considered assets but will never find their way onto an organization's balance sheet can include

♦ the value of a brand image (Dallas Cowboys being America's team),

♦ a well-known win–loss record,

♦ the historical significance of a team for a region,

♦ employee training that makes workers more efficient, and

♦ a process or strategy developed or implemented by the business that helps the organization run more effectively.

The key for intangible assets is they have significant value, if they can be nurtured and grown. Some of the most common brand names include Nike, Coca-Cola, and ESPN. Teams can also have significant value in their names, such as the Dallas Cowboys, the New York Yankees, or Manchester United. Each team has numerous—even millions—of fans around the world and on social media. Each team has numerous licensed goods sold to a thirsty public willing to pay for numerous trinkets bearing the team's name and logo. These are only a sample of the value associated with the intellectual assets for many teams.

Employees

One asset that is often overlooked is employees. They do not appear on a balance sheet as an asset, but money owed to employees in terms of wages owed or pension obligations might appear as liabilities. However, employees are often considered one of the most vital assets for a sports organization. We can use a professional sports team as an example. There could be 10 to 20 full-time sales people selling everything from tickets to sponsorship packages. Each employee has experience they bring to the job, and each might have received specific training from the team to make them more valuable. Expenses were incurred in the hiring, training, and promotion process for each employee. Each employee has been trained to generate revenue—an asset. Imagine if a company lost a piece of equipment that helps generate $1 million in revenue a year. The company would be devastated. The same holds true if an employee who generated over $1 million in revenue due to their wonderful sales techniques and rapport with customers leaves. That is why a great employee is an asset. Similar to other assets, they have value and need to be protected. When employees are not treated well they will leave. Employees that have left will need to be replaced, and that process costs money. When so much is invested in employees, it is important to treat them well, train them, manage them, and work with them to maximize the investment made in them. Similarly, if an asset is not taken care of it will break down. That is why it is so important to invest in assets—whether they be personnel, equipment, or facilities.

Besides the value of each employee, some employees are actually classified as assets by government taxing authorities. Professional athletes are considered assets by the U.S. Internal Revenue Service (IRS). The cost of player salaries can be depreciated from a team's tax obligations. This is a very unique attribute to professional sports that is not shared by any other industry. In no industry other than professional sports teams can employees be considered similar to fixed assets such as the plant, equipment, or furniture. This tax break was provided in part by famous baseball team owner Bill Veeck and his loophole is known as the roster depreciation allowance (RDA). Veeck first claimed the RDA with the IRS in 1946, following his purchase of the Cleveland Indians. Veeck assigned 90% of the team's value to intangible assets or player contracts. Veeck argued for depreciation because over time players' skills diminished, similar to other pieces of equipment. The tax rule was meant to address depreciations in the productive value of aging livestock used for work, breeding, and milk production. Veeck might have been the creative one, but he is not alone. In 1970, Bud Selig (the eventual commissioner of Major League Baseball) bought the Seattle Pilots and moved them to Milwaukee. Even though Selig bought the franchise for $10.8 million, he reported to the IRS a purchase price of $600,000, attributing the rest to depreciating player payroll obligation. Similarly, one owner of the Philadelphia Eagles bought the team in 1969 for $16.4 million, but he reported a $50,000 franchise sale price to the federal government (Lamberti, 2012). This is all legal and afforded team owners millions of dollars in tax benefits. It should be noted that this does not represent the price paid for the team, which could result in higher capital gains taxes when a team is sold but rather represents the use of asset depreciation to help reduce tax obligations.

Over the years, the RDA has become more complicated but not more stringent. For around 30 years (until 2004), new team owners could write off 50% of the purchase price over 5 years due to declining player values. In one example, Doubleday & Company sold the New York Mets to Nelson Doubleday Jr. and Fred Wilpon in 1986. Doubleday Jr., the head of Doubleday & Company, basically sold the team to himself, albeit this was technically a change in ownership. The sale occurred exactly six years after Doubleday & Company purchased the team from the Doubleday family so it could once again start the five-year depreciation clock all over again (Durso, 1986). Due to these financial gymnastics (which are all legal) teams could be operating in the red and then owners could transfer losses over to their personal income tax forms, resulting in millions of dollars in tax savings. Starting in 2004, the tax rules were changed so owners claiming the RDA could write off 100% of their franchise purchase price over 15 years of team ownership (Lamberti, 2012).

Similar to other assets, a professional player is not just an expense but an asset that can generate revenue beyond what normal employees might generate. When Real Madrid paid a then-world record for Cristiano Ronaldo in 2009, it was not just for his football (soccer) skills. The team was counting on increasing the sponsorship value and price and also selling numerous jerseys with his name. It was hoped that such revenue would add millions over the cost of his purchase and salary. Likewise, Manchester United signed Park Ji-Sung and Shinji Kagawa not only for their potential contribution to the team but also for their ability to grow the team's presence in Asia—opening up new revenue streams. Similar to other assets, a player can also become a liability. An injured pro player is still owed a salary, they are still technically an asset, but they represent a huge liability and may never reach their asset value potential in the future. That is why teams often purchase injury protection insurance that will compensate them if a player is injured.

Asset Valuation

While there are numerous types of assets, some assets are easier to value than others. As previously mentioned, cash is easy to value, while half-finished inventory might be difficult to value. A nonprofit organization has a charitable mission or objective, but being a nonprofit organization is also an asset. It can help generate more funds because people are willing to donate in order to receive a possible tax benefit. How much then is the nonprofit status worth compared to a similar company that is for profit? The answer depends on the organization. The ability to receive tax-deductible donations is a major benefit. However, the legal requirements and educational or community focus of a nonprofit organization might make many sports organizations incapable of going the nonprofit route. As an example, a YMCA (nonprofit) might be able to accept a donation of land to build a new gym. This reduces the cost of building the gym. In contrast, a for-profit organization would have to buy the land. In such an example, the nonprofit status has significant value.

Noncash assets aren't as easy to value. A building might have multiple valuations based on different perspectives. Someone might value the land a lot less if they want to tear down the existing building and put in a different building for a different use, such as replacing a warehouse with a condominium project. The **value (V)** could also be set by a local taxing authority at a certain rate. A real estate buyer or seller might value it at a rate comparable to similar buildings in the same area. Others might give the building an increased value if the business inside the building will be part of the deal. The value can also be affected by when the valuation was undertaken and numerous other variables. The primary asset valuation techniques are

- liquidation value,
- the difference between book value and market value, and
- the fair value option.

Liquidated value for a business is the value if all the assets are sold. This might be high if the business owns significant land or has valuable intellectual property. However, if the business leases its property and equipment, it might have very little liquidated value if all the assets were to be sold. Book value examines what a product is worth based on the balance sheet. This valuation often has a discounted rate in part due to depreciation of the asset, when it was purchased, the useful life of an item, and related variables. Book value can also refer to a published value of what the asset is worth. In contrast, market value is based on what people would pay for the asset. Thus, a car could have a Blue Book value of $10,000, but if someone really wants the car and is willing to pay $12,000 for it, then there is a $2,000 difference between book and market value. Most people would prefer selling the car for $12,000, while buyers would generally prefer to pay $10,000. The fair value option is what most people would consider to be the fair value of the asset. In our car example, the fair value might be $11,000.

One element that affects an asset's value is whether or not it is impaired. Impairment can take the form of various issues such as whether the asset is damaged, modified, under contract, or used as **collateral** to secure a loan. Any one of these issues affecting an asset will limit the asset's value or what can be done with an asset. For example, a sports organization might want to move an asset secured by a note from one location to another. However, the note holder (lender) might not agree with such a move and can force the organization to keep it where it is—thus limiting the ability to effectively use the asset. This might be done if the lender feels they will lose the ability to confiscate the asset if the borrower defaults on payment. An example could be a $1 million scoreboard where the lender would not want the team taking it to a new location without paying off the note.

Finding and Leveraging Assets

So far this chapter has examined the various types of assets and their value. The first part of the process is to find the assets. Every sports organization will have assets. Even a consulting company has the mental assets of the sports

consultant as an asset. There are numerous assets that need to be tracked, monitored, and evaluated, whether they are employees, equipment, facilities, or the like. For example, a team might think it has $1,000 of food in a fridge, but what if $200 worth of the food has spoiled? Thus, on the books, the asset might be valued at $1,000, but in reality, it is only worth $800. Once the asset is identified, the sports organization has to determine how to leverage that asset.

The next topic to consider is how to leverage existing assets to generate additional revenue. Think of it similar to having a star player and having that player warm the bench. If you know the team will win with the player in the lineup, why isn't the player playing? Similarly, if you know you can make money through using a certain asset, then you should use it. Assume a team has paid $1,000 for a mascot costume. That costume can be used at various games, and the team will probably get its money's worth if the costume will last around five years (assuming $200 a year for the **payback period** and that the costume can be used for around 20 games a year). The team could leverage that asset to generate much more revenue through allowing the costume (and wearer) to go to birthday parties, community events, and other events that can generate revenue and at the same time generate publicity and hopefully more revenue for the team.

In financial terms, leveraging a resource means to multiply the resource's productivity. The goal is to get a given resource to **yield (rate of return)** a greater return without additional input of effort. In the costume example just discussed, once the purchase is made, the team has the costume. If the costume just sits in a closet most of the year, it is wasted. If it is used for birthday parties and 200 event days a year, then the team is really maximizing the benefits of the asset. As an additional example, if you can show your ticket sales people how to get customers to increase their average ticket purchase amounts by 20%, then you have leveraged your sales staff and increased your revenue by 20%. This approach often entails **upselling**, which entails encouraging a purchaser to buy more or more frequently. Current customers are an asset, and they are being leveraged to generate more revenue. The same approach can be used for leveraging any asset to minimize future expenditures. The goal is to use the asset as much as possible. If a business normally replaces its car fleet every five years, instead of replacing all of the cars, maybe some cars can be used for a longer time period. This extends the life of the asset and can save money.

Every sports organization will have multiple assets, which are either not utilized or underutilized. One example is all the cardboard boxes that a stadium or arena will utilize. Numerous concession items will be brought in for every game in cardboard boxes. In the past, these boxes were just thrown away, and every arena already spends a significant amount of money on trash removal. Over the past 20 years, more and more facilities are now selling that cardboard. This turned a liability into an asset. Besides generating revenue, it also looked good for the facility and showed it was trying to be sustainable.

CONCEPTS INTO PRACTICE

Another way to turn assets into cash is by selling items that might have been filling up warehouse space. The Boston Red Sox have had several sales where they have sold old giveaway items, bricks, jerseys, and other old items that were sitting around in storage. In one such sale, they put items into a bag and sold the bags for $75 to $100, and they had lines around historic Fenway Park for people wanting to purchase a piece of history, regardless of what the item might be. This is in addition to selling old seats from the stadium, which can still be purchased for $795 a pair. In addition, historic Fenway Park, as part of its 100-year anniversary in 2012, sold bricks for two entrances where fans could pay to inscribe a personal message. Similar fund-raising strategies utilizing a facility's historical nature and the cost to construct or renovate the facility can be seen at the NASCAR Hall of Fame and many other facilities. NASCAR was using bricks anyway as part of its walkway, so it created a fund-raising opportunity as well.

A well-known event can be an asset. For example, the Special Olympics has regular events, and these events are a major asset for the Special Olympics organization. Many nonprofits tend to utilize assets at their disposal to generate revenue. These assets can range from

celebrity connections serving as fund-raising chairs to offering the use of their property for special events rather than the nonprofit having to pay to use another entity's facilities. Organizations can also utilize their facility to generate additional funds by renting the facility out for various external groups and hosting various dances, concerts, or fund-raising events. There are no limits to the imagination when deciding on what revenue strategies to pursue with assets under your control. The key issues to consider when examining how to leverage assets include

- whether the event is consistent with institutional goals;
- whether an event might run afoul of the law;
- whether an event might be inconsistent with existing contracts, leases, or insurance requirements;
- whether an event or asset usage will generate political conflict or possibly upset key stakeholders;
- whether an event might lead to an asset losing value or being damaged; and
- whether the event will be able to generate future **goodwill** or income.

If an event will satisfy these concerns, then an organization might pursue using its assets to generate additional revenue. Some organizations have valuable resources and decide not to use them. This decision can be made to preserve an asset or to prevent any decrease in the asset's value. Some organizations with a valuable resource might put that resource in a safe location and hope that the asset increases in value. In the Special Olympics example, the connection to the Kennedy family is a very valuable asset. Eunice Kennedy Shriver helped found the games in 1968, and the family is very connected. The Special Olympics needs to steward this asset and not abuse the relationship. While the Kennedy family might feel they need to stay involved, there is significant goodwill on Special Olympics' part when they do not center too many events or demand too much from the Kennedy family. Similar to the Special Olympics, many nonprofits have a famous spokesperson, and to avoid overusing them and the goodwill the spokesperson provides, the nonprofit might only use the asset (spokesperson) as a fund-raising chair every three years so they do not get burned out. A good way to examine this potential is if you have a valuable sports card. Assume you have a Mickey Mantle card worth $1,000. You can use that card as collateral to borrow money to buy more cards. You can sell the card for $1,000 and hopefully pocket some money. You can use that card as a way to market some less valuable cards you really want to sell. You might loan the card for dealers to use as a way to generate some rental income or goodwill with other dealers. Lastly, you might just put the card in a safe location and hope it increases to $1,500 in a couple of years. Similar decisions are made with assets every day by various sports organizations.

Lastly, assets can serve as one of the most important tools for obtaining financing. Any bank or lender will want to insure its loan or investment and will ask for some type of collateral. Having a valuable asset can serve as a great resource for a possible lender. As long as the asset is not overcollateralized (not having too many loans on the asset or having loans that almost reach the asset's resale value), a sports organization can use it to borrow money for possible future growth or cover expenses.

CONCEPTS INTO PRACTICE

As an example of an asset's value in financing, we can explore the concept of asset-backed securitization, where assets serve to secure a major debt. In 1999, Bear Stearns sold a $315 million asset-backed securitization financing package for the STAPLES Center in Los Angeles. The taxable notes (as compared to tax-free bonds issued by many municipalities) bore an interest rate of 7.653% and had a final maturity of 27 years with an expected average life of 14.5 years. The financing received great rating support from Moody's Investors Service and Fitch IBCA, Inc. As part of the deal, STAPLES' owners pledged the rights to specific revenues, including the right to renewals of the underlying contracts, to secure the notes. The future revenue streams used for securitization came from contractually obligated fees from the arena's naming rights, a portion of the luxury suite and premier seat licenses, the concession leases, 10 founding partner corporate sponsorships, and an exclusive ticket sales agreement with Ticketmaster,

Inc. Because the securitization structure dedicates only a portion of the arena's revenue streams, the STAPLES Center had significant financing flexibility to leverage other income sources if necessary (Roth, 1999). Similar financing was also used at the Pepsi Center.

IDENTIFYING LIABILITIES THROUGHOUT A SPORTS ORGANIZATION

While we have been exploring the benefit of assets, the flip side of the coin is liabilities. A sports organization can have no assets but significant liabilities. This can be seen with some technology start-up companies who blow through cash and have nothing to show for it until a product is actually produced—if a product is ever produced. Liabilities represent what a sports organization owes. These can be amounts owed to the founders, banks, investors, employees, customers, government entities, and other organizations.

Types of Liabilities

Similar to current assets, there are **current liabilities**. Current liabilities are debts that are owed in the short time period, normally less than a year. Long-term debts are obligations that are owed more than one year out—but could have some current payments. Thus, if a sports organization owes payroll to some of its employees, that would be a short-term liability, as employment law requires employees to be paid in a timely manner. A long-term debt may include bond obligations that were taken out when a facility was built. The bonds might need to be repaid within 20 years. The organization might pay monthly installments, but the majority of the debt is due in the future. Confusion might arise in classifying a liability if it is a possible long-term debt that can be demanded for early payment. A bank loan, for example, might provide that if revenue does not reach a certain point, the obligation is owed within 30 days, even if the loan was initially a 10-year loan.

There are numerous liabilities that any sports organization can have. That is similar to how an average person might have numerous liabilities. A typical person might have current liabilities such as rent obligations, monthly utilities bills, monthly Internet and phone bills, and weekly food bills. An average person might also have several long-term liabilities, including a **mortgage**, car loans, or a student loan. Some of the liabilities a larger sports organization might have include

- 401(k) payable;
- accrued expenses payable;
- accrued liability;
- bonds payable;
- common stock dividend distributable;
- dividends declared;
- federal income tax withholdings payable;
- income and other taxes payable;
- interest payable;
- lawsuit payable;
- mortgage payable;
- net payroll payable;
- payroll taxes payable;
- pension payable;
- salaries payable;
- short-term debt;
- unemployment tax payable;
- utilities payable;
- vacation pay payable;
- wages payable;
- warranty liability; and
- workers' compensation insurance payable.

The amount owed to government agencies in terms of taxes, unemployment insurance, and related expenses is often a substantial amount. While it might seem that construction-related debts are going to be the largest liability, the actual culprit is employee-related expenses. Over the long run, employee expenses such as salaries, employment benefits, pension obligations, or training costs, will generate significantly more liabilities over the life of a facility than the facility itself.

Some liabilities are very clear. If a bond for a shoe manufacturer requires monthly payments of $10,000, then management can plan for such expenses. Other expenses, such as **fixed costs**,

might be calculated. For example, the organization might know it has $3 from every shoe sold dedicated to fixed costs. The management might also know that variable costs can range from $5 to $10 per shoe, based on raw material used in the shoe. These basic expenses do not always bring into consideration other liabilities and costs that can affect profitability and amounts owed. For example, contingent liability might exist if there is a patent-related lawsuit associated with the shoe, and the manufacturer might be on the hook for millions of dollars if it loses the case or has to settle. Further potential liability can be associated with warranties associated with the shoes. If the shoes are guaranteed to last at least one year, the company will have to set aside resources to help fulfill such warranties, and that represents a potential liability. Other expenses might generate additional liabilities such as shipping costs, customs taxes, transportation-related expenses, and numerous other expenses that can create liability issues. One of the key liabilities might be the amount of money owed to manufacturers in other countries that might make part or all of a shoe. These submanufacturers might send the seller (such as Nike or Under Armour) material on a regular basis and might bill on a monthly basis. Nike or Under Armour would owe these suppliers or manufacturers money, but they might wait and pay them every 90 days. This creates an opportunity for the shoe company to invest its money and pay on a less frequent basis. This creates a very unique liability dance. Company A might owe Company B $1 million. Company B owes Companies C and D $500,000 each. Company D owes several suppliers over $100,000 combined. Company B might not be able to pay Companies C and D until it is paid by Company A. Thus, everyone in this chain might be waiting for Company A to pay. This represents a chain of liabilities with everyone owing everyone else.

Cost of Debt

It is very difficult to complete a large transaction without having some type of debt. Imagine wanting to buy a home, which is often the biggest purchase a person makes during their lifetime. Most people do not have the cash to make such a large purchase, and there will be significant up-front expense to purchase the house in addition to regular payments. The same issue arises in the sporting world where building a stadium might cost over a billion dollars and teams regularly sell for a billion dollars or more. One example was the purchase of Manchester United by Malcolm Glazer. Glazer bought United in 2005 for £790 million in a heavily leveraged deal (he utilized assets of the team to obtain the financing). Glazer then loaded the debt, £525 million worth, onto the team. Such a debt burden on most teams would push the team into bankruptcy because the debt payment would be close to £60 million a year. Through 2014, the team had spent over £680 million on debt service (interest fees, bank charges, and debt repayment), close to double what it had spent on players (Amir, 2014).

That is not the only liability for the team. It also has a dividend liability. Manchester United plc, the United holding company, is registered in the Cayman Islands, and shares of the team are floated on the New York Stock Exchange. In 2014 to 2015, Manchester United plc announced it will pay a dividend of $0.045 (£0.03) every quarter, for each share owned by a shareholder. After the death of Malcolm Glazer in 2014, his six children became the primary shareholders, owning 131 million shares, 80% of the total issued shares. Every three months the children will be paid $5.9m (£3.8m). Annually, the quarterly dividend payments will add up to $23.6m (£15.2m). Even when such dividend obligations were being announced, the team still owed over £400 million (Conn, 2015). Teams are not alone in being burdened by debt to pay for managerial decisions. The same debt concerns often arise when investment bankers purchase companies. In order to purchase the company the investment bankers need to borrow funds and then use the newly purchased company as collateral to secure the debt. This approach backfired several times and was highlighted in chapter 1 in the discussion of the closing of The Sports Authority.

Every debt obligation has an associated cost. Borrowing money from the bank takes time and resources. The borrower will have to repay the loan with interest. The money spent on the interest and debt repayment takes money away from other potential endeavors. Thus, a vicious cycle might arise as money is needed to grow, but as the company grows it is required to pay more for money borrowed to grow. A good example of this could be how some people get into debt using their credit cards. The amount they owe is a liability. In an attempt to lower their payments they might consolidate five different credit card debts under a new credit card that offers a great introductory rate for balance transfers. The new credit card company knows that if these people had not made full payments on past credit card debts, they probably will not be paying the new credit card in full. So it will turn what seemed like a wonderful promotion into a noose as after six months the new credit card would require high interest payments. Furthermore, due to the fine print specifying zero interest only if the balance is paid in full, the credit card company will charge interest on all the prior months. This will throw people into more and more debt—especially if they think they can find an easy solution to get out of debt (such as buying lottery tickets, gambling, or even illegal transactions).

Pressure to Repay Debts

One famous case of trying to reduce liabilities through illegal means involved John DeLorean. His car, famous for the *Back to the Future* movies, was initially launched in 1973, but delays had it leaving the production floor only in 1981. After a year, his company and its iconic car had failed to recoup its $175 million investment costs, and the company faced a dire financial situation. In 1982, DeLorean was charged by the federal government with trafficking in cocaine to help obtain money to keep his car company going. While he was later acquitted of the charges (due to entrapment), his desire to help reduce liabilities at almost any cost became well known, and his company ended up in bankruptcy (Cummings, 1982).

While the DeLorean example is sensational, there are several similar examples in the sports world. One famous example involved John Rigas, former owner of the Buffalo Sabers. Rigas was initially the founder and chief executive officer of Adelphia, once the fifth-biggest cable company in the country, but it went belly up after Rigas and others looted it and then concealed the debt. Rigas and his son, who was the chief financial officer, took cash advances of $1 million a month and used Adelphia's assets to pay $40,000 a year for a personal masseuse and to buy 17 cars and $500,000 worth of antiques. The senior Rigas was convicted in 2004 and sentenced to 12 years in prison, and his son was sentenced to 17 years (Gregorian, 2016). Adelphia disclosed in 2002 that it was on the hook for $2.3 billion in off-balance-sheet loans associated with the Rigas family. This included financing the family's $150 million purchase of the NHL's Buffalo Sabres. Adelphia paid a Rigas family partnership that owns the Sabres $744,000 for luxury-box rentals, hockey tickets, and other entertainment costs. The Sabers filed for Chapter 11 bankruptcy in 2003, and according to reports, the Sabres had more than $238 million in debts, with assets of less than $70 million at that time (UPI, 2003).

Whenever a sports organization undertakes liabilities, whether bonds, bad loans, loan sharks, credit cards, or any other means, the total cost needs to be analyzed. One of the often underanalyzed costs of liability is the psychological cost. Whenever you owe someone money, you might not sleep as well. Issues to consider are inability repay the debt, possible loss of collateral, and collapse of the business relationship. In business, these are legitimate concerns that will not appear on paper that can take a significant toll on an executive.

Lowering Liabilities

When examining assets, this chapter looked at how to appropriately leverage assets to generate the greatest amount of value or to protect an asset. The same analysis needs to be undertaken when examining liabilities, but it needs to focus on how to reduce liabilities. A good example of the dance around asset growth and liability reduction can be seen in calculating an organization's net worth. Net worth is calculated by subtracting liabilities from assets. If an organization has $2 million in assets and $1 million in liabilities, then it has a net worth of $1 million. To increase net worth, the organization will want to increase assets. However, to do that, the organization will probably need to increase liability. Assets normally do not increase without some investment. A company might have **retained earnings** that can be used to fuel future growth. However, those retained earnings might be better off paying dividends to owners (either directly to certain individuals or to shareholders). Growth can also come from issuing stocks. Stocks are not a liability similar to bonds or bank loans. Shareholders become owners and there can be some potential liability (such as required dividends for preferred stocks), but it is not a debt that needs to be repaid.

The main technique used by most organizations entails borrowing money. This can be done through specific loans or utilizing a **line of credit**. A line of credit is in essence a credit card type arrangement where a company can tap the line whenever it needs any money. The line is created in advance, and there is normally a fee to keep the line of credit open. The bank might require a larger organization to do its banking at a specific bank and might allow it to have an open line of credit for several hundred thousand to several million dollars. Whenever the organization needs money, it writes a check against the credit line and then it has to start paying back the principal (borrowed amount) with the interest on a monthly basis. If there is no money borrowed from the credit line, then the organization does not owe anything. It is important to have a good relationship with a bank to allow for flexibility in utilizing a line of credit.

Organizations can use different techniques to borrow, with issuing bonds being the most difficult due to the cost and time required to issue them. That is why bonds are only issued by the largest organizations, such as professional teams and large municipalities when building a stadium or arena. While costs associated with bonds and other borrowing instruments can be reduced, the amount of reductions is limited. The easiest way to reduce these liabilities is to pay off any borrowed funds. A homeowner's example of this is to pay off a mortgage early. Instead of repaying a 30-year mortgage over 30 years, a homeowner can pay back a certain amount of extra principal every month, and then in maybe 20 years the mortgage will be paid off—saving 10 years' worth of interest payments. Such repayment efforts take significant discipline and dedication. There will always be problems requiring financial assistance, but an organization needs to prioritize liabilities and determine what is critical.

Some liabilities can be reduced through repayment or even by negotiating reduced amounts with lenders. For example, a sports organization can negotiate with employees to reduce its owed benefits. A sports organization might be facing hard financial times and might approach employees to reduce the amount the company contributes to a retirement program and that can reduce future liabilities. Other liabilities are owed regardless of what a company wants to do. Taxes are a perfect example. Even if an organization wants to reduce taxes owed, the government rarely reduces tax obligations. If an organization has set aside $1 million to pay quarterly taxes, the organization cannot take that to reduce other potential liabilities without incurring significant penalties. Another example of a required liability that would be difficult to reduce would be a union contract. Under the terms of the contract, the organization might have certain obligations that can only be reduced through the contract negotiation process.

CONCLUSION

Assets and liabilities are critical for any sports organization. Assets represent the ability to generate future revenue and the ability to grow in the future. Liabilities represent investments to grow a business. Every organization needs to identify its assets and leverage them to generate the greatest amount of revenue. An asset that is not properly leveraged will create lost opportunity, which might not ever be received in the future. Similarly, liabilities need to normally grow for an organization to grow, but liabilities need to be effectively managed so that the organization doesn't become insolvent through having too many liabilities and not enough assets to cover the liabilities.

Class Discussion Topics

1. What do you think is the most important asset for a youth sports organization?

2. Develop a list of the liabilities a traditional fitness club would have (assume it does not own the facility but owns everything else).

3. Create a list of all your current assets and liabilities. Examine each asset and ask yourself if you are appropriately leveraging it. Can you find a way to reduce some of your liabilities?

4. Do you think professional athletes should be considered assets? Defend your position.

Part I Case Study

Financing Soccer Around the World

An important example to help tell the story of sport finance entails the World Cup. The World Cup, similar to the Olympics, is held every four years, and the process to win the rights to host the games has become very competitive and shrouded in controversy. The issue of FIFA (Fédération Internationale de Football Association) corruption reached a crescendo with sponsors and others in 2015 when FIFA's president for the prior 17 years, Sepp Blatter, resigned. He resigned several days after seven soccer officials were arrested and held for extradition to the United States on corruption charges (Borden, Schmidt, & Apuzzojune, 2105). The scandal embroiled numerous individuals and helped show how money had greased the wheels of awarding the World Cup games. While the scandal, and resulting criminal convictions, resignation of Blatter, and significant negative publicity ruled the news cycle, soccer games were still played and a large amount of money was earned. This case study will explore some of the financial issues associated with the World Cup and also how financial issues affect a major soccer organization sending its athletes to the World Cup.

FIFA has complete control over the World Cup because it is its event. FIFA's guide for the World Cup states,

> FIFA is the original owner of all of the rights emanating from the FIFA World Cup™ and any other related events coming under its jurisdiction, without any restrictions as to content, time, place and law. These rights include, among others, all kinds of financial rights, audiovisual and radio recording, reproduction and broadcasting rights, multimedia rights, marketing and promotional rights and incorporeal rights (such as those pertaining to emblems) as well as rights arising under copyright law whether currently existing or created in the future subject to any provision as set forth in specific regulations (FIFA 2014, p. 24).

In terms of revenue from preliminary matches, FIFA allows each host organization to collect revenue from ticket sales and commercial rights (broadcasting). From this amount, FIFA takes a levy of 2% of the gross revenue and allows host organizations to deduct up to 30% for renting stadiums and paying all applicable taxes. Besides those deductions, remaining funds, if any, are used to cover costs. The following guidelines spell out what expenses should be covered by whom:

- The visiting association shall cover its delegation's own international travel costs to the venue or the nearest airport, boarding, lodging, and incidental expenses.
- The host association shall cover domestic transport costs for the visiting team's official delegation.
- The host association shall also pay for first-class boarding and lodging and domestic transportation in the host country for the match officials, the match commissioner, the referee assessor, and any other FIFA officials (security officer, media officer, etc.) (FIFA, 2014).

For the World Cup, in contrast to qualifying events, FIFA pays certain amounts such as appropriate airfare to the games (based on FIFA's official airline sponsor charge; if a team wants to charter a flight, FIFA would pay the comparable rate for 50 tickets on its sponsor airline), hotel accommodations for five days before a team's first match through two days after the team's last match (for up to 50 people), match officials, winner awards, doping tests, and FIFA-associated insurance (FIFA, 2014). This does not include FIFA's costs for sending its own employees and stakeholders to the games.

One interesting element of FIFA's money distribution process is paying current and former professional teams for releasing players to play for the World Cup. FIFA set aside $70 million to distribute at a rate of $2,800 per player on World Cup duty per day. This money is shared among each player's current club and any other club the player had played for in the two previous years while engaged in qualification matches (Associated Press, 2014). Professional teams appreciate the payment, but they have significant risk if they release a player to play. If a player were to be injured, it could be a significant loss for a team. Of course, the team and the player would buy insurance, but soccer players can be very expensive. Heading into the 2014 World Cup, the Spanish squad was worth an estimated $921 million, almost $90 million more than Germany, which ended up winning the 2014 World Cup (Soergel, 2014).

The following paragraphs highlight some of the unique financial issues faced by some of the past and future World Cup hosts.

2014 World Cup

The 2014 World Cup was supposed to help Brazil shine on the international stage before hosting the 2016 Summer Olympics. The country was initially anticipating spending approximately $1 trillion on 12 stadiums and numerous infrastructure-related projects (Zimbalist, 2011). Brazil's projected budget for hosting the World Cup was initially estimated at $13.3 billion (compared with $18 billion for the Olympics). Such a huge budget for putting on the month-long tournament with 32 teams might seem like a great capital (long-term) investment for the host country. However, history has shown that the World Cup only generates approximately $3.5 billion in revenue (with most of the funds going to FIFA) (Zimbalist, 2011).

2018 World Cup

Russia hosted the 2018 World Cup and has increased government spending on the tournament by 19.1 billion rubles ($325 million). That additional amount announced in February 2017 brings the total projected government spending to 638.8 billion rubles (US$10.8 billion). All the increases were from federal budget funds, which resulted in almost 55% of the World Cup's total spending being funded by the Russian federal government (Associated Press, 2017).

These huge capital expenditures represent a significant expenditure to host the games, but they do not reflect the macro expenditures associated with a team.

2022 World Cup

The tiny oil-rich country of Qatar is set to host the 2022 World Cup. It initially was planning on spending $200 billion for the games, including $140 billion for transportation infrastructure (including a new airport, roads, and a metropolitan transit system) and $20 billion for tourism infrastructure. The award was controversial based on the country's size, population, and the summer heat, which exceeds 40°C (104°F) in the desert country (Associated Press, 2013). By 2017, Qatar was facing financial hardships (similar to Brazil) and was trying to slash its World Cup budget by 40% to 50% and was trying to reduce the number of stadiums from the planned 12 to 8 (Alkhalisi, 2017). These expenses are on top of the reported $17.2 billion spent on deals to help land the games, such as legitimate deals to purchase airplanes from France and numerous other questionable deals that purportedly paid decision makers millions of English pounds (Harris, 2015).

2026 World Cup

In 2017, FIFA announced that it would expand the World Cup field from 32 teams to 48 teams. This would increase the number of games played from 64 to 80. Besides the extra cost and possible extra revenue from increasing the tournament size, social media jumped on one aspect of the games—the popular Panini sticker albums produced for each World Cup. With the larger number of teams, it was estimated that collecting all the players from the 50-pence (US$0.65) packets (which have random stickers inserted) would probably cost a fan close to 500 pounds (US$656) (Curtis, 2017).

National Organizations Facing Financial Issues Such As Player Salaries

Besides the individual World Cup host- related expenses, other issues can include the individual costs associated with teams preparing for the games. For example, how much does it cost to house and train a team for several years? In addition to housing and meals, expenses include salaries for players, coaches, athletic trainers, nutritionists, sport psychologists, administrators, video recorders, travel coordinators, and numerous other individuals. Each team also plays a number of events in preparation for the World Cup such as exhibition games called friendlies and other events that can generate revenue from ticket sales and broadcast rights. These events also generate costs such as renting a large stadium, personnel, and administrative and marketing expenses.

Players' salaries can spark a controversy. There is one controversy associated with how much star players should receive compared with small role players. But another major controversy is how much female players should earn compared with male players. This controversy spun into a major lawsuit when some of the 2015 Women's World Cup Championship team members filed a complaint in the United States claiming wage discrimination since they earned less than the male athletes who did not do nearly as well. The salary information comparing some of the top U.S. players showed the following:

- Clint Dempsey pocketed almost $200,000 more than Carli Lloyd ($428,022-$240,019).
- Goaltender Tim Howard earned $398,495 while Hope Solo earned only $240,019.
- The men's team shared qualifying bonuses totaling $2 million while the women's bonus was only $300,000. While the men played more games (16 qualifying games compared with 5 for the women) that is still a difference of $125,000 per game vs. $60,000 per game.
- For being named to the final 23-player World Cup roster, the men received $55,000 each while the women earned $15,000 each.
- The women's national team flew economy class for most of its trips while the men flew only business class.
- For friendly matches, the men earned a salary of between $7,500 and $14,100 per win (based on their opponent's FIFA ranking), between $5,000 and $6,500 for draws, and $4,000 for a loss. The women earned $1,350 for each friendly win, draw, or loss.
- The men earned bonus money for every World Cup group stage point they earned and $5,500 for each group-stage match for which the players were rostered. The women were not lucky enough to earn any such bonuses (Davis, 2016).

These differences apply to money earned in the United States or for games under the auspices of the United States Soccer Federation (USSF). While at first it appears glaringly like discrimination and unfair payment based on gender, the complaint was filed in the United States and USSF could not be responsible for what FIFA paid out, which creates an even larger disparity. The men's prize money (for losing in the round of 16) was $9 million. This is $7 million more than the $2 million the women received as a team for winning the entire tournament (Davis, 2016). FIFA lets national soccer federations determine how to reward their players, and Germany, which won in 2014, distributed its $35 million victor purse by paying each player on the team a €300,000 (US$408,000) bonus (AP, 2014).

It should be noted that FIFA generated $4.8 billion in revenue from the 2014 World Cup while the women's revenue was significantly less (Davis, 2016). In fact, the 2011 Women's World Cup (hosted in Germany) generated $72,818,500. In contrast, the 2010 men's South Africa World Cup generated over $3.7 billion, which is 50 times greater than the women. Women also received 10% of revenue in prize money in 2011 while the men only received 7% of the revenue they generated. The difference could also be seen with attendance. In 2014, attendance in Brazil averaged 53,592 for the men's games, while the women's attendance in Canada averaged only 26,029 fans (Pfeiffer, 2015).

Additional Costs

Another issue beyond hosting the games is the cost associated with bidding for a game, even if the city is not finally chosen. These costs can run into the millions. These costs include putting together a plan, bringing in consultants and lobbyists, producing high-end videos and brochures promoting the region, bringing in investment bankers to help explore stadium funding options, and hosting various dignitaries and showing them the best of the area (five-star hotels and top dining options). Olympic bids are similar to World Cup bids. In fact, in a bid to host Olympic Games, cities such as Chicago spent over $100 million in a failed attempt to host the 2012 Olympics, and Tokyo spent $150 million in its failed bid to host the 2016 Olympic Games (Zimbalist, 2016). One of the more publicized failed World Cup bids was undertaken by England to host the 2018 event. England spent over £19 million on the bid and lost in the first round of bidding—only garnering 2 of 22 votes ("Dave Richards sorry for comments about Fifa and Uefa," 2012).

Political cronies can benefit from hosting or even bidding on a major event, but others can also profit. When South Africa hosted the World Cup in 2010, some major construction companies were the big winners. The five primary construction companies saw their profits rise from $25 million in 2004 to $200 million in 2009—a major World Cup bounce for them (Zimbalist, 2016).

United States Soccer Federation Budget

The U.S. men's soccer team lost in the round of 16 during the 2014 World Cup. The women's team won the 2015 World Cup. How did this translate to revenue and expenses for the USSF, which is the governing body of soccer in the United States? To answer this question, one would have to examine the three primary areas where they generate both revenue and expenses: the nonnational team, the men's team, and the women's team. Thus, the 2016 nonnational team budget called for a surplus of $4,488,547 based on projected revenue of $67,444,188 and expenses of $62,955,641. The projections were for over $69 million in revenue, and they were able to reduce expenses to around $60 million, which would produce a **variance** (difference between what was budgeted for and the final projected amount) of a positive $4.6 million.

The men's national team was budgeted to bring in $23,817,500, but the team was expected to cost $27,118,386 for a $3.3 million loss. However, revenue jumped almost $21 million more than projected. While revenue shot up, so did expenses, which increased $6.7 million. The result was an almost $11 million profit (a $14 million swing from the budgeted amount) for the men's team. The positive financials did not translate to the women's team, which was budgeted for a $1.6 million loss (based on budgeted revenue of $3,234,600 and expenses of $4,843,190). The projected revenue was almost at the revenue mark, but the expenses jumped almost $600,000, so the final projected loss from the women's team was $2.2 million. The result was an $18 million variance from the budget and a positive $17.7 million year for USSF. For the 2017 fiscal year (April 2016-March 2017), total revenue and expected expenses could be grouped in eight categories (see table 1).

The budget was broken down even further through national men's and women's events scheduled for the 2017 fiscal year. For the women, as an example, there were three friendlies scheduled where ticket prices were scheduled to average $44. It was estimated that 17,000 tickets would be sold, generating $750,000. After deducting $286,500 in event expenses and $111,900 in team expenses, USSF was anticipating a net profit of $351,000.

Besides looking at the possible revenue and direct game expenses, there are numerous other administrative expenses (salaries, benefits, medical care, nutritionists, etc.). For example, the May and January training camps cost $244,000 to run. Even the cost to go to the Olympics needed to be calculated. Because the women's team was supposed to do very well, six games were estimated. The International Olympic Committee (IOC) was supposed to pay the team $250,000. The cost to send the women's team to the Olympics was $2.1 million. Thus, the glory of trying to win the gold (the U.S. team lost in the quarterfinals) cost the USSF around $1.857 million. Part of this money was to be earned back in a post-Olympic, 10-game, victory tour that didn't happen Tickets were to be sold

Table 1   2017 Fiscal Year (April 2016-March 2017) Revenue and Expenses

REVENUE		
Category	**Amount**	**Explanation**
Broadcast and sponsorship revenue	$46.8 million	ESPN, Fox, Univision, and commercial sponsors
Event revenue	27.9 million	Tickets and merchandise sold at games
Player and membership registration	$6.0 million	Children and adults registering for soccer leagues
Referee-related revenue	$3.0 million	Courses, registration, and assignor fees
Coaching and other educational program revenue	$2.1 million	Various coaching training and licensing programs
Development and fund-raising revenue	$1.2 million	Focused on fund-raising efforts—especially large donors
Revenue from international games played in the United States	$5.2 million	
Copa América Centenario revenue	$15.0 million	16-team competition to be held in the United States
EXPENSES		
General and administrative costs	$12.5 million	Personnel costs, rent, information technology, and professional services
Annual meeting, board of directors, and committee expenses	$1.0 million	Hotels, travel, etc.
Marketing and sponsor services	$4.8 million	Videos, commercials, and web content
Coaching expenses	$4.0 million	Online coaches' education program and coaching instructors
Referee expenses	$3.1 million	Training programs
Player development spending	$20.2 million	Across all national teams
Development academy and associated programming expenses	$7.0 million	
Senior national team expenses	$38.2 million	

at $50 each and with an estimated 16,000 anticipated fans, the USSF budget anticipated $803,000 in revenue against $300,000 in event expenses and $266,000 in team expenses to generate $235,000 in profit. The squad was also supposed to host a domestic tournament in early 2017. While the ticket price for the three-game match was similar to other events ($47 each), the attendance was projected at 51,000 fans. This would generate $2.4 million in revenue and after subtracting $862,000 in event expenses and $367,000 in team expenses, these three games alone were anticipated to bring in a $1.175 million profit. This three-game series helps show the value of attendance and why it is critical to drive revenue for some sports with attendance rather than broadcasting revenue.

Overall, for the 2016 to 2017 year (based on the USSF fiscal year running from July through June), the women expected to generate $17.589 million in revenue. They expected $6.228 million in event expenses and $6.295 million in team expenses. Thus, the total expected profit was $5.066 million.

In contrast, the men's team budget was based on six home friendlies, two away friendlies, and six World Cup qualifiers. The overall projection for the men was to generate $9.05 million in revenue. Projections included $2.244 million in event expenses and $7.769 million in team expenses. Thus, the projected budget was for a $964,000 net loss (U.S. Soccer Federation, 2016).

This example helps show how funds vary across a wide variety of soccer-related organizations and events, whether the World Cup or individual countries preparing for the World Cup. Each budget will be different and will hopefully be as accurate as possible. The example shows that variances will always occur, but they are often minor. In the case of USSF, it was a very positive difference. Many cases are not the same and the result is often falling below or significantly below the anticipated numbers due to either revenue not being as expected or expenses rising too fast (U.S. Soccer Federation, 2016).

Conclusion

This case study has shown several financial issues such as anticipated revenue and expenses, actual revenue and expenses, budgeting, financial planning, and revenue distribution (and associated disputes). It has discussed how difficult financial planning can be when some revenue and expenses are controlled by a third party.

Class Discussion Topics

1. What do you think is the future of soccer around the globe and in the United States? Try to defend your position with hard numbers rather than an emotional argument.

2. Research the corruption scandal in more detail. How do you think the corruption scandals affecting soccer will change the landscape of global soccer and what ethical lessons can you learn from those scandals?

3. Do you think U.S. women's soccer players should be paid the same as male players? What information will you need to help defend your argument from a financial perspective?

4. If you were tasked with increasing revenue for the United States Soccer Federation, where do you think you could find money, and how would you attempt to generate that revenue?

Resources for Further Reading

Tannenwald, J. (2016, March 7). Details of U.S. soccer's budget for national teams, NWSL. *The Inquirer.* www.philly.com/philly/blogs/thegoalkeeper/Details-of-US-Soccers-budget-for-national-teams-NWSL.html.

U.S. Soccer Federation. (2016). *2016 annual general meeting.* www.philly.com/philly/blogs/thegoalkeeper/Details-of-US-Soccers-budget-for-national-teams-NWSL.html.

Revenue and Expenses

The next part of the text examines revenues and expenses—the heart of any sports organization. Besides identifying various elements of revenue and expenses across a wide variety of sport organizations, this section proposes strategies to help increase revenue and decrease expenses, both of which result in greater profitability for a sports organization.

Part II begins with an introduction from Nathan Grube, the executive director of the Travelers Championship. Mr. Grube goes into detail concerning how he examines revenues and expenses when hosting a major PGA tournament that is technically a nonprofit event but generates millions in donations.

Chapter 5 explores how revenues are generated in collegiate and professional athletics and in sporting goods companies.

Whether from ticket sales, broadcasting rights, licensed goods, donations, or sold products, every organization needs to generate revenue to survive.

In contrast, chapter 6 focuses on the other side of the coin, expenses. Every organization has expenses. The largest expense for most organizations, especially for professional sport teams, is salaries. Numerous other expenses—such as debt service, raw materials, insurance, marketing, and commissions—are covered.

This part ends with a case study exploring the various revenue and expense items from a real baseball team. Although the minor league's team name is not revealed, the revenue and expense categories is immense, giving the reader a great perspective into how broad the categories are for revenues and expenses.

©Nathan Grube

Nathan Grube

Executive Director of the Travelers Championship

My name is Nathan Grube, and I am the executive director of the Travelers Championship. For those not familiar with professional golf, our team manages Connecticut's PGA Tour event. We annually host what has been touted as the state's largest professional sporting event with a budget of close to $15 million, an annual economic impact (based on a 2017 study by the Connecticut Economic Resource Council) to the state of around $68 million. The tournament has generated more than $14.7 million for charity since Travelers took over as title sponsor in 2007. Our staff of 11 employees and more than 4,000 volunteers work year-round to produce the tournament.

My background is in liberal arts with a degree in mass communication and a concentration in political science from Auburn University. I am also a certified class A member of the PGA of America after completing the Golf Professional Training Program. My internships were unstructured and never counted for any class credit, but I wouldn't trade them for anything. I was a camp counselor, a cook, a dishwasher, and a river guide, plus I performed in a rodeo and was a horrible waiter. All of these experiences during the various summers while I was in college helped to shape my career in ways that I could never have imagined.

I have been the executive director of the Travelers Championship since 2005. I honestly thought this would be a two- to three-year position to gain some good experience, and then I would move on. I could not have been more wrong. This position has challenged me in ways that I never could have expected, and the event has grown in ways I never could have imagined. I am fortunate to be here, and I am literally thankful every day that I am able to do what I do. Prior to working with the PGA Tour, I worked for an event management company running various sporting events. We ran golf tournaments, college football games, motor sport events, celebrity softball games, and Olympic qualifiers. While all of these events were very different, there were similarities that tied them all together as well, particularly that they all focus on commitment and sound financial decisions. Prior to my time with the event team, I was a PGA professional working in the golf industry. Prior to that and right out of school, I failed miserably at an attempt to play professional golf. This was one of my harshest lessons in the area of managing revenues and expenses in sport. Golf was my sport and my only source of revenue; not playing well only piled the expenses up higher.

My experiences with finance (and more specifically with revenues and expenses) are ones that I live with daily. I remember the first time this hit me square in the face and became a part of my daily existence. I was a freshman at Auburn, and I had just moved into my dorm. My parents had made me a deal as a young man, and they were making good on their promise. They committed to all three of us (my brother, my sister, and me) that they would help us get our undergraduate degrees. They would cover the cost of our education as long as we kept our grades up and showed a true effort in our education. I asked them years later why they drove such old, beat-up cars. My father replied with a comment that left me silent for about a week: "Well son . . . I guess your mother and I thought that getting you through school was more important than driving a nice car." I was humbled, embarrassed, and also proud of my dad for shutting me up. There were only so many resources, and they had to be allocated according to priority.

So, there I was as an 18 year old beginning the journey on my own. My family was in San Diego, and I chose Auburn—seven states away. I was in the small kitchen in my apartment, and I was on the phone with my dad. Phones were connected to the wall in 1992 so I couldn't roam around. I was sitting on the kitchen counter, and my dad asked me how much money I had in the bank. I tried to remember what my checkbook log roughly said as online banking didn't really exist yet; the number startled him a little bit, and he asked me how I was going to live on that. I didn't have an answer. He then asked me to send him a budget of my monthly expenses. I was to put down everything I thought I would spend in a month. From rent to food to gas . . . every dime I thought I would spend. After poring over this for a few days, I sent it off (with a stamp), and he called me later that week.

"Are you sure this is right?" he asked me.

I thought he was calling me out for trying to squeeze some things in around miscellaneous or entertainment. I held strong and said, "Yes sir. That is what I will need each month."

I will never forget what he said next: "Deal."

"What?" I replied.

"Deal . . . I am going to send you a check for that amount every month from now until the time you graduate. Whatever you don't spend, you can save. If you are short, you will have to figure it out."

I thought I had just won the lottery.

To say that I had underestimated my expenses would not be an accurate representation of the truth. Not remotely. I never knew that an electric stove was more expensive than gas to operate, that not all restaurants offered free refills, that leftovers cannot sit for a week, that dry cleaning is way overpriced, that you can be fined for riding your bike on the sidewalk . . . that basically everything costs more than you think. I ran out of money in 14 days and had a job as a waiter within two months. This was my first real lesson that revenue had to exceed expenses if I wanted to live.

Fast forward to today. Running a professional sporting event is exciting, unique, stressful, exhilarating, and all consuming. I heard it said once that in running a professional sporting event, you are barraged with the "tyranny of good ideas." People who watch sports or who are involved in any way are passionate. They are in it because they want to be, not usually because they have to be. With that passion comes ideas, suggestions, comments, and feedback—good idea after good idea after good idea. If you try to chase every good idea and bring them to life without vetting them properly, they will indeed come to life and then take you down with them if they are not built on a strong financial foundation.

Whether it is bringing a new product to market, creating a new seating package in a venue, selling a new luxury box to a client, creating a new initiative or platform that you need sponsored, you must take the time to consider all the associated expenses and price your product accordingly to make sure you are bringing in the revenue you need. I worked with an event that had huge revenue numbers due to how much inventory it sold. They were master marketers and had some of the best-looking products when it came to engaging in a sporting event and taking in the experience. Their revenue was twice what my event was at the time, but they were barely breaking even while we were netting close to $1 million annually. They were selling a lot, but they had failed to price their inventory appropriately, were not disciplined with their expenses, and ultimately went out of business. Their entire team was removed, a new team came in, profit margins were analyzed, and expenses were benchmarked against other events. The budget was brought into line, and now the event is viable again. The previous team made the mistake of chasing every good idea and bringing it to life without doing the proper analysis of how to keep it alive. You can't pay the rent with passion. The revenue you bring in must exceed all the possible expenses for that product. It sounds simple, but you will be surprised by how many good ideas will get people fired. It won't be the failure of an idea, it will be the success of an idea that was not properly priced that will take down very smart people in your career.

Our mission should be to turn passion into sound business. We have to keep the events and industry viable financially so that passion can exist in our sports. If we fail the fans and our businesses are not sustainable economically, we have only ourselves to blame for being blinded by the passion and not respecting the environment that allows that passion to exist.

Understanding Revenue

Chapter Objectives

After studying this chapter, you should be able to do the following:

- Understand where revenue comes from for sport enterprises.
- Understand the various revenue sources for organizations in the professional sport industry.
- Understand sources of revenue for collegiate sport and other amateur sports organizations.
- Understand the various sources of revenue for sporting goods companies and other sports organizations.
- Understand the importance of revenue planning for sports organizations.

Revenues are a primary aspect of financial analysis. As stated in chapter 3, **revenues** represent money coming into an organization. All businesses revolve around money. In the sport industry, money is generated from sources such as ticket sales, product sales, corporate partnerships, membership fees, and concessions. Most information on the revenues for a sports organization can be found by examining its income statements, annual reports, and budgets. This chapter addresses the primary sources of revenue for organizations across a number of sport industry segments. We will start by briefly summarizing the topic of revenues in the sport industry. We will then move on to addressing the specific revenue streams for organizations in sport industry segments such as professional sport, collegiate sport, and sporting goods.

REVENUES
IN THE SPORT INDUSTRY

This section highlights how we make money in the sport industry. For professional sports teams and collegiate athletic departments, revenue can come from ticket sales, broadcast contracts, concession sales, sponsorship agreements, and a host of other opportunities. In comparison, a sporting goods company like Under Armour (UA) generates revenue primarily through the sale of tangible products like sneakers, shirts, equipment, and hats. Each business has different revenue sources, and the number of these sources is constantly changing. In another example, a health club may have revenue of $1 million a year from sources that include

- membership fees,
- locker rentals,
- fitness class fees,
- advertising and signage,
- equipment sales,
- concession sales,
- apparel and other merchandise sales, and
- personal training revenue.

Lastly, the revenues of a typical public high school athletic program can include

- local and city school taxes,
- federal tax subsidies for education,

- state taxes,
- participation fees,
- donations,
- booster clubs,
- concession revenue,
- attendance revenue,
- broadcasting revenue,
- advertising revenue,
- fund-raising revenue,
- licensing revenue, and
- sponsorship revenue.

As you can see, there are various revenue sources for most sports organizations. While a high school athletic department might have a dozen or more revenue sources, some professional sports teams might have 20 to 30 revenue sources, and other sports organizations might have only one revenue source. Having more revenue sources might require more work to manage them. However, it also protects the sports organization. If a sports organization only has one or two revenue sources, and if those revenue sources evaporate, the organization will probably have to close down. In contrast, if there are multiple revenue sources and one or two evaporate, then there are other possible revenue sources upon which a sports organization can turn to in order to stay in business. A successful sports manager must be knowledgeable of the sources of revenue for the organization and have the ability to effectively manage and grow them.

Understanding revenue is critical because a sports organization will constantly work to increase its revenue to keep operating. If revenues decline, an organization must find new revenue sources or slash costs. For a multitude of reasons, many revenue-generating techniques do not work for high school sports in a given community. Parents may not want to support a program. Local advertisers may be unwilling to spend their advertising dollars on the school, or city regulations may prohibit using certain fund-raising techniques. Although revenue-generating options may be limited, expenses normally do not share the same fate.

At this point, it is also important to address the financial motivations for different sports organizations. For for-profit sports organizations such as an English Premier League club or a sporting goods company, the financial goal is to maximize owner or shareholder wealth. This is usually done by maximizing profit, which is the difference between total revenues and total expenses. In financial and accounting terms, profit is often referred to as **net income**. For example, Under Armour undertakes business strategies to generate as much revenue as possible at the least cost. While this is the general strategy for the vast majority of for-profit organizations, the motivation may be a bit different for some for-profit organizations; this is especially true in professional team sports. This makes the finances of pro sports teams different from other businesses. For a billionaire owner such as Mark Cuban of the National Basketball Association's (NBA's) Dallas Mavericks, is his sole focus on maximizing financial wealth and profit? Perhaps not. Mr. Cuban may be willing to forgo some profit in exchange for putting a team on the court that has the potential to win an NBA championship. This aspect of the professional sport industry sets it apart from other for-profit industries. Each individual team owner must balance the desire to win versus the desire to make money. The two goals do not always work hand in hand. An owner may be willing to spend hundreds of millions on team salary to win, but that championship may come at a steep financial cost with respect to overall profitability. Thus, in order to win, a team owner may be forced to decrease their profit level.

Other sports organizations such as youth sports programs, intercollegiate athletic programs, and charitable sports groups are organized as nonprofit. For these organizations, the maximization of profit is not the financial goal. For them, the financial goal is to maximize revenue, which can then be reinvested, or spent, by the organization. For example, the University of Texas (UT) Department of Athletics has no owners or shareholders for whom it must maximize profit and wealth. However, finances are still very important to the organization. The revenue that it generates is reinvested back into the organization. So, if UT can make an additional $10 million a year through the sale of corporate partnerships, it can then spend that money in areas such as facility upgrades, increased coaching salaries, and better academic support services for the student-athletes. So while UT does not have a profit motivation, it does have a desire to increase revenue that can be reinvested into the organization. This is also true for other nonprofit organizations like Amateur Athletic Union youth sports programs, the United States Olympic Committee, and the Special Olympics.

REVENUES IN PROFESSIONAL SPORT

In professional team sports, revenues are derived primarily from ticket sales and broadcasting rights (Howard & Crompton, 2013). For most teams in major sports leagues, these two sources compose over 75% of total revenue. Regardless of the team or league, every sports team has the same basic revenue streams. While the forms of revenue across professional teams are similar, the size of them can be dramatically different. Table 5.1 provides the total revenue, by league, for the five largest worldwide sports leagues. As one can see, the National Football League (NFL) is the largest with $13 billion in revenue per year. Major League Baseball (MLB) comes in second with $9.5 billion in revenue, with the English Premier League being third. NFL Commissioner Roger Goodell has stated that he would like to see NFL revenues reach $25 million per year by 2027 (Kaplan, 2016).

While having knowledge of the overall levels of league revenue is valuable, it is also important

Table 5.1 Annual Professional League Revenue, 2016

League	Annual revenue
National Football League	$13 billion
Major League Baseball	$9.5 billion
English Premier League	$5.3 billion
National Basketball Association	$4.8 billion
National Hockey League	$3.7 billion

Source: Which Professional Sports Leagues Make the Most Money (2016).

to address the different sources of revenue and their size. The largest source of revenue for three of the four major pro sports leagues in North America (NFL, NBA, and MLB) is national broadcasting rights fees. Each league sells the right to broadcast its games to media companies such as ESPN, Fox, NBC, and ABC. Table 5.2 provides data on the annual national broadcasting rights fees that are generated by each of the four major professional leagues in North America. As you can see, the NFL and its team owners have over $4.5 billion in the bank before they sell a single ticket, corporate partnership, or piece of licensed apparel. In comparison, the NHL generates slightly over $400 million in revenue from its national broadcasting deals.

With respect to the broadcasting of these leagues, it needs to be mentioned that the NFL sells only national TV broadcast and video streaming rights for its regular and postseason games. In comparison, the NBA, NHL, and MLB sell national TV and video streaming rights fees, but it also allows each team to sell local broadcasting rights for their market. For example, in Philadelphia, the Phillies, Flyers, and 76ers sell local broadcast rights of their games to the NBC Philadelphia regional sports network while under NFL rules, the Eagles do not. Teams in major markets like New York, Los Angeles, and Chicago can sell these local TV broadcast rights for fees in excess of $100 million per year. For the national broadcast rights, it should also be noted that most North American professional sports leagues equally share this revenue among the teams. So, despite the fact that the NFL's Green Bay Packers are much more popular than the Jacksonville Jaguars, each team receives the same amount from the national broadcasting deals with CBS, NBC, Fox, and ESPN. For each NFL team, its share of the national broadcasting deal is in excess of $100 million per year. This revenue sharing plan is not in place for the revenue from local broadcast rights fees in MLB, the NBA, and the NHL. While some of the local TV revenue is shared across teams, most of it is kept by the individual team. The actual amounts vary across the professional leagues. Historically, the revenue from broadcasting rights has increased greatly with each new deal between the professional league and the TV network. However, it is uncertain if this will continue to be true. Networks such as ESPN have suffered some financial difficulties in recent years as some consumers disconnect from cable TV and view content online. This loss of revenue for networks may result in the amount of rights fees being paid by these networks to the leagues leveling off, or even decreasing. If this occurs, the professional leagues must develop strategies to increase revenue from other sources; online streaming may be a source of future revenue growth for these leagues.

Ticket sales are another important revenue source for professional sports teams at all levels of minor and major league sports. In 2017, the median ticket price for an MLB game was approximately $44 (Cabrera, 2017). If an MLB team drew 2 million paying customers over a season, it would have generated about $88 million in ticket revenue. In MLB, about 30% of overall league revenue comes from ticket sales ("Ticket sales," 2017). In comparison, ticket sales compose only about 16% of overall revenue in the NFL, despite the median ticket price being about $88 ("Gate receipts," 2017). This is largely due to the difference in the total number of games played across the two leagues, 162 vs. 16 per team per season, and the value of the national broadcasting deals. While ticket sales are important for major pro sports teams, they are perhaps even more important for minor league teams in sports like baseball, hockey, basketball, and arena football. Teams in these leagues generate very little, if any, revenue from

Table 5.2 Professional Sport National Broadcasting Deals

League	Partners	Years	Payment
NFL	CBS, Fox, NBC, ESPN	2014-2022	$4.5 billion/year
NBA	ESPN and TNT	2016-2025	$2.6 billion/year
MLB	Fox, TBS, ESPN	2014-2022	$1.4 billion/year
NHL	NBC and Rogers (CAN)	2013-2024	$418 million/year

Source: Total Sportek (2017a).

the broadcasting of their games. Thus, they must rely on other sources of revenue, specifically ticket sales.

The ticket sales process has seen dramatic changes over the current century primarily due to technological advances. The vast majority of sports ticket sales now occur over the Internet. This has permitted teams and leagues to get much more creative in how they distribute tickets. To do a better job of measuring demand for their games, many teams have moved to variable or dynamic ticket pricing. With variable ticket pricing, teams set the ticket prices prior to the season based on the expected demand for games. For example, the New York Yankees may charge a higher ticket price for a game versus the Boston Red Sox, a long-time rival, than they would for a game against the Tampa Bay Devil Rays. This variable ticket pricing strategy has the potential to generate additional revenue for the Yankees. Key games can be priced accordingly. However, less attractive games might have fewer potential purchasers even at a lower price. This has led to many teams creating packages with several high profile games and several lower profile games to try to sell the two together. This induces fans who want tickets to the marquee games to buy those tickets at a higher price and also purchase some tickets for games they might not want to attend. This generates additional revenue for a team, but it can also harm the team as some fans dump their unwanted tickets on the secondary market. With a flood of tickets on the secondary market, fewer fans will buy from the team, thus depriving the team of some possible revenue.

It must be remembered that with variable ticket pricing, the pricing decisions are made prior to the season. Many teams have moved

Sponsorship revenue can be one of the major revenue sources for all sport organizations, but the depth and quality of sponsorship activation is best seen at the collegiate and professional levels.

beyond variable ticket pricing to dynamic ticket pricing. With dynamic ticket pricing, teams use computer models to estimate consumer demand on a continual basis, even at multiple points during the season and sometimes right up to the time of the game. If a team sees that sales for a game are low, it can lower the ticket price in order to attract more customers. The basic economic principle of supply and demand tells us that if ticket prices are lowered, that will increase demand. Many professional sports teams have incorporated dynamic ticket pricing into their sales strategies with success. As with variable ticket pricing, dynamic ticket pricing ultimately should increase overall revenue for the sports team.

Other sources of revenue for a professional sports team usually include

♦ corporate partnerships, sponsorships, and signage;
♦ naming rights;
♦ licensed merchandise;
♦ luxury suites and club seats;
♦ ancillary activities (concessions, parking, and hosting other events); and
♦ transfer fees.

Corporate Partnerships

Corporate partnerships and naming rights can generate significant long-term revenue for pro sports teams and leagues. For example, in 2014, Microsoft and the NFL signed a five-year partnership deal worth $400 million. The NFL will receive $80 million per year from the deal, and in exchange Microsoft will receive benefits such as their tablet being used on the sidelines by players and coaches. Microsoft has also been designated as the official tablet of the NFL (Gaines, 2014). More recently, NBA teams have begun selling sponsorships on the team jerseys. In 2017, the Golden State Warriors cut a deal with a Japanese technology company, Rakuten, that is reportedly paying the team $20 million per year for the right to have its logo appear on the team jerseys (Rovell, 2017). This is a brand new source of revenue for the Warriors and many other NBA teams. This is an excellent example of pro sports teams finding a new source of revenue. While it is great to have a new source of revenue, such an action can generate controversy. While football teams in Europe have had shirt sponsors for many years, in the past, the practice has had a negative connotation in the United States and might alienate some fans. That is why teams such as the New York Yankees have refused to have a corporate name on their stadium, even though many other teams in the region have sold naming rights to their stadiums or arenas.

Naming Rights

Naming rights are a form of corporate partnership in which a corporation purchases the right to attach its name to some part of a sports facility or event. These deals are quite common in professional sport. Most pro sports facilities have a corporate name attached to them, like Citi Field in New York City, FedEx Field in Washington, District of Columbia, and the STAPLES Center in Los Angeles. Some corporations pay in excess of $10 million per year for these naming rights. As of 2018, the largest naming rights deal in North America was MetLife Stadium, the home of the NFL's New York Jets and Giants. MetLife is paying $450 million over 25 years for the naming rights. Table 5.3 provides a breakdown of the top five naming rights deals in North America. Some

Table 5.3 Most Expensive Naming Rights Deals

Stadium	Team	Sponsor	Total value (millions of dollars)	Length of deal (years)
MetLife	New York Jets/Giants	MetLife	450	25
AT&T Stadium	Dallas Cowboys	AT&T	400	20
Citi Field	New York Mets	Citigroup	400	20
Mercedes-Benz Stadium	Atlanta Falcons	Mercedes-Benz	310	27
Reliant Stadium	Houston Texans	NRG Energy	300	30

Source: Badenhausen (2016).

facilities have gone beyond the naming of the entire facility and are now also selling naming rights to facility features such as parking lots, entrance gates, and concourses. The NFL's New England Patriots have sold the naming rights to their facility, Gillette Stadium, and also the names of entrances (Bank of America Gate), pavilions (NRG Plaza), and suite levels (Dell Technologies Suite Level) ("Seating map," 2017).

Licensed Merchandise

The sale of licensed merchandise is another important source of revenue for many professional leagues and teams. Most licensed merchandise at the professional level is controlled by the league, not the individual team. For example, the NBA has a subsidiary, NBA Properties, which handles all of its licensed merchandise business. In most deals, the licensee—the company that is paying to be associated with the sports team or league—pays an upfront fee and royalty, to the team or league, which is referred to as the licensor. If we use MLB as an example, New Era produces and sells hats bearing the team logos. New Era pays MLB an upfront fee to obtain the right to use the MLB logos on their product. It also then pays a royalty, usually 6% to 18% of wholesale price, based on the number of hats that are sold. So if you buy a New Era MLB hat, its retail price may be $30. The wholesale price is the amount the retailer pays to the manufacturer for the product. If we assume that the retailer paid New Era $15 for the hat it sold to you for $30, then MLB makes 6% to 18% of that $15. If we assume a 10% royalty, then MLB makes $1.50 in royalty revenue for every $30 hat that is sold. The overall revenue generated from the sale of licensed products can be substantial. It is estimated that the sale of NFL, NBA, and MLB merchandise is in excess of $3 billion per year for each league, so the royalty fees for those leagues may be as much as $100 to $150 million—which would be shared among the league teams.

Luxury Suites and Club Seating

All pro sports teams sell tickets in the form of season tickets, partial plans, group tickets, and individual game tickets. Additionally, most major professional teams have luxury suites and club seats. Club seats are a high-quality seat location with added amenities such as private concourses, concession areas, and restrooms. Some club seats also include preferred parking and wait staff service at the seat location. This form of seating has become popular with teams due to the higher prices that can be charged for them. Also, while a typical fan at a baseball game might spend $15 on food and drink, fans in luxury suites, on average, spend at least twice that amount for higher end food and drinks. Customers may pay 100% to 500% more for luxury seats versus traditional forms of seating. Luxury suites are a bit different from club seats. Luxury suites are usually enclosed spaces that may seat anywhere from 10 to 30 people. They often include outdoor and indoor seating in open-air stadiums along with private catering and restrooms, multiple flat screen TVs, and luxury theater-style seats. The primary customers for these suites are corporations and super-rich individuals. Most teams sell luxury suites in the form of multiyear contracts. The length of these contracts is usually three to seven years, and the price of these suites can be quite high. In Dallas, Texas, a suite for the NFL's Cowboys in AT&T Stadium can cost in excess of $900,000 per season (Koba, 2012). In addition, teams also charge more for the food and beverages that are consumed in the suite—often based on a per person buffet (all you can eat and drink). While teams prefer to sell suites in the form of multiyear contracts, they will sell the unsold inventory on a game-by-game basis. The rental cost for a luxury suite for a single game can be in excess of $5,000. New, modern facilities like AT&T Stadium and MetLife Stadium may have more than 200 luxury suites.

Ancillary Activities

Another major source of revenue for most pro sports is from ancillary activities like parking, concessions, and hosting of other events. While they may seem small in comparison to broadcast fees, these revenue sources are still important. One reason these revenue sources are so important is because most of this revenue is kept by the team, not shared with other league members like national broadcasting and licensed merchandise revenues. Parking revenue can, however, vary greatly depending on what entity owns the parking facilities, the total number of parking spots, and whether the facility is served by public transportation. In some locations, parking lots and garages may be owned by local municipalities or other private companies. If this is so, the team may be limited in its ability to generate parking revenue. With respect to parking revenues, the NFL's Washington Redskins may serve as a good example. The Redskins own all of their parking spaces and charge about $50 per car. If they have 10,000 cars park in their lots for a game, they can generate $500,000 in parking revenue for each home game. Over the course of a season (two preseason and eight regular season games) that may be over $5 million in parking revenue.

With respect to concessions, many larger sports organizations contract out concessions sales to companies such as Levy, Aramark, Comcast Spectacor, and Delaware North. These companies supply all the concessions for a team or facility. In return, the team or facility usually receives an up-front payment and a share of concession revenues or profits. While some teams have the ability to generate more revenue by operating their own concessions, they are minimizing their financial risk by contracting out to a third party concessionaire. In addition, most pro sports teams do not have the knowledge and experience to operate concessions on a large scale for their events that can draw in excess of 75,000 fans.

Teams, if they own their facility, may also rent their physical space to outside users. For example, a WNBA/NBA arena may be used for other events such as concerts, circuses, corporate gatherings, and holiday shows. This can be a significant revenue stream for the team/facility owner. For example, after decades of Fenway Park, the home of the Boston Red Sox, being used for Major League Baseball games only by order of team ownership the facility has hosted several major music concerts in the last decade including Billy Joel, Pearl Jam, and the Foo Fighters. On a smaller scale, physical spaces can also be rented for events such as weddings, parties, and even high school proms.

Transfer Fees

The last revenue stream that we will discuss for pro sports teams is largely limited to international sport, especially soccer. Soccer teams such as Tottenham Hotspur and Manchester United (MU) can generate revenue through the sale of player contracts. For example, if Tottenham has a player who is coveted by MU, Tottenham can sell that player for a price, known as a transfer fee. It should be mentioned that transfer fees do not exist in most major North American professional sports. As an example, in August of 2016, MU paid Italian club Juventus £89 million (about US$115 million) for the transfer rights to Paul Pogba. One aspect of transfer deals is that a player can negotiate that they will receive a percentage of the transfer fee. So, not only can international soccer players receive a salary for playing but also they may also benefit financially from being transferred between teams (Thomas, 2014). In recent years, the transfer fees for the top international players have grown dramatically. Table 5.4 provides information on the five largest transfer deals in international soccer history. Transfer fees can be both revenues and expenses for team. If a team is selling a player to another team for cash, then it is a source of revenue. However, if a team is paying the transfer fee to acquire a player, it is an expense on that club's financial books. Many smaller teams view transfer fees as an important revenue source. They will develop young players with the strategy of eventually transferring those players to a larger team for a fee. These fees will help the club cover expenses like player salaries, facility expenses, and travel costs.

Table 5.4 Top 5 Largest International Soccer Transfer Deals (in British Pounds)

Player	Transfer	Fee
Neymar (2017)	FC Barcelona to PSG	£198 millions
Ousmane Dembélé (2017)	Borussia Dortmund to FC Barcelona	£97 millions
Paul Pogba (2016)	Juventus to Manchester United	£89 millions
Gareth Bale (2013)	Tottenham to Real Madrid	£85.3 millions
Cristiano Ronaldo (2009)	Manchester United to Real Madrid	£83.7 millions

Source: Total Sportek (2017b).

In any given year, a player might be a low-level performer for one team but blossom for another; NBA fans may remember Toronto's Kyle Lowry. Conversely, a player can be a star one day and washed up the next; MLB fans may recall Philadelphia's Ryan Howard. Likewise, sport revenues can be plentiful one season and scarce the next. The business of managing sports teams, organizations, or facilities includes both potential profit centers and traps that can lead to financial ruin. The convergence of numerous variables that can increase or decrease revenue in a moment makes professional sports team management traditionally more complex than financing in other business sectors.

By seeing how revenues change over time, students can learn much about an industry. For example, in the 1930s, professional sport was not as popular as it is today, and teams had to promote themselves constantly. To achieve this, teams often paid the travel expense of sports reporters who covered the team. Because the team was paying the way for the reporters, they were less likely to write negative stories. The resulting positive publicity was designed to help sell more tickets and generate revenue. Teams no longer have to pay reporters to travel to cover them, but they still need to include a line item in their budgets to pay for food that is given to reporters in the pressroom. Again, the goal is to garner positive media coverage by supplying the media members with free food and beverages at games and team events.

Financial planning can address immediate issues that affect the bottom line or the development of long-term strategies for professional sports teams. Spurred by a major decline in spring training attendance (12% decline in 2009), several MLB teams developed innovative strategies to sell more tickets. For example, the Toronto Blue Jays sold tickets for a little over $1 per game when fans bought a $95 pass for 81 games (Nightengale & McCarthy, 2009). Teams developed other innovative strategies such as allowing fans to bring in their own food and offering all-you-can-eat discount programs. The Los Angeles Dodgers developed an all-you-can-eat offer for the rarely full right-field seating section. For $35 ($40 on game day) around 3,000 fans received unlimited Dodger dogs, nachos, peanuts, popcorn, and soft drinks to enjoy during the game. The profitable beer, ice cream, and candy products were not included in the package. These seats became much more popular than the left-field seats, which sold for $10 without any food.

REVENUES IN INTERCOLLEGIATE ATHLETICS

The business of intercollegiate athletics is unique to the United States. Most nations do not mix the business of sport with higher education. In the United States, especially at the National Collegiate Athletic Association (NCAA) Division I level, athletics is a very big business for universities. Athletic departments at universities such as Ohio State, Texas, and Michigan can generate over $175 million in revenue annually. However, this is not true for all colleges and universities. The median revenue for an NCAA Division I institution that competes in the Football Bowl Subdivision (FBS) is $63 million. In comparison, the median annual revenue for Division II programs is only $6.5 million.

The vast majority of collegiate athletic programs do not generate enough revenue to cover all of their costs. Thus, they must rely on allocations from the overall university and student body. Many universities transfer funds from the general university budget to athletics to cover costs; in some cases this can be in the millions of dollars.

Some universities rely on student fees to defray the cost of collegiate athletics. At most universities, students pay a fee to cover the cost of campus activities such as student clubs and organizations, fitness facilities, and campus entertainment. A portion of the student fee also makes its way to the athletic department at some universities. For example, let's look at the finances of the athletic department at James Madison University (JMU) in Harrisonburg, Virginia. JMU's athletic department has annual expenses of about $47 million. Student fees contribute approximately $34 million to cover those expenses (Craig, 2016).

While JMU is a bit unusual in the amount of revenue that comes from student fees, many universities use some portion of the student fee payment to cover athletic department expenses. While these revenue totals for NCAA Division I athletic programs are quite large, at most universities the athletic department revenues only make up about 3% to 5% of overall university revenue.

Table 5.5 provides a summary of the primary sources of revenue for NCAA Division I athletic departments. Several of these sources are similar to those that were addressed earlier with respect to professional sports teams. Intercollegiate athletic programs generate revenue from sources such as ticket sales, broadcast rights, concessions, and corporate partnerships. However, the management of these revenue sources may be different. For example, given that there is no overall league office structure that directly oversees each team, broadcast rights are negotiated differently in collegiate athletics. For the most part, broadcast rights for Division I athletics are negotiated at the conference level. For example, member schools of the Southeastern Conference (SEC) permit the conference headquarters to negotiate broadcast deals for all conference regular season and conference tournament games. In 2014 to 2015, the SEC reported annual income of $311 million from TV and radio broadcasting rights fees. This money is then distributed to the league members such as Alabama, Louisiana State University, and Georgia (Solomon, 2016). The conference and its membership own the rights to the broadcast of all regular season home games and the conference postseason games such as the conference basketball tournament and football conference championship game.

In table 5.5, the revenue from these broadcast deals is included in NCAA and conference distributions. The broadcast rights line item in table 5.5 includes the sale of broadcast rights to out-of-conference games and the radio broadcast of games. In collegiate athletics, ownership of the broadcast rights is usually based on who is the home team. As we can see with the SEC, these conference broadcast deals can be quite lucrative. However, the big money is usually reserved for members of the so-called power five conferences (SEC, Atlantic Coast Conference, Big Ten, Big 12, and Pac-12 Conference). Broadcast revenues decrease dramatically for smaller Division I conferences like the Mid-American and are virtually nonexistent for Division I Football Championship Subdivision (FCS), Division II, and Division III members. The FCS level of Division I is a group of about 125 schools who are Division I in all sports but play at the lower FCS level in football. This level of competition in football includes programs such as Delaware, James Madison, Youngstown State, and North Dakota State.

With respect to the sale of regular season broadcast rights in collegiate athletics, there is one obvious exception. The University of Notre Dame is a traditional football powerhouse with a rich tradition and national fan base. Given its market power, Notre Dame competes as an independent with no football conference affiliation. Notre Dame is a member of the Atlantic Coast Conference (ACC) in most of its other sports. One of the reasons for Notre Dame's football independence is that it allows Notre Dame to negotiate its own TV broadcast deal for home games. For over 25 years, Notre Dame home games have been broadcast on NBC. Over the years, this deal has been highly lucrative for Notre Dame. Currently, it has a 10-year contract that goes through 2025 and pays Notre Dame $15 million annually. In

Table 5.5 Median Generated Revenue for NCAA Division I (FBS) Institutions, 2015

Source	Total
Total ticket sales	$8,992,000
NCAA and conference distributions	$6,080,000
Guarantees and options	$878,000
Cash contributions from alumni and others	$9,531,000
Concessions, programs, and novelties	$1,071,000
Broadcast rights	$2,568,000
Royalties, advertising, and sponsorships	$3,290,000
All other	$1,182,000

Source: Fulks (2016).

return, NBC has the right to broadcast all Fighting Irish home football games ("NBC's Notre Dame deal extended," 2013).

As mentioned previously, the revenue from conference TV and broadcast deals is part of NCAA and conference distributions in table 5.5. But what else is included in this line item? Other forms of revenue in this area may include the sale of tickets to conference championship events along with the sale of conference-level sponsorships and licensed merchandise. NCAA distributions are also a significant part of this line item. The NCAA generates revenue from several sources, and about 90% of this money is distributed to its member programs.

The largest source of revenue for the NCAA is the broadcast rights for the Men's Division I Basketball Championship. The NCAA currently has a deal with CBS and Turner Sports that runs through 2032. Under this deal, agreed upon in 2016, the NCAA generates in excess of $1 billion per year in broadcasting and marketing fees (Sherman, 2016). Most of this money is distributed to the member programs through a variety of funding plans. The largest of these plans is the NCAA Tournament Basketball Fund. The distribution of over $250 million a year occurs through the basketball fund.

The NCAA distributes this money to Division I conferences that, in turn, distribute the money to their individual members. The level of distribution is based on the overall NCAA tournament performance of each team in a conference. Every NCAA tournament team receives a unit for each game it plays in the tournament. The NCAA then adds up each unit that every conference has earned over the past six years with each unit having a dollar value. The current dollar value is about $275,000 per unit. So, for explanatory purposes, let's assume that over the past six years members of the powerful ACC have played a total of 100 games in the NCAA tournament. That means that the ACC would receive approximately $27.5 million (100 × $275,000) from the NCAA Basketball Fund. In comparison, let's say the Big Sky Conference, a much smaller conference that usually has one team quality for the tournament and often loses in the first round, accumulated only six units over the same time period. The Big Sky Conference would only receive $1.65 million (6 × $275,000) from the basketball fund.

Once the funds are distributed to each conference, the conference membership then decides how that money will be distributed to its member schools. In the Big Ten, all teams receive an equal amount regardless of team success. So, a team that doesn't even make the NCAA tournament over a six-year time period makes the same amount as a team that qualifies every year. Meanwhile, other conferences such as the Colonial Athletic Association often reward those teams that were more successful, including their conference champion, with a higher distribution amount.

Another revenue source that is unique to intercollegiate athletic programs is gifts from alumni and boosters. The median amount of annual donations from alumni and boosters to Division I programs is in excess of $9.5 million (Fulks, 2016). Athletic departments invest a great deal of time, energy, and resources into fundraising and development efforts. The donations that are made can take many different forms. The most common is a cash donation. Most of these cash donations are in rather small amounts such $100 to $1,000. However, there have been some noteworthy major donations made to athletic departments. Billionaire T. Boone Pickens gave Oklahoma State University's athletic department a gift of $165 million in 2006. At the time, it was the largest single donation to an athletic department in history. Not surprisingly, the football stadium at Oklahoma State now bears Mr. Pickens' name. In another case, Nike founder Phil Knight has donated approximately $150 million to the University of Oregon's athletic department over the past 20 years (Rogoway, 2016).

Donations made to athletic departments may be made for specific purposes such as facility construction or renovation, scholarships, coaching salaries, or expenses for a specific sport. The donations may also be placed in the athletic department's general account for use to cover any type of expense. One benefit to the donor is that a portion of these donations are deductible on their **income taxes**.

At major universities, if one wishes to have season tickets for sports like football and basketball, in addition to paying the ticket prices, there may be an additional minimum donation required. Also, the donations can take many forms. In addition to money, donations may be in the form of real estate, stocks, bonds, and commodities such as gold and silver. Several universities in farming states even have programs where farmers can donate livestock such as cows and pigs.

Game guarantees are another unique aspect of the financial model of collegiate athletics. A game guarantee is a payment made to entice a team to play another team in a sporting event. Guarantees are most common in football and basketball but they may be present in other sports as well. There has been a substantial increase in the size of guarantees paid in football and basketball. For FBS-level football, guarantees can exceed $1 million per game. In the fall of 2017, Nebraska paid Arkansas State $1.65 million to travel to Lincoln for a game. In that same season, Auburn paid Georgia Southern $1.3 million to play a game. Overall, during the course of the 2017 football season, over $150 million in guarantees were paid (Berkowitz, 2017). It must be remembered that while these payments are revenues for the team receiving the payment, they are expenses for those teams that are making the same payments. For smaller programs like Georgia Southern and Arkansas State, guarantees are a vital source of revenue. The amount of money these programs can make from playing guarantee games far exceeds the amount they can make from playing a home game. For the larger programs, it gives them another home game and the corresponding revenue, along with the game generally being an easy win. However, this is not always the case. In one of the most famous guarantee games in history, Michigan hosted FCS-level Appalachian State in 2007. Ultimately, not only did Appalachian State leave Ann Arbor with a $400,000 check, but it also left with one of the biggest upset wins in college football history (Kahn, 2017).

All collegiate athletic departments attempt to maximize their existing revenue streams and also look to develop new ones. The job of a collegiate athletic director has changed from being an administrator to being a fund-raiser. What does this mean? Athletic directors now spend a great deal of their time in fund-raising activities along with developing strategies to increase revenue from sources such as ticket sales, sponsorship, facility rental, concessions, and merchandise sales. This is true even with smaller programs

that compete at the Division II and III levels. As stated earlier, a collegiate athletic program is a nonprofit organization, thus the more revenue it generates, the more it can spend to improve the experience of their stakeholders such as student-athletes, alumni, and the overall fan base.

REVENUES IN THE SPORTING GOODS INDUSTRY

With respect to revenue sources, professional sports teams and collegiate athletic programs are different than other sport segments such as sporting goods, fitness centers, sports equipment, and sports agencies. These sport segments are much more traditional in their revenues. For the most part, companies like sporting goods companies and fitness centers sell a line of products and services. A fitness center may sell services such as memberships, spa sessions, fitness classes, and even laundry service. Additionally, it may sell tangible products such as food, beverages, and fitness equipment (shorts, T-shirts, yoga mats, and weights). Sporting goods companies such as Under Armour, Nike, Puma, and, Adidas primarily generate revenue from the sale of tangible products. The products may include shoes, shirts, hats, sweatshirts, yoga pants, and outerwear along with sporting equipment such as bats, balls, helmets, and gloves. As stated earlier, all sports organizations must understand the sources of their revenue and develop strategies to make them grow. In this section, we will use Under Armour (UA) as a case study for understanding the sources of revenue for a sporting goods company. This section will focus on the sources of revenue for sporting goods companies.

Under Armour is a global company that primarily sells sporting apparel and equipment. It is headquartered in Baltimore and as of 2016 had about $4.8 billion in annual revenues. It also has over 11,000 employees and its stock is publicly traded on the New York Stock Exchange ("Under Armour Annual Report", 2016). UA's financial statements, which provide general information on its level of annual revenues, are located in appendix A. The income statement shows that UA had considerable growth in revenue from 2012 to 2016. Revenue went from $1.835 billion in 2012 to $4.825 billion in 2016. This is an increase in revenue of 262% in only four years. However, beyond that, the income statement fails to provide a great deal of information on revenue. To obtain additional information, it is necessary to take an in-depth look at UA's annual report, also known as the **10-K** report (a quarterly report is known as the **10-Q**). As a global corporation, it is important for UA and its stakeholders to have knowledge of its revenue sources based on geography. As we can see in table 5.6, although UA is considered a global business, 83% of its total revenue is generated in North America. Sales of its products from all other parts of the world account for only 17% of revenue. If UA wishes to grow its revenue, it may need to develop strategies to increase sales beyond North America.

Table 5.7 provides a breakdown of UA revenue across product segments. For 2016, $3.2 billion of the company's $4.8 billion in total revenue come from the sale of apparel. The second largest source of revenue is from the sale of footwear.

Interestingly, while apparel sales are easily the largest source of revenue, on a percentage basis, footwear revenue is growing at a faster rate—49.1% to 15.3%. Thus, UA must make decisions on how to allocate its capital in the future. Does it invest in growing its largest product segment—apparel—or does it attempt to increase sales in the segment that is growing at the fastest rate—footwear? These are the types of financial decisions that sports managers must continually make. In this case of UA, the fortunes of a company can change quickly. Under Armour saw its stock hit an all-time high in July 2015, when its price was $49.67 per share. However, the stock tumbled to a low of $12.52 in October of 2017—a loss of over 75% of its value. Kevin Plank, UA's chief executive officer, blamed the stock drop on a decrease in demand for UA footwear and apparel in the North American market.

Seasonality can also play an important role in the size of revenues for many sports organizations. Sport segments that are greatly affected by the season of the year may include golf, skiing,

Table 5.6 Under Armour Revenue Sources by Continent, 2016

Area	Net revenues (in millions)	% of net revenues
North America	$4,005	83.0
Europe, Middle East, and Africa	$330	6.9
Asia-Pacific	$268	5.6
Latin America	$141	2.9
Connected fitness	$80	1.6
Intersegment eliminations	$1.4	<1.0
Total	$4,825	100

Source: Under Armour Annual Report (filed 2/23/17).

Table 5.7 Under Armour Revenue by Product Segment, 2016

(in millions)	Year ended December 31, 2016	Year ended December 31, 2015	% change
Apparel	$3,229	$2,801	15.3
Footwear	$1,010	$677	49.1
Accessories	$406	$346	17.2
Total net sales	$4,646	$3,825	21.5
License	$99	$84	18.6
Connected fitness	$80	$53	50.6
Intersegment eliminations	$1.4		
Total net revenues	**$4,825**	**$3,963**	**21.8**

Source: Under Armour Annual Report (filed 2/23/17).

and tennis. For example, the revenue for a golf course in New England will be very high in the late spring, summer, and early fall months. However, in the winter, revenue from the golf course may decrease greatly, and the golf course must plan accordingly. In another example, ski resorts traditionally generated the vast majority of their revenue in the winter months. In an effort to increase revenue beyond the ski season, many ski resorts have diversified into activities like mountain biking, water parks, and hiking.

Seasonality can even affect sporting goods companies. As we can see from table 5.8, UA has its largest levels of revenue in the quarters that end in September and December. In general, the fall is UA's largest sales season. This is most likely due to customers buying higher priced winter apparel in the fall along with an increase in sales as the holiday season approaches. UA must plan accordingly for the inevitable decrease in revenue that will occur as a new year begins. While we have concentrated the revenue of UA, a similar story can be told for other sporting goods and equipment companies. The value of the revenues may change, but the sources of revenue such as apparel, footwear, and equipment will not be different. However, just for comparison, Nike has annual revenue of about $32 billion, Adidas' annual revenue is approximately $20 billion, and Puma's is $4 billion.

REVENUE PLANNING

Revenue can come from numerous sources as highlighted earlier. Developing strategies to generate revenue is a key part of financial planning for any sports organization. The higher the stakes are, such as those that surround billion-dollar professional teams or companies like Under Armour, the greater the need for financial planning. For example, in 2016, Manchester United had a whopping operating profit of £68.9 million (about US$90 million) on revenue of £515.3 million (US$670 million). This sum is the largest revenue obtained by any pro soccer team in the world (Kelleher, 2016). In another example, the 2016 Olympic Games in Rio de Janeiro generated over $4 billion in total revenue. Of that revenue, 73% came from broadcasting rights; 18% from sponsorships; and 9% from ticketing, licensing, and other revenue sources ("How Rio," 2015). Given the large levels of revenue, a great deal of planning must go into maximizing these revenue streams and developing methods for finding new revenues.

Financial planning can address immediate issues that affect the bottom line or the development of long-term strategies. Spurred by a major decline in football attendance, several college athletics programs have developed innovative strategies to sell more tickets. For example, the University of Delaware initiated a deeply discounted young alumni season ticket package and a pick three promotion in which ticket buyers pick three of six home games they would like to attend. Another strategy that several college football marketers have initiated is the sale of alcoholic beverages in their stadiums (in luxury suites, concourses, and the sitting bowl).

Many administrators of high school programs, which have already tried using fees to help balance their budgets, have used financial planning to focus on where they can generate additional revenue. The Licensing Resource Group has signed over 7,000 high schools and was expected to add more than half of the 27,000 high schools in the United States. The program places school-licensed goods in national outlets such as Wal-Mart and Kohl's (Halley, 2010). The program was designed to tap into the 7.5 million high school athletes and their followers who might want to buy athletic-related apparel. Estimates are that schools in the program might generate as little as $30 but possibly several thousand dollars. The prospect of competing against high school logos for shelf space caused a rash of letters from prominent college programs to high schools demanding that they stop using logos that could impede on the copyrights owned by the colleges (Halley, 2010). The Licensing Resource Group

Table 5.8 Under Armour Net Revenue by Quarter, 2016

(in thousands)	QUARTER ENDED			
	3/31/2016	6/30/2016	9/30/2016	12/31/2016
Net revenue	$1,047,702	$1,000,783	$1,471,573	$1,305,277

Source: Under Armour Annual Report (filed 2/23/17).

was so successful that in 2014 it was acquired by the Learfield Group (Smith, 2014).

Sport companies like Under Armour and Nike may attempt to increase revenue by acquiring other sporting goods companies. Nike has purchased companies that owned footwear brands like Converse and Cole Hahn over the years. In 2017, a major collegiate sports agency merger was announced. Two of the leading collegiate media and marketing firms were the aforementioned Learfield and IMG College. The two companies competed against each other to acquire the rights to manage media and marketing opportunities for collegiate athletic departments. In total, the two companies had accounts with hundreds of universities across the United States. The companies announced in the fall of 2017 that they would merge and become one company (Smith & Ourand, 2017). The combined company has the potential to increase revenue while decreasing costs due to the elimination of duplicate systems and personnel. While this may be a benefit to the new Learfield/IMG College company, it could be a negative for the collegiate athletic departments due to the loss of competition between the two companies, leaving them with just one company to work with in the area of media and marketing rights.

CONCEPTS INTO PRACTICE

Revenue can be limited by various rules or regulations. For example, every sports organization would love to be associated with a casino as a sponsor. In most professional sports leagues, association with casinos can lead to significant penalties. Thus, in the 1960s, Willie Mays and Mickey Mantle were temporarily barred from Major League Baseball because they had endorsement contracts with casinos and were still involved with the game. This concern filters down to collegiate athletics; the NCAA is concerned about gambling and wants to protect its image. But this issue does not apply to individual universities, which are allowed to enter into contracts with casinos. Thus, the University of New Mexico signed a five-year agreement for $2.5 million that makes the Route 66 Casino Hotel the university's exclusive gaming sponsor (Appenzeller, 2011).

CONCLUSION

This chapter provided information on the variety of revenue sources that sports organizations can encounter. Sport finance is a numbers game. Numerous revenues constitute the game pieces. Profits and losses are highlighted in the outcome of the game. By understanding all the necessary moves and the various strategies available to the contestants, a sports organization can win the game.

Although this game metaphor may appear contrived, it represents a reality in sport finance. Sport finance is as much a game as the games played on athletic fields or courts. Sport finance professionals need to play a heads-up game to take advantage of various laws, economic conditions, or other variables to maximize value. Through intelligent financial manipulations, a skilled player can turn a loss into a profit. As Paul Beeston, former president of the Toronto Blue Jays, said, "Under generally accepted accounting principles, I can turn a $4 million profit into a $2 million loss, and I can get every national accounting firm to agree with me" (Howard & Crompton, 2004, p. 12). This text does not analyze the ethical issues associated with such conduct, but it raises the red flag so that you will understand that financial data can be manipulated. Thus, care should be exercised in reviewing all financial statements. Whenever an issue arises, you have the ultimate responsibility to ask questions and not just assume that others have done the analysis work for you.

This chapter provided an overview of revenue sources, but it cannot fully prepare any student to assume complete responsibilities in managing all facets of revenue generation. The process of increasing revenue is not only about being creative and providing lasting value but also entails forecasting future revenue streams and how to manage existing resources effectively. Although the skills discussed in this chapter are important, financial managers of for-profit sports organizations are judged primarily on whether they have been successful in maximizing a corporation's stock value. Increasing stock valuation is an immense task that requires every unit within the business to operate together (Brigham & Ehrhardt, 2014). This can be seen when revenue production might be fantastic, but if expenses (covered in chapter 6) are left unchecked, the company will suffer and stock prices will not increase. Thus, to increase stock value a company needs to balance increasing revenue while at the same time decreasing expenses. Similarly, not-for-profit sports organization financial managers may be judged by their ability to maximize existing revenue streams, develop new revenue sources, and decrease expenses.

Class Discussion Topics

1. What are the primary revenue sources for a nonprofit sports organization?
2. What are the differences between revenues at a Division I program and a Division III program?
3. Develop a list of revenue streams for a professional baseball team.
4. Develop a list of revenue streams for a publicly traded sportswear company.
5. Develop a list of revenue streams for a NASCAR racing team.
6. For a professional sports team, what revenue source(s) to you see growing the most in the next decade? Why do you think so?

6

Understanding Expenses

Chapter Objectives

After studying this chapter, you should be able to do the following:

- Appreciate all the various expenses that affect a sport enterprise.
- Distinguish where expenses come from for sport enterprises.
- Understand the various sources of expenses for organizations in the professional sport industry.
- Explain sources of expenses for collegiate sport and other amateur sports organizations.
- Interpret the various sources of expenses for sporting goods companies and other sports organizations.

In chapter 5, the topic of revenues in the sport industry was addressed. This chapter will focus on the other side of the financial equation: expenses. Expenses are costs that are incurred by an organization. Typical expenses for sports organizations include areas such as rent, utilities, raw materials, insurance, salaries, and benefits. Each sport industry segment may have different expenses. A fitness center will have different expenses than a collegiate athletic department or a professional sports team. For a fitness center, an expense can be the salaries and wages of its employees. If the fitness center pays these wage expenses as they arise, then it is covering its expenses. If it fails to pay these wage expenses, then it will accrue debt. Debt is the owing of money to others—in this case employees. However, as stated, if the fitness center pays all its expenses as they arise, then it will avoid employee-related debt. While most sports organizations can cover short-term expenses such as wages, rent, utilities, and insurance with the revenue they produce, many must use debt to cover long-term and capital costs. For example, a professional sports team may use debt to cover the construction cost for a new stadium or arena. The team simply does not have the revenue on hand to cover this large expense; thus, it uses debt that will be repaid over a longer time horizon.

This chapter will address the various types of expenses for sports organizations across a number of sport industry segments such as professional team sport, collegiate athletics, and the sporting goods industry. Additionally, the financial strategies for minimizing expenses while maximizing profitability will be covered.

EXPENSES IN THE SPORT INDUSTRY

As stated earlier, certain fixed expenses will normally exist regardless of the sport industry segment. Employee salaries and wages, utilities, travel expenses, office supplies, and equipment costs are present in almost every type of sports organization, and they occur on a regular basis. Because most expenses occur on a monthly or other periodic basis, a sports organization can normally predict, monitor, and, when feasible, reduce future expenses. During difficult macroeconomic times, such as a **recession**, sports organizations may dramatically alter their expenses by terminating coaches, reducing coaching contracts (from 12 months to 10 months), limiting facility usage hours, closing retail stores, and minimizing office supply usage. Expenses may also change due to other factors such as increased competition, player injuries, or other organizational changes.

One of the greatest expenses for any sports organization is personnel costs. The cost for employees from coaches to custodians adds a significant amount to the bottom line cost for any sports organization. For example, some Major League Baseball (MLB) teams such as the New York Yankees and Los Angeles Dodgers spend over $200 million on player costs alone. Meanwhile, in collegiate athletics, the student-athletes are not paid a salary but do receive an athletic grant-in-aid (scholarship) that covers tuition, room, board, books, and a small stipend. In intercollegiate athletics, like professional team sport, collegiate coaches receive a salary. Some big-time collegiate coaches in football and basketball such as Duke's Mike Krzyzewski and Alabama's Nick Saban earn in excess of $7 million per year. Although personnel costs are a critical component of any sports organization's bottom line, all expenses need to be examined. The adage is that it costs money to make money, and this belief can be seen in the cost to raise money through sporting events. Walkathons and other sport-based fund-raising events can raise a lot of money for a charitable organization, but they also can cost a lot. Walkathons typically cost 50 cents on the dollar compared with the average fund-raising cost of 15 to 20 cents per dollar for other nonprofit fund-raisers. Expenses for these events include event producers, consultants, trade shows, technology vendors, caterers, printers, and other fund-raising costs. A more precise breakdown for a typical one-day fun run could include runner supplies (19%), furniture (16%), including tents, rental toilets, and signage, security and safety (15%), and fund-raising commissions (2%). The remaining 48% would be the net proceeds to the charity (Kadet, 2011).

CONCEPTS INTO PRACTICE

Expenses can quickly grow and when left unchecked can generate significant negative publicity. One such example involved the University of Oregon's effort to recruit some top talent. The football team attempted to recruit 25 high school players and spent approximately $5,635 on each student (for a total of $140,875.99). The recruits stayed at a top-level hotel, dined on steak meals, and were whisked around by four jets. When several recruits missed their charter jets, they flew on commercial jets at a cost of $10,009.72 each (Appenzeller, 2011). Oregon is not alone with having a large purse for college athletics. Most major college teams spend a huge amount on lodging for players at hotels, even for home games, to avoid noise and distractions. For the 2010 season, North Carolina State University paid over $85,000, The University of North Carolina Chapel Hill spent over $78,000, and Clemson University spent over $110,000 on player accommodations (Appenzeller, 2011). This trend has spread to even the lower level football programs. In 2017, the University of Delaware, a Football Championship Subdivision program, began housing its football team in a hotel the night before all home games.

Although revenue-generating options may be limited, the expenses normally do not share the same limitation, as many sports organizations face constantly rising costs. The following examples present the expenses of a typical public high school athletic program and a fitness center.

High School Athletic Program Expenses

Facility repair and maintenance costs

Uniforms and equipment

Travel and lodging

Insurance

Umpires and referees

Utilities

Salaries and benefits

Advertising

Promotions

Office supplies

Fitness Center Expenses

Employee salaries and benefits

Rent

Equipment (purchases and leases)

Insurance

Advertising

Professional services (accounting, legal)

Maintenance and repairs

Utilities

General

EXPENSES IN PROFESSIONAL SPORT

Professional sports teams at all levels and in all sports incur a variety of expenses annually. For most teams, the largest expense is player salaries and benefits. In addition to the player costs, teams have expenses in areas such as travel, front office personnel, utilities, scouting and player development, insurance, taxes, and office equipment and supplies.

Player Expenses

Professional team sport can be separated into two segments: major league and minor league teams. In North America, for leagues such as MLB and the National Hockey League (NHL) a system of minor league affiliate teams exists. For example, MLB's Minnesota Twins have seven minor league affiliate teams that range from the rookie level up to the highest minor league baseball level, AAA. These minor league teams incur no costs for player salaries. The parent club, in this case the Twins, covers the player and coaching salary and benefits costs for all of its minor league affiliates. In the NHL, most teams have affiliate teams in the American Hockey League (AHL), and the parent team pays the salaries of those minor league players and coaches. There are a few rare occasions where the AHL team may have players on contract directly with it, and the AHL team bears the burden of the players' salaries. Not all minor leagues, however, are affiliated with major leagues, even in baseball and ice hockey. Leagues such as the Northern

League and Frontier League (baseball), the North American Soccer League, the Federal Hockey League, and the Canadian Basketball League are independently owned and operated. Each team must cover the player and coach expense. Overall, players at the minor league level earn a salary that is dramatically less than the major league salary amounts. A minor league baseball player may make as little as $2,000 per month during the six- to seven-month playing season. Minor league teams also have expenses in other areas such as sports medicine, meals, player equipment, and travel costs.

While the minor league sport system in North America is important, the major leagues in sports such as football, basketball, ice hockey, baseball, and soccer garner the vast majority of attention. For teams in leagues such as the National Football League (NFL), the NHL, the National Basketball Association (NBA), the Women's National Basketball Association (WNBA) and in MLB and Major League Soccer (MLS), the largest expense is player salaries and benefits. The same is true globally for professional sport such as soccer, cricket, and rugby. For many teams in these professional sports leagues, player expenses can exceed 50% of their total operating costs. The player compensation system for most major North American professional sports leagues is much different from other international leagues such as the English Premier League or La Liga in Spain. These international leagues will be addressed a bit later in this section.

Historically, most North American professional leagues operated under some form of a reserve clause for players. The reserve clause stipulated that a single team owned the contractual rights to a player for his entire career. When a player's contract ended, the team could re-sign him at a negotiated salary. If the player did not like the salary, his only option was to not play; the player was not free to negotiate with other teams unless his original team refused to offer him a contract. In short, the player did not have the right to become a free agent. For the most part, this system was in place from the time that North American professional leagues started until the late 1970s. Prior to the advent of player free agency, owners could keep player expenses low, and this increased the owners'

profit level. Beginning in the late 1970s, players slowly began to obtain free agent rights either through legal action or through collective bargaining between the players' unions and team owners. In North America, players in all major professional leagues are represented by a players' union. The union negotiates a collective bargaining agreement (CBA) with the league and its owners. This CBA governs the relationship between the players and owners and covers areas such as player compensation, health and retirement benefits, drug testing policies, and free agency. As the players' unions got stronger in the late 1970s and 1980s, the players began to win more contractual rights either at the bargaining table or through legal action. One result of this was an increase in player salaries. While this was great for the players, it resulted in a sharp increase in expenses for the owners. For example, the average salary of a MLB player in 1975 was $44,676. By 1985, the average MLB salary was $371,571. Ten years later it was up to $1.1 million, and in 2017 it had skyrocketed to $4.47 million (Shaikin, 2016). The institution of free agency was a major factor in the increase of MLB average player salaries.

Further evidence of the level of MLB player expenses can be seen in table 6.1. The table provides team salaries for seven teams in MLB for the 2017 season. The Los Angeles Dodgers had the largest team payroll at $242.07 million; meanwhile the Milwaukee Brewers had the lowest at $63.06 million. Thus, the Dodgers spent about four times as much on players as the Brewers. Also, according to *Forbes*, the Dodgers

Table 6.1 Select Major League Baseball Team Salaries, 2017

Salary rank	Team	$ amount (in millions)
1	Los Angeles Dodgers	242.07
2	New York Yankees	201.54
3	Boston Red Sox	199.81
10	Baltimore Orioles	163.68
15	Kansas City Royals	140.93
20	Miami Marlins	111.88
30	Milwaukee Brewers	63.06

Source: Perry (2017).

had approximately $440 million in total operating expenses. So, player salaries composed about 55% of overall team expenses ("The business of baseball," 2017). Professional sport teams also incur other costs related to their players such as health and retirement benefits. For example in MLB, benefits include health care, workers' compensation insurance, and insurance for career-ending injuries. The cost for workers' compensation insurance alone may be close to the salary for each player due to the significant injury risks for athletes. These benefits can add substantially to the overall cost of paying the labor that produces the game: the players.

In an effort to control player costs, major North American professional sports league owners and players' unions have negotiated salary systems such as team salary caps, individual player salary caps, or luxury taxes. By doing this, the owners have tied player costs to team and league revenues, or the team salary caps have been negotiated for future years. For example, MLB has a team salary luxury tax, also known as the competitive balance tax. If a team spends over the negotiated team salary limit, it must pay a luxury tax. This tax money is collected from those teams that spend over the limit, and about 50 percent is distributed to the compliant MLB teams. The other half of the tax money is used to fund player health and retirement benefits. Table 6.2 provides information on the tax limits and the corresponding tax penalties ("Competitive balance tax," 2017). Let's use the Los Angeles Dodgers as an example. As we stated, the Dodgers had a team salary of approximately $242 million in 2017, and the luxury tax level for that year was $195 million. Thus, the Dodgers were $47 million over the luxury tax

threshold. If this was the first time the Dodgers were over the tax threshold, the team would have paid a $9.4 million penalty to the league ($47 million × 20%). However, let's say this was the second time that the Dodgers had gone over the tax threshold. In that case, the penalty would have increased to $14.1 million. In fact, 2017 marked the fifth time that the Dodgers were over the tax threshold and thus paid a 50% penalty that equaled $23.5 million. In 2017, the Dodgers, New York Yankees, Detroit Tigers, Boston Red Sox, Chicago Cubs, and San Francisco Giants all paid the luxury tax (Nightengale, 2017). So, while the intention of the luxury tax is to limit teams from spending on player salaries, it has not been totally successful. In an effort to win the World Series, several teams have made the business decision to spend beyond the luxury tax threshold and pay the fine; however, 24 teams have made the financial decision that it is not in their best interest to exceed the luxury tax limit.

MLB is somewhat different with the institution of its luxury tax system. Other North American professional leagues have attempted to curb player salary expenses through the use of team and player salary caps. The NFL has perhaps the strictest team salary cap system in professional sport. Each team is limited to a total amount it can spend on its roster of players. That amount is calculated as a percentage of league revenues. Therefore, the team salary cap can only increase if the league revenue also increases. This system allows the NFL to control overall spending on players. Other leagues such as the NHL and NBA also tie the team salary cap to league revenues. In short, the owners are policing their own spending through the team salary cap. Under the CBA between the NFL owners and the NFL Players

Table 6.2 Major League Baseball Luxury Tax System

Year	Payroll amount (in millions)	% Tax 1st offense	% Tax 2nd offense	% Tax 3rd offense	% Tax 4th+ offense
2017	$195	20	30	50	50
2018	$197	20	30	50	50
2019	$206	20	30	50	50
2020	$208	20	30	50	50
2021	$210	20	30	50	50

Source: Competitive Balance Tax (2018).

Association, which was signed in 2011 and runs through 2020, the team salary cap is set at 47% of overall league revenue. So, let's assume that the NFL has overall annual league revenue of $12 billion. The team salary cap is calculated by taking 47% of $12 billion (which is $5.64 billion) and dividing that by the number of teams in the NFL (32). This would result in a team salary cap of $176.25 for one season. In reality, the NFL's team salary cap for 2017 was fairly close to that amount at $167 million.

The NFL has extensive rules related to how salaries and bonuses are counted toward the salary cap. Thus, the actual out-of-pocket expense for a team is often different than the amount of money that is counted toward the cap. Table 6.3 provides data on the actual cash amounts that several NFL teams spent on player salaries for the 2017 season ("NFL team," 2017). For example, the NFL cap rules allow a team to prorate a player signing bonus. So, if a team signs a player to a four-year contract and, as part of the contract, pays an $8 million signing bonus, NFL rules permit that bonus to be prorated over the life of the contract. In terms of cash outlays, the team will pay the player the $8 million in the first year. However, with respect to the cap, the bonus counts as $2 million toward the cap for each of the four years. In another example, the NFL permits teams to carry over unused cap money from one year to the next. Thus, while the cap for 2017 was $167 million, if a team carried over $10 million from the previous year, its actual cap limit was $177 million. These examples show how a team like the Detroit Lions can spend over $200 million in cash when the cap figure was

only $167 million without violating the salary cap rules. Despite the NFL salary cap, individual NFL player salaries can be quite large. Table 6.4 provides data on the top five player salaries in the NFL for the 2017 season. The average player salary for 2017 was $1.9 million.

Table 6.4 Top Five NFL Player Salaries, 2017

Player	Team	Salary (in millions)
Derek Carr	Oakland Raiders	$25.00
Andrew Luck	Indianapolis Colts	$24.59
Carson Palmer	Arizona Cardinals	$24.35
Drew Brees	New Orleans Saints	$24.25
Kirk Cousins	Washington Redskins	$23.94

Source: Martin (2017).

As we can see from table 6.3, the difference between the highest and lowest salary teams is rather small. The Detroit Lions spent $201.70 million in 2017 while the Jets ranked last at $136.80 million, a difference of only $64.9 million. In comparison, the difference between the highest and lowest team salaries in MLB for 2017 was $179.01 million. The disparity between the two leagues is largely due to the NFL's fairly rigid team salary cap while MLB has a luxury tax but no actual limit on team salary expenditures. The NFL team salary cap rules are quite complex and beyond the scope of this text. In fact, the rules are so complex that all teams employ a person, or persons, who are known as "capologists." These people have a thorough understanding of the NFL cap rules, have the ability to negotiate and structure contracts, and have knowledge of the financial implications of the player contracts that are signed. In short, a capologist must structure team contracts in a manner that keeps the team under the salary cap while also giving the team the highest probability of success on the field of play.

The NBA also has a team salary cap based on a percentage of league revenues like the NFL's cap. The NBA's salary cap has been in existence since the 1984 to 1985 season. In the NBA, the cap is based on 50% of basketball-related income, which includes most revenue streams that come to the league. In 2016 to 2017, the NBA salary

Table 6.3 Select NFL Team Cash Payroll Figures, 2017

Rank	Team	Total cap spending (in millions)
1	Detroit Lions	$201.70
2	Carolina Panthers	$193.13
5	Jacksonville Jaguars	$180.48
10	Minnesota Vikings	$172.08
20	Los Angeles Chargers	$159.68
32	New York Jets	$136.80

cap was set at $94.10 million. Table 6.5 provides data on the actual salary expenditures for select NBA teams. As we saw with the NFL, there are many teams that spend beyond the cap number. Again, this is due to the existence of several rules that permit a team to continue to spend money on players' salaries even if it means the team will be over the cap. Most experts consider the NFL's salary cap to be rather hard; meaning it is difficult to exceed it without breaking NFL rules. In comparison, the NBA has a soft salary cap that includes numerous exceptions that make it rather easy for teams to spend over the cap level. The most publicized of these exceptions is the "Larry Bird exception." Named after the famous Boston Celtics star, the Bird exception was established in 1984 so the Boston Celtics could re-sign their star player. If the rule was not in place, Bird might have been forced to move to another team via free agency (Cronin, 2010). The NBA believed it was in its best interest for Bird to remain in Boston green. Therefore, it established a rule permitting a team to re-sign its own player even if it meant that the team went over the salary cap. Over the years, the rule has been amended several times. Under the current CBA that runs through the 2020 to 2021 season, a team can re-sign its own player to a contract even if it means the team is over the salary cap if that player has been on the team for three or more years. More recently, an "early Bird exception" was added, allowing a team to re-sign a player with only two years of service with the team. In those cases, the team can only pay the player up to 117% of his previous salary or 104.5% of the league average, which was $6.2 million for the 2016 to 2017 season.

Table 6.5 NBA Team Salaries, 2017 to 2018

Rank	Team	Salary (in millions)
1	Golden State Warriors	$137.49
2	Cleveland Cavaliers	$137.08
5	Washington Wizards	$125.18
10	Minnesota Timberwolves	$117.47
20	New York Knicks	$106.75
30	Chicago Bulls	$84.05

There are several other exceptions to the NBA league salary cap that lead to inflated team payrolls. The minutiae of these exceptions and the CBA are beyond the scope of this text, but some of these exceptions include the midlevel exception, the designated veteran exception, and the rookie exception. All these exceptions permit a team to sign new players or retain current players even if the team is over the salary cap. The NBA has another mechanism to deter teams from dramatically spending over the salary cap. Similar to MLB, the NBA has a salary luxury tax. The tax level is calculated as 53.53% of basketball-related income. For the 2016 to 2017 season, the tax level was $113.30 million. Thus, if a team spent over that amount, it was required to pay a tax. The tax penalty in the NBA is much higher than in MLB. For the first $5 million that a first offending team spends over the tax level, it pays a 150% tax ($7.5 million). The penalty increases to 175% for the second $5 million over the tax ($8.75 million) and 250% for the third $5 million over the tax ($12.5 million). So, if a team spends $10 million over the tax figure as a first time offender, it pays a tax of $16.25 million ($7.5 million + $8.75 million). For the 2016 to 2017 season, only two teams surpassed the tax level—the Cleveland Cavaliers and Los Angeles Clippers. Thus, while it looks like the salary cap has not limited team spending, it does appear that most teams are budgeting their team salary expenditures in a manner to avoid paying the NBA luxury tax.

The NBA is also different from the NFL and MLB, through an individual player salary cap that is part of the CBA. The individual salary cap is based on the player's years of experience in the league. For players with zero to six years of NBA experience, the maximum salary was $25.5 million or 25% of the team salary cap for the 2017 to 2018 season. For a player with seven to nine years of experience, the contract maximum was $30.6 million or 35% of the team salary cap, and for players with 10-plus years of experience, the maximum contract was $35.7 million or 35% of the cap. An exception to these limits is that a player may sign for a 5% increase over his previous salary even if that amount takes him over the individual player salary limit (Venook, 2017). As with the team salary cap and luxury tax, the individual salary cap was another attempt by NBA owners to curb expenditures on player salaries. With respect to individual player salaries, Stephen Curry of the Golden State Warriors was the highest paid player for the 2017 to 2018 season with a salary of $34.68 million; LeBron James was next at $33.28 million.

Other leagues such as the NHL, MLS, and the WNBA also have salary caps. Similar to the NBA and NFL, the NHL cap is based on a percentage of overall league revenue. In the NHL, the team salary cap was instituted for the 2012 to 2013 season and runs through the 2021 to 2022 season. The cap figure is determined by 50% of hockey-related revenue, which encompasses most of the league revenue streams. For 2016 to 2017, the team salary cap was $73 million. This figure, which is considerably less than the NBA and NFL caps, shows that the NHL does not generate the overall revenue of these other leagues, thus the smaller amount. In comparison to this figure, the salary caps in MLS and WNBA are very small. The WNBA salary cap is approximately $1 million with an individual player maximum of $109, 500. The average player salary in the WNBA is about $51,000. In MLS, the team salary cap for the 2017 season was $3.845 million. Given that international soccer superstars such as Cristiano Ronaldo and Lionel Messi can make in excess of $25 million in salary per year, this low salary cap makes it very difficult for MLS to compete for the best players. But MLS believes that it must severely limit its spending on player salaries to stay financially viable. In the early 1980s, the North American Soccer League spent lavishly on player salaries, which ultimately led to its 1984 demise. MLS has attempted to avoid this same fate by greatly limiting its player expenses.

While it has made a concerted effort to limit player expenses, MLS has instituted a rule that allows it to maintain its salary cap while also attracting some top international talent. In 2007, soccer superstar David Beckham made it known that he was interested in playing for MLS's Los Angeles Galaxy. But given the strict salary cap, there was no way for the Galaxy to pay Beckham his market price. In response, team owners initiated the Designated Player rule, also known as the Beckham rule. The Beckham rule in its original context permitted each MLS team to sign one player to any amount it wished. Only the first $400,000 of the player's salary counted toward the cap. Thus, only $400,000 of Beckham's $6.5 million per year salary counted toward the Galaxy's salary cap of $2.1 million. Over time, MLS has expanded the Beckham rule. For the 2017 season, each team was permitted to sign up to three players using the Beckham rule. Kaka of Orlando FC had the largest salary at $7.17 million per year, which was about twice as much as the overall league salary cap (Wagner, 2017).

Internationally, most major professional sports leagues do not have a team or individual salary cap or luxury tax system. This is evident in European soccer where each team in leagues such as the English Premier League (EPL), La Liga in Spain, Bundesliga in Germany, Serie A in Italy, and Ligue 1 in France, have no limit on team payroll. Teams such as Chelsea, FC Barcelona, Real Madrid, Paris Saint-Germain, and Manchester United spend lavishly on players. These clubs spend in excess of $200 million per year on player costs. For example, in the 2016 to 2017 season, Chelsea's wage bill was approximately £224 million (about US$300 million) ("Chelsea players," 2017). While the larger teams generate enough revenue to cover these costs, the lack of a financial system to curb spending leads to a large disparity between the highest spending European soccer clubs and their competitors who do not have the financial means to pay these large salaries. Burnley, a small EPL club with limited financial resources, had a 2017 to 2018 season wage bill for that of only £33 million (about US$44.25 million). Given that player expenditures often lead to wins, it is no surprise that Chelsea won the EPL that year while Burnley finished 16th.

Other Professional Team Expenses

As we stated earlier, for most major professional sports teams, player salaries and benefits compose 50% or more of the overall expenses. Now that we have reviewed player salary systems across multiple leagues, it is time to focus on the other expenses for professional sports teams. Beyond the salaries of players, additional labor costs comprise a significant amount of the remaining costs. These other staff members include coaches, scouts, and front office staff in areas such as media and public relations, marketing and sales, the box office, community relations, social media and technology, facility operations, equipment, and administrative support staff. The top-level management positions such as team president, general manager, and head coach are often highly paid and thus a substantial expense to a major professional sports team. Most teams split their organization into two parts: team operations and business operations. The team side is usually overseen by the general manager, who manages the coaches, scouts, sports medicine specialists, and player development staff. Most general managers in the major sports draw a salary that is easily in excess of $1 million annually. Within the coaching ranks, coaches and managers such as Bill Belichick (NFL), Gregg Popovich (NBA), and Mike Scioscia (MLB) make in excess of $5 million per year. Additionally, salaries must be paid for assistant coaches and strength coaches. The total coaching salary expense for some teams may run in excess of $10 million. Beyond the coaching ranks, most teams also employ scouts who search for talented players and staff who work on developing the current players on the roster. The development staff can include strength and conditioning coaches, athletic trainers and doctors, dietitians, sport psychologists, and sport analytics experts. While these staff members can be expensive, they are an important aspect in fielding a competitive team.

On the business side, pro sports teams employ staff across a variety of areas including media relations, marketing and promotions, ticket and premium sales, technology, community relations, media relations, digital content, and finance. Let's take the Philadelphia 76ers as an example. The team has about 65 employees, not counting the players, in its basketball operations side and over 100 staff members on the business operations side. The 76ers employ over 50 staff members solely in the area of ticket sales ("Front office directory," 2017). While the staff size on the business side is quite large, the average salary is dramatically lower than that of the players, general manager, and head coach. While the natural inclination may be to save money by eliminating some of these business operations staff members, they are vitally important in generating revenue. The 76ers have one of the largest ticket sales staffs in all of the NBA, and this is quite costly. However, these staff members are generating revenue for the team through the sale of season, group, and individual game tickets. Without this staff, it is likely that the 76ers would see a decrease in ticket revenue. It is not surprising that through this extensive ticket sales staff, the 76ers have rank near the top of the NBA in season tickets sold. Each team must decide on the appropriate staffing level that will allow it to maximize profit.

Another important staffing area is game day operations. Teams must have hundreds of ushers, concessionaires, ticket takers, parking attendants, and security guards at home contests. While these positions are largely part-time and low wage, the overall expense can be sizable given the overall number of staff members for these roles. If the workers are unionized, the expense can be even higher. One option is to primarily hire low wage workers, even paying just minimum wage, in an effort to save money. Negative consequences of this strategy may be poor customer service, increased fan violence, employee theft, and criminal activity. Due to this economic and service quandary, many teams and facility operators outsource these services to companies such as Aramark (concessions) and CSC (security, ticket takers, and parking attendants). By outsourcing, costs may be reduced because a third party pays for hiring, training, workers' compensation, and other costs. The third party provider usually has more experience and training to operate these elements more effectively and a lower total cost.

EXPENSES IN INTERCOLLEGIATE ATHLETICS

Prior to addressing the specific item expenses for intercollegiate athletic programs the difference between professional and college team sport expenses needs to be mentioned. Intercollegiate athletic programs are part of a larger organization—the overall university. This is important because some expenses related to the operation of an intercollegiate athletic program may be covered by other departments within the university. For example, at some institutions, expenses related to areas such as utilities, rent, and facility management may be paid for by the university. Therefore, they do not appear on the athletic department's income statement. Unlike traditional businesses, there are no generally accepted accounting practices for universities. This leads to each school, and each athletic department, financially accounting for expenses in its own way. The result is that intercollegiate athletics accounting can be quite confusing. This is compounded by the fact that each team represents a different expense model. While most professional teams are for-profit entities and some intercollegiate athletic programs belong to for-profit universities (such as Post University and Grand Canyon University), many colleges and universities are nonprofit, and even more are government owned.

Another difference between professional sport and intercollegiate sport relates to the payment of their primary source of labor: the players. As we have seen already, salaries and benefits for players in the major global sports leagues are being determined in a relatively free market, and they can reach hundreds of millions of dollars. In National Collegiate Athletic Association (NCAA) athletics, programs are not permitted to pay their players a salary for performing on the field. In the place of salaries and benefits, student-athletes are permitted to receive a grant-in-aid, also known as an athletic scholarship. This grant-in-aid covers housing, tuition, food, and books. Some NCAA Division I institutions also provide a cost-of-living payment to their student-athletes in football and basketball. As table 6.6 shows, the average cost of grants-in-aid was $9.27 million for NCAA Division I Football Bowl Subdivision (FBS) programs in 2015. This is much less than the cost of salaries for major professional sports teams.

Another difference between professional team sport and intercollegiate athletics in the United States is the financial role played by the NCAA. The NCAA has instituted many rules and regulations for managing intercollegiate athletics. These rules have a variety of purposes such as ensuring competitive balance on the playing field, emphasizing the educational mission of NCAA member institutions, and promoting ethical conduct by players, coaches, and administrators. With that said, some rules have been implemented to minimize expenses. For example, there are rules related to the lengths of playing seasons for each sport, such as practice times and the number of games that may be played. While the primary intent of these rules is to allow the student-athletes ample time to focus on their academic studies, they also reduce expenses for athletic programs. For example, in Division I FBS football, teams are limited to 12 regular season games. Additionally, rules are in place with respect to the number of days that teams may practice in the spring and in August prior to the start of the season. Without these

Table 6.6 Median Selected Expenses for NCAA Division I (FBS) Institutions, 2015

Source	Total $ expenses (in millions)	% Increase since 2006
Salaries and benefits	22.84	102.50
Grants-in-aid (scholarships)	9.27	59.88
Facilities maintenance	7.52	192.72
Team travel	4.17	69.65
Game expenses	2.24	76.52
Recruiting costs	1.05	55.55
Fund-raising expenses	1.26	32.21
Guarantees and options	1.36	44.68
Equipment, uniforms, and supplies	1.76	90.89

Source: Fulks (2016).

rules, teams would possibly increase the practice time and the number of games played. While this may improve the quality of the team, this additional practice and game time would also increase program expenses. This is true for all sports beyond football as well. Other areas where the NCAA has regulations that can lower programmatic expenses are recruiting and the size of coaching staffs. Again, all of these regulations have a justifiable effect of promoting fair play and the educational mission of the universities, but they also have a financial impact on the cost of operating these programs.

A unique aspect of expenses in intercollegiate athletics is the presence of Title IX. Title IX is a portion of the United States Education Amendments of 1972. Title IX states that no person in the United States shall, on the basis of sex, be excluded from participation in, be denied the benefits of, or be subjected to discrimination under any education program or activity receiving federal financial assistance. With respect to college athletics, Title IX has led to increased spending on women's sports. Thus, when developing budgets and determining levels of department expenses, college athletics administrators must be cognizant of Title IX and the equity of spending across men's and women's sports.

Despite NCAA regulation, spending in intercollegiate athletics, especially at the NCAA Division I level, has increased dramatically. This is due in part to Division I athletic programs generating a lot more revenue over the past decade. As we stated in chapter 5, intercollegiate athletic programs are not for profit and thus generate revenue so that they can spend it. So it is no surprise that as these programs have generated more money, they have increased their expenses. Table 6.6 provides data on the top expense categories for NCAA Division I FBS programs and the increase in these spending items from 2006 to 2015. It should also be stated that most intercollegiate athletic departments do not generate enough revenue to cover all expenses. Thus, they must rely on fund transfers from the overall university along with student fees to pay for all of their expenses. This is especially true at the NCAA Division II and III levels, where there are no athletic programs that can generate enough revenue to pay all expenses.

Salaries and Benefits

As we can see from table 6.6, salaries and benefits are the largest expense for NCAA Division I FBS institutions. Salaries and benefits for coaches and top-level administrators are quite sizable in sports like football and basketball. For example, table 6.7 provides salary data for the top five paid coaches in college football for 2017. Alabama's Nick Saban led the way with a salary of $11.1 million. That amount makes Saban's salary competitive with any NFL coach. In NCAA Division I men's basketball, coaches like Duke's Mike Krzyzewski, Kansas' Bill Self, and Kentucky's John Calipari earn over $5 million per year ("NCAA salaries," 2017). These high salaries are not limited to head coaches in football and basketball. Top assistant coaches in these programs can also earn in excess of $1 million. While the salaries overall in women's basketball are not as large, there are a few coaches such as Geno Auriemma of Connecticut who make over $1 million annually. Interestingly, these salary and benefit costs increased over 100% from 2006 to 2015. Also, in most states, the highest paid public employee is either the head football or men's basketball coach for the flagship state university.

There have also been sizable salary increases in sports that most athletic departments classify as Olympic sports. This includes sports such as wrestling, baseball, swimming, track and field, golf, tennis, and volleyball. These sports do not garner the interest of football and basketball and therefore do not generate substantial revenue. Despite the lack of revenue in these sports, coaching salaries have increased especially at the Division I level. For example, Kevin O'Sullivan

Table 6.7 Top 5 Coaching Salaries, NCAA Division I FBS Football, 2017

Name	Institution	Salary (in millions)
Nick Saban	Alabama	$11.1
Dabo Swinney	Clemson	$8.5
Jim Harbaugh	Michigan	$7.0
Urban Meyer	Ohio State	$6.4
Rich Rodriguez	Arizona	$6.0

Source: Gaines (2017).

of the University of Florida is one of the top college baseball coaches in the country. In 2016, he signed a new contract that pays him a base salary of $1.25 million along with a $500,000 signing bonus (Thompson, 2016). This situation is limited to the NCAA's Division I level. Programs at the Division II and III levels are paying their Olympic sport team coaches much less. A Division II or III coach in sports like swimming or tennis may make as little as $25,000 per year.

One last item to address with respect to the salaries and benefits of coaches and administrators in intercollegiate athletic programs deals with the overall size of these staffs. Since about 2010, there has been a large increase in the overall staff sizes of coaches and administrators at major Division I programs. For example, 34 people are listed in the football staff directory for the University of Alabama. Titles beyond those of traditional coaches include football analyst, athletics relations coordinator, director of player development, football recruitment director, and special assistant to the head coach. None of these 34 positions include areas such as sports medicine and nutrition, or equipment and facilities management. While all of these positions can be justified, they all come with a salary expense. As we can see, it is has become very expensive to compete at the NCAA Division I level.

The increase in salary and benefit expenses has also become evident for intercollegiate sport administrators. Top-paid directors of athletics now make in excess of $1 million annually and have large staffs to support the overall operation of the athletic department. The average total amount spent on salaries and benefits at the Division I FBS level is over $22 million. That amount drops significantly for Division II and Division III programs, which are $2.05 and $1.59 million, respectively (Fulks, 2016). Most NCAA Division I FBS athletic programs currently have a staff size that exceeds 100 people. Again, these positions provide important services to the athletic department, but they come at a cost.

Athletic programs spend millions each year on salaries and benefits for staff in areas like media relations, marketing, fund-raising and development, facility operations, rules compliance, and ticket sales. In reality, such expenses are not a concern for major programs that generate over $100 million in revenue annually. However, it is troublesome for smaller programs that lack the ability to generate substantial revenue. A trend that we have seen in recent years has been the use of outside service contractors for some athletic department responsibilities in an effort to both increase revenue and defray expenses. For example, dozens of universities have contracted with the Aspire Group for ticket sales. In exchange for a percentage of the ticket sales revenue, usually about 25%, Aspire handles outbound ticket sales by reaching out to new and existing ticket holders. While the athletic department loses some control of its ticket sales, it also lessens its expenses for labor. Another area where we see growth in contract services in intercollegiate athletics is the sales of corporate partnerships. IMG College and Learfield have been two leading corporations that work with athletic departments in the sales of corporate partnerships and advertisement.

Grants-in-Aid

Beyond salaries and benefits, the largest expense for an NCAA Division I athletic program is grants-in-aid (scholarships). At the Division I FBS level, the average expense on scholarships is $9.27 million, a 59.55% increase from 2006 to 2015. This amount is $1.97 million at the Division II level. NCAA rules prohibit the use of athletic scholarships at the Division III level, and thus programs at that level do not incur this expense (Fulks, 2016). In order to better understand this expense category, we must review NCAA rules and regulations with respect to scholarships. As stated previously, the NCAA limits an athletic scholarship to tuition, housing, food, books, and a cost-of-living stipend. The student-athlete is not permitted to receive any benefits beyond these. Additionally, the NCAA limits the number of scholarships according to the sport and Division level. For example, Division I FBS football teams are limited to 85 scholarships. Meanwhile, Division I Football Championship Subdivision level football programs can provide a maximum of 63 scholarships, and Division II programs can issue 35 scholarships. The rule is in effect to balance the on-field competition and to minimize expenses. Each sport has its own scholarship limit. In another example, women's soccer teams at the Division I level are limited to 14 scholarships, and Division II teams are not permitted to provide more than 9.9 athletic scholarships. In women's basketball, Division I programs can provide 15 full scholarships while Division II programs can issue up to 10 scholarships. Despite these limits, athletic scholarships are still a significant portion of an athletic department's budget. It should also be noted that not all scholarships provide full benefits, especially in the Olympic sports and at the Division II level. Many student-athletes receive partial scholarships that may be worth only a few thousand dollars. Some smaller Division II and III institutions have added the expense of new sports as a strategy for increased undergraduate student enrollment. If they offer 10 partial scholarships for a sport and charge $40,000 a year in tuition, even scholarships of 50% will result in $20,000 a year of additional revenue from each student-athlete's tuition. Thus, the increased expense of adding new sports may lead to increased revenue for the overall university.

Transportation and Equipment

Two other major expense categories for intercollegiate athletic programs are team travel and equipment, including uniforms and supplies. To compete at the Division I level, an athletic program must sponsor a minimum of 14 sports (men and women combined), and some offer more than 30 sports. While it is commendable for these programs to offer a large number of sports, it increases expenses. Team travel and equipment are two areas where expenses are directly related to the number of sport offerings. Team travel becomes more expensive as more teams are fielded. The average amount spent by a Division I FBS-level program on team travel is $4.17 million, a 69.65% increase from 2006 to 2015. That amount is only $474,000 at the Division II level (Fulks, 2016). Team travel costs include planes, charter buses, hotels, and meal expenses. If we use a football team as an example, a team travel party may include over 100 people when factoring in coaches, players, support staff, and administrators. It becomes

quite expensive to travel with all these people to an away football game. A charter flight alone for a team can cost over $50,000 per round trip. The athletic department must also factor in other travel costs such as hotels, local transportation, and meals. At the Division I level, we have seen teams dramatically increase the quality of their travel and accommodations. Most teams now travel on charter flights, stay in high-quality hotels, and eat catered meals. Interestingly, the hotel usage is not limited to away games. Many Division I football and basketball teams now stay in hotels the night before home games despite the players having their own apartment or residence hall rooms just miles from the hotel in which they are staying. In Olympic sports such as fencing, squash, or wrestling, travel costs may be high due to the lack of other programs that have those sport offerings. The lack of competitors' schools often results in teams traveling farther to their opponents' home sites.

In addition to team travel, the cost of equipment, uniforms, and supplies is substantial, with the average cost being $1.76 million at the Division I FBS level (Fulks, 2016). Some of this cost is defrayed through partnerships with sporting apparel and equipment companies such as Nike, Adidas, and Under Armour (UA). In exchange for promotional and marketing opportunities, such as having its logo appear on all team jerseys, the apparel company will provide equipment, uniforms, and money. These deals can be worth tens of millions of dollars for the top programs and greatly decrease expenses. However, for smaller Division I and Division II and III programs, the apparel deals are much smaller. These programs usually pay the apparel companies for uniforms and equipment. The expense in sports like football and lacrosse can be over $1,000 per player when factoring in items such as game uniforms, practice apparel, helmets, sticks, balls, and cleats.

Event and Facility Expenses

The final areas to address with respect to the cost of competing in intercollegiate athletics are facility maintenance and game expenses. The average amount spent on facility maintenance at the Division I FBS level is $7.52 million, a 192.72% increase from 2006 to 2015. That

When hiring personnel for an event a facility does not want to hire too many employees who might not have enough work to do but needs to have enough personnel to meet expected needs.

amount is only $101,500 at the Division II level and $51,100 for Division III (Fulks, 2016). As with the other expense areas, we see a significant difference between Division I and the rest of the NCAA. This is due to the size and scope of Division I athletic facilities. Football teams like Penn State, Michigan, and Tennessee have stadiums with capacities over 100,000 seats. While this is a great form of revenue generation, the maintenance and upkeep of these facilities is expensive. The game expenses also increase significantly as these programs pay for parking attendants, ushers, ticket takers, and security personnel. Additionally, these athletic programs have individual facilities for many sports. In addition to the competition facilities like baseball and softball stadiums, basketball arenas, and swimming and diving pools, the top Division I programs also have extensive practice spaces. For

example, Penn State has in indoor turf facility that can be used for multiple sport practices like football, soccer, lacrosse, field hockey, baseball, and softball. Meanwhile, it has outdoor individual practice spaces for football and soccer. All of these facilities must be maintained and repaired when damaged. Beyond the playing surfaces, the athletic department also has physical facilities for strength and conditioning, academic support, sports medicine, and food services. Most recently, universities like Tennessee, Clemson, and Oregon have spent over $50 million each on constructing new practice facilities for their athletic programs.

As we can see from the financial data, operating an intercollegiate athletic program at any level comes at a considerable cost. This can be especially troublesome for programs at the Division II and III levels because they have limited ability to generate adequate revenue to cover all these costs. Thus, they must rely on institutional support and student fees to close the gap between the total expenses and the revenue the athletic program can generate. For some smaller schools, students have to pay mandatory athletic related fees that can reach over $2,000 a year. This situation is even true for many Division I programs. While estimates vary, it is believed that only about 25 to 50 athletic departments generate enough revenue to pay all expenses. Despite this situation, we have seen intercollegiate athletic program expenses increase substantially since about 2010. As we have addressed, the primary sources of these rising expenses come from areas such as salaries and benefits, grants-in-aid, team travel, and facility management.

EXPENSES FOR A SPORTING GOODS MANUFACTURER

Up to this point, our discussion of sport industry expenses has focused on professional team sport and intercollegiate athletics. We will now address expenses for a major segment of the sport industry: sporting goods manufacturers. The expenses of the sporting goods industry are similar to the expenses that are present in other traditional businesses. Because of this, salaries and benefits often make up the majority of their expenses. We will begin with an examination of expenses for UA. Before this we should identify the two primary types of expenses. Fixed expenses (or fixed costs) are those that do not change as production changes, while variable expenses (or variable costs) will be altered as production changes. In the short run, no matter how much UA produces, a chief executive officer's salary is fixed, while the cost of raw materials such as leather and fabric is variable as production levels change.

The expense data from UA serves as a great resource for addressing costs in the sporting goods industry. Remember that UA's financial statements for 2016 are in appendix A. A review of UA's income statement shows that it spent $2.584 billion to produce the goods that it sold. It generated a net revenue of $4.825 billion from these products. So, the cost of goods sold was about 53.6% of the total net revenue generated from the sale of those same goods. Cost of goods sold included materials, production, transportation, and royalty payments to endorsers.

UA's second largest expense was on selling, general, and administrative expenses. It spent $1.823 billion in this area in 2016. These expenses include costs related to marketing, selling, and product innovation. Employee costs come under this area and include salaries, benefits, bonuses, and stock-based compensation. By adding both expense lines together and subtracting them from net revenues, we see that UA had an annual income from operations of $417 million. That was a $9 million increase from the prior year. So, while expenses increased over $500 million from the previous year, the overall income from operations increased due to higher net revenue. While this general expense data is important, it is helpful to have more detailed expense information on the production costs for UA. Unfortunately, these data are not present within the income statement.

A review of a company's annual report (10-K report) can often provide additional information on expenses. For example, in order to reduce production costs, UA may look at its agreements with its manufacturers. According to its annual report, UA apparel and accessory products are currently manufactured by 39 different companies that operate in 18 different countries with about 60% of its products being made in Jordan, Vietnam, China, and Malaysia. In short, UA hires other companies to manufacture products for it. With respect to its footwear, seven different manufacturers were used. They operated primarily in China, Vietnam, and Indonesia. Many sporting goods products are manufactured by third party companies in such countries due to the relatively low labor costs. Thus, it appears that UA has invested a great deal of time in developing strategies to minimize the costs of production.

Another method for minimizing product costs can be inventory management. UA claims it manages its inventory levels based on existing orders, anticipated sales, and the customers' delivery requirements. It has put into place systems that improve customer demand forecasting and supply planning. The goal is to minimize production lead time and the amount of time that inventory sits in UA's warehouses. All of these inventory strategies should aid in minimizing UA's expenses and improving overall efficiency.

Selling, General, and Administrative Expenses

As we stated earlier, UA's selling, general, and administrative expenses were over $1.8 billion in 2016. UA had about 15,200 employees, and 6,500 of them were classified as full-time. Currently, most of its employees are located in the United States, and no employees are unionized. Any future changes to UA's business can have an impact on UA's expenses related to salaries and benefits. These changes could include the acquisition of other companies, the introduction or elimination of product categories, the unionization of segments of UA's workforce, or a dramatic change in the sporting goods industry. For example, a global recession may result in a large reduction in demand for sporting goods that could adversely affect UA. If this occurred, UA might look to reducing expenses by reducing its workforce. In fact, this occurred in August 2017, when UA announced that it would lay off 280 workers after it reported two consecutive quarters of financial losses. While in the long run, UA initiated these layoffs to reduce expenses, in the short term it actually increased expenses since the company had to provide severance packages to the workers that it laid off. Those severance packages cost UA about $45 million in 2017 (Wilen, 2017). In some cases it may take years, to cut expenses as manufacturing contracts in foreign countries may be difficult to cancel or union contracts may not allow reductions in salaries and benefits.

Marketing Expenses

Another area of expense for companies that sell either a product or service is product marketing. It is always beneficial for a company to have a product or service that is attractive to consumers, but that is only part of the sales process. The company must also develop a strong marketing strategy to entice the consumer to actually buy the product. Areas such as advertising, media placement, corporate partnerships, and product endorsement are highly effective marketing tools for most sports organizations. All these activities come at an expense. For example, UA spends millions of dollars each year on athlete endorsement deals with sports stars such as Stephen Curry, Cam Newton, Lindsey Vonn, and Jordan Spieth. These deals provide great exposure for the UA brand and increase consumer demand for their products, but they are costly. In 2016, UA paid Steph Curry about $12 million, including bonuses and royalties, to endorse its product. While this is a sizable amount, Nike is paying LeBron James over $30 million per year (Bowman, 2017). While UA does not release the total amount it spends each year on athlete endorsement deals, it can conservatively be estimated at over $100 million. UA also invests in corporate partnerships with sporting events. UA pays for the right to associate itself with sport properties Hendrick Motorsports, Boston College Athletics, the Southampton Football Club in the English Premier League, and the men's and women's USA Gymnastics teams, along with dozens of other sport properties. All of these deals are part of UA's marketing strategy to promote its brand. UA also utilizes several different media outlets to advertise its brand and products. These media outlets include online, print, radio, television, and social media placements.

Taxes

As with traditional nonsport companies, UA must also pay taxes. These taxes may occur at the local, state, and federal levels. Taxed areas include the sales of goods and services, ownership of property, and the employing personnel. From its income statement, we see that UA paid about $131 million in taxes on taxable income of approximately $388 million. The largest tax most companies pay is the federal income tax, a tax paid on the income that the company generates. In the United States, the federal tax rate was 35% for decades; however, with the passage of the 2017 Tax Cuts and Jobs Act the rate was dropped to 20%. This will greatly reduce the federal tax liability for most American companies. Beyond the federal income tax, businesses in the United States must also pay federal payroll and unemployment taxes. The payroll taxes include payments toward Medicare and Social Security, called FICA, which stands for Federal Insurance Contribution Act. At the state level in the United States, companies that sell their products or services at the retail level usually are required to pay a sales tax. Depending on the state, this tax is usually between 5% and 8% of the retail price of the product or service being sold. There are a few states, such as Delaware, that do not impose a sales tax. Most major sporting goods companies similar to UA sell their products globally. In most cases, UA must pay taxes in other countries where it sells its products. Additionally, given that UA produces most of its goods outside the United States, it may be liable for the value-added taxes (VAT) that are present in many nations; the United States does not have a value-added tax. The VAT is a tax collected at each stage of production or consumption of a good. Thus, if UA has its shoes produced in China or Vietnam, it may be subject to the payment of a VAT in each country the shoes travel through. Thus if the shoe soles are made in China, a VAT might need to be paid there, and if the shoe laces are made in Vietnam, a VAT might be imposed on the laces in Vietnam. These various taxes need to be considered as a major expense because they are imposed regardless of whether any shoes are sold.

One final expense area to address with UA is interest. In chapter 4 we addressed the topic of debt with respect to liabilities. The amount of interest that is paid on debt in the current year appears on the income statement as *interest expense, net*. This line item is the net amount of money that is either paid or collected from interest. Interest is a form of revenue if UA is generating interest on its assets. An example of this would be cash that is in a financial institution or the interest that is paid toward any bonds that UA may hold. Conversely, the amount of interest that UA pays on its debt is an expense. The difference between the two appears on the income statement as net interest expense. For UA, that amount was $26.43 million in 2016. While this may seem like a great deal of money, as we saw in chapter 5, debt and interest can be a positive for a sports organization. Debt allows a business to invest in activities that should produce revenue.

In closing, UA has a number of expense areas. The financial key for UA is to manage these expenses in a manner that will allow it to operate as efficiently as possible. Expenses are not a negative, they are necessary for UA to produce and sell its products. Without expenses like the cost of goods sold, it would have nothing to sell. Without marketing and promotional expenses, there would be little consumer demand for the goods that UA produces. Without salary and benefits expenses, UA would not have any employees.

OTHER EXPENSES FOR SPORTS ORGANIZATIONS

Up to now, we have covered most expenses related to managing a sports organization. However there are a few expenses that still warrant discussion. Some of these expense categories include rent, utilities, technology, and office supplies. Almost every sports organization has a physical space from which it operates. This may be an office building, a retail store, or team headquarters. In some instances, the sports organization owns the building and land from which it operates. In this case, the organization would not have rental costs. But it would have costs such as principal and interest owed on the mortgage, facility upkeep, and local property taxes. If the organization leases the space, then it must pay rent. It is important for a sports organization to determine what is best for it financially. Another aspect that is part of the decision of owning versus renting a facility deals with depreciation. If a facility is built there may be no business expenses but the facility can be depreciated for tax purposes. In contrast, if a business rents a facility, the rent cost can be deducted every year as a business expense. For example, if you want to open a fitness center, should you lease space or purchase a building? More recently, we have seen some startup and small sports organizations save money through operating the businesses from their private residences. With the advances in technology, a small business can conduct most of its activities through text, e-mail, phone, and video conferencing. If these small businesses must have face-to-face meetings, there are even places where they can rent meeting rooms on an hourly basis. Ultimately, by using improved technology and creative meeting spaces, a small business owner can greatly reduce expenses.

Utilities are another area where sports organizations must strive to minimize expenses. Utility costs include electricity, heat, water, and even Internet access. In some cases, sports organizations are becoming creative in their attempts to minimize utility costs. For example, the NFL's Philadelphia Eagles market themselves as an environmentally friendly "green" team. As part of this campaign, the Eagles have installed 14 wind turbines at the top of their stadium, Lincoln Financial Field, and 11,000 solar panels on the side of the stadium and in the parking lots ("Lincoln," 2017). These devices have also reduced the team's electricity costs. As the technology improves for solar and wind power, we may see more sports organizations opt for these in an effort to be environmentally friendly and to hopefully lower costs.

Technology can also lead to considerable savings in expense areas such as office supplies. Increased use of document scanning, e-mail, and web-based services has reduced the need for printed materials. This can result in considerable saving in areas such as paper supplies, copying, and mailing. While this may seem relatively minor, every dollar saved in expenses is a dollar added to the organization's profit or reduction in its losses.

CONCLUSION

This chapter addressed the primary sources of expense for sports organizations. There are several areas of expense such as salaries, benefits, utilities, and equipment, which are common across all segments of the sport industry. However, as you have seen, there are some expenses specific to different sport segments. For example, grants-in-aid (scholarships) are an expense that are unique to intercollegiate athletic athletics. Meanwhile, salaries and benefits for players are managed by North American major professional sports leagues through the use of salary caps and luxury taxes. Understanding the different types of expenses is critical for a sports manager. A greater understanding of one's expenses will lead to more effective financial planning and ultimately a more efficient organization.

Class Discussion Topics

1. Develop a list of sources of expenses for a professional baseball team.
2. Develop a list of expense streams for a publicly traded sportswear company.
3. Develop a list of expense streams for a nonprofit health club.
4. Develop a list of expense streams for an intercollegiate athletic program.
5. List and explain at least three exceptions that exist in the NBA collective bargaining agreement that permit teams to spend beyond the league salary cap.
6. Explain how free agency in professional sport has increased salary expenditures for professional sports teams.
7. Explain how increased technology has aided sports organizations in minimizing expenses.
8. Explain the difference between the structure of American professional sports leagues' costs and expenses and European leagues' costs and expenses.
9. Explain the objectives of a collective bargaining agreement and how it serves the owners and players of a league.
10. Explain how the NCAA supports college athletics funding. How are athletic departments able to cover expenses when they are losing revenue?

Part II Case Study

Minor League Baseball Revenue and Expenses

The best way to go through the revenue and expense process is to highlight a detailed example from an actual team. We cannot disclose the minor league baseball team but these numbers are accurate. More importantly, this case helps show how the numbers are taken from past years to project for future years based on various assumed variables. The assumed variables are highlighted in various data sets that break down, as an example, how much sponsorship revenue is expected based on the number of sponsorships sold and at what price points. The numbers also help show the timing of when revenue and expenses occur, but that will be discussed in greater detail in the part III case study.

The team was hoping that it could increase its revenue in 2018 as it had an increase from its first year in 2016 to 2017 but still carried a loss on the balance sheet Such projections are common with new teams. They get a bump in sales from being a new team, but that upward tick often ends very quickly when the team's novelty dries up. The team appeared to be closing the gap on its losses. However, the projected 2018 budget had some salaries, but did not include front office salaries, which-if paid, could significantly alter the budget.

Table 1 highlights the various categories of revenue and expenses. Having all revenue and expense items in a master chart of accounts (MCA) with identifiable codes makes it easier to assign revenue when it comes in and to record expenses when bills arrive or are paid (depending on how the business functions). Having a variety of dedicated accounts makes it easier to budget in the future and to see if certain areas have changes from one period to another. Thus, if ticketing revenue is going to be examined, it would be important to make sure that group revenue is identified (whether preseason or during the season) and examined so that way there is no confusion of whether individual walk-up sales are included in the analysis.

Besides understanding revenue and expenses for the team, it is important to calculate what these amounts are. This process is going to be critical in the second part of this case study (part III case study) as it relates to the budgeting process. For now we will explore each account from the master chart of accounts and determine how that amount is calculated. Table 2 provides a detailed breakdown

Table 1 Master Chart of Accounts (All the Revenue and Expense Categories)

REVENUE				EXPENSES		
MCA #				**MCA #**		
100	**Preseason**	**Account**		**500**	**Sales expense**	**Account**
	110	Advertising and sponsorships			510	Printing and brochures
					520	Advertising production
	120	Season tickets			530	Radio station access fee
	130	Group tickets			540	Ticket stock
	140	Player contract sales		**600**	**Salaries**	
	150	Skybox rentals			610	Front office
	160	Picnic area rentals			620	Game day staff
	170	Miscellaneous income			630	Interns
	180	Mall sales			640	Player salaries
200	**Game day**				650	Manager and coaches
	210	Individual ticket sales			660	Commissions
	220	Merchandise sales		**700**	**Insurance**	
	230	Program sales			710	Medical insurance
	240	Concession revenue			720	Workers' compensation
	250	Speed pitch revenue			730	Liability insurance

EXPENSES		
800	Administrative	
	810	Office supplies
	820	Office hardware
	830	Postage
	840	Telephone
	850	Dues, subscriptions, fees
900	Taxes	
	910	Payroll
	920	Sales
1000	Cost of goods sold	
	1010	Merchandise and novelty goods
1100	Promotions	
	1110	Promotional expenses
1200	Travel	
	1210	Front office travel
1300	Team	
	1310	Player per diems
	1320	Player travel
	1330	Hotels
	1340	Team travel
1400	Advertising	
	1410	Newspaper

	1420	Radio
	1430	Cable
	1440	Outdoor advertising
	1450	Cinema
1500	Team equipment	
	1510	Uniforms
	1520	Bats
	1530	Balls
	1540	Misc. equipment
	1550	Training equipment and supplies
1600	Rent	
	1610	Stadium
	1620	Mall
	1630	Player and manager housing
	1640	Field manager auto
1700	Concessions	
	1710	Family day coupons
	1720	Skybox food
	1730	Picnic area food
	1740	Umpires and press box food
1800	Consultation	
	1810	Legal fees
	1820	Accounting fees

Table 2 Detailed Revenue and Expenses

Revenue: preseason	Actual	Budgeted MCA: 110 Name: advertising and sponsorships
Outfield fence signs	$52,500	12 signs renewed @ $2,500, 12 new or renewed signs @ $1,875
Concourse signs	$4,000	4 signs sold @$1,000 each, 1 tunnel, 1 grandstand entrance, 2 visitors' dugout signs
Scoreboard signs	$0	1 panel @ $4,000, 1 panel @ $2,000 (2-year commitment)
Insert ad space	$4,000	1 front @ $1250; 4 inside @ $375 each; back page (full) @ $1,250
Radio	$0	$2,500 in renewals; $5,000 in 19 new sponsors packaged with new fence signs
Scorecard	$3,600	8 inside panels @ $600; 2 front panels @ $1,000; back cover @ $2,000
Ticket backs	$1,000	Back-of-ticket sponsorship @ $1,000
Pocket schedules	$1,000	$500 for pocket schedule; $500 for ticket sales brochure
In-game promo sponsors	$7,500	8 wheels of prizes @ $750 each; 2 other promos @ $750 each
Promotional giveaway sponsor	$5,750	Approximately 15 giveaway nights @ average package price of $1,150
Promotional night sponsors	$8,000	Approximately 7 promotionally sponsored nights @ average price of $650 + 3 fireworks shows @ $3,500 each
	$87,350	

(continued)

Table 2 *(continued)*

	Actual	Budgeted
Revenue: preseason		**MCA: 120** **Name: season tickets**
Full season tickets	$38,000	
21 game, half season plan	$6,050	
12 game plans	$4,290	
Coupon book	$4,200	
	$52,540	
Revenue: preseason		**MCA: 130** **Name: group tickets**
Group tickets	$32,400	
Specialty tickets	$2,600	20 tickets sold @ $130 per ticket
	$35,000	
Revenue: preseason		**MCA: 150** **Name: skybox rentals**
Nightly skybox rentals	$12,250	35 nightly rentals @ $350 per night; 15 sold as part of promotional night sponsorships
	$4,800	
Revenue: preseason		**MCA: 160** **Name: picnic area sales**
Group picnics	$16,000	25 picnics with 40 people each @ $16 per ticket
	$16,000	
Revenue: preseason		**MCA: 170** **Name: miscellaneous income**
Miscellaneous revenue sources	$2,000	Revenue mostly from gift certificate sales
	$2,000	
Revenue: game day		**MCA: 210** **Name: individual ticket sales** **Department: Ticketing**
Club seats*	$5,440	17 per game × 40 games × $8 Represents 10% increase over 2017 totals
Reserved seats	$58,800	245 per game × 40 games × $6 Represents 10% increase over 2017 totals
General admission seats	$11,520	72 per game × $4 + 3,733 reserved seats @ $6 Represents 10% increase over 2017 totals
Advance ticket sales—all tickets	$23,598	
	$99,358	*Club seats represent 5% of 2017 total individual tickets
Revenue: game day		**MCA: 220** **Name: merchandise sales**
Merchandise sold at game or office	$36,000	900 turnstiles × 40 games × $1 per cap
	$36,000	
Revenue: game day		**MCA: 230** **Name: program sales**
Game programs sold @ game	$3,600	900 turnstiles × 40 games × $0.10 per cap
	$3,600	
Revenue: game day		**MCA: 240** **Name: concessions**
Concessions commissions	$19,908	900 per game × 40 games × $3.95 × 14%
	$19,908	

	Actual	Budgeted
Revenue: game day		MCA: 250 Name: speed pitch
Speed pitch	$4,680	900 × 40 games × $0.13 per cap
	$4,680	
Expenses: sales		MCA: 510 Name: printing, brochures
Season and group ticket brochure	$3,000	
Direct mail campaign	$2,000	
Business cards	$258	$43 per person × 6 people
	$5,258	
Expenses: sales		MCA: 520 Name: advertising production
Outfield fence sign	$3,500	10 new signs @ $350 per sign
Concourse signs and banners	$1,500	For new and replacement banners
New ticket price signs	$500	2 new, large ticket price signs to be located at middle entrance @ $250 each
Wheel of prizes	$250	New 2018 between-innings promo
	$5,750	
Expenses: sales		MCA: 530 Name: radio station access fee
Game broadcast on radio	$4,200	$75 per home game × 42 + $25 per road games × 42
	$4,200	
Expenses: sales		MCA: 540 Name: ticket stock
2018 ticket stock	$2,000	Slight increase from 2017 price
	$2,000	
Expenses: salaries		MCA: 610 Name: front office Department: administration
President		
General manager		
Assistant general manager		
Director of marketing		
Director of sponsorship sales		
Director of group sales		
Special event planning		
Radio announcer	$8,400	$1,200 per month, March 1–September 30
Total	**$177,000**	
Expenses: salaries		MCA: 620 Name: game day staff
Ticket sellers	$2,284	3 people × $5.18 × 3.5 hours × 42 games
Ticket takers	$4,351	4 people × $5.18 × 5 hours × 42 games
Ushers	$8,702	8 people × $5.18 × 5 hours × 42 games
Batboys	$2,100	2 people × @ $25/game × 42 games
Mascot	$1,050	1 person × @ $25/game × 42 games
Merchandise	$2,175	2 people × $5.18 × 5 hours × 42 games

(continued)

Table 2 (continued)

	Actual	Budgeted
Expenses: salaries		**MCA: 620** **Name: game day staff**
Game program, speed pitch	$2,175	2 people × $5.18 × 5 hours × 42 games
Customer service	$2,175	2 people × $5.18 × 5 hours × 42 games
Security	$7,831	42 games × $109.24/police officer + 10% processing cost + 2 firefighters on 3 firework nights @ $265.30 per + $1,201.60 for 10 extra officers used during larger crowd nights
Press box staff	$5,363	3 people × $5.18 × 5 hours × 42 games + $50 per game for public address announcer × 42 games
	$38,206	
Expenses: salaries		**MCA: 630** **Name: interns**
Spring interns	$2,400	2 interns × $1,200
Summer interns	$4,200	3 interns × $1,500
	$6,600	
Expenses: salaries		**MCA: 640** **Name: player salaries**
22 players	$82,000	League salary cap
2 player–coaches		
	$82,000	
Expenses: salaries		**MCA: 650** **Name: manager and coaches**
Field manager	$17,000	
Coaches	$10,000	
Trainer	$5,250	
Clubhouse manager	$2,400	
	$34,650	
Expenses: salaries		**MCA: 660** **Name: commissions**
Season tickets	$2,012	$54,180 renewals × 2% + $23,220 new sales × 4% = (based on 70% renewals; 30% new)
Sponsorships	$8,613	Marketing responsible for 30% of sponsorship budget × 15% commission + remainder of budget obtained at 70% renewal × 2.5% commission + 30% new sales × 5% commission
Group tickets	$2,050	$41,000 × 5% All sales new or renewal
Picnic area tickets	$300	$1,000 tickets × $6 spirit profit × 5%
Skybox rentals	$188	15 individual tickets @ $250 spirit profits × 5% (other rentals are included in sponsor packages)
	$13,163	
Expenses: insurance		**MCA: 710** **Name: medical insurance**
Full-time employees medical	$4,000	
	$4,000	
Expenses: insurance		**MCA: 720** **Name: workers' compensation**
Workers' compensation	$31,000	$29,000 in 2017
	$31,000	

	Actual	Budgeted
Expenses: insurance		**MCA: 730** **Name: liability insurance**
Liability insurance	$7,000	
	$7,000	
Expenses: administrative		**MCA: 810** **Name: office supplies**
Paper, pens, markers, etc.	$5,000	
	$5,000	
Expenses: administrative		**MCA: 820** **Name: office hardware**
Photo copier, lease		
Binder	$300	
Computer software, maintenance	$2,000	
	$2,300	
Expenses: administrative		**MCA: 830** **Name: postage**
Meter lease	$430	Pitney-Bowes yearly lease
Postage	$1,200	
Direct and bulk mail	$1,000	Mailings and invoices to season ticket holders, groups, etc.
FedEx overnights	$1,000	
	$3,630	
Expenses: administrative		**MCA: 840** **Name: telephone**
Telephone lease	$1,188	$99 per month × 12 months
Monthly charges	$2,400	$200 per month × 12 months
Long distance	$11,662	10% increase from 2017 totals
MCI fax broadcast	$750	
	$16,000	
Expenses: administrative		**MCA: 850** **Name: dues, subscriptions, fees, etc.**
Chamber	$1,730	$700 membership, $550 business to business, $480 out for business
League	$32,000	
Team marketing report	$200	
Newspaper subscription	$182	
Baseball America	$75	
Entertainment	$1,000	
	$35,187	
Expenses: taxes		**MCA: 910** **Name: payroll**
Payroll taxes	$1,500	
	$1,500	
Expenses: taxes		**MCA: 920** **Name: sales taxes**
State	$898	Based on $449,000 in sales × 2% as in 2017 totals
Other	$449	Based on $449,000 in sales × 1% as in 2017 totals
	$1,347	

(continued)

Table 2 *(continued)*

	Actual	Budgeted
Expenses: cost of goods sold		**MCA: 1010** **Name: merchandise and novelty goods**
Merchandise, clothing, hats, novelty items	$17,000	Based on 60% of budget sales
Game program printing	$3,500	Estimated from 2018 cost of $3,300
	$20,500	
Expenses: promotions		**MCA: 1100** **Name: promotions**
Schedule posters	$0	Trade in 2017
3 entertainers or appearances	$3,850	$850 for Elvis impersonator, $3,000 for Blues Brothers
Logo baseballs	$1,100	$1,105 in 2017
T-shirts	$0	No 2017 cost, trade out
Mini bats	$1,700	$1,653 for mini bats in 2017
Hats	$0	$3,300 in 2017
3 Fireworks nights	$7,000	$3,500 per show × 2
Pennants	$800	Based on 2017 price
Insured contests	$0	
Fan appreciation day	$0	Use extra prizes from prize wheel promotions
Bingo nights	$0	
50 cent hot dogs and beer nights	$0	Expense paid for in MCA 1710
Batting gloves	$1,600	Based on 2017 price
Seat cushion	$1,000	
Softee baseballs	$1,000	$990 in 2017
Miscellaneous promotions to be determined	$750	
	$18,800	
Expenses: travel		**MCA: 1210** **Name: front office travel**
Travel to baseball winter meetings	$500	2 flights @ $250 each
Travel to Independent Congress	$500	2 flights @ $250 each
Hotels for winter meeting and congress	$702	Nashville ($117 per night, two rooms, three nights)
Per diems		
Registrations	$600	$300 per person (2) for baseball winter meetings
	$1,802	
Expenses: team		**MCA: 1310** **Name: player per diems**
Player per diems	$13,104	24 players @ $13 per day for 42 days
	$880	1 manager @ $20 per day for 42 days
	$572	1 trainer @ $13 per day for 42 days
	$572	1 radio announcer @ $13 per day for 42 days
	$4,524	Preseason per diems—29 players @ $13 a day for 12 days
	$19,652	

	Actual	Budgeted
Expenses: team		**MCA: 1320** **Name: player travel**
Player arrival and departure travel	$4,500	Based on 2017 expenditures
	$4,500	
Expenses: team		**MCA: 1330** **Name: hotels**
Road hotels	$23,760	1 manager, 2 coaches, 22 players, 1 radio announcer, 1 trainer, 1 bus driver = 17 rooms × $45 × 33 nights
Local hotel	$6,000	Hotel rooms for use by team, preseason, players, front office, etc.; $42 approximately 130 rooms
	$29,760	
Expenses: team		**MCA: 1340** **Name: team travel**
Motorcoach fees	$23,100	Bus travel for road trips
	$23,100	$535 per game = 2017; $525 per game = 2018 2017 budgeted $550 (increase due to Québec City travel and 2017 rate increase) × 42 games
Expenses: advertising		**MCA: 1410** **Name: newspaper**
Newspaper	$10,000	
Other print media	$0	
	$10,000	
Expenses: advertising		**MCA: 1420** **Name: radio**
Radio advertising	$18,500	Stations and formats to be determined
	$18,500	
Expenses: advertising		**MCA: 1430** **Name: cable**
Cox	$3,000	
Charter	$3,000	
Tele-Media	$6,000	
	$12,000	
Expenses: advertising		**MCA: 1440** **Name: outdoor advertising**
Outdoor	$3,500	
	$3,500	
Expenses: baseball equipment		**MCA: 1510** **Name: uniforms**
Uniforms	$2,000	Replacement uniforms—jerseys and pants as needed
Accessories	$1,000	Socks, stirrups, sanitary items, belts, mesh bags
New uniforms	$1,000	Batting practice tops
	$4,000	
Expenses: baseball equipment		**MCA: 1520** **Name: bats**
Baseball bats	$6,000	Louisville Slugger, Hillerich & Bradsby
	$6,000	

(continued)

Table 2 *(continued)*

	Actual	Budgeted
Expenses: baseball equipment		**MCA: 1530** **Name: balls**
League baseballs	$6,500	126 dozen Wilson A1010 @ $51.59 per dozen
Batting practice balls	$1,000	SSKs
	$7,500	
Expenses: baseball equipment		**MCA: 1540** **Name: miscellaneous equipment**
Various helmets and catchers' gear	$1,000	
	$1,000	
Expenses: rent		**MCA: 1610** **Name: stadium**
Stadium rent	$22,000	Municipal stadium rent as per lease
	$22,000	
Expenses: concession		**MCA: 1710** **Name: family day coupons**
Hot dog, soft drink, beer coupons	$6,500	30% increase from 2017 totals
	$6,500	
Expenses: concessions		**MCA: 1720** **Name: skybox food**
Food ordered in skyboxes	$2,450	Skybox food revenue is realized under MCA 150; expense comes out of concessions commission
	$2,450	
Expenses: concession		**MCA: 1730** **Name: picnic area food charges**
Food ordered in skyboxes	$10,000	Revenue from picnics is realized under MCA 160; expense comes from concessions commission
	$10,000	
Expenses: concessions		**MCA: 1740** **Name: press box, umpires, birthday food expense**
Postgame umpire food	$1,000	Must feed umpires after game and working media during game
Birthday cakes for birthday parties	$350	50 parties × $7 per cake
	$1,350	
Expenses: consultation		**MCA: 1810** **Name: accounting fees**
Accounting fees	$5,000	2017 fees totaled $4,800
	$5,000	

The budgeted column shows what the team expected to receive. The actual column shows the actual revenue and expenses.

of how each revenue and expense item is calculated. This process is critical for pro forma financial statements as it represents the first time an executive or analysts can break down the numbers and determine if they are accurate. For example, a team can say they are going to earn $1 million from ticket sales. Where does that number come from? Is it a hunch or based on solid numbers? Through a detailed process, an executive can determine if the numbers seem plausible.

Conclusion

There is no one best way to track revenue and expenses. The key is that they need to be tracked, identified, and calculated with a detailed system. Similarly, having a means to properly allocate expenses is important, especially if there are multiple units within a sports organization. For example, how would landscaping expenses be documented? Should landscaping for the grounds around a stadium be classified as external or as turf management expenses, which might be significantly higher because the team really wants the field to look great? If all the expenses were lumped together under landscaping, the team would not be able to properly analyze if it were spending its money wisely. It should be noted that some amounts were not added to the propose budget as the team was struggling and trying to determine if they could survive and where they could possibly minimize expenses, such as salaries. The team eventually folded under too much debt.

Class Discussion Topics

1. What revenue category(ies) do you think needs to be added to the master chart of accounts to reflect the new economy (how business is conducted) and new technologies?

2. What expense category(ies) do you think needs to be added to the master chart of accounts to reflect the new economy (how business is conducted) and new technologies?

3. If you had the responsibility of increasing revenues, what revenue category do you think you could realistically increase 20% in one year and how? Think about the possible consequences (positive and negative) of taking actions to increase revenue—such as selling more tickets incurs more selling expenses.

4. If you had the responsibility of decreasing expenses, what expense category do you think you could realistically increase 20% in one year and how? Think about the possible consequences (positive and negative) of taking actions to decrease expenses—such as reducing salaries decreasing morale and possibly reducing future revenues.

Developing a Budget

Part III is one of the more applied sections; it examines how to develop and track a budget and then determine compliance. A budget is a road map: It can either take an organization in the right direction or steer the organization to doom. This part starts with Josh Vanada, general manager for Thompson Speedway Motorsports Park, explaining how his racetrack relies on budgets to run financially successful races.

Chapter 7 explores the types of budgets that can be found in almost every business, including sport businesses. The best budget is customized to meet the needs of the specific organization. A budget is the key for future planning, and this chapter provides various options for developing the right budget for a specific organization.

Chapter 8 continues the topic of budgets but with more applied information. Chapter 8 explains how to develop a budget. The budgeting process, though not necessarily complex, is very detailed oriented—it requires obtaining the right data, generating forecasts, and conducting a variance analysis at the end of the budgetary cycle.

Part III ends with a case study that builds on the case study in part II. Expanding on the minor league baseball team's information, this case study provides a detailed budget for the team. The budget was actually developed by the team, but the team folded before they had the chance implement the budget. There are some holes in the budget, and some of the numbers do not add up; this often happens when a budget is developed on the fly or with guesses, which unfortunately is a frequent occurrence with many small organizations.

Clarus Studios Inc.

Josh Vanada

Former General Manager at Thompson Speedway Motorsports Park

(Mr. Vanada is now a motorsport executive and wrote this when he was the general manager at Thompson Speedway Motorsports Park.)

In 2008, I graduated from Gordon College in Wenham, Massachusetts with a bachelor of arts degree in theology and philosophy. I immediately continued on to Gordon-Conwell Theological Seminary seeking a master of arts in religion. Unfortunately, I ended my studies early after completing half of my course work. My father became ill, and in order to help him I decided to move closer to him.

This also forced me to look for a job. I immediately went to work for a friend who owned a branding and promotions company in Cumberland, Rhode Island. I worked for him for eight months. I then moved on to Nissan of East Providence, Rhode Island as a sales and leasing consultant. I was soon promoted to sales manager and finally to general sales manager, a position I held through September 2013. During this time, I was responsible for crafting and managing our sales process, forecasting, inventory management, and marketing, as well as the recruitment, hiring, retention, training, and motivating of our sales team.

In October 2013, I blended my managerial skills with my lifelong passion for motor sport by accepting the newly created general manager position at Thompson Speedway Motorsports Park. My duties include general and administrative oversight, event scheduling and management, and business development. An important part of my duties include introducing (with our chief executive officer) forecasting, financial reporting, and budgeting into the company.

These financial tools were new to the organization—and to me. My prior roles were focused on forecasting and generating revenue. As part of the budgeting process, I was required to focus on costs and best practices for controlling and mitigating them. This was a process of trial and error, as the classification of previous data did not have the level of detail and accuracy necessary to create future budgets. We learned early on that the quality of our budget was only going to be as good as the quality of our data, and so, in the first year, we began to focus on classifying and coding the revenue and expenses as accurately as possible to assist in creating meaningful future budgets that could have a real impact on the business.

Due to the nature of our business—being seasonal—we also had to decide how we would craft our budgets—whether on a cash or an **accrual** basis. The cash budget, of course, records revenue and expenses as they come in (i.e., you receive payment, or make a payment). Accrual budgets are based upon when the revenue and expenses are expected or realized. Obviously, the two should match as closely as possible, but we found in our business that this isn't always the case given many exigent circumstances that affect the park. We elected to create budgets on an accrual basis for accuracy, and our chief executive officer reconciled that against our cash flow to see if any budget adjustments needed to be made.

After we worked our way through the past reporting concerns and deciding on how to set up our budget, we uncovered another concern that needed to be addressed—namely, using the budget to determine our profit and expense centers. This information became critical to us, as it helped our management team to determine where our revenue was coming from and what our profit percentage was against the total of gross sales. This guides and affects decisions on what events to book for the future and which events need to be eliminated because of the amount of risk associated with them (balanced against the expected return), and it points us to the areas where we should focus our business development efforts.

In addition to the benefits we uncovered, there are some additional cultural and organizational value additions that came from creating and operating within a budget. When done properly, budgets are empowering. Contrary to what may be intuitive, budgets are not always restrictive and confining. They afford employees freedom—within a framework—to choose how they can spend their allotted funds. This provides employees with autonomy and empowers them to take personal responsibility over the funds they've been budgeted, allowing them the ability to choose how to effectively steward their funds.

After we had a good handle on the structure of our reporting, we invited our departmental managers to be involved in the budgeting process. I was delighted to have several of them approach me to share their astonishment at how much it cost to run the business. The reason I was delighted was their concern was a clear indicator that they understood the impact of their decisions and were personally vested in the company's success.

Particularly, our director of track services shared with me how he was going to make staffing and operational changes, following a review of his past year's spending. As he began to look at the operations of the company through a financial lens, he was able to identify ways he could be a better steward of the company's resources. This is something that couldn't have been done prior to him being brought in on the process. Because of the knowledge that he received, he could make better, more fiscally responsible decisions.

As a result, three things happened: (1) his job satisfaction improved, because he was personally responsible for the success, not only of his department but also of the whole company; (2) the process created deeper trust between managers and the executive team, as everyone was now rowing in the same direction; (3) the information provided some measurable key performance indicators for employees and managers to share in performance evaluations. In sum, it kept him engaged and focused on the impact of his decisions and gave him the freedom to operate his department within boundaries and without fear of reprisal.

Based on this experience, some of the best advice that I could give is do not to be afraid of budgets. They are just numbers. That's all they are. When done properly, budgets are a great tool to keep everyone focused, removing egos and personality from fact-based decision making. Like most tasks, the hardest part of budgeting is getting started. One shouldn't let the fear of what they may uncover, or the scope of the undertaking, deter them from beginning.

Similarly, include as many of the organization's key personnel in the process as necessary. Providing departmental leaders with this information gives them keen insight into the business and creates alignment across the whole organization. They will be a lot more effective in their positions with the widest field of vision possible. I would caution the reader to ensure that, prior to doing so, profit and expense centers are clearly identified and the quality of the data is good. Otherwise, employees and management might start questioning the process and think management is out to get someone.

It's important to take budgeting seriously. While cash is king, budgets provide organizations with a good gauge of how much money a business has or does not have at a given time. Obviously, as market conditions change, budgets may need to be adjusted, but, in my opinion, that should only be in extreme cases. It's hard for employees to view budgets as legitimate if they are constantly being adjusted without good reason. Instead, senior managers and executives should challenge budgets during the review phase so their employees can have freedom to operate following final approval. Furthermore, budgets are meant to be monitored consistently.

Like all data and reporting systems, accuracy is crucial. A laser-like focus is needed to ensure that revenue and expenditures are placed in the proper place within the chart of accounts. It's important to regularly view the company's performance against the budget. Managers need to have real-time access to curtail overspending and be able to measure return on investment. Budgets provide key insights, which allow companies and organizations the freedom to operate within certain parameters. An organization's ability to generate a budget and operate within it can significantly affect organizational morale and free executives up to focus on business development.

Budgeting: A Road Map for Sports Organizations

Chapter Objectives

After studying this chapter, you should be able to do the following:

- ♦ Appreciate the need and value of financial planning.
- ♦ Understand the value and use of budgets.
- ♦ Define the different budget types.
- ♦ Understand what a pro forma budget is and why it is an important part of a business plan.

This chapter starts with examining the importance of financial planning. Every coach goes into a game with a plan. That plan might focus on which players to start, what offense to use, and what defensive strategies to use. Some coaches are known for scripting most of the game and writing down every play that they expect to run during a given period or under certain circumstances. The same basic concept applies to financial planning. Every sports organization needs to determine before a new year or season starts what they want to accomplish and then develop a road map. The map that is used is a budget. The budget focuses on what the business wants to accomplish during a set period for a given product or industry unit. Financial planning entails examining future income and expenses to help steer a company in a given direction. Every business decision requires planning. Strategic planning has gained popularity as a way of critically analyzing given business scenarios to generate appropriate solutions. This same strategic planning perspective applies to financial planning. Every monetary issue needs to be examined for fiscal soundness. Every dollar needs to be planned for to maximize that dollar's impact. Planning for most typical contingencies can help a business operate smoothly and save money. While this chapter discusses basic issues and the need for budgets, chapter 8 covers the mechanics of developing, implementing, and evaluating a budget.

This chapter highlights the various components necessary to plan effectively. The process starts with understanding that a sports organization needs a plan. While there are many plans such as a marketing plan or a strategic plan, we are going to focus on a financial plan. That financial plan results in a budget. The budget is a road map for the organization. Through utilizing a number of different budgets, an organization can be better prepared for financial conditions that might arise. One of the most well-known budgets is a pro forma budget that is often developed when a business or organization is initially developed to explore where money will come from and where it will be spent. The pro forma budget is a key to writing an effective business plan.

IMPORTANCE OF FINANCIAL PLANNING

Financial planning can help provide appropriate solutions for the types of problems businesses face every day, such as the need to

- develop new products,
- pay bills as they become due,
- spend more money on research and development,
- retire a given product line,
- borrow funds for future expansion,
- issue commercial paper,
- issue more stock,
- issue more bonds,
- sell existing assets,
- purchase new assets,
- increase prices,
- decrease prices,
- move the business to another location,
- acquire a competing company, or
- file for bankruptcy protection.

As the list suggests, every future action that a business might undertake entails financial planning. Some are short-term issues while others entail long-term focus. The financial planning examined in this chapter is focused on everyday financial issues such as paying rent and salaries. The financial planning covered in chapter 12 is much broader and covers long-term financial ideas such as whether to build a new facility. Both short- and long-term financial decisions will require planning, yet many businesses do not undertake this simple process. Some executives go with a hunch or a feeling, but the truly successful executives have a plan. Normally, two major steps are explored. The first approach is to undertake minor changes such as reducing costs or raising prices a small percentage. The second approach is to undertake major projects. The first approach is often called "thinking at the margins." *Thinking at the margins* is an economic term focused on how to cover marginal costs and then add some profit to the mix. Assume a team sells a hot dog for $2 at the ballpark. That price is the standard price based on 30 cents for the raw material used (hot dog and bun) and 30 cents for the fixed costs (employees, kitchen equipment, signage, and other expenses incurred regardless of how many units are sold [see chapter 5]). At the end of the game, all unsold hot dogs need to be thrown away, composted, or donated. Thus, in the middle of the ninth inning the team might reduce the price of each hot dog to $1 and possibly earn 40 cents profit or it could stick with the $2 price and maybe throw away some possible profits. While there is the simple math, there is also a strategy component as some people might wait until close to the end of the game to buy hot dogs if they know the price will be reduced. Microeconomic theory indicates that the lowest offer you should take is the one that exceeds your **marginal cost**. Sunk costs cannot be recouped, so if the fixed costs are removed from the analysis (as the employees will be paid and the hot dog warmer will still be on), the key point is the 30 cents of variable costs. Thus, earning 70 cents would be a great return compared to losing the 30 cents if the bun and hot dog will need to be discarded. Whatever the price, through developing a budget based on sound numbers, a team can make this calculation and therefore make sound financial plans.

Small changes can provide significant impact. Walmart changed its plastic bag design in 2017, which resulted in saving $20 million. Walmart also shortened the receipt length, and that saved the company $7 million in one year. Not every company can save so much money, but if the team understands how much it costs to put on a game, it can undertake specific steps to reduce costs or increase revenue. This approach can be reflected in a game budget where all the expenses and revenues are projected.

In contrast, long-term budgets often focus on much more than just incremental changes (plus or minus a small percentage). Long-term budgets will often focus on transformative goals. The difference could be whether to undertake incremental activity that might increase market share by 2% to 5% or aim for a transformative goal that is much riskier but could increase market share by 25%. Much more information and the

quality of analysis are enhanced with long-term budgets and executive need to use information from accountants, economists, marketers, and others to successfully craft a budget that would have the greatest potential for accuracy.

In some areas, there is little room for error. For example, Churchill Downs is known for hosting the most famous horse race in the world—the Kentucky Derby. The publicly traded company (Churchill Downs, **NASDAQ** CHDN) generates around 55% of its profits in the week leading up to and including the race (Hall, 2013). If a storm or some other issue arose, then revenue could be significantly impacted. That is why it is so critical for the company to have an accurate budget and financial forecasts of various scenarios to avoid any surprises or miscalculations.

Significant change in an organization often leads to a new plan and a new budget. For example, when The Sports Authority went bankrupt, one of its top suppliers, Under Armour, had to develop a new plan and new budgets to reflect that reality. Similarly, when the National Collegiate Athletic Association allowed member universities to provide more benefits to students, this was seen as a great benefit for both student-athletes and universities. However, it also changed the dynamic of expenses for all these institutions. Tuition was already increasing at many schools, and that is often one of the biggest expenses for an athletic department. The new expenses needed to be added to the budget. This created an imbalance that needed to be corrected with additional revenue or reductions in other expenses. This is why the budgetary process is so important. A university cannot just hope they have enough money to cover all its expenses. While a state university might overspend and be bailed out by the state government, a private company normally does not have a sugar daddy to bail it out of trouble.

Sound financial planning and the budgetary process can be seen in the example of a company undertaking an advertising campaign. The company needs to develop an advertising budget that incorporates **forecasts** of future advertising expenditures and then examine the potential revenue from each advertising effort. Table 7.1 is an example of an advertising budget worksheet

Table 7.1 2019 Advertising Budget Categories

Category	Priority	Number of insertions	2018 budget ($)	2019 budget ($)	% difference
Magazines	2	200	8,000,000	5,500,000	−31.2
Newspaper advertisements	7	40	1,000,000	1,000,000	0.0
Newspaper supplements	5	26	2,000,000	2,300,000	15.0
Radio	11	900	1,300,000	850,000	−34.6
Television	8	150	2,500,000	2,000,000	−20.0
Endorsements	1	10	1,000,000	8,500,000	750.0
Posters	4	50,000	60,000	140,000	133.0
Special media	3	100	800,000	1,000,000	25.0
Agency fees	16	N/A	1,200,000	1,000,000	−16.7
Trade media	6	60	700,000	750,000	7.1
Consumer incentives	9	100,000	500,000	500,000	0.0
Sales conferences	10	12	230,000	250,000	8.7
Merchandising material	12	400	130,000	150,000	15.4
Trade allowances	13	N/A	100,000	100,000	0.0
Trade free goods	14	2,000	1,000,000	1,050,000	5.0
Sundries	15	N/A	120,000	130,000	8.3
Totals	N/A	153,898	20,640,000	25,220,000	22.2

that could help a company establish priorities for future advertising campaigns. This information is critical for financial planning because sales forecasts are based on the anticipated advertising campaign and the anticipated resulting sales. If a new product is launched and only a small marketing budget has been provided, the anticipated sales could be severely compromised. At the same time, a large marketing budget that is misspent on the wrong advertising medium can be counterproductive.

If a sport manufacturer, such as Under Armour, decides to switch from advertising primarily in magazines to using athletes as endorsers, this planning decision will be shown on a completed form that lets management know how the strategy will be implemented (see table 7.1). The worksheet would help a company develop appropriate strategies that reach the desired audience but takes into consideration the financial cost and value of each advertising option.

The marketing budget highlighted in table 7.1 reflects a new emphasis on endorsement athletes,

along with a dramatic cut in the magazine advertisement budget. Note that some high-priority areas may have a lower budget than certain lower priority items. For example, posters have one of the lowest allocations in the budget, but they are a high priority. Because the new campaign emphasizes endorsing athletes, giving away posters of the athletes may be a major initiative, but it does not represent a major expenditure. Other items that have higher budgeted amounts may have a lower priority. For example, the company might purchase certain ads even though they are not a major part of the marketing effort because they have a long-standing relationship with the advertising medium or wish to avoid an image backlash. The major declines in the marketing budget are in radio (−34.6%), magazine (−31.2%), and television advertisements (−20%).

Advertising variables may not be as clear to upper management if different segments of the business submit different marketing budgets. A large business may have several segments, each with its own budget; if these budgets are not consolidated into a final marketing budget, upper management will not have a correct picture of the marketing goals and associated costs. For example, a professional sports team might have separate marketing budgets for ticket sales and for the team's web page or souvenir store. If the various budgets are not consolidated into a simple-to-read document, management will make decisions without all the relevant facts. The planning process cannot be accomplished without this information, and the information paves the way for the overall corporate budget. Although it might appear that examining individual budgets might be easier for some executives, the inability to compare and contrast each budget in a synthesized manner can reduce the effectiveness of various techniques such as zero-based budgeting. Thus, some executives like to examine the budgets for individual units but insist on examining a consolidated budget to see what effect any changes in one budget will have on other units.

Management can examine the chart shown in table 7.1 to determine where the marketing emphasis will be in the coming year and what areas will have the greatest spending growth and decline. This information can be correlated with sales forecasts to help management understand why a certain advertising strategy is being suggested. For example, if sales stemming from magazine advertisements increased 20% in the past year, it would make sense for the advertising campaign to show an increase in magazine ads to help spur additional sales from that outlet. But if the sales force informed management that using athletes as endorsers was expected to produce the greatest surge in exposure, management could understand why magazine advertising was declining despite an expected increase in advertising and sales. The marketing budget chart serves as a tool that management can use to make a logical plan for the future. The marketing budget, along with any other budgets, is critical for financial planning.

DETERMINING FINANCIAL OBJECTIVES

For many managers, making the highest profit possible is a financial objective. But profit is not the only criterion for financial success. Most corporate managers are interested in one primary overall objective—keeping stockholders happy, in which case management should focus more on earnings per share than on total corporate profits (Brigham & Gapenski, 1994). A company that earned $10 million and had over 100 million outstanding shares would generate earnings of $0.10 per share. In contrast, a company that earned $1 million but had only 100,000 outstanding shares would generate earnings of $10 per share. The shareholders of the second company would have higher earnings per share and would probably think that they had a better investment. This evaluation assumes that the criterion for analysis used by the shareholders was earnings per share rather than stock price appreciation or total earnings.

Earnings can also be reflected in increased stock value. Especially for stocks that do not pay dividends, the increase in share value will be the hallmark for determining financial success. Thus, if two companies (company A and company B) have earnings of $50 million each, the hallmark of yearly success could be the companies' stock values. If company A's stock rose $2 per share from $28 to $30 and company B's shares rose $1 from $4 to $5 per share, most analysts would consider company B more successful. Because the earnings were identical, the focus turns to increased stock value, and company A's 7.125% increase in stock value pales in comparison with company B's 25% rise.

Earnings per share is just one of the factors that influence the health of a corporation. A corporation is a business entity that is incorporated under state law and is entitled to issue ownership interests in the form of stock certificates (see chapter 10 for more information on stocks). People interested in investing in stocks, also called shares in a corporation, want to know whether their investment will generate a return, such as dividend payments or an increased stock price. Besides knowing whether the stock will pay a dividend, a potential investor might want to know the following:

♦ How often the dividends are paid
♦ How risky future earnings might be
♦ How much debt the company carries

◆ What the corporate policies are (e.g., whether the company is going to try to purchase a competitor or what dividend rate it pays)

All these questions become critical for financial analysis because corporate policies concerning stocks and bonds help dictate stockholder and analyst interest in the stock. Stocks are only one criteria of success. Nonprofit sports organizations will have different financial objectives. But every organization has a financial objective, and the budget planning process is designed to help an organization reach those goals.

Every sports organization will also go through good and difficult financial times. Through preparation, a sports manager can possibly position an organization for the rough times by stashing away money. For years, high school sports programs have been facing financial challenges. These challenges seem to occur almost every 10 years, as evidenced by incidents in the 1980s, 1990s, and more recently, the 2008 recession and its impact on high school sports. These incidents have ranged from drugs in sport to Title IX compliance to pay-to-play requirements due to strapped budgets. Financial planning can help high school athletic administrators prepare for what they know will be tough times in the future. When the years are good, expenses start increasing as more services or programs are offered. When times become rough, administrators cry foul and ask for help in balancing their budgets. This example shows that slow, steady growth is much easier to plan for than a yo-yo cycle of rapid growth and rapid decline. This can be reflected in a budget.

An example of appropriate financial planning entails large colleges bringing in small schools to play in the larger school's stadium or arena without a corresponding return contest. Traditionally, teams play home-and-home series in which each team hosts a game. But schools such as Ohio State University can hold a crowd of around 100,000 at their home stadium, and a return away game might be played in front of a crowd of just 40,000, the capacity of their opponent's stadium. To generate greater revenue for both, teams often agree to play in the larger stadium without a return game being scheduled. For larger universities, this kind of scheduling generates revenue and usually (but not always) results in a win before a tough conference schedule begins. Playing an away game in a big arena gives smaller schools significant revenue and helps them recruit better players by letting them know that they will play against national-caliber competitors. Thus, both sides in such an arrangement generate significant revenue and other benefits. The best financial plans benefit both sides to an agreement. Again, such a decision will need to be based on a budget, and the budget is based on the organization's objectives. If the objective is to increase revenue 100%, then that will need to be reflected in the budget through reducing expenses and increasing revenue.

THE ANATOMY OF A BUDGET

Revenues and expenses are included in various types of financial statements, such as budgets, income statements, and balance sheets. As previously mentioned, a budget is a road map that shows where the sport business intends to spend its money. The budget helps show the right path for a business, but it is much more. A budget helps anticipate the future, so it is a strategic planning tool. The budget also gives a clear picture of the resources that are needed, indicates where revenue shortfalls might arise, allows for better financial monitoring, helps communicate plans to various stakeholders, and allows more precise measurement of financial performance.

All members of the business can use the budget to help make decisions. If the budget allocates a certain amount of money for marketing and the marketing department reaches that limit halfway through the year, it may be difficult for the department to receive additional funds for the rest of the year. The only way that additional funding is likely to become available is if sales exceed the sales forecast or if another area in the budget, such as customer service, is reduced to free up money for the marketing department. A good example associated with sport budgeting is the process of going to a postseason football bowl game. Most schools would love to have a chance at a bowl game and the resulting positive publicity, but if they do not properly budget for such an opportunity, it can quickly change from a blessing to a curse. The university will generate some appearance fees and possible broadcasting revenue that is shared with its conference. Expenses include transportation, housing, food, and related expenses. Often excluded from this analysis is the cost to purchase tickets. Every major bowl game requires participants to purchase a certain number of tickets at a set price to participate in the game. For that reason bowl organizers prefer to have strong universities such as Big Ten or Pac-12 schools that have large numbers of loyal alumni who will travel to games and buy tickets. Such was not the case with some schools that have had the financial misfortune to make it to a bowl game. In 2011, the University of Connecticut, as the Big East champion, was invited to play in the Fiesta Bowl, a New Year's bowl game against Oklahoma. UConn was supposed to sell thousands of tickets. It was able to sell only 4,600 tickets for around $646,000 against a guarantee of $3.35 million. Only 2,771

of those tickets went to the general public, who paid from $105 to $255 per ticket. The remaining tickets were given to fulfill sponsorships or given to athletes' families. Many fans did not want to pay the high list price and instead purchased tickets on the secondary market, where tickets were plentiful and cheap. When all the dust settled after the game, UConn generated around $3.2 million from the game but incurred $4.86 million in expenses, resulting in a loss of $1.66 million ("Bowl no bonanza for UConn," 2011).

Budgets are often developed by examining existing business successes or failures. These business stories are found in income statements and balance sheets. An income statement highlights a company's income and expenses over the past year. A balance sheet shows the worth of a company at a specific time. These documents are just two of the types of financial state-

A budget can help identify how much product to stock at an arena before a game or event to maximize the possible profit while not overspending on products or personnel.

ments discussed initially in chapter 3 and will be discussed in detail in chapter 11. Investors, stakeholders, analysts, and government officials are the primary readers of most financial statements. By examining past financial statements, a business can help plan for its future budget and also determine whether or not its prior budget was accurate.

Almost all businesses need to start the budgeting process by initially developing a rough budget based on assumptions. These numbers will normally be a best guess, so the first-year budget for most organizations or business units will be vague and often inaccurate. After one or several years, however, the organization will be able to craft a more accurate number based on information received through the process. Businesses have to track compliance closely with a budget to make sure that expenses are not out of control or that revenue is not growing too quickly. Although increased revenue might appear to be a favorable outcome, it can spell doom for a business. For example, a sport manufacturing company might develop the latest must-have product and see sales skyrocket. With increased sales, the company might have to increase production. To do so, it will have to find a larger manufacturing location, hire more workers, and purchase more raw goods (inventory). If sales drop significantly, the company will have assumed significant new expenses and will not have the revenue stream to pay for all its growth. Thus, a budget helps an organization manage growth in a more effective manner. This is accomplished through budgeting small amounts to riskier or unknown efforts or budgeting more to known money-generating ideas.

The same concern can be raised with overspending or not timing spending accurately. One such issue that often affects public schools and university athletic departments is that a budget might need to be spent by a given date, often June 30 if the budget year is from July 1 through June 30. To meet the expenses allocated for their programs, many managers spend every penny they have on June 30 purchasing office supplies and other items. This annual dance occurs because managers want to show that they needed all the money that they were allocated. If they had any money left over, the organization might cut their budget in subsequent years, surmising that the department does not need as much money. One way to deal with this issue is to have an incentive and a penalty. If a department exceeds its budget one year, the money would be taken out of its next budget. But if the department was able to spend less than what was budgeted, the amount would roll over to the next year, offering the department an incentive to save and giving it more money to work with in the future. This process can occur only if a department has a budget and has properly documented all its revenue and expenses.

If a manager was asked to indicate the benefits for a budget, they would probably indicate the following:

EXPLORING TWO SPORT-SPECIFIC BUDGETS

Many universities have a separate nonprofit [501(c)(3)] foundation in charge of raising money through hosting various events and fund-raising drives. Assume that an athletic foundation reported $7.1 million in income and expenses in its 2018 annual report. The 2018 athletic foundation income statement shows how the numbers could break down in amounts and percentage of total funds for various categories (table 7.2).

Among the stories these numbers tell are the following:

- More than 50% of all moneys raised helped pay for program services.
- Investment income will increase on an annual basis if the foundation continues increasing its net assets, because the primary assets are investment securities that will generate future income.
- Only 6.6% of expenses were dedicated to managerial tasks, whereas 26.5% of expenses helped raise operating funds. Thus, over a quarter of the expenses were used to raise money.

Table 7.2 2018 Athletic Foundation Income Statement

INCOME ($)	
Fund-raising and annual campaign (45.4%)	$3,220,266
Direct mail and telemarketing (27.2%)	$1,936,589
Investment income (11.8%)	$838,773
Program services (5.6%)	$395,540
Game sponsors (5.2%)	$366,930
Foundations and grants (3.0%)	$215,007
Souvenir sales (1.8%)	$126,895
Total income	$7,100,000
EXPENSES ($)	
Program services (52.8%)	$3,742,385
Revenue development (17.6%)	$1,252,106
Net asset increase (14.1%)	$1,001,196
Direct mail and telemarketing (8.9%)	$634,965
Management and general (6.6%)	$469,348
Total expenses	$7,100,000

- Although direct mail and telemarketing costs were $634,965, this investment helped raise almost $2 million.
- The greatest revenue source came from fund-raising efforts and donations by individuals to the annual campaign.

Based on these numbers, a budget could be developed for 2019 highlighting possible additional anticipated revenue from programs that are doing well. Expected expenses also might increase if priorities are different or if additional expenses are anticipated, such as a significant increase in the cost of postage. If those working in the fund-raising area anticipated a major gift, the future budget could reflect that opportunity. But if they anticipate a change for the worse, such as a decrease in gifts brought about by a tough economy, they might have to reduce the budget. If they anticipate a 10% decline, the income and possibly the expenses will both be reduced by 10% in the next budget.

Another example of a budget involves the University of Alabama and its famous football program. The university reported a school-record $164 million in athletics revenue for the 2015 to 2016 academic year. This represents a 142% increase from the $67.7 million the department brought in from 2004 to 2005 (Casagrande, 2017). The athletic department transfers a good amount of any excess revenue back to the university. The numbers in tables 7.3 and 7.4 help show what the expenses and revenue numbers were for 2015 to 2016 and how they represent a significant part of the total athletic budget. Similarly, the numbers help show that some revenue areas are more important than others. These numbers can be used as a template for future budgets and to see if the prior year's budget was relatively accurate. The numbers can also be compared to what other schools in the conference or across the country generated. Lastly, these numbers can be compared from year to year over multiple years to identify any potential trends. For example, in 2012 to 2013, Alabama spent $11.766 million on coach salaries for football. By 2015 to 2016, that had risen to just over $14 million. Coach salaries represent almost 25% of all expenses for football and increased 19% over four years. This increase and the percentage of the budget can be compared from one time period to another. The budget can give a good picture of where money is spent and what expenses can be controlled. For example, bowl expenses are the second largest expense, so maybe fewer

Table 7.3 University of Alabama Athletic Department Expenses

Major expenses	2015-2016 total	% of total
Scholarships	$4,577,797	8.1
Guarantees	$3,600,000	6.4
Coach salary	$14,019,693	24.9
Support staff	$2,949,321	5.2
Severance	$299,100	0.5
Recruiting	$1,676,631	3.0
Team travel	$1,882,143	3.3
Equipment	$1,508,530	2.7
Game expenses	$3,831,759	6.8
Fund-raising, marketing	$4,528,759	8.1
Overhead, admin	$3,191,634	5.7
Medical and insurance	$1,593,862	2.8
Meals	$512,656	0.9
Other	$3,236,370	5.7
Bowl expenses	$8,806,120	15.7
Total expenses	$56,214,375	

Reprinted M. Casagrande, *How Alabama Football Makes Its Money* (Birmingham, AL: Alabama Media Group). By permission of Michael Casagrande, Alabama beat reporter.

Table 7.4 University of Alabama Athletic Department Revenues

Top revenues	2015-2016 total	% of total
Ticket sales	$37,314,723	35.9
Contributions	$20,442,909	19.7
Media rights	$20,822,783	20.0
Conf. distribution	$7,265,720	7.0
Royalties	$1,395,547	1.3
Bowl revenue	$5,310,405	5.1
Total revenue	$92,552,087	
Total profit	$36,337,712	

Reprinted M. Casagrande, *How Alabama Football Makes Its Money* (Birmingham, AL: Alabama Media Group). By permission of Michael Casagrande, Alabama beat reporter.

boosters or administrators should travel with the team to help reduce expenses in the future.

While these numbers are very impressive, the bowl game was actually a $3 million loss for the team. This does not mean that in the future Alabama should not go to a major bowl game, but a budget can be prepared to anticipate that a successful year would include losing some money on going to a bowl game. Many businesses and organizations lose some money on some elements of a business but make up for such losses from other areas. Thus, losing money by going to a bowl game has little impact on the entire athletic department when going to the bowl game actually helps increase broadcast revenue, ticket sales, and merchandising unrelated to going to the bowl game.

- Assist in strategic planning
- Anticipate potential future results
- Highlight what resources are needed and why
- Highlight potential revenue shortfalls
- Communicate future financial plans to key stakeholders (employees, management, stockholders, and government agencies)
- Assist management in monitoring spending
- Help produce more accurate analysis and performance measurement

As highlighted earlier, a budget is a map. A map has the points that the traveler wants to reach. Normally, various routes could be taken. Some of these routes might be scenic, whereas others might get the traveler to the destination quickly. Some people might use tools such as a GPS to help, but a GPS device might lead a driver astray or might not highlight specific concerns such as road construction or accidents. Furthermore, a map has a legend that shows what various symbols or colors mean on the map. This information helps the map reader understand the issues that might affect the planned trip. Note that just as GPS devices have revolutionized travel, computerized budgeting has changed the way that budgets are developed and changed. Electronic systems make it easier to track and predict trends for planning purposes. Current inventory tracking systems (utilizing bar codes as an example) are an example of how technology can help with budgeting. By knowing what inventory is in stock, a company can reduce the inventory it carries, the cost to monitor inventory, and the cost to order new supplies. Besides reducing costs, the information can be plugged into a budget.

BUDGET TYPES

Sports organizations can use several types of budgets. The two primary budgets are **operational budgets** and **capital or financial budgets**. An operational budget reflects the day-to-day operations of the organization and lists sales and expenditures for normal operations. The operational budget is possibly composed of other budgets such as a sales, production (often

broken down with categories such as direct material, direct labor, manufacturing overhead, and variable cost budgets), and administrative expenses budget. The numbers produced in this budget are entered into a budgeted income statement. A capital or financial budget is oriented more to the long term and often focuses on future expenditures such as spending for a new building or purchasing other major assets. The financial budget is often made up of smaller budgets such as a capital expenditure and the cash budget (produced with input from the budgeted income statement). The numbers from the capital or financial budget are entered into a budgeted balance sheet.

An operational budget often uses a line-item approach in which each revenue and expenditure amount is highlighted on a separate line. Some companies use a numerical code to reflect each line item so that aggregating similar revenues and expenses is easier. For example, all revenue from ticketing sources might start with a 100 code and be further specified with a code of 101 for season tickets and a code of 102 for individual game-day tickets. Such a breakdown facilitates the identification of out-of-place or inconsistent reporting in budgets.

Budgets can also be organized based on programs, such as an athletic department budget that is separated by sports. This can sometimes be hard to implement. For example, if only one sport uses a field, then it is easy to assign lawn care expenses to that sport. However, if three sports use the field, how should the expense be distributed to each sport? Should each sport be responsible for one-third of the cost or should such an expense be considered a general administrative expense? These are the types of managerial decisions that need to be explored to properly produce an appropriate budget. A program budget can also evolve into a **performance budget** in which each revenue or expenditure is related not just to a program but also to how it furthers an organization's strategic plan.

While operational and capital budgets are the two primary budget types, there are several additional budget types. They all strive to convey the same basic information such as anticipated expenses and possible revenue, but not every budget will have a revenue component. A budget for a part in a larger product might not generate any specific revenue, but the part's budget can focus on reducing costs through efficiency or using different raw product suppliers. For example, a park and recreation department budget might entail numerous subbudgets such as for each individual sport and even playground equipment where there might not be any revenue generated (but possible government funds dedicated to a specific program). These budgets can focused to accomplish a given role so a park's baseball budget can be asked to reduce expenditures by 10%. Regardless of how much tax revenue the city collects, the baseball budget would need to be reduced across the board or specific elements might need to be eliminated such as the planned purchase of new field fencing.

In this section, we will explore the different types of budgets that are used by numerous businesses. There are many budgets out there. Our focus is on master, capital, operational, cash flow, financial, static, line item, and performance budgets and zero-based budgeting.

Master Budget

The master budget is a comprehensive projection of how management expects to operate all aspects of the business over the designated budgetary period (typically a fiscal year but possibly a different time period). A clear, broad perspective can be created through using summarized projected activities from a cash budget, budgeted income statement, and budgeted balance sheet. Most master budgets contain various interrelated budgets from the various departments or areas such as marketing, ticketing, facilities, and other departments. These subset budgets are used to plan and set performance objectives. Not all organizations have departmental budgets, and they might just have one master budget.

Capital Budget

Capital budgeting focuses on major future expenses and how to finance them. For example, if a team wants to build a stadium, it will need to show how much money will be required, from what sources (bonds, cash, government financing, etc.), and how revenue will be generated to help pay for the stadium. A capital budget

can utilize tools such as the payback rule or the accounting rate of return for a project.

Operational Budget

The operational budget shows revenue and expenses associated with the day-to-day operation of a business. Operating budgets are usually broken down into shorter reporting periods, rather than just annual operating budgets. These shorter term operating budgets allow management to respond quickly to an issue that might arise. For example, the cost of raw goods could increase significantly, and such added expense requires immediate attention, such as finding new suppliers, reducing expenses, or increasing prices.

Cash Flow Budget

A **cash flow budget** examines the inflows and outflows of cash on a day-to-day basis. The cash budget will help highlight a company's ability to pay bills with the money it receives. Such a process can identify cash shortfalls and if and when financing might be necessary. Cash flow budgets can also pinpoint production cycles and inventory levels so a sport manufacturing company does not have idle resources.

Financial Budget

A **financial budget** outlines how an entire organization spends and receives money. Revenue from the core business is analyzed along with the costs and income associated with capital expenditures. **Capital assets** such as facilities and equipment can have a significant impact on an organization, and managers need to closely monitor whether they have extra cash or might need to raise money through other means.

Static Budget

A **static budget** shows expenditures that remain unchanged regardless of sales levels. For example, overhead (fixed) costs will not change regardless of sales. This provides a fixed amount around which a more accurate budget can be produced. In addition, some departments or programs might receive a fixed amount for the designated period. For example, if a ticketing department only receives $1 million for the coming year, regardless of any changes to the attendance number, then that is a static amount.

Line Item Budget

Every item is listed on a line with a corresponding amount associated with it. A typical **line item budget** has a number code, item description, and the amount associated with it. Some line item budgets can also indicate whether the amount has increased or decreased from prior budgets or past budgeted amounts. See table 1 in the part III case study.

Performance Budget

A performance budget might not actually utilize in-depth numbers but rather explores a goal for the organization, the anticipated outcomes, and the cost to achieve the outcome.

Zero-Based Budget

Zero-based budgeting (ZBB) focuses on proving the value of an expense. Using ZBB, all expenses must be justified for each budgeting cycle or period. The process starts with each division or unit having to start its budget with zero dollars and then prove the value of its anticipated expenses. Ideally, every function within a sports organization should be analyzed to make sure it is producing true value rather than just relying on historical allotments in past budgets. ZBB does not examine revenue but only expenses.

Table 7.5 summarizes the different budget types highlighted as well as some of their key benefits.

PRO FORMA BUDGETS AND BUSINESS PLANS

Budgets represent the key to financial planning. Budgets help establish a means to forecast future performance based on past results and expected external changes such as changes in the market or the economy. The budget also helps management establish goals and objectives for the business. Thus, a budget is first and foremost a financial plan for the future. The financial plan highlights what results are anticipated if certain financial actions are taken. For example, if you want to buy a car, you might examine your financial position and determine that you can afford only $100 a month. You can develop a financial plan based on how much of a down payment you can make and your $100 a month available for monthly payments.

A financial plan is often a key component of a **pro forma** budget and a business plan. A pro forma budget is simply a future budget based on past financial results and expected future financial results. The pro forma budget contains a financial plan for the business, and the two are often combined to help complete the business plan. The business plan is the road map for the business; it contains financial analysis along with other key components such as marketing and production that help an executive or lender determine the potential for future success of the business.

Table 7.5 Basic Budget Types

Budget type	Explanation
Master budget	Provides an overall analysis of organizational revenue and expenses
Capital budget	Serves as a long-term financial plan
Operational budget	Shows the day-to-day operations of the organization
Cash flow budget	Examines the cash going in and out of an organization
Financial budget	Outlines how an organization spends and receives money
Static budgets	Examines fixed costs regardless of any change in revenues
Line item budget	Provides easier analysis with items listed on separate lines and the lines grouped together
Performance budget	Explores how set funds help achieve organizational goals
Zero-based budget	Forces every unit to prove the value of its expenditures

Before considering the pro forma budget as part of the planning process, we should note the significant difference between forecasting and budgeting. A forecast is an estimate of anticipated operations, such as how many hours given machinery will operate. The sales force could be asked what sales they would forecast for the coming quarter. In contrast, a budget is a target agreed on by management as an indicator of success; for example, management might agree that a successful year would entail selling one million tickets. On the basis of this distinction, it is often best to view profit planning and appropriate budgeting from a product or division perspective in which less profitable products or divisions can be isolated for more thorough analysis.

Typical extensive pro forma budgets might incorporate the following:

♦ A sales budget

♦ A promotion budget

♦ A materials, labor, and overhead budget

♦ A cash flow budget

♦ A capital appreciation budget

Each one of these budget elements could be included in an operational budget or a capital budget. These are all just examples of the types of budgets that could be included in a pro forma budget, but there are no set rules as to what should be included. The key is that the pro forma is designed to provide basic understanding of how an organization will move forward, and these budgetary elements might help highlight the anticipated sales (the sales budget) or the product marketing (the promotion budget, which highlights where the product will be promoted and the costs for such promotions). The cash flow budget might be considered the most critical to help determine where the money is as many new companies do not realize where all their money is going or coming from.

All the budgets in the previous list are contingent on developing a focused strategic plan. All the numbers in the world are meaningless if the business has no direction. Although this book does not focus on strategic planning (but chapter 14 covers strategic implementation of financial directives), the hallmark of any business is a concise corporate purpose or mission. This overall mission for the business leads to the development of the corporate scope—a definition of the business' area of concentration. The area of concentration is further refined through developing corporate objectives, strategies, and plans that focus on how the business can achieve its corporate purpose. The financial plan is a key document produced after significant foresight has shaped the future direction of the business.

The financial plan can be developed in five steps (figure 7.1). The first step is to develop a system of projected financial statements, which can help a company analyze how the operating plan will affect the projected profits. The next step requires analysts to determine the funds that will be needed to help support the long-term plans. The third step entails forecasting what funds will be available over the long term and how much of the funding will be generated internally and externally. The fourth step requires a business to establish and maintain a system of controls governing how funds are allocated and used. The last step requires analysts to examine the results and develop procedures for adjusting the plan if the forecasts are not met (Brigham & Gapenski, 1994).

INCORPORATING THE PRO FORMA BUDGET INTO THE BUSINESS PLAN

The hallmark of a successful business involves a detailed business plan that accentuates the pro forma budget. This chapter has focused so far on

Figure 7.1 Financial plan developed in five steps.

developing a financial plan or road map. After this plan is developed, it has to be communicated. Some individuals with a strong financial background can examine the pro forma budgets and get a decent picture of a business, but most people need a little more guidance. That guidance comes from a business plan that expands on the financial plan and communicates the business' vision using both words and pro forma budgets. Thus, a business plan blends a financial plan and a business strategy analysis to examine both long- and short-term goals and objectives.

Although a business plan can be written in several ways, the following framework provides the most critical elements of a business plan that you might write to submit to a bank or other investors. Within the business plan, the pro forma budget is the concise document used to show that the plan makes financial sense and is viable and accurate. An example of the first page of a pro forma budget is shown in figure 7.2 (numbers are rounded for ease in calculation). The initials used in this table are discussed in later chapters but to help read the material. ROE refers to return on equity, which represents the profitability returned in direct relation to shareholder investments. ROA refers to return of assets, which indicates how profitable a company is relative to its assets.

The following components found in a typical business plan were developed by Florida Atlantic University's Small Business Development Center. Potential variations are countless, however, and software to help with writing business plans is widely available. The Small Business Administration also offers sample forms for writing a business plan at www.sba.gov

▸ The plan summary should be written after all other sections are finished. It describes

- the purpose of your plan,
- the product or service that you will sell and why it is unique,
- second- or third-generation products or services to help maintain sales,
- the market potential,
- specific highlights in the marketing plan,
- the skills provided by the management team,

- the financial projections for the first several years,
- your funding needs, and
- an exit strategy to be implemented if the business does not succeed.

▸ The industry section should highlight the economics in the industry, industry trends, and potential legal or regulatory concerns, and it should critically analyze the competitive forces that you might face. This section requires objective, verifiable information. Most of the information should be documented through secondary data from reliable sources. Sources of secondary data could include government reports, Better Business Bureau reports, reports from national or international trade organizations, research conducted by competitors, and even magazine or newspaper articles. Primary data, as discussed earlier, are data generated by the business itself (e.g., results of a customer satisfaction survey of a competitor's customers to determine whether the customers would prefer a different option or service). Any data used to substantiate statements in the industry section should be copied and attached to the business plan as exhibits.

▸ The company section describes the history and background of the business. It can include the mission statement, objectives, goals (long term and short term), and strategies. This section should also list the current principal owner or owners or majority stockholders, all members of the board of directors (if applicable), and all key executives. Last, this section should include the business' address; form of organization (sole proprietorship, partnership, limited liability company, or corporation); and any pertinent local, regional, or federal license requirements (such as requirements for handling pool chemicals).

▸ Any special circumstances concerning the company should be specified in this section, such as what stock purchase options exist if the company goes public or whether key employees have **noncompete contracts**. Any data that an investor would need to make an investment decision should be included. For example, if a company-owned patent is about to expire, meaning that competitors could start manufacturing the previously protected item, the company could face significant hardships. Similarly, if a

Profit and loss summary ($000)	Year 1	Year 2	Year 3	Year 4	Year 5	Year 6	Year 7	Year 8	Year 9	Year 10
* CONFIDENTIAL *										
Net revenue: sports core (schedule A)	0	0	6,167	8,543	10,334	11,183	11,252	11,265	11,265	11,265
Leasing (schedule B)	0	0	1,782	2,158	2,214	2,247	2,278	2,310	2,310	2,310
Total net revenue	0	0	7,949	10,701	12,548	13,430	13,530	13,576	13,576	13,576
Net margin	0	0	4,210	6,659	8,288	9,013	9,007	8,947	8,947	8,947
Net margin %	0	0	53.0%	62.2%	66.1%	67.1%	66.6%	65.9%	65.9%	65.9%
Period costs:										
General and administrative (worksheet 2)	486	709	1,183	1,227	1,245	1,245	1,245	1,245	1,245	1,245
Depreciation (worksheet 2)	51	586	1,139	1,157	1,174	1,192	1,068	937	816	684
Vacancy cost (worksheet 2)	0	0	99	46	42	44	45	47	47	47
Total period costs	537	1,295	2,421	2,430	2,461	2,481	2,358	2,229	2,108	1,976
Income from operations	(537)	(1,294)	1,788	4,230	5,827	6,532	6,648	6,717	6,838	6,970
Other income/(expense) (see schedule E)	0	(1,446)	(218)	(834)	(720)	(553)	(371)	(178)	12	209
Charge-out to capitalizing organizational costs (except depreciation)	486	709	0	0	0	0	0	0	0	0
Pretax income	(51)	(2,031)	1,571	3,395	5,106	5,979	6,278	6,539	6,851	7,179
Provision for taxes (N/A due to LLC status)	0	0	0	0	0	0	0	0	0	0
Net income	(51)	(2,031)	1,571	3,395	5,106	5,979	6,278	6,539	6,851	7,179
Ratios and valuation (assumes owning land vs. leasing)										
ROE	N/A	N/A	30.0%	46.7%	49.4%	42.9%	35.5%	30.2%	26.6%	23.9%
ROA	N/A	N/A	22.5%	36.8%	40.9%	37.0%	31.5%	27.4%	24.5%	22.3%
Net income or net revenue	N/A	N/A	19.8%	31.7%	40.7%	44.5%	46.4%	48.2%	50.5%	52.9%
Book value	449	3,668	5,238	7,276	10,339	13,927	17,694	21,617	25,727	30,035
Liabilities to net worth	2.28	5.09	0.33	0.27	0.21	0.16	0.13	0.10	0.09	0.07
Interest coverage	N/A	N/A	16.26	38.45	52.97	59.39	60.44	61.06	62.17	63.37
Debt service coverage	N/A	N/A	25.64	42.38	58.10	66.19	67.88	68.97	70.69	72.48

Notes: Information on this and accompanying pages is confidential. It is being provided to the reader with the understanding that it shall not be shared with others without express permission.

As of this date, the numbers provided here are preliminary and still undergoing analysis and revision. They are best, current, conservative estimates. We are in the process of refining the financial model and testing the investment, revenue, and expense projections as well as exploring various capitalization strategies.

Interest expense based on assumption that mortgage principle payments are level over the life of notes, with interest payments declining.

Pro forma assumes organization as an LLC. In future years the company may elect to change to a corporate structure.

Figure 7.2 The first page of a pro forma budget.
Adapted from The Peak Experience, LLC.

fitness center is leasing a fitness facility and the lease is about to expire, meaning that the center could be without a facility, that fact would need to be disclosed. The plan needs to highlight such hardships even if they hurt the prospects for raising capital. The failure to include critical data can lead to allegations of fraud or of negligent or intentional misrepresentation.

▶ The analysis of the product or service is a thorough analysis of the unique qualities of the product or service, which will help distinguish the product or service from those offered by competitors. You want to analyze the risks associated with the product or service and the reasons that purchasers might not buy your product or service. You will need to analyze any market surveys or other research that helps you draw conclusions about your product or service or that of the competition. Last, this section should identify any ancillary products or services that might be produced to develop a more expansive product or service line. If you were developing an indoor rock-climbing facility, for example, you would examine that facility in relation to

- any home-based climbing apparatus,
- any club-based climbing apparatus,
- options available at health clubs,
- the uniqueness of the industry,
- the demand for leisure sports or recreational activities in a given community,
- the availability of other climbing facilities within a 20-mile (32 km) radius of the proposed facility,
- the availability of natural climbing areas nearby and how weather patterns will affect usage,
- the availability of safety-related products, and
- the availability of trained instructors to work with patrons.

▶ The market section focuses on the demographic characteristics of the proposed market. Who is in the target market? What is its size? Can those people be reached? And do they have the funds necessary to purchase the product or service? You will need to examine the market critically to determine whether the potential customers or clients buy on a regular basis or seasonally, whether they respond to sales or coupons, and whether other locations can more effectively reach the intended market. Look through a general telephone directory such as the yellow pages and identify the competition by name, address, and phone number. Visit the competition to see how big it is, what products or services it offers, whether it is busy, and when it

is busy. After you analyze the potential market and the competition, you should establish one-year and five-year sales goals.

▶ The marketing strategy section of the business plan applies the product or service characteristics to the customers' demands. This section focuses on how to sell or distribute the product or service to potential buyers. It requires applying the four Ps of marketing—product, place, price, and promotion. Sample brochures, advertisements, announcements, product packaging, product or service guarantees, and related materials should be included. The price for the product or service should be clearly explained and compared with prices charged by competitors. This section should include all relevant information obtained through the marketing research process and used as a basis for the marketing decisions.

▶ The operation section describes how the product will be developed and produced or how the service will be delivered. Here you should discuss critical dates, such as when production will begin, as well as who will produce the products, where the inventory will come from, what shipping schedule will be followed, how the products will be delivered to clients, and so on. Writing this section requires that you have analyzed the financial and managerial control mechanisms for tracking production, inventory, and shipping, as well as accounting procedures and the like. This section should conclude by specifying the steps that will be taken if the sales goals are not reached (e.g., inventory liquidation) and the revenue that such procedures can realize.

▶ The management and personnel section lists all the key individuals necessary for the business to be successful, including brief biographies of accomplishments and potential references. This section should highlight the key skills required for the business to succeed and indicate how the key individuals fit within the necessary skill areas. In addition to discussing qualifications, you will typically analyze the compensation packages of key individuals.

▶ The financial projections section addresses when investors can make their money back and what profit they can realize. Anyone who might be interested in investing in your business will probably view this as the most important section of the business plan. Although the product or service, marketing strategy, and personnel are critical areas, investors are likely to be most interested in the return on their money. Projected cash flow needs to be calculated on a month-to-month basis for the first year until a positive cash flow can be realized and then maintained. The cash flow should also be calculated annually for five years. These projections should be augmented with pro forma income statements and balance sheets. From these pro forma statements, potential investors can start making calculations to determine critical points for business growth and expansion, such as the break-even point or return on investment.

▸ The capital needs section covers what funds will be needed to launch the business and when the funds will be needed. To help establish potential collateral, the plan should highlight what the funds will be used for. Thus, if the funds will be used to purchase a building, a lending institution will probably be more willing to extend the loan knowing that the loan proceeds could be secured by the building. This section also needs to detail how the money will be repaid, over what period, and what penalties might apply for late payments. Last, this section should cover any ownership potential that might be available. If you are willing to sell a 10% stake in the business to the right investor, you need to explain the potential deal in great detail. Details are required, especially if someone else can purchase a controlling interest or can assume liability for financial obligations.

▸ A miscellaneous section that contains relevant pictures, price lists, facility diagrams, a listing of necessary equipment, or a discussion of any unusual risks can be added (Pounds, 1997).

Business plans are written every day, but most businesses never receive funding. Most business plans fail because of lack of research, preparation, and presentation. The following is a top 10 list of characteristics seen in successful business plans:

1. Clear and realistic financial projections are the most important element.
2. The plan contains detailed and documented objective market research.
3. The plan includes a detailed analysis of all competitors.
4. The plan demonstrates that the management team is more than capable of leading the company.
5. The plan has a "killer" summary of two or three pages that includes critical projections such as income statements.
6. The plan provides proof of the writer's vision by clearly differentiating the product or service from that of the competition.
7. The document follows a clear plan and, most important, is written in proper English that is clear, precise, and free of grammatical mistakes.
8. The plan is short, not exceeding 40 pages. Documents longer than this can become too cumbersome to read.
9. The writer clearly explains the bottom line—why the money is needed and how investors will be repaid.
10. The writer has taken the time to make the plan their own. When people write business plans using their own words, instead of hiring an outside writer or using canned computer software, the reader has a better feel for their sincerity (Elkins, 1996).

CONCLUSION

Every organization needs an accurate plan, and the budget serves as the plan. The previous chapters highlighted various forms of revenues and expenses; this chapter discussed how to examine revenues and expenses in a way to plan for the future. Vigilance is the key to effective financial planning. Managers must take the time to research all prior actions and potential future actions. Planning cannot focus just on the past; it also requires a critical analysis of the future. By doing their homework, managers can learn a great deal about their businesses. The research required to prepare budgets and develop business plans can provide a significant education about a company. All the people in the planning process have valuable information about the business. Their insight can be of great help. If chief financial officers meet with individual salespeople, they may uncover reasons why certain products do not sell as well in particular regions and can use this knowledge to help allocate resources more effectively. Thus, the planning process is not designed just to keep employees busy; it is the only technique available to prepare a business for the future. The hurdles and opportunities identified in the planning process lead to finalizing the capital budgeting process, which is covered in chapter 12.

Class Discussion Topics

1. Discuss a rough budget for your personal finances. What hurdles might you face in preparing and following the budget?

2. What things can prevent a team from meeting its budget projections?

3. What is the value of budgeting?

4. Analyze the revenue and expense projections for a local college or university and try to determine some of the potential financial objectives for the athletic department.

5. What key items need to be documented so that a business can accurately analyze its financial performance?

6. What are some of the difficulties that can be encountered when trying to project the future profitability of a team-sport franchise?

7. Why is it advisable to use multiple scenarios to project the future financial profitability of a business?

The Budgeting Process

Chapter Objectives

After studying this chapter, you should be able to do the following:

- Create a budget.
- Distinguish between long-term and short-term financial planning and understand how to minimize risk.
- Utilize break-even analysis to examine whether a budget is accurate.
- Respond to financial changes in real time.
- Undertake variance analysis.

Chapter 7 explored the importance of financial planning and how that transformed into a budget to help guide an organization. Various types of budgets were discussed, and the chapter ended with a discussion of pro forma budgets and business plans. What was not discussed was how to develop a budget. This chapter goes through the process of identifying what is involved in creating a budget, focusing on the data collection process and how to develop both short- and long-term budgets. Part of the analysis includes break-even analysis to determine what minimum benchmarks are needed for an organization to cover its expenses. The chapter then goes into determining whether the budget was appropriate and if changes need to be undertaken—through a process called variance analysis. The key is data—accurate data.

CREATING A BUDGET

By collecting all the appropriate data (see the next section), an organization can conduct a variance analysis to determine whether the budget is being followed or whether the organization is overspending or not generating enough revenue. The key to collecting data is to identify the proper classification of data. As an example, expenses are often categorized as either variable or fixed costs. Variable costs are those costs that change in direct relation to the number of items or products that might be consumed or the number of fans in attendance. Concession food costs might fall into this category. Fixed costs remain constant and are independent of the level of organizational activity. Using the concession example, the fixed costs would include the refrigeration and cooking equipment that incur an expense regardless of how many food items are sold.

While various budgets were discussed in chapter 7, some budgets are simple exercises of basic math. Budgets can be manipulated based on possible changes that could affect the business. **Incremental budgeting** takes an existing budget and increases it based on expected changes. If sales are expected to increase 5% in the future, then the incremental process would increase all line items in a budget (both revenue and expenses) by 5%. A **decrement budget** is one in which the revenue and expenses are decreased based on expected lower revenue. A

sports manager can really stand out in this circumstance. Sports managers who can properly administer and maintain a budget to avoid financial losses will set themselves apart from others in the industry. The key for sports managers is to have a system in place to track costs. Having such a system is contingent on obtaining and properly analyzing appropriate data.

Data

Companies and organizations cannot develop financial plans without appropriate data. Planning data should be compared against internal projections and external projections such as industry standards. The information from which spending and revenue sources can be identified includes internal data and external data. Internal data are often referred to as primary data because the business itself generates the information. External data, or data obtained from other sources, have already been developed and published and are referred to as secondary data. As an example, a professional sports team could develop its own data on ticket prices for other entertainment venues in the area to price its tickets appropriately. The team could then identify revenue for the future budget based on such research. This source of information is an example of internal data. In contrast, secondary data could be obtained from industry research that might track how much game tickets are sold for on the secondary market. If a report published by a local business magazine highlights that tickets are selling for significantly less on the secondary market, the team might be pricing the tickets too high compared with the demand.

Collecting data is the first step in the budgetary process. The process is normally straightforward with the data leading to a forecast. That forecast can focus on either a short- or long-term budget. Data, whether internal or external, are the driving force.

Internal Data

Forecasting cannot be accomplished without reliable internal data. An internal audit could have significant value, but if the underlying numbers are not accurate, then any reliance on the data would be erroneous. Having reliable internal and external data is critical to making good decisions. Internal data can include past balance sheets and income statements, audited financial records, annual reports, research and development reports, and countless other documents generated by employees or consultants. Paper trails should not be used to the exclusion of other data. For example, e-mails may contain valuable data that researchers may miss if they examine only printed materials.

Internal data can come from various other sources. Information can be derived from personal observation or through conversation around the water cooler. Additional sources may include surveys conducted by the business to analyze customer concerns. Many sports teams conduct fan surveys to determine why people attend games and how the organization can provide more valuable services. Information about how much and what types of soft drinks or beer are sold can be useful. By analyzing the sales figures in the grandstands and at concession stands, a team can plan its strategy for increasing beverage sales. Similarly, by breaking its operation down into its basic elements, the team can develop a more appropriate budget. This process is often seen in zero-based budgeting (ZBB). While ZBB was discussed in chapter 7 as a type of budget, it can serve as a useful example of how a budget is created.

Many companies use ZBB as a technique to justify future expenditures. In ZBB, every expenditure is justified in comparison with other potential projects. If a team will have $1 million for its marketing budget, every department that wishes to receive some of that money needs to indicate how much money it is requesting and provide justification for the request. If a department has been successful in a particular campaign, those numbers can be used as a justification for receiving a given amount of the funds. Each unit, division, or department might be required to produce formal documentation to justify requested expenditures.

Objective documentation is the key. If the existence of a department is under review, there may be a temptation to manipulate data to ensure continued employment. As an example, a head coach can be evaluated on their win–loss record as very measurable data. However, it might be more difficult to evaluate the success of a farm team system. The success of a farm system will be evaluated based on developing strong future players, but such success might be hard to evaluate or take years to develop a solid return. The farm teams might have losing records, but they can develop some strong future stars. Some areas are easier to review while other areas are harder to review. Will the future stars be stars regardless of the contribution from the minor league coaches? The minor league coaches might try to enhance their success to avoid the proverbial budgetary ax. People in an affected program might try to paint a picture that is better than what really occurs. But objective data can help eliminate potential bias or distortion. An excellent way to uncover objective information is to go to external sources.

As part of the information-gathering process, defining the target markets of the business is imperative. Key questions that must be answered include the following:

♦ Who are the past customers?

♦ How many customers are out there?

♦ What are the buying patterns of the customers?

♦ How big are the target markets?

♦ What is the business' penetration of these markets?

♦ What potential is remaining for the business to exploit in these markets?

♦ Who are the competitors, what are their market shares, and what is their pricing strategy?

While some of these topics entail external data, significant data are internal data or external data that are manipulated through internal processes to acquire usable information. Answers to the listed questions are important in generating accurate revenue forecasts.

As a business projects its revenues, including a reality check is important. In particular, is the future projected sales growth truly sustainable? High growth will consume substantial sums of internal cash and capital, as well as any capital provided by lenders and investors. Managers need to determine whether the firm has sufficient resources to sustain the level of growth built into revenue forecasts.

Information also needs to be obtained about the extent to which expenses vary directly with revenues. If the expenses of the firm are primarily variable, profitability may be improved significantly by reducing the costs per unit produced.

FINANCIAL NUMBERS FROM A MINOR LEAGUE BASEBALL TEAM

The following are excerpts from an interview with Chris Canetti, the general manager (GM) of a minor league baseball team at the time of the interview several years ago. The information reflects the importance of internal data and how the internal data can generate strategies for future growth.

I receive a lot of resumes where someone says in the cover letter that they love sports, and that's great. You have to love baseball to work in baseball, and you have to love sports to work in sports, but the bottom line is that it is a business. When I have to hire someone I couldn't care less if they played Little League baseball; I want to know what positives they can bring to my business and me, and how they can benefit the bottom line. This might encourage or discourage you, but when I went to college I was a communications major. I never took an accounting, marketing, or finance course. For a bachelor's degree in my school the only thing I needed was Economics 101. I wish differently now that I had taken those courses, but a few years ago before I became general manager, the former GM came to me one day and said, "I want you to do the budget." A minor league baseball team makes millions a year in revenue, and I have to make a budget. You can't tell your boss no, so you have to figure it out. I wish I had a course like this [sport finance]; it would have made my life a lot easier.

A budget is a model that is set by the team to try to forecast the goals they want to meet for the coming year. If you look at some budgets, they might show a cash-positive year. However, if the team has debt service that is amortized out over the course of time, it will show up as an expense, even though it is not a hard cash expense. With the debt service expense included in the budget, the budget could show a loss. I use a piece-by-piece approach to developing the numbers in this budget. The primary source for these numbers is from historical data. History describes what occurred last year and serves as the base for predicting what might happen in the coming year. For example, if we look at fictitious numbers for last year, we see that the team had

$1.4 million in (game-day) concession sales. Assume 200,000 fans attended games last season. By dividing the $1.4 million by the 200,000 fans, we can calculate that an average fan spends $7 each game on concessions. If we anticipate a 10% increase in attendance, then our budget should also reflect that 10% increase. Our ticket sales would increase 10% and our concession sales would also increase. If fans once again spend on average $7 each, then we can multiply $7 by 220,000 fans (200,000 fans plus the 10% increase in fans), resulting in a budgeted $1.54 million for concession revenue for next season.

A team's stadium lease will always be a major factor in determining an organization's financial picture. The lease is a key consideration when going through the budgeting process. The lease outlines how the parties involved will split the responsibility and control of major expense and revenue categories. These elements often include things such as concession revenue, suite revenue, parking revenue, ticket taxes, stadium maintenance, and utilities. The factors within a lease are unique in almost every team's case. In some instances, a team's lease is written so that a percentage of annual revenues are used to pay debts incurred from stadium construction or renovation. Such cases will affect the team's annual financial statement.

When asked about profit centers, Canetti responded:

Concessions represent one of the greatest profit centers for a team. While a minor league team makes a significant amount on ticket revenue and does not pay players' and coaches' salaries, which are paid by the parent club, concessions are still the best profit center. A team can generate between 50% and 60% profit on concession sales. A team could possibly outsource concessions to another company but then would only receive 35%. This significant potential decline in concession revenue has encouraged us to keep taking care of concessions ourselves to maximize the revenue and flexibility.

Hypothetical Minor League Baseball Team Budget for the 2020 Season

Category	(In $000s)
Revenue	6,140
Direct costs	1,758
Gross profit	4,382
Park and game expenses (schedule 1)	992
Team expenses (schedule 2)	196
General and admin. expenses (schedule 3)	2,422
Debt service (schedule 4)	840
Total expenses	4,450
Operating income	–116

SOURCES OF REVENUE	
Ticket revenue	2,000

DIRECT TICKET COSTS	
Facility fee	200
Payment to MLB	60
Ticket production	14
Total costs	274
Gross profit	1,726
Advertising revenue	1,400

DIRECT COSTS	
Paint and material	–
Printing	–
Radio	10
Promotional spots	200
Total costs	210
Gross profit	1,190
Game day concessions	1,400
Group concessions	600
Total concessions revenue	2,000

DIRECT COSTS	
Food	380
Soft drinks	70
Beer	80
Supplies and uniforms	60
Equipment leasing	8
Payroll	240
Payroll taxes	30
Total costs	868
Gross profit	1,132
Merchandise revenue	340

DIRECT COSTS	
Beginning inventory	70
Purchases	130
Payroll	14
Total costs	214
Ending inventory	48
Final costs	166
Gross profit	174

Category	(In $000s)
OTHER REVENUE	
Parking	40
Programs	40
Other	320
Total other revenue	400
DIRECT COSTS	
Program	80
Other	160
Total costs	240
Gross profit	160
Total gross profit	4,382
DEPARTMENTAL GROSS PROFIT MARGIN	
Ticket department	1,726
Advertising department	1,190
Concessions department	1,132
Merchandise department	174
Other departments	160
Total gross profit	4,382
Gross profit margin	71.37%
SCHEDULE 1—PARK AND GAME EXPENSES	
Stadium rent	150
Real estate taxes (waived)	0
Utilities	130
Maintenance—grounds	280
Security	110
Umpires	70
Game day payroll	190
Game day payroll taxes	18
Equipment rental	16
Miscellaneous	28
Total park and game expenses	992
SCHEDULE 2—TEAM EXPENSES	
Transportation	80
Lodging	96
Laundry and clubhouse	10
Uniforms	10
Total team expenses	196
SCHEDULE 3— GENERAL AND ADMINISTRATIVE EXPENSES	
Salaries	800
Payroll taxes	74
Office operations	4
Dues and fees	60
Promotion and advertising	550
Other (schedule 5)	984
Total general and admin. expenses	2,422

(continued)

Hypothetical Minor League Baseball Team Budget for the 2020 Season *(continued)*

Category	(In $000s)	Category	(In $000s)
SCHEDULE 4—DEBT SERVICE PLUS OTHER EXPENSES		Insurance	160
Interest	180	Professional fees	60
Depreciation	260	Miscellaneous	2
Amortization of contracts	400	Outside services	16
Total expenses	4,450	Postage	40
SCHEDULE 5—OTHER EXPENSES		Rent	2
Amortization	370	Repairs	16
Auto expenses	18	Supplies	32
Bad debt expenses	10	Taxes—others	60
Bank service charge	40	Telephone	80
Contributions	2	Travel	16
Entertainment	10	**Total other expenses**	934
		Total debt service	840

Although we often use Under Armour as a real-world example in this book, here we use the fictitious Sport Manufacturing Company (SMC). Inventory numbers are rarely publicly available because companies do not want their competitors knowing what manufacturing cycles they are following. In this example, SMC manufactures and sells golf clubs and skis. Variable costs for SMC include the cost of labor and material. If the company finds that it is selling fewer golf clubs, it will reduce production. As production is reduced, SMC can reduce the number of people employed in production as well as the purchase of materials used to manufacture the golf clubs.

As for fixed costs, we assume that SMC has extensive machinery and equipment in its manufacturing facilities. The machinery and equipment, along with the manufacturing premises, are long-term capital assets whose costs are considered fixed over any particular period. If the machinery and equipment are used in a facility that fabricates golf clubs, the annual expense is incurred even if no golf clubs are produced. When expenses are mostly fixed, higher profitability will be associated with higher sales because the cost per unit sold will fall as sales increase. If we assume that most of SMC's expenses are the fixed costs associated with its machinery and equipment, the company needs to maximize golf club sales to boost profitability by lowering the cost per golf club sold.

In the short run, a major constraint in SMC's attempts to maximize profitability through increased golf club sales is the maximum production capacity of the manufacturing facility. A production constraint is also a sales constraint. If SMC can produce only 800,000 golf clubs in a year, it will be unable to sell more than 800,000 golf clubs annually. Even if the demand for golf clubs is one million per year, SMC will be unable to sell that many unless it can find some way to increase production. SMC could conduct break-even analysis using the fixed and variable costs to help determine the initial manufacturing run consistent with the research data it would have on projected sales.

In contrast to a manufacturing company that has numerous variable costs, the major cost for a professional sports team is the salaries of players and coaches, which are fixed costs. No matter how much revenue is derived from attendance at games or broadcast rights, the team will be paying the same salaries, so it needs to make sure that the budget covers at least those expenses.

External Data

By knowing how successful internal operations are, a business can plan more appropriately. External data can serve the same purpose. External data and documentation are critical for successful planning. External data can be used to help shape various decisions to reflect the true business environment. For example, some leagues have league-wide data available to teams where they can examine their costs and revenue against competitors and league-wide averages. Similarly, a football team in Europe might face relegation (or promotion) and will be faced with brand new budgetary challenges. They might face a significant decline in broadcast revenue or they might have new revenue streams they had not had in the past along with new expenses such as higher priced players. To help create a budget based on these new challenges and opportunities, the team might contact other teams or league offices to obtain additional information. Such information is considered external data. Once the budget is produced for the team, it will be considered internal data for that team. These are only two examples of the use of external data to help shape sport business decisions.

External data can help shape decisions in many other ways as well. The following are examples of gathering external data:

- Monitoring international terrorist activities to determine whether an event needs to be canceled
- Analyzing industry trends to develop appropriate pricing for concessions items
- Tracking culinary advances to determine the most effective means of packaging and selling food items
- Reading current articles in trade publications to stay abreast of industry changes
- Attending conferences to hear what other executives are saying about the industry
- Reviewing government census reports to understand demographic changes in the possible fan base

Publications such as *Barron's*, *Forbes*, *Business Week*, and *The Wall Street Journal* provide useful general information. More specific information can be obtained from such sources as Dun & Bradstreet's *Key Business Ratios*, which analyzes 14 key ratios for various industries. Both state and federal governments produce significant useful data such as statistical abstracts. Industry trade groups can also produce valuable data to assist with financial planning. The suggested resources section contains information on these publications and how to access them.

Among the best information sources for the sport industry are industry publications such as *Athletic Business*, *Athletic Management*, *Fitness Management*, and *NCAA News*. Each has unique special features, reports, and surveys that can provide invaluable assistance. One of the premier publications in the industry is Street & Smith's *Sports Business Journal*. This weekly publication has special sections devoted to attendance numbers, a stock **market index** for sport-related companies, and information on sponsorship deals, among other features.

Regular newspapers often list the payrolls for every professional team in leagues such as the MLB, the NFL, and the NBA. Such data can help a team compare itself with others, which is called **benchmarking**. Benchmarking allows a business to see whether it is paying more for similar work or results. For example, a basketball team can compare its salary range with other teams in the league or examine specific statistical variables such as the cost per rebound or assist for each player.

Organizations regularly research specific industry benchmarks that can help establish criteria for success or failure. Although the data are only as good as the techniques used to retrieve them, the information can help shape many financial decisions. Numerous managers focus on the bottom line, and the bottom line can be examined by looking at what others in the same industry do to determine whether a facility is operating as effectively as similarly situated facilities.

Industry-related data come from a variety of sources and appear in a variety of formats. The Small Business Administration publishes free business plan formats online to help businesses understand what data they will need and what to do with the data. More specific data are often needed from specific industry groups or associations.

Regardless of the type of external data, the reader of such reports needs to compare apples with apples. Some publications calculate return on equity as net income divided by average common equity, but others divide net income by the year-end common equity. Comparing data that have been obtained using different equations will lead to inaccuracies. One example of inaccuracies could be when two teams are discussing a player transfer and have agreed on a price, but one team is thinking about dollars and the other team is thinking about euros. Similarly, incorrectly analyzing an internal rate of return or price–earnings ratio can destroy an investment decision. Thus, all financial statements should be carefully scrutinized to determine what equations and measurement techniques were used and when the data were collected to ensure proper comparisons.

Proper Documentation

The key to success in data collection is proper documentation. Although record keeping is stressed throughout this text as an integral component of financial success, it should not be seen as an end in itself. It is simply a tool. If too much emphasis is placed on developing the right documents, managers will not be able to see the forest for the trees and may make decisions that look great on paper but become major disasters. Nevertheless, the documentation process is critical and is highlighted throughout this text. At the same time, documentation is only one of the many functions required by law or contract for obtaining necessary funds. For that reason, analyzing revenues and expenses is critical. Finance necessitates analyzing the financial feasibility of various projects based on the projected revenues to be gained, the expenses that will be incurred, and the availability of moneys to fund projects through to completion. When potential income from a project is properly documented, a potential investor is more inclined to back that project.

The ability to make appropriate financial decisions is predicated on proper documentation. Every publicly traded corporation, such as Nike or Under Armour, has to pay an accounting firm to develop an audited financial statement that could be shown to the government and other stakeholders. When a sport business finds itself in a financial plight, the only way that it can analyze the situation accurately is through proper documentation. Did someone fudge the sales numbers? Is someone embezzling money? Is the company carrying too much inventory? Are the costs of employee benefits out of control? Is extra cash just lying around in unknown accounts? Proper documentation enables you to find the answers to these types of questions because a company can trace when dollars come in and when they go out. Thus, when examining a balance sheet or income statement, people need

CONCEPTS INTO PRACTICE

When a sports organization examines a budget, managers must use the right information and compare apples with apples. Under the Equity in Athletics Disclosure Act of 1994, the U.S. Department of Education requires all colleges that receive federal funds and have intercollegiate athletics to report their spending on an annual basis. The problem is that the information can have errors or omissions and is not specific. After years of work, a database called the financial dashboard is now available for NCAA Division I and II. The database uses the Equity in Athletics Disclosure Act data to examine 26 indicators in multiple formats and what-if scenarios (Goldstein & Alden, 2011). Colleges can examine other colleges in their conference or across the nation to get a better idea of how they are spending and earning money.

Comparison is critical to understanding what it takes to be competitive. Sport administrators can use the information to be proactive rather than reactive and to construct a better strategic plan. The numbers are useful, however, only if they are analyzed correctly. For example, one school might list every expense associated with recruiting in the recruiting budget, whereas another might put air travel for recruiting in a travel budget. Other differences include salaries that likely vary with the cost of living at colleges in large cities compared with those located in rural areas. Several other areas need to be carefully examined:

- *Team travel.* Some programs take buses everywhere, some take commercial air carriers, and others take chartered flights.

- *Equipment and supplies.* Although some schools need to pay a lot for equipment and supplies, other schools have a contract with a sports apparel company and would not have to buy any equipment.

- *Ticket sales.* Some schools have large facilities and huge ticket demand, whereas other schools let students in free.

- *Donations.* Some institutions let the athletic department record gifts, whereas others record the donations for a general institutional fund (Goldstein & Alden, 2011).

to ask themselves if they can trust the numbers. If the financial statements are not audited or otherwise certified by an independent party as accurate, the reader should be cautious.

APPLYING THE DATA

After data are obtained, from whatever source, they need to be evaluated. Data will be evaluated based on organizational mission, goals, and objectives, as well as any competitive analysis that could help shape future organizational activities. The data combined with potential future directions will help in developing a financial plan, which is a budget. Financial planning requires two major activities: forecasting potential revenues and budgeting for future expenses. After the appropriate data are collected, management must act on the data. They cannot hide behind the numbers and fail to make a decision. Stockholders and voters demand that a business or government entity make decisions that will maximize their investments. The most common managerial decisions have to do with maximizing revenue sources and minimizing expenses.

Financial planning is often based on behavior learned from previous bad habits or mistakes. Failing to turn over inventory quickly enough or not collecting overdue bills in a timely manner leads to reduced income and higher expenses. Both inventory levels and uncollected accounts can significantly decrease profitability if they are high. If excess inventory and uncollected accounts receivable appear on the balance sheet, then a significant amount of money may be unusable. Both of these problems can be corrected through the implementation of efficiency control mechanisms such as posting systems (based on the due dates of outstanding accounts receivable) or the establishment of guidelines for inspecting the inventory. Many steps that people might categorize as financial planning are just commonsense tactics. For example, companies can stretch out the repayment to suppliers or pay bills early to take advantage of any positive financing terms. Companies can also reduce inventory, increase prices, and other strategies to help meet financial objectives.

These simple strategies are in fact decisions that can be reached through the planning process. A business can decide to pay bills within 10 days if a discount is offered and then reinvest the savings into interest-bearing Treasury bonds.

Such a planning process appears simple, but numerous managers live by the seat of their pants when making decisions and do not consider the long-term consequences. Planning helps determine potential long-term ramifications.

One of the most important planning issues is determining the capital structure for a business. The planning process can help determine the most appropriate structure for a given year based on economic variables and countless additional pieces of information acquired in the data-collection process. If Nike is overburdened by bond obligations, it might not be able to generate enough return to interest potential stockholders. But if Nike's equity is overdiluted, the company may find it difficult to buy back its shares. Nike could be in trouble if it has issued so many shares that its equity is composed primarily of shareholders' equity rather than retained earnings. This situation could be a problem if Nike ever wanted to buy back its stock to go private or buy back some of its shares to reduce the number of shareholders and increase the share value for the remaining shareholders.

Economic conditions are an excellent example of the concerns raised in the planning process. **Inflation** and prosperity typically cause a sharp need for corporate capital so that the company can continue to produce more. If bonds and preferred stock are issued too quickly, however, a company can go bankrupt if the economy changes and the company owes too much in interest, principal, and required dividend payments. Furthermore, during periods in which interest rates are low, bank borrowing may be more economical than issuing bonds. If a bank loan is obtainable at a relatively low interest rate, the main savings will be the costs associated with issuing bonds versus the minimal costs associated with obtaining a bank loan. If the long-term bond interest rate is lower than the obtainable bank interest rate, then it may be worthwhile to issue the bond because the issuing cost can be recouped over the long term. The opposite result is seen when interest rates are high, in which case a business would have more difficulty issuing long-term bonds. The business would have trouble selling long-term bonds to investors if the interest rate is lower than what an investor might be able to obtain in the short run from other investments. Planning helps prevent making the wrong decision and issuing securities that might not be attractive to investors.

Forecasting

Forecasting is the key to financial planning. If a plan is to work, the sports organization will need to look toward the future. The more distant the forecast period is, the greater the difficulty is in making the forecast and the lower the likelihood is that the results will be accurate. Thus, a 1-year forecast will be much more accurate than a 5- or 10-year forecast. Forecasts also involve uncertainty and historical performance. They are usually less accurate than desired, and experience is often the best teacher of what really works (Schmidgall, Singh, & Johnson, 2007). Information for forecasting can come from quantitative data (such as regression analysis, econometrics, naive estimation, and smoothing) or qualitative data (market research, sales force estimates, and focus groups). The most common approach for forecasting is the prior year's actual revenues adjusted subjectively. This somewhat naive approach is one of the most commonly used approaches. Thus, if the budget for one year entails revenue of $1,000,000 from ticket sales and sales are estimated to increase 10%, then the next year's budget would have estimated revenue of $1,100,000. Smoothing is another key technique in which a sports organization uses an estimated percentage for future growth or decline. Instead of applying it for one year, however, the manager uses several years of past sales data for a more realistic estimate. Thus, if over three years the team sold $1,000,000, then $1,100,000, and lastly $900,000 in tickets, the average smoothed over three years would be $1,000,000. If sales are projected to increase 10%, the estimate for the next year would be $1,100,000 in revenue.

To generate sales forecasts for an established business, the starting point is sales from the most recent full year. It is useful to list sales separately by product line, by sales distribution method (e.g., direct sales, retail sales, online sales), or by geographic market.

Assume that Under Armour sold four million apparel units in a given year. If Under Armour charged $15 per unit sold, its total revenues for those units would be $60 million. In table 8.1, Under Armour's 2019 revenues of $60 million are broken down by sales distribution channel (i.e., by the method for distributing the products to the final customers). Under Armour, in this hypothetical example, relies heavily on sales to retail chains, with 60% of sales through that distribution channel. Sales to independent stores and abroad are also significant. Under Armour has invested in distribution on the Internet, although online sales in 2019 were only 6% of total sales.

After sales force and marketing executives analyze potential sales from various projections, historical sales are examined to project future sales. At a minimum, three to five years of the most recent sales figures should be reviewed. This approach allows analysis of recent trends that can be useful in forecasting future sales growth for the budget. Even though forecasting often looks to both the short term and long term, for most budgets, you will examine short-term forecasts, normally less than one year. However, long-term forecasts can help allocate resources more effectively for long-term efforts, such as a capital budget.

The research process, specifically an examination of historical sales data, has shown that over the last 10 years, Under Armour has maintained its position as a sporting goods manufacturer with seasonal sales patterns, and those sales have grown an average of 8% per year. In individual

Table 8.1 Under Armour's 2019 Sales (Hypothetical)

Distribution channel	2019 sales ($)	% of total
Chain stores	36,000,000	60
Independent stores	12,525,000	21
Individual (direct)	375,000	1
Internet	3,750,000	6
Foreign	6,000,000	10
Other	1,350,000	2
Total	60,000,000	100

years, sales have been dependent on the strength of the U.S. economy. The forecasts for 2019 sales will be based on the historical information, supplemented by the experience and research of Under Armour's analysts.

In table 8.2, three scenarios are presented for forecasting purposes. These include a best-case scenario, a worst-case scenario, and a most likely scenario. The most likely scenario is based on pulling together the best and worst cases. The two extreme cases give the analyst a way to understand opportunities as well as potential barriers to success (Koller, Goedhart, & Wessels, 2005).

The worst-case scenario assumes that most of Under Armour's sales are stable and that 90% of 2019 sales is a reasonable assumption. The 90% range is designed as a cushion in case sales are lower in a subsequent year. If Under Armour's historical sales had fluctuated substantially from year to year, a worst-case scenario could involve sales of even less than 90% of 2019 sales. In the case of sales over the Internet, that distribution channel is still relatively small and is subject to greater risk, particularly if other manufacturers decide to use the Internet as a distribution medium. Thus in a worst-case scenario, sales over the Internet are shown as a 40% decline. Sales to individuals are expected to remain the same, even in a worst-case scenario, because Under Armour does not devote any marketing effort to individual sales and annual sales to individuals have stayed relatively constant over the last decade.

Note that historical sales were used to determine the worst-case scenario. In the event of a new trend that is not reflected in the historical sales information, the potential sales decline under the worst-case scenario would be easy to underestimate. For example, if a new movement toward consolidation took place in the retail sporting goods sector and certain retail chains that had been Under Armour customers went out of business, Under Armour's sales might be subject to unforeseen declines. Furthermore, if Under Armour made nothing but snowboarding and skiing jackets and winter snowfall was poor or if it missed the snowboarding jacket trend, then sales could plummet. While this is a hypothetical example, in 2017, Under Armour was facing significant hardship and sales declines across multiple lines and the sudden drop reflected consumer changes that were probably not reflected in any internal forecasts.

The best-case scenario assumes that with properly focused marketing efforts, chain store, independent store, and foreign sales can increase by 20%. By contrast, because the Internet distribution channel was relatively new in this example, a best-case scenario includes Internet sales growing by a multiple of 2.5 in the event that Under Armour's efforts to enter this market segment begin to bear immediate fruit. The increase of 2.5 times is an estimate based on either an educated hunch or market expectations.

The most likely scenario represents a composite of the worst-case and best-case scenarios. The best- and worst-case scenarios do not have to be weighted evenly. Instead, the weight applied to each should represent subjective judgment about the relative likelihood that each of these scenarios will occur. In terms of a reasonableness check, note that Under Armour's sales in its traditional chain store, independent store, and for-

Table 8.2 Under Armour's Sales Forecast for 2020 (Hypothetical)

Distribution channel	2019 sales ($)	Worst-case sales ($)	Most likely sales ($)	Best-case sales ($)	Most likely sales ($), % change
Chain stores	36,000,000	32,400,000	38,880,000	43,200,000	8
Independent stores	12,525,000	11,272,500	13,527,000	15,030,000	8
Individual (direct)	375,000	375,000	375,000	375,000	0
Internet	3,750,000	2,250,000	6,525,000	9,375,000	74
Foreign	6,000,000	5,400,000	6,480,000	7,200,000	8
Other	1,350,000	1,350,000	1,350,000	1,350,000	0
Total	60,000,000	53,047,500	67,137,000	76,530,000	12

eign distribution channels are expected to grow at rates that match recent historical growth rates for the business as a whole. Because the Internet is a relatively new distribution channel (in this hypothetical example) with a lot of upside potential for growth, Internet sales are projected to grow 74% in 2020 under a most likely scenario. The Internet sales growth causes overall projected sales growth to be 12% for 2020, which would surpass the 8% historical norm.

So far, we have developed a sales forecast using a bottom-up approach. Essentially, we have separately forecasted each component of sales and then summed up the total sales across components (or distribution channels in our example) to determine total sales.

Short-Term Planning

The Under Armour example is a short-term forecast for one year. Short-term planning dictates how a business should proceed within a short time frame, usually less than two years. Short-term planning cannot be undertaken without examining the potential implication of current decisions on the long-term profitability or success of any business. Long-term planning is more oriented toward the future and allows executives to be more creative because many options and uncertainties play into such decision making. Short-term planning is based on specific research and requires people to meet specific goals.

Regardless of the time frame used for planning, accuracy and the ability to interpret internal and external data properly are the keys to success. For example, if the short-term analysis does not adequately examine internal debt-related issues and the external borrowing environment, a business may not last more than several months before creditors file for involuntary bankruptcy.

The short-term planning process requires close scrutiny of internal variables such as cash flow and debt-related issues. Key aspects of short-term planning include knowing how to make decisions based on **working capital**, net working capital, current ratio, quick ratio, and the cash budget. Most of these ratios are discussed in chapter 13.

Deciding whether to hire a new basketball coach is normally a long-term planning process. Most coaches are not hired for the short term;

they are hired to build a program using their skills and strengths. This intention does not mean that short-term planning will not influence the decision. Ticket sales and player recruiting still need to be undertaken during the hiring process to ensure continued success or prevent falling further behind rival programs. Thus, the hiring process, like almost all planning decisions, entails a blend of short- and long-term planning.

There have been several examples over the years of a university hiring a former NBA star with hopes they can turn around the school's basketball program, sometimes investing significantly in the program with the hopes that hiring and facility renovations would pay off. One recent example was Mark Price (NBA player from 1986 to 1998) who coached for three years at the University of North Carolina at Charlotte. He lasted there three years and had a win-loss record of 30–42. As another example, the University of Houston hired a former star basketball player at the university and one of the top 50 players in NBA history, Clyde Drexler, as the head basketball coach a number of years ago. Almost immediately thereafter, the university spent a considerable sum to remove several rows of seats and install luxury boxes in their arena. Although the initial demand for the boxes was high based on the prospect that the new coach would develop a winning team, those hopes quickly faded. The team performed unremarkably during Drexler's tenure, and after two years he resigned. This account serves as an example of poor short-term planning and inadequate capital management. The athletic department was hoping for a miracle with a new coach, but it would have been better served by waiting for the coach to succeed and the business to grow rather than hoping that growth would be immediate.

Effective planning would have included a cost–benefit analysis of installing the luxury boxes based on the possible failure of the coach rather than just on the expectation that a miracle would occur and that the hiring would erase years of debt. Similarly, a break-even analysis would have been appropriate for any investment. In fact, attendance had been abysmal for years before the hiring, and during the two years thereafter it improved. Still, there were no guarantees that attendance would not return to its previous level if the basketball team did not deliver a high-quality product. Short-term planning might have focused on examining the attendance trends associated with the new coach for at least several years after he came to the University of Houston to see whether his hiring would, in fact, increase attendance. After collecting some empirical data based on actual ticket sales and revenue for a one- or two-year period after the coach's hiring, the university could have made a more accurate short-term plan for capital expenditure during a deficit.

The University of Houston example highlights how most business decisions entail an element of both short- and long-term planning. Another example of how short-term planning can blend into long-term planning is the futures market. The futures market primarily involves commodities such as metals, meats and other foods, and currencies. Most commodities sales are conducted in the spot market, where an item is bought and sold for cash and the exchange is completed immediately.

But in the futures market, transactions involve delivery and payment at some future date. A sports team could pay a significant amount of money for a player, but the player might be delivered at a future date because of other contractual obligations. This future obligation often happens with foreign athletes who might be drafted and signed by North American teams but still have to complete their contracts with their foreign teams. If a player is playing in Europe, the payment amount could be affected by fluctuations in the value of the U.S. dollar against the European currency during the waiting period.

Floating means paying a certain amount to buy future dollars or other currencies on the currency markets. Some people are betting that currency values will increase, and others are betting that the values will decrease. A similar type of gamble occurs when people buy or sell stock with the expectation that the shares will either increase or decrease in value. This process is often called hedging, which entails purchasing futures contracts in situations in which a price change could positively or negatively affect profits. A business could purchase a long hedge when it anticipates a price increase. With a short hedge, a business sells futures contracts to guard against price declines (Brigham & Gapenski, 1994).

The short sale is also used in the stock sale context when someone sells short with the intent of borrowing the stock from a broker and waiting for the price to decline before actually buying the stock. The difference between the value of the borrowed stock and the final amount the investor paid for it when the stock price declined is the profit generated by this short sale. But if the stock increases in value, the investor will have to pay the higher price, which could result in a significant loss for the investor. Purchasing stocks is covered in greater detail in chapter 10.

When purchasing a futures contract, the purchaser only needs to put up an initial margin, which for certain Treasury bonds is only $3,000 for each $100,000 in contracts (Brigham & Gapenski, 1994). Although the purchase price is low, investors need to maintain a certain value in their margin account, called a maintenance margin. If the contract value declines, the futures owner is required to pay more money to cover the maintenance margin.

A futures contract can be satisfied by the actual delivery of the commodities. A farmer could sell a futures contract for 5,000 bushels of oats for a September delivery. A sport nutrition bar company might buy the contract in March so that the company knows how much it will need to pay for ingredients and the farmer knows how much they will be paid for the future delivery of oats. Thus, a futures contract is a definite agreement on the part of a given party to buy something on a specific date and at a specific price. No matter how the price might change, the contract guarantees that the purchaser has locked in a price to protect against such price fluctuations. Futures can be used speculatively or for hedging. People buy speculative futures if it appears that a price might decline or rise, resulting in profits.

By carefully examining financial markets, a business can increase its profitability and reduce its chances of losing money through inactivity. For that reason, a business needs to scrutinize short-term strategies related to all facets of its operation. Long-term strategies also help guide businesses, as discussed next.

Long-Term Planning

In contrast to short-term forecasts, long-term goals are often less clear because the large number of variables reduces the accuracy of projections. Even so, obtaining additional research results on which to base decisions can result in projections that are more accurate. Long-term planning focuses on planning for the future and places greater emphasis on external variables, such as industry trends and technological advancements. A fitness center's long-term analysis might focus on developing new exercise techniques or programs that combine some of the hottest fitness trends.

The long-term plan serves as the backbone for developing the documentation needed to secure capital support. Potential lenders such as banks or venture capitalists look to the managerial foresight highlighted in the plan. But no matter how much information the plan contains, a lender will not invest a penny without getting a picture of the business' future profit potential, which is reflected in the pro forma budget.

Earlier we examined a one-year hypothetical sales forecast for Under Armour. Most companies develop both a short-term forecast (for sales and other parts of the business) and a longer term forecast. Typically, lenders and investors require at least a three-year projection, as shown in table 8.3.

In the case of Under Armour, we assume that in the chain store, independent store, and foreign distribution channels, sales will continue to grow at their historical 8% average annual growth rate. In the case of the Internet, we assume that growth will decline from 74% in 2019 to 40% in 2020 and 20% in 2021. This projection is consistent with the notion that a new business line will demonstrate extremely high sales growth that declines over time (Ross, Westerfield, & Jaffe, 2008). We also continue assuming that sales to individuals and other sales will remain constant over time.

As discussed earlier in this chapter, numerous decisions in the sport industry entail both short- and long-term planning. An excellent example involves the Extreme Football League (XFL), launched by World Wrestling Entertainment (WWE) in 2001. WWE went public in 2000 and is listed on the New York Stock Exchange. The launch was undertaken with a broadcast partner, NBC, and had the intent of capitalizing on the young male audience that dominates in wrestling. The games, scheduled for prime-time Saturday nights, were a complete disaster. The shows had declining ratings each week, and the experiment ended with WWE taking a $37 million charge to earnings (Grover & Lowry, 2001). A *charge to earnings* is a fancy term for a loss. Instead of a steady loss from poor sales, a charge represents a one-time loss that the business does not expect to occur again in the future.

Wall Street did not take the news well. Some analysts were skeptical about how WWE could expand in a saturated market after the XFL collapsed (Grover & Lowry, 2001). The concern was also reflected in a drop in the WWE stock price from $21 per share to around $12 per share after the XFL folded. By November 2001 the company had laid off almost 10% of its employees because lower-than-expected revenues resulted in year-end losses ("WWE fires COO," 2001). In 2018 shares of WWE were selling for around $28 per share. This significant increase could be attributed, in part, to developing more content sold directly to customers over the WWE Network, which was launched in 2014. The network initially was viewed as possibly another blunder, but WWE has been able to generate significant revenue from the venture and by 2017 had around 1.6 million subscribers, with around 1.1 million subscribers being from the United States.

This example highlights how a long-term plan, such as attempting to increase revenues by

Table 8.3 Under Armour's Three-Year Sales Forecast (Hypothetical)

Distribution channel	2018 actual sales ($)	2019 estimated most likely sales ($)	2020 forecasted sales ($)	2021 forecasted sales ($)
Chain stores	36,000,000	38,880,000	41,990,400	45,349,632
Independent stores	12,525,000	13,527,000	14,609,160	15,777,893
Individual (direct)	375,000	375,000	375,000	375,000
Internet	3,750,000	6,525,000	9,135,000	10,962,000
Foreign	6,000,000	6,480,000	6,998,400	7,558,272
Other	1,350,000	1,350,000	1,350,000	1,350,000
Total	60,000,000	67,137,000	74,457,960	81,372,797

launching a new football league to compete with existing leagues, can backfire. With a significant amount of hype and planning, the league had a decent first night because of the novelty of the event. When advertisers started complaining about the low ratings and the general lack of interest in the new league, a short-term exit planning process had to be undertaken. As the XFL crumbled, WWE had to engage in short-term planning to find other options for continued growth and to fill the void of expected revenue. WWE started pursuing other projects such as music sales, cookbooks, and children's storybooks. It expanded overseas broadcasts and launched a two-hour, magazine-style show (Grover & Lowry, 2001). WWE was not resting on its laurels and was pursuing long-term growth through new consumer product launches, new television programming, and international growth. The company was also exploring the acquisition of entertainment content companies and the outsourcing of WWE's core competencies—television and film production, live event production, and licensing.

Break-Even Analysis

Part of the in-depth analysis and forecasting will entail break-even analysis. Break-even analysis focuses on determining the price and cost point at which expenses will cover expected revenue. Similar to the best case, worst case, and most likely analysis, a sports organization cannot develop an appropriate budget without identifying what will be appropriate cost and price points. For example, if a team has player payroll of $1 million, administrative expense of $500,000, and all other expenses of $500,000, then it will need to generate at least $2 million in admission fees or other revenue to break even. This is a very simple example. A more complex example would include the break-even analysis for concessions, parking, broadcasts, and related revenue and expense areas. For example, with concessions, the break-even analysis will need to examine the projected sales, the cost to purchase, store, cook, and sell items. In the end, there will be wasted food that will not be sold and such food will need to be thrown away (or hopefully donated) and thus any break-even analysis will need to include wiggle room for such losses.

Special Situations

In our discussion of preparing sales forecasts, we have not considered the following special situations:

- ♦ Start-ups
- ♦ Ownership changes
- ♦ Fast growth

Start-Ups

Sales forecasts for start-ups are particularly difficult because such a business has no established track record. In addition, trade group and industry data make up sales figures for ongoing and successful businesses, which are not necessarily relevant for a new business. New businesses tend to have lower sales than those of an established business but have the same level of expenses. In addition, new businesses tend to be strapped for the capital necessary to generate sales sufficient to translate into profitable financial results. Consequently, pro forma balance sheets and income statements for new businesses are speculative.

Ownership Changes

When an ownership change occurs, the operating history of the business may not be a useful guide for developing future sales forecasts. If the ownership change resulted from poor business performance, new ownership is probably going to institute changes in management. The business must halt its negative momentum and engineer a turnaround before sales growth can occur. Ownership changes can also result in the loss of customers or key employees, especially in smaller, closely held businesses in which the company's success is tied to the efforts of a key person. Under these circumstances, businesses tend to need to reexamine their product lines and markets.

To avoid possible conflict with a previous owner, buyers of existing small businesses often insist that the sales agreement includes a noncompete clause. Noncompete clauses prevent the sellers from competing in the same line of business from a location within the same geographic region for a specified number of years. Another way around this problem is for the buyer of the business to retain the seller of the business as a consultant for a specified time after the sale is completed.

Fast Growth

Businesses characterized by fast-growing sales should not assume that this fast growth will continue forever. For example, if corporate sales in the economy have been growing annually at a rate of 6% per year over the past five years and a particular business has been growing at a rate of 20% per year, it is unreasonable to assume that this divergence will continue. Typically, successful start-ups have extremely high growth rates that slow as businesses mature. Businesses seizing new market niches or entering new and growing markets are typically the ones associated with abnormally high growth. These businesses are at risk as other entrants, having witnessed the explosion in growth, try to steal market share (Pratt & Niculita, 2007).

BUILDING THE BUDGET FROM THE GROUND UP

So far in this and the prior chapter we have reviewed various budgets and the information that goes into making a budget. While there has been an in-depth look at these two major concepts, it is imperative once a manager knows what budget to produce and what the available information is to actually produce a budget. Once it is determined which budget to use (such as an incremental, marketing, or long-term budget or a ZBB), then the internal and external data need to be gathered. These two primary components discussed in this and the prior chapter are not analyzed in a vacuum. There are several pretty straightforward steps in the budgetary process, which are as follows:

1. Examine the organization's mission, vision, goals, objectives, and other guiding information to make sure the budget is consistent with such material.
2. Undertake intensive research into the organization's strengths and weaknesses—especially in terms of resources that might be needed as part of the budget.
3. Bring together all relevant stakeholders.
4. Review all the data collected in step 2 along with past financial statements and other information as discussed earlier in this chapter.

5. Develop a budget and then examine it for accuracy and feasibility.
6. Have key stakeholders examine the budget, which is often examined through a formal presentation process.
7. Obtain approval for the budget.
8. Educate all key personnel about the budget and make sure employees understand their role in the process.
9. Implement the budget.
10. Audit the process through variance analysis to track whether the budget is being followed and to identify any potential concerns.
11. Document the process for ease in launching the next budgetary cycle.

While the steps seem simple, each step can have multiple parts. For example, in developing a new budget, a manager might utilize increment or decrement budgeting. This approach either develops a budget with various line items increased by a certain percentage or decreased by a certain amount. For example, by using decrement budgeting, a team might know its revenue will be declining, and it might reduce all expense lines by 5% a year for three years in an effort to slash expenses and stay viable.

Similarly, in the budget development phase, besides collecting past budgets and related material, there will be a political process that involves a prioritization process. Some items might be key priorities, such as annual money for an owner's favorite charity. There will also be a number of items that can easily be removed from a budget. Such a process can be complicated and might entail a significant amount of political infighting.

VARIANCE ANALYSIS

So far we have covered various budgets and how they are created. Step 10 in the budgetary process relates to auditing the budget. The auditing process is called variance analysis. Variance explores why a budget worked or did not work. There will always be a difference between what was projected and the actual results. The difference might be cents or might be millions of dollars. It would be impossible to nail a budget 100% correctly, as there will always be variations in total expenses, amount of electricity utilized, and hundreds or thousands of other variables.

Cost and revenue tracking are often examined through various cost and revenue centers. The most effective way to track revenue and expenses is through a cash budget, where revenue is applied to revenue centers and money is also applied to expenses centers, often on a percentage basis. As revenue is generated, it reduces the future amount of revenue needed before the budget is close to balancing. Thus, if a team generated $1 million in revenue and budgeted for $20 million, then there would be only $19 million more revenue needed to meet the budgeted goal. Similarly, as the expenses keep adding up, the amount allocated towards expenses will decrease until the expenses possibly zero out. Thus, if $1 million in expenses had occurred and there was a budgeted amount of $10 million, then after $9 million more is spent the team would have reached the budgeted expense amount. If revenue exceeds $20 million, the team would have a budgetary surplus. Likewise, if expenses exceed $10 million, then the team would have gone beyond the expensed amount and would need to explore how to either generate additional revenue or cut expenses.

CONCLUSION

Chapter 7 covered some basic budget types. This chapter has examined the types of internal and external data that will be critical when developing a budge. A manager needs accurate information; a budget built on faulty data will always be wrong. The data then need to be combined and referenced against shot-term and long-term plans as a one-year budget would require different data than a five-year budget. Once the data are uncovered, whether through developing a break-even analysis or looking at special situations that can affect a budget, the budget will need to be built. A manager's work is not done once the budget is completed. The budget needs to be examined and evaluated, and a variance analysis needs to be done to make sure the budget was somewhat accurate and what managerial decisions will need to be undertaken if the budget was incorrect.

Class Discussion Topics

1. Discuss a short-term plan for a perennially losing team and identify specific steps that could be taken to increase income or generate victories.

2. Discuss a long-term plan for a perennially losing team and identify specific steps that could be taken to increase income or generate victories.

3. What do you think is the most important primary data for a sport business to develop, and how can the business find this information?

4. What do you think is the most important secondary data for a sport business to develop, and how can the business find this information?

5. Develop a sample survey you believe could be used to obtain critical information on which financial decisions could be made.

Part III Case Study

Minor League Baseball Operational Budget

The best way to go through the budgeting process is to highlight a detailed example from an actual team (as in the part II case study). In this case, which continues from part II, we discuss a minor league baseball team, but we cannot divulge the name of the team. Using an actual team helps show how the numbers are taken from past years to project for future years based on various assumed variables. The assumed variables are highlighted in various data sets that break down, for example, how much sponsorship revenue is expected based on the number of sponsorships sold previously and at what price points. The numbers also help show the timing of when revenue and expenses occur. This is often one of the most critical components that people do not remember when examining budgets. A team will often earn a majority of its revenue over a period of several months and have expenses all year. This could force the team to borrow money or engage in other forms of short-term cash management to cover bills as they come due.

Table 1 shows two years of actual expenditures and one year representing the budgeted amount based on past expenses. Having two years to compare allows an executive to determine whether an entry is an anomaly or a possible trend. The 2018 budget shows that the team was trying to cut its losses, but some key issues such as payroll for front office employees was not listed in detail so there could be significant wiggle room. This could reflect that the team was willing to not pay front office staff to keep the team afloat. The only time such an option might be plausible is if the front office staff are also part of the ownership group and might be willing to forgo pay to keep the team alive.

Table 1 2017 Budget Comparison

REVENUE			
MCA categories	**2016 actual**	**2017 actual**	**2018 budget**
Advertising and sponsor	$62,225	$80,729	$115,400
Season tickets	$20,644	$52,540	$74,300
Group tickets	$0	$27,113	$44,600
Skybox rentals	$0	$2,130	$12,250
Picnic rentals	$0	$6,948	$16,000
Miscellaneous income	$3,374	$3,700	$1,000
Individual tickets	$30,171	$87,360	$116,000
Merchandise sales	$31,002	$23,695	$36,000
Program sales	$5,389	$3,936	$3,600
Concession revenue	$9,337	$3,726	$21,567
Speed pitch revenue	$0	$4,094	$4,680
Total	$162,142	$295,971	$443,738
EXPENSES			
Printing	$13,000	$25,000	$6,758
Advertising and sponsor production	$11,000	$7,000	$5,500
Radio access fee	$0	$0	$4,200
Ticket stock and printing	$3,680	$11,595	$2,000
Front office salary	$84,000	$132,000	$???
Game-day staff	$27,000	$78,000	$29,693
Interns	$0	$0	$7,600

EXPENSES			
MCA categories	2016 actual	2017 actual	2018 budget
Player salaries	$65,000	$0	$82,000
Medical insurance	$1,314	$721	$4,000
Workers' comp	$25,680	$14,584	$31,000
Liability insurance	$5,100	$12,448	$9,000
Office supplies	$5,178	$2,291	$5,000
Office hardware	$7,000	$0	$2,650
Postage	$1,340	$4,537	$3,630
Telephone	$11,285	$14,329	$16,000
Dues and subscriptions	$19,121	$27,847	$34,117
Payroll taxes	$16,647	$1,490	$1,500
Sales taxes	$0	$476	$1,347
Cost of goods sold (COGS)	$23,168	$0	$26,900
Promotions	$0	$16,237	$32,000
Front office travel	$1,404	$1,200	$4,766
Player per diems	$16,233	$20,093	$20,978
Player travel	$37,269	$50,523	$6,000
Hotels	$23,203	$0	$30,462
Team travel	$0	$0	$23,100
Newspaper advertising	$25,000	$34,250	$10,000
Radio advertising	$0	$0	$18,500
Cable advertising	$0	$0	$12,000
Outdoor advertising	$0	$0	$3,500
Cinema	$0	$0	$5,000
Uniforms	$10,575	$1,943	$4,000
Bats	$0	$0	$6,000
Balls	$3,000	$0	$7,500
Miscellaneous equipment	$3,012	$0	$1,000
Training equipment	$0	$0	$3,000
Stadium rent	$20,000	$21,000	$22,000
Manager housing	$0	$0	$2,400
Manager auto	$0	$0	$800
Family day coupons	$0	$0	$6,500
Skybox food	$0	$0	$2,450
Picnic food	$0	$0	$10,000
Umpires and press box	$0	$0	$1,000
Legal fees	$2,620	$0	$0
Accountant fees	$0	$$4,800	$5,000
Total Profit or loss	$461,829 -$299,687	$482,364 -$186,393	$510,851 -$67,113

The team was hoping that its revenue increase was not just a one-year event due to the team's novelty. The team appeared to be closing the gap on its losses. However, the team was taking some drastic steps to stay alive. These steps did not work, as the team eventually folded under a weight of expenses and low revenue. The budget could have been the first hint that there was a problem. Another major hint could have been the cash flow statement discussed later in this case study.

The team's strategy included changing some of the seating from box seats to club seats, which would be sold at a higher price ($8 rather than $7) and the walk-up gate tickets would also increase from $5 per ticket to $6. The team also decreased season ticket sale price points by 12% to 21%. The pricing strategy for tickets is reflected in table 2 and table 3.

Table 2 2017 Ticket Prices, Sales, Revenue

	Gate price	Full season price	Full season sold, number	Gate sold, number	Season ticket revenue	Gate ticket revenue
Club	$9	$360	76	598	$26,386	$5,382
Box	$7	$250	45	3882	$10,825	$27,174
Reserved	$5	$190	13	5251	$1,661	$26,255

Table 3 2017 Total Ticket Revenue

Club	$31,768
Box	$37,999
Reserved	$27,916

Based on these numbers, the team developed a budget based on proposed new pricing strategies for tickets. The 2018 proposal included eliminating all box seats. All the grandstand seats were to be renamed as reserved seats and priced at a different rate. Such a strategy represents a minor tweak designed to help increase revenue by eliminating some seating options. These strategies are highlighted in table 4.

Table 4 2018 Price Proposal

Full season changes		New price	New revenue @ 2018 price	Shortfall	New sales needed to match 2017 revenue
Proposal	Club seats	$320	$24,320	$(2,066)	7
	Box or reserved	$215	$12,470	$(16)	1
Gate ticket sales	Club seats	$8	$4,764	$(598)	75
	Box or reserved	$6	$54,798	+$1,369	

Other Changes

The team also wanted to expand the club seating area by 112 seats by converting several current box seats to club seats. General admission seating would remain the same (unless they could find a better use for that area). The team was discussing the possibility of making that area into a children's playground. That project was a long shot, given the various intangibles facing the venture. For example, any structural changes would require the stadium to comply with the Americans with Disability Act, which could be very expensive.

According to this budget, approximately 25 season tickets or mini plans would be affected by the expanded club seats and the increase in reserved seat prices. Some of the seats might have needed to be grandfathered for one season. The impact on revenue, though, would be minimal.

Furthermore, youth, senior, and group pricing would reflect reserved prices of $5 and $4 for groups of 100 or more. The total estimated number of tickets the team expected to sell at each category is highlighted in table 5.

Table 5 Total Number of Seats in Each Price Level

Seat type	2017	2018
Club	184	296
Box	1310	0
Reserved	1080	2278
Total	2574	2574

It is possible to massage these numbers, because 112 box seats became club seats—in effect going from $9 to $8, not $7 to $8. The numbers in table 5 reflect changes made to the price before changes were made to seat classification. Based on these changes, ticket sales could be estimated in the 2018 budget as highlighted in table 6.

Table 6 Season Ticket Sales, 2018 Projections

Level	2017 price	2018 price	Total reduction	% decrease
Club 1	$360	$320	$40	11
Club 2	$360	$285	$75	21
Box	$250	$215	$35	14
Reserved	$190	$215	($25)	Only 14 sold in 2017

New Price Motivators and Derivations

The simplification of grandstand seating into two price levels would have helped when selling tickets at the gate, through telephone orders, and through brochures and sales materials. It would also alleviate the problems associated with sections A and B, which had very similar seats, with a $2 price difference. Under the new pricing structure, fans could decide where to sit for themselves regardless of price. The revenue difference to the team was minimal. Full-season ticket plans were priced at a discount as shown in table 7, compared with game-day sales.

Table 7 Ticket Pricing Options, 2018

FULL-SEASON PRICES		
Level	Price	Comments
Club number 1	$320	5% discount from gate—same as 2017
Club number 2	$285	15% discount from gate price—same as for reserved seats
Reserved	$215	15% discount from gate price—same as 2017
GATE TICKET PRICES		
Club	$8	Lowered to reduce gap between club and reserved—need to sell 75 more seats to match 2017 revenues
Reserved	$6	$6 is middle ground between 2017 box and reserved prices, which would create an increase in gate ticket revenues from 2017 sales numbers

Summary of Budgeted Changes

- In the 2017 season, 56% of fans purchased box, club, or general admission seating. In 2018, these fans would see a cumulative price reduction of around 15% or no price increase at all.
- In 2017, 44% of fans purchased reserved seats; these fans will see a $1 increase in the price of their seats but for 2018 would be able to choose from among 88% of grandstand seating versus only being able to choose from 44% of the grandstand the previous season.

- These price changes are fan friendly and a public relations dream from nearly every standpoint. The lost revenue will not be hard to recoup. In order to sell more season tickets, the team would need to price them to sell, not to maximize revenue.
- The only negative to this structure was the $1 increase on nearly 1,000 reserved seats. However, only 14 of these seats belonged to season ticket holders, and 10 of them belonged to the city parks and recreation department. The team assumed that many of these tickets were sold at the gate in 2017, not because they were priced at $5 but because they were the cheapest available in the grandstand. For 2018, the team anticipated needing a special spin to pull off this price increase. The front office could claim those seats did not sell well due to location. The team would also need to communicate to stakeholders that 1,300 seats received a $1 price reduction.

Timing and Rollout for Price Changes

The team would need to make a decision quickly on 2018 ticket pricing for several reasons. Over the next several weeks, it could have a tremendous amount of news to release, all of which was positive. Some examples of positive news stories included

- the return of the entire front office for the 2018 season,
- a new manager for the 2018 season,

Table 8 Cash Flow Over a Year, 2017

MCA							
Revenue	Account	Projected ($)	Jan ($)	Feb ($)	Mar ($)	Apr ($)	May ($)
Sponsorships	110	87,300	2720	3,000	10,510	14,430	25000
Season tickets	120	44,540	2585	2,131	6,539	12,738	1,1517
Group tickets	130	35,000	0	0	0	1,300	
Player sales	140	0	0	0	0	0	0
Skyboxes	150	7,500	0	0	0	0	0
Picnics	160	12,800	0	0	0	0	0
Miscellaneous income	170	2,000	180	20	297	100	325
Mall sales	180	0	0	0	0	0	0
Individual tickets	210	99,358	0	0	0	0	16,560
Merchandise	220	36,000	0	0	0	0	2,571
Programs	230	3,600	0	0	0	0	270
Concessions	240	19,908	0	0	0	0	1,494
Speed pitch	250	4,680	0	0	0	0	351
Total revenue		352,686	5,485	5,151	16,986	28,568	58,088
Expenses	Account	Projected ($)	Jan ($)	Feb ($)	Mar ($)	Apr ($)	May ($)
Printing	510	3,200	81	958	1,159	0	0
Advertising and sponsors	520	5,750	349				5,750
Radio access fee	530	0					
Ticket stock and printing	540	2,000				1,875	
Front office salary	610	168,600	13500	14,837	9715	14,625	14,625
Game-day staff	620	41,196		50			2,730
Interns	630	6,600					1050

- a continuation of the planned municipal stadium improvements,
- any new stadium news that the team could announce through the city's cooperation, and
- any third-season improvements the team wanted to highlight.

Coupling these announcements with the major reduction in ticket prices should give the team plenty of terrific off-season public relations coverage and help boost any renewal sales. The team could also announce that 2018 season tickets have been put on sale. This coverage, coupled with the Major League Baseball playoffs, could result in increased renewal sales as well as new season ticket sales. These assumptions help show that most budgets are based on numerous assumptions.

Timing of Cash Flow

A minor league baseball team would generate most of its revenue from May through August. This can be reflected on the monthly revenue projections and actual amounts. For example, all individual tickets, merchandise, programs, and concessions sales were during these months. The projected budget for 2017 was -$321,008, with the actual result being a loss of $256,516. Part of this large loss was based on front office salaries of $158,375 in 2017. The timing for revenue generation is a critical issue when it comes to cash management. The team would possibly need a line of credit or cash available to cover expenses during the slow periods. This cash timing dance is very delicate and requires significant planning and analysis. Table 8 reflects the cash flow for 2017.

MCA								
Jun ($)	Jul ($)	Aug ($)	Sept ($)	Oct ($)	Nov ($)	Dec ($)	Current pace ($)	
25,000	7,000	0	0	0	0	0	87,300	
7,000	0	0	0	191	1,386	453	44,540	
1,1233	11,233	11,233	0	0	0	0	34,999	
0	0	0	0	0	0	0	0	
2,500	2,500	2,500	0	0	0	0	7,500	
4,266	4,266	4,266	0	0	0	0	12,798	
325	325	0	0	0	0	0	1,972	
0	0	0	0	0	0	0	0	
33,119	33,119	16,561	0	0	0	0	99,359	
11,143	11,143	11,143	0	0	0	0	36,000	
1,110	1,110	1,110	0	0	0	0	2,600	
6,138	6,138	6,138	0	0	0	0	19,908	
1,443	1,443	1,443	0	0	0	0	4,680	
103,277	78,277	54,394		191	1,386	853	351,656	
Jun ($)	**Jul ($)**	**Aug ($)**	**Sept ($)**	**Oct ($)**	**Nov ($)**	**Dec ($)**	**Current Pace ($)**	
0	0	0	0	169	0	146	3,108	
				0	0	0	6,099	
1,400	1,400	1,400	0	0	0	0	4,200	
				0	0	0	1,875	
14,625	14,625	14,625	14,625	9,976	11,601	10,960	158,375	
11,825	11,825	11,826	0	0	0	0	38,256	
1050	1050	1,050	0	0	0	0	4,200	

(continued)

Table 8 *(continued)*

		MCA					
Expenses	**Account**	**Projected ($)**	**Jan ($)**	**Feb ($)**	**Mar ($)**	**Apr ($)**	**May ($)**
Player salaries	640	82,000					
Manager, coach salaries	650	37,450			3,091	2,240	3,290
Commissions	660	7,133	169	124	475	808	
Medical insurance	710	4,000	351	351		333	333
Workers' compensation	720	31,000	1500	1,976	2730	2,584	2,584
Liability insurance	730	9,000	76	99	129	750	750
Office supplies	810	5,000	232	222	467	416	416
Office hardware	820	2,3000	200	220	48		
Postage	830	3,630	216	242	247	291	391
Telephone	840	13,000	859	527	762	1,333	1,333
Dues, subscriptions	850	35,187	1367	2,051	3975	2,782	2,707
Payroll taxes	910	1,500	900	1,186	1,536	125	125
Sales taxes	920	1,347					112
Cost of goods sold (COGS)	1010	20,500			156		
Promotions	1100	18,800	1000				
Front office travel	1210	1,802			237		
Player per diems	1310	17,839					3,000
Player travel	1320	4,500					4,000
Hotels	1330	29,760					6,000
Team travel	1340	19,300			1,930		4,000
Newspaper advertising	1410	10,000	70	61			2,500
Radio advertising	1420	10,000					
Cable advertising	1430	12,000					
Outdoor advertising	1440	3,500				1,166	1,166
Cinema	1450	0					
Uniforms	1510	4,000				1,430	
Bats	1520	6,000				6,000	
Balls	1530	7,500			725	7,500	
Misc. equipment	1540	1,000			393	1,000	
Training equipment	1550	0					
Stadium rent	1610	22,000					22,000
Mall	1620	0					
Manager housing	1630	0					
Manager auto	1640	0					
Family day coupons	1710	6,500					465
Skybox food	1720	2,500					
Picnic food	1730	10,000					
Umpires, press box	140	1,350					
Legal fees	1810						
Accounting fees	1820	5,000	230			417	417
Total expenses		694,444	21,100	22,904	27,775	45,675	79,744
Profit or loss		(321,008)	(15,615)	(17,789)	(10,789)	(17,814)	(21,656)

	MCA						
Jun ($)	Jul ($)	Aug ($)	Sept ($)	Oct ($)	Nov ($)	Dec ($)	Current Pace ($)
27,333	27,333	27,333	0	0	0	0	81,999
4,341	4,341	4,341	2,240	0	0	0	23,884
1,487	683	683		0	0	21	4,450
333	333	80	0	0	0	0	2,447
2,584	2,584	2,584	2,584	0	0	0	21,710
750	750	750	750	0	0	0	4,804
416	416	416	416	37	0	20	3,474
							468
291	291	291	291	0	67	230	2,848
1,333	1,333	1,333	1,333	948	569	1,333	12,996
2,707	2,707	2,707	2,707	50	0	985	24,745
125	125	125	125				4,372
112	112	112	112				672
1,3847							14,003
4500	4050	5,800					15,350
						330	567
5,000	5,000	5,000					18,000
0	0	0	500				4,500
7,920	7,920	7,920					29,760
4,000	4,000	4,000	1,370				19,300
2,500	2,500	2,500					10,131
5,000	5,000	5,000					15,000
4,000	4,000	4,000					12,000
1,166							3,498
							0
							1,430
							6,000
							8,225
							1,393
							0
							22,000
							0
							0
							0
2,011	2,011	2,011					6,498
817	817	817					2,451
3,334	3,334	3,334					10,002
450	450	450					1,350
							0
417	417	417	417				2,732
125,674	109,407	110,905	27,470	11,180	12,237	14,025	609,172
(22,397)	(31,130)	(56,764)	(27,550)	(10,989)	(10,851)	(13,172)	(256,471)

Conclusion

This and the prior case study help demonstrate how closely connected revenue and expenses analysis is to a budget. Every team or organization needs to know all the various revenue components and how many of each unit is sold. The same applies to all expenses. Once these numbers are understood, they can be incorporated in a budget. The budget would be based in part on numbers from prior years and strategies designed to increase revenue or decrease costs—or both. It does not end with a budget. The budget would need to be monitored to determine if the strategy was actually working. The cash flow needs to be analyzed in light of the budget. A budget reflecting new strategies will need to be closely monitored (variance analysis) to see if key dates for expected revenue and expenses are as accurate as possible. No team would want to go through a full season to only find at the end that their revenue was not as hoped or that expenses ran out of control.

Class Discussion Topics

1. If you had seen the cash flow for this team not meeting expectations, what would you have done?

2. If you were trying to examine the cash flow for a hockey team, how would you anticipate the revenue and expenses to be generated over the course of a year?

3. What do you think about the team's ticket price strategy, and what would you have done to generate additional revenue without alienating fans?

4. Do you think it is ethical to change the name of a seat and charge more just due to the name change? What could be the impact of such a decision?

PART

IV

Cash Management

Part IV explores the cash needs of a sports organization. Although some sports organizations are flush with cash, most are not. Sport executives perform a balancing act when determining how, where, and when to search for cash to keep the organization running.

The industry spotlight is written by Ken Wajda, the senior vice president of finance for Spectra. Spectra is part of Comcast, which has a significant sport presence, including owning the Wells Fargo Center, the Philadelphia Flyers, the Maine Mariners (ECHL), the Philadelphia Wings (National Lacrosse League), and the Philadelphia Fusion (Overwatch League). He discusses how his company handles cash-related concerns.

Chapter 9 starts by exploring short-term cash needs, the need for cash to pay an organization's regular bills, and how a company can get money when there is not enough in the bank account. In addition to short-term financial needs, most organizations also have long-terms needs, and various financial strategies for the long run are discussed. Knowing how much money is available (and from where) is one of the most challenging financial tasks for any manager.

Chapter 10 explores what many corporations do to raise necessary funds. When it is too difficult to borrow from a bank or when the amount of needed funds is high, corporations can issue stocks or bonds. Stocks represent ownership interest in corporations. Bonds represent borrowing by large corporations.

Part IV's case study explores the issues involved in funding and building major college football stadiums. Stadiums can cost several hundred million dollars, and most schools do not have this much money lying around. Colleges have to undertake various strategies to obtain the cash, with the hope (often misplaced) that the facility will eventually pay for itself.

©Ken Wajda

Ken Wajda

Senior Vice President of Finance for Spectra

My name is Ken Wajda, and I am the senior vice president of finance for Spectra. Spectra is a sport and entertainment industry leader in venue management, food services and hospitality, and commercial rights sales. Spectra's parent company is Comcast Spectacor, which owns the Philadelphia Flyers of the National Hockey League and the Wells Fargo Center arena in Philadelphia. Spectra is headquartered in Philadelphia and today delivers services to more than 400 properties around the world, including arenas, stadiums, and convention centers that collectively host millions of fans and visitors every year.

I have worked in the sport and facility business for 18 years. After graduating with a degree in accounting, I started my professional career in public accounting where I earned my CPA designation. Then I joined Comcast Spectacor, which allowed me to apply my accounting skills in the sport and entertainment field. I spent my first several years doing tax work for each of Comcast Spectacor's divisions, including professional teams, arenas, television production, facility management, food and beverage, ticketing, and commercial rights sales. I then transitioned into a more operational role with Spectra and its venue management and food services divisions.

Having a trained background in finance and accounting has helped me to succeed in the sport and facility industry, as you will find that finance is a discipline that is highly regarded in the field. Though many do not have an accounting degree like I do, those that have a high degree of financial acumen often have more success than their counterparts who do not. Financial skills will serve you well and will help you in almost every aspect of the sport and entertainment field.

The topic of cash management is critical to success in any business, and the sport and entertainment business is no different. Things happen every day that have implications on a company's cash—deciding what bills to pay, reviewing what scheduled payments are due to be received, reviewing outstanding accounts receivable, deciding whether or not to extend credit to a customer, assessing what capital needs are present, and so forth. Additionally, many sport and entertainment businesses have a busy season and an off season, in which cash considerations are much different at different times of the year. All of these factors will influence a company's ability to have the cash necessary on a daily basis to achieve its goals and grow its business.

Many people look at a company's income statement and view its profitability as the sole measure of its financial health. However, there are other parts of the financial statement package that are equally important in assessing financial health, including the balance sheet and the statement of cash flows. The balance sheet represents the company's assets and liabilities as of the financial statement date. Cash is typically the first item listed among the assets. The statement of cash flows represents the cash activity during the given period and demonstrates the various cash inflows and cash outflows that contributed to the change in the cash balance from the beginning of the period to the end of the period. Be sure not to ignore these pages of a financial statement when reviewing the operational performance of a business.

One common error in cash management is overlooking the amount of accounts receivable on the balance sheet. Though some cash is received at the time of sale, there is generally also a significant portion of revenue that involves extending credit to customers. This may involve extending credit to large corporations or possibly to individuals. In either case, it is important to issue credit wisely and to hold your customers to the payment schedule outlined. Often times, people make the mistake of letting receivables get too large and too old, making them more difficult to collect and putting the ultimate collection at risk. Even if they are ultimately collected, slowness in collections puts a drain on the cash available for use in the business. As such, it is important to stay closely connected with the amount of outstanding receivables and stress timely collection.

In the business of venue management and food services, cash for capital purchases is equally as important as cash for operating needs. This is because a business does not only need operating capital but also requires access to capital for investments that are necessary to maintain current operations and also to invest in new areas of the business or new revenue-generating concepts. Use of cash for capital purchases and acquisitions requires a special review of the return on investment that can be expected from the cash investment made. An investment should not only return the same amount of cash that was spent but also return cash above and beyond the investment amount, which will serve as the return on the investment. If an investment is not expected to make a large enough return, then a business needs to consider a different use of the cash. Cash is a commodity that can be used in various ways, each yielding a different return and perhaps achieving a different objective. The challenge for any business is finding the best use of its cash resources in order to maximize its returns and to grow the business and achieve the business' goals and objectives.

In our business we make decisions every week on how much capital to commit to new potential projects and opportunities. Factors that influence this decision are things like the internal rate of return on the investment, the net present value of future cash flows from the investment, and the payback period for the investment. If the payback period is too long or the rate of return is not sufficient, then the amount of the investment may need to be decreased or perhaps there may be a better use of the cash. You also need to consider any opportunity cost of using cash for a particular capital project. For instance, if an investment yields a 10% rate of return but it prevents you from using that same available cash for another investment that will yield a 15% rate of return, there is an opportunity cost because the cash is already tied up in the lower yield investment.

Executives often think of forecasting in terms of sales and profitability forecasting, but a business needs to forecast its cash as well. Running out of cash is a problem all sports organizations want to avoid. Most books are kept on an accrual basis of accounting, which means that the operating profit does not necessarily correlate with the amount of available cash. For this reason, it is important to forecast not just your profitability but your cash as well. A cash forecast provides insight into your upcoming cash inflows and outflows. If a cash forecast indicates that the business is going to run out of money due to the timing of various receipts and disbursements, many businesses turn to a line of credit for assistance. Lines of credit are very common and can help to smooth out cash flow especially in a seasonal business like many in the sport and entertainment world. Of course, the business will need to pay interest to the lender for any borrowings, but the line of credit provides much-needed financial flexibility to the operation.

Equally as important as managing and forecasting your cash is safeguarding and protecting the cash on hand in your operation. A sports organization can produce high volumes of cash from customers at an event. It is imperative that strong internal controls are in place and being enforced to ensure that there is no opportunity for anyone at any level to steal or misappropriate cash. Strong internal controls include various levels of checks, balances, and counts from multiple personnel at various stages of the collection cycle. The mere presence of strong controls will deter staff members from considering any bad intentions. In addition, prompt use of a secure safe (or drop box) and subsequent immediate deposits into a bank will limit the amount of cash on hand and reduce risk. Likewise, having numerous transactions through credit cards can change the dynamic for collecting and processing payments. Do not underestimate the importance of strong cash management controls.

Cash is the fuel that makes an operation go and is vital to the ongoing viability of a sports venue or other business. It is important that you manage the business' cash as if it were your own money and take pride in your responsibility as custodian of the cash management. The more you understand about the role of cash in your business, the more successful you will be as an operator and professional.

Methods for Funding a Business

Chapter Objectives

After studying this chapter, you should be able to do the following:

- Describe where money comes from.
- Compare various short-term borrowing strategies.
- Understand how to use personal funds and private financing as a source of capital.
- Understand how government-backed borrowing can spur economic growth.
- Understand how to use existing resources to leverage the financial position of a business.
- Distinguish between leasing and other financial vehicles.

There is no one correct method to fund a sport business. Some people acquire a sport business through inheritance and do not need any funds to become owners. This is the case for many professional team owners, such as the Rooney family, who have owned the Pittsburgh Steelers for several generations. Other owners have tapped numerous sources such as their credit cards, relatives, and bank **loans** to keep a business alive. Each business is different and requires its own unique blend of financing. The various funding techniques will be addressed in this chapter.

The total number of options and techniques that can be used to obtain funds is limitless. Some people have made their fortunes through luck, whereas others have relied on hard work. Arthur Rooney, the famed owner of the Steelers, bought the franchise for $2,500 in 1933. It is rumored that he obtained the money for the franchise by winning $250,000 at the horse track in 1932 (Pro Football Hall of Fame, 2007). John Moores, former owner of the San Diego Padres, founded BMC Software in 1980. By working hard, designing innovative products, and making a strong marketing push, he made a fortune ("Company," 2012). With these funds, he purchased the Padres. Dallas Mavericks owner Mark Cuban; Microsoft cofounder, Portland Trail Blazers, and Seattle Seahawks owner, Paul Allen; and Los Angeles Clippers owner, Steve Ballmer, made their fortunes in computer software before buying their teams.

A person lucky enough to win the lottery could use their winnings to start a business. Former athletes have taken the money that they earned in professional sport and used those funds to launch or buy a business. One example is Magic Johnson, who turned his winning form and smile into a major fortune in real estate and movie theaters. In 2012, he became a part owner of the Los Angeles Dodgers in a record-breaking, $2.15 billion deal. Another basketball legend, Michael Jordan, turned his fortune into owning a majority share of the Charlotte Hornets and has made hundreds of millions of dollars from his collaboration with Nike on the Jumpman brand. In yet another example, Mario Lemieux was owed a fortune by the Pittsburgh Penguins and was the largest debt holder for the team. He purchased the team in bankruptcy proceedings. Most recently, retired baseball legend Derek Jeter used the fortune he accrued throughout his playing career to become a part owner of the Miami Marlins.

Although this chapter and chapter 10 on stocks and bonds highlight for-profit businesses, we make some references to funds used by government and tax-exempt businesses. As with for-profit businesses, both government and nonprofit organizations can use countless techniques to raise funds. One of the major differences between government and nonprofit organizations is the opportunity to receive gifts and the potential tax consequences associated with such funding techniques.

Most fund-raising for sport businesses follows established patterns that countless organizations have used for years. This chapter highlights the basic approaches to raising funds without necessarily having to incur significant costs or sell owners' equity. Early in the chapter we examine basic funding sources for starting a business, such as personal bank loans, credit cards, and government assistance. The chapter then covers open markets and short-term borrowing options, followed by several long-term borrowing options. The chapter concludes with an analysis of funding options for minority-owned businesses, including advice on how to obtain funding.

WHERE THE MONEY COMES FROM

Most consumers have faced a financial crisis in which they needed money but found that sources of funds were lacking. Some people can approach their parents and ask for a loan. Money sometimes comes from an inheritance or in the form of a raise. Increased monetary streams are sometimes expected—such as an annual cost-of-living salary increase to keep a salary at pace with inflation. At times money might not come in when it is expected. You might anticipate receiving a tax refund by a certain date and have to change your plans significantly if a delay occurs. But what happens when you need a substantial amount of money and your likelihood of receiving a major gift is astronomically small? You need to analyze alternative approaches for raising the needed capital.

Not all capital needs arise from emergencies. Numerous capital structuring changes occur because of anticipated growth—growth that can occur only through the exploration of various capital financing options. This chapter deals with the various capital options available to those seeking to raise needed capital. We give special attention to individual borrowing, SBA (Small Business Administration) loans, commercial lending, and venture capital. Other chapters will cover issuing various types of stocks, issuing bonds, and obtaining capital assistance from the government. There is no one correct method of raising funds, and this chapter presents the diverse techniques available.

Personal Resources

Sometimes people accumulate money from a current job with the intention of someday starting their own businesses. Often these sums are wholly inadequate for that purpose. Industry professionals highlight the need to set aside at least two years' worth of living expenses in preparation for starting your own business. This sum is necessary because most new full-time businesses take at least a year, and sometimes many years, to earn enough profit to pay the business owner a salary. Proper financial planning can help eliminate numerous hurdles that might arise during the formative years of a business. But the planning process needs to begin long before a business starts up, and sufficient capital reserves are required to sustain the business through cyclical and seasonal downturns.

If you do not have enough cash or investments that could be liquidated to start the business, you might consider a home loan. Home equity financing requires a borrower to use their house as collateral when obtaining a loan from a bank or other lending institution. The loan amount is based on the equity that the borrower has in the home. Suppose that you have a house that is worth $300,000 on the market today. You paid $180,000 for the house 10 years ago, with $30,000 down and a $150,000 mortgage. You have paid off $60,000 on the mortgage and still owe $90,000. The difference between the value and the amount owed is $210,000, which represents the equity that you have in the house and

is the maximum amount that you could borrow from a lending institution.

Home equity loans are traditionally favored over other loans because they carry a lower interest rate. Furthermore, some banks are willing to lend more than 100% of a home's value, depending on what the loan proceeds will be used to purchase. New businesses are highly speculative, and only 20% of new businesses survive. Therefore, some banks require substantial equity before loaning to a new business; established businesses with significant financial history are more reliable, and owners of these businesses can obtain larger mortgages.

Although most financial advisers do not recommend borrowing on a credit card because of the high interest rates, credit cards can also generate funds from which to start a business. But anyone using this method of borrowing must be careful to repay the debt as quickly as possible because the interest charges will negate any potential benefits that could have accrued from not having to approach other lenders such as banks. Furthermore, the high rate of small business failures should serve as a warning that a business owner could be paying off debts for years after a business fails. With a high interest rate, the repayment obligation could force an individual into bankruptcy.

The key to using credit cards is to maintain a good **credit rating**. Especially if using personal credit cards, borrowers need to be vigilant in ensuring that purchases and repayments do not hurt their credit rating. A credit rating can plunge if the credit card bills are not paid on time or if payment is always late (see How Credit Card Applicants Are Rated sidebar).

Can the Government Help You Get a Bank Loan?

A spotty credit history might limit a person's ability to obtain bank financing. The government, however, has developed several programs to help small businesses borrow funds, even if the owner does not have an unblemished credit history. The federal government realized the need for helping small businesses in the 1950s. In 1953 it created the Small Business Administration to "aid, counsel, and protect the interest of

HOW CREDIT CARD APPLICANTS ARE RATED

When determining whom to issue credit cards to, companies often use complex computer programs to score applicants. Table 9.1 shows one scoring system. The scoring technique analyzes distinct credit patterns to determine the likelihood that a borrower will repay any debts. Scores range from 375 to 900; higher scores indicate lower likelihood of default (Sichelman, 1998). The key factors that can lower a score are late payments, collections, bankruptcies, outstanding debts, a short or nonexistent credit history, credit inquiries, and applications for new credit (Sichelman, 1998).

AnnualCreditReport.com is the only government-authorized (Federal Trade Commission) source for a free annual credit report that is yours by law. The Fair Credit Reporting Act guarantees

Table 9.1 Percentage of Points Given to Help Determine Your Credit Score

Category	Percentage
Payment history	35
Amounts owed	30
Length of credit history	15
New or attempted credit accounts	10
Variety of credit types	10

you access to your credit report at no cost from each of the three nationwide credit reporting companies—Experian, Equifax, and TransUnion—every 12 months. A high number of identity theft crimes affect college students and young adults so checking your credit history is important.

the nation's small business community" (SBA, 2002). SBA accomplishes this mission by working with lending institutions to encourage and promote loans and other financing to small businesses. For example, SBA started its Microloan Program with the express purpose of helping people realize the American dream of owning their own businesses. The microloans range from $100 to $50,000; the average loan is around $13,000. These loans need to be paid back in six years, and the current maximum interest rate is 8.50%. SBA created more than 100 loan outlets throughout the United States through various nonprofit organizations. The only requirement is that the company requesting funds must prepare a business plan that can meet the loan criteria.

SBA also offers various other programs to encourage investing in small businesses. Its 7(a) Loan Guarantee and Certified Development Company programs provide a guarantee for approved lenders if the borrower defaults on the SBA-backed loan. SBA will not repay the loan; instead, it requires the lender to go after the borrower's collateral and then will supplement any remaining shortfall that might have been guaranteed.

The SBA does not loan money to everyone. SBA lends money to people starting a business if they have

- excellent credit, including no collection letters in the past 3 years;
- no bankruptcies in the past 10 years;
- a business plan;
- some type of collateral, such as a home;
- up to one-third of the required capital to put into the business;
- 24 months of experience in the same field as the current business;
- at least 12 months of training or special certification required for the business;
- an explanation of hardship that caused any blemishes to personal credit; and
- a personal expense plan to satisfy the lender that the borrower can meet his or her own living expenses.

Self-Funding

Funds for a business can also come from the business itself. An established business might use depreciation allowances and profits not paid out as dividends as a way of fueling further expansion. For example, if a golf course lawn mower purchased for $10,000 has a four-year life, it can be depreciated at $2,500 a year. The $2,500 deduction reduces total tax obligations and represents funds that should be set aside to help purchase another lawn mower in the future. Most businesses also retain a percentage of their profits, whether at regular or random intervals, for future needs. These retained earnings are for future use and are not intended to pay salaries or other current expenses.

Companies often have extra cash that might be sitting around for one day or several months. Liquid assets can be invested in a bank, in commercial paper, or in **Treasury bills (T-bills)** for a short period and then withdrawn for any fiscal needs. The interest earned from such investments can be used for future development.

CONCEPTS INTO PRACTICE

An example of a self-funding concept is raising ticket or membership prices. If a professional sports team wants to hire two new star players, it can anticipate a payroll increase of several million dollars a year. Borrowing funds from a bank or other lending institution can be risky. The Pittsburgh Penguins filed for bankruptcy in 1998, and part of their debt was attributable to players' salaries. Other teams face a similar problem when they attempt to cover their payrolls. A standard industry technique for covering such expenses is to raise ticket prices. If the team raises ticket prices 10%, the resulting increased income might be enough to fund both players. Although the funds for the new players' salaries come from customers and constitute external funds, they are generated from internal marketing efforts rather than from debt or equity sources. However, teams that engage in such activities must also recognize the basic tenets of supply and demand. If the team raises ticket prices, it is highly likely that attendance will decrease, and thus the overall increase in revenue may not be 10% as expected. Economic and financial analysis must occur when sports teams make decisions on the prices of items such as tickets, parking, concessions, and merchandise.

CONCEPTS INTO PRACTICE

A fitness center could also try to raise funds before the center even opens. It can hold a membership drive to sign up prospective members who will be entitled to pay $500 for a two-year membership and $200 a year in subsequent years. If the center sells 200 such memberships, it will have $100,000 to pay for construction costs. Some states, however, require clubs to keep preopening revenue in escrow until the club is opened (Caro, 2000). Even if it cannot touch these initial funds, the center would have 200 membership contracts that could be used as collateral for a loan. Such collateral is often called contractually obligated revenue or contractually obligated income. Large stadiums and arenas use naming rights, pouring rights (for beverage companies), personal seat licenses, and luxury box contracts as collateral to secure loans.

Although business owners will find it difficult to finance capital growth by themselves, it can be done. Through savings, credit cards, government assistance, or internally generated funds, a business owner can find the means to grow. More often than not, however, the business owner will need help from relatives or external investors.

Relatives and Friends

Some people are fortunate to have wealthy family members or friends who are willing to invest in a business. But most people do not have a Mark Zuckerberg or Bill Gates in their circle, so they must go elsewhere for funding. If you are able to obtain money from a parent or relative, you should take specific steps to maximize the benefits for you and the other parties. Many people regularly borrow money from friends or relatives, and most of these arrangements are never documented. Most people do not think that their own flesh and blood or best friend would fail to pay a debt. But courtrooms are filled with people who have broken such promises.

To avoid any improprieties, a business owner should take the following steps when borrowing money from family members or friends who might have to write off a bad debt in the future (Marullo, 1998):

◆ Document the loan with a formal agreement.

◆ Develop a formal repayment schedule.

◆ Pledge security or collateralize the loan.

◆ Keep accurate records of all repayments.

◆ Make sure that there is proof that the business was solvent when the loan was made.

◆ Provide the lender with a detailed business plan specifying how the loan will be repaid.

A relative or friend could also play the part of an angel who comes to the rescue. An angel is a major investor who can give a small amount or several million (Ambrosini, 2002). One of the most well-known angel investors in the sport industry is Paul Allen, a founder of Microsoft and owner of the Portland Trail Blazers and Seattle Seahawks. Allen operates an angel investment firm that has invested in sport-related entities such as electronic ticketing businesses and Charter Communications, a major cable operator ("*Paul Allen*," 2002). Unlike venture capitalists, who want the business to go public and who invest only in larger projects, angel investors often come into a project before venture capital investors do or when they anticipate being part of a smaller but still profitable business. No matter who provides the capital, risks are always associated with accepting money from others. Some concerns are

◆ whether the lender requires an ownership interest,

◆ whether the lender will demand a say in management decisions,

◆ whether an exit strategy is in place after the business is sound enough to repay the investor and regain control, and

◆ whether interest payments will be tax deductible as a business expense.

Friends and acquaintances can also be a good source of funds. People often think that they need to approach someone with a luxury car or big house for a loan. However, as of 2016, there were over 10.6 million millionaires in the United States, with many of them owning and operating mundane businesses and living well within their means in midpriced homes and driving midpriced cars. So, instead of attempting to meet potential investors at the private country club or five-star restaurant, one may have more success attending industry trade shows to meet people who might be willing to invest.

Loyal customers also represent a potential funding source. The Mad River Glen Cooperative is one of the nation's smallest and oldest ski resorts, but it is financially sound. Loyal skiers are willing to pay $2,000 a share for stock in the cooperative and $200 a year thereafter. These funds and the dedicated following of loyal skiers help make the single-lift facility successful. The resort's management has critically examined expenses and determined that the resort needs to be open only 90 days a year to make a profit. Because the top customers are also owners, the resort understands its investment options and maintains a lower run price than that of other resorts. The company does not invest a significant amount in new equipment, such as chairlifts or snow-making machines that could cost $1,000 an hour to operate.

Although family and friends can be a source for capital infusion, many business owners do not want to risk souring a good relationship. What happens if the initial capital infusion is not enough? What happens if more funds are needed, but the business owner does not want the initial investor to lose any money? What happens if the lender needs the money back immediately? Such issues associated with exit strategies are critical. People who do not want to make enemies of family members or friends might try to find funding through external sources such as the open market.

One of the most innovative means to raise funds is the Internet. *Crowdfunding* is the term used to describe using the Internet to gather investors into a company. Under laws in place in 2011, new companies using this approach through various online platforms such as Kickstarter, GoFundMe, and Indiegogo can collect start-up funds from people all over the world. Some sites collect the money and release the funds to the start-up when the desired goal is reached. If the desired funding amount is not reached, the donors get their funds back. Other sites give the start-ups the money right away. In contrast, current laws do not let the start-up give any equity to these investors, so the companies give products or other items in exchange for the funding.

OPEN MARKETS AND OTHER SHORT-TERM BORROWING

Several effective techniques can be used for raising funds on either a short- or long-term basis. Long-term equity or capital funding techniques are discussed later in this chapter. Short-term funding techniques include borrowing to purchase inventories, supplies, or other items or to pay expenses in situations in which the repayment period is expected to be less than 90 days. For purchases that require longer funding commitments, midterm, start-up, or long-term funding strategies might be needed.

People often find short-term and long-term funds in the open market. The open market is a free-enterprise environment where anyone who wants to borrow and anyone who wants to lend money can enter into a relationship—somewhat similar to the traditional bazaar in which sellers and customers come together and negotiate the price of goods. A bank is part of the open market because anyone can enter a bank and, with collateral or a good credit history, borrow money. Likewise, a successful business can be approached by numerous lenders interested in lending it money.

A professional sports team might rely on long-term funding options such as issuing stocks or bonds to buy a new scoreboard or renovate its arena. It might require short-term funds to pay expenses or salaries if the players are on strike. In contrast, a fitness facility might need to use short-term borrowing to meet current accounts payable but need long-term funding to buy expensive equipment. A company such as Under Armour, for example, might turn to short-term funds to buy inventories or pay unexpected expenses such as the settlement of a lawsuit. Such a company also might need long-term funds to buy manufacturing equipment or lease a new facility. Every business at times experiences a need for long- or short-term funds.

Short-term funds may be required for a business to meet monthly, seasonal, or other temporary financial needs. A business does not want to obligate itself to several years of interest payments if the money will be available to repay the loan in several months. A major advantage of short-term borrowing is the relative ease of completing such transactions.

Banks and other lending institutions are accustomed to providing short-term loans, whether the money is required for several hours or several months. Many companies maintain a line of credit with a lending institution that allows them to borrow short-term funds on a preapproved basis.

Another major benefit of short-term borrowing is that this strategy can be used to postpone long-term financing. Economic conditions or interest rates sometimes do not justify issuing bonds or stock. A bridge gap lending option such as short-term borrowing can help cover any financial obligations until conditions are more favorable for obtaining long-term funding. Regardless of the purpose, short-term borrowing is critical for all businesses.

Accounts Payable

One of the primary techniques for obtaining short-term funding involves accounts payable. **Accounts payable** represent amounts owed to vendors and suppliers for services or products.

Many people use accounts payable daily. The most common approach is through a credit card. People make purchases with a promise that at the end of the month they will pay for them. Businesses do the same thing, whether they are purchasing items on a corporate credit card or buying office supplies and inventory with the expectation that they will pay a bill coming at the end of every month. Normally these accounts need to be repaid within 30 days of receiving the bill. This example demonstrates that accounts payable can be more complex than a credit card arrangement. Most businesses use a blend of short-term borrowing that includes accounts payable and other short-term borrowing options.

Assume that a sport business completes an account contract with an information technology service to pay the bill every month. At the end of the first month, it receives a bill for the prior month's service with specific repayment instructions. The information technology service might give a discount if the bill is paid within a week, offer no benefit if the account is paid in full within 30 days, and assess a penalty fee or an interest obligation on the owed amount if the required payment is not made within 30 days. This type of account payable is called a trade credit that one business issues to another. In this example, the trade credit is being offered pursuant to a cash discount option.

A major problem with accounts payable is that the turnaround time for repayment is often slow. If a business buys season tickets for a team's games but does not pay at the time of purchase, the team may have a problem with this receivable account if it never gets paid or is paid months later. Some suppliers do not mind slow repayment because they can obtain interest payments from the borrower. Other suppliers, however, may count on repayment to help pay other obligations. In this case the supplier may reduce the total amount owed to encourage fast repayment.

The most common technique for encouraging fast repayment is the **cash discount**. A supplier might provide a business with a cash incentive for paying the obligation within 10 days. Cash discounts are often expressed in the formula 2/10/30. This notation refers to a 2% discount if the buyer pays in cash within 10 days and full payment if paid after the 10th day. If payment is not made within 30 days, the buyer has to pay interest or other penalties as defined by the purchase agreement. Although a 2% discount may not seem large, calculated out for the entire year it represents 36%. To calculate the opportunity lost by not paying early, divide the 20 days each month that you do not receive a 2% discount into 365 days a year. The resulting 18.25 is then multiplied by the 2% discount that you could have obtained to find the annualized loss of 36.5%. This discount encourages purchasers to pay their bills quickly, which can reduce collection fees for the supplier. The purchaser receives a significant benefit in obtaining a 30-day interest-free loan. For those reasons a cash discount is a popular short-term funding technique.

CONCEPTS INTO PRACTICE

Assume that Under Armour needs to buy some supplies. After working out an agreement with a local supplier, Under Armour purchases 10 pieces of material for $50 each with sales terms of 10/10/30 (10/10/30 means payment in full is due in 30 days, but the buyer may take a 10% discount if payment is made within 10 days). If payment is made during the discount period, Under Armour will save $50 (10 × 50 × 0.10). If payment is not made within the discounted period, it will owe the entire $500.

Bank Financing

Banks are among the cornerstones of the finance system. Banks provide numerous levels of financial assistance, whether through personal banking or comprehensive business banking services. Although accounts payable are a critical tool for commerce and most businesses use accounts payable on a daily basis, bank loans are the most economical and flexible means of short-term financing. Banks provide various services, from savings accounts and business checking accounts to night deposit and automatic bill payment services. They often offer flexible short-term loans ranging from 30 days to several months. If a 30-day loan comes due, a bank has the flexibility to renew the debt. If the loan is for a longer period, such as three to five years, it is referred to as a **term loan**. Banks prefer to issue short-term loans to get their money back as quickly as possible (Spiro, 1996). Unlike short-term loans that come due at the end of the designated period and are discharged with one payment, term loans often entail regular periodic payments and one balloon payment.

CONCEPTS INTO PRACTICE

If a university borrows $5 million from a bank for five years, the university might be required to pay $500,000 a year in principal and interest for four years and make a large balloon payment approaching $4 million in the fifth year. For a conventional loan, the university might make the $500,000 payment for 14 years to cover both the principal and the interest.

No matter what services are used, a bank is more willing to negotiate and customize accounts with businesses that already have an established account. Some banks require businesses with active loans to maintain an average deposit balance equal to 20% of the loaned amount. Such a deposit is often called a compensating balance. This protective balance may not seem significant, but it does represent a cost of borrowing.

CONCEPTS INTO PRACTICE

Suppose that a sport business borrows $100,000 from a bank but has to maintain $20,000 in a savings account at the bank throughout the life of the loan. If the business pays 10% on the loan, maintaining the $20,000 in the bank at a low interest rate or with no interest would in essence bring the cost of borrowing to 12.5%, which is calculated as follows:

$$I / (L - B) = \text{cost of borrowing}$$

I = interest paid on loan

L = amount borrowed

B = compensating balance that needs to be maintained

$$\$10,000 / (\$100,000 - \$20,000) = 12.5\%$$

A loan that is contingent on maintaining a minimum balance at a bank is a type of secured loan. Many loans require the use of collateral. Anything of value can be used to secure a loan. Some businesses pledge physical property such as land, buildings, inventory, or equipment. Other businesses pledge intangible assets such as accounts receivable or the rights to an invention or patent. Because loans against accounts receivable or inventory are often riskier, some banks do not offer such loans, and businesses need to go to nonbank lenders for those loans.

Many businesses use real estate or machinery as collateral for a loan, but assets such as inventory, investment assets, or accounts receivable can be pledged if other assets are already being used for collateral. In some instances, businesses do not want to encumber an asset because they want to be able to sell it. A company that has pledged a factory as security cannot sell the factory because it does not have a **clear title**—the title is clouded. Because most debt instruments with any security (especially real property) are recorded by a city or county clerk, potential buyers can determine whether a property has a clouded title. If someone tried to buy the pledged factory, the title could not be passed as free and clear of any encumbrances. After the obligation was paid in full, however, the factory could be sold. This same process operates when people buy a house. The mortgage on the house is recorded with a government agency and is discovered when a title search is conducted. The buyer can clear the title by paying the mortgage and having the mortgage company release its claim to the property.

Using current inventories as collateral is a technique that maximizes current value while affording the option to raise additional funds. Asset-based borrowing entails a revolving line of credit secured by accounts receivable, inventories, or both (Hovey, 1998a). Bally Total Fitness expanded its business by acquiring debt, and the debt was secured by accounts receivable (Caro, 2000). Because the chain had numerous members throughout the world, it was guaranteed a certain amount each month from dues. These dues were part of the accounts receivable and were also called contractually obligated revenue or contractually obligated income because they were required by the membership contracts. Bally could use these prospective assets to secure debt obligations, similar to the way that a stadium can use the contractually obligated revenue from naming-rights contracts as collateral for a bond or other debt instruments.

Standard & Poor's raised its corporate credit rating on Bally Total Fitness to B− from CCC+ and removed it from credit watch, after placing it on the list on August 17, 2005 ("*Club hopping*,"

2004). Bally obtained limited waivers relating to its 10.5% senior notes due 2011 and 9.875% senior subordinated notes due 2007 ("*Club hopping*," 2004). As of September 30, 2004, Bally's debt was $747.7 million. To restore investor creditability, Bally Total Fitness was to commence a search for a new chief executive officer as part of its financial structuring process ("*Liberation Investments delivers*," 2005). Bally was accused of indenture violations that originated from its failure to file with the SEC its financial statements for the quarter end of June 30, 2004, as well as its failure to deliver the financial statements to the board trustee and lenders ("*Liberation Investments delivers*," 2005). By 2007, Bally had been delisted from the **New York Stock Exchange (NYSE)** and filed for Chapter 11 bankruptcy protection. Bally was then on the **over-the-counter exchange**, but its legal woes about stating income and expenses continued through 2008, when it finally reached a settlement with the **Securities and Exchange Commission (SEC)**. The commission issued a press release with the following language:

> The Securities and Exchange Commission today filed financial fraud charges against Bally Total Fitness Holding Corporation, a nationwide commercial operator of fitness centers that has recently emerged from bankruptcy proceedings under new, private ownership. The Commission alleges that from at least 1997 through 2003, Bally's financial statements were affected by more than two dozen accounting improprieties, which caused Bally to overstate its originally reported year-end 2001 stockholders' equity by nearly $1.8 billion, or more than 340%. The Commission's complaint further alleges that Bally understated its originally reported 2002 net loss by $92.4 million, or 9,341%, and understated its originally reported 2003 net loss by $90.8 million, or 845%. As a result, the Commission alleges that Bally violated the antifraud, reporting, books and records, and internal control provisions of the federal securities laws. (U.S. Securities and Exchange Commission, 2008)

Bally had been a public company and generated annual revenues over $1 billion until 2007, when it filed for bankruptcy protection. In 2009, after Bally's second bankruptcy in 17 months, J.P. Morgan received 50.5% of Bally's equity and Anchorage Advisors received 33.7% in a reorganization plan approved in bankruptcy court based on the owed debt (Goldman, 2011).

LA Fitness, based in Irvine, California, acquired 171 clubs from Bally Total Fitness for $153 million in 2011. The acquisition involved Bally clubs in 16 states and the District of Columbia. Between 2012 and 2014, Bally sold the remainder of its fitness centers to Blast Fitness and 24 Hour Fitness.

If a borrower, such as Bally, defaults on secured loans, the lender can seize the assets as with any other collateral. Because of the potential difficulty that a lender might have in collecting receivables or selling inventory, the lender might loan only up to 85% of the value in receivables and 55% of the value of the inventories (Hovey, 1998b). Asset-based loans are normally provided at the prime rate plus 2% for a creditworthy business. Although these loans are not especially hard to obtain, they do require significant paperwork. A borrower typically needs to provide three years of profit-and-loss statements, current and past financial statements, inventory aging reports, personal financial and tax return statements for the past three years, and sales projections for the coming year (Hovey, 1998b). After receiving a loan, the borrower must comply with additional paperwork requirements such as providing monthly reports on accounts payable and receivable.

Some commonly used documents that provide security for an asset-backed loan are bills of lading, trust receipts, and warehouse receipts. A bill of lading pledges commodities or merchandise in transit as collateral for a loan. Goods covered by a trust receipt are held in trust for the lending institution but could be housed in a separate area at the borrower's business. After those goods are sold, the cash from the sales is first paid to the bank to satisfy the debt. A warehouse receipt performs the same function as a bill of lading, but it applies when the inventory is stored in a bonded warehouse to protect the

COLLATERAL VALUES

Table 9.2 shows common collateral values needed to secure credit from financial institutions. According to these industry standards, if a company has accounts receivable of $100,000 and allows the bank to monitor the receivables, it could possibly obtain an $80,000 loan secured by the receivables.

Table 9.2 Value of Factored Assets in Obtaining Loans

Collateral	% loaned
Accounts receivable, monitored	80
Accounts receivable, unmonitored	70
Inventory, monitored	50
Inventory, unmonitored	40
Owned equipment, % of book value	50
New equipment, % purchase price	80
Used equipment, % purchase price	75
Real estate	65-90
U.S. government securities	90
Investment-grade municipal bonds	80
Bonds or preferred stock	75
Stocks below AA grade	50
NYSE, AMEX, NASDAQ shares	65
Cash value of insurance policies	100
Cash	100

Data from "Planning for success," *CampBusiness* (2000): 8-11.

bank's collateral. Title to the assets rests with the lender until a release document is provided to the warehouse. The warehouse can then release the specified assets. Although secured loans provide significant protection for the lender, collateral may not be required if a business has a strong credit rating or a good relationship with the lending bank.

Banks have significant flexibility, within federal guidelines, to offer various customized services. Decades ago, banks were typically smaller than they are today and often had strong personal relationships with customers. Banks could provide a broader range of services for business owners whom the bank employees knew and had done business with in the past. Having a personal banker is less common today. Recent mergers along with technological advancements have resulted in more impersonal banking experiences for individuals and businesses. But even with larger banks, businesses need to communicate with bank employees on a regular basis. Loan officers and their supervisors are important contacts. Knowing several bank employees in these positions provides protection if bank personnel move to different locations (Nelton, 1998a). Developing personal relationships can help if you ever need to apply for a loan—it is to your advantage if you are more than just a name on an application but possibly a friend and someone whom the bankers would judge as highly credible.

Banks frequently expect the owner of a proposed new business to put some of their own money at risk. The underlying thinking is, why should the bank invest in a project if the owner is not willing to risk his own money? Equity capital represents a firm commitment by the owner to work for the best interest of the business. The owner wants to succeed to avoid losing their own money, as well as the bank's money. A bank could require equity capital to approach approximately 40% of the amount needed to fund the new business (Horine, 1999). Even if no equity is required to obtain the bank loan, banks traditionally require audited financial statements to help calculate standard ratios, such as debt–equity and quick ratios, and these figures can help determine the prospect for default. Banks may also require business plans, pro forma budgets, personnel profiles, sample products, and other information to make a lending decision. Most banks require a borrower to complete a formal application, which could include a sum-

---

THE FIVE CS OF CREDIT

Regardless of the requested loan amount, people should not quit their jobs before obtaining a loan. A bank will check to see whether an applicant is currently employed to help establish her ability to repay, or service, the loan. The potential borrower's employment status is just one variable that banks and other lending institutions might investigate. Banks commonly refer to the five Cs of credit when deciding whether to loan someone money. The five Cs are character, capacity, collateral, capital, and condition.

1. *Character.* This refers to the applicant's credit history and truthfulness. Did the applicant disclose all outstanding debt? Did she list any prior bankruptcy? Does the applicant have favorable business or professional references? Does it appear that they are willing to repay the loan? The answers to such questions help determine whether the lender can trust the applicant.

2. *Capacity.* This represents the lender's determination about whether the potential business has the right management team and philosophy to become a profitable enterprise that will earn more than enough money to pay the loan.

3. *Collateral.* This refers to anything of value that can be pledged to guarantee final repayment of the loan. Collateral can include a home, property, equipment, collectibles, a legal judgment, or even a lottery payoff.

4. *Capital.* This represents the equity that the applicant will put into their own business. A lending institution will not be interested in loaning money to help launch a new business if the business owner does not think that the business will succeed. If the applicant believes that the business will be a success, they must support that conviction by investing some of their own money. Banks typically require a 30% to 35% equity or cash investment in the business by the loan applicant (Pounds, 1997). Capital also refers to any excess cash that might be available to pay unexpected expenses.

5. *Condition.* This is the applicant's primary opportunity to sell the lender on the value of the business. The lender will want to know whether the industry is growing, whether there are competitors, whether the product has a long life cycle, whether a location or distribution channel is available to sell the product, and so on. By thoroughly researching the proposed business and presenting the lender with a comprehensive business plan that addresses those issues, the applicant greatly increases the chance of securing a loan.

mary of the business, profiles of the top executives, financial statements, pro forma budgets, and a detailed repayment plan (Griffin, 1991).

After the loan papers have been approved, the parties sign an agreement. This document is called a promissory note. The note specifies the amount borrowed, the interest rate to be charged, any repayment terms, whether the loan is collateralized, and all other terms and conditions that the parties have agreed on. After the note is signed, the borrower receives the loan proceeds.

Whether the loan is backed by a personal guarantee, collateral, or a mortgage, banks offer numerous financial options that make short-term borrowing fairly simple. Lines of credit are more complicated but still represent an effective use of bank resources to cover immediate fiscal needs. A lending institution charges interest only on the amount actually borrowed from the credit line but can also charge a commitment fee that could range from 0.05% to 1% (Battersby, 1999). The commitment fee can be waived if the borrower has compensating balances in other accounts. Three types of lines of credit are available:

1. A nonbinding line of credit is an open account for the business to borrow from. If the business experiences hardships and has financial trouble, however, the line of credit can be revoked.
2. A committed line of credit requires the potential borrower to pay a commitment fee to lock the line of credit into place, thus guaranteeing needed funds.
3. A revolving line of credit requires the borrower to undergo an annual review and renewal of the credit line (Battersby, 1999).

A revolving credit agreement is similar to a line of credit in allowing a company to borrow a specified sum, but there is a major distinction. A line of credit allows the borrower to access a certain amount of money if needed, but the bank or the company can withdraw from the agreement at any time. A revolving credit agreement is a contract whereby the borrower agrees to pay an annual commitment fee, a small percentage of the unused amount, to compensate the bank for entering into the commitment (Brigham & Gapenski, 2017). If the company uses only half the available credit, it is charged the commitment fee for the unused amount and is charged the agreed-on interest for the amount borrowed. Because the revolving credit agreement is a contract, both parties need to undertake formal contract cancellation steps to end it. An example of a sports organization using a line of credit may be a professional sports team that has a line of credit to cover short-term expenses, utility costs, player and staff salaries, and vendor expenses. If the team is low on available cash, it can take funds from its line of credit to cover these expenses.

Private Placement Through Nonbank Lenders

Various options are available for obtaining cash from other sources. Private placement refers to the process of obtaining funds from private parties such as investors, venture capital investors, or other companies interested in investing in a business. These investments can take the form of debt instruments, equity interest, or a blend of the two.

Nonbank lenders—which do not include angel investors, family members, and friends—are the most frequent source other than banks for financing smaller businesses. Nonbank lenders can be independent businesses or can work in conjunction with the government. Some companies that offer nonbank loans include AT&T Small Business Lending Corporation, Heller First Capital, Business Lenders, Money Store Investment Corporation, and GE Capital Small Business Finance Corporation. Nonbank loans often have a higher interest rate based on risk factors, which might have been what dissuaded a bank from providing the loan in the first place. These loans are often attached to special purchasing deals offered by suppliers.

The list of potential lending sources is almost limitless. This section covers private companies, factoring, installment sales, and leasing. These financing methods do not entail selling any equity position in the business. Thus, no ownership interest is given up to obtain the funds.

We discuss mergers and acquisitions in chapter 14, but every business owner has the option of selling a portion of the business or the entire business to acquire funds. Several **buyout** funds established for the sport industry provide funds to businesses or purchase businesses. Chase Manhattan joined with International Management Group to form the IMG/Chase Sports Capital fund. The fund had $170 million to help finance sport businesses and used some of those funds to purchase the Skip Barber Racing School in Connecticut (Tan, 2000). Although selling an entire business entails obtaining funds for the sellers, the process should not be thought of as selling out. The owner may have sold the business, but the potential cash infusion from a financially stronger business might have been what was necessary to finance further expansion. Many businesses would have failed had they not been purchased by a buyer who funded future growth.

Private Companies

Other nonbank lenders include private companies that are licensed by the U.S. Small Business Administration. These small business investment companies (SBICs) can provide either debt financing by issuing long-term loans or equity financing by acquiring an ownership interest in a company (Pryde, 1998). The SBIC structure is unique in that the investment funds are privately owned and managed and regulated by the SBA. An SBIC uses its own capital plus funds to make debt and equity investments in qualifying small businesses. Many investments are in specialized companies, which might include minority-owned businesses and socially or economically disadvantaged companies. To qualify for an SBIC loan or equity investment, a company's net worth must be less than $19.5 million, and the business must have had after-tax earnings of less than $6.5 million in the two previous years (SBIC Program Overview, 2018).

Most cities have local brokers, bankers, or regional brokerage firms that can help coordinate private-placement deals. These individuals or firms typically are paid a percentage of the money that they help raise (5%-15%). Caution is required when working with anyone who is trying to help you raise funds. Because deals are contingent on getting funding, numerous scams and incomplete deals can cost a company both money and time. If any broker or investment banker asks for money up front, there is no guarantee that you will receive anything (Reynes, 1998). In contrast, people who receive a percentage after a deal has been completed are more likely to engage in prudent conduct to guarantee payment for themselves and their firms.

Through private placement, an investor might purchase convertible debentures, in which a borrower pays a certain predetermined interest rate to the investor. After a specified period, convertible debentures can be converted into stock or maintained as a loan. The opportunity to convert the loan to stock is a choice made by the loan holder, the issuer, or both (Reynes, 1998). In one example involving a company that manufactured drug-screening kits, investors had the option to purchase convertible debentures in $5,000 blocks. The company's shares were selling for $0.38 each. After three years, the lenders could choose to get their money back and all interest owed or convert their debenture to stock at $0.75 a share. Converting to stocks would have been the best option for the lenders because three years later the stocks were selling for $3 to $4 per share (Reynes, 1998). Debenture offerings are discussed further in chapter 10.

Factoring Accounts Receivable

Private parties can also provide short-term funds through factoring. Factoring entails selling assets. The assets sold are either inventories or accounts receivable, and they are purchased by a specialized financing company.

Factoring of receivables can be accomplished in several ways. One way is for a company to purchase the receivables and another is for a company to purchase only the rights without transfer of actual administrative duties. The first technique is called factoring without recourse. A factor (the company that purchases the receivables) that purchases without recourse assumes complete responsibility in debt collection. Customers are instructed to send their payments to the factor. The factor receives a commission on the accounts that are paid and charges interest on the money loaned to the business until the accounts are paid.

Concepts Into Practice

Assume that a sport business is owed $100,000 and that Eagle Factoring purchases the accounts receivable without recourse. Eagle might receive 10% of the $100,000, or $10,000, as commission and might loan the sport business $70,000 on the remaining receivables at 5%. If Eagle collects the entire $100,000, Eagle profits from the $10,000 commission and from receiving 5% interest on the $70,000 loan. The remaining $30,000 might be returned to the sport business according to the negotiated contract provisions.

In the second type of factoring—factoring with recourse—the original holder of the receivables is still responsible for obtaining repayment and collects all payments but sends those payments to a finance company. This technique is also called accounts receivable financing. A finance company might advance money contingent on the borrower's agreeing to collect and manage the receivables. The factoring company might advance 70% to 95% of all receivables sold to it and then pay the remaining percentage when the last receivables are collected (Bogen, 1966). Again, the factoring company makes money by charging interest on the money advanced to the company selling the receivables. Regardless of the technique used, factoring accounts receivable is more expensive than bank borrowing because the factor charges a higher interest rate based on the potential risk factors.

Installment Sales

Installment sales are common in the auto sales industry. A buyer makes a down payment and makes monthly payments of principal and interest for a specified number of months or years. These contracts are typically for three or four years. The purchaser's failure to make timely payments gives the installment contract holder the right to repossess the car. Thus, the person holding the installment contract has title and true ownership.

Installment sales contracts can be found in the sporting goods industry (e.g., when someone buys an abdominal workout machine seen in an infomercial for three installments of $19.99 each). The purchaser has obtained the opportunity to receive the product contingent on future payments. Similar deals are made in almost all businesses, by which a party to a contract can make several payments. If a university sells its broadcasting rights to a television station, the station might pay 33% when the contract is signed, 33% before the season starts, and 33% when the season ends.

Operating Versus Capital Leases

Leasing, whether from the selling company or from a leasing agent or corporation, can also provide the funds needed to obtain equipment or other assets. By leasing equipment, money can be saved to buy other assets or equipment.

Fitness equipment does not depreciate as quickly as other assets, such as vehicles, and thus often serves as collateral for the lease. A fitness center may obtain either a capital lease or an operating lease for equipment. Under a capital lease, the fitness center would make its monthly lease payments and at the end of the lease term could pay a specified price, normally $1, to acquire the ownership rights for the equipment (Cohen, 1999). In contrast, an operating lease allows the lessee to return the equipment at the end of the lease or to buy it for a percentage of the original cost. Operating leases are often called service leases because the contract normally requires both financing and maintenance. Operating leases are not fully amortized, which means that the lease payments are insufficient to recover the full cost of the equipment.

A major advantage of the operating lease is a cancellation clause that gives the lessee (the fitness center) or the lessors (the equipment company) the opportunity to terminate the lease within a specified period. The cancellation clause could call for a 30-day written notice. Regardless of the time requirement, the benefit for the facility would be that they could, within 30 days, switch to a less expensive equipment supplier or one that provides equipment that is more advanced.

In contrast to the operating lease, the capital lease has one major advantage: the right to own the equipment when the lease ends. A capital lease, however, does not have any maintenance provision, the lease is not cancelable, and the lease payments will equal the cost of the equipment. A capital lease is often called a finance lease because of the nature of the lease arrangement.

Several issues require examination when determining whether to purchase or lease new assets. Leasing new assets has the following advantages:

- Funds that would normally be used to purchase assets could be used for working capital and other needs.

- No external financing is required, or the amount of such funds would be minimal.

- The corporation's financial picture is strengthened because investments in fixed assets are reduced and debt service is not increased (although additional debt obligation would be required to pay for the lease).

- No significant capital outlay is required, because most leases do not entail a significant down payment.

- Corporations can often avoid a large maturity payment such as that involved when a corporation retires a bond issue.

- The shareholder's equity is not diluted through leasing as it would be with stock sales.

- The entire lease payment is deducted from **taxable income**, which often produces a significant benefit over asset ownership.

Other assets such as buildings and equipment can be depreciated if purchased, but the land is not deductible.

- A company can avoid technological obsolescence because it can rapidly replace older leased equipment.

- Leasing equipment can eliminate numerous repair and upkeep expenses that could be covered by the lease agreement.

- A company's credit rating can improve.

Some distinct disadvantages are also present:

- Gross lease costs are traditionally higher than financing costs if extended over the life of the asset.

- The lessee still makes regular lease payments throughout the lease period after the point at which an asset would have been paid for if purchased.

- Modifying the asset requires the lessor's permission, eliminating the lessee's ability to control the asset.

- A lessee loses the benefits associated with inflation, increased values, or increased salvage values because the asset is turned over after the lease period ends. The lessor gains these benefits.

- A long lease obligation may force a company to keep using older equipment covered by the lease to avoid paying penalties for breaching the lease.

- Some companies lease too much equipment, not realizing that their fixed lease obligations are growing significantly and that the lease obligations would still be owed even if their sales stopped.

- A lessor can always confiscate the equipment upon default, leaving the company without machinery.

Whichever leasing technique is used, there are specific effects on taxes and the balance sheet. The big tax benefit of a lease is the ability to deduct lease expenses as a business expense. If a company buys the equipment instead, it will be able to depreciate the equipment cost over five years only as set forth by IRS regulations. The tax benefit is available only under specific circumstances if the lease meets the following conditions (Brigham & Gapenski, 2017):

♦ The initial lease term cannot exceed 80% of the estimated useful life of the equipment, which means that when the lease ends the equipment still should have at least 20% of its useful life remaining.

♦ The residual value of the equipment at the end of the lease must equal at least 20% of its initial value.

♦ No party can be allowed to purchase the equipment at a predetermined price when the lease ends. This concern can be eliminated by allowing the lessee to purchase the equipment at the equipment's fair market value after the lease ends.

♦ The lessee cannot make any investments in or improvements to the equipment other than through the lease payments.

♦ No contractual provision can limit the use of the equipment until after the lease expires.

An example of the depreciation versus business expense deduction highlights the value of a lease to the bottom line.

CONCEPTS INTO PRACTICE

Assume that a fitness center bought $2 million in equipment with a three-year class life. It would receive a depreciation allowance of $660,000 in the first year, $900,000 in the second year, $300,000 in the third year, and $140,000 in the fourth year. If the center was taxed at 40% (federal and state taxes combined), the purchase would provide a total tax savings of $800,000. Assuming a discount rate of 6%, the present value of the tax savings would be $671,680. If the center leased double the amount of equipment for one year for a $2 million lease payment, it would likewise have an $800,000 tax savings ($2,000,000 multiplied by 40%). But because the lease option benefits are derived in the first year, the savings are $42,559 compared with the present value from the purchase option (Brigham & Gapenski, 2017). The problem with this analysis is that the $2 million lease obligation appears extremely high when the purchase price is also $2 million. The example makes sense only because we are supposing that the fitness center would lease twice as much equipment as it would have purchased. If it were to lease the same amount of equipment, the tax savings as a function of present value would be significantly less. Obviously, proper comparisons must be made between items to be leased or purchased.

Leases also affect financial statements. Leases were called off-balance-sheet financing for many years because neither the leased asset nor the lease liability (payment requirements) appeared on a company's balance sheet. Because leased assets and obligations did not appear on the balance sheet, an investor might not know that all the equipment in a business was leased and that the business owed, for example, over $1 million annually in lease obligations. These facts would be critical for any investor. On the basis of this concern, the Financial Accounting Standards Board issued a ruling that leased assets need to be reported as fixed assets and that the present value of future lease payments needs to be recorded as a liability (Brigham & Gapenski, 2017). An operating lease is now recorded on the balance sheet. A capital lease is recorded on the books as either an asset or an obligation. An asset is considered part of a capital lease if ownership of the asset is transferred to the lessee when the lease expires, if the lease contains a bargain purchase option, or if the lease term exceeds 75% of the asset's economic life (Spiro, 1996).

LONG-TERM BORROWING

This chapter has covered various financing techniques that are often short-term solutions. Borrowing on a credit card is not a long-term option because of the high interest rates. Furthermore, factoring is a stopgap solution, and other funding options would need to be pursued in subsequent times of financial need. Other funding options, such as a bank's line of credit, can be either short term or long term. Installment contracts can be short term for a car or long term for equipment that might last longer than 10 years.

The most traditional forms of long-term funding are stocks and bonds (discussed in chapter

10). Whereas these two options are normally available for larger businesses, smaller or new companies often do not have these alternatives. Various long-term funding options, such as mortgages or long-term loans, exist for medium-sized businesses. Mezzanine financing (discussed next) is also available as a bridge loan. This section covers mezzanine financing and venture capital financing.

Mezzanine Financing

Although raising short-term start-up capital is often difficult, the scenario for existing companies is different. A company with a successful track record has fewer problems raising money because it should be able to show sustained income. Such a company can use mezzanine financing, a type of financing available to established companies that show growth potential but that are not yet ready for a capital stock offering. Companies can typically use mezzanine financing to raise between $1 million and $20 million through a combination of borrowing money from an investor and selling stocks to the same investor (Hovey, 1998b).

Financing typically works through payment of interest on the borrowed amount for about five years. After that time, the business can cash out the investor by going public or can refinance for a longer period. The investor has the benefit of earning a good rate of interest, typically the prime lending rate plus 2 to 4 points, or, if the business has increased in value, selling the stock for a capital gain (Hovey, 1998b). No set amount needs to be raised. So the sports organization, after operating the business for several years, could possibly raise $2 million in unsecured, partially secured, or secured debt financing and perhaps $1 million in equity financing. Such deals typically take between three and five months to complete, and the total fee cost (attorneys, accountants, and investment bankers) can equal 5% of the deal (Hovey, 1998b).

The rule of thumb for mezzanine lending is that a company can

> leverage two to three times its cash flow in senior secured debt. It can raise total debt four to five times cash flow with

a mezzanine deal. So if the company is doing $2 million in cash flow, it can probably raise $4 million to $6 million in senior debt and $4 million to $5 million more in mezzanine financing, for a total debt of $10 million or five times cash flow. (Hovey, 1998c, p. 42)

Although mezzanine lending can help a company grow before a possible **public offering**, some businesses need a larger boost to expand more rapidly or to position themselves more expediently for a public offering. Whereas the previously discussed angel investor might stay with an investment for the long term, a venture capital investor normally remains with an investment until the business goes bankrupt, is purchased by someone else, or goes public.

Venture Capital

Venture capital represents an opportunity for people with marketable ideas or products to raise funds from private investors willing to take a risk in owning part of the company in exchange for their investment. Venture capital, commonly called VC, is similar to mezzanine financing in that it blends debt-based loans with the potential for equity interest if the borrower's company goes public. In 2000, capital investments of more than $120 billion were made in U.S.-based companies. Investments went up and down over the next 17 years, and in 2017 venture capitalists invested over $71 billion ("Value", 2018).

VC investors are primarily interested in technology-based industries in which a winning company can pay off many times over rather than industries in which a successful company will show only marginal profits. Venture capitalists like to see gross margins over 50%. A company that makes a 30% profit a year represents too great a risk and does not attract the strong investor interest that could make an **initial public offering** successful.

Venture capital investors have shied away from the sport industry in the past, but sport-related Internet companies are starting to garner VC interest. But not all Internet businesses are drawing VC interest. Venture capitalists are attracted to companies that have clear access to a channel of distribution, whether it is the company's own or someone else's. A unique product with significant demand has priority over a flashy new product that might be harder to sell. The ultimate goal for any VC investment is for the company to go public. Through a public offering, the VC company can make many times over its investment. A VC investor might invest in 10 companies with the hope that one will hit it big and more than make up for their initial investment in all 10 companies.

Regardless of the method used to obtain initial funding or short-term funding, any successful business will also require long-term financing. VC and mezzanine investors may pay a premium for the ability to transfer their investment from a debt instrument to an equity interest. The equity interest is developed through giving the investor a share of the business. Providing a share of the business is made easier with stock. The preferred approach is to give a VC investor one million shares of two million outstanding shares instead of a contract stating that the investor owns 50% of a business. That is, a contract indicating a 50% ownership in a business is often much harder to sell than stocks, especially stocks listed on an organized exchange.

FUNDING FOR SMALL OR MINORITY-OWNED BUSINESSES

This section expands on previous analysis to look more closely at other capital options for smaller or minority-owned businesses and indicates where to go for help if you are having difficulty finding funding.

Small Business Association Loans for the Inner City

A government source to look to is the SBA, discussed earlier in the chapter. The SBA can offer assistance in obtaining various types of loans, including 7(a), 504, microlender, small business lending company, bank-regulated certified development company, and SBIC-related loans or programs. In addition, the SBA can provide assistance in conjunction with other capital efforts. For example, the city of Detroit obtained $100 million from the federal government to develop an empowerment zone (Detroit Empowerment Zone Transition Office, n.d.). The empowerment zone is designed to foster revitalization of a community. Businesses moving to such a zone may receive wage credits, tax-exempt bonds, section 179 (depreciation) expensing, and assistance in obtaining SBA-backed loans. Property taxes also were to be frozen for those new businesses for five years. In conjunction with this effort, the Detroit Recreation Department put forth an empowerment zone initiative that received more than $10 million in Title XX funding for such projects as Roving Recreation and the Recreation Facilities Enhancement Project (Detroit Empowerment Zone Transition Office, n.d.). Blending various government levels and agencies can help develop innovative capital acquisition programs and reduce operating costs, especially in the context of minority-based programs.

A Helping Hand for Minority Business Owners

Although the capital sources just mentioned all present some strong opportunities for a new or established business to obtain funds for growth, other companies might not have the same opportunities. Minorities and women have traditionally faced hardships in acquiring capital for their businesses. Some of these hardships were attributable to minimal or nonexistent credit histories for business owners who had never had credit cards in their own names or who represented too high a risk for traditional capital lenders. To prevent potential continued discrimination—whether disparate impact (unintentional) or disparate treatment (intentional)—numerous support opportunities have been established to help minorities and women obtain funding. A female-owned business could become eligible for specific government set-aside contracts.

Female-owned companies can use the Women's Prequalified Loan Program, guaranteed by the SBA, to borrow up to $250,000. Guarantees are for 80% of loans under $100,000 and 75% for loans over $100,000 (Broome, 2001). To qualify for the SBA-guaranteed loan, the business needs to be a female-owned business (at least 51% of the business needs to be owned, managed, or operated by women), have less than $5 million in sales, and employ fewer than 100 workers (Broome, 2001). If a loan under $100,000 is sought, the process requires only a one-page application. For loans over $100,000, the applicant needs to submit an expanded application, business plan, resumes of the primary officials, recent financial statements or tax returns, and a personal financial statement (Broome, 2001). Loans over $50,000 have an interest obligation at the prime rate. Loans under $50,000 can cost the prime rate plus up to 4% interest (Broome, 2001).

The following paragraphs describe some minority-oriented funding programs.

The National Minority Supplier Development Council has 23 regional affiliates and works with 1,750 businesses to help minority-owned companies acquire goods and services. Such assistance is not meant to be charity. Rather, the companies involved in the council participate to help generate additional sales. Through the provision of flexible payment options or collateralized sales to minorities who otherwise might not obtain such preferential treatment, new sales and potential clients can be developed. The National Minority Supplier Development Council has proceeded one step more to create the Business Consortium Fund, which helps minority business owners obtain financing for raw materials, employee salaries, and other contract-related expenses (Nelton, 1998b). The Business Consortium Fund limits loans to $500,000 over a maximum of seven years and requires the borrower to have a purchase order specifying where the funds will be spent.

Apart from the Business Consortium Fund, minority-owned companies may obtain capital from specialized small business investment companies licensed by the SBA. Local chambers of commerce, economic development committees, and various national associations can also help minorities and women find needed capital.

CONCLUSION

This chapter covered the basic resources available for the short- and long-term funding of a business. Numerous options exist for finding necessary funds, but even people with business experience can face rejection. A businessperson may approach multiple lenders and be refused by all. This does not mean that the individual is a bad businessperson; it may mean that the economic environment is not right, that the lending market is tight, or that collateral is insufficient to secure the obligation, among a host of other things.

No matter what capital source you attempt to tap, you will need several key tools. The primary tools are either audited financial statements or pro forma statements along with a realistic road map for your business (i.e., a business plan) that will help investors determine what direction you will be taking to guarantee a strong likelihood of success. Although the proper documentation is important, you also need a strong team of professionals to help you through the process. An accountant, attorney, and financial planner or investment banker might be critical for your capital acquisition success.

Selling investors on your project is significantly different from selling potential customers. Customers may be interested in product features, customer service, and warranties. In contrast, investors are interested in margin (profit), market size, a competitive environment, return on investment, product development opportunities, and related financial issues (Evanson, 1997). The financial planning process helps identify these issues.

Persistency is the key to securing capital. This chapter focused on short-term funding in situations in which quick decisions are necessary and when time is not available to pursue long-term funding options. Having the funding sources in place, such as a line of credit, is always important in case you need money and do not have time to try various options.

Class Discussion Topics

1. If you have ever applied for a credit card, what were you required to show to obtain credit?

2. If you have ever borrowed money to buy a car, what was involved in that process?

3. If you have ever borrowed money for college, what steps were involved in that process?

4. What would you want from a friend (e.g., collateral, a contract) if you loaned the person $1,000?

5. If a friend asked you for a $10,000 loan to start a business, what information would you want to help you make your decision?

6. Have you ever defaulted on a loan? What were the ramifications?

7. If you had the money, would you lend it to someone to help start a business if you knew that the business had a 75% chance of failing? What are the issues that you would need to address in making this decision?

Stocks and Bonds

Chapter Objectives

After studying this chapter, you should be able to do the following:

♦ Compare the different classes of stock available.

♦ Describe the rights of a stockholder.

♦ Describe how a smaller sport business can issue stock.

♦ Understand how stocks are issued.

♦ Understand the evolution of sport stocks.

♦ Describe what types of bonds are available and how they are secured.

♦ Understand how a company repays bondholders.

♦ Understand the dynamics of using government-issued bonds to finance sports facilities.

A major form of capital acquisition is selling the business to a group of individuals who purchase stock in the company. **Stocks**, which represent ownership in the business, can be sold on the open market or through private transactions. Whereas some businesses are owned by thousands of shareholders, others are owned by only one shareholder. Each business is different, and the number and types of **shares** sold are based on the capital needs of the company, initially and later.

Another financial tool used by both the private and the public sectors to raise funds is bonds. A bond is an obligation that needs to be repaid with interest, similar to a loan from a bank. The difference is that bonds are typically issued by larger corporations or government entities with a good repayment history and are sought after by investors because of either favorable interest rates or tax benefits. The high desirability of these bonds creates a market for their purchase and sale that is similar to the **stock market**. Thus, bonds have the financing characteristics of loans as well as a market in which they can be bought and sold, like stocks. This chapter will address both stocks and bonds and provide information on how they are used to raise capital for sports organizations.

STOCKS

Stock certificates represent an investor's ownership right in a business. A stockholder pays a designated amount to acquire an ownership interest in a company. Each share represents an ownership interest, so a stockholder is also referred to as a shareholder. If you own 1,000 shares of a company's stock and 100,000 shares were issued, you own 1% of the company. This section covers the types of stocks that can be purchased and the ways in which shareholders participate in a business.

Common Stock

As the name implies, the type of stock that is most frequently issued and used is **common stock**. Under Armour (UA), for example, has issued millions of shares of common stock. UA's largest shareholder is its founder, Kevin Plank. Common stocks represent an equity ownership right in a company. Each share denotes a percentage ownership of the corporation. If we use UA as an example, let's suppose that Plank owns approximately 30% of the outstanding shares of stock. As a partial owner, Plank is entitled to a proportional share of profits earned by the company. If UA had a $250 million profit and the board of directors decided to pay the entire amount to its common shareholders, then Plank would be entitled to a dividend of $75 million.

Plank has certain rights, risks, and obligations as an owner. His rights include the right to help set the direction of the corporation through voting his shares. He also faces risks, such as the possibility of losing his investment and the prospect of any recovery if UA ever goes bankrupt and no money is left after the bondholders are repaid. Common stocks are low on the repayment list after secured creditors are repaid and holders of preferred shares are paid. Also, Plank has obligations to the business, which could include the prohibition of self-dealing or taking a business opportunity for himself.

Because of the potential for significant losses and because investors are often risk averse (not wanting to invest in risky stocks for fear of losing precious money such as a retirement fund), investors try to minimize their risks. One technique that reduces the risk of purchasing stock is to purchase shares in a mutual fund. A mutual fund normally represents millions of dollars from investors who want to spread their risk and opportunity for gain over many stocks. Specialized **mutual funds** can invest in sport stocks, social equity stocks, global stocks, or aggressive growth stocks. A mutual fund might have millions of shares in hundreds of stocks, and professional administrators of each fund analyze each stock and try to pick the best time to buy or sell the fund's shares.

Preferred Stock

Preferred stock earns its name from the dividend preference that it carries in relation to common stock. Although a corporation might not issue a dividend to common stock shareholders, it may be bound to provide dividends to preferred stock shareholders. The dividend is cumulative in that if it is not paid to holders of preferred stock in a given year, the corporation will owe two years' worth of dividends the next year. The dividend to the preferred shareholders needs to be paid before common stockholders can receive their dividends. The requirement to pay a dividend, if one is issued, makes a preferred stock a blend of a bond with a required interest payment and a stock with its associated equity benefits. The requirement to pay a fixed dividend increases the issuing company's **financial leverage**. In the eyes of lenders, preferred stock represents equity and is shown in the equity section of the balance sheet.

Other benefits that are available for preferred stockholders can include

- reference as to assets in distribution;
- voting power for preferred stock, available under limited circumstances;
- strong redemption provisions;
- subscription privileges to future stock offerings; and
- the right to convert preferred stock to common stock.

Some investors rely on dividend income as their primary return on an equity investment. For these investors, preferred shares would be the most prudent investment because preferred stock shareholders are entitled to a dividend payment before common stock shareholders receive any dividends.

Regarding preference in distribution, some corporations specifically authorize preferred stockholders to receive the first of any return upon liquidation of a corporation's assets. If no such preference is provided for in the corporate bylaws, all classes of stock share equally in any distributions. Preferred stockholders often perceive their investment as riskier than bonds because the preferred shareholders' claims are subordinate to those of bondholders in the event that the company is liquidated. Furthermore, bondholders are more likely than preferred shareholders to continue receiving disbursements during hard times (Brigham & Gapenski, 2017).

The conversion privilege attached to some preferred stocks can be an attractive feature. Assume that UA issues a preferred stock that can be converted two to one. Such a provision means that one preferred share can be exchanged at a given time for two common shares. Assume that UA's common stock is selling at $20 but management decides to raise $5 million by selling 100,000 shares of preferred stock at $50 par value. At the $50 price, converting the preferred stock to common stock would not be worthwhile.

If the common stock subsequently rose to $30 a share, however, converting the preferred stock to common stock would be advantageous, because the shareholder would receive two common shares valued at a combined $60, compared with the initial investment of $50 per preferred share. A $10 per share profit would result from the conversion.

SHAREHOLDERS' RIGHTS

In the United States, the basic rights and obligations of stockholders are set forth in the laws of the state in which the business is incorporated. Incorporation is the formal process of applying to be registered as a stock-issuing corporation. Each state has different laws. A disproportionately large number of businesses are incorporated in several states, including Delaware and Nevada, because they offer favorable tax or liability laws designed to attract corporations. Besides being spelled out in specific state laws, stockholders' rights can also be found in the corporation's bylaws, charter, or articles of incorporation.

Stockholders have the following legal rights (Investopedia staff, 2010):

- To receive evidence of ownership such as a stock certificate
- To transfer the stock freely, within limited rules
- To exercise the right to vote in person or by **proxy** as set forth in the corporation's bylaws
- To receive dividends and other disbursements on a pro rata basis according to the number of shares held
- To receive disbursements on a pro rata basis when a partial or complete liquidation of corporate assets occurs
- To bring action on behalf of the corporation against board members who do not act in the corporation's best interest (commonly referred to as stockholders' derivative actions)
- To obtain information from the corporation to help safeguard the stockholders' investment (such as an annual report)
- To subscribe pro rata to new shares of company stocks when authorized by law (commonly referred to as stockholders' **preemptive right [or preemption]**)

SPONSORSHIPS INCREASE STOCK VALUES

Is sponsoring a major professional league worth the investment? A sales increase is one positive indicator, but stock values can also increase. According to a 2005 study, sponsoring a professional league can result in increased stock prices for the sponsors. The study examined 53 publicly traded companies whose stocks gained $257 million in market value ($13.6 billion in economic value) in the first trading week after announcing sponsorship deals with the National Basketball Association (NBA), the National Football League (NFL), the National Hockey League (NHL), Major League Baseball (MLB), or the Professional Golfers' Association (Howard, 2005). Companies that sponsored the NFL or MLB had slight gains (because of the high costs of such deals) compared to the larger spikes for companies that sponsored the other leagues. Smaller companies, those with smaller market shares, and those associated with products that had a clear connection to the league being sponsored had larger increases in stock value (Howard, 2005).

As an owner of the business, a stockholder has the right to receive a share of profits earned by the company if the board of directors approves such a payment. Whether to issue a dividend is an important decision for the board. If a dividend is declared, most investors see that decision as a sign that the business is doing well, because the business is able to cover its internal fiscal needs and still have money available to pay the shareholders. In contrast, some investors and analysts view paying a dividend as a sign that the business has no good investment prospects in which to reinvest its additional capital.

The board of directors is responsible for making the final determination about where the extra funds, if any, should be invested, and shareholders assume that the board makes those decisions with the shareholders' interest in mind. The board of directors is elected by the shareholders to run the company on behalf of the shareholders. A successful board does more than just pay dividends to shareholders. A board is judged according to whether its decisions increase the value of the stock.

SPORT STOCKS

Stock offerings in professional sport are not new. The Green Bay Packers sold their first 1,000 shares in 1923 for $5 each (Lascari, 1998). In 1935, the company went into receivership and was reorganized as a Wisconsin nonprofit stock corporation; it then issued another 3,000 shares at $5 each. In 1950 the Packers had another stock offering that raised $118,000. By 1997 there were 4,627 stockholders, who were given 1,000 shares for every share owned, which resulted in 4,627,000 shares outstanding. After amending their articles of incorporation, the Packers were able to sell an additional 5,373,000 shares. A fourth sale was consummated in 1997. Each new share sold for $200 plus a handling fee of $15 (Lascari, 1998). (See The Case of the Green Bay Packers sidebar.)

Significant restrictions prohibited almost all transfers of the new stock except transfers back to the Packers for $0.025 per share, to family members as gifts, or as a bequest after death. Additional rules prohibit a stockholder from making any profit or even receiving a dividend. Furthermore, to comply with NFL rules, each stockholder had to pledge that he or she had not been involved in any litigation alleging fraud, had not been convicted of a felony, and had not participated in sport gambling. Even with all these restrictions, the Packers sold 120,000 shares and raised over $24 million. Most purchasers bought the stock as a novelty to claim ownership in the Packers.

The last sale raised $24 million to renovate Lambeau Field. The stock is **illiquid** and pays no dividend, and no one is allowed to own more than 200,000 shares. As with previous sales, resale is prohibited, except to the club at a fraction of the original value. The success associated with the 1997 sale spurred the Packers to issue stocks again in 2011. The Packers leveraged team interest in choosing to sell their last two offerings

THE CASE OF THE GREEN BAY PACKERS

The Packers, the city of Green Bay, and the Green Bay and Brown County District financed the $295 million stadium renovation that took place over four years (2000-2003) in four major ways: sales tax, stock sale, sale of naming rights, and premium seat licenses. According to financial records, when the Packers sold stock in 1997, they raised nearly $24 million and increased the number of shareholders from 1,940 to 109,723. Although the Packers have not sold naming rights to the stadium itself, they have successfully sold naming-rights deals for multiple entrances to Lambeau Field (Frey, 2011). The Packers also financially capitalized on the NFL's G-3 loan program. Initiated in 1999, this program, now called the G-4 fund, provides financial assistance to franchises using the money as collateral to issue bonds for stadium development. This money is taken from the league's national television revenue, which is shared equally among the teams. Between 1994 and 2004, the league loaned $725 million to facilitate the building or renovation of 20 NFL stadiums including Lambeau Field (Frey, 2011). Yet despite the fact that the Packers are the only publicly traded NFL organization and have one of the most passionate fans bases in professional sport (over 100,000 people are currently on a season ticket waiting list), whenever there is public allocation of scarce resources involving professional sports franchises, opposition and controversy arise. As noted by Frey (2011), the initial resistance came from the Wisconsin legislature after the team sought legislation to create the Brown County Stadium District. Specifically, the board was to issue $160 in bonds for the stadium project, subject to voter approval of a half-percent sales tax increase. A sales tax is a regressive tax; consequently, every taxpayer is charged the same amount to pay, regardless of overall income.

In addition to the challenges presented by the state legislature, the Packers were also confronted with issues locally in Green Bay. For example, several key elements within the lease kept the team and the city from reaching an agreement. Included among these issues were user fees, ticket tax surcharges, rent, and the city's usage of the stadium (Frey, 2011).

---

immediately after winning Super Bowls. Thus, after winning the 2011 Super Bowl, the team organized another stock offering similar to the 1997 offering. Fans could pay $250 per share (plus a $25 handling fee) for stocks that basically had no value, received no rights, and paid no dividends. The stock offering was designed to help the team offset an expected $143 million renovation to its stadium. In the first two days of the offering, the team sold 185,000 shares, which generated over $43 million and represented selling three-quarters of the entire offering ("*Packers sell*," 2011). The stock sale occurred in December, at a time when many fans were excited about the team's outstanding play (they were 12-0), and the stocks made a nice Christmas gift. Since 2011, the Packers have not had any additional public sales of team stock.

Because of its ownership structure, the Packers is the only NFL team to reveal annual financial results. Consequently, the Packers offer a rare glimpse into league finances. Intuitively, NFL owners are reluctant to open their financial books for public scrutiny for several reasons including establishing ticket prices, trying to get stadium subsidies, and managing payroll costs.

The Cleveland Indians have also sold stock to the public. The Indians were unusually lucky with the timing of their stock offering. The year the Indians went public (1998), they went to the World Series. The **prospectus**, which showed income through December 31, 1997, highlighted $140 million in revenue and $22.5 million in net income (see table 10.1) (Much & Phillips, 1999). Those numbers were much inflated; almost 90% of the income that year came from postseason and nonbaseball activities. If interest income, gains from player transactions, league expansion proceeds, and postseason income had been removed from the team's net income, the net income would have dropped to $1.76 million (Much & Phillips, 1999).

Table 10.1 Cleveland Indians' 1997 Adjusted Net Income

Income item	$ amount (in millions)
Reported net income	22,570
Interest income, net of interest expense	(2,371)
Gains on player transactions	(2,696)
League expansion proceeds	(9,286)
Playoff game revenue	(5,700)
Pretax income (adjusted to highlight only traditional revenue)	2,517
Pro forma income taxes	(755)
Pro forma adjusted net income	1,762

Data from Much and Phillips (1999).

The $15 per share initial public offering, which implied a $232 million franchise value, priced the stock at 131.7 times the adjusted earnings from regular-season revenue (Much & Phillips, 1999). By pricing themselves so high, the Indians provided virtually no opportunity for stock price appreciation. Thus, when the 1998 revenue numbers for the quarter ending September 30 showed a 37% increase in third-quarter operating profit, the stock price barely budged (Much & Phillips, 1999).

Stocks in professional teams have had a mediocre reception from the investing public. Pure-play investments that include only a professional sports team have several major problems, such as seasonal revenue streams, potential labor strife, limited investment liquidity, reliance on other business owners to generate a product, and intense media and government scrutiny (Much & Phillips, 1999). A pure play refers to a corporation that participates in only one industry segment. For example, the Indians were exclusively a sports team and thus was a pure play. In contrast, a blended company could encompass a team and other unrelated businesses; an example is the Florida Panthers hockey team and their resort holdings. Other examples include diverse companies such as Disney, Tribune, Comcast, and Time Warner. Even with blended companies, the presence of a sports team can significantly affect stock prices. In 2010, Madison Square Garden, Inc. (NASDAQ: MSG), which became its own public company that year, had various revenue streams, but when the team was in the running for acquiring LeBron James, its share prices spiked 12% and then fell when he chose to play elsewhere (Flamm, 2010).

Although a **pure-play stock** offering for a team might not be a sound investment option for stockholders other than the primary team owner (because of significant risks), blends may produce significant revenue streams through the addition of other revenue-producing units to a professional team. In the case of the NHL's Florida Panthers, additional units were combined with a pure play, producing a comprehensive business entity with the potential of using additional revenue to offset potential losses associated with a professional team. However, in the long run, this blended strategy, which combined a pro sport team with holdings in arena management, resorts, and golf facilities, was not successful. In 2001, the team portion was spun off into a separate company.

The Panthers are not alone in their inability to develop a blended structure. Poor performance also hounded Ascent Entertainment Group, which owned several businesses including the NHL's Colorado Avalanche and the NBA's Denver Nuggets. After enduring double-digit losses for years, Ascent's parent company, Comsat Corporation, divested its remaining interest in Ascent in 1996. Ascent suffered operating losses of $42.4 million in 1997 (Much & Phillips, 1999). In 1999, the Avalanche and the Nuggets were tentatively sold, along with their arena, for $400 million, and the buyer assumed some debt associated with the arena ("Two Denver franchises," 1999). The sale did not go unchallenged; a potential suitor sued, saying that Ascent shareholders would make more money from a different offer to buy the team and that a potential conflict of interest had not been made public (Lewis, 1999). After several lawsuits were filed, the original team sale was nullified. The original buyers returned with a $450 million offer, which appeared to be enough to close the deal ("Wal-Mart heir," 2000). The teams and the Pepsi Center were eventually purchased for $450 million by Stanley Kroenke ("*Owner*," 2002).

In addition to pure-play and blended professional sport-related corporations, another variation emerged in the first two decades of the 2000s—a vertically integrated combination whereby the sports team benefits other corporate units. Some examples of such combinations were Walt Disney (Mighty Ducks of Anaheim), Tribune (Chicago Cubs), and Fox Entertainment Group (Los Angeles Dodgers and a minority interest in the New York Knicks, New York Rangers, Los Angeles Lakers, and Los Angeles Kings) (Much & Phillips, 1999). The Ducks, Cubs, and Dodgers have all subsequently been sold, highlighting that sometimes a sport property will not benefit the corporate bottom line. These vertically integrated combinations were thought to be more effective than pure-play sport businesses because the broadcasting arms of each company can generate significant sport advertising income without having to pay significant fees for broadcasting rights. The sale of these teams might indicate that purchasing sport media is easier than operating a team at a profit. Comcast Spectacor (now called Spectra) is an example of a vertically integrated company that has a sports team holding—the Philadelphia Flyers.

Sport stocks are not focused just on professional teams, whether as a pure play or part of a larger organization. Golf-related companies are an active area for sport stocks. Ely Callaway took his golf company public in 1992 and was one of the few to succeed. The landscape has been littered with various golf companies that failed in their efforts to go public, including Orlimar, TearDrop, CoastCast, and Natural Golf (Foust, 2008). Part of the problem is that only a limited number of dedicated golfers are willing to spend money on expensive golf gear. Only 13 million golfers account for 91% of equipment spending (Foust, 2008).

Also, there have been some new types of sports organizations that have been involved in the stock market to raise funds. One example involved Boise State University, which started selling stocks in 2009 for $100 a share. Because the university is a nonprofit organization, the athletic department started a separate nonprofit organization called Boise State Broncos, Inc. that has a 12-person oversight board. The fundraising effort was designed to raise $20 million to help fund facility renovations. The shares do not pay dividends, provide any financial reward, or provide privileges for purchasing tickets. The only benefit to owners, besides pride in supporting the school, is the ability to vote on future oversight board members ("Boise State sells stock," 2009).

BONDS

We now focus on a tool used by both the private and the public sectors—bonds. In this section, the types of corporate bonds available will be addressed, followed by the costs associated with issuing such bonds, as well as various repayment methods. Next, we consider government bonds used to finance stadium and arena construction and related projects; this section highlights the various types of bonds issued by government entities and the manner in which they are issued.

There are two general categories of bonds: secured and unsecured bonds. Secured bonds are secured by the issuer's pledge of a specific asset, which is a form of collateral on the loan. In the event of a default, the bond issuer passes title of the asset onto the bondholders. Plant, property, and equipment would all be examples of bond collateral. Unsecured bonds are not backed by a specific asset but instead backed by the full faith and credit of the issuer. While it may initially seem like secured bonds would be the safer of the two bonds for investors, this is often not the case. Major companies can issue unsecured bonds because they are so financially stable that bond investors have faith in the repayment of the bonds. For example, U.S. Treasury bonds are considered the lowest risk bonds, and these are unsecured.

Bonds issued by businesses are often referred to as **corporate bonds** because bonds can normally be issued only by the largest corporations. Similar to a mortgage loan, a mortgage bond is a bond backed by specified real estate. If the bond issuer defaults, the **bondholders** can foreclose on the property and sell the property to satisfy the claim.

A bond is similar to a long-term loan in that it is a contract under which a borrower agrees to make specified interest and principal payments on specified dates for a specified period. Every bond has some restrictions attached. These restrictions (called bond covenants) are similar to typical contract terms that limit both parties. A company issuing bonds might attach restrictions that allow the company to pay a lesser amount if the investor tries to redeem the bond before its maturity date. Similarly, investors might demand restrictions on a company to protect their investment. These restrictions could include limiting the extent of acquisition activity and capital spending, requiring minimum levels of liquidity, restricting a company's right to issue additional equity, and limiting the size of the debt–equity ratio.

Besides the bonds already discussed, there are convertible bonds; income bonds that pay interest only when income is earned; indexed bonds whose interest rates increase if inflation rises; and **zero coupon bonds** or original issue **discount bonds**. For indexed bonds, the index typically tracks a well-regarded index such as the **consumer price index (CPI)**. Discount bonds which carry no interest rate but are originally sold at a price lower than **par value** and appreciate in value over time (Brigham & Gapenski, 2017).

Bond Financing

People often do not appreciate how important it is to choose the right funding vehicle for a business. If an owner makes a quick decision and the business has some poor years, the debt obligation could turn a strong investment into a fiscal disaster. An example can be seen with the Memphis Redbirds minor league baseball team and its AutoZone Park. The Redbirds built an extravagant $80.5 million stadium and made ambitious attendance projections that led the team into its financial struggles. The Memphis Redbirds Foundation, which owns the team and stadium, defaulted on a $1.625 million bond payment in March 2009. In 2010 the foundation entered into a deal with bondholders for reduced annual bond payments of just over $1 million that year because they could not afford to make the payments. In 2010, the bonds were consolidated from five or six bondholders to one private equity firm, Fundamental Advisors of New York (Morgan, 2010). But even with the downside associated with a financial obligation that can last more than 30 years, bonds have significant positive attributes (see Advantages and Disadvantages of Bond Financing sidebar).

Other factors that affect the decision of a business to issue bonds include the general business environment and the prevailing interest in the specific business that is issuing bonds. If interest rates are generally low, then every business may have difficulty issuing bonds. But a specific business that is facing a potential hardship may find it impossible to issue bonds. For example, if a labor dispute arises within the players' association, a the team might face a difficult market in which to issue its bonds even though other businesses may not be having a problem in this regard. One way of avoiding such a problem is to provide some type of pledge to guarantee repayment (e.g., by issuing a secured bond).

ADVANTAGES AND DISADVANTAGES OF BOND FINANCING

Advantages

- Interest on bonds is tax deductible (versus stock dividends, which are not deductible).
- Bond financing can be reasonably inexpensive for an established company with a good credit rating.
- The market for trading and issuing bonds is strong and established.

Disadvantages

- Interest is a fixed charge that needs to be paid regardless of whether income was earned.
- The principal loaned amount must be paid in full when the bond matures.
- Issuing bonds can harm a company's credit rating and make it more difficult for the company to borrow money in the future.
- If the bond is secured by collateral, a corporation might not be able to sell or otherwise dispose of the asset without bondholder approval.
- Bondholders have the upper hand whenever a company declares bankruptcy.

Secured Versus Unsecured Bonds

One disadvantage of **secured bonds** is related to a corporation's ability to control secured assets. If an asset is secured by the terms of the security agreement, the corporation does not have exclusive use of the asset and might need to obtain approval before using the asset for various activities. Unsecured bonds provide the greatest flexibility for the issuing corporation but minimal protection for the bond purchaser. A secured bondholder receives preferential treatment over subsequent bondholders, whether those subsequent bondholders are secured or unsecured.

Debentures

A **debenture** is an unsecured bond, meaning that no assets secure the bond (guarantee repayment) if the bond issuer defaults. Normally, because of the lack of protection for debenture bondholders, only companies with the best credit rating can issue such bonds. Although debenture bonds are generally unsecured, several techniques are used to extend protection to such bondholders. To provide investors with additional security that a debenture will be repaid, some companies issue **subordinate debentures**. These bonds provide some security because assets are pledged to back them. Claims on these assets, however, are subordinate to senior claims against the assets.

For example, a mortgage bond issue could be secured by a company's manufacturing equipment, and any amount of the equipment value that is not securing the mortgage bond issue (senior claim) can be used to secure repayment of the subordinate debentures. Assume that a company backs a $10 million mortgage bond issue with property valued at $15 million. The company issues subordinate bonds in the amount of $10 million several years later, after the property has appreciated. If the company were to file for bankruptcy protection, its land and buildings might be worth only $16 million. The mortgage bondholders would recover their $10 million. The subordinate bondholders are still in a better position than unsecured creditors because $6 million is still available from the assets after the mortgage bond is satisfied. The $6 million would go to the subordinate bondholders, who would probably be paid on a pro rata basis ($600 for each $1,000 bond that they held).

Regardless of the asset used to secure a debt instrument, the security helps increase the liquidity of the instrument, lowers the cost of capital to borrowers, and helps develop greater efficiency through the financial marketplace (Brigham & Gapenski, 2017). Thus, whether a homeowner pledges her home to secure a mortgage or a team uses contractually obligated revenue from its broadcasting contract, the security helps seal the deal and allows the flow of needed capital.

Whether they are secured or unsecured, bonds are covered by a contract called an indenture. The indenture is issued to a trust company that acts as a trustee for the bondholders. The indenture must follow specific Securities and Exchange Commission guidelines related to the trustees and their duties: Trustees must have no conflict of interest and must have financial responsibility, make periodic reports to bondholders, provide appropriate default notice, protect bondholders after default, and fulfill related obligations.

Most bonds are **bearer bonds**, which means that the bondholder retains possession of the bond document. Bonds typically have **coupons** attached to them that the bondholder can redeem to receive the specified interest payment. Such bonds are called coupon bonds. Coupon bonds are the easiest to transfer to other purchasers because the person in actual physical possession of the bond is entitled to redeem the coupon. In contrast, a registered bond is issued in the name of the bondholder. If such shares are transferred, the registered bondholder needs to endorse the bonds to the new owner, and the new owner has to have their name added to the corporate books. Because of the registration requirement, such bonds are less marketable.

Some corporations have issued income bonds during reorganizations or in exchange for preferred stock. Income bonds pay interest only if the corporation earns income. If no income is earned, no interest is paid. Such a contingency requirement reduces the fixed costs that would normally be allocated for paying the interest on a coupon or registered bond. Thus, if a company is facing tough financial times, it does not need to worry about paying interest to the bondholders. This provision frees up a significant amount

AN UNUSUAL WAY TO SECURE A BOND

In 1998, in an effort to acquire considerable cash in advance of his payday, Chicago White Sox slugger Frank Thomas, working with a New York City investment banking firm, was attempting to raise $20 million. The money would be raised through an offering of bonds in Thomas' name backed by his guaranteed annual salary of $7 million per year through 2006. The bonds would have probably paid a rate of approximately 9%. It was assumed that Thomas could earn more than 9% by reinvesting the $20 million somewhere else. Otherwise, borrowing the money would be of no benefit to him ("Thomas secures," 1998). But shortly after an attempt was made to launch the bond, the idea was scrapped because the player's contract included too many inhibitive conditions, such as a morals clause, that could limit repayment. Furthermore, players can lose their entitlement to compensation if they are injured in a nonteam-related event or if players go on strike. Thomas would also lose his entitlement to compensation if he decided to not play anymore (Kaplan, 1998). After 1998, Thomas was often injured and he performed sporadically at times, which justified the nervousness of potential investors back in 1998.

But Thomas rebounded. In 2006, the 38-year-old slugger led the Oakland Athletics with 39 homers and 114 runs batted in (RBIs). Thomas hit .301 with 521 homers and 1,704 RBIs in 19 major league seasons—16 with the Chicago White Sox. His success with the Athlet-

ics prompted the Toronto Blue Jays to reach a tentative deal with him for the 2007 and 2008 seasons. Under the $18.12 million contract, Thomas received a $9.12 million signing bonus, a $1 million salary in 2007, and $8 million in 2008. The deal included a $10 million vesting option for 2009 that would become guaranteed if Thomas made 1,000 plate appearances in the next two seasons or 525 plate appearances in 2008 ("*Blue Jays sign Thomas*," 2006). Thomas retired in 2008.

In February 2001, William Andrews securitized the remaining $5 million that he was owed by the NFL's Atlanta Falcons. Andrews had last played in the NFL in 1996. But as part of his playing contract, he was still owed $200,000 per year over the next 25 years. Instead of waiting for those annual payments, Andrews decided to sell the deferred compensation in the form of a bond to Hanleigh, a sport insurance company. Hanleigh paid $2 million to Andrews for the right to the future compensation stream. This deal marked the first sale of a bond securitized by an individual athlete's deferred compensation in the history of professional sport. Although the $2 million was only 40% of the amount that Andrews was to be paid over the next 25 years, the securitization gave the athlete immediate access to a large sum of money. He then had the ability to invest and grow that $2 million. The transaction was overseen by NDH Capital, a small Connecticut financing company (Kaplan, 2001).

of money to help the business staff in an operation. But when the company starts turning a profit, it is required to start paying interest to the bondholders. An indenture specifies the formula for calculating the required payments under an income bond. One rule typically applied to income bonds is that the interest is cumulative. If interest is not paid in a given year because income is low, it must be paid the next year, when income is greater, along with the interest for that next year.

Issue Size and Maturity

One of the primary concerns associated with bonds is determining the appropriate interest rate to attach to the bonds and determining how many bonds should be issued. When corporations are seeking millions of dollars, they do not resort to guesswork to determine the appropriate interest rate. Long- and short-term forecasting becomes a serious matter—a difference of one-tenth of a percentage point can cost millions in interest or may make an offering so unattractive that no one purchases the issue.

Several agencies, such as Moody's Investors Service and Standard & Poor's, rate bonds. These entities examine the bond issuer and determine the potential for default based on factors such as the revenue stream to repay the bonds, current economic conditions, interest rates, and past repayment history. After analyzing all the relevant criteria, the rating agency establishes a rating for a bond. The highest rating is typically AAA or Aaa depending on the agency. Bonds with such a rating have the lowest risk for default and do not need to pay as high an interest rate. Bonds that have a low rating are sometimes classified as **junk bonds** and need to pay a much higher interest rate to attract investors. Even if Moody's and Standard & Poor's give a bond a high rating, the potential for default exists and needs to be considered.

To help reduce the potential disaster associated with choosing an inappropriate interest rate, corporations appraise the supply and demand for money, which affect interest rates. Interest rates represent a true example of supply and demand in that if a glut of money is on the market, whether because of government actions or market forces, interest rates are lower than when the money supply is tighter. If the money supply is tight, however, interest rates are higher because more corporations are fighting to obtain scarcer funds, and the competition drives up the interest rates.

The demand for long-term funds arises from four major sources: mortgage borrowing, corporate bond financing, state and local government bond financing, and long-term U.S. Treasury borrowing. The various entities that have money available and those that need funds are all affected by the Federal Reserve. The Federal Reserve can control the supply and demand and affect interest rates through monetary policies. The Federal Reserve tends to relax the money supply during recessionary times and restrict money during prosperous times. Such a strategy is designed to foster stable growth without significant fluctuation.

The diverse suppliers for long-term funds include

- life insurance companies,
- savings and loan associations,
- mutual savings banks,
- commercial banks that might acquire bonds,
- insurance companies (fire, property, and casualty),
- corporate pension funds,
- state and local government retirement funds,
- union retirement plans, and
- mutual funds that buy bonds.

COSTS OF ISSUING BONDS

Although bonds can raise substantial funds, they are expensive to issue. The primary cost associated with issuing bonds is the required interest payments. Such payments are due on a semiannual basis for as long as the bond is outstanding. A 20-year, $100 million bond issued with 10% interest would require semiannual payments of $5 million for 20 years.

Another cost associated with issuing bonds is the discount or risk premium at which they are sold. The discount for the $100 million bond issue might be $5 million, which means that the issuing or selling entity for the bonds would take $5 million (5%) as a fee to process and help sell the bonds. Every transaction is different, but the typical issuing fee for bonds is around 5%. This cost effectively increases the interest rate because the $10 million annual interest obligation is based on $100 million. So the company would still owe $100 million for the bonds but receive only $95 million after paying the fee. This added cost must be built into the bond's repayment schedule. Thus, the actual interest cost for such a bond would be 10.25%. The $5 million cost for the bond issue can be amortized over the bond's life by putting aside $250,000 a year for 20 years. Thus, the actual cost to the bond issuer is $10.25 million a year. Additional expenses could include legal fees for preparing the indenture, recording the mortgages, and general legal advice, as well as marketing expenses.

LOAN REPAYMENT

Up to now we have looked at the types of bonds that can be issued. In this section we turn our attention to repayment and refunding mechanisms. Normally, bond repayment occurs when the bond matures and the issuer repays all remaining obligations. Most bonds are redeemable when they mature. At that point the issuing company pays the bondholder the cash value of the bond. Some bonds are redeemable at par, at the holder's option. The par value is the arbitrary initial value that the bond was issued for, and that helps establish its value. These bonds are often sold at a lower interest rate. If the prevailing interest rate for bonds is 10%, the redeemable bonds might pay only 9.5%. The lower interest rate is justified in that the bondholder has the option of redeeming the bond before it matures and is then able to take the proceeds and invest in another bond. If the interest rate increases, then the investor may want to take the proceeds and purchase a bond with a higher rate. If the interest rate declines, the investor still has a bond paying 9.5% interest.

Sometimes a company faces hardships that can force it to pay off the bondholders before the bonds' **maturity**. If interest rates drop several percentage points, a company may not be able to afford the prior interest rate. Normally, changes in interest rates do not affect the maturity date, and the issuer is stuck with the higher rate. But if the bond was issued with a call provision, the issuer can exercise the call provision after a specified number of years. The call allows the issuer to pay the **face value** of the bond plus a fixed payment, such as a year's worth of coupon payments. After a bond is called and paid, the company can issue new bonds at the lower interest rate. Callable bonds have higher interest rates than noncallable bonds to compensate investors for the risk of the bonds being redeemed by the issuer before they mature.

Repayment can be accomplished through the following techniques:

♦ Sinking funds
♦ Serial bonds
♦ Bond redemption before maturity
♦ Convertible bonds

Sinking Funds

Bond repayment can be accomplished through several techniques. The most common technique for repaying a note is to use a sinking fund in which moneys are set aside, either in preset amounts or on a variable basis. For example, a professional team could deposit a preset amount of $1 million a year into a sinking fund account.

The amount can grow to well over $20 million in 20 years, and the funds can be used to repay loans, bonds, and notes as they mature. In certain instances, the price of a bond may decline because the associated interest rates are unfavorable. In those instances, the sinking fund account can be used to buy bonds on the open market and retire them at an earlier date. This practice can save significant interest obligations.

Sinking funds can be created through various means. Annual payments of a fixed amount or a percentage of profit can also be used. Bonds issued for the purpose of acquiring fixed assets could also be retired through the establishment of a sinking fund using annual depreciation allowances for the asset. In that case the tax savings associated with depreciating an asset can be set aside to repay the bond. No matter what approach is used, the key is that a sinking fund is a way to set aside funds to repay the bonds in the future—a much better approach than trying to obtain funds at the last minute when the company wants or needs to buy the bonds back.

Bond Redemption Before Maturity

The sinking fund is a technique that companies can use to redeem bonds. Corporations can also issue newer bonds with more favorable interest rates and use the proceeds to buy older bonds on the open market. Numerous corporations issue bonds on a regular basis in an effort to take advantage of favorable interest rates and avoid the potential effect if interest rates rise. Such bonds often have a call provision to allow the corporation to repurchase the bonds at a moderate premium if interest rates change drastically. Some bonds are **convertibles**, which means that they can be redeemed when the bondholder converts the bonds to stocks (see the next section). Other bonds are retired through retained earnings, the selling of assets, or the issuing of more equity. If all these techniques fail, the corporation can ask the bondholders for a voluntary extension of the bond's maturity date.

As just mentioned, a corporation may issue callable bonds that it can repurchase before the maturity date. If a bond is not callable, there are two other means of repurchasing. The company can purchase a bond on the open market or from a bondholder who is willing to exchange it voluntarily. Note that even if a corporation issues callable bonds, the callable provision typically does not take effect on a 20-year bond until at least the 10th year. Until then, the bondholder is protected from an attempt by the corporation to call the bond when interest rates decline or if the corporation attempts to issue new bonds with a lower interest rate. The protection against having a bond called can encourage larger investors such as life insurance companies to accept a lower yield on the express condition that a bond will not be callable.

Serial Bonds

Serial bonds are a series of bonds issued with maturity dates at predetermined redemption dates. These types of bonds could include $1 million in bonds due in 20 years, and a company can issue such bonds every year for a 10-year period so that the bonds would need to be repaid in a series 20 to 30 years later. Serial bonds for a $50 million bond offering could include $5 million of bond obligations that mature in the 15th year and increased retirement obligations in subsequent years until the final bonds are retired in the 30th year.

Convertible Bonds

Some corporations issue bonds that can be converted to common stock. These bonds are designed to redeem themselves and retire the debt through converting the debt to equity ownership. This approach increases equity ownership while reducing the total corporate debt. Reducing the corporate debt can dramatically increase the corporate credit rating, which can make it easier for the company to borrow additional funds or issue additional bonds. But when a bond is converted to stock, it does not bring any new funds into the business; it merely redistributes debt obligations to owners' equity.

Convertible bonds have some strong benefits for both the issuing company and the potential bond buyer. Buyers often prefer convertible bonds because investors can obtain interest payments on their investment but can also choose to switch to the equity ownership option if the corporation starts to experience significant growth. Buyers might also prefer convertibles because they retain the position of a secured creditor but also have an option to purchase stock. This feature might not be an important reason to purchase the bond, but if the stock price soars, it can suddenly become a key benefit.

Corporations can also benefit from convertibles. When bonds are converted, the conversion usually occurs at a share price that is higher than it would have been if the shares had been purchased earlier. Thus, if the conversion occurs, the corporation can lower its debt obligation by exchanging that obligation for shares that are valued significantly lower on the corporate books. This helps the corporation because it can sell its own shares at a higher rate compared with the bondholder, who might buy stock on the open market that might not directly benefit the corporation. But this benefit is also one of the primary reasons that some corporations do not want to issue convertible bonds. Some corporations do not want to dilute the stockholders' equity. Furthermore, because it is uncertain whether or when a bondholder might wish to convert bonds to stocks, convertible bonds add a degree of uncertainty to the corporation's capital structure.

GOVERNMENT-ISSUED BONDS

Corporations and government entities are the most frequent issuers of bonds. Government-issued bonds for building sports facilities have several unique attributes. Special laws, elections, or referendums are often required for the bonds to be issued. After the legal hurdles have been overcome, numerous additional steps need to be taken, from entering a lease agreement with a professional team to acquiring funds for infrastructure repairs. Also, the various sources of bond repayment must be determined and approved. The following example depicts this complex process.

In 2017, the Atlanta Braves moved into a new ballpark in Cobb Country, Georgia. As part of the financing deal for construction of SunTrust Park, the county agreed to finance approximately $276 million of the construction cost through the issuance of government **revenue bonds**. These bonds are to be repaid over 30 years. The money to repay the revenue bonds will be generated through the following sources:

- $400,000 from a new rental car tax
- $940,000 from an existing hotel and motel tax
- $2.74 million from a new hotel and motel fee

♦ $5.15 million from a property tax increase

♦ $8.67 million from relocation of funds from a preexisting property tax

In total, over 30 years about $870 million will be necessary to repay the $276 million in bonds. The extra expenses are used to cover other finance-related costs such as issuing the bonds and bond insurance. In turn, this feature allowed the bonds to be issued at a lower interest rate (Petchesky, 2013). Interestingly, as construction costs continued to soar, the final estimate was that Cobb Country would contribute over $400 million to the construction project (Snyder, 2017).

Types of Government-Issued Bonds

Numerous types of bonds can be issued in the sport industry. Earlier sections of this chapter cover several types of bonds that can help sport corporations. This section centers on bonds issued by various government entities. Bonds represent the most likely funding source for publicly financed projects such as stadiums and arenas.

Although bonds for stadiums and arenas are the type of bonds most typically studied, sports facilities are low on the list of total expenditures for bond proceeds. Other public projects garner a greater amount of bond money. The greatest amount of funding is directed to school projects. Other major projects funded by bonds include park and recreation departments, convention centers, and administrative offices. Although this section focuses on stadiums and arenas financed with bonds, the same principles that relate to securing and repayment of bonds apply to all projects funded with government-issued bonds. The primary types of bonds considered here are general obligation bonds and revenue bonds. Other financing techniques, such as lease-backed financing (lease revenue bonds) and certificates of participation, can be used by the government entity, which then leases the facility to another government entity or sports authority (Greenberg & Gray, 1996).

General Obligation Bonds

General obligation bonds (GOBs) are among the instruments most commonly used to fund facilities. These bonds are often called **full faith and credit** obligations because the city, county, municipality, state, or other government unit pledges to repay the obligation with existing tax revenues or by levying new taxes. General obligation bonds and other bonds are rated by independent companies such as Moody's and Standard & Poor's based on the issuer's ability to repay the loan. General obligation bonds are often highly rated because currently existing and future sources of tax revenue can be tapped for repayment. **Bond ratings** can be influenced by a multitude of factors, including

♦ the level of coverage (ability to repay the loan with existing revenue streams);

♦ the strength, breadth, and reliability of the tax base;

♦ the historical performance of the revenue stream;

♦ the risk associated with the project;

♦ the underlying economic strength of the stadium or arena or the community;

♦ political volatility; and

♦ whether the project is economically viable.

The strength of the tax base is one of the most important criteria for general obligation bonds. A small city with a low tax base might suffer significantly if property values decrease or sales drop significantly. In contrast, a large city with hundreds of thousands of properties can experience downturns in the economy but still have a large enough tax base that the damage could be minimal.

Raters often look at the purpose of the project and the anticipated long-term benefits. Projects such as Baltimore's Camden Yards or Denver's Coors Field revolutionized the manner in which stadiums were viewed. These stadiums could be seen as catalysts for change that could revitalize an entire downtown community. If the downtown was revitalized, property values would increase. The increased property values would result in higher tax revenue, which would generate additional funds from which to repay bonds.

The Florida Marlins built a stadium in 2009 (which opened in 2012) with a price tag of approximately $525 million, and the stadium was to cost taxpayers more than $2.4 billion in debt service over the next 40 years. The project managers looked at three bond-backing strategies from general obligation bonds to convention center tax-backed bonds and sports tax bonds.

About $91.2 million in convention development tax-backed bonds was to cost almost $1.2 billion in debt service (principal and interest) by 2047. Of the $91.2 million, $80.8 million was structured to go to the stadium. The rest covers expenses such as debt service reserve deposits. An additional $319.3 million in professional sports tax bonds was to be used for the project, which would cost a total $1.3 billion by 2049. The project required an additional $50 million in county general obligation bonds for the stadium. The county commissioners approved up to $563 million in bonds to back the planned ballpark. The county planned to sell about $454.6 million in new and refunding bonds. The total county contribution was estimated at $347 million just for the new stadium. The city of Miami contributed $23 million, and the team owners contributed $155 million. The county had a hard time selling all the bonds within the commission-set 7.5% interest cap. Professional sports tax bonds sold below the ceiling. In contrast, the convention development tax-backed bonds went for nearly 8.2%, yielding proceeds $6.2 million short of what the county was hoping to raise (Polansky, 2009).

Revenue Bonds

A more specific type of bond is the revenue bond; here the tax revenue to support repayment may come from the project itself. For example, an entrance tax of $1 per ticket could be charged, and all revenues from this tax would first be allocated to repaying the revenue bond. These bonds traditionally have a lower credit rating than other bonds because significant financial risks are associated with limiting repayment requirements to a specific tax source. An example of this risk could be an elongated players' strike or owner lockout. If games are not played, revenue from game-related sources such as ticket sales, parking, and concessions is not generated. If bonds are to be repaid from these sources, then the risk of bond default is heightened.

Sometimes a public entity targets a specific tax to finance a bond. Cleveland used a sin tax on alcohol and tobacco sales to help finance Jacobs Field and Gund Arena. The state of Minnesota used a gambling tax–based bond issue to help finance building U.S. Bank Stadium, the home of the NFL's Vikings. **Special tax bonds** are repayable from a specific pledged source and are not backed by the full faith and credit of the issuing entity. Thus, if the specific revenue source is inadequate, tax revenue may be insufficient to repay the bondholders. Tax and revenue anticipation notes can be issued to fund the project before revenue starts arriving. Similarly, a bond anticipation note or tax-exempt commercial paper can help bridge the gap during construction until revenue is generated to repay the interim note and start repaying special tax bonds (Greenberg & Gray, 1996).

Repayment Sources

Whichever type of bond is issued, repayment will always be the key concern for investors. Other factors can be important to a potential investor, such as whether the bond is tax exempt, whether the government entity purchased bond repayment insurance, and whether contractually obligated revenue (COR) is sufficient to repay the bond. Even with these variables, investors will look toward a stable and adequate repayment source as an additional assurance that the bond will be paid. Significant funding sources include (Greenberg & Gray, 1996)

- utility taxes,
- ticket surcharges,
- car rental taxes,
- real estate taxes,
- specific sales taxes,
- possessory interest taxes,
- tourist development taxes,
- restaurant sales taxes,
- excise or sin taxes,
- lottery and gaming revenue,
- nontax fees such as permits,
- general appropriations, and
- general sales and use taxes.

A utility tax, for example, is a cost added to an electric, water, or gas bill to help pay for the debt service of the bond. In the 1990s, the San Francisco Giants were considering a move to San Jose, California. The proposed stadium was to be partially financed by a utility tax. Opponents of the stadium distributed light-switch covers to communicate the idea that every time people turned on the lights, they would be paying for the proposed stadium. The stadium ballot measure was defeated by the strong activists against the tax.

A possessory interest tax designed to tax the primary facility user is charged to whoever possesses control of the facility. Tourist development taxes and car rental taxes are designed primarily to tax out-of-towners who visit the city. This technique is popular because it is easy to tell a voting population that out-of-towners will pay for the facility (Howard & Crompton, 2013).

Excise taxes are general taxes added to various products. Sin taxes are more specifically set up to be added to the cost of alcohol and tobacco products.

Nontax fees are special expenses (e.g., permit costs) passed on to particular parties. Such a tax can stimulate a backlash from citizens who do not want to pay a greater share of the funding for the facility than others are paying. General appropriations are among the most favored funding options. **Appropriations** are funds that are set aside for specific purposes. Through political dealings, a municipality might convince the state legislature or federal government to give an appropriation from the budget to help pay the facility construction expenses or to fund bond repayments. Construction of the San Antonio Alamodome included a bus stop to help secure a federal appropriation for interstate transportation. In March 1994 VIA Metropolitan Transit started collecting a five-year half-percent sales tax to help fund the $197 million construction of the Alamodome in 1990 to 1993.

Although these revenue sources can often support significant repayment obligations, CORs can also provide a significant guarantee that a debt will be repaid. Contractually obligated revenues are any contract whereby a party agrees to pay a specific sum for a guaranteed number of years. Typical long-term contracts that form the basis of COR backing include (Greenberg & Gray, 1996)

- premium seat contracts,
- luxury box contracts,
- concession and novelty rights contracts,
- naming rights contracts,
- pouring rights (beer and soft drink) contracts,
- personal seat licenses, and
- parking rights contracts.

CORs have two primary functions. They can be used as a source of revenue to guarantee repayment of bonds or other loans. They also can be used as an independent funding source. If the bonds are all covered through other revenue streams, the team or facility may be able to sell the naming rights and use those funds to enhance its bottom line.

Two examples will suggest how stadium and arena builders can use a blend of bonds and CORs to finance a stadium. U.S. Bank Stadium in downtown Minneapolis opened in 2016 as the home of the Minnesota Vikings. Its total construction cost was estimated at $1.1 billion. That money was raised through both public and private sources. The Vikings raised about $572 million through sources that included the sale of naming rights and seat licenses, contributions and loans from the NFL, and bank loans. The public sector (the state of Minnesota and city of Minneapolis) contributed the remaining funds. The state of Minnesota contributed $348 million through the issuance of bonds. The bonds are being repaid by a charitable gambling tax and state corporate tax revenue. The state of Minnesota permits and taxes nonprofit organizations to run gambling games such as raffles, pull tabs, bingo, and paddle wheels. The city of Minneapolis contributed $150 million to stadium construction along with $7.5 million annually that goes toward stadium operations and maintenance. The city's costs are being funded through a city-wide sales tax (Roper, 2016).

In another example, the Golden 1 Center is the home of the NBA's Sacramento Kings. The 17,608-seat facility was opened in 2016 at a cost of $558 million. Similar to U.S. Bank Stadium, the Golden 1 Center was funded through a public–private partnership. In this deal, the city of Sacramento generated $273 million through a bond sale. The 35-year bonds had a 5.67 percent interest rate and will be repaid through lease payments, property taxes from the new arena, and increased revenues from city parking meters and garages. The annual debt service on the bonds is about $18 million (Kasler, 2015).

After it has been determined where potential tax revenue can be found to repay the bonds, a public entity considering issuing bonds needs to examine the potential municipal bond rating. Bond ratings for stadium projects are normally fairly high because of the backing of major cities that presumably will not go bankrupt. Lenders, however, have become more leery of these deals in recent years because of the possibility that the oversaturated television market will reduce future broadcast contracts. Lenders can also be concerned when teams and leagues face a multitude of challenges, from fickle fans to legal challenges of league policies. For example, suppose that a public university issues $50 million in bonds to fund new buildings and a new stadium. If bond repayment is tied to student tuition revenue, the university could be in serious trouble if student enrollment decreases significantly. If student tuition drops by 20%, the effect on bonds could be significant, and the lender might speed up the repayment schedule.

CONCLUSION

This chapter highlighted various capital acquisition techniques. Sport businesses, whether for profit or nonprofit, need to acquire funds to keep operating or to expand. Finding capital is often the most difficult task for both new and established businesses.

The ability to reach more potential investors is a major advantage for a company issuing stock. Investors who might never express interest in a company might be willing to gamble and invest a small amount to be part of the ownership team. Large mutual funds could also purchase a large number of shares. No matter who owns the shares, a publicly traded company has greater access to capital than almost all nonpublicly traded companies.

Although shareholders have some obligations and significant rights, a publicly traded company needs to comply with numerous regulations and reporting requirements, which can make the decision to go public unattractive—regardless of how much money could be raised. In fact, because of the quick decisions that often need to be made in sport, public ownership may not be an attractive option. If the issuance of stock is not available as a capital acquisition tool, a company can entertain the idea of issuing bonds.

A significant amount of work is required to issue a bond, and typically only the largest companies do so. Most sport businesses use stock or bank financing rather than bonds. But major privately financed construction projects, such as stadiums or arenas, can be financed through bonds secured by the facilities. Furthermore, stadiums and arenas built with public funds are almost always built using bonds guaranteed by a variety of taxes or revenue streams. Thus, bond financing is often the most visible form of capital acquisition in the sport industry.

Class Discussion Topics

1. Have you ever purchased stocks yourself or been given stocks? If you purchased them yourself, what factors went into buying those shares?

2. Would you ever buy any sport stocks? Why or why not?

3. What sport stocks would you consider purchasing? Why?

4. Have you ever lost money on an investment? Explain what happened and what you learned from the process.

5. Do you think that buying the publicly available shares in the Green Bay Packers is a good investment?

6. Should the general population pay the debt service for bonds issued to pay for a stadium or arena that is used primarily by a privately owned professional team? Debate the topic, citing all the pros and cons associated with the question. What innovative ideas could be used to help repay the bonds?

7. What is the value of bonds versus stocks?

8. What happens when a company defaults on paying a bond?

9. Is a bond a safer investment for an investor than other investing options such as stocks?

Part IV Case Study

Financing a College Football Stadium

While significant attention is often paid to building stadiums and arenas for professional teams, the same cannot be said for some college facilities. There are often contentious political battles between those who want to spend public funds to become or stay a big time sport city and those who do not want to spend scarce public funds to help make a wealthy team owner even wealthier. Similarly, debates often rage around city halls as to whether to put in a new field (whether soccer, football, baseball, etc.) at a local park and whether the financing makes sense. Each facility needs to be built based on financial metrics. For example, a professional sports team might want to build a stadium to increase its revenue stream. It is hoped that such a project would be cash positive. In contrast, a local park might need more fields to meet public demand, and there might not be little or no potential revenue. That project is not motivated by revenue but to serve a perceived public need. As such, the field project would either be cash neutral or, more realistically with maintenance costs, cash negative. It is important to examine the two extremes of a stadium for profit generation and a stadium to benefit stakeholders' nonfinancial needs as a college facility falls in between. A college stadium needs to generate revenue, but it also must meet the needs of a nonprofit educational institution. Every facility project will have some impact on cash flow. Whether it is a city helping to fund a $500 million stadium or spending $500,000 to install a new artificial turf field and drainage system, the impact on a local budget could be significant. The city might have to borrow funds, reallocate funds, issue bonds, or try to find funding from a state or federal government. The budgetary impact could be significant, and that is why there are so many intense battles around building sports facilities with public funds.

Political battles might not be as public with college facilities, but building and operating these facilities is no easy task when it comes to college campuses. There are numerous stakeholders with a vested financial position. If it is a public university, then elected officials might want to promote their benevolence by agreeing to build a new stadium with public funds. Loyal alumni who want the new stadium might chip in. Local businesses might get into the action as well. Those opposed to such an effort might argue that funds are needed for classrooms, labs, or teacher salaries. Others might argue that a large chunk of the expenses will be borne by students who will have higher fees to help subsidize the facility or athletic department. All these arguments are valid and have merit as building a large facility is an expensive undertaking that will affect cash flow for years to come. It is not just the initial building cost that affects cash flow and possible debt service. A majority of the costs associated with the lifetime (typically 30- to 50-year facility life span) cost of a facility will be employee salaries and maintenance costs such as daily cleaning, heating, or electricity. Thus, the decision to build a new stadium has serious financial implications for years to come.

Financial Implications

Wealthy alumni might be able to single-handedly provide a university with enough funds to build and or maintain a stadium. In December 2005, T. Boone Pickens made a $165 million gift to his alma mater, Oklahoma State University. He has given close to $1 billion over the years to the school, including over $265 million to OSU athletics. Due to his donation, the stadium is now called Boone Pickens Stadium.

Not every stadium-related story is such a happy one, and not all schools have a sugar daddy to help them out of trouble. From 2009 to 2013, public universities in the United States reported increasing their annual expenditures on football to more than $1.8 billion, a 21% jump in inflation-adjusted dollars. The latest numbers available from the Knight Commission (Knight Commission, 2013) on Intercollegiate Athletics highlight that Football Bowl Subdivision schools paid on average over $69,000 in yearly debt obligations associated with athletics. Students interested in tracking college sport finance can utilize the Knight Commission's database to critically examine university athletic expenditures (www.knightcommission.org). During the 2009 to 2013 time period, public universities' reported debt on their athletic facilities had grown to $7.7 billion, a 44% jump in inflation-adjusted dollars (Sirota & Perez, 2016). Every year, universities collectively must pay more than a half billion dollars to pay down athletic-related debt—roughly double the annual debt service payments for public universities' athletic facilities from 2008. If revenues from ticket sales, merchandising, and fund-raising do not cover the bills, which is normally the case, students and the general public are on the hook by way of higher student fees, higher tuition, and taxes. This provides less incentive to be accurate with financial projects. This is not meant to imply that universities do not care, but similar to other public projects it is not their money. In contrast, a wife–husband team opening a small fitness studio using their own money would not have large public coffers to bail them out of trouble if financial projections are wrong.

There are several glaring examples of poor financial planning associated with building college facilities. One such example is the University of California, Berkeley, which was trying to reduce athletic subsidies and then took a gamble to increase revenue by expanding sports facilities. UC Berkeley incurred $445 million of debt to renovate its football stadium and build a new student athletic center. The result was weaker-than-expected attendance and ticket sales. The football team suffered a drastic attendance drop to 36,548 fans per game in 2017, a 22% drop from the 2016 average of 46,628 fans. This resulted in a decrease in ticket revenue of close to $200,000 (delos Santos & Weinstein, 2017). Projections were for increases rather than decreases, which made it more difficult for the university to repay the debt it undertook to renovate and build the facilities.

University of Akron Stadium

Some examples of colleges spending to make it big entail smaller schools who want to move up to a higher conference or division. This is a risky gamble. While it has paid off for some schools, it has not for others. As an example, the University of Akron completed construction of a $62 million stadium in 2009. To build the new stadium, several dormitories had to be demolished, and the properties of local tenants were acquired using eminent domain. Displaced students were put into a local hotel converted from an old Quaker Oats Company oat silo and surrounding area purchased for over $22 million. The Zips, who now play at 30,000-seat InfoCision Stadium, reported drawing a total of 55,019 fans for six games (less than 10,000 per game—the lowest in Division I college football, according to the NCAA) in 2014. It was the lowest number reported by the university since 2005, when the team attracted 54,464 and played at their old off-campus stadium named the Rubber Bowl (Armon, 2015). The attendance average for 2016 was 10,337. As of 2013, the school faced more than

Table 1 University of Akron Total Athletic Debt Balances

Year	Debt total
2006	$18,810,873
2007	$15,100,158
2008	$14,342,130
2009	$14,169,365
2010	$84,749,805
2011	$80,607,145
2012	$77,391,565
2013	$73,371,134
2014	$68,086,688
2015	$66,425,689

Source: Knight Commission (2013 and 2018).

$73 million in debts for its athletic facilities. That is part of the more than half-billion in debts which, school officials told local media, has led to layoffs and to higher fees for students. Table 1 highlights the total athletic debt balances owed by the University of Akron athletic department.

In 2013, Akron had annual debt service obligations of $5,267,482. Table 1 shows the potential impact of a major capital expenditure where the debt increased over fivefold from 2009 to 2010 due to building the new stadium. While the university is making payments on the debt obligation, the strain on finances can affect the university's ability to borrow funds for other projects or to spend. Obviously the university felt that an investment in the stadium would produce a positive net cash flow. Maybe it would have helped them gain a coveted invitation to a bigger conference, maybe it could have helped with recruiting, maybe it would have made the student body happy, or maybe it would have made some alumni happy. There are numerous maybes—every financial projection requires some maybes. However, proper financial planning will minimize the maybes and try to find the most likely scenarios. It would be interesting to see if the university undertakes a worst case, most likely, and best case scenario analysis as to future attendance and revenue streams and compare those projections to actual revenue amounts.

Colorado State University Stadium

Akron is not alone in its effort to spend money hoping to generate additional revenue. While the stadium was supposed to help the university move to a better conference, it needed to also generate enough revenue to justify the expenditure. Colorado State University (CSU), in the sleepy city of Fort Collins (population 158,000), decided to spend $238 million to build a new football facility that opened in 2017. With principal and interest payments, the school of 32,000 students will be forced to pay close to $400 million ($12 million every year for over 30 years just for the new stadium and not counting any future repairs or renovations). Even before the facility was planned, the school was already using tuition, student fees, and taxpayer money to subsidize its football program. The expected cost to maintain the new stadium was estimated to be around $3 million a year.

CSU's athletic department, similar to most public universities, operates at a deficit. It spent more than $38 million on operations but generated only $18 million from ticket sales, donations, concessions, and advertisements in 2016. The football program itself ran a $6 million deficit in 2016. An independent analysis by journalists found that from 2012 to 2016, roughly half of CSU's athletic department budget, approximately $83 million, came from student fees and general fund subsidies. Between 2010 and 2014, the amount of CSU student fees going to athletics has jumped 10% (Sirota & Perez, 2016). CSU students pay around $115 in athletics-associated fees every semester. CSU tuition also increased over 130% from 2006 to 2016, while per-athlete spending on football went up by 70%. Such a huge increase in spending is consistent with the larger trend of football-spending increases outpacing academic-spending increases over the past 20 years (Sirota & Perez, 2016).

As with any cash flow analysis, it is not just about the total revenue or expenses. There is a cost to raising capital. In CSU's case, potential construction cost overruns and the lag in $110 million in fund-raising goals could harm CSU's future credit rating. In 2015, Standard & Poor's (a major credit rating agency) downgraded the school's credit outlook to negative. The primary concern was the university's new debt levels. It was initially hoped that in the first two years of fund-raising, the university could find $30 million for the project, but after breaking ground and a year from opening, donors had only committed around $26 million (Sirota & Perez, 2016).

Convention Sports and Leisure International (CSL) issued a market analysis as part of a full financial feasibility study commissioned by CSU in 2012. Feasibility reports are often conducted to ascertain whether a project is feasible, possible financial issues, and what economic impact could be expected. CSL has undertaken hundreds of such reviews for universities and their athletic departments. The CSL report was very positive about the stadium and its potential benefit to the university. Thus, it can be argued whether such reports are appropriate if each and every one of them showed a positive impact for each project (Maxcy & Larson, 2014).

CSL undertook capital budgeting analysis to project low, base, and high revenue projections for the new stadium. CSL's report increased the annual cash flow by 3% each year over the course of the 30-year period to help reflect inflation, even though inflation had not been near 3% in a number of years. It also adjusted its cash flow estimates by assuming a 4% increase in attendance for each of the first five years of the facility's life, which is unrealistic since the normal honeymoon period for a new facility is only one to three years. CSL's projected revenue increases alone led to CSL net stadium revenue projections that would more than double (would increase by 119.5%) for the lowest revenue scenario projection, more than triple (210%) for the base scenario, and more than quadruple (344%) for the high revenue projection (Maxcy & Larson, 2014).

An academic article examined this stadium deal. The researchers examined the net present value and associated discount rates based on some CSL projections. Of course, only time will tell if the feasibility report was anywhere close to being a reliable instrument upon which a major investment could be made. The researchers offered the following two interpretations of the initial capital cost of the investment:

1. The entire cost of $259.05 million was calculated as the sum of the estimated stadium cost plus the estimated cost of the parking and transportation upgrades ($226.5 million + $32.55 million).

2. The initial cost of capital at $146.05 million reflected the university's promised fund-raising goal of $113 million, which was mandated to be raised in gifts and donations before the project was supposed to proceed (Maxcy & Larson, 2014).

The researchers concluded that the financial projections only worked if the most optimistic revenue projections were met and the university was able to work around the lowest chosen discount rate. Thus, only in the most unlikely positive situation would CSL's projection pan out. The article went on to explore how five other college football stadium projects fared (including the University of Akron). The results showed that revenue due to the new stadiums increased between 29% and 86%. These numbers appear impressive, albeit not as generous as CSL had suggested. However, what is often not taken into the consideration with increased revenue is possible increased costs. The stadiums studied each saw stadium expenses increase from 30% to 60%, which would eliminate most purported gains associated with the new stadiums (Maxcy & Larson, 2014). The primary added costs entailed bond repayment obligations for the new or revised stadium.

Besides the economics behind the new stadium, the following list highlights some of CSU's stadium facts by the numbers (Stephens, 2015).

- $220 million—Cost of stadium
- $18.5 million—Cost of the attached 82,975-square-foot academic and alumni center
- 17.56—Acres on campus the stadium occupies
- 41,000—Total capacity, including standing room
- 36,000—Total seats
- 10,000—Seats reserved for students, the same as at CSU's old Hughes Stadium
- 800—Club seats
- 210—Box seats
- 150—Seats in the Ram's Horn Club that provides views of the field and scenery
- 22—Suites with open air seating
- 5—Stadium retail shops
- 9,100—Square footage of the stadium's weight room
- 3,700—Square footage of player lounge

These numbers highlight that the university was more focused on alumni and boosters with less than 25% of the seating capacity dedicated to students. Many other large public universities have a greater percentage dedicated to students, who are helping to foot the bill for the stadium. This could possibly lead to upset students who are paying for the facility but might not be able to enter.

The cost for a season ticket pass for 2017 was $225 for students. Those wanting the premium seats had to join the Ram's Club, which has an added expense of $100 to $500 to receive the opportunity to *purchase* tickets. Approximately 13,000 season tickets were sold for 2017. Also, there was significant attention placed on the stadium's luxury seating. The stadium is small compared to many D-I stadiums in the 60,000-plus range, but the average attendance for 250 D-I programs was around 28,500 in 2016. Can the Fort Collins market sustain so many corporate or wealthy supporters? It might be easier to find such large donors in a big city such as Denver than in a smaller city. That is where having solid contracts in advance can be a significant benefit. Contractually obligated revenue from major donors willing to sign a 10-year lease on a suite, as an example, could help finance the facility or can be used by the lender as collateral to obtain better lending terms.

CSU's new stadium opened in 2017. Attendance for the first game was 37,583. Over the course of the season the attendance average was 31,169 over seven games. The average in 2015 was at a 10-year high of 26,575. Thus, the new stadium drew more fans, but every facility has a honeymoon period drawing new and more fans over the first three years.

An anonymous donor paid $20 million to name the playing field after former coach Sonny Lubick. The university is still seeking a sponsor for the stadium naming rights (Lyell, 2017). That means that the Denver Broncos' Mile High Stadium, Colorado University's Folsom Field (named after a former coach) and CSU's stadium do not have naming rights deals, and the prospects would look very weak for any such future sponsorship. If the university was counting on naming right funds to help cover debt service, it was surely barking up the wrong tree. According to one source, the Rams' stadium project was fully bonded in March 2015 with an array of football revenues (contractually obligated revenue) planned to meet and exceed the annual debt service. Thus, any major gifts or sponsorship deals would be set aside in a stadium rainy-day fund that could be accessed if football revenues dipped, according to the university's athletic director (Frederickson, 2017).

Conclusion

These two detailed examples help show that financial planning can have a variety of uncertainty. Revenue streams might not be enough, and additional cash might be needed. Where such cash comes from can be very controversial. A winning record can sometimes help (CSU's record from 2014 to 2017 was 21-18), but fund-raisers cannot control that. That is why consistent revenue streams are needed. Similarly, programs need to invest to grow and generate more revenue, but adding too much debt can doom even a great program. This case helps highlight why managing cash flow, capital expenditures, and monitoring revenue streams is so important not just for professional sports teams but also collegiate teams.

Class Discussion Topics

1. If you were asked whether a large university such as Tennessee or Michigan, with a large seating capacity in their football stadiums, should build a new football stadium, how would you respond, and what additional information would you need to make this decision?

2. If you overspent on building or renovating a stadium, what can you do after the fact to minimize the damage done by the bad deal?

3. What do you think Akron should do to turn things around and to help repay the bonds issued to build the stadium?

4. Can a university default on a loan or bond repayment, and what could be the ramifications of such an action?

PART V

Financial Statements and Strategic Planning

The fifth part of this book examines financial statements and how sport organizations make decisions that take into consideration various financial issues.

Ralph Willis, the managing partner of EFA Partners, wrote the industry spotlight for this part. His financial consulting expertise has helped raise hundreds of millions for various sport organizations, and he explains where organizations need to focus to actually make money or meet their budget.

Chapter 11 reexamines financial statements (introduced in chapter 3). The chapter provides more depth to help the reader understand the various elements within the balance sheet, income statement, and cash flow statement. The chapter also covers annual reports, which are used to share financial information with stakeholders.

Chapter 12 explores financial planning. After an organization has developed a budget and studied all financial statements, it needs to develop a plan for the future. Financial plans are based in part on financial forecasting, which explores what might occur in the future by examining what has happened in the past. Besides planning, this chapter explores several managerial accounting concepts that help an organization run more effectively, including the balanced scorecard and triple bottom line.

One way to explore a corporation's financial performance is through financial ratios. Chapter 13 explores financial ratios and other tools that can be used to determine whether a corporation is doing well. Financial ratios can help an organization compare its performance over various periods or compare its results to those of similar corporations.

Chapter 14 focuses on moving from strategy to action. It is one thing to develop a plan; it is another thing to actually execute the plan successfully. Successful execution is very difficult, and the sport landscape is filled with companies that have failed. This chapter covers how to create a sport organization, how to expand that organization, and how to dissolve the organization if necessary. The entire business life cycle is covered.

Part V ends with a case study that explores how several industries have undergone very difficult situations. The music industry, circuses, and theme parks are all examples of industries that have undergone significant changes, and the sport industry can learn from these challenges.

Ralph Willis

Founder and Managing Partner of EFA Partners

In early 2009, my two business partners and I founded EFA Partners, a financial advisory firm in New York and Atlanta that provides financial consulting services for entertainment and media companies such as arranging senior debt and junior capital. In addition, we advise on mergers and acquisitions, and we complete comprehensive industry analyses. The first year of our business was difficult given the economic decline in 2009, but we have now been retained by over 125 clients and have advised and arranged for over $3 billion of capital. Our clients are in many sectors including motor sport, movie theaters, water parks, family entertainment centers, film services, digital media, and television.

Prior to forming EFA, I had almost 25 years of experience in the financial sector with various New York–based companies. I graduated from the Whitman School of Management at Syracuse University with a bachelor of science degree in marketing and also attained the chartered financial analyst designation from the CFA Institute, both of which provided me with a strong foundation to build my career.

I started my finance career in the mid-80s and have held various positions with CIS Corporation, Gilman Financials Services, and Heller Financial. In 2001, I joined GE Capital after that company acquired Heller Financial. In 2004, GE acquired NBC Universal, and a group of us put together a business plan to form a new financing unit within GE Capital dedicated to financing entertainment and sport as an alignment with NBC Universal. This plan resulted in the formation of GE Capital's Sports & Entertainment Group in early 2004. I led that group as managing director from its formation through to 2009. We closed transactions across numerous sectors including sports (such as the National Hockey League, the National Football League, Major League Baseball, and the National Basketball Association), movie theaters, digital cinemas, theme parks, water parks, family entertainment centers, casinos, ski resorts, film production, and film services.

Over the years, I have been involved in closing and managing finance transactions across numerous sports and entertainment sectors and advised a wide variety of companies ranging from small start-up ventures to large mature companies. These organizations typically need financing for working capital, equipment purchases, refinancing existing loans, and acquisitions. Transaction sizes have ranged from $1 million to over $200 million.

Given my finance career, it's been imperative for me to fully understand the analysis of historical financial statements as well as projections. However, even if you foresee a different career path, an understanding of financial statements is still important to provide the ability to analyze the strength of your own company, competitors' businesses, and industries as a whole. All too often, I've met with management teams who have great passion for their businesses but are surprisingly unsophisticated with financial statement analysis, preparing projections, and understanding the ongoing financial needs of their businesses.

With this in mind, there are many key aspects of analyzing financial statements (balance sheets, income statements, and cash flow statements) that should be part of your business foundation. These include the following:

1. *Closely examining the financial statements.* While it's important to understand the basics of assets, liabilities, equity, revenue, expenses, and the general outlook these can provide for a business, it's also just as important, if not more so, to be able to more closely examine the financial statements and ascertain the true prospects of a business.

2. *Considering the source of the data.* The very first item to check when analyzing financial statements is the source of the data. Statements that have been certified by an accounting firm are much more reliable than statements from a company's management team. An accounting firm's analysis of company financial statements should ensure that there are no mistakes (or, in rare instances, fraud) in the statements. Even when an accounting firm has certified the statements, it should be checked to determine if the accounting firm conducted a full audit or only conducted a review. While reviewed statements are more reliable than internally prepared statements, the accounting firm's scope is less extensive when it is only preparing reviewed statements.

3. *Having a specific focus.* When reviewing financial statements, it's good to have a specific focus, whether it's to examine the company's working capital needs, its ability to pay its loan obligations,

its long-term equity value, or, in some instances, all of these. Good starting points are equity value on the balance sheet and net profit on the balance sheet; however, true analysis needs to go much, much further.

4. *Being aware of generally accepted accounting principles' limitations.* While generally accepted accounting principles (GAAP) rules are good as they provide a common methodology for preparing financial statements to make it easier for comparing companies, there are many aspects of GAAP rules such as depreciation, **amortization**, goodwill, and leases that can result in the financial statements not providing the full picture of a company's strengths or weaknesses.

5. *Using earnings before interest, taxes, depreciation, and amortization (EBITDA) to analyze profitability.* A common measure of a company's strength is EBITDA. This is not a GAAP accounting measure, but it is often utilized to analyze profitability. Enterprise values are often based on a multiple of EBITDA with such multiples varying by industry. For example, companies in mature industries such as movie theatres and restaurants may be valued at 6 to 10 times EBITDA while companies focused on new technologies may be valued at well over 10 times.

6. *Reviewing items that affect cash flow.* Determining short-term working capital needs are essential for any business analysis so it's important to review accounts payable, accounts receivable, and all other items that can affect operating cash flow. Financial ratios that measure company liquidity such as the current ratio (currents assets compared to current liabilities) will assist in this analysis; however, additional analysis is needed such as the amount of cash available to meet near-term needs or identifying potential bad accounts that make it unlikely that certain accounts receivable will actually be received. In addition, review whether relatively few customers make up a disproportionately large percentage of the company's revenue. In such cases, losing one customer could have a significant impact on the company.

7. *Analyzing capital expenditure needs.* An analysis of short- and long-term capital expenditures needs is also key to determining potential future outlays of cash to replace or grow the asset base. In this regard, it is important to review management's budget and projections (neither found in the financial statements) to determine their view of the capital needed to meet their goals.

8. *Reading the footnotes.* Read the footnotes. Read the footnotes. The numbers in a financial statement only tell part of the story. The footnotes are needed to determine the details, calculations, and assumptions behind the numbers. Items such as the details for loans (interest rates and maturity), ongoing lease payments due for property and equipment, and many other items will be disclosed in the footnotes, not on the balance sheet or income statement.

9. *Meeting with management teams.* After an assessment of the financial statements and related information, it's also important to meet with company management teams if they are accessible and willing to discuss the company history and future outlook. During such discussions, it's important to be prepared with a specific agenda and specific questions since such discussions need to be focused and relatively short as management teams are busy running their businesses.

As an example to illustrate the previous list, one of our clients operated entertainment venues in much of the United States. Based on an initial review of the financial statements, revenue and profits seemed good and debt obligations were relatively low. Then, upon a more in-depth examination, there were a few items that provided a different outlook for the company, as follows:

- Property rent for its many sites was shown on the income statement based on GAAP accounting rules rather than the actual cash paid.
- Over 20% of the company's EBITDA was needed for annual capital expenditures to maintain revenue.
- About 20% of the company's sites generated over 70% of total EBITDA.

Even with these items, the company remained viable and profitable, but the detailed review provided a different picture than the initial review.

As another example, one of our clients in the film production sector had growing revenue and EBITDA; however, from a more in-depth analysis of the company and during discussions with management, the following was learned:

- Over 75% of EBITDA was needed for capital expenditures.
- These capital expenditures were needed just to maintain, not grow, current revenue and EBITDA levels.

The capital expenditures were not anticipated to continue for the long term but did change the near-term outlook for the company.

Whatever your career path, it's essential to have a solid foundation of financial statement analysis to provide insight on your own business needs or analyzing the strengths or weaknesses of other businesses in your sector. In the end, after all of your financial statement reviews, it is also essential to speak with management teams to understand their backgrounds, the company history, and the prospects of the business.

Reprinted by permission from Ralph Willis.

Financial Statements

Chapter Objectives

After studying this chapter, you should be able to do the following:

- Identify the key elements of the balance sheet and income statement.
- Discuss the cash flow statement as it relates to the income statement and the balance sheet.
- Understand the importance of communicating the key elements from financial statements.
- Discuss how sports managers can use information from financial statements to communicate both internally and externally to various stakeholders.
- Understand the key elements of an annual report and its utility.

Financial statements are essentially report cards for your business. The information contained within financial statements is compiled using generally accepted accounting procedures (GAAP). A business should strive to continually update its financial statements to capture fluctuations in the economy, financial markets, and the business itself. To achieve success in their ventures, sports managers must know how to analyze financial statements and develop skills in financial forecasting and planning. In this chapter, we will discuss the key parts of financial statements and the subsequent benefit of analyzing these financial statements to help managers further understand the health and viability of a business. In addition, we describe the basic accounting statements that businesses use for reporting purposes. The techniques we discuss are critical for starting new businesses, investing in new equipment, and making appropriate operating decisions. This chapter addresses the following key concepts underlying financial analysis:

♦ Understanding the types of financial statements

♦ Understanding financial statements

♦ Reading an annual report

TYPES OF FINANCIAL STATEMENTS

Similar to how a team's general manager will review statistics of an organization's players to help determine player productivity, financial managers will use financial statements that are compiled from a firm's accounting records to assess how a company is performing. These financial statements include the balance sheet, income statement, and statement of cash flows. While no one individual financial statement provides all of the meaningful information, when examined collectively, they do provide relevant information to various stakeholders. Financial statements are intended to deliver information about a business in a consistent manner as a result of efforts by accountants to follow GAAP.

Two private organizations, the American Institute of Certified Public Accountants and the Financial Accounting Standards Board, as well as the Securities and Exchange Commission, an agency of the federal government, are the authoritative bodies determining GAAP. For example, GAAP establish policies concerning how to categorize depreciation or to properly record losses. Although GAAP are considered appropriate standards, they were criticized because of loopholes that allowed accounting scandals involving such companies as Enron, WorldCom, and Wells Fargo to occur. Consequently, Congress passed the Sarbanes-Oxley Act in 2002 to ensure the financial operations of public companies were more transparent to the investing public. One significant element of this new legislation prohibited auditors from doing consulting work for their auditing clients to alleviate any conflict of interest. Following this legislation and the ease which information for publicly traded companies is readily available, individual businesses would be applauded to be as transparent as possible in presenting their financial information.

The **balance sheet** displays the financial condition of a business at a single point in time, presenting information about assets, liabilities, and **owners' equity**. Comparatively, the **income statement** describes a business' operating performance and more specifically, profit or loss over a given length of time, such as a month, quarter, or year. Finally, the **statement of cash flows** indicates how the cash position of a business has changed over a given period. For example, the firm may see its cash position depleted through the purchase of machinery or supplies or by paying down debt or by paying **dividends** to **stockholders** The statement of cash flows can be used to determine what happened to the business' cash. When examining financial statements, remember that *sales* and *revenues* are identical terms; *profits*, *earnings*, and *income* are the same; but *costs* refers to money spent on manufacturing a product or service, whereas expenses refers to money spent on developing, producing, selling, and managing the product or service.

Balance Sheet

The balance sheet is used by accountants to give a snapshot of the business at a single point in time, as if the business was stationary. Here is the basic equation all balance sheets follow:

Assets = Liabilities + Owners' equity

The asset or left side of the balance sheet (debit side) lists what a company owns; the right side (credit side) indicates how the assets were financed. Given the preceding equation, when any two variables of the equation are known, we can always solve for the third using basic math. For example, when a company purchases new equipment with cash, cash is reduced on the asset side of the ledger while property is increased under long-term assets. Comparatively, if this same equipment is purchased with credit, then we need to make two entries on the balance sheet; one entry would be to increase equipment on the assets side and the other entry would be to increase accounts payable on the credit side. Obligations to creditors are known as liabilities.

The balance sheet lists assets of the firm according to the length of time needed to convert them to cash (**liquidity**). The asset side is normally determined by the nature of the business, the industry it operates in, and financing and operational decisions made by management. In many businesses, management has to decide whether sales are cash or credit transactions, whether equipment should be purchased or leased, and whether cash balances should remain as cash or be invested in short-term securities to earn a **return**.

The entries listed under current assets are the most liquid because they are expected to be converted to cash within one year or less—or it already is cash. Cash is the ultimate measure of an organization's short-term purchasing power and ability to pay **short-term debt**. Other current assets include **accounts receivable (A/R)**, consisting of the dollar amounts not yet collected from customers for goods and services sold to them (after adjustments for bad debts). Inventory consists of raw materials used for manufacturing, work in process, or finished goods. Because inventory can include unfinished goods, some inventory can be categorized as not liquid. Fixed assets are the assets on the balance sheet with the least liquidity that are expected to last longer than a year. These assets include property, plant, and equipment. *Property, plant, and equipment (PPE)* is a term describing an account on the balance sheet. The PPE account is a summation of all a company's purchases of property, manufacturing plants, and pieces of equipment to that point in time, less any amortization.

Unlike current assets, fixed assets normally are not converted to cash for such day-to-day activities as meeting payroll or paying vendors. The balance sheet also lists intangible assets including goodwill and patents. These assets are not physical in nature but do have real value. For example, a business such as the Coca-Cola Company has become a worldwide global business in part because of its brand-name recognition. Although brand recognition is not a tangible asset, its positive effects on bottom-line profit are the driving force behind Coca-Cola's annual global sales.

A 2017 balance sheet for apparel company Under Armour (UA) is shown in appendix A. Here we can see how assets are equal to liabilities plus owner's equity:

$$\text{Assets} = \text{Liabilities} + \text{Owner's equity}$$
$$\$3,644,000,000 = 1,613,000,000 + \$2,031,000,000$$

Most of the current assets consist of accounts receivables, cash, inventories, and cash equivalents. UA also reports prepaid expenses such as insurance premiums as a current asset. Prepaid expenses are listed as an asset because the good or service has been paid for but not yet received by UA and is expected to earn income for the company in the future. UA reports equipment and property as fixed assets.

Liabilities consist of the obligations the company owes to creditors for products and services purchased. They are listed in the order in which they must be paid. Current liabilities (bills to vendors, interest and principle) consist of obligations that must be paid down within a year, and long-term liabilities (such as land leases, mortgages, deferred income taxes, and some loans) will take longer to be repaid. Accounts payable is generally the largest category of short-term liabilities. The liabilities and stockholders' equity (capital provided by investors) typically reflect decisions about the sources of financing for the business. Therefore, decisions concerning the mix of financing provided by debt versus stockholders' equity, as well as short-term versus long-term debt financing, are reflected in the entries shown in the liabilities and stockholders' equity section of the balance sheet.

UA's primary current liability is accounts payable—unpaid bills sent to vendors. In addition, UA lists the current portion of its long-term debt as a current liability because it must be paid within the year. Because Under Armour is not required to pay all of its long-term debt immediately, it discloses exactly how much of it must be paid in the current year and reports that amount as a current liability. For UA, the investment in the business by its owners is denoted by the term *stockholders' equity*.

The **net working capital**, or working capital, of any business is current assets less current liabilities. When net working capital is positive, the firm expects the cash paid out over the next year will be less than the cash that will become available over the next year. UA had positive net working capital of $1.279 billion in 2016 and $1.020 billion in 2015, representing an increase of $259 million in net working capital, indicating the company's short-term assets have been exceeding the company's short-term obligations. Positive net working capital is an indication of strong liquidity. Strong liquidity means that UA has the cash available to pay bills, expand operations, or sign endorsement deals with new athletes. A lack of liquidity is one of the most frequent causes for a sports organization to fail.

Income Statement

The income statement measures a business' profitability over a specific period—such as a year or a quarter—and is also called the profit and loss statement. Similarly, the income statement is a report card for a business as it is issued from time to time and gives an overview of how the business is doing for that time period. Since this statement reflects business activity over time (not like the balance sheet, which is a snapshot of a business for one segment in time), it is usually developed monthly, quarterly, and annually. Specifically, the income statement will show

- if sales (revenues) are going up or down,
- the gross profit—how much money remains for the business after deducting what it costs to produce or purchase the product,
- all expenses for the time period covered,
- increases and decreases in net income,
- how much money is left to grow the business, and
- how much money is left for the owner(s).

Also, while the income statement does report income generated over a specific time period, the true earnings or profits reported can fluctuate, perhaps seasonally. A baseball team, for example, will typically have several months where income levels are much higher than months during the off season.

Income is defined as follows:

$$Income = Revenue - Expenses$$

Under Armour's income statement is shown in appendix A.

The income statement typically consists of three sections. The first section includes the revenues and expenses from the company's operations. Second, a nonoperating section of the income statement includes financing costs and any income earned by financial investments. For UA, the interest expense represents financing costs. Typically, the nonoperating section of the income statement includes all taxes paid by the enterprise. The third section of the income statement is the net income of the business.

Under GAAP, revenue is generated when an exchange of goods or services occurs. In addition, revenues and expenses are reported when they occur, although cash inflows or outflows may or may not have occurred. For example, when goods and services are sold for credit, associated sales and profits are reported even if payment has not yet been received. This system is known as **accrual basis accounting** as opposed to **cash basis accounting**, in which revenues and expenses are not recognized until actual cash inflows and outflows occur.

The value of a firm's assets is linked to the future incremental cash flows that they will generate, but cash flows do not show up on the income statement. As a result, some expenses appearing on the income statement are not actual cash outlays. One such expense is depreciation. Depreciation represents an estimate by the firm's accountants of the cost of equipment and property that are used up by the organization in the process of producing and distributing goods and services.

Companies report as the cost of goods sold those expenses that are directly related to the production and distribution of goods and services. Such costs include raw materials, direct labor, and manufacturing overhead. Other costs are allocated by the accountants preparing the financial statements to the period covered by the income statement. Such costs are reported separately as selling costs and as general and administrative costs. For example, a team with a call center to sell tickets might have additional selling costs while adding an extra secretary would be an administrative cost.

UA has a noncash expense related to the amortization of its property, plant, and equipment and intangible assets. Intangible assets are nonphysical fixed assets of the business that provide value, such as patents, licenses, trademarks, and copyrights (Investopedia, n.d.). Unless one is ready to assume an intangible asset has unlimited life for accounting purposes, amortization must be claimed over a reporting period because of either obsolescence or the wearing out of the intangible asset. As with depreciation, this amortization of intangible assets does not result in a cash outflow for UA. While the balance sheet and income statement are generally acknowledged to be the two most prominent financial statements, the statement of cash flows also plays an important role and will be discussed in the next section.

Statement of Cash Flows

The statement of cash flows summarizes a firm's cash flows resulting from operations, financing activity, and investment activity. Financial statements are important due to their ability to provide information about an organization's cash flows. Cash flows for investors adds value to the firm. By *cash flows*, we are referring to cash flowing into the business as well as to cash flowing out of the business. As a reminder of the distinction between cash flows and accounting measures of income, income statements include noncash expenses such as depreciation.

The amount of depreciation reported on a business' income statement has no effect whatsoever on the cash generated by the business. When the business reports depreciation, the dollar amount reported as depreciation is not directly paid to any vendors or employees, as would be the case with other operating expense categories. The statement of cash flows is a financial statement that reports changes in a company's cash holdings over a particular period. Tracking cash for a business is an important part of the business operation particularly with newer

companies. As an example, when a business has early success with a product it may hire more employees, expand too quickly, and purchase additional inventory. However, if the product's demand begins to fade faster than expected, this can create financial stress on a company. Under Armour's statement of cash flows is shown in appendix A.

Under Armour has three primary sources of cash flows as a result of business activities. These include cash flows from operating activities, cash flows from investing activities, and cash flows from financing activities. Cash flow refers to the difference between what a company brings in and what it pays out. Thus, cash flow from operating activities refers to both positive and negative cash flows resulting from the firm's basic operating activities. These include operating revenues less all operating expenses other than noncash operating expenses, such as depreciation. When a firm earns revenue, positive cash flows occur, whereas cash expenses such as payments to a manufacturer are associated with negative cash flows. In addition, operating cash flows include the positive cash flows resulting from increasing current liabilities (other than short-term debt) and the negative cash flows associated with increases in current assets (other than cash).

The cash flows associated with financing activities are cash flows to and from **creditors** and owners. Such cash flows include changes in the firm's debt and equity. When the firm increases its borrowings, it creates a positive cash flow. By comparison, paying off a loan results in negative cash flow. When dividends are paid out to stockholders, negative cash flow occurs, whereas proceeds from stock issues result in positive cash flow. When a sports team receives its share of a national television deal, a positive cash flow occurs.

Most companies choose to use the indirect method of cash accounting, and UA is no exception. Rather than add up every cash revenue and expense, the indirect method begins with the year's net income, adds back noncash expenses, and deducts noncash revenues. This approach saves considerable time and effort because all the cash revenues and expenses are already accounted for in the net income figure.

UA reported positive cash flows from operating activities for the years ending December 31,

2015 and December 31, 2016. The cash flows from investing activities are associated with the business' making additions to fixed assets. Purchases of current and fixed assets lead to negative cash flow resulting from the use of cash to purchase those assets. When current and fixed assets are reduced (e.g., sold) during the year, a positive cash flow occurs because of the cash generated by the sale of the assets. In addition, when current liabilities are increased, a positive cash flow occurs from investing activities because of the postponement of cash use.

In this section, we introduced the three primary financial statements including the balance sheet, income statement, and statement of cash flows. We discussed the elements of the balance sheet, which summarizes the firm's financial condition at a particular point in time, and the contents of the income statement, used to measure the profitability of a business over a specified period. The balance sheet and the income statement provide a lead-in to explain changes in the cash position of a firm over a given period. Specifically, we described changes in cash flows resulting from operations, investing activity, and financing. The elements of the balance sheet and income statement are used to compute financial ratios summarizing the firm's liquidity, activity, financial leverage, profitability, and market value.

Understanding the information contained in financial statements is critical to projecting future profits. When we forecast future sales and profits, we make various assumptions requiring extensive analysis of company financial statements, as well as knowledge of typical financials in the industry the company represents. This analysis is especially important because sales and profit forecasts are used in the planning process to determine capital needs and break-even sales.

FINANCIAL STATEMENT ANALYSIS

Interpreting the key elements of financial statements allows management to evaluate areas of growth and opportunity while also identifying concerns about the overall future stability of the business. Financial statement analysis is an evaluative process used to estimate current and past financial positions and the subsequent results of an enterprise. Similarly, the primary objective is to determine the best possible predictions about the future. This is accomplished by the grouping and analysis of information provided by financial statements to establish relationships and identify strengths and weaknesses of a business. Additional implications complement the decision making involving comparison with other firms (cross-sectional analysis) and with a firm's own performance over a time period (time series analysis).

Financial analysis is the selection, calculation, and understanding of financial data to help managers choose investments and guide decision making affecting their respective organizations. Specifically, financial analysis examines the relationship among data contained in several financial statements and the subsequent interpretation to gain insight into the profitability and operational efficiency of the firm. Likewise, financial analysis may also be used to evaluate employees, efficiency of operations, and external business operations such as borrowing money or interactions with creditors. In order to achieve success in their ventures, sports managers must know how to analyze financial statements and subsequently be able to tell a story. While seeing the different classifications of assets is important in terms of understanding what a company owns, examining the role these assets play in the company's long-term financial position is possibly more important.

Interpreting Financial Statements

Financial statements provide significant value to both internal and external stakeholder groups. Moreover, the ability to effectively communicate the information contained in these statements is an important skill, and organizations would be well served to ensure those individuals who are responsible for disseminating key financial information are adequately prepared to do so. Internal constituents include management, while external stakeholders include stockholders, analysts, customers, suppliers, and creditors. Internal uses might include planning, evaluating, and controlling company operations while external practices might include assessing past performance and current financial position, as well as subsequently making predictions about the future profitability and solvency of the company and evaluating the effectiveness of management. Specifically:

- *Investors.* Current and future investors in a company evaluate if the company is a good investment. If a company's financials and performance indicate the company is a worthy investment, the investor can expect a good rate of return by sharing in the company's profits. In addition, investors will monitor the financial performance of a business because it is important to know when to sell a losing investment, and investors could be limiting themselves by tying up capital that could be invested in more attractive opportunities. Investors should pay close attention to signals given by key company executives, ratings provided by analysts, and reviewing the financial statements of companies.

- *Creditors.* Creditors want to know if a company is a good risk to loan money to and if the company will be able or likely to pay a loan back in a timely manner. If a company defaults on a loan, that is a bad risk for the creditor; if the company pays back the loan plus the interest, the creditor receives a profit.

- *Customers.* Customers are concerned about a company's financial health because they want to ensure the company will be sustainable if they plan to continue purchasing products. In addition, customers prefer to do business with a company that will be able to service the products purchased. Prudent customers considering engaging in a long-term relationship with a company and planning to purchase high volumes may ask for financials to determine whether or not such a relationship is advisable.

- *Suppliers.* Suppliers look to build long-term relationships with their customers and want to align themselves with financially sound companies they can grow with and bring added value to the products they sell. Furthermore, suppliers can often attract investors or impress creditors by their customer list.

Industry analysts and fund managers advise others as to whether or not to invest in a company. The information they provide can give them satisfied customers and greater credibility as industry analysts. These examples illustrate how various stakeholders may be interested in the financial health and reporting of a company. Consequently, sports managers should understand the importance of carefully and accurately prepared financial statements as they affect the ability of a company to do business, receive credit, and attract investors and customers.

Management can benefit from financial statement analysis to help determine which distribution channels are the most cost effective. Owners assess financial information from their operations to gauge whether their business is profitable and in some regards assess whether to exit the business altogether. Investors in the business rely on certain information to assist with deciding if and when the time is good to buy, sell, or hold their shares of stock. Finally, creditors are interested in knowing the overall financial health of their partners to ensure they are able to honor their payments when due.

When assessing a company's financial statements there are several questions to consider. While the following list is not exhaustive, some of these questions might be:

- How is the company distinguishing itself from the competition?
- How does it compete? For example, on price, quality, responsiveness, and availability?
- Is the company's strategy viable given the marketplace economy?
- Is management adapting its strategy to a changing environment?
- Is the business model sustainable?

Limitations of Financial Statements

Financial statements are normally prepared on the basis of accounting principles, settlements, and past experiences. Consequently, they do not communicate key firm information such as profitability, solvency, stability, or liquidity, and financial statements virtually ignore qualitative information. With some businesses, the intellectual knowledge, brand equity, and customer relationships are significant value-added qualitative factors. Furthermore, despite the various policies to help provide some measure of consistency among various businesses, there are still many conventional reporting techniques that can vary how a particular financial statement is composed. The following are among the limitations:

- *Verifiability.* An audit provides reasonable but not absolute guarantees of the accuracy of the financial statements.
- *Use of historical cost.* Using historical cost to measure assets fails to account for changes in values over time. This causes the relevance of accounting information to be subjective, because the assets may be significantly less valuable today.
- *Measurability.* Financial statements cannot account for nonmonetary resources. Some of these, such as goodwill, cannot be assigned a numeric value.
- *Predictive value.* Because financial statements present the accounting snapshot of a company in a previous time period, there is limited insight for future prospects and predictive value essential for investors.
- *Timing.* Financial statements can be reported monthly, quarterly, or annually. In addition, the numbers are often listed in different denominations (hundreds, thousands, or millions) or percentages.

Horizontal analysis is the comparison of the financial information of a company with historical information of the same company over a number of reporting periods (Accounting Coach, 2018). For example, an analyst examining the short-term performance of UA may examine annual balance sheets from three to five consecutive years in order to make informed decisions. Similarly, this historical information can be used to compare and contrast financial trends within the organization and subsequently allow management to make necessary adjustments to help keep the business viable.

Comparatively, vertical analysis reports each amount on a financial statement as a percentage of another item (table 11.1). For example, the vertical analysis of the balance sheet indicates every amount on the balance sheet is restated to be a percentage of total assets. Therefore, if inventory is $150,000 and total assets are $1,000,000 then inventory is presented as 15% ($150,000 divided by $1,000,000). As another example, if cash is $100,000, then it will be presented as 10% ($100,000 divided by $1,000,000). The total of the assets will add up to 100%. This type of analysis allows an analyst to compare the operating and financing characteristics of two companies of different sizes in the same industry. Thus, common size statements are useful for both intrafirm comparisons over different years

Table 11.1 Vertical Analysis of the Balance Sheet

	Totals ($)	Percentage
Cash	100,000	10
Accounts receivable	350,000	35
Inventory	150,000	15
Total current assets	600,000	60
Fixed assets	400,000	40
Total assets	1,000,000	100
Accounts payable	180,000	18
Accrued liabilities	70,000	7
Total current liabilities	250,000	25
Notes payable	300,000	30
Total liabilities	550,000	55
Capital stock	200,000	20
Retained earnings	250,000	25
Total equity	450,000	45
Total liabilities and equity	1,000,000	100

and also for making interfirm comparisons for the same year or for several years.

The information provided by this balance sheet format is useful for noting changes in a company's investment in working capital and fixed assets over time, which may indicate an altered business model that requires a different amount of ongoing funding.

Some of the more common types of financial analyses include the following:

▶ *Comparative statements.* These statements show the profitability and financial position of a firm for different periods of time in a comparative form to give insights about two or more periods. Generally, this applies to two financial statements—the balance sheet and the income statement. However, the financial data will only be comparative when the same accounting principles are used in preparing these statements. This analysis is an example of a horizontal analysis.

▶ *Trend analysis.* This is a technique of studying the operational results and financial position over a series of years. By using the data of a business' previous years, trend analysis can show percentage changes over time. The trend percentage is the percentage relationship, in which each item is compared from each year to the same item in the base year. Trend analysis is an important tool because of its long-run view and helps identify where fundamental changes in the business are happening. For high-growth companies, this is an area that managers should carefully monitor. For example, Under Armour experienced significant increase in annual sales in its first few years as it grew and increased its market share. However, these annual increases are generally short term due to consumer demand, competitors, and changes in market demand.

▶ *Ratio analysis.* This type of analysis describes the significant relationship existing among various items of a balance sheet and a firm's statement of profit and loss. As a technique of financial analysis, accounting ratios measure the comparative significance of the individual items on the financial statements. Table 11.2 is an example of the market cap and current ratio of several related companies. Market cap is one metric to value a company and is calculated by taking the number of outstanding shares by the shares price. The current ratio is calculated by taking current assets divided by current liabilities.

ANNUAL REPORTS

Annual reports are formal financial statements published annually and distributed to company stockholders and other interested stakeholders. Investors today have easy access to annual reports through the Internet. An annual report assesses the year's operations and discusses the company's view of the upcoming year, the market, and future prospects. Both for-profit and nonprofit organizations produce annual reports. Annual reports have been a Securities and Exchange Commission (SEC) requirement for publicly owned businesses since 1934, and companies meet this requirement in many ways. An annual report includes the following basics:

♦ A general description of the industry in which the company is involved

♦ Audited statements of income, financial position, and cash flow, with notes that provide details for various line items

♦ A brief description of the company's business in the most recent year

Table 11.2 Competitive Comparison Data

Ticker	Company	Market cap	Current ratio
UA	Under Armour, Inc.	$7,760.61	2.31
RL	Ralph Lauren Corp.	$6,865.05	2.54
HBI	Hanes Brands, Inc.	$8,773.00	2.01
PVH	PVH Corp.	$9,590.63	1.93
CRI	Carter's, Inc.	$4,088.87	3.19
COLM	Columbia Sportswear Co.	$4,036.26	3.67
UNF	UniFirst Corp.	$2,840.41	4.67

- Information related to the company's various business segments
- A list of the company's directors and executive officers
- The market price of the company's stock and information about dividends paid
- A letter from senior management

Some companies provide only the minimum information necessary to be in compliance with SEC regulations. Such annual reports are usually only a few pages in length and are produced relatively inexpensively. The final product often resembles a photocopied document. For these companies, the primary purpose of an annual report is simply to meet legal requirements and do so in the most cost-efficient way.

Other companies view their annual report as a potentially effective marketing tool to disseminate their perspective on the company fortunes. Thus, many midsize and large companies spend significant money making their annual reports as attractive and informative as possible. In such instances, the annual report becomes a forum through which a company can inform, influence, opine, and discuss any number of issues and topics.

An opening Letter to Shareholders section often dictates the tone of annual reports prepared for publicly held companies. This section typically focuses on the past year's results, strategies, market conditions, significant business events, new management and directors, and company initiatives. The chairman of the board of directors, the chief executive officer, the president, the chief operating officer, or a combination of these four usually sign the letter on behalf of company management. Although some of these letters may run a dozen or more pages and include photographs of the CEO, the majority of these letters are significantly shorter. The annual letters written by Warren Buffett, generally recognized as perhaps the greatest investor ever, have become an industry standard. Buffett's letter in the Berkshire Hathaway annual report is always brutally honest in his assessment of both the company's performance and his leadership. He identifies both strengths and weaknesses of the company and refuses to turn his letter into a marketing document.

Under Armour's 2016 annual report is an impressive 112-page document (http://investor.underarmour.com/annuals.cfm). The report begins by showcasing several iconic athletes who endorse Under Armour, including two-time NBA champion Stephen Curry, five-time Super Bowl champion Tom Brady, and three-time major golf champion Jordan Spieth. Next, there is a letter from CEO and company founder Kevin Plank. He highlights the company's 20th anniversary in 2016 and mentions various new partnerships and business agreement.

Promoting a long, successful track record is often appealing to shareholders and various audiences, because it connotes reliability and quality. Some companies have developed traditional formats for their annual reports, with little deviation from year to year except data updates. Whatever the theme, concept, or format, the most successful reports clearly delineate a company's strategies for profitable growth and cast the firm in a favorable light.

Current shareholders and potential investors remain the primary audiences for annual reports. But employees (who may also be shareholders), customers, suppliers, community leaders, and the entire community are also targeted audiences. The annual report serves an employee-relations purpose, because it provides management with an opportunity to praise employee innovation, quality, teamwork, and commitment. Often times, an annual report is used to publicize significant company successes such as a new contract, a product innovation, cost-saving initiatives, new applications of products, or expansions into new territories. The annual report can help increase employee understanding of the different parts of the company. For example, many manufacturing locations are in remote areas, and an employee's understanding of the company often does not go beyond the facility where he or she works. An annual report can be a source for learning about each of a company's product lines, its operating locations, and who is leading the various operations. Finally, the annual report can show employees how they fit into the company's big picture; because employees also are often shareholders, the annual report can educate employees how their contributions has added value to the company's stock.

Business-to-business customers pursue working relationships with quality suppliers of goods and services, and an annual report can help a company promote its image with customers by highlighting its corporate mission and core values. As customers reduce their number of suppliers, one criterion on which existing suppliers are judged is financial strength; businesses want committed and capable suppliers that will be around for years to come.

For some companies, suppliers are an integral part of the overall success. A company's ability to meet its customers' requirements will be seriously compromised if the company has inept or undependable suppliers. By highlighting internal measurements of quality, innovation, and commitment, annual reports can send an implicit message to suppliers about the company's expectations of outside vendors. An annual report may elect to profile an exemplary supplier. This recognition serves two purposes. First, it rewards the supplier for its work and serves to further cement the business relationship. Second, it provides the company's other suppliers with a better understanding of the level of service desired (and the rewards that can be reaped from such service).

Reading an Annual Report

Individuals read annual reports for extensively different purposes and at dramatically different levels. For example, a stockholder with five shares might not be as discriminating a reader of an annual report as the financial analyst representing a firm owning a million shares. Although it may require an MBA to understand all the specific details buried in an annual report's footnotes, a good understanding of a company is possible by focusing on some key sections of the report.

Management's Discussion and Analysis

This section of an annual report provides a summary of the company's performance over the previous three years. Specifically, it makes a comparison of the most recent year with prior years and discusses sales, profit margins, operating income, and net income. In addition, other sections discuss capital expenditures, cash flow, changes in working capital, and anything extraordinary happening during the years under examination. The management's discussion and analysis narrative is also supposed to be forward looking, discussing anything the company may be aware of that could affect results either posi-

tively or negatively. There usually is a page listing the company's address and phone number, the stock transfer agent, dividend and stock price information, and the next annual meeting date. This information is helpful for anyone wanting additional data on the company or more information about stock ownership.

Packaging the Annual Report

For most companies regardless of size, the financial information and the corporate message are the most important aspects of an annual report. The challenge for producers of annual reports is to disseminate pertinent information in a comprehensible fashion while simultaneously communicating the company's primary message. In many ways, the annual report serves as an advertisement for the company, a reality that is reflected in the fact that leading business magazines now present awards to company reports deemed to be of particular merit. In recent years, companies have also chosen to make their annual reports available in a variety of electronic media, lending themselves to creative, visually interesting treatments.

Finally, annual reports are cyclical. Certain techniques, formats, and designs that are popular at the time they're issued will often times be replaced by new ideas in later reports. Other more traditional formats are classic—never seeming to go out of style. A key to a successful annual report is understanding what works best for conveying the message of the respective organization.

CONCLUSION

Collectively, financial statements and the annual report represent important documents to any business and can serve multiple purposes. Both internal and external stakeholders use these documents to make current and future decisions that have both short- and long-term consequences. Sports managers represent a group of professionals who would be well served to have the necessary skills to interpret and subsequently make informed decisions for their respective organizations regarding both their current and projected financial positions.

In this chapter we discussed the rudiments of financial statements and financial statement analysis. Specifically, we provided an introduction to financial statements by introducing the elements of the balance sheet, which summarizes the firm's financial condition at a particular point in time, and the contents of the income statement used to measure the profitability of a business over a specified period. The balance sheet and the income statement provide a lead-in to explain changes in the cash position of a firm over a given period. Also, we described changes in cash flows resulting from operations, investing activity, and financing. The elements of the balance sheet and income statement are used to compute financial ratios summarizing the firm's liquidity, activity, financial leverage, profitability, and market value.

Understanding the information contained in financial statements is critical to projecting future profits. When we forecast future sales and profits, we make various assumptions that require extensive analysis of company financial statements, as well as knowledge of typical financials in the industry that the company is part of. This analysis is especially important because sales and profit forecasts are used in the planning process to determine capital needs and break-even sales.

Finally, the annual report serves as an important communications document for various stakeholders including current shareholders, analysts, and potentials investors.

Class Discussion Topics

1. Discuss the pros and cons of using the various measures of profitability to examine a company's performance.
2. Differentiate between the balance sheet, income statement, and statement of cash flows.
3. Identify three external stakeholders of an organization who management should be prepared to communicate the key elements of the financial statements.
4. What type of annual report should a company produce and why?

Financial Planning

Chapter Objectives

After studying this chapter, you should be able to do the following:

- Explain what financial forecasting is.
- Identify financial planning strategies.
- Survey various cash management strategies.
- Project expected cash flows across an investment opportunity.
- Explore break-even analysis to identify financial needs.
- Summarize managerial accounting concepts such as balanced scorecard and triple bottom line.

This chapter continues with our in-depth analysis of an organization's ability to analyze itself and its future financial needs. Similar to how people always need a plan to pay their bills, every company needs a plan to cover its expenses. That plan is predicated on future revenue streams and expected expenses. This text has covered financial planning in several different ways so far. In an earlier chapter, it explored assets and liabilities and whether assets were being maximized and liabilities undertaken in a strategic matter. The text then examined revenue and expenses and how much planning is required to increase revenue while trying to reduce expenses. The text then examined budgets and all the forecasting required to properly plan for any budgetary increase or decrease. In this chapter we revisit financial planning with some examples and briefly discuss how sometimes planning needs to focus on more than just the numbers.

Once a baseline is developed, different strategies can be explored to increase income or reduce expenses. For instance, someone might need to borrow money to pay bills or charge something with their credit card. Such an action can lead to liabilities spiraling out of control. At that point, someone might undertake more detailed analysis to see if they can afford the car they want. That same person might explore public transportation options or other options that might provide an opportunity to benefit other core values such as saving the environment or supporting a local transportation effort. Those are the types of issues covered in this chapter from a much broader perspective than just a financial one.

FINANCIAL FORECASTING

Financial forecasting explores what financial needs will be required in the future to meet short- and long-term needs. This is similar to an individual's changing financial needs. When someone is a child they might not have any financial needs because someone is already covering those expenses. However, as the person gets older they start needing money to buy food, pay for gas, and cover school expenses. Those financial obligations grow over time. Whether a person is going to college or joining the workforce, expenses start increasing, and revenue sources need to be found. Most people will eventually realize they need a budget. They will also need to increase their revenue and assets and decrease their expenses and liabilities. In order to be effective in this exercise the person will need to develop a financial forecast. That forecast can be built upon the back of a budget, but it will need to explore more detailed information such as the timing of various events and how they might affect revenue and expenses in the short term.

A good example of the need to critically examine the timing of revenue and expenses was highlighted in the budgeting case study where a minor league baseball team would have expenses all year round but income only during a four- to five-month window. If the forecast is off, the team could find itself in significant trouble. What if season ticket buyers wait until the last second or just do not buy? The financial forecast can be significantly off when assumptions are incorrect. That is why so much care is taken to critically track the numbers. The Under Armour versus Nike sidebar highlights how two companies in the same industry segments charted different paths and whose financial forecasts were either correct or miscalculated—and the resulting impact.

Financial forecasting will force an organization to critically examine its future direction. One such example entails NASCAR. NASCAR was a sport juggernaut through the first decade of this century. Those who looked at the great trajectory might assume or argue that the organization would keep doing well. However, the numbers started showing a decline. Forecasters and others might have been caught off guard, or warning signs might have been misunderstood. Forecasting is similar to doing a jigsaw puzzle, with one key difference. People working on the puzzle have a picture of the finished puzzle and know what they need to complete it as they try to put the pieces together. However, what if someone was to work on a puzzle where they had numerous pieces but no picture of the final project? There will be numerous assumptions and guesses as to what pieces fit together and how they fit into the big picture. Financial forecasting is like that. There are numerous data points, and those data points can be misconstrued—resulting in an unfinished or incorrect final puzzle.

NASCAR is under a 10-year, $8.2 billion contract (negotiated in 2012) to broadcast races on

UNDER ARMOUR VERSUS NIKE

Under Armour (UA) was forecasting that by 2018 it would have $7.5 billion in revenue with $800 million in earnings before interest and taxes (EBIT). Such a lofty projection was reduced in late 2016 when **Wall Street** analysts anticipated that the company's profits would only increase 20% rather than the projected 28% to 30%. While EBIT rose 28% in the third quarter of 2016, revenue only rose 22%. While such strong revenue numbers would be great for any company, they were not great for UA, which had such strong prior growth that this amount (which surpassed expectations) was not good enough for the future. Investors avoided the company, and the stock tumbled 13% in one day and declined 30% over a six-month period in 2016 (Snider, 2016). Investors were hoping for stronger returns, and the decline in growth worried investors. Company Chief Executive Officer Kevin Plank acknowledged numerous challenges and disruptions and even replaced the company's chief financial officer (CFO) in early 2017 with a new CFO (Bomey, 2017). In 2017, the 2016 numbers came in showing revenue was up 22% to $4.83 billion and the projections for 2017 decreased to only 11% to 12% growth, reaching nearly $5.4 billion. Operating income was also projected to decrease from $420 million in 2016 to $320 million in 2017 (Bomey, 2017).

Part of the decline that continued into 2017 was based on bad performance associated with Stephen Curry as his shoes did not sell as well as expected. Too much fanfare, UA won Curry away from Nike in 2013. Nike had paid him $4 million a year and UA was willing to pay around the same amount, but Curry felt UA offered a greater opportunity. Steph Curry's UA line of SC30 shoe was selling for $139.99 a pair. In contrast, Nike sells Michael Jordan's Air Jordan shoes for $185 a pair.

One of the major expenses for a shoe or apparel company is sponsorship deals. UA had entered into the largest sponsorship deal in the history of college sport when it signed UCLA to a 15-year contract for $280 million (Monroe, 2016).

The cost to grow a company can also represent a significant investment. To build a company costs a lot of money, but when changing or growing a business, expenses can skyrocket. UA was interested in moving from downtown Baltimore to another part of the city with a UA-planned 50-city block development. The development was meant to highlight Baltimore and was more than a corporate office but a planned community with 7,500 housing units, a hotel, shopping center, and even two light rail stops. Such an ambitious plan is not without detractor, both in the political and financial world. For example, the development was seeking $1.1 billion in support from local, state, and federal government agencies including $535 in tax increment financing from the city of Baltimore (Monroe, 2016). During planning meetings, members of the city's Urban Design and Architecture Review Panel were impressed with the proposed project's bling, such as a whiskey distillery, but there were no post offices, fire stations, libraries, or schools. These deficiencies were corrected in a subsequent plan. While UA was trying to receive significant city funding to help build the community, such a massive project exposed the company to significant financial risks. The financial forecast for such a project had to include real estate markets and lending markets, and it had to maintain certain financial costs and projections.

At the same time, UA was pursuing other initiatives. Technology was another key investment strategy pursued by UA. It spent $150 million on exercise app MapMyFitness in 2013, $475 million for MyFitnessApp in 2014, and $85 million for Endomondo in 2015—a European fitness app (Olson, 2015). This resulted in an investment of almost $1 billion on apps, and two of the three companies were not profitable (Foster, 2016). Morningstar retail analyst Paul Swinand felt such an investment for UA was very risky (Foster, 2016). UA was hoping to leverage the information from 150 million fitness app users to help design better products for them (Foster, 2016). This included the fact that more than 60% of connected fitness users

(continued)

are women, while only 30% of UA sales were to women. Furthermore, while only 11% of UA sales are international, 35% of those using fitness apps owned by UA were from outside the United States (Foster, 2016). Thus, it was hoped that purchasing these apps would help UA grow revenue from sales to women international customers. Through building more e-commerce into its apps, UA was hoping to leverage the fact that fitness enthusiasts purchase more right after a workout, and UA orders from app users were 26% higher than purchases from other options (Foster, 2016).

It was expected in 2015 that mobile health apps and gadgets would hit sales of $120 billion by 2020 (Olson, 2015), and 2015 sales had 45.7 million units sold with an estimate that 126.1 million units would be sold by 2019. Wristwear was expected to slightly drop in its dominance (from 89% to 80%) and smart clothing was expected to grow from less than 1% of all such tech sales to 4% (Olson, 2015). Those numbers are across the entire industry, and UA was hoping to take a big chunk of that market. However, sales have not been as strong for the wristwear and related tech market. For example, Apple faced disappointing sales of its Apple watch (three to four million units by 2015) (Olson, 2015). This investment represented a significant amount of **cash** and was not viewed favorably by some analysts.

Personnel is another big issue. In 2016 UA had a quarter of a million people making something associated with the brand. Kevin Plank was expecting that to increase by another 200,000 by 2019 (Monroe, 2016). Having so many employees might sound impressive, but it creates a significant financial drain in terms of salaries, benefits, office space, human resources departments, and so on.

UA has tried to be as cutting edge as possible. It entered into a partnership with DuPont to custom design and manufacture a midsole that makes the shoe partially a 3D-printed shoe and could help reinvent UA's supply chain (Monroe, 2016). These innovative options are possibly great opportunities, but they can also represent major financial risks if they do not generate significant sales. This is where break-even analysis comes into play.

What was the result of all these steps? Not positive for investors who shunned UA stock through 2017 with stock ending the year at around $13 per share, half its early-year value. In March 2016, the stock was trading at around $85 per share.

Nike

Nike has been the biggest player in the sports shoe and apparel industry for a number of years. Its shares increased over 505% from 2006 through the end of 2015 (Lashinsky, 2015). Nike's profits in 2015 totaled $3 billion—or 11% of sales. Nike's growth since 2008 has been fueled by adopting an approach called category offense, where Nike divides the world into categories of sporting endeavors (golf, basketball, soccer, etc.) rather than geographic regions (Lashinsky, 2015). Also, due to its significant presence in some shopping areas, such as being in two or three stores in the same mall, Nike decided that some stores with a focus would not sell other Nike products, so maybe only one or two stores in a mall would sell basketball shoes while others would specialize in soccer or running shoes. This approach increased Nike sales in English malls by nearly 20% (Lashinsky, 2015).

Similar to UA, Nike had developed a wearable technology product, which it called a FuelBand, but it discontinued the product after disappointing sales. The FuelBand was released in 2012 and discontinued in 2014 (Statt, 2014).

Similar to UA, Nike has its own corporate campus—394 acres in Oregon. Nike has spent the past couple of years changing how it markets in products and has, as an example, cut print and TV advertising by 40% and shifted that spending to advertising on digital platforms. This has resulted in Nike.com expecting $7 billion in sales by 2020, up from $1 billion in 2015. Such an increase has to be pursued very carefully as such a huge chunk of business being taken away from retail establishments selling Nike products can backfire on Nike (Lashinsky, 2015). If Nike sells more shoes and apparel directly online that might increase sales, but it can also harm the sale of Nike in malls, and these stores purchase a significant number of items from Nike to resell to consumers.

Supply chain innovations are also being examined and implemented by Nike. The shoe leader had expressed interest in increasing domestic production and was looking at hiring up to 10,000 engineering and manufacturing employees through 2026 (Monroe, 2016). Being nimble in its supply chain is critical with trade pacts and agreements under fire. Nike has 1.1 million manufacturing employees in 645 factories located in 42 countries. This includes over 400,000 workers in Vietnam, 202,000 in China, and only 7,000 in the United States (Townsend, 2017). About 1,300 employees in the United States (Oregon and Missouri) help make air-filled soles, but once the soles are finished they are shipped overseas for the shoes to be completed. With the threat and actual cancellation of various trade pacts, companies were exploring ways to move production back to the United States. The problem is that sneakers have many parts that need to be stitched or glued together, and that is labor intensive. Robots could be a solution. Nike has deployed a robot that paints a midsole without having paint affect any other part of the shoe, saving time and money (Townsend, 2017).

UA is trying to manufacture more in the United States, and in 2017, Adidas opened a robot-based facility outside of Atlanta that uses only 160 employees to produce 50,000 pairs of shoes each year, a number that can possibly increase to close half a million in the future. That might seem like a lot, but Adidas manufactures over 300 million pairs of shoes a year (Townsend, 2017).

While UA and Nike have pursued different growth strategies requiring different financial strategies, Nike has shown significantly more stability with its stock price remaining between $50 and $65 per share over the 2016 to 2018 time frame and was near the 53-week high at the end of 2017 ($62.50 per share). Share prices fluctuated in 2018 with the launch of the Colin Kaepernick advertisement and with Nike not meeting the high sales expectations sets by analysis. This example helps highlight how financial strategies from two different large shoe companies have resulted in significantly different results and different returns on an investor's shares.

Fox and NBC. In 2005, *Fortune* magazine claimed that NASCAR was America's fastest growing sport. However, in 2015, TV ratings were down. Attendance at races also declined. International Speedway Corp and Speedway Motorsports Inc. are both publicly owned and 20 of the 23 Cup series races are run at their tracks. International Speedway Corp's and Speedway Motorsport's attendance-related revenue were both down between 47% and 48% from highs in 2007 and 2008 through 2016 (Gluck, 2016). Attendance revenue from all three publicly traded NASCAR track owners totaled $215.1 million in 2017, a drop of 54 percent from 2007, when the companies hit an all-time high of $467.4 million. While some might say that ticket costs were affecting attendance numbers, ticket costs only represent a small percentage of the total costs to attend a race. For a family going to a race, the outing is not one day but several days leading up to the main race, generating significant bills for things such as travel, hotels, and food for several days and nights. Attendance declines drove some venues to remove a significant percentage of their available seating capacity.

While attendance might have been declining, digital and social metrics were growing. In 2016, NASCAR's social media channels generated nearly 2 billion social impressions and more than 92 million fan engagements. NASCAR's website in 2016 averaged 9 million unique viewers every month (Gluck, 2016).

While attendance numbers and social media reach are numbers that can be forecast with a certain degree of accuracy, the same cannot be said about possible social issues that could significantly affect an organization. That is exactly what happened in 2014 when the U.S. government cut funding for advertisements for military recruiting during NASCAR events by $13.8 million when it was learned that the advertising program was not successful in attracting future personnel (Brook, 2014). The impact of an injury to a star athlete, a major scandal, political backlash from an action or statement (e.g., NFL national anthem protests and the scandal around several professional team owners allegedly making racist statements or engaging in sexual harassment), and numerous other issues are sheer speculation. However, insurance is one strategy to help minimize the potential roller coaster associated with hard-to-quantify future events. Sports organizations can also undertake strategic financial planning to help reduce future issues.

FINANCIAL PLANNING STRATEGIES

Financial planning activity involves assessing the business environment; confirming the business mission, vision, and objective; identifying the resources needed to achieve the objectives; quantifying the amount of resources (labor, equipment, and material); and identifying additional risks and opportunities associated with financial targets. One way to look at it is a box with the board of directors, employees, senior leaders, and investors in each corner. Financial planning and analysis are in the center, with strategy and financial management on either side (see figure 12.1).

The financial management process will require a CFO to undertake tasks such as the following:

♦ Developing operating and three-year plans

♦ Forecasting cash flow and liquidity

♦ Structuring capital (dividends and debt facilities)

♦ Delivering monthly and quarterly progress updates

♦ Reviewing operations monthly and updating the executive committee on the status

♦ Making sure the technology and process are in place to monitor analytics and benchmarks

♦ Managing special projects as assigned

Every CFO and financial executive will have different responsibilities, but the previous list helps identify typical jobs faced by CFOs on a regular basis. A CFO or any other executive will normally undertake several types of analysis. The basic comparative analysis will include:

♦ *Intracompany analysis.* In this type of analysis, financial statements and records from the current and past periods of the company are examined. For example, the current cash amounts can be compared to where the company's cash level was the prior year or even several prior years.

♦ *Intercompany analysis.* In this analysis, one company is compared to another. This is often seen when benchmarking occurs between publicly available information (such as annual statements). Thus, sales levels (especially on a percentage basis) can be compared between two different companies to see if they are growing or shrinking together or if they are headed in different directions.

♦ *Industry analysis.* Some organizations are able to examine industry-related data to explore how they are doing financially. In many professional sports leagues, the teams within the league share some financial

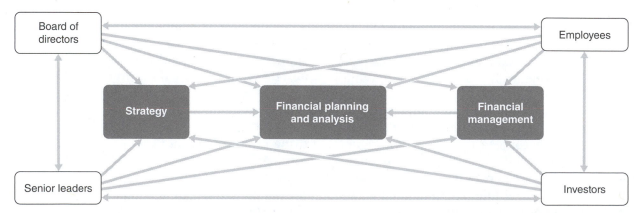

Figure 12.1 Intersection of financial planning, financial management and stakeholders.

information. This shared information is especially important for revenue-sharing agreements. One team can compare its merchandise sales to another team's sales. Industry trade associations often undertake various surveys and then share these anonymous survey results with members. An international association such as the International Association of Venue Managers might undertake some member surveys and share the results. These results can provide per capita comparison of concession sales at various facilities so one facility can see if they are doing well compared to similar facilities.

These tools can examine numbers in several different approaches such as horizontal analysis (trend analysis over a period of time such as comparing sales from 2016, 2017, and 2018), vertical analysis, and ratio analysis (covered in chapter 11). Vertical analysis is often called common size analysis, and every element on the financial statement is reflected as a percentage of a base amount—thus such analysis might say that current assets represent 40% of current assets or that cost of goods sold (COGS) represents 50% of all income. Financial ratios make examining financial changes and conditions easier not by looking at a specific number but by using a calculated ratio that makes it easier to compare with past ratios or the ratio of competitors. To put this into a sport-related context we can use Under Armour. Assume a company's executive wants to examine what strategies to pursue in the future. The first thing she would do is a horizontal analysis of UA from the past three years. This could then morph into looking at a vertical analysis of the financial statements to get a better

feel for the percentage change in different key metrics. Lastly, she would examine some ratios based on UA's actual numbers—such as liquidity ratio. Using hypothetical numbers to make the example easier to read, her initial analysis might look like the data in table 12.1.

This simplified fictional analysis of internal financial conditions shows that UA has increased revenue by $100 million (or a 20% increase) from 2016 to 2018. The cost of revenue has also increased $100 million, possibly from raw materials being more expensive. While the numbers are both $100 million, the increase in expenses represents a 28% increase. Thus, this example shows that expenses are rising faster than revenue. UA would have to examine whether it needs to raise prices, reduce costs, or undertake other financial steps to make sure this trend does not continue. Similarly, the information shows that the gross profit is actually decreasing as a percentage of total revenue. Lastly, the general and administrative expenses also seem to be increasing significantly as a percentage of the gross profit. This raises a question—*why?* Could it be advertising expenses increased? Could it be payroll or benefit related? We do not know the answer. However, this brief overview of some internal numbers provides an example of what an executive would want to examine when exploring internal financial information. The executive would also want to examine ratios produced from the financial statements to see what story they might tell.

After examining internal data, our fictitious UA executive would want to compare UA's numbers to those of competitors such as Nike or Adidas. Through using published financial statements for publicly traded companies (shared with the government and public as

Table 12.1 Revenue (in Millions of Dollars)

	2016		2017		2018	
	Millions	Percentage	Millions	Percentage	Millions	Percentage
Total revenue	500	100	510	100	600	100
Cost of revenue	350	75	380	75	450	75
Gross profit	150	25	130	25	150 (percent of total revenue)	25
OPERATING EXPENSES						
General and admin.	50	33	55	42	75 (percent of gross profits)	50

required by law), the executive could compare various areas to see if Nike and Adidas are similarly facing increased raw material costs and how are they responding to those increases. If competitors are able to minimize the impact of those rising costs better than UA, the executive would have to undertake some research to determine what is going on and why. Maybe the executive can contact colleagues at other companies to obtain some information. Maybe the competitors have locked in long-term supply contracts that have insulated them. Maybe the competitors are using less material, using different manufacturing facilities, or a slew of other cost-cutting efforts. The UA executive would need to examine whether any similar strategies might help UA.

Lastly, the executive would probably contact any trade associations in the sporting goods industry to see what information is circulating within the industry as to how other companies are doing and what trends the industry might be seeing. For example, if survey results and news articles highlight that more companies are utilizing 3D printers to reduce costs, then maybe the UA executive would explore whether such a technology might save UA money.

The key for every executive is to make smart decisions based on numbers. Whether using internal or external data, the data need to be put into a format that makes it easier to process and analyze. Strategic analysis allows decisions to be made concerning the direction the company might need to pursue. The company might need to free more cash, sell assets, reduce prices in an effort to increase sales, or invest more in research and development. The team might need to reduce payroll or increase concession prices. There are many different techniques that can be undertaken to address financial concerns. Whatever decision is made needs to be based on solid information.

An executive should be able to prove their decision is the best decision, as we'll illustrate. Assume an executive wants to increase prices by 10% in an effort to generate new revenue. That sounds great, but what would the other ramifications be? If such an effort might infuriate suppliers, customers, regulators, or others, then what seems like a no-brainer is actually a very difficult decision. Before making any such decision, the executive would need to be able to prove their case as a lawyer might prove a case in court. A lawyer cannot just list facts, make conjectures, and hope to win. The lawyer has to lay out a meticulous case with proof that cannot be rebuffed. Even the best trained lawyer might face a surprise in the courtroom, but the groundwork undertaken before court will hopefully minimize those surprises. While there might be some financial surprises in the future, an executive can try to prove their case with all available data and show why a given strategy is more likely than not to produce a given result.

Once all the information is analyzed, the next step is to take action. There is little value in analyzing cost-cutting measures utilizing numerous personnel over many weeks and then not undertaking any action on that analysis. Analysis needs to segue from figuring out what to do to actually doing something. For example, if UA in our prior examples wants to reduce costs, where should it start? It might be simple for someone to say UA should not spend as much money on athlete sponsorship, but how much sales revenue is generated by such sponsorship? The company can possibly renegotiate a contract with a manufacturer. However, what if it contracts with a new company to reduce costs but the new manufacturer is in a country where new tariffs are imposed or where the monetary exchange shifts? The cost benefits can be lost or the decision can actually result in higher costs.

A *Harvard Business Review* article from 2010 explored the approaches that could be undertaken to reduce costs and what strategy to take when expenses need to be reduced 10%, 20%, or 30% (Coyne, Coyne, & Coyne, 2010). The article's first suggestion was to not look for a single idea that would radically change the cost structure. Such an action would undoubtedly come with a significant amount of risk and would probably not be successful. The authors instead suggested taking 10 or more smaller actions with the idea being cumulative small savings with much lower risks. Any cost cutting efforts need to be undertaken with a close analysis of what disruption will occur. Letting go of one inside sales person might not kill a team, but if the commission for each person is reduced 5% to save money, the backlash could be brutal and several key sellers might leave. That is why small incremental reductions reduce the amount of backlash and could lead to a cumulative 10% saving over time. What are these small incremental reductions? They could be anything including purchasing in bulk, joining a co-op to save on purchases, consolidating expenses (such as one office birthday party a month for everyone with a birthday that month rather than an individual party each time), terminating ineffective employees, reducing the number of managers and meetings, analyzing and then reducing miscellaneous spending, asking for cost-sharing ideas from employees (and implementing several), and postponing pay increases. For deeper cuts a company might need to reorganize, eliminate programs or product lines, or possibly close a factory or office (Coyne, Coyne, & Coyne, 2010). Reducing expenses is one of just many financial decisions which will require significant analysis to make sure a decision is appropriate. Another major strategy is cash management and break-even analysis, which are covered next.

CASH MANAGEMENT STRATEGIES

One of the more critical strategic decisions for any sport business entails managing cash. This entails identifying how much cash an organization might have and what the forecast cash needs are. Cash management is one of the most intricate activities for any business. The company does not want to have too much cash on hand (so it will put some extra into CDs), but it does not want too little available cash in case it owes a lot of money and needs to immediately make a payment. An individual might also face the same concerns on a regular basis. At times they might have some extra cash and at other times they might owe a lot of money. That is where planning comes into play. Assume this person has $500 in their bank account, they are going to be paid their salary of $1,500 in two weeks, but in five days they will owe over $1,000 in rent. How will they pay the rent? Will the landlord be flexible? Can the person borrow some money—and if so how and at what cost? Will they just pay late and hope nothing happens? Each one of these options would add stress to this individual's life. In order to more effectively manage this stress, many people carefully choreograph when they pay their bills and when they might ask others for money. The same applies to every business.

The key focus for analyzing this dance is the statement of cash flows mentioned in chapters 3 and 11. The cash flow statement helps an orga-

nization appreciate its current cash position. A great way to think about a cash flow statement is to think of your typical bank account. If you have automatic deposit from your job, then you know money will be deposited every payday. If you have bills that are automatically paid from the account, then you will know when those bills are paid. At any time, you can check on your bank balance and find out how much cash you have. Likewise, a business has at least one and sometimes many accounts that need to be regularly checked. Besides examining the actual amounts in your account, you will need to track if you are owed any other money and what outstanding bills still need to be paid. Some larger bills might be delayed if the cash is not there on time. You might also ask to pay part of the bill right now and more at a later date. A business will have the same cash management issues. It will have money owed to it, and it will have bills it owes and has to pay. This is referred to as accounts receivable (AR) and accounts payable (AP). Many businesses will have one or more dedicated individuals working in AR and AP departments where they spend their time coordinating paying bills and collecting payments.

Cash timing is important in many different areas, but in international sport it is even more critical. One example is the National Hockey League (NHL). There are a number of NHL teams in both the Unites States and Canada. This is great for the sport but is not great in that there are two different currencies that might go up and down at mismatched times. The NHL and the NHL Players' Association inserted a clause in their collective bargaining agreement to address this concern. Mentions of money in all NHL contracts are in U.S. dollars, and players are paid in U.S. dollars. Prior to the change in the bargaining agreement, this issue came to light when the Canadian dollar was at a 13-year low against the U.S. dollar at 68 U.S. cents. The revenue from the NHL's seven Canadian teams come in to the league in Canadian dollars. Since there is an agreement between the players and the owners to split revenue 50/50, some money is withheld from player paychecks every year and put into an escrow account. If revenue targets are not met, money is taken from the escrow account and given back to the owners. In 2011 to 2012 the players lost only around 0.5% of their annual salaries. As the Canadian dollar declined in 2015 to 2016, the players were scheduled to lose 18% of their salaries because about 33% of the league's revenue comes from Canadian teams, broadcasters, and sponsors. One such contract is the $5.2 billion, 12-year, Canadian broadcast agreement paid in Canadian dollars (Novy-Williams & De Vynck, 2016). This example shows how changes in cash can affect a league and how such potential changes need to be included in contracts.

When examining accounts payable, most companies try to delay payment as much as possible. Think of it similarly to how you might pay bills at the end of the month rather than when they arrive. The amount you owe is accounts payable for you, but for the company you owe money to it is an account receivable Thus, a team could have $1 million owed to it by various companies who purchased luxury suites for the year. This amount is a receivable for the team. In contrast, for the companies renting the suites, it is an account payable. These companies would probably be very motivated to pay before the first game begins, but they might delay payment as long as possible to earn as much interest as possible on the cash in the bank.

Accounts Receivable

Chapter 9 highlighted how accounts payable can help provide some funding flexibility. Accounts receivable can serve as a more advanced funding technique. On the balance sheet, accounts receivable represent money owed and as such are a positive asset. The problem is that this positive can quickly turn into a negative. Almost everyone has loaned money to a friend. When the friend does not pay you back in a month you might ask them several more times for repayment. However, what if they do not have the funds or never intended to repay you? Would you ever get the money back? If you will not get the money back, what will your response be? That is where cash management comes into play.

The amount of accounts receivable held by the business is determined by the extent to which that business sells on credit, as opposed to cash. In addition, the terms of credit become important in determining the amount of accounts receivable appearing on the balance sheet. For example, if UA offers its customers the terms of net 30 days, customers have 30 days from the date of purchase to pay the amount owed. Under these circumstances, most of UA's customers will pay near the end of the 30 days. To encourage its customers to pay earlier, UA may offer terms of 1/10/30, which means that customers have 30 days to pay the balance owed, and they receive a 1% discount if payment occurs within 10 days of purchase. Another formula for credit terms is 2/10/30, which means that the discount is 2% if payment occurs within 10 days.

CONCEPTS INTO PRACTICE

In the case of 1/10/30, the customer who pays after 10 days is in effect receiving 20 days of credit at interest equal to the 1% forgone discount. Because about 18 such periods occur in a year (360 days a year divided by 20 days in each period), the annual interest equals 18 times 1%, or 18%. If UA changed the terms to 2/10/60, the cost of credit for 60 days minus the cost for 10 days (for paying early) would equal the cost for 50 days, which is 2% in lost discounts. About 7.2 periods would occur each year (360 divided by 50), so the annual interest would be 7.2 multiplied by the 2% forgone discount, or 14.4%.

To summarize thus far, the terms of a sale define the amount that the cash customer pays for the merchandise. In addition, the terms of sale set the interest rate charged for credit. If UA increases the discount from 1/10/30 to 2/10/30, the price for the cash customer has been reduced, but the interest rate charged to the credit buyer has been increased.

If a customer has a poor credit record, UA may insist that the buyer pay either cash on delivery or cash before delivery. UA can assess the creditworthiness of a customer in various ways. One way is to have a credit agency such as Dun & Bradstreet perform a credit check. Credit agencies typically report the experience that other firms have had in collecting payments from the customer. Credit bureaus also provide this kind of information.

The business' own bank can do a credit check by contacting the customer's bank, which will provide information on the customer's average bank balance, access to bank credit, and reputation.

BENEFITS OF ELECTRONIC FUNDS TRANSFERS

One of the most important developments in collections management over the past 20 to 30 years has been electronic funds transfers (EFTs). EFTs are now used by 80% to 90% of all health clubs in the United States. The EFT systems withdraw funds automatically from a customer's bank account. Because the withdrawals are done electronically and at set times, such as the fifth day of each month, the process streamlines the collection and accounting process (Ernest, 2002). This process can save a significant amount of time and lost cash caused by payment delays. A third party, which can also provide additional support such as membership retention and marketing assistance, often administers the process. A health club could also use EFTs to establish an accurate flow of revenue on which a bank loan or other borrowing could be secured.

Another benefit of such a payment system is the time lag for terminating the service. If someone wants to cancel the service, she has to give advance notice; otherwise, she would have to make an additional payment, which represents additional cash that the health club might not otherwise have received from that customer. Furthermore, if a customer breaches the contract, the health club could keep collecting the disputed amount until the matter is resolved without incurring a significant collection problem. This can also represent a problem and unethical conduct when some clubs know a contract has ended, but they try to keep collecting for as long as possible hoping the former customer might not know or drag on the process to get some more money from the client.

If the customer is a publicly traded firm, there are inexpensive ways of collecting information about how this customer is assessed in the financial markets. Although a precipitous drop in a company's stock price does not imply that the firm is going into bankruptcy, it indicates that the company's future prospects are no longer as bright as they were previously.

CONCEPTS INTO PRACTICE

UA may be supplying its sporting goods apparel and shoes to a publicly traded chain of sporting goods stores and can easily look up the company's Moody's or Standard & Poor's rating. Moody's and Standard & Poor's rate the outstanding bonds of publicly traded companies in terms of the likelihood of default. Given the availability of stock price data on the Internet through such sites as Yahoo! Finance, UA can look at the recent performance of the customer's stock price. If the customer appears to be in financial distress, UA might require some cash in advance or secure the goods as collateral.

Collections Management

Besides managing credit, sport businesses need to manage collections. Collections management focuses on converting receivables to cash and refers to efforts made to obtain payment of past due accounts. In addition, the credit manager needs to have records of the collections experience of the company in dealing with customers who currently have credit terms. This information is relevant for determining whether credit should continue to be extended in the future.

A sport business also needs to monitor its general collections experience to determine whether its terms are appropriate. One reporting tool involves the average **days sales outstanding**, or days in receivables. Our example involving Under Armour can illustrate the use of this tool.

CONCEPTS INTO PRACTICE

Assume that the terms on all UA sales to customers are 1/10/30. Assume that 65% of the customers take the 1% discount and pay on day

10 and that the remaining 35% pay on day 30. The average days sales outstanding is 65% multiplied by 10 days plus 35% multiplied by 30 days, which is 17 days ([0.65 × 10] + [0.35 × 30]).

Because payments to a business tend to arrive more sporadically than in our example, calculating average daily sales is necessary. To make our calculations simple and easy to understand, let's assume that UA's annual sales are $4 million. Thus, its average daily sales are $10,959 per day ($4,000,000 divided by 365 days). That number is divided into the existing accounts receivable to obtain the average daily sales outstanding. If accounts receivable is $186,300, then average daily sales outstanding is 17 days ($186,300 divided by $10,959). This means that when making a purchase, the average UA customer pays in 17 days.

If UA analyzes daily or weekly data on sales and accounts receivable and finds that average daily sales outstanding stays at 17 days over a 1-month period, then some customers are paying later. In addition, some accounts may be overdue. With sales outstanding staying at 17 days, a significant number of UA customers are not paying their bills immediately or taking advantage of early payment discounts. Keep in mind that for a company such as UA that has seasonal sales patterns, the calculated average daily sales outstanding will fluctuate during the year. For such businesses, receivables are low before the major selling season and high afterward. As a result, average daily sales outstanding on a particular date may need to be compared with past averages for the same date.

An aging report, which tabulates receivables by the age of accounts, can provide more detailed information. Table 12.2 presents an example. Note that a significant number of customers are past due (40% of accounts are outstanding more than 30 days). Any sport business that displays a report like the one shown in table 12.2 has serious collections problems and should be reviewing its collections policies.

The rules governing the deduction of bad-debt losses are complicated. Whether a company has to go to court to obtain a judgment against the **debtor** depends on the particular situation. For example, if the company can show that the court would return a judgment of uncollectible, then going to court is unnecessary. Bankruptcy

Table 12.2 Sample Aging Report

Age of account	% of total accounts receivable
0-30 days	60
31-60 days	15
61-90 days	15
90-120 days	6
121 days or more	4
Total	100

is generally considered evidence by the Internal Revenue Service that at least a portion of the debt can be viewed as bad. The deduction of bad-debt losses is summarized in Internal Revenue Service Publication 535, Business Expenses (Internal Revenue Service, 2010).

For smaller businesses, employing someone in credit management and collections may be too expensive. Under these circumstances, the business may sell its accounts receivable directly to a financial institution, called a factor. The factor buys the receivables of the firm at a discount, which is typically 1% (Brealey, Myers, & Marcus, 2008). The company and the factor agree on credit terms for each customer. The customer sends payments to the factor, which bears the risk that the customer will not pay.

Capital Budgeting for Long-Term Cash Management

So far in this this section we have been examining planning associated with short-term needs, normally needs that might arise in the next month or several months. We transition now to long-term needs. That is where capital budgeting comes into play. Short-term financial planning might entail a sports team trying to determine how to meet payroll this month or what will happen when ticket sales dry up at the end of the season. Capital budgeting for the same team would focus on building a new stadium or practice facility, which normally cannot be paid for with cash on hand. That is when a more intensive and elaborate strategy needs to be developed and implemented to avoid overpaying or not raising enough money.

The goal of capital budgeting is to select investment opportunities that are worth more than they cost. Also, sport businesses should initially

GETTING THE CASH TO FLOW

In a 2016 article on how small businesses can avoid cash flow issues, the author provided the following suggestions:

- Get money to come in before money has to be spent via presales to book revenue and cash.
- Hold early sales events.
- Sell gift cards (which will generate contractually obligated revenue).
- Demand payment on delivery (if customers will not prepay) so you do not need to wait 30 to 90 days for payment.
- Accept credit card, mobile payment, or debit card payments, which will result in faster payment.

- To provide more time to repay bills, try to negotiate favorable repayment terms when possible.
- Ask if installment payment options are available.
- Pay by credit card, but make sure you have the ability to pay credit card balances in full to avoid interest charges.
- Have vendors fill the order in your place, but you do the marketing and get the difference between the manufactured price (plus shipping) and the sales price (Abrams, 2016).

invest in those projects that provide the greatest return for their investment. Given the long-term effects associated with any investment, we can see why capital budgeting is a primary focus for sports organizations.

A sport business can raise and spend capital funds in countless ways. An integral part of financial management is determining the best capital sources. Efficient capital spending leads to growth and success for a sport business. To grow, a business must invest some of its available capital in fixed assets such as land, equipment, or machinery. For example, a fitness center cannot improve its recreational offerings without investing in new equipment and facilities. Although a for-profit business should invest in those projects that will result in the largest return on investment, this concern may not always be true for government or nonprofit organizations.

CAPITAL SPENDING

Before critically analyzing capital budgeting any further, we must focus on the meaning of capital spending. **Capital spending** is the net spending on fixed assets. Net spending is the total money that a business uses to acquire real assets, less the sale of previously owned real assets (Brigham & Ehrhardt, 2011). During the first decade of

the 2000s, many businesses invested heavily in fixed assets. This trend carried over into the sport industry as well. A boom occurred in construction of new sport stadiums and arenas such as AT&T Stadium in Dallas and Citi Field in New York. The construction boom was fostered by several circumstances. On the financial side, team owners believed that capital expenditures for facility amenities such as luxury suites, club seats, concessions, and parking would result in new income streams. Additionally, new facilities were needed to replace older structures that required major repairs, such as Veterans Stadium in Philadelphia and Busch Stadium in St. Louis. The building boom slowed down, however, with the recession of 2007 to 2008 because many teams either had trouble securing financing for these projects or decided to wait until the end of the recession. More recently, with the United States and many other countries growing out of the recession, new stadiums, such as Mercedes-Benz Stadium in Atlanta were built.

Capital budgeting and purchasing capital items are long-term endeavors. When we refer to items as long term, the period involved is usually greater than one year. For equipment and facilities, this refers to their productive life. With respect to capital, a business is usually unable to allocate the amount of money necessary for purchasing high-priced fixed assets in a single year. Therefore, the business must develop capital budgets that detail how the funds will be raised and allocated over an extended period. For this reason, current, or short-term, items are separated from capital items in financial statements.

The funding mix required for capital expenditures is referred to as the **capital structure**. In general, the traditional corporate capital structure includes debt (bonds and long-term loans), preferred stock, and common stock (Ross, Westerfield, & Jordan, 2008). All these capital sources have an accompanying cost. If a sport business wishes to borrow funds from a bank to construct a new facility, it must pay interest on the borrowed amount. The interest that is paid in addition to the principal being borrowed is referred to as the cost of the debt. The next section deals with each form of capital and covers methods to measure the accompanying costs.

For nonprofit organizations such as university athletics departments, additional sources of funding include donations and gifts. Supporters of nonprofit organizations often make financial donations toward new capital projects. For example, a university alumnus may donate a significant amount of money toward constructing or renovating a sports facility, such as when T. Boone Pickens donated over $175 million to the Oklahoma State University Department of Athletics. Many nonprofit organizations rely on these donations for a portion, or all, of the funds necessary to complete capital projects. These donations are important to nonprofit organizations because unlike corporations, they cannot raise capital through equity ownership.

COST OF CAPITAL

Sport businesses can use four traditional forms of capital, known as capital components, to fund growth: debt, common stock, preferred stock, and retained earnings. These components all have one common trait: The persons or institutions that provide the capital expect, or demand, a return on investment (Brigham & Ehrhardt, 2011). A bank or financial institution that loans money to a sport business expects to be repaid the loan principal plus interest. A common stockholder or investor expects the firm to invest in capital-spending projects that will increase the

value of the company and ultimately result in increased stock value. This expected return on the investment means that the business incurs a cost to acquire the capital funds. In the case of a bank loan, the cost of capital is the amount of interest owed to the creditor. This section develops methods to measure the cost of capital for debt and equity. Sport businesses need to understand and appreciate the fact that any capital acquisition technique has a cost, and that cost will dictate how much capital can be raised.

We must make a quick point about retained earnings before moving forward. Retained earnings are funds that are kept by a business to be used for **reinvestment** in the company. This reinvestment often takes the form of capital spending. Management believes that the stockholders will benefit more from this reinvestment than from having the money returned through dividend payments. Because the retained earnings can be used by the sport business to purchase additional stock, the cost of retained earnings is considered to be the cost of common stock. Therefore, we will discuss the cost of retained earnings along with the cost of common stock.

Note that companies develop strategies for structuring their capital. For example, Speedway Motorsports may have 50% of its capital in the form of debt, 30% in preferred stock, and 20% in common stock. These proportions, referred to as a target capital structure, may vary greatly across businesses and industries (Ross et al., 2008). Within some professional sports leagues, capital structure is controlled by the league to some extent. For example, the NFL has restrictions on the level of debt that each team can maintain. The NFL set the debt limit as a financial safeguard to ensure that none of its teams has excess debt that will lead to financial difficulties.

Most larger sport businesses finance their capital budgets through a combination of debt and equity. Each form of capital has an associated cost. Some businesses decide to structure their capital budgets such that they rely on one form of capital, but this approach is uncommon for large corporations. For government-owned and -operated institutions such as a university athletic department, the sources of capital are primarily debt and money raised through gifts and donations. State-funded universities such as Florida State University and The University of Iowa have no individual private ownership rights. Their income comes from sources such as donations, ticket sales, sponsorships, student fees, and broadcast fees. These funds are used to cover the current expenses involved in operating a collegiate athletic program. The university usually raises money for capital projects from donations or the issuance of debt. The state government is ultimately responsible for paying the bondholders if the university defaults.

Privately held sport businesses such as fitness centers, pro sports teams, and apparel companies can also raise capital by selling equity ownership rights or borrowing funds. For example, Under Armour may raise money by issuing common stock to the public, but it may also borrow from banks or issue bonds.

Several factors can influence capital-structuring decisions. For example, a weak stock market such as that seen in 2007 and 2008 may make the issuance of stock less attractive than it might be otherwise. As stock prices fall, a business needs to issue more shares to raise the necessary capital funds. In addition, a cost is associated with issuing new stock. Most businesses work with a financial institution to help with a public offering, and they pay for those services. The expenses related to issuing new stock are known as **flotation costs** (Ross et al., 2008). Immoo, Lochhead, Ritter, and Zhao (1996) found that a company that wants to raise $2 million to $10 million in capital through a common stock offering will have flotation costs of approximately 13.28% of the total amount of capital being raised. Thus, if a business wants to have $2 million in capital, it will need to raise approximately $2.26 million.

Immoo et al. (1996) also found that the average flotation cost is significantly less when capital is raised through debt. In this case, in the $2 million to $10 million debt range, the average flotation cost is 4.39%, one-third the level of flotation costs for common stock. Whether debt or equity is used, many of the flotation costs, such as attorneys' fees, are fixed and are not greatly affected by the amount of capital being raised. Therefore, most businesses do not like to raise capital in small quantities. Other businesses also elect to raise capital through a single debt or equity source each year in an effort to minimize flotation costs (Ross et al., 2008).

A professional sports team example will illustrate average cost of capital for debt. Assume that the Atlanta Braves decide to go public by issuing stock. The team raises $300 million in its initial public offering. If the average flotation cost for such an offering is 8%, then $24 million will be paid to float the shares, and $4.5 million to $6 million of that amount might represent attorneys' fees. The attorneys' fees need to be paid even if only $100 million had been raised through the offering.

Selecting one capital source each year has short-term effects on a target capital structure, so maintaining the target structure is difficult. A business' target capital structure may also be affected by outside economic forces such as the stock market or interest rates. Interest rates have an effect on the cost of issuing debt. Therefore, a business may want to select debt as its capital source (to maintain its capital target), but issuing new stock may be more cost effective, especially when stock prices are relatively high.

Thus far, we have discussed the general principles of capital, the forms of capital, and the importance of capital cost. The next step is to develop a method for accurately measuring new capital costs. The most commonly used method to measure the cost of capital is the **weighted average cost of capital (WACC)**. The WACC focuses on determining the average cost of each capital component and weights each based on its contribution to the total capital amount. In general, a sport business will maximize its value when it minimizes its WACC (Ross et al., 2008).

To calculate the WACC, we must separate capital into each of the three potential capital sources available for a business: debt, preferred stock, and common stock. As stated earlier, the cost of retaining earnings and the cost of issuing common stock are calculated similarly. In doing the calculation of the WACC as outlined in this chapter, retained earnings are implicitly included in the value of common stock. Whether new shares of stock are issued or whether retained earnings are used to finance a capital project, the cost of funds is identical (ignoring underwriting and flotation costs). Because most sports organizations do not issue preferred stock and very few issue stocks and bonds, we decided to mention this process, but it is so detailed that we defer anyone interested in the topic to take a finance course.

Cost of Debt

Debt is important because many smaller businesses raise most of their capital through this capital component, usually in the form of bank loans (Brigham & Ehrhardt, 2011).

CONCEPTS INTO PRACTICE

Suppose that you own a relatively small business, such as a local health and fitness center. You may borrow money from a bank or similar financial institution to fund new capital spending. The principal amount that you borrow must be repaid over time with interest. The interest is the cost of borrowing the funds. If you borrow $200,000 at an interest rate of 8%, the cost of debt, excluding taxes, is also 8%. But the cost of debt is misleading unless the potential tax implications are extracted. Because the debt repayment of 8% is probably tax deductible, you will not pay 8% per year. The true cost will be $16,000 (8% multiplied by $200,000) minus what tax savings can be generated by reducing your income by $16,000. Assuming a 30% combined federal and state tax rate for the business, the potential cost could drop from $16,000 to $11,200 ($16,000 minus 30% of 16,000).

Many large corporations also issue debt through bonds and debentures. A bond is a long-term promissory note issued by a business. For most bonds, the business agrees to pay back the amount borrowed at a specified future date (usually in 10 to 30 years for long-term bonds) in addition to a coupon payment, which is a percentage of the bond's value. The coupon payment for most corporate coupon bonds is made semiannually. For example, a sport business can sell 25-year bonds with a value of $1,000 and a semiannual coupon payment of 6%. Anyone who purchases a bond will receive semiannual payments of $60 for 25 years. Also, at the end of the 25 years, the creditor will receive $1,000. In this example, the annual cost of debt for the life of the bond would average around 12%.

A debenture is a long-term bond. But unlike regular bonds that are secured by corporate assets, a debenture is unsecured. The only protection that a debenture holder has to guarantee repayment is the good name of the company that issues the debenture. If the corporation faces financial hardship, the debenture holders are similar to all other unsecured lenders in that they are often the last group to be repaid, if they are paid at all.

From these examples, measuring the rate of return required by debt holders appears to be relatively straightforward. How much will debt holders demand in future payments to make the necessary funds available today? For a small business like an independently operated sporting goods store, ascertaining this number may be as simple as determining the annual interest rate on a bank loan. But the process can be a bit more complex for a large corporation such as Under Armour. Given that the WACC is used in the planning process for the issuance of future debt, a financial manager is making a prediction or estimation of the future cost of debt. Determining the coupon payment that must be offered to attract future bond purchasers is not always easy. A business that issues a new bond at a time when interest rates are on the rise will have a hard time selling the bonds without increasing the interest rate paid to purchasers. Therefore, determining the appropriate rate of return is not an exact science. Nevertheless, by using the correct information, the analyst can make a credible estimate.

What Is the Correct Information?

A financial manager can analyze historical data on debt instruments to make a prediction about the future. Suppose UA wants to issue new 25-year bonds to raise capital. Through experience, the financial manager knows that similar bonds have been issued for each of the past five years. She also knows that the financial position of the business has not changed over that period and that the previous bonds were issued with a 10% coupon rate. Additionally, the financial manager would look at the **current yield** on a bond with the same maturity and credit rating, as determined by Moody's or Standard & Poor's, as well as the current debt costs for similar businesses. For example, suppose UA is investigating issuing debt to build a new warehouse. The financial manager would gather information on the cost of debt incurred by other businesses that have recently financed facility construction.

Calculating the Cost of Debt

One other important debt feature is crucial to the cost-of-debt calculation. To encourage capital investment in the United States, the federal government and most state governments provide a tax deduction on the interest payments made to debt holders. For most corporations, the federal tax rate for interest deductions is 35%. Most states also give tax allowances for interest deductions, usually at about a 5% rate (Brigham & Ehrhardt, 2011). In total, the average tax rate for interest deductions is approximately 40%. This tax savings reduces the overall cost of debt for a sport business.

Assume that we want to calculate the cost of debt for UA. The cost of debt can be written as a mathematical formula:

$$D = R - (R \times T)$$

D = cost of debt

R = interest rate paid to debt holder

T = marginal tax rate on interest payments

The rate of return required by debt holders is the interest rate, or R, that is paid on the debt. The tax savings is the rate of return required by debt holders multiplied by the **marginal tax** rate on interest payments, which we will abbreviate as T. We can rewrite the cost of debt this way:

$$D = R \times (1 - T)$$

CONCEPTS INTO PRACTICE

In our example, we assume that UA borrows $1,000,000 at an interest rate of 6% and has a marginal tax rate of 40%. Their cost of debt is calculated as follows:

$$D = 6\% \times (1 - 0.4)$$
$$D = 3.6\%$$

Therefore, UA's cost of debt is 3.6% annually. Multiplying 3.6% by $1,000,000 shows that the cost of debt in dollars is $36,000. The tax deduction associated with making interest payments will save UA 2.4%, or $24,000 each year, of the original $1,000,000 that was borrowed.

Cost of Equity

Capital can also be acquired by selling ownership in the business, also known as the issuance of equity. Equity is separated into two different classifications: preferred stock and common stock. As mentioned previously, we will not go into preferred stock, but rather we will focus just on common stock.

Cost of Common Stock

With respect to common stock, a sport business can raise capital through two methods. First, it can issue new common stock. To attract new common stock shareholders, the sport business must sell the stock shares at an attractive price. Prospective stockholders will buy the stock if they believe that the value of the stock will increase in the future. The annual percentage return (holding period return) associated with annual dividend payments and increases in the stock price must exceed the returns on investments of equivalent risk. If it does not, people will invest their money elsewhere.

A sport business can also raise capital through retaining earnings that would otherwise be used to pay dividends to common stockholders. By not paying dividends, the firm is retaining funds for use in capital spending. The capital-spending goal is to increase the value of the business. If the value of the business grows because of the capital spending, the common stock price should also increase. Most common stockholders will gladly forgo current dividend payments if the retained earnings will lead to an increase in the firm's stock price that is greater than the expected dividend payment.

Dividend policy is an important part of corporate finance. Financial managers continually struggle with the trade-off between dividend payments and retained earnings. They are looking for the appropriate levels of each that will both keep the stockholders happy and allow the firm to grow. Making every investor happy is impossible, and there are never any guarantees. For example, Speedway Motorsports could pour $100 million into retained earnings and build a new racetrack. Investors might be ecstatic with the prospects of future increased value as new track revenues develop. But a year after the track opens a competitor may build a better facility and send

Speedway's stock into a dramatic tailspin. Thus, retained earnings represent a potential risk, but all business decisions contain an element of risk.

Ultimately, the important aspect of common stock is that common stock shareholders require a return on their investment. This expected return on investment is vital for calculating the cost of common stock. In the simplest terms, the cost of common stock is the rate of return demanded by stockholders.

We must include several factors in calculating the cost of common stock. As with preferred stock, flotation costs are incurred when new common stock is issued. Likewise, issuing new common stock increases the overall supply of common shares available in the market. The increased supply of stock will cause the price of all shares to drop. The price decline often forces the firm to sell the new stock at a lower price and reduce the amount of capital that is raised. All these additional costs discourage some businesses from issuing new common stock. Most established larger businesses do not regularly offer new common stock on the open market. Instead, they elect to raise capital through retained earnings that would otherwise be paid as dividends or by issuing bonds or commercial paper.

Shareholders incur an opportunity cost, also known as implicit cost, if a business retains earnings to raise capital. The shareholders are forgoing dividends when earnings are retained. Shareholders could have reinvested those dividend payments in stocks, bonds, and other opportunities that may have resulted in a positive return. Therefore, the retained earnings should result in an increase in the value of a business that is greater than the amount that a shareholder can expect to earn if the money is paid out as dividends. The difficult task for a financial manager is to calculate this amount. As with issuing new stock, the amount that shareholders could make by investing their dividend payments in the best alternative can serve to help measure the cost of common stock. Thus, the cost of common stock involves many factors, such as dividend payments, flotation costs, the rate of return of other investment opportunities, and the risk involved in investing in common stock. There are three primary techniques for valuing common stocks that are beyond the scope of this text—the **capital asset pricing model**, **bond yield** plus risk premium model,

and the dividend growth model. These models examine risks of various investments and the costs of issuing common stock compared to other investment options.

Once the cost of issuing bonds, preferred stocks, and common stocks is calculated, the numbers can be used to help calculate the WACC. The analysis is beyond the scope of this text, but it is an important concept to know because the WACC uses the targeted levels, or proportions, of the three components along with the cost measures developed for each. Most firms have a targeted capital structure. The target is the proportion of debt to preferred stock to common stock that the business believes will be best for its future success. The proportions of target capital are represented by weights that are given to each capital type. When added up, the weights must equal 1. For example, if the debt portion has a weight of 0.1, then 10% of the business' targeted capital structure is funded through a debt instrument. The WACC is for the cost of new capital only in an attempt to develop cost measures as part of the capital-budgeting process. This estimate should not be used to make statements about the cost of previously issued capital. Previous capital was raised under different economic and financial circumstances, and such circumstances can greatly influence the cost of capital. Note that the weights used are based on a targeted capital structure. If the firm raises capital in proportions that vary from the targets, the WACC will vary as well. Again, the WACC is a method used to estimate the cost of capital. Any changes in the variables used in the model will change the WACC.

Our discussion of WACC and the cost of capital has focused primarily on publicly held businesses. Numerous businesses in the sport industry are small businesses, privately held companies, or both. Neither of these types of businesses has stocks that are openly bought and sold. This circumstance presents some unusual problems when determining the cost of capital. The price of preferred and common stock is not easily obtainable because the stocks are not traded on the open market. Overall, the same principles for the cost of capital determination apply for small businesses and privately held companies. Obtaining accurate and usable financial data, however, is difficult. Moreover, many small firms do not pay any dividends.

Earnings are often retained and used to grow the company, adding to the difficulty of calculating accurate costs of preferred and common stock.

In addition, most small businesses do not have publicly traded bonds. The bond yield plus risk premium method for determining the cost of common stock relies on knowing a business' bond yield. Applying this method to small businesses is usually not appropriate.

Another consideration when examining any capital-related decision is the concept of time. Capital spending and obtaining the returns from capital projects occurs over many years. Therefore, the timing of the costs and revenues is critical.

CONCEPTS INTO PRACTICE

Let's assume that a university athletic department, such as the one at The Ohio State University, is approached by a wealthy philanthropist who would like to make a large donation. The philanthropist offers two options for how the money will be paid:

1. The athletic department can receive a $500,000 check today to help build a new practice field.
2. The athletic department can receive a $550,000 check in one year for the field.

The decision is based on which option is more valuable. If the value of $550,000 in one year is expected to be greater than the value of the $500,000 check received today the athletic department should select option 2. But how do we determine which option is more valuable? Obviously, $500,000 today is worth more than $500,000 a year from now, but is $500,000 today worth more than $550,000 a year from now? The athletic department can invest the $500,000 today in an interest-bearing account and have more than $500,000 in one year. But can it make an additional $50,000 from the investment? Suppose that it investigates the payoff from the best risk-free investment opportunity—probably a U.S. government security—and learns that the annual interest rate is 7%. Therefore, $500,000 invested in a U.S. government security will give the athletic department $35,000 in interest in one year. Under these circumstances, the university should obviously select option 2 and take the $550,000 in one year.

Net Present Value

Another method for making this decision is to calculate the present value of option 2. Using this process, the athletic department will determine the dollar value of receiving $550,000 in one year. To make the decision, the university will need to know the expected rate of return. The rate of return is the reward demanded by investors for waiting one year to receive a payment. Assume that the athletic department would expect no more than a 7% return from its best alternative risk-free investment. Therefore, we will use 7% as the rate of return. The rate of return is then used to develop a discount factor. The tables in appendix B can help calculate the discount value of the $550,000 next year in today's dollars. This analysis would also show that option 2 is the better option as the higher a positive net present value (which will be explained shortly), the more attractive the investment.

Although the calculations in this example help establish which choice will be the most beneficial, they do not take into account other variables. For example, if the athletic department does not build a field with the $500,000 this year, inflation and increased building costs might force the university to pay $575,000 next year. Furthermore, the future contains numerous variables that might make budgeting decisions more difficult. The athletic department might approve an additional $500,000 for a new field, but those funds might not be available if the athletic department waits a year to receive the $550,000 from the philanthropist.

While the time value of money is an important concept, it is even more important when examining future financial decisions, especially expensive decisions. Using current values and present value analysis can help clarify the financial ramifications for various decisions. For all capital investments, a sports manager should calculate the present value of the expected future income related to the project. An investment is considered wise if the present value of this future income is greater than the necessary investment. The financial term associated with this process is **net present value (NPV)**. The NPV is the difference between the present value of the future income and the required investment. It can be represented as follows:

$$NPV = PV - RI$$

NPV = net present value

PV = present value of future income

RI = required investment

The following concepts into practice sidebar highlights how to apply NPV.

CONCEPTS INTO PRACTICE

The same university athletic department from the previous example must decide whether it wants to spend $1 million to construct 10 new luxury suites in its basketball arena. Each suite should last for 10 years. At the end of 10 years, we will assume that the suites will need to be replaced and will have no salvage value. For simplicity, we will also assume that each luxury suite can be rented for $30,000 per year and that no other income will be made from the suites. The construction project will take one year. Therefore, the first income from the suites will be earned one year from today. If we think of one year from now as the end of year 1, income will flow into the athletic department at the ends of years 1 through 10. Even though this example is not completely accurate, it offers a good depiction of the concept of NPV.

The athletic department must calculate the NPV of this investment opportunity before making the decision. So starting next year, assuming all 10 suites are rented for all 10 years, it will have $300,000 in income for each of the next 10 years. Overall, the project will generate $3 million in income, but the present value of the income stream must be calculated. Unlike the situation in the previous example, in which one payoff was to be received one year into the future, here there is a stream of future payoffs. Thus, the present value of the payoff in each future year must be calculated. The following mathematical formula is used to calculate cash flows in future years (Brigham & Ehrhardt, 2011):

$$PV = \left(\frac{1}{1+r} \times FP_1\right) + \left(\frac{1}{(1+r)^2} \times FP_2\right) + \left(\frac{1}{(1+r)^3} \times FP_3\right) + \ldots\ldots + \left(\frac{1}{(1+r)^{10}} \times FP_{10}\right)$$

FP_1 = future payoff one year from now

FP_2 = future payoff two years from now

r = rate of return

And so on for FP_3 through FP_{10}

These calculations will continue up to the end of year 10. We will assume that the rate of return for the athletic department is 8%. We can rewrite the equation as the following:

$$PV = \left(\frac{1}{1.08} \times \$300,000\right) + \left(\frac{1}{1.08^2} \times \$300,000\right) + \left(\frac{1}{1.08^3} \times \$300,000\right) + \ldots\ldots + \left(\frac{1}{1.08^{10}} \times \$300,000\right)$$

$$= \$2,013,000$$

The present value of $2,013,000 can then be used to calculate the NPV of the capital expenditure. Note that these calculations can be done manually, but if the rate of return and stream of income are constant throughout a project, an annuity table, such as table B.3 in appendix B, can be used. The table will save a great deal of time and frustration by allowing the user to arrive at the correct amount without the need for mathematical calculations because the math has already been done. As stated previously, the initial investment is $1 million, and the present value of the stream of income is $2,013,000. So, we can calculate the NPV as follows:

$$NPV = \$2,013,000 - \$1,000,000 = \$1,013,000$$

The NPV of the construction of 10 luxury boxes is positive and slightly over $1 million. The project definitely is worth more than it costs the athletic department.

Net present value is an important capital-budgeting component. Ordinarily, a project that has a negative NPV should not be undertaken because the cost of the project is higher than the projected income—financially, it is a losing proposition. But not all projects that have a positive NPV must be undertaken. It should be noted that some negative NPV projects are undertaken anyway because they are important projects for political or other reasons. Thus, NPV analysis is a great mechanical tool. However, some decisions are based on intangible issues and benefits.

It is important to note other methods besides NPV can be used for making capital-budgeting decisions. All these methods have strengths and weaknesses. The NPV method was presented first because it is the most often used and is regarded as the best. Although it is important to recognize and discuss these other methods, the NPV method is strongly recommended.

Payback Rule

A second method of analyzing the value of a capital project is through using the payback rule. The payback rule analyzes how long it will take a business to recoup its money after investing in a capital project. The money is paid back through the stream of future income related to the project. The payback rule may be best explained through the concepts into practice sidebar.

As you can see in the example, the capital-budgeting decision method that is used can have a major effect on the decision. The difference occurs because the payback rule weighs all cash flows equally, ignoring the importance of time. This rule centers on which investment option will repay the initial outlay in the shortest time. The NPV method discounts future cash flows based on the opportunity cost of capital. It also looks at the entire cash flow over the life of the project, in this case four years. The university's payback rule of three years means that only the cash flows in the first three years are important; even if project A had a projected cash flow of $1 billion in the fourth year, it would not be selected. Ignoring the cash flows after the arbitrarily selected payback date is an obvious weakness of the payback rule.

To account for the failure of the payback rule to recognize the time value of money, the **discounted payback rule** has been developed.

Discounted Payback Rule

The discounted payback rule discounts the future cash flows based on the opportunity cost of capital, as highlighted in the concepts into practice sidebar.

CONCEPTS INTO PRACTICE

Assume that a university athletic department has $1 million that it wants to invest in a capital project. The initial investment will result in a future cash flow into the university. The university has two possible capital projects that cost $1 million each. It must decide which one to select. These are the two choices:

Project A is a new outdoor aquatics facility. The facility is expected to produce $250,000 in revenue in the first year and $300,000 per year for two subsequent years. In the fourth and final year (as the building in this example would be abandoned or torn down after four years), the cash flow will be $400,000. For simplicity, we will assume that there are no other costs or revenues. The total revenue for the next four years will be $1.25 million.

Project B is a new recreational gymnasium to be used for adult and youth sports leagues. This facility should produce $100,000 in the first year and $450,000 per year for the two subsequent years. Because of an expected decrease in future demand, the cash flow for the fourth year will be only $100,000. The total revenue for the next four years will be $1.1 million.

The question is, *which capital project should the athletic department select?* The university is going to use the payback rule to make this decision. The university has decided that all of the initial $1 million investment must be paid back within three years. If this cannot occur, capital funds will not be allocated for the project. Table 12.3 depicts the cash flows over time, the expected payback periods, and the NPV for each project.

Examining table 12.3, we see that it will take four years for project A to repay the investment, whereas the investment for project B will be repaid within three years. Given the university's payback rule of three years, project B is the one to select. The projected cash flow from this project can repay the $1 million initial investment in three years.

The decision would change dramatically if we used the NPV method. To determine NPV, we assume that the opportunity cost of capital is 8%. We find that the NPV of project A is $20,842, and the NPV for project B is −$90,880. Using the NPV method, project B would be rejected and the athletic department would select project A.

Table 12.3 Timeline of Cash Flows for Projects A and B

Project	P_0	P_1	P_2	P_3	P_4	Payback period	Net present value at 8%
A	−$1 million	$250,000	$300,000	$300,000	$400,000	4 years	$20,842
B	−$1 million	$100,000	$450,000	$450,000	$100,000	3 years	−$90,880

CONCEPTS INTO PRACTICE

To return to our previous example, table 12.4 shows the cash flows when the athletic department applies the discounted payback rule, incorporating an 8% rate of return.

Using the discounted payback rule, the payback period remains at four years for project A. Project B is not expected to produce enough cash flow in four years to cover the initial investment. Therefore, using the discounted payback rule and a predetermined three-year maximum payback period, both projects are rejected. Remember that using the NPV method would lead to the selection of project A, and the original payback rule would result in the selection of project B. This illustrates that which capital-budgeting decision method is used has a major effect on the disbursement of long-term capital.

Table 12.4 Timeline of Discounted Cash Flows for Projects A and B

Project	P_0	P_1	P_2	P_3	P_4	Payback period	Net present value at 8%
A	–$1 million	$231,481	$257,210	$238,150	$294,009	4 years	$20,842
B	–$1 million	$92,593	$385,802	$357,225	$73,502	>4 years	–$90,880

Internal Rate of Return Method

The last method for making capital-budgeting decisions is to use the **internal rate of return (IRR)**. As with NPV and the discounted payback rule, IRR relies on the opportunity cost of capital and the time value of money. As stated earlier, the opportunity cost of capital is the return obtained by investing the capital in the next best alternative. For example, if you can place $100,000 in an interest-bearing investment that will result in you having $110,000 at the end of one year, the rate of return is 10%. Therefore, you would invest only in projects that can return more than $110,000. The IRR method emphasizes finding the rate of return for which NPV equals zero. Table 12.5 displays a situation in which a $1,000 capital investment results in a $750 cash flow in one year and a $500 cash flow in two years.

Table 12.5 Timeline of Cash Flows

Time 0 (P_0)	In one year (P_1)	In two years (P_2)
–$1,000	$750	$500

The goal of the IRR method is to find the rate of return for which NPV equals zero. The mathematical model for our example in table 12.5 is as follows:

$$\text{NPV} = P_0 + \frac{P_1}{1+r} + \frac{P_2}{1+r^2} = 0$$

NPV = net present value

P_0 = cash flow at time zero

P_1 = cash flow in first year

r = rate of return

P_2 = cash flow in second year

To complete the formula, we need to solve for r, the rate of return. This can be difficult without the proper computer software. If you attempt to solve the formula manually, it will be a matter of trial and error. The trial-and-error process for manual calculation requires you to estimate for r and keep lowering or raising r until the equation equals zero. With a computer you can perform the analysis almost instantaneously. If we input the information from table 12.5, the equation can be rewritten as follows:

$$\text{NPV} = -\$1,000 + \frac{\$750}{1+r} + \frac{\$500}{1+r^2} = 0$$

We must now solve for r. Using trial and error, let's start with a 10% rate of return. If we solve the equation when $r = 0.10$, we find that the NPV equals $95.10. We now know that the IRR for which NPV will equal zero is greater than 0.10. We continue this trial-and-error process until we find the rate of return at which NPV equals zero. In our example, NPV will equal zero when *r* equals 0.175. A wise sports manager will undertake this capital project if she believes that its opportunity cost of capital is less than 17.5%. In other words, she will go ahead with the project if no other investment choices have an expected rate of return greater than 17.5%.

It should be noted that all the examples in this section have used terms such as *expected* rate of return. That is because each decision has an element of risk. When you are calculating the return on investment for capital expenditures, risk is important. Different capital projects have different levels of risk. To accept a higher level of risk for a project, the investor must expect the returns to be higher. In every case, a wise sports manager faced with the choice of selecting one of two capital investment opportunities with equal returns will select the one with the lower risk.

PROJECTING CASH FLOW

The discussion to this point has centered on capital budgeting from the cost side. The calculation of capital costs is an integral part of capital budgeting, but it is only half the story. The other half deals with income and with developing methods to estimate future income that results from capital investment. The combination of expenses and income is known as cash flow. The accurate projection of cash flows, both expenses and income, is a key to making wise capital-budgeting decisions. Although no projection of future income will be totally accurate, a sports manager needs to make the best and most accurate attempt.

The future cash flows that result from capital investment depend on many business factors. For example, if an athletic department plans to spend $100 million on a new 30,000-seat football stadium, the future cash flow resulting from this spending may be difficult to estimate accurately. The following is a list of factors that may affect future cash flow for such a project:

♦ Is there demand for 30,000 tickets to the football games? Before construction, an in-depth market analysis should be undertaken to determine spectator demand.

♦ How important is ticket price to the spectators? Would an increase in the ticket price affect spectator demand?

♦ The athletic department cannot assume that it will always put a winning team on the field. How will winning and losing affect spectator attendance?

♦ If the project succeeds and the 30,000 seats are filled on a regular basis, can the stadium be expanded in the future?

♦ If the capital is raised, in part, through booster donations, how will fund-raising efforts for other parts of the athletic program and university be affected? Will other projects or budgets be affected by the stadium project?

♦ How much additional cash will flow into the athletic department? If the new stadium is built, will it have an effect on future cash flow compared with the current cash flow from football games?

♦ Besides football games, what other uses would the facility have, and what would the cash flow be from those uses?

♦ If luxury seating or boxes are included, is there a demand from corporate clients for those seats? What is the fair price for the luxury seating or boxes?

♦ How much will it cost to maintain and repair the stadium after it is built?

♦ What will the cost be for the capital required to construct the facility?

All the factors listed are important when projecting the cash flow from a new university sports facility. It is necessary to ask questions related to market demand, sales projections, operating costs, and capital costs when attempting to project future cash flow. Remember that projecting cash flow is not an exact science. A financial manager makes the best possible estimation based on available data and research.

We will define the cash flow of a project as the net cash inflows and investment expenditures associated with the project (Brigham & Ehrhardt, 2011). Again, projecting cash flow is the most difficult facet of capital budgeting.

For a sports organization, many people and departments should be involved in any major capital projects. For example, when a university athletic department constructs a new stadium, several departments will be involved in the process. The ticketing and marketing departments need to make projections about ticket

When Yale University was renovating the Payne Whitney Gym, the process took so long that the university ended up having to buy all the scaffolding around the building for several hundred thousand dollars—an unexpected expense.

sales and pricing. The university's construction planners and outside construction firms need to estimate construction costs. The university's physical plant department should be consulted to estimate maintenance costs. An event planner or promoter can help determine what revenues will be generated from other events being held in the stadium. The university's advancement or fund-raising office can estimate the effect of stadium fund-raising on other university fund-raising endeavors. The focus should be on obtaining relevant and accurate information. Any projections made based on poor information will be a disaster.

An organization's financial staff must play a prominent role in projecting the cash flow. The financial managers have the job of taking all the information obtained from other departments and developing accurate projections. Several common pitfalls must be avoided. For a number of reasons, such as career advancement, emo-

tional ties, or possible benefits to their departments, some people in other departments will be strong supporters of specific capital projects. This bias may affect the accuracy of the information that they provide to the financial staff. The financial staff needs to ensure that projections are as accurate as possible. Unfortunately, doing this is not always easy.

All businesses have a limited capital budget and many alternatives for capital spending. Each project must be evaluated on its own financial worth and needs to be compared with other options. Those investment opportunities that fit within the capital budget and have the highest NPV are the most attractive. The process of quantifying the NPV of investment choices is not easy because many confounding factors come into play. One capital-spending project may affect another, and some may need to happen simultaneously to be successful. Management has the job of deciphering all this information.

Measuring Relevant Cash Flow

The first step in projecting cash flow is to measure the relevant cash flow for a capital project. All existing firms have a cash flow. The key to obtaining an accurate measurement of the cash flow of a single project is to include only new cash flow. The new, or incremental, cash flow is the additional future cash flow, either internal or external to the business, which results only from the decision to undertake a project. Any cash flow that occurs regardless of the presence of a new project should not be included in the calculation of relevant cash flow. You need to remember this important concept throughout this discussion. With respect to measuring incremental cash flows, financial managers make several common errors.

The first common error relates to measuring **sunk costs**. Sunk costs are costs that have already occurred and do not change regardless of the decision to undertake a project. Let's go back to the example of a university. The university may pay $20,000 for a feasibility study on the construction of a new student recreation building. If, because of this report, the university decides not to construct the building, it would still have to pay for the feasibility study. The cost is incurred regardless of the outcome. According to our definition of incremental cash flow, the $20,000 is not important in making the capital-spending decision.

The second common error concerns **opportunity cost**, another important aspect of projecting relevant cash flow. Opportunity cost refers to the most valuable alternative that is forgone if a particular capital project is undertaken. Returning to the university example, the recreation building must be built on a piece of land. The university has a parcel of land that can be used, but the land could also be used for new playing fields or a swimming pool. Initially, you might think that the cost of land is zero because the university already owns it. This assessment is not accurate. An opportunity cost is associated with using that piece of land; the university is forgoing its next best alternative use of the land. The next best alternative may be to build a swimming pool. The university must estimate the value of the land and include it in its projection of project costs. This point is especially important if the university will need to buy a new piece of land in the future to build a pool.

Failure to analyze the effect of any funding decision is a third common error. Most new capital-spending projects have an effect on the overall organization. If the athletic department elects to build the new student recreation building, other parts of the university may feel some side effects. Perhaps student fees will increase for activities that do not take place in the new recreation center. Visitors to the new facility will learn more about other activities at the university and might pay to attend them. This result is an example of a positive side effect, also known as a spillover effect. But negative spillover effects can also occur. Students may decide to decrease their activities at other university venues or events to go to the new facility. This drop in attendance—and most likely a loss in income at other locations—is directly related to the new project. These types of spillover effects must be factored into projecting cash flows.

The failure to appreciate the effect of a decision on net working capital is another common error. New projects normally result in an increase in net working capital. Most projects need some cash on hand to pay for short-term expenses that arise. For our example, the university may need to buy a scoreboard for the new facility using net working capital. Additional net working capital

must be allotted for any new project. We could expect the increased investment in net working capital to be recouped by the university at the end of the project's life span. If the new facility has a life span of 30 years, at the end of that 30 years, the scoreboard will no longer be needed. The scoreboard can possibly be sold for scrap value, and some of the initial investment in net working capital can be recouped. The increase in net working capital could be viewed as a loan that will be repaid at the end of the project's life span.

The last common error is including interest payments in the cash flow projections. We are interested only in the cash flows, both income and expense, that result directly from the project's assets. Interest payments and dividends are payments to creditors and shareholders. They are not expenses that result from the assets themselves. But perhaps more important, as already discussed, interest and dividend payments were included in calculating capital costs. If we also include them as cash outflows, we would be double counting these payments, so they do not need to be included as expenses (Brigham & Ehrhardt, 2011).

As you can see, some aspects of projecting cash flow are complex. The easiest way to explain the projection of cash flow for a capital project is probably through an example.

Example of Projecting Cash Flow: New Fitness Facility

Pro forma financial statements must be developed to project cash flow for a small business owner who wants to construct a new health and fitness center. Pro formas are the easiest and most convenient method for projecting cash flow. To develop these statements, we need estimates of items such as fixed costs, variable costs, unit sales, and sales price per unit. Information must also be obtained on the change in net working capital and the total required investment. For our example, several numbers will be simplified. We will limit the life span of the facility to four years. A four-year life span is somewhat unrealistic (the facility would probably last much longer than that), but it will make our example of projecting cash flow much easier to understand. The important thing is to understand the concepts of projecting cash flow.

Several assumptions will be made for the new facility. The new facility will be built on land valued at $250,000. The fitness center owner currently owns the property and has already had an offer from another business to buy the land for this amount. The construction cost of the building will be $400,000. The equipment that will be required, such as fitness machines, weights, and computers, will cost $100,000. The equipment can be fully depreciated over four years. For simplicity we will assume that the new facility can be constructed in one year and will open for business the following year. Therefore, all the land, building, and equipment costs will occur in the same fiscal year (2018), and income from the facility will occur from 2019 to 2022. This assumption is also somewhat unrealistic, but it will make the example easier to understand. Table 12.6 provides an overview of the investment costs for the project.

At the end of the building's four-year life span, the land should still have a value of $250,000, and the building is projected to be worth $200,000. Therefore, straight-line depreciation will be used to depreciate the $200,000 loss in value over the four years. The value of the equipment will be equal to the cost of removing it from the site; therefore, we will state that the overall value of the equipment in four years will be zero.

The owner believes that 1,000 memberships can be sold at an average price of $500 per year. She estimates that they will incur about $100 per person in variable costs (e.g., staff salaries, benefits, and supplies such as towels). For a membership level of 1,000, fixed costs such as rent, electricity, and water will be approximately $70,000 per year. Again, for simplicity, we will assume that there is no inflation and that the level of sales will remain at 1,000 memberships for each of the four years of operation.

To open the new facility, the owner must initially increase her net working capital. The net working capital for the entire organization

Table 12.6 Investment Outlays for 2018 (Year 1)

Fixed assets	Cost ($)
Land	250,000
Building	400,000
Equipment	100,000
Total initial investment	750,000

will be increased from its prior level of $65,000 to $75,000. The additional $10,000 in the first year must be included as a cash flow. The $10,000 will be retained at the end of the project, and that sum must also be included in the projections of total cash flow. The new facility will be subject to federal, state, and local taxes. The total cumulative tax rate will be 35%. Last, the WACC for the owner is 9.5% (if she raises $1 million, then $950,000 of that is associated with using debt or equity), and we will assume an interest rate (r) of 5%.

From all this information, we can construct our pro forma statement of cash flows as shown in table 12.7. As you can see, a pro forma cash flow statement is complex. But it captures the expected inflows and outflows of cash for the new facility during its four-year operational life span. Several important aspects must be discussed here. First, notice that depreciation is added back into the calculation of cash flow. Depreciation is an item that is included as part of the balance sheet of a business to calculate its accounting value. But depreciation is not a flow of cash into or out of a firm. Therefore, although it is initially deducted in the cash flow statement, depreciation is ultimately added back into the cash flow.

This important point is worth reemphasizing—the cash flow statement measures the inflows and outflows of cash for a firm, and depreciation is not a cash flow (therefore the $75,000 is added back into the cash flow statement in our example). The important result from the cash flow statement is that it provides a projection for the amount of cash that will accrue from operating the new facility. The cash flows range from $230,750 in 2019 to $250,750 in 2022. The difference in cash flows occurs because the owner must increase her net working capital in 2019 to start the operation. She will get this $10,000 back in 2022 when the facility closes.

The next step for the fitness center owner is to make the decision about undertaking this project. At this point, she has a projection on the cost of construction for the facility and the projected cash flows during the life of the operation. The importance of the time value of money must be mentioned. The owner is using capital today to construct a facility that will increase future cash flow. The future cash flow must be discounted to account for the time value of money as highlighted in the concepts into practice sidebar.

Table 12.7 Pro Forma Statement of Cash Flow

	2019 (year 2)	2020 (year 3)	2021 (year 4)	2022 (year 5)
Unit sales	1,000	1,000	1,000	1,000
Sales price	$500	$500	$500	$500
Net sales	$500,000	$500,000	$500,000	$500,000
Variable costs	$100,000	$100,000	$100,000	$100,000
Fixed costs	$70,000	$70,000	$70,000	$70,000
Depreciation (building)	$50,000	$50,000	$50,000	$50,000
Depreciation (equipment)	$25,000	$25,000	$25,000	$25,000
Earnings before taxes	$255,000	$255,000	$255,000	$255,000
Taxes (35%)	$89,250	$89,250	$89,250	$89,250
Projected net operating income	$165,750	$165,750	$165,750	$165,750
Add back noncash expenses*	$75,000	$75,000	$75,000	$75,000
Cash flow from operations	$240,750	$240,750	$240,750	$240,750
Investment in net working capital	($10,000)			$10,000
Total projected cash flow	$230,750	$240,750	$240,750	$250,750

*Depreciation is used for tax purposes. However, it is not a cash flow, and therefore the $75,000 is added back into the cash flow statement.

CONCEPTS INTO PRACTICE

In this example, we will assume that there is no inflation. The timeline in table 12.8 captures the cash flow analysis. Additionally, the value of the land must be included in the cost of the project.

Using the assumptions that have been made and the projected cash flows that are presented in tables 12.7, 12.8, and 12.9, we can calculate the net present value, internal rate of return, and discounted payback period. You should be able to make these calculations on your own.

Table 12.8 Timeline of Net Cash Flows (2018-2022)

Year	Net cash flow ($)
2018	−750,000
2019	230,000
2020	240,740
2021	240,740
2022	250,740

Table 12.9 Discounted Payback Period (5% Interest Rate)

	2018	2019	2020	2021	2022	Discounted payback period
Cash flow	−$750,000	$230,750	$240,750	$240,750	$250,750	
Discounted cash flow	−$750,000	$219,762	$218,367	$207,969	$206,293	
Aggregate discounted cash flow		−$530,938	−$312,571	−$104,602	$101,691	Approximately 4.5 more years

(continued)

(continued)

Net Present Value

$$NPV = P_0 + [P_1 / (1 + r)] + [P_2 / (1 + r)^2] + [P_3 / (1 + r)^3] + [P_4 / (1 + r)^4]$$

Assume $r = 5\%$.

$$NPV = -\$750,000 + [\$230,750 / (1 + 0.05)] + [\$240,750 / (1 + 0.05)^2] + [\$240,750 / (1 + 0.05)^3] + [\$250,750 / (1 + 0.05)^4]$$

$$NPV = -\$750,000 + [\$230,750 / 1.05] + [\$240,750 / 1.1025] + [\$240,750 / 1.1576] + [\$250,750 / 1.2155]$$

$$NPV = -\$750,000 + \$219,762 + \$218,367 + \$207,969 + \$206,293$$
$$= \$102,391$$

Internal Rate of Return

$$NPV = P_0 + [P_1 / (1 + r)] + [P_2 / (1 + r)^2] + [P_3 / (1 + r)^3] + [P_4 / (1 + r)^4] = 0$$

$$NPV = -\$750,000 + [\$230,750 / (1 + r)] + [\$240,750 / (1 + r)^2] + [\$240,750 / (1 + r)^3] + [\$250,750 / (1 + r)^4] = 0$$

Through trial and error, we find that for NPV to equal 0 in the previous equation, r must equal 0.1066, or 10.66%.

Table 12.9 presents the calculations for determining the discounted payback period. For each period, the discounted cash flow values, which were calculated when determining the NPV, are deducted from the initial investment. The discounted payback period is the estimated length of time required to repay the investment after discounting the value of the cash flows because of the passage of time. In this case, approximately 3.5 years is needed to generate the cash flows necessary to repay the initial $750,000 investment.

As the calculations show, the NPV of this project is $102,391. Because the NPV is positive, it appears that this capital project could be undertaken. Additionally, the IRR is higher than the weighted average cost of capital (WACC), 10.7% versus 9.5%. Therefore, a sports manager who uses IRR as a basis for capital-budgeting decisions would also accept this project. Finally, through use of the discounted payback method, the manager would learn that it would take approximately 3.5 years to pay back the initial capital outlay of $750,000. Thus, someone basing her decision on the discounted payback method may elect to pass on this project and search for other business opportunities. As stated earlier, the owner wants to recoup her investment within four years. As this example clearly shows, the various capital-budgeting decision techniques can support different conclusions.

A financial manager can use all these measures—IRR, NPV, and the discounted payback method—in making the capital-budgeting decision for this project.

You should note that a project should not be undertaken solely because it has a positive NPV or an IRR that is higher than the WACC. Capital budgeting is one part of a sports organization's overall financial management strategy. The capital project must fit into the organization's long-term objectives. A sporting goods company may have an opportunity to invest in a capital project involving athlete representation that will result in a positive NPV, but if this project does not fit into the overall organizational objective, it should not be undertaken.

The previous example explores trying to make a decision where the goal is to make the most amount of money or to undertake a difficult long-term decision. Decisions are also made for everyday types of activities every business might undertake. For noncapital issues, a company might utilize break-even analysis.

BREAK-EVEN ANALYSIS

In chapter 8 we explored break-even analysis in terms of the budgetary process. When developing a budget, an executive wants to make sure the projected revenue will at least cover the expected expenses. The same approach is used for everyday and large capital expenditures. Every day, executives need to make decisions critical for running their business. For example, how would a fitness facility price its yoga classes? The executives could look at what other facilities in the area charge. They could look at national standards. They can also just come up with a number they feel is reasonable. There are many techniques, but most organizations will try to price the class at more than the cost. Businesses are around to make money, not lose money. Even a government agency will need to generate positive cash flow or risk being cut due to tight budgets. If the class needs to generate more money than it costs, the facility is going to utilize break-even analysis. Break-even analysis is a financial tool used to determine the level of unit sales required for the business to cover its expenses. In other words, break-even analysis provides the base sales level needed to ensure profitability. The **break-even point** occurs when EBIT equals zero (i.e., when pretax operating profits, independent of financing considerations, are zero).

Before discussing the formula, it is important to remind the reader about the difference between fixed and variable costs. Fixed costs refer to costs that occur regardless of any units being made or sold. Office rent, managerial salaries, and research and development costs are all examples of fixed costs that need to be considered regardless of any other sales or production. Variable costs, on the other hand, are associated with the volume produced. Raw material, electricity for specific equipment, and personnel costs for the builders all might be examples of variable costs. In the yoga example, the costs to open and staff the gym are examples of fixed costs. Paying the independent contractor yoga instructor is a variable cost, as he is paid $100 for every class he teaches. If he teaches three classes one day, then the variable cost is $300 that day. If the fixed cost for the facility is $500 a day (just for a simple analysis), then the total costs are $800 per day. If 100 people attend the classes on an average day, then the facility would need to charge $8 each to break even. Thus, to make a profit and protect the facility from any low attendance days, it will probably charge at least $10 per class, per participant. The break-even point can be expressed in the following way:

$$EBIT = revenues - variable\ costs - fixed\ costs\ of\ production = 0$$

The preceding equation can also be expressed as follows: $EBIT = PQ - VQ - F = 0$ where:

EBIT = earnings before interest and taxes

P = selling price per unit sold

Q = sales

V = variable cost per unit sold

F = fixed costs of production

The break-even point of unit sales (QBE) follows:

$$QBE = F / (P - V)$$

QBE = break-even point of unit sales

F = fixed costs of production

P = selling price per unit sold

V = variable cost per unit sold

The break-even formula states the break-even point of unit sales will be higher if fixed costs are higher. The difference between unit price and unit variable cost (P − V) can be viewed as the gross profit per unit sold. The higher the level of gross profit per unit sold, the lower the number of units needed to be sold to break even. The break-even formula can be demonstrated using assumptions about Under Armour. For example, assume the company's per shirt price (P) is $15 and the per shirt variable cost (V) is $8.25, which is the sum of the direct manufacturing costs ($7 per shirt) and the selling and administrative costs ($1.25 per shirt). The fixed cost of production is $15 million, which is the sum of the $10 million depreciation expense and the $5 million interest expense. Plugging these values into the break-even formula, we get the following:

$$QBE = \$15,000,000 / (\$15 - \$8.25) = 2,222,222\ shirts$$

Thus, to break even, UA would need to sell over 2.2 million shirts to cover its costs. Also note UA's per shirt gross profit margin on each sale is equal to $15 minus $8.25, or $6.75 per shirt sold. If fixed costs remain at $15 million per year, the per shirt gross profit margin would have to fall to $3.75 for UA to be breaking even at four million shirts. This calculation indicates that UA is in good shape because any reduction in per shirt profits could come about only through severe price reductions, significantly reduced sales, or substantial increases in variable costs.

This analysis can be used for all facets of a professional sports team. A professional sports team, will take into consideration all expense and revenue items, so the analysis is more complex. That analysis is made more difficult by variable components that will need to be explored, such as a revenue-sharing agreement with players, which can change on a regular basis based on ticket sales and sponsorship contracts.

While a majority of this chapter has focused on identifying hard numbers upon which to make decisions, financial planning is about more than just money. Some financial related plans will be based on nonfinancial variables. Customer satisfaction, as an example, is a key metric that is hard to assign a financial number to. Any plan that does not take customer satisfaction into consideration will probably result in failure. That is where some managerial accounting comes into play.

MANAGERIAL ACCOUNTING

Managerial accounting entails providing managers with both financial and nonfinancial information to assist in decision making. The managerial accounting process entails identifying, measuring, analyzing, and interpreting information from various sources and communicating with those sources to help analyze critical information for achieving an organization's goals.

While we have covered financial information, it is imperative to examine nonfinancial information. Nonfinancial information can be measured in various ways. Oral comments from salespeople, customer satisfaction surveys, just-in-time inventory management (lean accounting), risk management strategies, and other techniques can be explored. The primary focus we will examine in this text are the balanced scorecard and triple bottom line. Each technique attempts to examine some key performance indicators to help demonstrate whether a company is operating effectively and meeting its goals.

Balanced Scorecard

The balanced scorecard is a set of measures (financial and nonfinancial) related to a company's critical success factors. The question being asked and analyzed is, *what will make the company successful?* The balanced scorecard attempts to analyze different elements of an organization and hopefully present the analysis in a manner that helps employees understand that what they are doing helps the organization reach its goals. The approach examines audiences, governance, internal resources, and staffing issues. The areas overlap and help explore the current and future prospects of the company. Thus, vision and strategy are central to any analysis.

The four interconnected areas of analysis are the financial, customer, internal business, and learning and growth perspectives.

1. *Financial perspective.* This perspective asks and answers the question, *what type of financial performance should we provide for our investors?* This could be answered in terms of sales totals, cots of goods sold, company profitability, company debt, and related measures.

2. *Customer perspective.* This perspective asks and answers the question, *how should our customers perceive us in order for us to reach our company's goals?* To answer this question, the company will need to explore its products and services in terms of quality, price point, on-time delivery, customer support, customer satisfaction, and frequency of shipping.

3. *Internal business perspective.* This perspective asks and answers the question, *at what business process must we excel at to satisfy our customers and shareholders?* To answer this question, the company will need to critically analyze its manufacturing process, how new products are developed and introduced, how new business is developed, how to keep a competitive advantage, and what sales presentations are utilized to secure new customers.

4. *Learning and growth perspective.* This perspective asks and answers the question, *to achieve our company's vision, how will we as a company sustain our ability to change and improve?* The primary focus of this perspective is around employees and what is being done to make sure salaries are competitive and that growth opportunities (job advancement and learning opportunities), award recognition, and good corporate citizenship exist.

These areas are the four primary perspectives, but others can be added as necessary to develop the best all-around analysis of the company. Numerous elements can be examined and numerous questions can be asked, but each perspective will be different because each company is different. To launch a successful balanced scorecard, a company should have a retreat with all key stakeholders to examine the company's vision and examine strategic issues affecting the company. From these perspectives, a committee should be formed to formulate specific objectives and tasks addressing each of the perspectives. The scorecard can then be used as a communication tool highlighting what is expected from all company stakeholders. Results are obtained, and feedback is incorporated in analyzing the scorecard to determine what changes need to be undertaken to make sure the company is heading in the right direction. The scorecard becomes a living document that will be revised several times. Based on results, a strategic plan is adopted for the future. There is no magic score or number but rather a focus on continual improvement in all key areas that affect the company's vision and what will hopefully make the company successful.

In a sport example, the financial perspective can examine player salaries, concession sales totals, national broadcast contract revenue, and related items. The customer perspective will explore whether fans are enjoying the concession food, are happy with the parking experience, and feel part of the team, as well as related customer-centric perspectives. The internal process will examine the effectiveness of the farm team system, the value of the coaching staff, the players' medical care, and related areas. Lastly, in terms of organizational effectiveness, the team would look at the players, the quality of the field, quality of the players' equipment, and related issues.

The focus of the balanced scorecard is on combining financial and nonfinancial information to get the true perspective of a company. Income statements, balance sheet, and cash flow statements are not the only criteria upon which to develop and execute plans, and the balanced scorecard is one tool that can help transcend just the key financial statements. Another tool, especially for those interested in sustainability, is the triple bottom line analysis.

Triple Bottom Line

The **triple bottom line** analysis examines how people, the planet, and profit intersect. There are numerous decisions a business might undertake that can increase profits, but at what costs can they do so? What if a concession stand dumps its used grease down the drain? That will save the company some money in the short term, but it will harm the planet in the long term. Many business decisions in the past have been made with a primary focus on profits rather than looking at the impact on people and the planet. While the triple bottom line is not required by any law or governing authority, it represents a potential best practice to make sure an organization is acting in the best interest of people and the planet, not just in the interest of profits. This does not mean that profits are not important, but an organization needs to balance the three.

The first leg of analysis is people. *People* does not just refer to employees and customers. People refers to how the organization affects people at various levels. Is the organization trying to connect with the local community? Is the organization trying to promote social programs such as those that benefit homeless or battered women? A team might have players go to local schools and read books to kids. A fitness center might offer free or discounted membership rates for the poor. A college athletic department might open its doors for displaced people during a disaster. These are all examples where a sports organization undertakes efforts that will benefit others—outside of the organization and in addition to key stakeholders.

The second element explores the planet. We have a finite amount of resources and cannot overuse them. Is a team wasting resources such as throwing away trash that can be recycled? How much electricity is a team using, and can they reduce such usage—perhaps by using LED light bulbs or utilizing renewable energy sources? Water waste is often overlooked. Imagine how many toilets are flushed during a professional sporting event or how much water is used to keep a pitch or field healthy and green. There are numerous small strategies that can help the planet and help reduce expenses. Some facilities sell their extra oil, cardboard, and scrap food. By selling the items to recyclers, the facility is doing something good for the environment and might simultaneously generate some money and reduce its trash hauling expense.

The last element examines profit. A company still should be able to make a decent profit. However, everything is relative. Should a health club overcharge for services as a way to maximize profits? Many people would say that sounds reasonable. However, what if the health club is the only fitness facility in a town? Furthermore, what if there are numerous poor people in the town who have health problems and the gym could undertake programs that can help improve their lives?

What is the best way to balance the need for profit and a good return on an investment versus doing what is right for people and the planet? The triple bottom line approach forces an organization to examine these tough questions and hopefully develop a strategy to help balance people, planet, and profits.

CONCLUSION

Financial planning is a process of deciding what steps need to be taken to help a sports organization survive the hard times and hopefully grow for the future. This chapter has examined a number of financial strategies such as how to effectively manage cash, how to make capital-intensive decisions, and how to determine the break-even point to properly price products and services, as well as several managerial accounting approaches to aid in planning efforts. There is no one correct financial plan. However, having the right information and making decisions based on solid information can help a company grow and hopefully thrive.

Capital spending is an integral part of financial management and was a key part of this chapter. Ultimately, it ensures the long-term success of the organization. Sport businesses must develop capital budgets that will increase the stock value. The primary sources of capital for private or public sport businesses and organizations are debt and equity. Equity can take the form of preferred stock, common stock, and retained earnings. Government-owned and nonprofit sports organizations do not have ownership rights and therefore cannot raise capital through the sale of equity ownership interests. But these organizations can raise money through donations and gifts. Many college athletic departments rely on donations as a major source of capital for

spending in areas such as facility construction and equipment.

The cost of capital is only one piece of capital budgeting. Managers must also determine the additional revenue that will be generated from a capital project. Only new or marginal revenue should be considered when making this projection. Because of risk and uncertainty, the best approach is to establish a range of expected revenues. Best-case, worst-case, and most likely (also called middle-of-the-road) estimates of future revenues are recommended.

The next step is to use the cost and revenue estimates to project cash flow statements. These pro forma statements are critical for making a final capital-budgeting decision. They allow a sports manager to organize and analyze a wealth of data related to a capital project.

A wise sports manager must analyze the validity of the projections that are included in calculating cash flows. If poor or inaccurate projections are used, the results are worthless. Accurate financial data are critical for the success of capital-budgeting decisions. Businesses often develop several measures for projecting cash flows. For example, they might make several projections based on different economic conditions. Perhaps a business develops worst-case, best-case, and most likely projections. The worst-case projection would capture a situation in which sales are low, economic conditions are poor, and costs are larger than expected.

The final step is to make a decision on the capital project. The capital-budgeting decision, whether it be constructing a new facility, signing a professional athlete to a long-term contract, or purchasing new technology, can have a major effect on the future value of a sport business. Three models used in capital budgeting are NPV, the discounted payback rule, and IRR. Each has inherent strengths and weaknesses. Financial managers should use the method or methods that they believe are most appropriate for their organizations. While the financial analysis is critical, any decision will also require nonfinancial analysis such as applying the balanced scorecard or triple bottom line to see if a given investment is appropriate or consistent with an organization's goals.

Class Discussion Topics

1. Why is the capital structure of a business important?

2. Why is cash management important for a sports organization?

3. Which funding option would be the most economical to issue if you were trying to raise $200 million?

4. What does flotation cost mean?

5. Why is the time value of money important?

6. Why is the payback rule important when analyzing financial issues?

7. If you were to make a capital-budgeting decision based on project cash flows, would you prefer to use NPV, the IRR method, the payback rule, or the discounted payback rule? Why would you use the method that you have selected? What is the advantage of using multiple methods?

8. Try to determine the break-even point for selling 500 hot dogs at a game knowing the fixed costs are $250 for the game. Look up the cost for hot dogs, condiments, buns, and paper plates to help determine what the variable costs will be.

9. If you were to develop a managerial accounting approach to measure the nonfinancial success of your school's athletic programs, what would you measure, how will you get that data, and how will you respond to the information you would uncover?

Financial Ratios

Chapter Objectives

After studying this chapter, you should be able to do the following:

- Understand the importance of financial ratios to a business.
- Interpret the key financial ratios as they relate to a business, competitor, and industry.
- Discuss how sports managers can use ratios to communicate both internally and externally to various stakeholders.
- Understand the key liquidity, activity, leverage, and profitability ratios.

While sports fans can relate to the voluminous amount of statistics calculated including batting averages, touchdown–interception ratios, and field goal percentages, in business, stakeholders are also interested in specific metrics, including financial ratios. Specifically, financial ratios are mathematical comparisons of financial statement accounts or categories. Information from financial statements is used to compute financial ratios providing insight into the stability of a business. The relationships between financial statements help investors, creditors, and internal company management understand how well a business is performing, identify areas needing improvement, and they can serve as guidelines in helping management with key decisions. For ratios to be useful and meaningful, they should be

- calculated using reliable and accurate financial information,
- calculated consistently from period to period,
- used in comparison to internal benchmarks and goals,
- used in comparison to other companies within the industry,
- viewed both at a single point in time and as an indication of broad trends over time, and
- carefully interpreted in the proper context, considering there are many other important factors and indicators involved in assessing performance.

Management should develop and utilize specific ratios relative to their individual organizations and the business sector they identify with. While the following list is not exhaustive, the more commonly used financial ratios focus on these areas:

- *Liquidity.* Provides information on a company's ability to meet its short-term obligations.
- *Activity.* Relates to a company's ability to manage its assets efficiently.
- *Financial leverage.* Provides information on a company's ability to satisfy financing obligations.

- *Profitability.* Provides information on the amount of income generated from each sale.
- *Firm valuation.* Provides information on the overall value of a company.

Financial ratios are important for companies because they serve as a barometer against three different benchmarks:

1. *Previous company ratios.* Is the business improving or declining?
2. *Competitors' ratios.* How does the company compare to its competitors (such as Under Armour to Nike)?
3. *Industry ratios.* How does the company compare to other firms of similar size and scope?

Ratios can be invaluable tools for making investment decisions. However, new investors may elect to leave their decisions to fate or intuitions rather than dealing with the intimidation of financial ratios. Fundamentally, ratios are not intimidating even if you do not possess a business or finance degree. Using ratios to help make informed decisions about an investment or evaluate the position of a company is good business. To help you understand how various ratios are compiled, we have the balance sheet, income statement, and statement of cash flows of Under Armour as of December 2016 in appendix A.

LIQUIDITY RATIOS

Liquidity ratios measure the ability of a business to meet short-term (less than one year) financial obligations. Liquidity ratios are associated with a firm's net working capital, and a common liquidity ratio is the **current ratio (CR)**, which is computed by dividing current assets by current liabilities. Consequently, a current ratio can be improved by either increasing current assets or decreasing current liabilities. This can be accomplished by paying down debt, selling a fixed asset, or putting profits back into the business. These numbers are derived from a company's balance sheet (see appendix A).

$$\text{current ratio} = \text{total current assets} / \text{total current liabilities}$$

One ball club can compare attendance, concession, ratings, and other numbers to evaluate if they are comparable to similar teams (i.e., benchmarking).

The current ratio for Under Armour as of December 31, 2016, is 2.86.

$$\text{current ratio} = \$1,965,000,000\ /\ \$686,000,000 = 2.86$$

The company's current ratio of 2.86 is greater than 1, indicating current assets can cover current liabilities. If the current ratio drops below 1, Under Armour may be unable to pay its bills on time without borrowing more money or receiving more cash from the owners. For manufacturing companies, a ratio of 2.0 or greater is favorable. While a higher current ratio is generally preferred, if a company's current ratio is unusually large it may signal that management is not sufficiently utilizing excess cash or is carrying excess inventory—neither of which is ideal for long-term company viability. Before determining if Under Armour's ratio is too high, it would be best to compare this ratio to a competitor like Nike. For the same time period, Nike had a current ratio of 3.06.

A second measure of liquidity is the **quick ratio**, which is obtained by subtracting inventories from current assets and dividing the resulting difference by current liabilities. Because inventories are the least liquid of any current assets, the quick ratio indicates whether a firm can pay its current liabilities without relying on the sale of inventory, which can be a time-sensitive issue.

$$\text{quick ratio} = (\text{total current assets} - \text{inventories})\ /\ \text{current liabilities}$$

For UA, total current assets were $1,965,000,000, inventories were $917,000,000, and current liabilities were $686,000,000. Thus, its quick ratio was 1.52.

$$(1,965,000,000 - 917,000,000) / \$686,000,000 = 1.52$$

Comparatively, Nike's quick ratio was 2.10 for a similar time period. Because Under Armour has significant inventory, its quick ratio is generally going to be lower than its current ratio. Comparatively, a professional sports organization like the Green Bay Packers football team would more than likely have a current ratio and a quick ratio that are similar to each other because the Packers carry little inventory relative to Under Armor.

Net working capital is not a ratio, but it helps determine the available current assets after all the current liabilities are paid. Net working capital shows how much cash or other liquid assets might be available if the business had to repay all the liabilities due in the next several months. Net working capital is calculated as follows:

$$\text{net working capital} = \text{current assets} - \text{current liabilities}$$

Liquidity ratios are important since every business has various expenses that are required to operate. While some are daily, others are longer term or sporadic. Therefore, every business must have a minimum amount of liquidity to keep the business operating. Understanding this concept will help you see why liquidity ratios are so important. While having liabilities exceed assets is not in any way sustainable, a company in that situation could theoretically continue to run for several months by issuing more debt or increasing earnings in a short period or by making other tough but necessary decisions. This could continue for several months until something unexpected arose but eventually would result in the business either failing altogether or making significant changes.

Imagine a situation if the world economy moved into a recession. During a typical recessionary time, earnings at companies across the exchange would lower as spending decreased. Consequently, highly leveraged companies would start to default on their loans as lowered earnings made them unable to make minimum payments. As a residual effect, the financial banks that are the most leveraged industry in the market would also lose earnings from consumer loan defaults. Finally, banks without sufficient liquidity would also default, causing a ripple effect with enormous ramifications across the broader economy.

ACTIVITY RATIOS

Activity ratios measure how effectively and aggressively a firm manages its assets. Specifically, this ratio measures the speed with which various asset accounts are (or can be) converted into sales (accrual income) or cash. For example, if a firm keeps an inventory of only 10 units and sells 100 units during the financial year, inventory must entirely turn over and be replaced 10 times. The **total asset turnover ratio** is computed by dividing total revenues for a particular period by the average total assets for that period.

$$\text{total asset turnover ratio} = \text{revenues} / \text{total assets}$$

For the year ending December 31, 2016, the total asset turnover ratio for Under Armour was 1.09. The average level of assets was obtained from its income statement shown in appendix A. We need to compute the average of Under Amour's assets in the period ending December 31, 2015, and the period ending December 31, 2016, to obtain the average level of assets during 2015 to 2016. The average level of assets is equal to ($3,963,000,000 + $4,825,000,000) / 2 = $4,394,000,000.

$$\text{total asset turnover ratio} = \$4,825,000,000 / \$4,394,000,000 = 1.09$$

The asset turnover ratio gives an indication of how effectively a firm uses its assets to generate sales. If the asset turnover ratio is relatively high, the firm is efficiently using its assets to generate sales. If the ratio is relatively low, the firm is not using its assets effectively and may wish to consider selling off assets if sales do not increase. Comparatively, Nike's asset turnover ratio for a similar period was 1.50.

FINANCIAL LEVERAGE RATIOS

Financial leverage ratios provide information about the extent to which a business relies on debt (loans) rather than equity (stocks) for financing. Firms with high financial leverage ratios relative to other firms in their industry have a greater likelihood of financial distress and bankruptcy.

Generally, the more debt a company has, the riskier the stock becomes since debt holders have first claim on company assets. Thus, once creditors are paid there may not be anything left over to pay stockholders (Morningstar, 2015). One measure of financial leverage is the debt ratio, which is calculated by dividing total liabilities by total assets.

$$\text{debt ratio} = \text{total liabilities} / \text{total assets}$$

The December 31, 2016, debt ratio for Under Armour was 0.44.

$$\text{debt ratio} = \$1{,}613{,}000{,}000 / 3{,}644{,}000{,}000 = 0.44$$

Under Armour is not highly leveraged because its total assets are greater than total liabilities. The term *leveraged* refers to the extent to which a company relies on borrowing to finance its operations. Because Under Armour is not highly leveraged, it is paying lower interest costs relative to the value of its assets than highly leveraged companies are paying. Most businesses cannot survive with high debt ratios relative to their competitors. A higher debt ratio indicates a company is effectively paying more for its assets than its competitors.

An alternative to the debt ratio is to measure the extent to which a company is leveraged by calculating the ratio of long-term debt to net worth. The difference between the debt ratio and the ratio of long-term debt to net worth is that the ratio of long-term debt to net worth excludes current liabilities. Similar to the debt ratio is the debt–equity ratio, which analyzes a business' leverage but from the standpoint of the owners' equity rather than all assets. The debt–equity ratio is calculated as follows:

$$\text{debt–equity ratio} = \text{total debt} / \text{total shareholders' equity}$$

This ratio highlights how much of the debt is financed by shareholders (in the case of a private company, individual or equity partners). The higher the ratio is, the greater the reliance on shareholder support is. A low ratio might indicate the debt is being purchased through retained earnings or internal sources rather than through shareholders.

PROFITABILITY RATIOS

How efficiently is a company running a business? **Profitability ratios** help answer this question. One of the most critical figures for examining a company's success is **corporate earnings**. The bottom line for companies is their ability to generate sufficient earnings to continue growth and reward shareholders. Earnings are calculated by subtracting total costs from total sales. The earnings or the corporate losses are the key point of analysis for future progress, dividend payments, bankruptcy, and any other potential corporate decisions. In the year ending December 31, 2016, Under Armour had a net income of $257 million.

Several measures of profitability are commonly used. These include profit margin (gross and net profit margin), return on assets, return on equity, and return on investment. Profit margins are calculated by dividing profits by revenues. Net profit margin is computed using net income (earnings after interest and taxes) as a proxy for profits; gross profit margin uses **earnings before interest and taxes** to represent profits. It should be noted that gross profit margins will vary substantially by industry. For example, a high-volume grocery store may be profitable despite having many items with small margins. The store may be able to sell large enough quantities to offset its slim margins. Comparatively, an apparel company such as Under Armour has much larger margins on the sale of its clothing. These numbers are derived from Under Armour's income statement and are typically quoted as percentages.

$$\text{net profit margin} = \text{net income} / \text{sales or revenues}$$

$$\text{gross profit margin} = \text{earnings before interest and taxes} / \text{sales or revenues}$$

Under Amour's profit margins for the year ending December 31, 2016:

$$\text{net profit margin} = \$257{,}000{,}000 / \$4{,}825{,}000{,}000 = 5.32\%$$

$$\text{gross profit margin} = \$562{,}000{,}000 / \$4{,}825{,}000{,}000 = 11.65\%$$

When a firm's net profit margin is high relative to other firms in its industry, the firm is able to provide its products at either a low cost or a high price. If Under Armour has a 5.32% net profit but a competitor has only a 4.50% net profit margin, there could be multiple explanations. For example, the difference could be attributable to better sales or payroll differences. Nike's gross and net profit margins over a similar time period were 44.21 and 11.61% respectively.

Stockholders are primarily concerned about the return on their investment; thus the **dividend per share** is an important calculation. If the stock price increases, stockholders can realize a gain only if they sell the stock, known as **capital gains**. In contrast, if the corporate board of directors decides to issue a dividend, then stockholders can earn an immediate return on their investment without having to sell their shares of stock. Other measures of profit do a better job than profit margins in reflecting the investment in capital by the firm or its shareholders. One such measure of profitability is return on assets (ROA), which is defined as profits divided by average assets for the reporting period in question. The average assets can be found on the balance sheet.

$$\text{return on assets} = \text{net income} / \text{total assets}$$

For the year ending December 31, 2016, the return on assets for Under Armour was the following:

$$\text{return on assets} = \$257{,}000{,}000 / \$3{,}644{,}000{,}000 = 7.05\%$$

Return on assets (often referred to as ROA) is also known as return on investment because it reflects the amount of profits earned on the investment in all assets of the firm. Any new asset purchased by the firm should be able to generate increased returns over and beyond what could have been earned had the funds been placed in an equally risky financial investment.

A profitability measure related to ROA is the **return on equity (ROE)**, which is net income divided by average stockholders' equity. Return on equity measures profitability in terms of profits earned on investment in the firm's assets by stockholders only—as opposed to ROA, which measures profitability earned on investments in a firm by all providers of funds, including lenders and creditors as well as stockholders.

$$\text{return on equity} = \text{net income} / \text{stockholders' equity}$$

For UA, the return on equity would be 12.65%, based on the net income and stockholders' equity found in appendix A.

$$\text{return on equity} = \$257{,}000{,}000 / \$2{,}031{,}000{,}000 = 12.65\%$$

DETERMINING THE COMPANY'S VALUE

As discussed, financial statements give information about the basic condition of the firm, but they do not tell us anything about the firm's market value. Market value is based on what stock buyers and sellers establish when they buy and sell shares in the business. For a publicly traded company, the market value is simply the price per share of common stock as noted on the **stock exchange** multiplied by the number of shares of common stock outstanding.

$$\text{market value} = \text{price per share of common stock} \times \text{number of outstanding shares}$$

On October 20, 2017, Under Armour traded at $20.80 per share. Because 440.32 million shares of common stock were outstanding, the market value of the company can be expressed as follows:

$$\text{market value} = \$20.80 \times 440{,}320{,}000$$
$$\text{outstanding shares} = \$9{,}160{,}000{,}000$$

Whereas market value tells an investor what the investing public thinks a company is worth, a company's book value presents a different version of the company's worth. Book value is based on the historical cost of assets minus accumulated depreciation. Although book value represents the value of assets on paper, it does not necessarily represent the true value because an asset might have a **replacement cost** that is higher than its book value. An asset might cost $1 million to replace, but the book value could be only $500,000 ($2 million purchase price minus $1.5 million in accumulated depreciation). Book value is calculated by subtracting total liabilities from total assets.

$$book\ value = total\ assets - total\ liabilities$$

For Under Armour, the book value on October 20, 2017 was $2,030,900,000.

$$book\ value = \$3,644,331,000 - \$1,613,431,000 = \$2,030,900,000$$

The book value of a company is also called owners' equity because it represents the value the owners have in the business. Owners' equity is also calculated by adding retained earnings and the value of common stocks. Because owners' equity is a measure of a company's value, it is also called the **net worth**. **Book value per share** is another measure of a company's value based on the owners' equity obtained from the balance sheet. The easiest way to increase book value is to increase the value of the share of common stock.

TECHNIQUES TO DETERMINE THE VALUE OF AN INVESTMENT

Besides all the calculations that a corporation can make concerning its value, earnings, and liquidity, investors can use several techniques to determine whether it was profitable to invest in the company. These techniques include **annual return**, holding period return, **simple rate of return**, and dividend payout ratio.

The annual return per share and the annual rate of return for an investment analyze whether any increase or decrease occurred in the value of a stock and whether any dividends were distributed to stockholders. Assume an investor purchased a stock on January 1, 2018, and sold it on December 31, 2018. The stock was purchased at $8 per share and was sold for $10 per share.

During the year the company paid dividends of $0.04 per share. The annual return per share and annual rate of return would be calculated as follows:

$$annual\ return\ per\ share = increase\ or\ decrease$$
$$in\ value + dividends = (\$10 - \$8) + \$0.04 = \$2.04$$

$$annual\ rate\ of\ return = annual\ return\ /$$
$$initial\ investment = \$2.04\ /\ \$8.00 = 25.5\%$$

The 25.5% return highlights how profitable the investment in the stock was that year. But this analysis is useful only for a quick snapshot in time and only if the stock was sold. If the stock price fell the next day, then the annual return would still be an accurate reflection of the value for the prior year but would not reflect the true value of the investment. The relevant concept here is paper profit (because the profit is shown only on paper). That is, the stock might have produced an excellent annual return, but if the stock is not sold, the profit could vanish in an instant if the stock price declines.

In contrast to annual return, the holding period return takes into consideration the fact the stock was possibly not sold. For the stock being analyzed, the holding period return indicates what happened to the investment, independent of what might happen in the future. Because the return on the investment during the one-year holding period was 25.5%, that is the holding period return rate. The **dividend payout ratio** examines the dividends per share relative to how much the company earned per share. The formula is as follows:

$$dividend\ payout\ ratio = dividends\ per\ share\ /$$
$$earnings\ per\ share$$

If dividends per share are $0.50 and earnings per share are $3.00, the dividend payout ratio is 0.1667 ($0.50 / $3.00). This number means that 16.67% of earnings were repaid to the stockowners as dividends. Company management must decide if any dividend will be paid and if so, how much per share will be returned to shareholders. However, once a company decides to pay dividends, management should try to do so in perpetuity, as stopping this practice can send a signal to investors there may be difficult challenges for the company in the near future.

FINANCIAL POSITION OF MANCHESTER UNITED AND TOTTENHAM HOTSPUR

To illustrate some additional examples of how financial ratios can be used to evaluate the financial position of a sports organization, we compare and contrast two English Premier League (EPL) franchises—Manchester United and Tottenham Hotspur. The EPL, consisting of 20 franchises, is widely regarded as the top football league in England. Started in 1992, the EPL is the most watched professional sports league in the world (Premier League, 2017). Furthermore, Manchester United football club is one of the most recognizable and successful sport brands worldwide. The team has won the most EPL championships and reported a franchise record $515.3 million dollars in revenue for fiscal year 2016. Using data from its 2016 consolidated balance sheet (table 13.1) we can derive several ratios. Their current ratio is 0.91—this was calculated by taking current assets (£366,665,000) current liabilities (£403,744). As noted earlier in the chapter, a current ratio below 1 could signal a concern as this might indicate a potential financial solvency issue. Comparatively, another successful EPL team, Tottenham Hotspur football club, had a current ratio of 0.87 calculated by taking current assets (£172,560,000) divided by current liabilities (£198,991,000). This was calculated from the club's balance sheet (table 13.2).

A key financial leverage ratio is the debt ratio, which measures how much debt financing (risk) the business has taken on. The debt ratio for Manchester United was 0.68 and was calculated by taking total liabilities (£993,622,000) / total assets (£1,451,904,000). Comparatively, the debt ratio for Tottenham was 0.67 and was calculated by taking total liabilities (£419,298,000) divided by total assets (£625,348,000). In this example, the two clubs were essentially equally leveraged.

Net profit margin is a key performance metric to assess how much money, if any, an organization is making and is calculated from the income statement. Using the figures from Manchester United's income statement (table 13.3), we calculate the club's net profit margin to be 7% by taking net income (£36,371,000)

Table 13.1   Manchester United Consolidated Balance Sheet

	As of June 30, 2016	As of June 30, 2015
ASSETS		
NONCURRENT ASSETS		
Property, plant, and equipment	245,714	250,626
Investment property	13,447	13,559
Intangible assets	665,634	660,397
Derivative financial instruments	3,760	—
Trade and other receivables	11,223	3,836
Deferred tax asset	145,461	133,640
	1,085,239	1,062,058
CURRENT ASSETS		
Inventories	926	—
Derivative financial instruments	7,888	27
Trade and other receivables	128,657	83,627
Tax receivable	—	124
Cash and cash equivalents	229,194	155,752
	366,665	239,530
Total assets	1,451,904	1,301,588

	As of June 30, 2016	As of June 30, 2015
EQUITY AND LIABILITIES		
EQUITY		
Share capital	52	52
Share premium	68,822	68,822
Merger reserve	249,030	249,030
Hedging reserve	(32,989)	4,729
Retained earnings	173,367	155,285
	458,282	477,918
NONCURRENT LIABILITIES		
Derivative financial instruments	10,637	2,769
Trade and other payables	41,450	48,078
Borrowings	484,528	410,482
Deferred revenue	38,899	21,583
Deferred tax liabilities	14,364	17,311
	589,878	500,223
CURRENT LIABILITIES		
Derivative financial instruments	2,800	2,966
Tax liabilities	6,867	2,105
Trade and other payables	199,669	131,283
Borrowings	5,564	485
Deferred revenue	188,844	186,608
	403,744	323,447
Total equity and liabilities	1,451,904	1,301,588

Unaudited; in £ thousands.

Reprinted by permission from Manchester United PLC.

Table 13.2 Tottenham Hotspur Balance Sheet as of June 30 2016

	Notes	2016 £'000	2015 £'000
NONCURRENT ASSETS			
Property, plant, and equipment	9	287,969	217,859
Intangible assets	10	98,476	108,564
Trade receivables due after one year	12	990	24,984
		387,435	351,407
CURRENT ASSETS			
Inventories	11	4,179	4,037
Trade and other receivables	12	61,174	43,076
Cash and cash equivalents	13	172,560	10,723
		237,913	57,836
Total assets		625,348	409,243

(continued)

Table 13.2   *(continued)*

	Notes	2016 £'000	2015 £'000
CURRENT LIABILITIES			
Trade and other payables	14	**(188,909)**	(142,835)
Current tax liabilities	14	**(4,085)**	(1,101)
Interest-bearing loans and borrowings	14	**(1,354)**	(19,360)
Provisions	14/16	**(4,643)**	(9,009)
		(198,991)	(172,305)
NONCURRENT LIABILITIES			
Interest-bearing overdrafts and loans	15	**(122,526)**	(11,978)
Trade and other payables	15	**(68,585)**	(9,315)
Deferred grant income	15	**(1,852)**	(1,923)
Deferred tax liabilities	15/16	**(27,344)**	(30,709)
		(220,307)	(53,925)
Total liabilities		**(419,298)**	(226,230)
Net assets		**206,050**	183,013
EQUITY			
Share capital	18	**10,646**	10,646
Share premium		**34,788**	34,788
Preference shares	19	**20,000**	30,000
Capital redemption reserve		**642**	642
Retained earnings		**139,974**	106,937
Total equity	19	**206,050**	183,013

Reprinted by permission from Tottenham Hotspur Limited, *Annual Report and Consolidated Financial Statements* (London: Tottenham Hotspur Limited, 2016), 10.

Table 13.3   Manchester United Consolidated Income Statement

	TWELVE MONTHS ENDED 30 JUNE		THREE MONTHS ENDED 30 JUNE	
	2016	2015	2016	2015
Revenue	**515,345**	395,178	**134,575**	105,777
Operating expenses	**(436,709)**	(387,179)	**(126,131)**	(102,315)
(Loss)/profit on disposal of intangible assets	**(9,786)**	23,649	**(4,948)**	5,445
Operating profit	**68,850**	31,648	**3,496**	8,907
Finance costs	**(20,459)**	(35,419)	**(7,534)**	(17,038)
Finance income	**442**	204	**152**	68
Net finance costs	**(20,017)**	(35,215)	**(7,382)**	(16,970)
Profit/(loss) before tax	**48,833**	(3,567)	**(3,886)**	(8,063)
Tax (expense)/credit	**(12,462)**	2,672	**2,929**	1,153
Profit/(loss) for the period	**36,371**	(895)	**(957)**	(6,910)
Basic earnings/(loss) per share (pence)	**22.19**	(0.55)	**(0.58)**	(4.22)

	TWELVE MONTHS ENDED 30 JUNE		THREE MONTHS ENDED 30 JUNE	
	2016	2015	2016	2015
Weighted average number of ordinary shares outstanding (thousands)	**163,890**	163,795	**163,892**	163,798
Diluted earnings/(loss) per share (pence)	**22.13**	(0.55)	**(1)**	(4.21)
Weighted average number of ordinary shares outstanding (thousands)	**164,319**	164,132	**164,319**	164,132

Unaudited; in £ thousands, except per share and shares outstanding data.

Reprinted by permission from Manchester United PLC.

Table 13.4 Tottenham Hotspur Income Statement for the Year Ended 30 June 2016

	2016			2015		
	Operations, excluding football trading*	Football trading*	Total	Operations, excluding football trading*	Football trading*	Total
	£'000	£'000	£'000	£'000	£'000	£'000
Revenue	209,770		209,770	196,377		196,377
Operating expenses	(162,443)	(31,785)	(194,228)	(162,361)	(38,562)	(200,923)
Operating profit (loss)	47,327	(31,785)	15,542	34,016	(38,562)	(4,546)
Profit on disposal of intangible fixed assets		27,109	27,109		21,182	21,182
Profit from operations	47,327	(4,676)	42,651	34,016	(17,380)	16,636
Finance income			2,978			4,207
Finance costs			(7,179)			(8,790)
Profit on ordinary activities before taxation			38,450			12,053
Tax			(5,413)			(2,657)
Profit for the year			33,037			9,396

*Football trading represents amortization, impairment, and profit on disposal of intangible fixed assets and other football trading-related income and expenditure.

Reprinted by permission from Tottenham Hotspur Limited, *Annual Report and Consolidated Financial Statements* (London: Tottenham Hotspur Limited, 2016), 9.

divided by sales (£515,345,000). Using table 13.4, we calculate Tottenham's net profit margin to be 16% by taking net income (£33,037,000) / sales (£209,770,000), which is more than double Manchester United's profit margin. This comparison is especially noteworthy considering Manchester generated over 240% of the revenue Tottenham generated but also had significantly more operating expenses (£436,709,000).

Finally, another profitability ratio that measures the ability of a firm to generate profits from its shareholders' investments in the company is return on equity (ROE). Here, we can determine the ROE for each football club. The ROE for Manchester United was 8% and was calculated by taking net income (£36,371) divided by stockholder's equity (£458,282). Consistent with the difference in net profit margin, Tottenham's ROE was 16% and was calculated by dividing net income (£33,037) by stockholder's equity (£206,050).

To understand how the stock market is valuing a company, we can compute the **price–earnings ratio (PE ratio)**. The PE ratio is equal to the price per share of common stock divided by the **earnings per share** of common stock. Earnings per share is calculated as follows:

$$\text{earnings per share} = \text{net income} / \text{average number of shares outstanding}$$

If Under Armour and a competitor each reported earnings per share of $5, but UA's sell for $15 and its competitor's shares sell for $20, then the PE ratio for UA is 3.

$$\text{price–earnings ratio} = \text{price per share} / \text{earnings per share} = \$15 / \$5 = 3$$

By contrast, the PE ratio for UA's competitor is 4.

$$\text{price–earnings ratio} = \$20 / \$5 = 4$$

Note the stock market is valuing UA's competitor's shares at a higher multiple of earnings than it is valuing UA shares. This disparity in PE ratios is usually related to differences in how the financial markets view the quality of earnings, past profitability, expected future earnings growth, or a combination of two or more of those factors. Besides noting the PE ratio, some financial analysts also report a company's **price–earnings growth (PEG) ratio**. Because the PE ratio is historical in nature, the PEG ratio has become another metric to gauge company performance. Although the PEG ratio and traditional PE ratio have similarities, they conceptually have one fundamental difference. Specifically, the PEG ratio estimates what the future quarterly earnings will be as well as the previous three trailing estimates. This ratio offers a forward-looking perspective to investors.

Here is one example of how to calculate a PEG ratio using Under Armour. In this example, we know the stock is trading with a PE ratio of 3 and we assume the company's earnings per share (EPS) have been and will continue to grow at 15% per year. By taking the PE ratio (3) and dividing it by the growth rate (15), we can compute the PEG ratio to be 0.20.

PE Ratio of 3 / Growth rate of 15 = PEG ratio = 0.20

However, because of market fluctuations and other noise, estimates are not so straightforward when it comes to determining which growth rate should be used in the calculation. Suppose instead Under Armour had grown earnings at 20% per year in the last few years but was widely expected to grow earnings at only 10% per year for the near future. To compute a PEG ratio, you would first decide which number to plug into the formula. In theory, you could take the future expected growth rate (10%), the historical growth rate (20%), or an average of the two years.

Financial statements provide important information about the condition of a firm. By using numbers in financial statements, we can extrapolate key information allowing us to summarize an organization's liquidity, activity, financial leverage, and profitability. These ratios also allow a firm to examine its operations and ratios in comparison with publicly traded firms in the same industry. But when appropriate information is available, the market value of the firm should be used as a supplement to these accounting-based ratios. Market value is the true street value for a business (i.e., what someone would pay for a business today). Such a value is based on investor perceptions and the quality of available information about the company.

CONCLUSION

Financial ratios provide a business with valuable information to use as a tool to assess firm performance. However, when assessing financial ratios and their utility, it is important to remember these ratios are significantly more useful when compared to a company's own figures as well as to competitors' ratios. Ratios examined in isolation are of little value. In this chapter, we examined the key financial ratios and compared and contrasted four different businesses in two completely different sectors. In addition we covered the different methods for determining a company's value and the techniques used to determine the value of an investment.

Class Discussion Topics

1. Discuss three comparative benchmarks a company can use to assess its financial performance.

2. Discuss the four key categories of financial ratios.

3. Identify three companies you would compare Under Armour's financial ratios against?

4. Who would be three external stakeholders interested in a company's financial ratios?

Moving From Strategy to Action

After studying this chapter, you should be able to do the following:

- Identify strategies associated with business formation to provide the best tax and fund-raising opportunity for a new business.
- Explain how much funding will be needed to start a sports organization.
- Explain how a sports organization can maintain an even financial position.
- Analyze various expansion strategies to leverage any profits such as mergers and acquisitions.
- Understand various exit strategies from selling a business to declaring for bankruptcy.

Many people think that strategy is focused on what to do to make a business or organization run smoothly and meet its goals. While this is true, one of the most important facets of financial strategy is dealing with the unexpected or plans that backfire. Instead of resigning in defeat, financial strategists need to identify possible solutions to the unexpected. If everything goes as planned and the right amount was borrowed, producing the expected results, then the entire plan worked like a charm. In reality, rarely does a plan go exactly as envisioned. That is when strategy really comes into play. For example, the business models for many online retailers focused on convenience, and free shipping was part of the business plan. While an average brick-and-mortar store has a return rate of 9%, online retailers are seeing around a 30% return rate. These customer returns wreak havoc on margins and eat up between 20% and 65% of an online retailer's cost of goods sold ("The bottom line," 2017). Similarly, some bicycle-sharing companies launched over the past couple of years have attempted to reduce costs as a way to increase profits. That is not an unusual strategy. However, what was different is that some of these companies sacrificed following rules and safety in order to launch a disruptive service. Traditional bike-sharing companies have docking stations where bikes can be checked out and then returned to the same station or other docking stations. In contrast, other companies felt it would be more convenient (and less costly) to allow riders to pick up and drop off their bikes wherever they wanted. This led to bikes piling up on sidewalks, interfering with traffic, and creating a significant liability concern. The strategy was to take an existing system and streamline it, make it more user friendly, and reduce costs . . . but the result was cities trying to ban these companies and levying large fines.

CABELA'S LAUNCH TO FORTUNE

One example of the ups and downs can be seen with the sporting goods store, Cabela's. The company was founded by husband and wife team, Richard and Mary Cabela, in 1961 around their kitchen table. The company was started when the Cabela's bought $45 worth of fishing flies at an expo and then took out an advertisement in a local paper to sell them. With only one response, the couple thought they had a flop. They took out another advertisement in the nationally published *Sports Afield*, and things took off from there ("Random shots," 2014). The company grew over the years, primarily as a direct marketer to outdoors people through the millions of catalogs they sent out every year. The mail order business helped spur the building of brick-and-mortar stores around the United States. Even though the company started out focusing on fishing, it grew through firearms sales. In 2004, it went public. The stock was originally priced at $20 per share but jumped to $27 per share when the stock market opened. The stock offering raised $156 million to lower company debt and provide capital to open new stores. Those who were stockholders before the initial public offering were able to cash in four months after the stocks started selling by purchasing $270 million in shares at a set price of $22.50 each. Things were going very well until Richard Cabela passed away in 2014. In 2015, Paul Singer's Elliott Management purchased 11% of the shares—giving the investment company significant say in the business. Elliott Management pushed the company to sell its lucrative credit card business or the company itself in a leverage buyout. Cabela, similar to many other retail establishments, offer credit cards for customers, and they can generate significant revenue from people who rack up credit card debt and pay high interest rates. In 2016, Bass Pro Shop founder John Morris offered to take the company private for $5.5 billion, and Cabela's agreed (Schaefer, 2017). This example helps show how a company can start small , grow slowly at first, then expand rapidly, and then experience an exit strategy such as being sold, going public, going bankrupt, or just closing. At each point, strategic decisions were made—some good and some bad—but that is the life of any business.

These two examples help show how bumps can arise in the roadway to financial success for any business. Whether a wealthy donor passes away, a new competitor enters the market, or a massive recession occurs, there are many reasons why strategy is so critical. Every organization will face challenges, and how they respond to such challenges reflects the strength of their strategic planning to deal with the good and bad times.

Everything in the book to this point has focused on various information, ratios, documents, formulas, and related material to help readers understand the financial numbers. It is not enough to just know the concepts. The concepts need to be applied for a sport business from start to finish. Thus, this chapter will examine the financial strategy from starting a business through closing a business and the entire business life cycle. The chapter starts with examining the creation process and resulting funding needs. The chapter then examines how a business needs to remain steady in its growth. Every business will face growing pains and might merge with another entity or purchase another business to help with growth. The text ends with exploring what happens things go wrong and what is required to contract—either through **bankruptcy (or bankrupt)** or possibly by selling the business.

CREATION STRATEGY

One of the first strategies when forming a sport-related business is to examine the business structure. Every business structure has benefits and possible drawbacks. Some businesses start

as a sole proprietorship, turn into a partnership or LLC, and then convert to a publicly traded stock company as the company grows. The most common form of business used to be sole proprietorships with a single owner. However, this business structure limits the amount of money a business might be able to raise and exposes the owner to potential personal liability. Partnerships are also a relatively simple business form, requiring only a contract. While more money could be raised than by a sole proprietorship, unlimited personal liability still exists.

Since the late 1990s, many businesses, even large businesses, have formed as limited liability companies (LLCs). An LLC has the best elements of a small business with minimal paperwork and simple pass-through taxes and the major benefit of limited liability. When businesses want to obtain more significant financing, they often file to incorporate as a publicly traded company issuing stocks. While the paperwork is more complex and there is double taxation (both for the business' profits and the dividends paid to stockholders), corporations have an easier time raising money and have liability protection for investors. Thus, this brief overview helps show that the financial strength of a business will depend on how it is formed and continues. It should be noted that many sports organizations are nonprofit organizations and can raise money through donations. Other organizations are affiliated with government entities, and they can rely on public coffers and possibly government immunity as significant benefits.

There is no one best business form. There are benefits and detriments to every type of business structure, as highlighted in table 14.1. Every

Table 14.1 Benefits and Detriments of Various Business Structures

Organizational type	Benefits	Detriments
Sole proprietorship	Simple to form Simple taxes Complete control	Harder to raise money Ends when person dies/quits Unlimited personal liability
Partnership	Easy to form Simple taxes	Unlimited personal liability Ends when person dies/quits Still hard to raise money
Corporation	Limited liability Easier to raise money Can issue stocks Easy ownership transfer	Double taxation Need audited financials
LLC	Simple to form Simple taxes Limited personal liability	Not as easy to raise money

business or organization will pursue a strategy that works best for them, and it might change its structure over time. The key is the organization's goals and mission. If an organization is ready to meet all the requirements of a nonprofit organization, then it could start that way and enjoy the tax-benefit opportunities. However, under law, it would need to provide services to the community, and if it does not have a plan to offer those services, it can run afoul of the law.

Tax considerations are an important component of forming a business. Some businesses have simple pass-through taxes where the income from the entity passes through and is declared on

KEY STRATEGIES FOR LAUNCHING A SPORT BUSINESS OR ORGANIZATION

- *Be open to discovery.* When you start an organization, you will make many assumptions, including who the customers will be, what the financial needs will be, what the marketing strategy will be. This provides significant opportunity for creativity.

- *Be social.* You will need to bounce the idea around a number of people, run focus groups, and implement other strategies that will get people involved. It is critical to obtain relevant feedback from as many people as possible. Two of the important questions are, *what problem are you solving?* (sport solves an entertainment problem) and *what are you bringing to the market that is not already out there* (e.g., are you the third minor league team in a market?)?

- *Line up mentors and advisors.* No matter how smart you are, you can always use more guidance and information. Bring aboard top-notch professionals (accountants, lawyers, etc.) from the start to help navigate potential problems.

- *Conduct a stress test on all of your assumptions.* This can be done through looking at what was done in the past. If you are launching a minor league team, examine what previous, unsuccessful minor league teams in the area did right and what they did wrong. Then identify what you *think* will be the market reaction. For example, if you want to build a new sports facility and think there will be a lot of interest, bring a schematic drawing to some sports organizations and see if they would sign a commitment to pay and play at the facility. This will also represent contractually obligated revenue for a possible lender.

- *Explore where the money might come from and how to pay bills.* Many entrepreneurs dream of starting a business but normally do not have enough funds saved to cover their new venture's start-up expenses and pay living expenses. They might quit a full-time job, forgoing a salary and benefits. Many recommend having at least one year's salary available in savings before launching a new venture.

- *Test the founders' commitment.* If there are multiple founders, test the commitment for each person, as there might be some dedicated and others who are less interested. It is important to share financials with potential lenders and investors, but these individuals will also be looking at vision and commitment from the founders. Founders can be tested by asking for more time, effort, or funds.

- *Test the market with pricing strategies.* Fitness provider ClassPass initially launched with unlimited memberships, but people took so many classes that it lost money, so it had to eliminate that category.

- *Pursue sales soon after launching to show success.* Aim for the first sales no later than 90 days after launching. While getting prelaunch sales from Kickstarter might be a tempting approach, you have to consider what will happen if you cannot deliver the product on time. Some analysts discourage pursuing online funding campaigns as a way to test the market. It is better to test the market in other ways and only pursue such campaigns after the discovery phase is over (Buchanan & Marikar, 2017/2018).

the owner's income statement. Other organizations are much more complex. Businesses need to pay a variety of taxes including the following:

- *Income tax*. Based on the amount of money the business earns
- *Estimated tax*. Quarterly payments of the amount estimated to be owed to the government
- *Self-employment tax*. A Social Security and Medicare tax for individuals who work for themselves
- *Employment taxes*. Various taxes for Social Security, unemployment, and other withholding
- *Excise taxes*. Special taxes on specific types of products or businesses

All prior editions of this text have utilized a 35% federal tax rate and a 7% state rate resulting in total tax obligations of 42% on average for most businesses. However, the tax laws were changed in December 2017, and the federal tax rate decreased from 35% to 21%. This could significantly change financial strategies because in the past individuals might have pursued an LLC for the benefit of the pass-through taxation (in contrast to double taxation with corporations). However, the new rules might make it more beneficial to be charged at the corporate rate and retain money (to reinvest) rather than pay a higher individual rate (maximum of 37%).

FINDING FUNDS AND INVESTORS

After identifying what type of structure to use, the organization will need to obtain funds. Some organizations are established from the beginning with certain funds, such as a spin-off business division of an existing company. Most businesses, though, have an idea and then try to find necessary funds.

Initial Funds

The simplest way to fund a business is through cash. That cash might be funds in a bank or possibly personal funds. Many small businesses are self-funded, but large businesses can be funded by wealthy individuals. Some businesses fund development and growth through funds from family or friends. Strangers can also help fund a business. The recent growth of **crowdfunding** has allowed complete strangers to prepurchase items or become early investors in a business. Lastly, funds can be obtained from angel or venture capital investors who feel that a company is worth the investment risk. Angel investors are the first major investors in some businesses, and they will demand some ownership equity for their initial investment. Venture capital investors will demand a lot of input and governance power if they invest in the business. Due to the competitive nature of companies vying for venture capital investments, it is very hard to obtain such financing. Very few companies receive venture capital funding, and even with such funding, many new businesses do not succeed.

While many businesses have received funding through the founder's cash, friends, and family members, the Internet has served as a great tool for raising funds. When exploring using a crowdfunding technique, a new business needs to identify if it wants to give away an equity (ownership) or nonequity opportunities. Nonequity options could include a discounted price to prepurchase the potential product or other benefits. Kickstarter is an example of a site that focuses on nonequity rewards. Selling equity through stocks can cost millions and has numerous regulations. Crowdfunding also has specific rules such as:

- Only $1 million can be raised in a 12-month period.
- Most investors cannot invest more than $2,000.
- The funds must be raised through a Securities and Exchange Commission–registered portal (there are around 25 such portals).
- The business must have a specific business plan.
- The company must be based in the United States (for U.S. crowdfunding sites).
- Individuals with greater than 20% interest in the company must disclose ownership interest in the company.
- If the owners are raising more than $500,000, the required detailed financial statement needs to be audited (if it is between $100 and $500,000, it needs to be reviewed by a CPA).

♦ The business needs to file an annual report (Abrams, 2016).

♦ The business needs to pay the portal 5% to 9% of the raised amount.

The primary benefit of crowdfunding is the ability to reach many more potential investors, and it can also help expose an idea to input and scrutiny. A con of crowdfunding is that the idea is now known to the public, and a new business might spend a lot of time focusing on raising money rather than growing. With that said, businesses are not the only ones utilizing crowdfunding. Some athletes have started crowdfunding campaigns as a way to help cover travel and other related costs. In preparation for the 2016 Rio Olympic Games, 94 GoFundMe campaigns were running by various athletes, and they raised a total of $420,000. Athletes were trying to raise funds to qualify for national teams, as traveling around the world to reach a certain level of competence or world ranking can be very expensive, depending on the sport. Besides GoFundMe, athletes have raised money on Kickstarter, RallyMe, and Puru.It (Peterson, 2016). Besides athletes, numerous youth sports organizations and community sports organizations have flooded various crowdfunding sites. The success rate is not that high due to the large number of entities seeking funds, but with a compelling story, you never know what might happen.

There are several ways to raise necessary funds, but there is a cost to doing so. This can be a loss of business ownership or control; the actual cost of hiring lawyers, accountants, and others to do the necessary paperwork; and possibly adopting significant liability that can expose the business to harm. That is why every organization needs to carefully consider what steps it will take involving fund-raising. For example, a nonprofit organization might be offered a multimillion-dollar gift. While most organizations would be excited about such an offer, what if there are strings attached? What if those attached strings run counter to the future direction of the organization? Should the organization still accept the gift (and possibly sell its soul), or should it stand its ground and refuse to compromise? This is not an easy decision and requires significant analysis before the decision should be made.

A school might need funds to put in lights, but if there are no funds available, creative strategies might need to be undertaken to raise the necessary funds.

Ongoing Fund-Raising

After initial funds are obtained, a business will normally require funding throughout its existence. As highlighted in chapter 7, covering capital budgeting, and chapter 9, covering funding a business, organizations are always looking for both short-term cash and long-term capital funding. At times there will be enough funds in the bank or cash reserves, while at other times the business will need to borrow funds. Many businesses time their cash flow to anticipate future directions. A team might set aside some money knowing it has a major expense in the future. This is similar to someone putting aside some money every month with the idea of putting a down payment on a car. They might not have enough money for the down payment right now, but if they saved $100 a month for a year, they would have enough money. This is called a **sinking fund**, and many organizations follow this practice to make sound financial decisions—sometimes before they make a purchase but more often when they are trying to pay back a liability. Tapping a line of credit or borrowing from a bank are often the simplest means to obtain funds. If a business still needs funds, it might obtain them from the open market where various organizations are willing to lend money at a little higher interest rate or for an equity ownership stake in the business. A nonprofit organization could also try a bank, other short-term borrowing, or obtaining funds from major donors or board members willing to help the organization.

If additional funds are needed, the business might start selling assets or look for other sources. One such source is accounts receivables. While a company or organization can delay paying its accounts payable to conserve cash, an organization can also be on the receiving end of others not paying their bills in a timely manner. If necessary, an organization can be more aggressive in trying to obtain owed funds more quickly. An organization can examine its accounts receivable and determine when accounts are being paid, who is not paying on time, techniques to expedite payments, or when to write off an account as unpayable. Some accounts will not be paid regardless of what an organization does while others might have to be pursued through litigation. Some accounts might be repaid after a phone call or e-mail. Other accounts might need to be sent to a collection agency that might pay the company a percentage of the funds owed, and then the company does not need to spend time and energy trying to collect funds. This process is called factoring of accounts receivable.

One strategy utilized to obtain funding is growth. One team might generate some interest. In contrast, a company composed of several teams has more diversity and more potential synergy, so it can attract more investors. Similarly, various companies over the years have expanded through acquiring other companies and creating a larger entity that could then be sold for a premium. One such example occurred with endurance events. In 2015, Chinese mega-conglomerate Dalian Wanda purchased the World Triathlon Corporation (which runs the Ironman and similar events). In 2017, Wanda also purchased the Competitor Group, Inc. (CGI), which operates the Rock 'n' Roll marathons and other races in 28 markets. The combined entity has over 250 events throughout the world. The combined events allow Wanda to market to larger sponsors and create packages involving more events and eyes (potential customers). The process entailed several mergers over several years. For example, Elite Racing owned the Las Vegas-based Rock 'n' Roll Marathon. In 2008, Elite Racing was purchased by Falconhead Capital (an investment firm), which merged that event with other events to form CGI. Then CGI went on a buying spree and purchased a number of other marathons around the world. CGI's revenue rose significantly until marathon participation numbers decreased around 2015. While the marathon participating numbers are decreasing in some parts of the world, the numbers are actually increasing in China, where there were 134 marathons in 2015 and 328 in 2016 (Wahba, 2017). That is where Wanda came to the rescue with a large growth strategy. Other businesses have grown in the same manner through acquiring other similar entities. This trend can be seen with a number of NFL team owners purchasing English Premiere League soccer teams.

Whatever method is used to find additional funds, they will need to be repaid. As previously mentioned, many organizations utilize a sinking fund to set aside money to repay borrowed money. Others just repay on a monthly basis. This is similar to an individual's credit card debt. Someone can make the minimum monthly

Olympic Coin Program

The lineage of Olympic coinage is formidable. Anaxilas, a ruler of Sicily, ordered the first recorded minting of a coin struck especially to commemorate a sporting event in about 480 BC. The silver coin honored his victory in a historic chariot race and appropriately depicted the winner bearing a laurel wreath. Since the 1950s, several Olympic host countries have issued a variety of commemorative coins to defray costs of the Games. Canada's coin program for the 1976 Summer Games was considered one of the most successful (*Charlton standard catalogue*, 1990).

The program was aimed at selling collections of 28 specially minted silver $1, $5, and $10 (Canadian) coins. Canada was also the first Olympic host to issue a gold coin in the denomination of $100 in its own currency.

The margin between the cost of production and the face value of coins is known as seigniorage. According to the Canadian legislation authorizing the coins, the seignior, or issuing authority, had the right to retain that difference as profit. Profits from sales of the Olympic coins were initially expected to reach between $125 and $500 million (Canadian). The coin program was successful, but the coins were issued at the height of an internationally depressed economy. Even so, through 1977, sales of the coins had reached $386 million (Canadian). Of the $386 million, $278.7 million represented the face value of all coins delivered and had to be held in reserve by the Canadian government. The expenditures over and above the face value of the coins totaled only $8 million (Canadian). Thus, the program netted a profit of close to $100 million (Canadian).

Olympic Stamp Program

The Olympic Stamp Program was yet another unique fund-raising effort designed to help finance the 1976 Olympic Games. Canada Post's fund-raising focused on four areas: Olympic action stamps, commemorative stamps, stamp sculptures, and stamp souvenirs. In 1974, Canada brought out its first set of semipostal issues—postage stamps that carried a surcharge. The purpose of the surcharge was to give the public a convenient opportunity to support the Olympic Games on a voluntary basis. Germany, France, and Japan all have used semipostal stamps when hosting the Games. Additional sets were issued by Canada in 1975 and 1976 (Gandley & Stanley, 1978).

The Olympic action stamps bore two different prices, separated by a plus sign (+). The first price on each stamp indicated the postal value of the stamp, the other the amount of the surcharge; the two amounts combined gave the sale price of the stamp. Thus, a stamp with a 15 + 5 marking included $0.15 of postage and a $0.05 contribution to the Olympic effort. Canada Post collected $0.20 (Canadian) for each one of those stamps sold.

To support the Olympic Stamp Program, Canada Post developed a promotional program under the umbrella theme, Help It Happen. Advertisements were published in all major Canadian newspapers and magazines and in specialized publications the world over; commercials were aired on television and radio networks. Display stands, posters, and decals were used in post offices to attract the customers' attention. In spite of all the promotion, the stamps did not generate the target figure of $10 million (Canadian). Potential buyers were either opposed to the idea or hesitant to try anything new.

The United States Postal Service (USPS) used a similar approach in the 1990s to raise funds for breast cancer research. Since 1998, the USPS has raised over $86.7 million for breast cancer research. In 2011, the USPS issued the Save Vanishing Species semipostal issue (the fourth semipostal in U.S. history), and through 2017 the stamp had raised over $4.3 million to help protect threatened and vanishing species.

payments and will repay the debt over time with a significant amount of interest paid (assuming the organization does not need to borrow any future funds and has a strong steady income stream). That same person can also try to repay their entire bill as soon as possible to minimize interest rates. The key is to repay amounts owed as soon as possible to minimize interest payments. One way to approach this repayment is to issue more stocks. Ownership might be diluted, but cash can be raised through this process to pay debts and possibly grow the business. This approach was undertaken after Manchester United was purchased by the Glazers and taken private. The team then issued shares with the Glazers controlling most of the class B voting shares. Funds raised from the offering helped repay, in part, some of the team's debt obligations.

When examining initial and subsequent funding options, it is important to consider undercapitalization and overcapitalization. **Undercapitalization** is when a company raises an insufficient amount of money. This would force the company to raise money again. Since there is a cost for raising capital, there will be wasted money because some of these same costs would have been covered in the initial funding round. Thus, if it cost $1 million to raise $100 million and the company has to raise another $100 million six months later (at the same $1 million cost) the company would have wasted $1 million and some additional time and energy. **Overcapitalization** occurs when a company raises too much money. If the company in the previous example raises $300 million to be cautious but only needed $150 million, then it has borrowed too much. This represents more debt service costs and stockholders and analysts wondering what the company is doing. The most dangerous type of overcapitalization is issuing too much bond. This debt can saddle a business for 10 to 20 years with interest and principal payments, which would be a major, unnecessary financial burden.

KEEPING AN EVEN KEEL

While some organizations are hoping for meteoric increases once they launch, others are hoping for slow and steady. In fact, rapid growth can be a major problem. A small company with significant new sales might be at a disadvantage. Rapid growth entails a rapid increase in expenses (such as buying more products or hiring new employees to process orders). In a rush to meet all these new potential orders a company might hire more employees, purchase more raw materials, and rent new facilities. If sales decline (due to a fad, competition, regulations, etc.) the company could be saddled by significant debt. That is why slow and steady is often the preferred way to grow a business or organization. While businesses might not have a choice in the matter, keeping an even keel by controlling growth as much as they can is better for the organization.

Financial Problems

The key to dealing with a financial problem is to plan ahead. Funds can be obtained to address potential issues before they become actual problems, but most financial problems could be spotted in advance and minimized by reading the right financial signals and communicating concerns with all stakeholders before they become too problematic. The stakeholders can be fans, unions, employees, government officials, stockholders, and others. Most publicly traded companies have an investor relations department. This person or department will reach out to board members, internal stakeholders, external stakeholders, investors, research analysts, financial press, and government agencies. The investor relations department will attempt to increase awareness and understanding across four different dimensions: operations, strategy, performance, and customers. These dimensions can be reached through management scripts (given during earnings calls), social media, website information, communications with institutions to promote stock sales, communications with institutions that buy significant shares, and staging road shows to promote the company. This communication needs to synthesize key financial drivers such as revenue numbers, total sales, earnings before interest, taxes, depreciation, and amortization (EBITDA), net income, and free cash flow into plain English and other appropriate languages. While so many folks are interested in the numbers, an annual statement and other communications are often read by individuals without significant financial acumen. Both internal and external stakeholders might not admit they do not understand all the numbers, so it is critical to effectively communicate with relevant stakeholders. This is especially critical when some people think the company is making money because there is a nice profit from a given item, but the cash flow or number of units sold might be showing the company is actually losing money.

Financial Planning

Misconstruing what the numbers really show is where financial planning comes into play. If a sports organization knows it is going to have a major expense on the horizon, it can plan for it by setting aside money or planning a stock or bond issue if it cannot borrow the necessary funds. When something is planned, it can be managed more effectively. However, as highlighted throughout this text, many financial issues occur as immediate disasters that need to be addressed. Think about it from a personal perspective. Imagine if you have a two-year-old car that you take every couple of months for an oil change. You follow all the manufacturer recommendations and take care of your "baby." Then the transmission blows out. You did nothing wrong and invested appropriately to keep everything running fine. Maybe the car warranty will cover the expense, but if not, where will you get the money to make the necessary repairs? Similarly, every business will face challenges like this. That is why even a company that is running smoothly needs to prepare for possible bumps and protect itself from income stagnation that can affect the bottom line.

The most frequent message many hear from executives facing financial challenges is that they did not see the sign. This could be that they did not want to think about the good or the bad. It could also be that they just did not notice the subtle signs—similar to people with serious health issues. Eventually, a person or business manager can trace a big problem to some previously minor issue that they did not really appreciate at the time. Other times, employees could have informed management about some potential problems before they became actual problems. That is why it is so critical to communicate even small issues so that management can put together information from various sources to help predict the future. Some signs that a business might be in financial distress include the following:

- *The business has trouble paying bills as they become due.* This is where understanding cash flow is so important to figure out why the money is not there.
- *Sales drop significantly.* This is where the company can reduce prices or launch other incentives to increase sales.
- *Employees keep quitting.* Exit interviews can be helpful, but if key employees are leaving, they might see the writing on the wall.
- *The number of competitors keeps dwindling.* Maybe the industry is dying.
- *Larger entities are taking over.* If so it might be time to reinvent the business.
- *The business is in constant turmoil.* This might be a sign that the management team might be the issue.

Companies are constantly trying to find ways to generate additional funds, and new technologies is one such approach. Disney is spending $7.3 billion on content through ESPN. In order to leverage this expenditure and keep up with Netflix and other streaming platforms, it will work with BAMTech (started by Major League Baseball and now majority owned by Disney) to stream content on its app. Besides ESPN, other proposed entertainment for the APP includes Disney, Pixar, Marvel, and Lucasfilm movies to go along with the sport content. The entry of new technologies and new competitors in the broadcasting and streaming field has also changed the dynamics of each deal. In the past, many broadcasters wanted to get an exclusive lock in a property for many years (such as the NBC long-term lock on Notre Dame football games and Olympic broadcasts with contracts spanning several decades). The new contracts, though, are often very short-term digital agreements. As an example, the NFL is hoping that a one- or two-year contract will be such a success that other entities will battle for the rights when they open in a year or two. This approach can create a more competitive environment, but it can also backfire. If the digital broadcasts are not drawing the fans, then the NFL would be hard pressed to find a buyer at the same price in the future. It is a gamble, but it is one the league feels comfortable it can leverage for a higher payday.

Companies are also exploring ways to reduce costs. The Green Bay Packers are a publicly owned, nonprofit, team established in 1923. The team can generate a profit but was formed as a non-for-profit community organization over 80 years ago. The public ownership provides the city with a degree of protection, because if the team was ever sold, all the proceeds would go to the Green Bay Packers Charitable Organization. The local nature of the team can also be seen in the concession stands. While food is prepared by professionals (Delaware North), most of the food and beverage sellers are actually volunteers from local nonprofit organizations. These organizations receive 10% of the net revenue for the permanent concession stands and 5% of the net revenue from the portable beer stands and hawkers. Such an effort can reduce the total overhead costs for employees, but it also helped return $4.16 million to the Green Bay community in 2016 (Ryman, 2016). Such efforts can help create a loyal following. Lambeau Field season ticket packages have been sold out since 1960, and the fan base is so loyal that the team has a 10-year waiting list for season tickets. This is that much more impressive when examined in light of the population of Green Bay, which is only around 105,000. The volunteer corps can also help reduce the total payroll costs for the team.

These are just two examples of strategies undertaken to either reduce expenses or increase revenue as highlighted in earlier chapters in the book. One important strategy to maintain stability is purchasing insurance. Most people are familiar with automobile, homeowner's, or medical insurance. Such policies are designed to protect the insured from sudden losses or expenses. There are numerous types of insurance that can be purchased such as automobile, comprehensive general liability, workers' compensation, employment practices liability, prize coverage, business interruption, and almost any other insurance people are willing to pay for. This text cannot identify every potential strategy that can help an organization progress at a steady pace, but some areas to possibly explore include

- maintaining strong relationships with customers and suppliers as they can help identify potential issues and opportunities;
- communicating the organization's financial position with key stakeholders so they can help make effective decisions;
- maintaining strong relationships with banks and other financial institutions in case funds are needed;
- keeping abreast of as many changes as possible in the organization's business field; and
- monitoring the cash flow as it can be the first sign of potential trouble.

Dividend Payments

While exploring reducing costs or growing revenue, a company will also spend significant effort determining whether to reward owners or reinvest any excess funds into the business. Keeping the owners happy by paying a dividend has value. Not paying a dividend also has value as the reinvested funds can help grow the business' overall value. There is no one correct decision, but when there are any profits, a business needs to have a strategy in place to deal with what hopefully is a regular occurrence.

A dividend is a payment made out of earnings, in the form of either cash or stock, to the owners or shareholders of a business (Brigham & Ehrhardt, 2011). Dividends are paid to reward stockholders for staying with the corporation. Some stocks steadily appreciate in value, and that capital appreciation is the reward that stockholders need to justify their investment. Other corporations may have a steady stock price but reward stockholders by paying a regular dividend.

Paying dividends is one method of distributing profits. For many corporations, it is a major cash expenditure. Large companies such as IBM and Microsoft spend millions of dollars in dividend payments to their shareholders. Many other companies, however, elect to make no dividend payments. A firm's board of directors determines the amount of dividend payments and makes all other dividend decisions not otherwise specified in the corporate bylaws or on the stock certificates.

Initially, you would think that a firm would want to give as much money back to its shareholders as possible. But it also makes financial sense for the firm to take the money and invest it for the shareholders. Deciding which option to select can be both difficult and controversial for financial managers. Shareholders and financial analysts can be critical if they believe that management is pursuing a poor dividend policy. Such negative feelings can affect a stock's performance.

A sport business may also make distributions to its ownership. A distribution is similar to a dividend, but it is paid out of sources other than current or accumulated retained earnings. For simplicity, we refer to any payment by a firm to its shareholders as a dividend. Typically, dividends are paid by large corporations. Smaller corporations often need to reinvest the money so that they can grow.

CONCEPTS INTO ACTION

How Much Dividends to Pay

In the late 1990s, Speedway Motorsports was a growing company involved in the motor sport industry. It owned and operated several racetracks across the United States. In its 1998 annual report, the company stated that it would not pay dividends for the foreseeable future so that it could reinvest money for company growth. By 2003, however, Speedway Motorsports had enough cash on hand to feel comfortable in paying dividends to its shareholders. The company paid out dividends of $0.31, $0.32, and $0.33, respectively, for the years 2004 through 2006 (Speedway, 2006). By 2010, Speedway was making quarterly dividend payments of $0.10 per quarter, which increased to $0.15 per quarter through 2017. In contrast, Nike paid a $0.36 quarterly dividend per share in December 2011, and at the end of 2017 the dividend was $0.20 per quarter.

Dividend policies can be somewhat confusing. A corporation may have many good reasons to pay high dividends, but there are as many good reasons to pay relatively low dividends. This section covers the ways that dividends are paid, the various types of dividends, and reasons for the payment of high and low dividends.

A company that is doing well can pay a cash dividend, or it can pay a **stock dividend**. A stock dividend can include a company buying back shares, therefore increasing the value of remaining shares, or a business can give shareholders additional shares. Many stockholders actually prefer to have their dividend paid in stocks, and with small dividends an investor might get share fractions in lieu of payment.

GROWTH AND EXPANSION

If a business is doing well, it has multiple options for the future. It can stash money away in investments or in the bank. It can give employees bonuses. It can reduce the price of products or services. It can also pay the owners (as dividends to shareholders or as a salary for an individual business owner). These are just some of the strategies the business could undertake. Such decisions are not made in a vacuum. A business owner might pay themselves millions of dollars in order to claim the wages as a business expense in order to reduce the business profit and ultimate tax liability. Paying off a debt might be a good use of extra money, as it will reduce future interest obligations. Extra money can be put aside to invest in new research and development—critical to develop future products.

If an organization or business is doing very well, it might explore expansion. Expansion can include building more stores, launching new sports, opening new facilities, or buying competitors. The goal is that at some point the organization feels it can provide more services to more people or generate more income. Expansion efforts do not necessarily need to only entail growing but can entail morphing the business. The organization can change its focus from one product to another, or it might change from one industry to another. One such example was the Florida Panthers, who issued stocks in 1997. They were morphed into a real estate company (purchased by Boca Resorts, Inc.), and the focus moved to real estate. The entire company was subsequently purchased for $24 a share by Blackrock Group and taken private.

Companies can also expand through gaining recognition in new areas. Some organizations become certified as a way to distinguish themselves from others. Some organizations pursue ISO 9000 certification, which is a quality assurance protocol to show the organization has policies and procedures to insure high quality. Organizations can pursue differentiation through B Corporation status, which is a new designation sought by some for-profit companies to show they are following sustainable business practices.

One way to grow is to purchase other business units or assets. If a person or company is interested in buying another company, they need to undertake a due diligence analysis to determine what they are buying and what it is actually worth. Part of this process would include examining:

- ♦ financial information, including all appropriate financial statements and bank records;
- ♦ corporate data such as articles of incorporation, corporate minutes, and employment charts;
- ♦ legal documentation such as all existing contracts, insurance, and pending litigation;
- ♦ distribution and marketing information to gauge how strong and loyal the customers are;
- ♦ product-related information such as any patents or other protections; and
- ♦ government information such as tax records, abatements, zoning information, and the like.

Mergers and Acquisitions

In a **merger**, one business blends its business with the acquired business. Thus, company A can merge with company B, and the new entity could be called company C. In contrast, in an **acquisition**, the acquiring company maintains control of the acquired company and serves in a dominant position over the acquired company. Thus, in an acquisition, company A can acquire company B and still be company A. A merger can be part of an acquisition, such as the merger of accounting departments from two different companies.

A merger is an investment, made under uncertainty, in which the goal of the acquiring business is to increase its value or its shareholders' wealth. As with other investment opportunities, a business should acquire another business only if it believes that a positive gain in net present value will occur. Unfortunately, given the level of uncertainty, calculating the net present value of an acquisition candidate is extremely difficult (Ross, Westerfield, & Jaffe). Unlike the situation when a company decides to invest in long-term capital, placing a value on the additional expenses and income associated with a merger is difficult.

A number of important mergers have occurred in the sport industry since about 2008. For example, sport and entertainment companies such as Disney and Comcast acquired other companies to increase the scope of their operations. Then Disney acquired part of Fox, and

Disney is known for not just launching theme parks and Wide World of Sports but acquiring other businesses that can help them grow revenue.

Comcast acquired SKY, which has the Premier League broadcast contract. These acquisitions have been somewhat controversial due to larger firms gobbling up other firms which can significantly reduce competition and may have a large effect on the future financial landscape within the sport industry.

Not only can the largest entities do well in mergers but also the small ones can, too. Conversely, some companies actually lose significantly from overextending themselves financially to swing a merger. One example that shows how the little guys can win is the merger of the National Basketball Association (NBA) with the American Basketball Association (ABA) in 1976. The NBA absorbed four ABA teams (the Nets, Nuggets, Pacers, and Spurs), which meant the ABA had to eliminate two teams (the Kentucky Colonels and the Spirits of St. Louis). The Colonels owner was paid $3.3 million and walked away. The Spirits owners refused that deal and worked out a deal where they were paid $2.2 million up front and a percentage of future TV revenue. At that time the NBA received very little in TV revenue. However, the deal allowed the owners and their descendants to receive a percentage of the TV revenue for as long as the other ABA teams are in the NBA. This amount has totaled over $180 million so far, even though they only owned the franchise for several years (Pells, 2006).

Company acquisition for the sole purpose of diversification is normally not a wise financial strategy. Companies normally should merge only if they believe that the new company will result in some additional value that is not possible if separate enterprises are maintained. If no additional value is earned through a merger or acquisition, the action may not be in the best financial interests of either side. But not all mergers have financial growth as the goal. Some companies want to eliminate or reduce competition by purchasing a competitor and then shutting it down. Other companies buy a competitor for leverage with unions so that the unions cannot use the other business as an example of concessions that they want. Still other businesses merge to avoid a takeover by another company.

We need to remember that many mergers are unwelcome. Although the purchase of a small corporation by a large corporation may make the owners of the small company wealthy, some owners do not want to sell. In this circumstance a **hostile takeover** may occur. Hostile takeovers can also occur when one corporation is trying to buy another one and a third corporation arrives on the scene, offering more money.

Not all hostile takeovers are successful, however, because companies can undertake various steps to protect themselves. Among these steps are issuing new shares to dilute the market, selling key assets, and approaching a "white knight" to make a counteroffer (Cheeseman, 2010). Other approaches include adopting "poison pills" that require the would-be buyer to pay executives a large fee if it purchases the company or require the would-be buyer to pay more for the shares. In fact, poison pills have increased the value of the companies that have adopted them by 35.9% versus only a 31.9% premium for companies that did not have them (Thornton, 2002).

A successful sports manager must be attentive to the possibility of acquiring other companies or possibly becoming the target of an acquisition attempt. The discussion that follows focuses on the types of mergers, justifications for mergers, the legal forms of acquisition that occur within sport, and other forms of acquisition.

Types of Mergers

Ross, Westerfield, and Jaffe (2008) separate mergers into three categories: horizontal, vertical, and conglomerate. Each type has potential benefits, but each could also generate some concerns.

Horizontal Mergers

A **horizontal merger** takes place when two companies in the same line of business are joined. The sports shoe industry has seen two mergers that have dramatically changed the business landscape. In 2003, Nike spent $350 million to acquire one of its competitors, Converse. This merger brought together two traditional shoe manufacturers. In a much bigger deal, Adidas-Salomon spent $3.8 billion to acquire Reebok in January of 2006. Reebok and Adidas together have about a 15% to 20% market share in the sports shoe industry. In deals such as these, management believes that the new merged company will have a higher value than the two separate businesses. Another example of horizontal mergers in the sport industry include ESPN buying ABC and ESPN. Comcast launched several sport-related companies and also bought ticketing company Paciolan Inc. (formerly part of Ticketmaster) in 2010. IMG Worldwide, a sport marketing and athlete representation company, acquired ISP Sports, a collegiate sport marketing firm, in the summer of 2010. Later on IMG Worldwide split, and IMG College became a dominant player in the college sport marketing space. Then in 2017 IMG College merged with Learfield to create a super college sport marketing company (Smith & Ourand, 2017).

Vertical Mergers

In a **vertical merger**, a buyer expands operations forward toward the final consumer or backward in the direction of the source of raw materials. Livingstone (1997) refers to these different market levels as upstream and downstream. A downstream market is further along in the production process, whereas an upstream market is closer to the original raw materials. In either situation, a business expands by acquiring other companies that are part of the production process. In 1998, Intrawest, the operator of several mountain resorts in North America, acquired two companies, Breeze and Max Snowboards. Both companies rented ski and snowboard equipment. By acquiring these two businesses, Intrawest was able to extend its operations upstream because rental equipment is a necessity for many consumers who want to ski. Intrawest not only has control of the ski mountains and the corresponding income streams but also rents the equipment needed to ski on its mountains ("For the record," 1998). But given that sporting events are simultaneously produced and consumed, the frequency of vertical mergers is much less common in sport than it is in other industries.

Conglomerate Mergers

A **conglomerate merger** occurs when companies in unrelated lines of business come together. One example of a company that was involved in conglomerate mergers was SFX Entertainment during the late 1990s. SFX had traditionally been in the entertainment industry through the ownership of amphitheaters and concert halls,

as well as through participation in the music promotion business. With its acquisitions of the Marquee Group, Integrated Sports International, and FAME, SFX expanded into sport marketing, sports event production, and athlete representation. It appeared that with these deals, SFX was attempting to become the largest integrated sport and entertainment conglomerate in the world. In 2000, however, SFX was bought by an even larger entertainment company, Clear Channel. Another conglomerate merger occurred in 2005 when Quicksilver, a famous surfboard manufacturing company, bought Rossignol, a ski company, for $320 million. Although the deal involved different sports, both are outdoor sports, and both companies had various lines of equipment and apparel (Grant, 2005). A more recent example is Dalian Wanda, from China, which has purchased various sport entities through 2017 such as part of a Spanish football (soccer) team (Atlético Madrid), the Ironman Triathlon series, and the Competitor Group, which owned numerous races such as the Rock 'n' Roll Marathon series.

Credible Justifications for Mergers

Credible justification must be in place for a merger to occur. As stated earlier, if no additional value is generated through a merger, then maintaining the status quo and keeping the companies independent is probably wiser. Perhaps the best justification for a merger, especially in the case of a horizontal merger, is **economies of scale**. A company achieves economies of scale by increasing its size. The adage, "bigger is better," is a good way to summarize the idea of economies of scale. Two companies that duplicate activities may be more profitable if they merge operations. If a fitness center owner acquires another fitness center, economies of scale may result. Corporate responsibilities such as accounting, staff development, and office management for the two facilities could be combined, offering the potential for substantial cost savings. Although the consolidation of these operations would have little effect on revenues, it would likely lead to a decrease in expenses. The result would be an increase in earnings and in the value of the merged company.

CONCEPTS INTO ACTION

The recent (2017) acquisition of some Fox sport entities by Disney is an example in which economies of scale may be achieved through a merger. Disney and Fox revealed details about the $52.4 billion merger agreement in a massive 455-page filing with the Securities and Exchange Commission in 2018. Under the agreement, which is expected to close in late 2019, if approved by regulators, Disney would acquire the Twentieth Century Fox film and TV studios, cable networks such as FX Networks and Fox Sports Regional Networks. Not included in the deal would be other Fox networks such as FS1 and FS2. Fox Sports Regional Networks (often referred to as FSN) had numerous rights contracts throughout the United States involving a number of Major League Baseball, NBA, and National Hockey League teams and owned a larger percentage of the YES network—which broadcasts New York Yankees and Brooklyn Nets games. FSN actually was a combination of previously independent sports channels that were compiled into a network. Some original networks that went into forming FSN include SportsChannel Florida, SportsChannel Ohio, Prime Sports Midwest, Prime Sports Southwest, Prime Ticket, and Sport South. It is a perfect example of an entity building a strong network through acquisitions and then being acquired itself.

Another credible justification for a merger in the sport industry is the prospect that a company can save on costs not related to economies of scale. For example, Cablevision, the New York–based broadcasting company, had paid over $40 million annually for the local television broadcast rights of the New York Yankees. The 12-year, $486 million broadcasting deal between the Yankees and Cablevision ended in 2000. In the fall of 1998, Cablevision made a reported bid of $525 million to purchase 70% of the Yankees (King & Brockington, 1998). Part of the rationale for the acquisition was that it would allow Cablevision to save $40 million per year. Instead of paying local broadcast fees to the Yankees annually, Cablevision wanted to purchase part ownership of the team and use the ownership rights to reduce or eliminate the broadcasting

payments. Cablevision would have owned both the television outlet and the team. Ultimately, the two sides were unable to agree on some details regarding the acquisition, such as team control, and the deal was abandoned. Ironically, the New York Yankees then decided to begin their own regional sports network, the YES Network. So Cablevision was not only unable to acquire ownership interest in the Yankees but also lost the television rights to broadcast Yankees games.

A merger or acquisition is also a wise financial endeavor if the merged entity can generate revenues that are not possible if the firms remain separate. Two firms may have complementary resources or products that when combined will result in substantial revenues. As a consequence of the merger, the combined company may have a very successful future. For example, the merger of IMG and ISP Sports Marketing that was mentioned earlier has allowed IMG to be involved at a much greater level in collegiate marketing and sponsorship sales. Although IMG had a small interest in these activities before the deal, it became the largest player in collegiate sport marketing.

A corporate acquisition may also be a wise maneuver if a business believes that the targeted company is poorly managed. A business may view the other company as underperforming because of poor management and believe that it can transform the targeted company into a financially successful business. The business believes that, through acquisition, it can improve its own value by instituting more effective management in the underperforming company.

Last, a merger can be the most effective way to invest surplus funds. As mentioned earlier, a successful business with a substantial amount of net income has several options. It can distribute the income to shareholders by increasing dividend payments, or it may repurchase its stock. A third option is for the business to invest its surplus cash by purchasing the stock of other companies. Often, businesses with surplus cash and a lack of good alternative investment choices redirect their capital toward purchasing other companies. The strategy may be wise in that a business that fails to redirect its cash may itself become a target for takeover. Businesses with significant excess cash face the possibility of acquisition because other companies may believe that they can acquire the business and redirect the cash in a profitable manner.

When examining merger and acquisition options, the two interested companies can just decide to fold themselves together. To reduce expenses, some employees in redundant areas might be terminated. For example, if both companies have large accounts receivable departments, then the merged company might lay off some of the people in the new department to become more efficient and save money—one of the key drivers for any merger. Another approach when acquiring a company is to purchase all the stocks so the purchaser becomes the owner. This might seem like a good idea, but if the acquired company has any potential legal liability, then the acquiring company will be responsible for any such payments. To avoid this potential liability concern, some acquiring companies will just purchase the assets of the company they want to acquire.

Just as there are numerous strategies to grow, there is an equally large number of strategies that might need to be explored to reduce costs if they reach a critical level.

CONTRACTION

Contraction refers to the process of either shutting down (possibly closing a division) or closing the entire company a business or business unit. Sports organizations sometime face significant financial issues and cannot solve them. That is what happened to The Sports Authority, and the company had to file for bankruptcy protection. Strategy comes into play when a sports organization starts facing pressure from various sources such as competition, government entities, changes in laws, or changes in markets. It could be as simple as a fad. For example, some readers of this text might remember when inline skating was popular in the late 1990s and the turn of the century, but that seems to have been a fad. According to the Sporting Goods Manufacturing Association, there were 22 million people in 2000 who went inline skating at least once that year. By 2010 that number had declined more than 64%. Such a quick rise and subsequent fall is a classic example of a fad. Similarly, trampo-

line parks were popular through the 1960s, and then they were basically sued out of existence. More recently, trampoline parks have popped up again, but the number of injuries and resulting suits might once again jeopardize this industry segment.

NASCAR was facing issues with a decline in viewership and sponsors. In 2017, multiple teams moved to reduce costs by hiring younger drivers or renegotiated contracts with veteran drivers. Changing drivers or contract terms was one of the first steps at shedding costs as a driver could represent one-third of the annual budget for a team (Stern, 2017). It used to be that star drivers were the primary focus for sponsors, but sponsors are focused now more on return on investment. Top driver salaries can range from $5 to $10 million a year compared with junior drivers who might be closer to $500,000. A base salary is complemented by a portion of race winnings and a portion of sponsorship dollars. With some sponsors leaving the field or reducing their sponsorship amounts, teams are now fighting for the sponsorship crumbs (Stern, 2017).

While financial planning has previously been discussed, such efforts normally focus on trying to achieve a positive result such as launching a new business unit or trying to increase sales. Sometimes planning has to focus on another goal—avoiding going out of business. Such a scenario requires different analysis and strategies. When exploring possible financial hardships, a sport business has several options. The organization can reduce salaries, delay paying some bills, ask for additional funds from lenders, slow production, sell a business unit, sell some assets, or sell the business. Most organizations attempt one approach and see if it makes any difference. Then it can explore other efforts or a combination of efforts. Sometimes the efforts will work and the organization can get back on its feet. At other times, all these efforts to stay alive might not work. If efforts do not work in reducing expenses, an organization might need to liquidate or file for bankruptcy (or be pushed into bankruptcy). Even nonprofit organizations can face bankruptcy protection when their assets are not enough to cover debts. That is why it is so important to identify signs of trouble and then to act quickly to prevent further harm.

Red Flags

Before deciding to terminate operations, a business needs to know when it is in trouble. Most businesses cannot just decide to close their doors; they usually have financial obligations such as accounts payable, long-term labor contracts, long-term lease obligations, repayment to equity investors, and debts. The decision to close is neither an easy one, nor is it made without significant managerial forethought. Most executives take pride in their managerial skills and would not want to be remembered as the person who lost a business.

Fortunately, a number of indicators can help signal financial trouble and provide adequate warning to an executive. For example, if orders start declining significantly, a business can examine the reasons and take corrective action to avoid losing market share. If a new competitor comes into the market with a more advanced and cheaper product, then the business needs to adjust to stay competitive. Key factors associated with business failures include economic weakness, industry downturns, poor location, too much debt, too little capital, and countless others. These concerns can lead to temporary cash flow problems that can often be worked out. Sometimes, however, the concerns indicate a permanent problem.

One sign of trouble is a lender's request for early repayment of a loan. A bank or other lender may call the loan under certain conditions; the primary reason is poor financial performance. If a sport business has been losing money steadily for several years, banks may feel uncomfortable with their loans and demand immediate repayment. The following are other conditions under which a bank might call a loan or not renew a line of credit (Broni, 1999):

◆ Loan covenants have been repeatedly violated.

◆ The bank is losing money on the relationship.

◆ New bank managers favor a different loan mix or institute new policies.

◆ The bank does not understand or is uncomfortable with the industry segment.

◆ The bank's credit exposure in the industry segment is too great.

◆ A loan guarantor's financial condition has deteriorated.

◆ The bank has lost faith in the business' management team.

If a bank or lending institution pulls the plug, the business needs to establish a policy to deal with the lost cash. The first step is often to negotiate a short-term extension to try to resolve any problems or secure new funding. If the business is on strong financial ground, approaching another bank might be easy. If a problem caused the bank to call the loan or pull the funds, asking the bank what the problem was might be worthwhile. If the problem is one that can be fixed, such as untimely reporting, then the business owner can explain this to another potential lender and take measures to correct the problem.

If the business has assets, the assets could help secure needed funds. Asset-based loans, as the name implies, can be obtained on the basis of the existing inventory or accounts receivable. If the business owns a valuable asset such as buildings or land, these could be pledged as collateral to secure more funds. If these options are not available, the business might need to approach a commercial finance company that specializes in unbankable loans. Because these loans are riskier, they entail a higher interest rate. The business may also need to report earnings frequently to keep the lender abreast of financial conditions. After the business can show sustained success and compliance with loan terms for one to two years, the owner can usually apply again for conventional bank loans.

Losing a bank loan is just one sign that a business is in trouble. A business that cannot pull itself through the hard financial times may have to resort to informal or formal attempts to satisfy debt holders. Debt holders can be satisfied through informal reorganization or liquidation, bankruptcy, removal of assets, or selling the business.

Informal Reorganization

Informal reorganization allows a business to recover and reestablish itself after facing a temporary financial crisis. These voluntary plans, in which all parties try to come to an agreement, are often called workouts. Workouts are successful only if the debtor is a good moral risk, if the debtor can show the ability to recover, and if the general business conditions are favorable for recovery (Brigham & Gapenski, 1994).

The informal reorganization process comprises extensions and composition. Extensions allow additional time for repaying a debt. If a debt is owed and due in one year, an extension could be worked out for the borrower to repay the debt in two years instead. Composition is the process of asking to repay a lower amount. A debt holder would rather receive $900 from the company versus only $500 in bankruptcy proceedings from a $1,000 debt. Most often a workout involves a combination of these two methods.

CONCEPTS INTO PRACTICE

Assume that Under Armour (UA) owes several lenders $10 million. The company might be able to develop a workout in which it pays 25% of the debt immediately and 20% a year for the next three years. Thus, in four years, UA will have repaid 85% of the original debt, and the debt will be discharged. Although lenders might not receive the entire amount they are owed, most lenders would be happy to recover 85% of the original loaned amount versus possibly nothing, or a much smaller amount, if the borrower goes bankrupt.

Not all banks are willing to engage in workouts, but most understand the value of negotiating the best deal they can to receive the largest possible share of their initial loan. The lenders might demand interest payments during the payback period to help cover the extension and might also demand additional security, such as personal pledges or asset-backed pledges.

Informal Liquidation

Informal liquidation is effective if the company can turn around, but some companies cannot fix their problems. If the company's debt is larger than its net worth, the company will probably need to go through bankruptcy protection (discussed later). But if the company has more assets than debt, it is "worth more dead than alive." Assignment is the term used for the informal liquidation process. Lenders normally obtain a greater return through assignment than through bankruptcy. For that reason, lenders should focus on encouraging informal reorganization or liquidation rather than trying to force a company into bankruptcy.

Banks and other lenders are not the only options available when times become rough. When financial concerns arise, a business can sometimes look inside itself to find an answer. One such answer lies in liquidating assets such as stocks. If no such assets exist, the business might have to sell other assets such as property.

Removal of Business Assets

A business owner might decide to condense a business by removing assets. Selling assets can reduce business costs or raise cash. Such transactions are often highlighted on annual reports as a footnote indicating a one-time write-off. Otherwise, the transactions would appear to boost the company's income when there is no likelihood of ever generating those levels of funds again. Selling assets, or downsizing, occurs frequently. The Boston Celtics once owned their own television and radio stations but sold them because those assets did not fit into the team's business plans.

Owners can use several techniques to downsize a business and remove assets so that the new business will be smaller. The primary reason that a company would want to downsize is reduced expenses, which will hopefully generate future higher profits. Instead of closing the business, a business owner might wish to downsize and hope that at a later date it could grow again. The first technique is taking out profits as dividends. Owners can also pay themselves more, sell assets, give bonuses, or effect other strategies to right the ship. All these efforts, though, can take a toll on a business owner, and they might decide to exit the game by selling their business.

SELLING A BUSINESS

Any business goes through ups and downs, but owners are sometimes not willing to accept the stress associated with such cyclical patterns. Business owners may decide to sell their businesses for a number of reasons, including the following:

♦ Wishing to retire

♦ Wanting to make a profit

♦ Wanting to change careers

♦ Wanting to get out while they can

♦ Finding the level of competition unacceptable

One trend that is helping to foster business sales is the fact that many baby boomers who own businesses want to retire, travel, or manage their pensions or investments. Furthermore, many older people are not ready to retire and are looking for a second career and might want to purchase a small business. Note that not all business transfers entail a sale. For example, a business owner can die and her heirs can inherit the business. Assume that a fitness center is owned by a husband and wife team. If one spouse passes away, the surviving spouse should value the club as highly as possible because there is no federal estate tax when an asset passes to a surviving spouse; but if the surviving spouse wanted to sell the center, they would have to pay taxes on the difference between the selling price and the gym valuation at the time of the deceased spouse's death. This will normally be a significantly lower taxable value compared with using the initial purchase or development cost (Battersby, 2003). To avoid these issues, many business owners plan for succession to allow their heirs to continue owning the business rather than being forced to sell the business.

If an owner does need to get rid of the business but does not want to give it away, the options include shutting down or selling the business. The first step in selling any business is to gather together all relevant financial information. If an independent auditor has reviewed the company's financial condition, the audited statements are the best tool to use in selling a successful business. Having several years' worth of audited financial statements shortens the time that the buyer needs to conduct a due diligence investigation and can accelerate the process of acquiring financing to buy the business.

A key component of any purchase decision is establishing exactly what will be purchased. For example, in 2000, Footstar purchased some assets of Just For Feet for $66.8 million. Footstar purchased 79 Just For Feet superstores, 23 specialty stores, the Just For Feet name, and its Internet business ("Footstar," 2000). Footstar made a business decision by choosing to purchase specific assets rather than the entire company. This decision might have been based on a number of factors, such as Just For Feet's debt obligations from lease agreements or numerous other debt and liability concerns. Similarly, with the Sports Authority bankruptcy highlighted in chapter 1, Dick's explored possibly buying some stores and some other assets before letting the bankruptcy process proceed to make any purchases at the end—hoping for a rock bottom price.

If a business owner wishes to sell a now-successful business, they face a major challenge—determining how much the business is worth. Owners put so much sweat equity into a business that they typically think that it is worth much more than it is. Owners may have a misconception based on sales of large, publicly traded companies, which can sell for up to 20 times their earnings (Livingston, 1998). Sales of smaller, closely held companies rarely reach such multiples of earnings. Larger corporations have a strong track record, can maintain consistent sales for extended periods, and have significant goodwill associated with their product or service. An NFL franchise is valuable even when the team has a losing record because of the inherent value of an NFL team. The strong value of NFL teams is based on the strong broadcast agreement and shared revenue. In contrast, a small mom-and-pop gym has a less stable product, and customer loyalty might not transfer over in the same manner as it does with a large company. Some gym members might have bought memberships just because they were friends of the owner. Fans of the Dallas Cowboys or any other NFL team would still be fans even if their franchise changed ownership several times over a decade.

Four options exist for selling a business: a taxable sale of company stock, a tax-free sale of company stock, a taxable sale of company assets, and a tax-free sale of company assets (Lee, 1999). Each option involves different concerns. A cash purchase takes less time than a stock deal because there are fewer compliance issues. A sale can raise concerns for the buying company. For example, if a company issues more stock to buy another company, will the new shares give rise to preemptive rights to current shareholders? A sale can also raise concerns that are normally not considered when making a typical asset purchase such as a car, in which the only issue might be determining whether there is a clear title.

Calculating Business Value

Valuing a business correctly is important for entrepreneurs who are trying to acquire a sport business. Valuation is also important for current business owners, who need to make sure that they are selling a business for the right amount. Chapter 13 highlighted how a business' value can be found in financial statements and associated ratios focused on valuation. A selling price that is too high will drive away potential purchasers, and underlisting a business can result in a significant financial penalty. Last, valuation is important for lenders who are attempting to establish the borrowing ability of the proposed business owners. Thus, everyone involved in the potential sale of a sport business needs to make sure that the value is accurate.

Value represents the monetary worth of an item. Value can be expressed as what you could obtain on the open market if you had to sell an item (Siegel, Shim, & Hartman, 1992). The value that individuals place on various items will vary significantly. A family heirloom could be priceless for someone in a family but valueless for someone buying the item at a garage sale. Similarly, a baseball card could be listed in a price guide with a $100 value, but a sports card dealer might offer only $10 for the card. This disparity in interpretation of value also affects businesses.

Valuation is the process of determining the value of a business. Although a vast amount of literature has been published about valuing businesses, little specifically addresses valuation concerns associated with the sport industry. Sport business valuation can represent unique challenges, such as determining membership numbers for service organizations, the value of intellectual property, and the value placed on a business because of the demand associated with people wishing to enter the sport industry. These concerns foster the need to conduct a critical analysis of sport businesses and their value.

Sport valuations must incorporate numerous factors beyond those used to value other businesses, such as total risks, the competitive environment, the business' assets, the timing of the valuation, and the ownership structure. These factors can significantly alter a sport business'

value even if an analysis of historic revenues and earnings suggests that two competing businesses are otherwise similar.

As highlighted in this section, a number of variables affect the final value that can be placed on a sport business. Because these variables can be interpreted in various ways to affect the final value assigned to a business, several valuation approaches should be used to develop a potential range of values.

A typical valuation may include the following steps:

♦ An estimate of the future benefits of the business based on some combination of earnings, cash flow, revenues, assets, and the potential future value of the business

♦ An estimate of the capital required between the purchase price and expected future investments

♦ A risk-adjusted estimated cost of capital or discount rate to be used in the valuation

♦ An analysis of the timing, taxes, personalities, and other nonfinancial factors that may influence a valuation (Pratt, Reilly, & Schweihs, 2000)

Critical financial information will normally come from available business reports and records. These data will probably require adjustment before they are suitable for valuation purposes. Such adjustments might be required to ensure accuracy or to reflect changes since the reports were completed. Mentioning such adjustments is important so that someone does not think that financial documents are without potential problems or blemishes.

Documentation essential for valuation purposes includes the following:

♦ Complete financial statements (balance sheet, income statement, statement of cash flow) for at least three years, including **disclosures** about leases, related-party transactions, and any pending legal issues

♦ Supplemental financial statement schedules such as compensation schedules for employees and officers, ownership distributions, dividend payment schedules, and key-person life insurance policies

♦ Federal and state income tax returns for the same period

- Operating information such as company history; marketing materials; brochures; copyrights, trademarks, and patents; organizational charts; customer and supplier databases; contractual obligations; and industry-related information concerning association membership
- Planning information regarding current budgets and forecasts, particularly of capital requirements such as future capital expenditures, deferred maintenance, and future working capital requirements
- Business formation documents such as corporate or partnership agreements, employee contracts such as noncompete agreements, and employee stock option purchase (ESOP) agreements (Pratt et al., 2000)

In addition, general economic or industry information can come from secondary sources such as various private (industry) and government entities or publications. Some examples include the U.S. Industrial Outlook, Standard & Poor's Industry Survey, Moody's Investors Industry Review, and the Almanac of Business and Industrial Financial Ratios.

The techniques presented here in no way represent a definite science. There is no one correct way to measure the value of a business. Someone who loves golf might be willing to pay a premium to buy a golf-related business just so they can own a golf business. This emotional element makes it almost impossible to create a foolproof valuation. Similarly, given the difficulty in valuing goodwill, a subjective element is always part of valuing a business.

Several techniques can be used to calculate the value of a business. The most common are asset-based valuation methods, the asset accumulation approach, the excess earnings method, the market-based approach, and the income-based approaches. Next we briefly consider each of these. The asset accumulation approach and the excess earnings method are generally accepted for valuing sport businesses, but due to their infrequent use, we will only briefly cover them.

Asset-Based Valuation Methods

In asset-based approaches to valuation, the value of a business is determined based on the value of tangible and intangible assets minus any liabilities attached to those assets. In essence, the net worth is computed based on factoring in assets that appear on the balance sheet along with assets that might not be recorded. Intangible assets, such as goodwill, might not appear on a balance sheet because of the difficulty in determining an accurate value, but nevertheless they add value to the business. Asset-based approaches (in particular the asset accumulation approach discussed next) are most relevant for valuing an established sport business or in cases in which the valuation is being done in response to the sale of an ownership stake that exceeds 50%.

Two asset-based approaches are generally accepted for valuing sport businesses: the asset accumulation approach and the excess earnings method.

Asset Accumulation Approach

The asset accumulation approach is simply the identification and summation of the current economic values of all assets—tangible and intangible—that are controlled by the sport business as of the date of the valuation. Because the objective of the valuation is to determine the current net worth, or equity value, of the business, all liabilities existing at the date of the valuation must be deducted from the estimated value of the business' assets.

Excess Earnings Method

In the excess earnings approach, the value of net tangible assets is estimated based on the return that those assets can earn. As a separate process, intangible assets are valued based on the value of excess earnings that can be attributed to the intangible assets. The steps in the excess earnings approach can be summarized as follows:

1. Estimate the value of the tangible assets of the sport business, net of liabilities.
2. Estimate the normal level of earnings for the sport business after a historical review of the business' financial results and subject to forecast of future results. To measure normalized earnings, the compensation of all equity owners, including salary, bonus, and profit sharing is adjusted to reflect what the cost would be to hire a manager with nonownership status to perform the same tasks as owners.

3. Estimate the annual income that an owner would require to be interested in investing in the net tangible assets of the sport business.

4. Deduct the annual income computed in step 3 from the normal earnings estimated in step 2. This remainder can be viewed as the excess earnings that are attributable to the business' intangible assets.

5. Convert this remainder to an economic value by applying a capitalization rate that reflects the inherent riskiness in relation to the ability of the business to generate the excess earnings over the long run. Capitalization refers to the conversion of a single value of economic income to a current economic value by dividing the measure of economic income by a capitalization rate that is expressed as a percentage. As an example, if the excess earnings generated by the intangible assets equal $400,000 per year and the appropriate capitalization rate is 20%, then the value of the excess earnings equals the following:

$$\frac{\$400,000}{0.20} = \$2,000,000$$

6. Add the value of the tangible assets to the value of the excess earnings to produce the value of the sport business.

Market-Based Approach

The market-based approach gives the value of the sport business based on a multiple of operating results, such as profits or revenues. The multiples are based on market transactions involving similar sport businesses. The inherent appeal of this approach is that the value of the business based on market-derived multiples reflects informed decisions negotiated between parties in transactions. When transactions are identified, notions of risk and return are incorporated into the multiples. Thus, the multiplier would vary within the same industry if one business has significant competition whereas a second business has no competition and is in a great location; the second business should have a higher multiplier.

For many types of closely held businesses, market multiples are derived based on multiples of earnings and revenues that are obtained either from analysis of publicly traded companies simi-

lar to the business or from data on actual transactions involving acquired or merging public and private companies. When market values of publicly traded companies are used to establish the value of a closely held business, a discount should be applied for lack of marketability to the value of the publicly traded companies. The lack-of-marketability discount results from a privately held company's being less valuable than a comparable public company because it is not as easy to quickly convert a business ownership position to cash (i.e., a private company is less liquid). The appropriate lack-of-marketability discount should be between 40% and 63% based on a recent survey of empirical studies (Pratt et al., 2000). For valuation analysis, limited information is available on transactions that involve sport businesses, and few sport businesses are publicly traded.

Many people believe that simple rules of thumb concerning the market multiple should be applied. This approach would mean applying an arbitrary multiple based on anecdotal information to current annual revenues, rather than analysis of empirical data. Such rules do not adjust multiples to reflect differences in operating characteristics and should not be used for any purpose other than as a reasonableness check on the values obtained from the use of other methodologies.

Income-Based Approaches

In income-based approaches, the value of a business is estimated based on the present value of all earnings and cash flow that the company provides to the owners during the time that it is owned. The appeal of this approach for valuing a sport business is that such a business is an operating entity that generates cash flow and earnings for the owners. The value resulting from the revenue- and profit-generating ability of the business is more relevant than the value that can be obtained from selling the assets of the business, because many sport businesses are not capital intensive.

One income-based approach, called the **discounted net cash flow** approach, estimates the present value of future economic income that is expected to result from the operations of the business. Also commonly used is the net cash flow to equity formula, which requires the following steps:

1. Determine net income after taxes.
2. Add noncash charges (e.g., depreciation).
3. Subtract net capital expenditures necessary to support business operations.
4. Subtract changes in net working capital necessary to support business operations.
5. Add net changes in long-term debt necessary to support business operations.

Net cash flow is used because conceptually it represents all income that an investor can hypothetically take out of the business. Generally, annual net cash flows are projected over a 5- to 10-year period. At the end of the projection period, a terminal value is estimated on the basis of the cash flows that are expected to be earned after the projection period.

The value of the business is then computed as the sum of the present value of the annual net cash flows over the forecast period plus the present value of the terminal value (Shapiro, 1999). The present value of any single annual cash flow received in the future is computed by discounting the future cash flows. The concept of discounting recognizes that money received in the future is worth less than it would be today because money invested today can accrue interest over time. Under the assumption that the investor can earn an interest rate of i, the present value of net cash flow (CF) received n years (CFn) in the future is as follows:

$$\frac{CF_n}{(1+i)^n}$$

For example, if the interest rate (i) is 10%, the present value of $1 million received five years from now is $620,921.

$$\frac{\$1,000,000}{1.10^5} = \$620,921$$

The tables in appendix B can help with such calculations.

A useful way to examine these various approaches is to use an example of a hypothetical martial arts studio to illustrate how a sport business valuation might be calculated in the real world. Because little inventory, capital equipment, or long-term debt is involved in this scenario, the simplified focus will use the basic income-based valuation approach.

John Lee is the owner and primary instructor at Kung Fu-R-Us Studio in New Haven, Connecticut. He started the business in 1989 and now has 200 clients. Each client signs a one-year membership agreement and pays $1,000 a year for lessons. The retention rate is high, and John often has new students wishing to join. The business is located at a strip mall, and 10 years are remaining on the lease. The lease calls for $2,000 a month in rent and includes a small yearly escalation clause. Utilities are included in the lease payment.

Staff salaries (not including Mr. Lee's salary) and benefits are $40,000, and miscellaneous expenses, such as phone, janitorial expenses, and increasingly expensive liability insurance are approximately $1,000 a month. Mr. Lee sells $2,000 each year in martial arts clothing and carries approximately $500 in inventory. He has $10,000, net of accumulated depreciation, invested in fixed assets such as protective mats, specialized martial arts equipment, lockers, and office equipment. Advertising and promotion in the community costs approximately $4,000 a year. The corporation has a $20,000 bank loan payable at a 10% interest rate.

As with many small businesses, Mr. Lee withdraws a significant amount of corporate profits as personal salary. Although many students enjoy Mr. Lee's personal instruction, he estimates that he could probably hire a high-quality instructor to teach his classes for him for about $50,000 per year. Mr. Lee estimates that a new owner could continue to grow profits by 5% per year for the next five years with minimal additional capital investments. Mr. Lee wants to enter into another business venture and is willing to sign a noncompete agreement stating that he will not open a competing business.

The balance sheet and income statement of the business are highlighted in tables 14.2 and 14.3.

As previously stated, because Kung-Fu R Us is clearly a service business that has few assets, an income-based approach is the most appropriate valuation technique. Adjusting net profits by replacing Mr. Lee's $110,000 compensation with a hired instructor gives a pretax return on the business of $68,500 ($8,500 [profit] plus $110,000 [owner's compensation] minus $50,000 [new instructor's salary]). Adjusting for an expected tax burden of $23,975 (35% tax rate)

Table 14.2 Balance Sheet as of December 31, 2017

ASSETS		LIABILITIES AND NET WORTH	
Cash	$5,000	Note payable	$20,000
Accounts receivable	$17,000	Accounts payable	$2,000
Inventory	$500	Taxes payable	$500
		Other accruals	$500
Total current assets	$22,500	Total current liabilities	$23,000
Equipment	$10,000	Retained earnings	$9,500
Total assets	**$32,500**	**Total liabilities and net worth**	$32,500

Table 14.3 Income Statement 2017

Sales	$202,000
COSTS OF GOODS AND SERVICES SOLD	
Cost of goods sold	$500
Depreciation expense	$1,000
Staff salaries and benefits	$40,000
Rent and utilities	$24,000
Miscellaneous	$12,000
Loan interest	$2,000
Advertising and promotion	$4,000
Total expenses	**$83,500**
Profit before taxes and owner's compensation	$118,500
Owner's compensation	$110,000
Profit before taxes	$8,500
Taxes	$1,275
Net profit after taxes	**$7,225**

leaves an after-tax net profit of $44,525 ($68,500 minus $23,975).

The next step entails assessing the value of expected future returns at present value. If a risk-adjusted 18% discount rate is used on the cash flow for a seven-year period, the net present value would be $169,708. This figure is calculated by multiplying the $44,525 net profit by 3.8115, which is found by looking up seven periods (representing seven years) at 18% on an annum table as found in appendix B.

An industry rule of thumb for buying and selling businesses is five times net income, which would give a value of $222,625 (5 multiplied by $44,525). The often-used professional service rule of thumb of 1 times revenues gives a value of $200,000 (Shapiro, 1999).

Because the value of the inventory and receivables is offset by accruals and the banknote, little adjustment would be required in this example. In a situation with no debt and substantial strong receivables or valuable inventory, some adjustment should be made to increase the valuation.

The numbers highlighted demonstrate that various valuation methods can provide a wide range of values, from $169,708 to $222,625, for the buyer and seller to start the negotiation process.

Bankruptcy

If a sport company is not doing well and has not found an entity to merge with or to buy it out (whether just assets or in its entirety), the company might limp along for a while. If the company limps along, it might be able to survive for a little bit, but it also could be hemorrhaging cash—often forcing the business to borrow more and go further in debt. At a certain point the debt becomes too much and the business will have to close. Some companies can pay off the bills and close. However, most have much debt that cannot be repaid, which results in the company filing for bankruptcy—either voluntary or forced.

Chapter 7 bankruptcy has the most common types of bankruptcy an individual or a company can pursue in the United States. Every country has bankruptcy-related laws so the issues are common, but the legal implementation is different. Chapter 7 is sometimes called straight bankruptcy or liquidation bankruptcy. Once bankruptcy is filed for (either voluntarily or by creditors), the court appoints a trustee to oversee the bankruptcy case. The trustee is responsible for taking the assets, selling them, and distributing the money to creditors who file proper claims. It should be noted that not all property is taken and bankruptcy laws protect certain items such as a basic home, retirement accounts, and other items protected in that jurisdiction. The goal of Chapter 7 is to give the debtor a fresh start.

In contrast, Chapter 11 bankruptcy focuses on trying to renegotiate existing debt to allow a business or person to stay in business. Courts provide monitors and protection so the debtor can stay in business. An ongoing business has the potential to turn things around and repay lenders. Lenders have the option of pushing a business into bankruptcy, or the business itself can apply for bankruptcy protection.

Bankruptcy is not only seen in the United States but all over the world. This can be seen with various football teams in Great Britain. When teams are liquid (such as after selling a star player) they might have excess cash. Illiquid teams do not have the extra cash. Insolvent teams are unable to pay their legal obligations as they become due. Lastly, in England, bankruptcy entails a team's management moving to an appointed external administrator or receiver who liquidates the team with an eye on protecting the interest of the creditors. From 1986 through 2008, 56 clubs in the English leagues became insolvent, based on a 2008 study, with three of the teams being Welsh clubs (Beech, Horsman, & Magraw, 2008). Since 2008, at least 17 more English clubs have entered administration. The majority of clubs from the 2008 study were tier 2 to 5 clubs. While no tier 1 clubs became insolvent, some of the lower tier teams were previously tier 1 and after relegation became insolvent. A club could have a payroll of several million dollars and could have earned millions from tier 1 broadcasting contracts, but if it were relegated, it would not have the large broadcast contracts anymore and still owe millions in player salaries. **Relegation** is the process of teams at the bottom of a tier being sent to the next tier of play. Thus, a tier 1 team that finished at the bottom of the league rankings will be relegated to tier 2 the next season and the top tier 2 team would move up to tier 1. In essence, if you win you keep making money, but if you lose, you lose your ability to generate as much money. This is a risk their U.S. pro sport counterparts do not worry about. The financial picture for these teams with formerly large broadcast contracts that have evaporated include Middlesbrough FC, which was relegated in 1982 and went bankrupt in 1985 owing £2 million. Since then the money spent and gained in football has grown quickly, so when Leeds United was relegated in 2004 and went into bankruptcy in 2006, it owed £35 million. The average amount owed by the 13 tier 2 teams that filed for bankruptcy was £10 million. In contrast, the 35 tier 4 to 6 teams only owed £1 million on average when they filed for bankruptcy. Relegation in the prior 12 months was the primary factor in a football club declaring bankruptcy in 30% of the 56 bankruptcy cases. Relegation in the prior three years was the primary factor in 48.5% of the study's bankruptcies. The most frequent debtor in these cases was typically the government—often owed significant taxes. Of the 56 studied bankruptcies, only 11% resulted in complete liquidation. The rest were able to satisfy debtors' demands within a five-year period and return to the pitch in better financial health. One of the common causes for the bankruptcies was fraud by chairman or directors (10 of the 56 bankruptcies)—such as in the cases of Darlington and Derby County. One of the other major factors associated with bankruptcies in English football was that many of the teams were dependent on one major donor (Beech et al., 2008). The lesson that can be learned is that football clubs who might be forced into relegation need to develop a plan, such as contracts contingent on the team staying in a given tier. Also, being reliant on one major sponsor is very dangerous.

One last element to consider in relation to bankruptcy is a league taking over a team to keep the league stable. This has happened several times with several teams. Such efforts were undertaken by the National Hockey League with the Phoenix Coyotes (in 2009 after the team moved from Winnipeg and incurred hundreds of millions in losses and was sold by the league to a new owner in December 2010) and the NBA with the New Orleans Hornets (which the NBA bought in 2010 for around $300 million to prevent the team from going bankrupt) (King & Lombardo, 2012). While teams going bankrupt is not unheard of, there are only three examples (the two previously mentioned and the Montreal Expos) where the leagues made the decision to take ownership of a team. The moral of the story is that even professional teams can go bankrupt. Thus, owners of smaller organizations or businesses facing financial trouble are going down a road that other, bigger organizations have gone down for years.

CONCLUSION

There is no one strategy to be successful in the sport business. Someone interested in starting a business in this exciting field will need to create the appropriate business structure, find necessary funding, run the business effectively, navigate around potential hurdles and opportunities, and hopefully grow. If the company can grow, then it might expand and purchase another business or launch new business lines. If the company cannot maintain or grow as needed, it might need to scale back. This could entail slowing production, selling a business unit, selling the business, or even going bankrupt. Each decision is a strategic decision based on financial variables.

The text has tried to cover various financial tools and ideas that have ranged from understanding financial statements to developing a budget and numerous other concepts. However, a concept is only one piece of the puzzle. The best budget in the world would not help if there is a significant economic downturn, a new technology, or any of numerous other variables. That is why there is such a difference between theory and practice. Finance is a combination of science and art. Executives are tasked with balancing what seems best with what will really work. Even if all the financial signs indicate that a company will do great, there is still no guarantee. That is why executives need to constantly evaluate what they are doing to avoid financial pitfalls. This chapter has attempted to identify some points where those pitfalls might arise and then suggest some strategies moving forward.

Class Discussion Topics

1. What is the most important part of the financial strategy process?
2. If you were to start a sports facility business, what business model would you use and why?
3. What do you think is the future of the Pilates industry and why? Examine the industry as a strategic investor who might want to invest money in opening a Pilates studio.
4. If you owned a professional team in the United States and were thinking about expanding internationally, where might you attempt to purchase a similar sports league–based team? Support your decision with sound research and advice.
5. If you ran a bowling alley that was struggling financially to pay the bills, what strategy would you pursue if you start falling further and further behind in paying your bills?

Part V Case Study

Tracking Industry Changes

What was the most popular spectator professional sport through the early 1970s? If you guessed professional baseball, you would be wrong. The correct answer is actually horse racing. Back in the 1990s, one study showed that horse racing drew 54 million fans to race tracks in 1990 to 1991 compared with only 52 million for Major League Baseball (Sports Law Center, 1992). However, over the past 20+ years attendance at horse racing tracks in the United States has significantly fallen on average race days, but attendance remained strong at major races such as the Belmont Stakes, the Preakness, and the Kentucky Derby (Minkel, 2015). The state of New York's racing handle in 2009 was approximately 20 percent of what it was in 1974 (Liebman, 2010). So why has the sport of kings fallen so much? This is a key strategy question and something that we can often examine in hindsight. However, why weren't we able to identify this trend in time to take different steps, or would the decline have happened regardless of any steps that might have been taken? These are issues of concern that affect those in sport finance fields because they need to produce and analyze numbers and make decisions on the course of action. All the evidence can point to a given strategy as being correct, and it can still turn into a money loser. In the case of horse racing, some claim the decline was due to variables such as demographic change (people moving away from the inner cities), other gambling options (casinos, Internet gambling, and lotteries), change in sport preference, modernization (off-track betting), corruption and drugs in the sport, and the knowledge base necessary to bet on horse racing (compared with a slot machine where all you need to do is push a button) (Liebman, 2010).

All is not bad for horse racing. Horse racing moved up to the second most popular spectator sport in Britain in 2016 with six million fans, just passing rugby but still far behind football (soccer) (*London Times*, 2017).

Music Industry

Similar to horse racing going through some dynamic changes, the music industry has also undergone significant changes. In the golden years (1960s through 1980s) album sales were king. Concerts were used to promote the artists and increase album sales. Technology kept affecting the industry with the transition from vinyl to eight track tapes, then cassette tapes, then to CDs, and then to online streaming. In the same vein, technology affected how music was listened to from record players, to tape recorders, to boom boxes, to Sony Walkmans, and then to iPods. Similar to how the phone, computer, and television industries have gone through significant changes, so did the music industry. Artists were able to also circumvent the big record labels and go to sites such as Pandora or Spotify (Sisario, 2013). That switch allowed them to make more than the 7 to 10 cents earned from a regular download, reaping instead around 40 cents per play at direct-to-consumer sites. The numbers do not make most artists rich, and the way for stars to make money is live acts, and only the top acts can make money on the concert circuit (Sisario, 2013). The big acts, though, can make a lot, and one, Live Nation, has significantly grown its control over the outdoor music industry (through buying many competitors and locking in acts to large tours of Live Nation locations). The company's revenue increased more than 50% from 2009 to 2013, when it had $1.44 billion in revenue, and it was expected to reach $1.7 billion at the end of 2016.

While there was a significant growth in the early 21st century for music festivals, that successful run started changing as price, competition, and other variables started having an impact on the industry. For example, one of the more famous festivals, Bonnaroo (named best music festival in 2008 by *Rolling Stone* magazine) saw its attendance drop 46% from 2011 to 2016 (Shaw, 2017). Other festivals shut down. However, the Coachella festival in 2015 over two weekends grossed over $84 million through selling 198,000 tickets costing from $400 for general admission to $900 for a VIP ticket (Puente, 2016). By 2017 the Coachella festival grossed almost $115 million.

Thus, the music industry needed to undertake significant transformation in a relatively short time frame to deal with technology, demographics, trends, listening habits, and even copyright infringement to help identify what would be the best strategies to generate revenue and keep the industry moving forward.

Other Entertainment

Horse racing and the music industry are not alone in facing changes. Other entertainment-based entities have also been facing a changing landscape requiring significant changes in how they operate as a business to protect the bottom line. SeaWorld made a major decision in 2017 to stop its killer whale shows in California. This step represented a concern because it was one of the park's most popular attractions. The company felt pressured to stop the killer whale show due to animal rights activists. Several months earlier SeaWorld reported a 7.7% drop in attendance, from 6.5 to 6 million. This knocked more than $16 million off SeaWorld's quarterly earnings—which spooked analysts and investors, sending the company's shares down 14.2% to $12.74 (Neate, 2016). SeaWorld hoped that dropping the whales would help spur a major turnover. However, by late 2017, the company's stocks were selling for under $12.00, and the company had just let go of 350 employees.

The circus also faced similar challenges from animal rights groups. Based on activist pressure, the famous Ringling Bros. and Barnum and Bailey Circus stopped its elephant act in 2016. While this made activists happy, it did not help the circus. The circus was facing several challenges from a lack of interest to kids not having the attention spans they used to have. This led to Feld Entertainment (owners of Ringling Bros.) scuttling the circus in 2017.

Theaters are also facing challenges. Netflix and other streaming sites are making it easier for people to watch what they want, when they want to. Shares of the United States' largest theater chain, AMC Entertainment, fell 27% on one day alone in 2017 after reporting a net loss of around $175 million for the key summer period (April-June), compared with a profit of $24 million during the same period in 2016 (Snider, 2017). Other theater chains were facing revenue pressure as well from weaker than expected summer block busters. Such lackluster movies have put pressure all across the movie industry as evidenced by the United Kingdom–based Cineworld finalizing a deal in December, 2017 for $3.6 billion to buy fellow theater chain Regal Entertainment. That would normally be positive news, but Cineworld shares declined. That could be in part because consumers were spending around $13 billion on streaming services in 2017 compared with only $11 billion at theaters (Snider, 2017). Thus, new technologies and new fan interests are significantly changing strategies used by various entertainment companies.

While there might be some challenges in the United States, international movie growth has been strong. Movies are now a huge industry in China. The number of movie tickets sold in the United States has declined by 80 million over the past decade and per capita attendance fell 14% (from 2007 to 2017) which means that the average person goes to four movies a year (Lev-Ram, 2017). China, on the other hand, has been growing like crazy in the movie industry. In 2016 alone, 7,500 screens opened, bringing the country's total to 40,917 screens. These 40,917 screens is more than double the number of screens in 2013 and surpasses the 40,759 screens in the United States. Similarly, China's box office revenue has increased 144% since 2012 while the North American growth during the same time period was just 6%. In total, the Chinese media and entertainment industry as a whole was estimated to be $180 billion in 2017 (Lev-Ram, 2017). Things started changing in China in 2017 when the country started promoting its own films rather than U.S.-produced films. This could represent a major concern for international films as such films can be dubbed into Chinese and still do well, while the U.S. market is not as strong for foreign films.

Beer Suds Are Falling Flat

An example of how quickly fortunes can change is the craft beer market. Many invested in their beer-making hobbies and launched numerous craft breweries. They were unique and offered a different option. However, most good things end, often due to everyone trying to chase the same dollars. Craft beer sales increased 6% in 2016 to 24.6 million barrels. However, that was a significant decline from prior great years where growth often was 20% a year. To try to take advantage of this trend, the number of breweries that opened in 2016 increased 17% to 5,301 breweries. So many breweries and types of beers can paralyze consumers and often cause confusion, as many customers do not know what is truly a small batch brewery or a division of a larger brewer trying to look similar to a craft brewery (Kell, 2017). This cautionary tale is especially relevant to the sport and fitness industry where it constantly seems like new fads or products (such as fitness trackers) are launched and quickly lose their luster. That is why it is so critical to undertake research to determine market strength and ability to reach a market before launching a new product.

Professional Sport

The same transitions affecting other entertainment companies are affecting sport as well. Every sport faces some financial- and strategy-related issues like those affecting horse racing and the music industry. Baseball is facing a major hurdle with the aging of its fan base. According to 2015 research results, 50% of baseball viewers are 55 or older, up from 41% 10 years earlier. It is not just the fans attending games, but baseball viewers on ESPN now average 53 years old. National Football League (NFL) fans are also getting older (average 47 years old) while the National Basketball Association (NBA) has a relatively young viewer base at an average age of 37 (Fisher, 2015). To deal with the aging baseball demographics, the league is exploring different strategies to speed up the game. If a game lasts for three hours, that might be over an hour more than many younger fans can stand. It is similar to how the circus was too long. In the 1950s, people sat and enjoyed the game, but now distractions such as large scoreboards, mascots, swimming pools, hot tubs, merry-go-rounds, and numerous other distractions, including the all-important Wi-Fi, are used to entertain fans.

The NFL is not immune to issues. A *Bloomberg Businessweek* front page headline in 2016 highlighted a litany of problems faced by the league such as Sunday night football games, concussions, domestic violence, Colin Kaepernick (then with the San Francisco 49ers) leading a protest by refusing to stand for the national anthem, lousy football, millennial cord cutting, and even the presidential election (Gillette, 2016).

All of professional sports are concerned about the bubble associated with rights fees. ESPN spent $15.2 billion when it renewed the NFL rights package in 2011 (running through 2021), and in 2012 it signed the NCAA football playoffs for 12 years for $7.3 billion. Many of the recent large sports team transactions were predicated on large nationwide and local media contracts. When Steve Ballmer bought the Los Angeles Clippers for $2 billion, he was anticipating a share of the NBA's league-wide, nine-year, $24 billion TV deal. Similarly, the Ultimate Fighting Championship was purchased for $4 billion in 2016 based in part on what was hoped to be a rights renewal contract of $450 million to $500 million with Fox. However, in 2017 Fox reportedly only offered a reported $200 million for the rights (Deitsch & Wertheim, 2017). Such a shakeup will result in various strategies to reduce the potential for losses. ESPN has undertaken several rounds of layoffs, including some on-air personalities. ESPN has also centralized a significant amount of its production. Thus, by having feed sent directly to Bristol, Connecticut and having a central unit to edit and send out the broadcast, ESPN was able to reduce costs associated with bringing all the trucks and production crews to every broadcast. Only the top events needed significant production teams, and ESPN would be able to leverage some freelancers or smaller crews for smaller events while utilizing assets in Connecticut. ESPN also entered into a massive contract to purchase assets for around $52.4 billion from 21st century Fox in late 2017. As part of the deal, Disney (ESPN's parent company) would acquire the Fox Regional Sports Network (RSN) comprising 22 regional networks. Excluded from the deal were Fox Sports,

FS1, FS2, and the Big Ten Network. The deal gave ESPN local broadcast deals for 17 NBA teams, 15 Major League Baseball teams, 12 National Hockey League teams, Major League Soccer, and the Women's National Basketball Association, as well as college sport contracts. No NFL rights were involved as the NFL does not allow local broadcast deals. One analyst valued the Fox RSN package as worth around $20 billion. The deal gives ESPN a broad regional network to go along with its various national channels. While national channels have had some shrinkage through cord cutters, regional sports networks have not seen the same trend yet due to loyal local viewers who want to see their local teams and might not see them as frequently on national channels (Bonesteel, 2017).

Dealing with these financial challenges is where strategy comes into play. For example, the NFL is not resting on its laurels or large broadcast contracts. The NFL is trying to leverage technology and new media companies to generate new revenue. Thus, in December 2017, Twitch, the Amazon-owned social video service popular among e-sport fans, began hosting Thursday Night Football games through twitch.tv/primevideo. The Thursday night games had been broadcast on Twitter before the Amazon deal came to fruition. Also in December 2017, Twitch announced that it would begin streaming up to six NBA G League games a week. Also in December, the NFL announced a multiyear deal with Verizon Communications to live stream in-market and national games, including playoff games and the Super Bowl. The deal worth $2 billion also allows broadcasting across Verizon's digital and mobile media properties to users across the United States (Booton, 2017).

Broadcasters such as ESPN also need to explore other ways to maximize the return on their significant investment. Strategies can include

- revenue enhancement such as increasing subscribers' fees, utilizing more direct to consumer strategies, developing new mobile and digital products, and conducting more frequent audits of additional streaming multichannel video programming distributors; and
- expense reductions such as pursuing rights-free bartering to reduce rights fees, slowing down the growth of rights fees, trimming overhead costs, replacing big-name on-air talent with cheaper talent, and consolidating, which occurred when Disney purchased Fox (Desser, 2017).

There is no one correct strategy when faced with a challenge. Whether starting a company, managing a company through growth or slowdowns, or even when dissolving a company, every organization will face challenges. What separates the successful companies from those that are not as successful will be how they perceive potential challenges and success. As highlighted in the text, growing too quickly can raise significant cash-related challenges. Similarly, facing unexpected downturns can destroy a company. In between the extremes is a zone where business as usual occurs. It is in this zone where many businesses get in trouble as they can become complacent and not be as vigilant in tracking risks and opportunities.

When faced with potential concerns, there are numerous efforts to pinpoint the issue and possibly to fix blame on someone or something. The process can be very enlightening and liberating for a company. To tear apart a business and find the strengths and weaknesses is an intense process. Some employees might feel resentful or fudge data to protect their jobs. Only through accurate information can the right decision be made. That is why it is important to track data on a regular basis in real time to constantly work on tweaking a strategy. Obtaining turnstile information only on a monthly basis will not provide good information for the rest of the season. However, having turnstile information on a nightly basis can help an administrator determine if there are tweaks that can be undertaken for the next night or day to increase revenue or decrease costs. Imagine having to hire 150 workers to work a game as concessionaires, ushers, and ticket takers. Is that number required for every game? What if 10,000 fans are expected one night and 20,000 the following day? The deployment numbers will have to change for the different events. If the employees are unionized, they might require 24-hour notice if they are working a given game. If employees are called in at the last minute, the employment costs can increase over $50,000 in the blink of an eye. That is why constantly tracking the right information is so important. It will help with long-term plans such as where the industry is going. It will also help with daily planning and cash management efforts.

Conclusion

The examples above help highlight how various industry segments go through positive and negative cycles. Each organization plans for possible growth or survival, but technology, consumers, and other changes can dramatically alter the best laid out plans. That is why there is a significant difference between initial financial plans and subsequent analysis of what really happened. It is not often that the financial projections work exactly as planned, but when proper research and accurate numbers are used, a financial executive can get a close approximation as to what will happen in the future.

Class Discussion Topics

1. Where do you think your sport (whatever is your favorite sport to watch or play) is going in the United States, and what financial or strategic challenges do you foresee?

2. What do you think will be the next big international break-out sport or entertainment trend, and how can a company or team take advantage of those potential opportunities?

3. If you had to make the game of baseball more attractive for viewers and fans, what would you do, and what do you think will be the impact?

4. What current trend in the sport or entertainment area do you think will fall into disfavor with the consumer population? What supports your argument, and what would you do to possibly reverse that downward trend?

Appendix A

Under Armour Financial Statements

The tables presented in appendix A show the financial statements for Under Armour. Table A.1 presents the Under Armour balance sheet. Table A.2 shows the Under Armour income statement. And table A.3 shows the Under Armour cash flow statement.

Table A.1   Under Armour Balance Sheet

Fiscal year ends in December USD in million except per share data	2012-12	2013-12	2014-12	2015-12	2016-12
Assets	1,157	1,578	2,095	2,869	3,644
Current assets	904	1,129	1,549	1,499	1,965
Cash	342	347	593	130	250
Cash and cash equivalent	342	347	593	130	250
Total cash	342	347	593	130	250
Receivables	176	210	280	434	623
Inventories	319	469	537	783	917
Deferred income taxes	23	38	52		
Prepaid expenses	44	64	87	152	175
Total current assets	904	1,129	1,549	1,499	1,965
Non-current assets	253	449	546	1,370	1,679
Property, plant and eq ...	181	224	306	539	804
Gross property, plant ...	326	396	522	832	1,201
Accumulated Depreciation	(145)	(172)	(217)	(293)	(397)
Net property, plant and equipment	181	224	306	539	804
Goodwill		122	123	585	564
Intangible assets	4	24	26	76	64
Deferred income taxes	23	31	34	92	137
Other long-term assets	46	48	57	79	110
Total non-current assets	253	449	546	1,370	1,679
Total assets	1,157	1,578	2,095	2,869	3,644
Liabilities and stockholders	1,157	1,578	2,095	2,869	3,644
Liabilities	340	524	745	1,201	1,613
Current liabilities	252	427	422	479	686
Short-term debt	9	105	29	42	27
Accounts payable	144	165	210	200	410
Accrued liabilities	85	134	148	193	209
Other current liability	14	22	35	43	40
Total current liability	252	427	422	479	686
Non-current liabilities	88	98	323	722	928
Long-term debt	53	48	255	627	790

(continued)

Table A.1 *(continued)*

Fiscal year ends in December USD in million except per share data	2012-12	2013-12	2014-12	2015-12	2016-12
Other long-term liabilities	35	50	68	95	137
Total non-current liabilities	88	98	323	722	928
Total liabilities	340	524	745	1,201	1,613
Stockholders' equity	817	1,053	1,350	1,668	2,031
Common stock	0	0	0	0	0
Additional paid-in capital	321	397	508	637	823
Retained earnings	493	654	857	1,077	1,259
Accumulated other compensation	2	2	(15)	(45)	(52)
Total stockholders' equity	817	1,053	1,350	1,668	2,031
Total liabilities and equity	1,157	1,578	2,095	2,869	3,644

Reprinted from Morningstar. Available: http://financials.morningstart.com.

Table A.2 Under Armour Income Statement

Fiscal year ends in December USD in million except per share data	2012-12	2013-12	2014-12	2015-12	2016-12	TTM
Revenue	1,835	2,332	3,084	3,963	4,825	4,895
Cost of revenue	956	1,195	1,572	2,058	2,585	2,630
Gross profit	879	1,137	1,512	1,906	2,241	2,265
Operating expense	671	872	1,158	1,497	1,823	1,875
Sales, general and administrative expenses	671	872	1,158	1,497	1,823	1,875
Total operating expenses	671	872	1,158	1,497	1,823	1,875
Operating income	209	265	354	409	417	390
Interest expense				15		
Other income (expense)	(5)	(4)	(12)	(7)	(29)	(33)
Income before taxes	203	261	342	387	388	358
Provision for income	75	99	134	154	131	122
Net income from continuing operations	129	162	208	233	257	236
Net income	129	162	208	233	257	236
Preferred dividend					59	59
Net income available	129	162	208	233	198	177
EARNINGS PER SHARE						
Basic	0.31	0.39	0.49	0.54	0.45	0.40
Diluted	0.30	0.38	0.47	0.53	0.45	0.40
WEIGHTED AVERAGE SHARE						
Basic	417	421	426	431	436	438
Diluted	426	432	439	442	445	444
EBITDA	252	316	426	502	562	544

Reprinted from Morningstar. Available: http://financials.morningstart.com.

Table A.3 Under Armour Cash Flow Statement

USD in million except for per share items	12 months ending 2016-12-31	12 months ending 2015-12-31	12 months ending 2014-12-31	12 months ending 2013-12-31
Net Income/Starting Line	256.98	232.57	208.04	162.33
Depreciation/Depletion	144.77	100.94	72.09	50.55
Amortization				
Deferred Taxes	-43.00	-4.43	-17.58	-18.83
Non-Cash Items	130.54	134.68	94.16	59.37
Changes in Working Capital	-184.80	-507.87	-137.68	-133.34
Cash from Operating Activities	304.49	-44.10	219.03	120.07
Capital Expenditures	-387.62	-301.48	-141.39	-88.31
Other Investing Cash Flow Items, Total	6.48	-545.99	-10.92	-149.80
Cash from Investing Activities	-381.14	-847.48	-152.31	-238.10
Financing Cash Flow Items	36.59	44.97	35.25	17.17
Total Cash Dividends Paid	-2.93			
Issuance (Retirement) of Stock, Net	15.48	10.31	15.78	15.10
Issuance (Retirement) of Debt, Net	156.85	384.80	131.28	94.53
Cash from Financing Activities	206.00	440.08	182.31	126.80
Foreign Exchange Effects	-8.72	-11.82	-3.34	-3.12
Net Change in Cash	120.62	-463.32	245.69	5.65
Cash Interest Paid, Supplemental	21.41	11.18	4.15	1.50
Cash Taxes Paid, Supplemental	135.96	99.71	103.28	85.57

Reprinted from Google Finance.

Appendix B

Time Value of Money

The tables presented in appendix B illustrate the time value of money. Table B.1 shows the future value of $1 at the end of **t** periods. Table B.2 shows the present value of $1 received at the end of t periods. And table B.3 shows the present value of $1 per period for t periods.

Table B.1 Future Value of $1 at the End of t Periods

Period	INTEREST RATE										
	1%	2%	3%	4%	5%	6%	7%	8%	9%	10%	11%
1	1.0100	1.0200	1.0300	1.0400	1.0500	1.0600	1.0700	1.0800	1.0900	1.1000	1.1100
2	1.0201	1.0404	1.0609	1.0816	1.1025	1.1236	1.1449	1.1664	1.1881	1.2100	1.2321
3	1.0303	1.0612	1.0927	1.1249	1.1576	1.1910	1.2250	1.2597	1.2950	1.3310	1.3676
4	1.0406	1.0824	1.1255	1.1699	1.2155	1.2625	1.3108	1.3605	1.4116	1.4641	1.5181
5	1.0510	1.1041	1.1593	1.2167	1.2763	1.3382	1.4026	1.4693	1.5386	1.6105	1.6851
6	1.0615	1.1262	1.1941	1.2653	1.3401	1.4185	1.5007	1.5869	1.6771	1.7716	1.8704
7	1.0721	1.1487	1.2299	1.3159	1.4071	1.5036	1.6058	1.7138	1.8280	1.9487	2.0762
8	1.0829	1.1717	1.2668	1.3686	1.4775	1.5938	1.7182	1.8509	1.9926	2.1436	2.3045
9	1.0937	1.1951	1.3048	1.4233	1.5513	1.6895	1.8385	1.9990	2.1719	2.3579	2.5580
10	1.1046	1.2190	1.3439	1.4802	1.6289	1.7908	1.9672	2.1589	2.3674	2.5937	2.8394
11	1.1157	1.2434	1.3842	1.5395	1.7103	1.8983	2.1049	2.3316	2.5804	2.8531	3.1518
12	1.1268	1.2682	1.4258	1.6010	1.7959	2.0122	2.2522	2.5182	2.8127	3.1384	3.4985
13	1.1381	1.2936	1.4685	1.6651	1.8856	2.1329	2.4098	2.7196	3.0658	3.4523	3.8833
14	1.1495	1.3195	1.5126	1.7317	1.9799	2.2609	2.5785	2.9372	3.3417	3.7975	4.3104
15	1.1610	1.3459	1.5580	1.8009	2.0789	2.3966	2.7590	3.1722	3.6425	4.1772	4.7846
16	1.1726	1.3728	1.6047	1.8730	2.1829	2.5404	2.9522	3.4259	3.9703	4.5950	5.3109
17	1.1843	1.4002	1.6528	1.9479	2.2920	2.6928	3.1588	3.7000	4.3276	5.0545	5.8951
18	1.1961	1.4282	1.7024	2.0258	2.4066	2.8543	3.3799	3.9960	4.7171	5.5599	6.5436
19	1.2081	1.4568	1.7535	2.1068	2.5270	3.0256	3.6165	4.3157	5.1417	6.1159	7.2633
20	1.2202	1.4859	1.8061	2.1911	2.6533	3.2071	3.8697	4.6610	5.6044	6.7275	8.0623
21	1.2324	1.5157	1.8603	2.2788	2.7860	3.3996	4.1406	5.0338	6.1088	7.4002	8.9492
22	1.2447	1.5460	1.9161	2.3699	2.9253	3.6035	4.4304	5.4365	6.6586	8.1403	9.9336
23	1.2572	1.5769	1.9736	2.4647	3.0715	3.8197	4.7405	5.8715	7.2579	8.9543	11.0263
24	1.2697	1.6084	2.0328	2.5633	3.2251	4.0489	5.0724	6.3412	7.9111	9.8497	12.2392
25	1.2824	1.6406	2.0938	2.6658	3.3864	4.2919	5.4274	6.8485	8.6231	10.8347	13.5855
30	1.3478	1.8114	2.4273	3.2434	4.3219	5.7435	7.6123	10.0627	13.2677	17.4494	22.8923
40	1.4889	2.2080	3.2620	4.8010	7.0400	10.2857	14.9745	21.7245	31.4094	45.2593	65.0009
50	1.6446	2.6916	4.3839	7.1067	11.4674	18.4202	29.4570	46.9016	74.3575	117.3909	184.5648
60	1.8167	3.2810	5.8916	10.5196	18.6792	32.9877	57.9464	101.2571	176.0313	304.4816	524.0572

*Future value interest factor exceeds 99,999.

INTEREST RATE									
12%	14%	15%	16%	18%	20%	24%	28%	32%	36%
1.1200	1.1400	1.1500	1.1600	1.1800	1.2000	1.2400	1.2800	1.3200	1.3600
1.2544	1.2996	1.3225	1.3456	1.3924	1.4400	1.5376	1.6384	1.7424	1.8496
1.4049	1.4815	1.5209	1.5609	1.6430	1.7280	1.9066	2.0972	2.3000	2.5155
1.5735	1.6890	1.7490	1.8106	1.9388	2.0736	2.3642	2.6844	3.0360	3.4210
1.7623	1.9254	2.0114	2.1003	2.2878	2.4883	2.9316	3.4360	4.0075	4.6526
1.9738	2.1950	2.3131	2.4364	2.6996	2.9860	3.6352	4.3980	5.2899	6.3275
2.2107	2.5023	2.6600	2.8262	3.1855	3.5832	4.5077	5.6295	6.9826	8.6054
2.4760	2.8526	3.0590	3.2784	3.7589	4.2998	5.5895	7.2058	9.2170	11.7034
2.7731	3.2519	3.5179	3.8030	4.4355	5.1598	6.9310	9.2234	12.1665	15.9166
3.1058	3.7072	4.0456	4.4114	5.2338	6.1917	8.5944	11.8059	16.0598	21.6466
3.4785	4.2262	4.6524	5.1173	6.1759	7.4301	10.6571	15.1116	21.1989	29.4393
3.8960	4.8179	5.3503	5.9360	7.2876	8.9161	13.2148	19.3428	27.9825	40.0375
4.3635	5.4924	6.1528	6.8858	8.5994	10.6993	16.3863	24.7588	36.9370	54.4510
4.8871	6.2613	7.0757	7.9875	10.1472	12.8392	20.3191	31.6913	48.7568	74.0534
5.4736	7.1379	8.1371	9.2655	11.9737	15.4070	25.1956	40.5648	64.3590	100.7126
6.1304	8.1372	9.3576	10.7480	14.1290	18.4884	31.2426	51.9230	84.9538	136.9691
6.8660	9.2765	10.7613	12.4677	16.6722	22.1861	38.7408	66.4614	112.1390	186.2779
7.6900	10.5752	12.3755	14.4625	19.6733	26.6233	48.0386	85.0706	148.0235	253.3380
8.6128	12.0557	14.2318	16.7765	23.2144	31.9480	59.5679	108.8904	195.3911	344.5397
9.6463	13.7435	16.3665	19.4608	27.3930	38.3376	73.8641	139.3797	257.9162	468.5740
10.8038	15.6676	18.8215	22.5745	32.3238	46.0051	91.5915	178.4060	340.4494	637.2606
12.1003	17.8610	21.6447	26.1864	38.1421	55.2061	113.5735	228.3596	449.3932	866.6744
13.5523	20.3616	24.8915	30.3762	45.0076	66.2474	140.8312	292.3003	593.1990	1,178.6772
15.1786	23.2122	28.6252	35.2364	53.1090	79.4968	174.6306	374.1444	783.0227	1,603.0010
17.0001	26.4619	32.9190	40.8742	62.6686	95.3962	216.5420	478.9049	1,033.5900	2,180.0814
29.9599	50.9502	66.2118	85.8499	143.3706	237.3763	634.8199	1,645.5046	4,142.0748	10,143.0193
93.0510	188.8835	267.8635	378.7212	750.3783	1,469.7716	5,455.9126	19,426.6889	66,520.7670	*
289.0022	700.2330	1,083.6574	1,670.7038	3,927.3569	9,100.4382	46,890.4346	229,349.8616	*	*
897.5969	2,595.9187	4,383.9987	7,370.2014	20,555.1400	56,347.5144	*	*	*	*

Table B.2 Present Value of $1 Received at the End of t Periods

Period	INTEREST RATE										
	1%	2%	3%	4%	5%	6%	7%	8%	9%	10%	11%
1	0.9901	0.9804	0.9709	0.9615	0.9524	0.9434	0.9346	0.9259	0.9174	0.9091	0.9009
2	0.9803	0.9612	0.9426	0.9246	0.9070	0.8900	0.8734	0.8573	0.8417	0.8264	0.8116
3	0.9706	0.9423	0.9151	0.8890	0.8638	0.8396	0.8163	0.7938	0.7722	0.7513	0.7312
4	0.9610	0.9238	0.8885	0.8548	0.8227	0.7921	0.7629	0.7350	0.7084	0.6830	0.6587
5	0.9515	0.9057	0.8626	0.8219	0.7835	0.7473	0.7130	0.6806	0.6499	0.6209	0.5935
6	0.9420	0.8880	0.8375	0.7903	0.7462	0.7050	0.6663	0.6302	0.5963	0.5645	0.5346
7	0.9327	0.8706	0.8131	0.7599	0.7107	0.6651	0.6227	0.5835	0.5470	0.5132	0.4817
8	0.9235	0.8535	0.7894	0.7307	0.6768	0.6274	0.5820	0.5403	0.5019	0.4665	0.4339
9	0.9143	0.8368	0.7664	0.7026	0.6446	0.5919	0.5439	0.5002	0.4604	0.4241	0.3909
10	0.9053	0.8203	0.7441	0.6756	0.6139	0.5584	0.5083	0.4632	0.4224	0.3855	0.3522
11	0.8963	0.8043	0.7224	0.6496	0.5847	0.5268	0.4751	0.4289	0.3875	0.3505	0.3173
12	0.8874	0.7885	0.7014	0.6246	0.5568	0.4970	0.4440	0.3971	0.3555	0.3186	0.2858
13	0.8787	0.7730	0.6810	0.6006	0.5303	0.4688	0.4150	0.3677	0.3262	0.2897	0.2575
14	0.8700	0.7579	0.6611	0.5775	0.5051	0.4423	0.3878	0.3405	0.2992	0.2633	0.2320
15	0.8613	0.7430	0.6419	0.5553	0.4810	0.4173	0.3624	0.3152	0.2745	0.2394	0.2090
16	0.8528	0.7284	0.6232	0.5339	0.4581	0.3936	0.3387	0.2919	0.2519	0.2176	0.1883
17	0.8444	0.7142	0.6050	0.5134	0.4363	0.3714	0.3166	0.2703	0.2311	0.1978	0.1696
18	0.8360	0.7002	0.5874	0.4936	0.4155	0.3503	0.2959	0.2502	0.2120	0.1799	0.1528
19	0.8277	0.6864	0.5703	0.4746	0.3957	0.3305	0.2765	0.2317	0.1945	0.1635	0.1377
20	0.8195	0.6730	0.5537	0.4564	0.3769	0.3118	0.2584	0.2145	0.1784	0.1486	0.1240
21	0.8114	0.6598	0.5375	0.4388	0.3589	0.2942	0.2415	0.1987	0.1637	0.1351	0.1117
22	0.8034	0.6468	0.5219	0.4220	0.3418	0.2775	0.2257	0.1839	0.1502	0.1228	0.1007
23	0.7954	0.6342	0.5067	0.4057	0.3256	0.2618	0.2109	0.1703	0.1378	0.1117	0.0907
24	0.7876	0.6217	0.4919	0.3901	0.3101	0.2470	0.1971	0.1577	0.1264	0.1015	0.0817
25	0.7798	0.6095	0.4776	0.3751	0.2953	0.2330	0.1842	0.1460	0.1160	0.0923	0.0736
30	0.7419	0.5521	0.4120	0.3083	0.2314	0.1741	0.1314	0.0994	0.0754	0.0573	0.0437
40	0.6717	0.4529	0.3066	0.2083	0.1420	0.0972	0.0668	0.0460	0.0318	0.0221	0.0154
50	0.6080	0.3715	0.2281	0.1407	0.0872	0.0543	0.0339	0.0213	0.0134	0.0085	0.0054
60	0.5504	0.3048	0.1697	0.0951	0.0535	0.0303	0.0173	0.0099	0.0057	0.0033	0.0019

*The present value factor is zero rounded to four decimal places.

INTEREST RATE									
12%	14%	15%	16%	18%	20%	24%	28%	32%	36%
0.8929	0.8772	0.8696	0.8621	0.8475	0.8333	0.8065	0.7813	0.7576	0.7353
0.7972	0.7695	0.7561	0.7432	0.7182	0.6944	0.6504	0.6104	0.5739	0.5407
0.7118	0.6750	0.6575	0.6407	0.6086	0.5787	0.5245	0.4768	0.4348	0.3975
0.6355	0.5921	0.5718	0.5523	0.5158	0.4823	0.4230	0.3725	0.3294	0.2923
0.5674	0.5194	0.4972	0.4761	0.4371	0.4019	0.3411	0.2910	0.2495	0.2149
0.5066	0.4556	0.4323	0.4104	0.3704	0.3349	0.2751	0.2274	0.1890	0.1580
0.4523	0.3996	0.3759	0.3538	0.3139	0.2791	0.2218	0.1776	0.1432	0.1162
0.4039	0.3506	0.3269	0.3050	0.2660	0.2326	0.1789	0.1388	0.1085	0.0854
0.3606	0.3075	0.2843	0.2630	0.2255	0.1938	0.1443	0.1084	0.0822	0.0628
0.3220	0.2697	0.2472	0.2267	0.1911	0.1615	0.1164	0.0847	0.0623	0.0462
0.2875	0.2366	0.2149	0.1954	0.1619	0.1346	0.0938	0.0662	0.0472	0.0340
0.2567	0.2076	0.1869	0.1685	0.1372	0.1122	0.0757	0.0517	0.0357	0.0250
0.2292	0.1821	0.1625	0.1452	0.1163	0.0935	0.0610	0.0404	0.0271	0.0184
0.2046	0.1597	0.1413	0.1252	0.0985	0.0779	0.0492	0.0316	0.0205	0.0135
0.1827	0.1401	0.1229	0.1079	0.0835	0.0649	0.0397	0.0247	0.0155	0.0099
0.1631	0.1229	0.1069	0.0930	0.0708	0.0541	0.0320	0.0193	0.0118	0.0073
0.1456	0.1078	0.0929	0.0802	0.0600	0.0451	0.0258	0.0150	0.0089	0.0054
0.1300	0.0946	0.0808	0.0691	0.0508	0.0376	0.0208	0.0118	0.0068	0.0039
0.1161	0.0829	0.0703	0.0596	0.0431	0.0313	0.0168	0.0092	0.0051	0.0029
0.1037	0.0728	0.0611	0.0514	0.0365	0.0261	0.0135	0.0072	0.0039	0.0021
0.0926	0.0638	0.0531	0.0443	0.0309	0.0217	0.0109	0.0056	0.0029	0.0016
0.0826	0.0560	0.0462	0.0382	0.0262	0.0181	0.0088	0.0044	0.0022	0.0012
0.0738	0.0491	0.0402	0.0329	0.0222	0.0151	0.0071	0.0034	0.0017	0.0008
0.0659	0.0431	0.0349	0.0284	0.0188	0.0126	0.0057	0.0027	0.0013	0.0006
0.0588	0.0378	0.0304	0.0245	0.0160	0.0105	0.0046	0.0021	0.0010	0.0005
0.0334	0.0196	0.0151	0.0116	0.0070	0.0042	0.0016	0.0006	0.0002	0.0001
0.0107	0.0053	0.0037	0.0026	0.0013	0.0007	0.0002	0.0001	*	*
0.0035	0.0014	0.0009	0.0006	0.0003	*	*	*	*	*
0.0011	0.0004	0.0002	0.0001	*	*	*	*	*	*

Table B.3 Present Value of $1 per Period for t Periods

| Period | INTEREST RATE | | | | | | | | | | |
	1%	2%	3%	4%	5%	6%	7%	8%	9%	10%	11%
1	0.9901	0.9804	0.9709	0.9615	0.9524	0.9434	0.9346	0.9259	0.9174	0.9091	0.9009
2	1.9704	1.9416	1.9135	1.8861	1.8594	1.8334	1.8080	1.7833	1.7591	1.7355	1.7125
3	2.9410	2.8839	2.8286	2.7751	2.7232	2.6730	2.6243	2.5771	2.5313	2.4869	2.4437
4	3.9020	3.8077	3.7171	3.6299	3.5460	3.4651	3.3872	3.3121	3.2397	3.1699	3.1024
5	4.8534	4.7135	4.5797	4.4518	4.3295	4.2124	4.1002	3.9927	3.8897	3.7908	3.6959
6	5.7955	5.6014	5.4172	5.2421	5.0757	4.9173	4.7665	4.6229	4.4859	4.3553	4.2305
7	6.7282	6.4720	6.2303	6.0021	5.7864	5.5824	5.3893	5.2064	5.0330	4.8684	4.7122
8	7.6517	7.3255	7.0197	6.7327	6.4632	6.2098	5.9713	5.7466	5.5348	5.3349	5.1461
9	8.5660	8.1622	7.7861	7.4353	7.1078	6.8017	6.5152	6.2469	5.9952	5.7590	5.5370
10	9.4713	8.9826	8.5302	8.1109	7.7217	7.3601	7.0236	6.7101	6.4177	6.1446	5.8892
11	10.3676	9.7868	9.2526	8.7605	8.3064	7.8869	7.4987	7.1390	6.8052	6.4951	6.2065
12	11.2551	10.5753	9.9540	9.3851	8.8633	8.3838	7.9427	7.5361	7.1607	6.8137	6.4924
13	12.1337	11.3484	10.6350	9.9856	9.3936	8.8527	8.3577	7.9038	7.4869	7.1034	6.7499
14	13.0037	12.1062	11.2961	10.5631	9.8986	9.2950	8.7455	8.2442	7.7862	7.3667	6.9819
15	13.8651	12.8493	11.9379	11.1184	10.3797	9.7122	9.1079	8.5595	8.0607	7.6061	7.1909
16	14.7179	13.5777	12.5611	11.6523	10.8378	10.1059	9.4466	8.8514	8.3126	7.8237	7.3792
17	15.5623	14.2919	13.1661	12.1657	11.2741	10.4773	9.7632	9.1216	8.5436	8.0216	7.5488
18	16.3983	14.9920	13.7535	12.6593	11.6896	10.8276	10.0591	9.3719	8.7556	8.2014	7.7016
19	17.2260	15.6785	14.3238	13.1339	12.0853	11.1581	10.3356	9.6036	8.9501	8.3649	7.8393
20	18.0456	16.3514	14.8775	13.5903	12.4622	11.4699	10.5940	9.8181	9.1285	8.5136	7.9633
21	18.8570	17.0112	15.4150	14.0292	12.8212	11.7641	10.8355	10.0168	9.2922	8.6487	8.0751
22	19.6604	17.6580	15.9369	14.4511	13.1630	12.0416	11.0612	10.2007	9.4424	8.7715	8.1757
23	20.4558	18.2922	16.4436	14.8568	13.4886	12.3034	11.2722	10.3711	9.5802	8.8832	8.2664
24	21.2434	18.9139	16.9355	15.2470	13.7986	12.5504	11.4693	10.5288	9.7066	8.9847	8.3481
25	22.0232	19.5235	17.4131	15.6221	14.0939	12.7834	11.6536	10.6748	9.8226	9.0770	8.4217
30	25.8077	22.3965	19.6004	17.2920	15.3725	13.7648	12.4090	11.2578	10.2737	9.4269	8.6938
40	32.8347	27.3555	23.1148	19.7928	17.1591	15.0463	13.3317	11.9246	10.7574	9.7791	8.9511
50	39.1961	31.4236	25.7298	21.4822	18.2559	15.7619	13.8007	12.2335	10.9617	9.9148	9.0417
60	44.9550	34.7609	27.6756	22.6235	18.9293	16.1614	14.0392	12.3766	11.0480	9.9672	9.0736

INTEREST RATE									
12%	14%	15%	16%	18%	20%	24%	28%	32%	36%
0.8929	0.8772	0.8696	0.8621	0.8475	0.8333	0.8065	0.7813	0.7576	0.7353
1.6901	1.6467	1.6257	1.6052	1.5656	1.5278	1.4568	1.3916	1.3315	1.2760
2.4018	2.3216	2.2832	2.2459	2.1743	2.1065	1.9813	1.8684	1.7663	1.6735
3.0373	2.9137	2.8550	2.7982	2.6901	2.5887	2.4043	2.2410	2.0957	1.9658
3.6048	3.4331	3.3522	3.2743	3.1272	2.9906	2.7454	2.5320	2.3452	2.1807
4.1114	3.8887	3.7845	3.6847	3.4976	3.3255	3.0205	2.7594	2.5342	2.3388
4.5638	4.2883	4.1604	4.0386	3.8115	3.6046	3.2423	2.9370	2.6775	2.4550
4.9676	4.6389	4.4873	4.3436	4.0776	3.8372	3.4212	3.0758	2.7860	2.5404
5.3282	4.9464	4.7716	4.6065	4.3030	4.0310	3.5655	3.1842	2.8681	2.6033
5.6502	5.2161	5.0188	4.8332	4.4941	4.1925	3.6819	3.2689	2.9304	2.6495
5.9377	5.4527	5.2337	5.0286	4.6560	4.3271	3.7757	3.3351	2.9776	2.6834
6.1944	5.6603	5.4206	5.1971	4.7932	4.4392	3.8514	3.3868	3.0133	2.7084
6.4235	5.8424	5.5831	5.3423	4.9095	4.5327	3.9124	3.4272	3.0404	2.7268
6.6282	6.0021	5.7245	5.4675	5.0081	4.6106	3.9616	3.4587	3.0609	2.7403
6.8109	6.1422	5.8474	5.5755	5.0916	4.6755	4.0013	3.4834	3.0764	2.7502
6.9740	6.2651	5.9542	5.6685	5.1624	4.7296	4.0333	3.5026	3.0882	2.7575
7.1196	6.3729	6.0472	5.7487	5.2223	4.7746	4.0591	3.5177	3.0971	2.7629
7.2497	6.4674	6.1280	5.8178	5.2732	4.8122	4.0799	3.5294	3.1039	2.7668
7.3658	6.5504	6.1982	5.8775	5.3162	4.8435	4.0967	3.5386	3.1090	2.7697
7.4694	6.6231	6.2593	5.9288	5.3527	4.8696	4.1103	3.5458	3.1129	2.7718
7.5620	6.6870	6.3125	5.9731	5.3837	4.8913	4.1212	3.5514	3.1158	2.7734
7.6446	6.7429	6.3587	6.0113	5.4099	4.9094	4.1300	3.5558	3.1180	2.7746
7.7184	6.7921	6.3988	6.0442	5.4321	4.9245	4.1371	3.5592	3.1197	2.7754
7.7843	6.8351	6.4338	6.0726	5.4509	4.9371	4.1428	3.5619	3.1210	2.7760
7.8431	6.8729	6.4641	6.0971	5.4669	4.9476	4.1474	3.5640	3.1220	2.7765
8.0552	7.0027	6.5660	6.1772	5.5168	4.9789	4.1601	3.5693	3.1242	2.7775
8.2438	7.1050	6.6418	6.2335	5.5482	4.9966	4.1659	3.5712	3.1250	2.7778
8.3045	7.1327	6.6605	6.2463	5.5541	4.9995	4.1666	3.5714	3.1250	2.7778
8.3240	7.1401	6.6651	6.2492	5.5553	4.9999	4.1667	3.5714	3.1250	2.7778

Appendix C

Formulas

The following balance sheet and income statement are interpreted through the financial analysis formulas and industry ratios in this appendix.

Additional facts include a fictitious Sport Manufacturing Company's (SMC) having one million outstanding shares currently selling for $10 a share. The stock was selling for $8 per share at the start of the year. SMC also has $10 million in outstanding bonds. The bonds are $1,000 face-value bonds redeemable in 20 years, paying 10% interest and currently selling for $1,100 each.

Balance Sheet

ASSETS	($000)	LIABILITIES AND NET WORTH	($000)
Cash	100	Note payable	0
Accounts receivable	60	Accounts payable	150
Inventory	300	Taxes payable	40
Total current assets	460	Other accruals	30
Plant and equipment	500	**Total current liabilities**	220
Less depreciation	100	Mortgage payable	150
Net	400	Common stock	250
Total assets	860	Retained earnings	240
		Total liabilities and net worth	860

Income Statement

	($000)
Sales	500
Less: Material and labor	300
Manufacturing costs	30
Cost of goods sold	330
Gross profit	170
Depreciation	20
Selling expense	20
Profit before interest and taxes	130
Interest payments	10
Taxes	40
Profit after taxes	80
Dividends	40
Retained earnings	40

Profit

profit margin = profit after taxes / sales (i.e., $80,000 / $500,000 = 0.16, or 16%)

corporate earnings = sales – costs (i.e., $500,000 – $330,000 = $170,000)

earnings per share = earnings / total shares (i.e., $170,000 / 1,000,000 = $0.17)

PE ratio = price per share / earnings per share (i.e., $10.00 / $0.17 = 59 times earnings)

Liquidity

acid test ratio = liquid assets / current liabilities from cash and accounts receivable (i.e., $160,000 / $220,000 = 0.73)

current ratio = current assets / current liabilities (i.e., $460,000 / $220,000 = 2.09)

solvency ratio = net worth / total assets (i.e., $490,000 / $860,000 = 0.57)

working capital = current assets – current liabilities (i.e., $460,000 – $220,000 = $240,000)

Company Value

book value = total assets – total liabilities from total current liabilities plus mortgage payable (i.e., $860,000 – $370,000 = $490,000)

owners' equity = common stock + retained earnings (i.e., $250,000 + $240,000 = $490,000)

book value per share = owners' equity / outstanding shares (i.e., $490,000 / 1,000,000 = $0.49)

dividend payout ratio = dividend per share / earnings per share (i.e., $0.04 / $0.17 = 0.235, or 23.5%)

net worth = common stock + retained earnings (i.e., $250,000 + $240,000 = $490,000)

turnover = sales / assets (i.e., $500,000 / $860,000 = 0.58)

Indebtedness

debt–equity ratio = total liabilities / shareholders' equity (i.e., $370,000 / $490,000 = 0.76)

interest coverage (IC) = (pretax income + interest expense) / interest expense (i.e., [$130,000 + $10,000] / $10,000 = 14 times)

Return on Investment

return on assets (ROA) = net income / total assets (i.e., $80,000 / $860,000 = 0.09, or 9%)

return on equity (ROE) = net income / owners' equity (i.e., $80,000 / $490,000 = 0.16, or 16%)

return on investment capital (ROIV) = net income / long-term debt + owners' equity (i.e., $80,000 / [$150,000 + $490,000] = 0.125, or 12.5%)

bond yield = 10%

Investor Information

annual return (per share) = increase or decrease in value + any dividend (i.e., $2.00 + $0.04 = $2.04 per share).

On a percentage basis, the annual return would be divided by the initial investment (i.e., $2.04 / $8.00 = 0.255, or 25.5%).

current yield = annual interest payment / current market value (i.e., $100 / $1,100 = 0.0909, or 9.09%)

Annual interest payment = bond face value × bond interest rate (i.e., $1,000 × 10%).

dividend per share = dividends / outstanding shares (i.e., $40,000 / 1,000,000 = $0.04 a share)

holding period return (HPR) = (current income + capital gains) / purchase price (i.e., $0.04 + $2.00) / $8.00 = 0.255, or 25.5%)

simple rate of return (SRR) = investment's annual income / initial investment (i.e., $0.04 / $8.00 = 0.005, or 0.5%)

Glossary

10-K—An annual report required by the U.S. Securities and Exchange Commission (SEC) that shows specific information about a company.

10-Q—Specific quarterly report featuring comprehensive financial statements of a publicly traded company required by the **SEC**.

accountant—A person who practices accounting or accountancy, which is the measurement, disclosure, or provision of assurance about financial information critical for making financial and managerial decisions.

accounting—The art of tabulating financial numbers to determine how much money someone earned and spent during a given period.

accounts payable—Outstanding obligations that are owed by a business to vendors, lenders, or anyone else from whom credit was received and goods were purchased on such credit.

accounts receivable (A/R)—Moneys that are owed to a business from customers who purchased merchandise or services on credit. Many customers do not have sufficient funds to make cash purchases and thus need credit in order to purchase necessary products or supplies. Accounts receivable are not bad; they represent significant sales and can be used as collateral to borrow money. However, accounts receivable can become a burden if they are not repaid in a timely manner.

accrual—Anticipated future expenses and revenues. For example, in some accounting systems (accrual accounting), expenditures and revenues are recorded at the time of the transaction, regardless of when the money is actually disbursed or received. In contrast, in the **cash basis budgeting** (or accounting) system, expenditures and revenues are recorded at the time they are actually disbursed or received.

accrual basis accounting—Accounting process in which expenses are matched with the related revenues or are reported when the expense occurs, not when the cash is paid. The result of accrual accounting is an income statement that better measures the profitability of a company during a specific time period.

acquisition—Gaining control of a corporation through stock purchase or exchange.

activity ratios—Measures how effectively a firm manages its assets.

allowance—A credit that a creditor allows a debtor to take for any of a number of reasons, such as compensation for defective products.

amortization—Repaying a loan in installments. As such payments are made, typically on a property mortgage, the debtor's equity in the property increases because each installment comprises both interest and principal. Goodwill can also be amortized over several years instead of just the first year after a business has been purchased.

annual report—A report produced at the end of a fiscal year to inform shareholders about the company's financial position. Annual reports are carefully scrutinized by more than just shareholders; potential investors, creditors, lenders, and other interested parties rely on the audited information to help make investment decisions.

annual return—The return from a given investment over the course of a year, calculated as follows:

total return = $(s - p) + d$

where s = sale price that year, p = purchase price that year, and d = dividend that year.

The percentage annual return calculation is:

percentage annual return = total annual return / initial investment

annuity—A savings account or a retirement account with an insurance company or other investment placement company into which the investor can deposit a lump sum or scheduled deposits. When a particular event occurs, such as retirement, the investor receives regular repayments such as monthly distributions until the entire invested amount is repaid. Annuities have several significant benefits and drawbacks (Siegel, Shim, & Hartman, 1992).

appropriation—An amount of money set aside in a budget to cover a particular expense such as inventory or expected wages.

asset—Any resource or goods that might offer future benefits to a business and have value. Examples of assets are buildings, machinery, land, inventory, business goodwill, and related resources. Hard assets (*see also* **tangible assets**) include such items as inventory and equipment that are tangible (can be touched). Intangible assets such as a company's goodwill, which has value but is hard to quantify, are called soft assets.

audit—An inspection by an independent, external entity of all a company's accounting records and business operations. The primary purpose of a company audit by a certified public accountant is to validate all financial statements for accuracy so that the government, lenders, shareholders, and others can obtain an accurate view of the company. An independent audit is conducted by a neutral auditor who can certify the accuracy of an audit.

auditor—Someone who conducts an audit.

average day sales outstanding—The average amount of time it takes a business to collect outstanding accounts receivable. The longer the average, the more money is lost because of the inability to use such outstanding funds for investment or other growth opportunities. Furthermore, if the average is long, that means there is a greater likelihood that some accounts receivables might be difficult to collect.

balanced scorecard—A strategic planning and management system that businesses and organizations use to communicate strategy, align employee activity, prioritize projects, measure performance, and monitor progress toward specified goals.

balance sheet—A statement of financial condition prepared at the end of a set time period that lists a company's assets, liabilities, and owners' equity. The balance sheet is bal-

anced when assets equal all liabilities plus the owners' equity.

bankruptcy (or bankrupt)—Protection from creditors or an attempt by creditors to protect any remaining value when a business' debt exceeds its assets' fair market value. Bankruptcy may be voluntary or forced by the courts. Three categories of bankruptcy are available: Chapters 7, 11, and 13. Chapter 7 allows an individual's or business' property to be sold and the proceeds to be divided among creditors. Any debts that are not covered by the sale proceeds are discharged. Chapter 11 allows a company to reorganize and maintain control over its assets and operations while it attempts to resolve repayment schedules and amounts with debtors. Once the courts confirm a reorganization plan, all debts not included in the plan are discharged. Chapter 13, which is sometimes called the wage-earner plan, allows a debtor to repay debts in installments over a three-year period (Cheeseman, 2010).

bearer bonds—Bonds that do not require owners to register their names with the issuing company or government unit. The person who bears the bond can clip a coupon when it becomes due and cash it in. Also known as a coupon bond.

benchmarking—The process of analyzing statistical data to compare companies against one another or against industry standards.

bond—A legal instrument through which a company or government entity promises to repay the bond purchaser both the principal and a specified interest rate; in return the bondholder receives a pledge of assets or can rely on the **full faith and credit** of the issuer. The full faith and credit of a company can back bonds not backed by assets. If the company collapses, there will be no collateral from which to repay the investment.

bondholder—Anyone who holds legal title to a bond.

bond rating—Evaluation by one of two companies, Moody's or Standard & Poor's, ranging from C or D to Aaa or AAA, respectively. An AAA- or Aaa-rated bond is the highest quality bond, while ratings at the other extreme (C or

D) indicate a lower chance that bondholders will be able to recover their investment. Blue-chip companies or strong government entities (financially strong cities, municipalities, or states) typically have AAA or similar ratings.

bond yield—A bond's effective rate of return. One means to measure the yield is the **current yield** method, which is calculated by dividing the annual interest payment by the bond's current market value, expressed as:

coupon rate × par value) / current market value.

Two other more complex formulas, yield to call and yield to maturity, can help provide a more detailed analysis if the bond is held for a set time period or held until it matures.

book value—Total assets less total liabilities.

book value per share—The value of each share of stock based on its cost when the stock was originally issued. We can calculate book value per share by dividing total **stockholders' equity** by the number of outstanding shares.

break-even budget—*See* **break-even point.**

break-even point—The level of revenue generation at which total revenue exactly matches total costs. The break-even analysis is used to help determine when profit could be made on a given product.

budget—A road map or plan expressed in monetary terms that highlights all anticipated assets, debt, expenses, revenue, and net worth. Can also be called **budgeting.**

budgeting—The process of creating a budget.

buyout—Situation in which one or more investors or a business acquires a controlling interest in a company through buying a majority of that company's stock. Various professional sports teams have gone public and issued stock, and some of these teams were subsequently bought out by an individual investor or investment group and became privately owned teams.

capital—Wealth used to produce additional wealth.

capital asset pricing model—A method of measuring the cost of common stock.

capital assets—Fixed assets such as buildings, fields, stadiums, equipment, and other assets that can be depreciated.

capital budget—*See* **financial budget.**

capital budgeting—The process of creating a budget specifically developed for large investment such as building a new factory or stadium where the financial plan might take years.

capital gains—The total gains in value of an investment, excluding dividends. However, dividends can be included in the capital gains if the dividends are reinvested in additional shares of the same stock. Long-term capital gains are investments that have matured for more than one year and result in capital gains that must be reported to the IRS. Short-term capital gains apply to investments held for less than one year.

capital spending—The net spending on fixed assets.

capital structure—The blend of stocks, bonds, and other borrowing (both short-term and long-term) required to help a business grow and finance its overall operations.

cash—Money. In the business world, it includes paper money, coins, checks, bearer bonds, bank accounts, negotiable instruments, and related liquid assets. There are many synonyms, including *legal tender* and numerous slang terms.

cash basis accounting—Method of recording transactions for revenue and expenses only when the corresponding **cash** is received or payments are made. Thus, you record revenue only when a customer pays for a billed product or service, and you record a payable only when it is paid by the company.

cash discount—A reduced payment that manufacturers or wholesalers often offer those who purchase items with cash. The terms of a cash discount may be indicated by the expression 2/10/30. This formula means that the buyer has 30 days to pay the net amount. However, a buyer who pays the bill within 10 days will receive a 2% discount. Sellers can use multiple discounts in addition to cash discounts, such as seasonal or volume discounts, to offer even greater savings.

cash flow—The difference between what a company brings in and what it pays out.

Companies can keep track of cash payments and receipts with a cash flow statement. *See also* **statement of cash flows**.

cash flow budget—A budgeting process that recognizes income and expenses when cash is actually received or paid and does not recognize accounts receivable or accounts payable.

cash management—The process of managing cash within an organization so the company does not run out of cash and can pay its bills.

certificate of deposit (CD)—A type of savings account that pays more than traditional passbook or other savings accounts. They earn higher interest because the depositor has to keep the money in the CD for a longer maturity period than for other types of accounts.

clear title—When real or personal property is sold, the buyer normally wants the property to have a clear title, which means that no liens (a claim against property) or other claims exist against the property. If the property is subject to a court-ordered lien, it can still be resold but with a clouded title.

collateral—Either real or personal property pledged as security for repaying a loan.

common stock—Shares in either privately held or public companies, representing an equity interest in those companies. Although common stock shareholders own an equity share in the company, if a company goes bankrupt, they are paid only after bondholders and preferred stock shareholders are paid. Stockholders have specific rights, including the right to elect the board of directors and the right of preemption, which entitles them to buy any new stocks from the company before other investors can.

compounding—Retaining an investment's return from subsequent years after the initial investment, which results in accruing more revenue than if the investment's return was withdrawn immediately upon receipt. Thus, compounding can significantly increase an investment's total return.

compound interest—Interest added to the principal loaned amount over the loan's life.

conglomerate merger—Form of merger that occurs when companies in unrelated lines of business come together.

consumer price index (CPI)—Number published monthly by the Bureau of Labor Statistics. The number represents an average of the prices of various goods and services that consumers typically purchase in various urban areas. The CPI provides insight into the purchasing power of the U.S. dollar.

contraction—The process of either shutting down a division of a company or closing the entire company, a business, or a business unit.

convertibles—Bonds, debentures, or preferred stocks that can be converted to common stock or other securities. An investor might convert the bonds or preferred stock to obtain an ownership interest or to benefit from dividends or continued growth. Convertible preferred stock can be converted according to a preset conversion price formula at a specified date. Debentures can also be converted to stocks if they are convertible debentures.

corporate bond—A company can issue a debt security (bond) with semiannual interest payments that is traded on the major exchanges. These bonds typically have a $1,000 face value. Bonds are backed by either collateral or the full faith and credit of the corporation.

corporate earnings—Sales less costs. If earnings increase, stock prices should increase; and if earnings decrease, stock prices should decrease. This happened in late 1998, when corporate earnings slid, causing the Dow Jones Industrial Average to drop almost 2,000 points.

cost share—Determining the total cost for an item and allocating the cost to different units.

coupon—Part of a bond that can be clipped so that the bondholder can present it to a designated institution such as a bank to obtain payment of interest.

credit—Any purchase made on account, which means it is paid at a later date. In accounting terms, a credit represents an increase in funds and is usually listed on the right side in the T-account system. *See also* **debit**.

creditor—Anyone who is owed money is a creditor. This can include secured creditors (who have collateral securing their debt) or unsecured creditors.

credit rating—Score that lenders use to determine the risks associated with any given loan or extension of credit. Factors such as job history, housing, income, assets, and credit history help determine an individual's credit rating. Credit rating is a process that tracks an individual's or company's ability to repay borrowed money. Lenders use credit ratings to determine if any new moneys might be advanced.

crowdfunding—Using the Internet to obtain initial funding for a business.

current assets—Assets that are expected to be converted to cash in one year or less. Examples of current assets that appear on balance sheets are cash and short-term financial assets.

current liabilities—Liabilities that are expected to be paid within a year. Wages, rent, and utilities are examples of current liabilities as they are due every month.

current ratio (CR)—A company's ability to cover current liabilities with current assets. To calculate current ratio, we divide current assets by current liabilities.

current yield—An investment's return in relation to its current value. For a bond, the annual interest payments are divided by the bond's current market value.

days sales outstanding—The average collection period, which represents the length of time it is taking customers to repay debt owed to the company. A high number of days sales outstanding means that a company is not effectively collecting its accounts receivable or that credit is being extended to inappropriate customers.

debenture—Long-term bonds that are not secured by any collateral. Because these bonds are backed by a company's good name and credit history, companies need good credit ratings to issue debentures.

debit—Any decrease in revenue or net worth. It is documented by being listed on the left side of a T-account. *See also* **credit**.

debt—Any money, goods, or services owed to someone else on the basis of a prior contractual agreement.

debtor—Anyone who has a legal or moral obligation to pay a debt to a creditor.

debt service—The repayment of an obligation. The debt service on some new stadiums will be about $20 million per year for approximately 30 years.

decrement budget—A budget that is decreased a certain percentage from prior budgets.

default—The failure of someone to pay their financial obligations.

depreciation—A charge against earnings to write off the costs of a deteriorating asset based on a specified formula. Every item deteriorates over time, and a business must replace items as they deteriorate. Depreciation reduces earnings and a business can better afford to purchase new equipment if it depreciates the old assets. The formula is derived from the depreciation base.

disclaimer—A notice that some uncertainties exist (e.g., a pending IRS audit or a lawsuit that can significantly jeopardize the company's financial position). Accountants or auditors who have not had enough time or received enough information to make a conclusive decision about a company's financial statement can prepare a report with a disclaimer.

disclosure—Notification in all financial statements, including a company's annual report, of all relevant facts such as contractual terms, debt issues, and equity adjustments. Under **SEC** regulations, a publicly traded company has to fully disclose to stockholders any disastrous event that could affect the company's financial condition, such as the death of a key executive or major research and development failures.

discount bond—A bond that is sold in the marketplace below its **face value**.

discounted net cash flow—A means to determine an investment's value by examining after-tax cash flows and return on an investment. By examining income streams and reducing them to represent the present value of money, an investor can critically examine how much should be paid for a given investment in order to generate a given rate of return.

discounted payback rule—A rule that analyzes how long it will take a business to get its money back after investing in a capital project while also factoring in the opportunity cost of capital by discounting the future cash flows.

discount factor—An arithmetic calculation that is used to help calculate the **present value** of a given investment. Also called a **present value factor**.

discounting—The formula used to determine the present value of a sum of money to be received in the future. Comprehensive tables allow individuals to easily determine the **present value** of given sums assuming various interest rates.

discount rate—The interest rate or percent return that can be earned from an investment. The discount rate is used when determining the **present value** of an investment option.

dividend—A portion of the company's net income set aside by the company's board of directors to benefit the shareholders. Cash dividends can be given, but once received by the shareholder they are taxable. This double taxation (the company pays taxes on income, then taxpayers get taxed on their dividends) is one of the key drawbacks of the corporation structure of business. **Stock dividends** consisting of additional shares of stock can also be allocated by the board of directors and are not taxed upon receipt by the shareholder. When additional stocks are given as a dividend, the stockholder pays taxes only when selling them.

dividend payout ratio—An expression of dividend payments as a percentage of net earnings: Dividends per share are divided by earnings per share.

dividend per share—Represents how much dividends each shareholder receives for each share. As an example, if a $1 million dividend is declared and there are one million shares outstanding, the dividend per share is $1.

earnings before interest and taxes—A company's earned income, not taking into consideration any owed interest or taxes.

earnings per share—A measure of how much each share of stock is earning in dollar terms and one of the most important tools to mea-sure a company's success. To calculate earnings per share, the company's net income is divided by the total number of outstanding shares.

economics—A blend of art and science to help explain and chart the most effective and efficient use of scarce resources. Microeconomics analyzes individual markets such as baseball, football, or basketball. Macroeconomics analyzes the big picture, such as the national economy or global economy.

economic impact—Measure of how a dollar spent will impact an entire community—often referred to as a ripple effect because a dollar thrown into an economy will have a ripple effect on the surrounding economy.

economies of scale—A reduction in cost per unit resulting from increased production, realized through operational efficiencies.

elasticity of demand—A measure of the degree to which a change in pricing affects the unit sales of a product. If a change in price does not impact demand, then the demand is inelastic while an elastic demand changes significantly when prices change.

equity—An individual's net worth or a company's stock ownership value.

excise taxes—Numerous taxes for various consumed goods that are generally lumped under the designation excise taxes and are sometimes added to the purchase price of such items as gas, alcohol, and tobacco.

expenses—Any payments, any reduction in value (such as depreciation), or any new legal obligations (such as entering into a binding contract).

face value—The stated value for a bond or other security. Most bonds, for example, have a $1,000 face value but can be sold for an amount higher or lower than the indicated value. In addition to a face value, a security has a face interest rate, which is the interest rate guaranteed for the security when the security was issued.

finance—The study of how investors and entities allocate their assets over time under conditions of certainty and uncertainty. The focus is on how to strategically deal with financial certainty and uncertainty.

financial accounting—The process of recording, summarizing, and reporting the financial transactions of an organization. The end result of this process is the creation of three primary financial statements: balance sheets, income statements, and cash flow statements.

financial budget—A basic budget that examines all revenue and expenses.

financial leverage—The portion of a company's assets that are financed with debt rather than equity. It is normally beneficial to reinvest your own money (equity) rather than borrow funds; if you can reinvest borrowed funds and obtain a rate of return greater than your interest and principal payments on the borrowed funds, then leveraging is a potential strong option for growth.

financial leverage ratios—Various ratios that help identify how a company is financed and whether it has undertaken too much debt to grow. These ratios include the acid test ratio, current ratio, debt ratio, and debt–equity ratio.

financial statements—Reports of corporations' financial condition annually, semiannually, and quarterly. The reports contain numerous financial statements such as balance sheets, income statements, and cash flow statements.

firm valuation ratios—Ratios that inform us of the value of sport organizations. In general, this is achieved through two methods: market value and book value.

fiscal year—A one-year period used as a basis for analyzing the company's financial performance and creating new budgets for the coming year. Many companies have August 31 as the first date of the fiscal year and the following August 30 as the last day of the fiscal year.

fixed assets—Permanent assets, attached to the ground, such as buildings or equipment required to run a business. Ice rinks, locker rooms, rental counters, spectator seating, and a Zamboni are all examples of fixed assets.

fixed costs—Regular expenses that are incurred regardless of level of activity. Rent is a fixed cost because the same amount is owed regardless of potential business activity. Other examples are taxes, insurance premiums, and fixed salaries. Also called fixed charges.

flotation costs—The cost of a publicly traded security to issue new securities such as stocks.

forecast—An estimate, based on hopefully sound data, of what might happen at a future time. Forecasting is the process of using a forecast to plan for the future.

full faith and credit—*See* **bond**.

future value (FV)—The value that a given investment or security might have at a given time in the future. An investment's future value can be determined through various means, including the use of a future value table. FV_n is the future value at a specific (n) period. The opposite of future value is **present value**.

generally accepted accounting principles (GAAP)—Industry rules developed to ensure uniformity by accountants. If an accountant follows these principles, others will know that there are standards behind how the numbers were calculated and that other accountants would come up with the same results using the same numbers.

general obligation bonds (GOBs)—Municipal bonds issued for such projects as stadiums or arenas, with the interest and principal payments backed by the **full faith and credit** of the municipality that issues the bonds. This means the bonds are backed by all the taxes collected by the municipality even if such taxes are not used for the facility. Under such a bond, a stadium could be constructed from a bond backed by a ticket surcharge. If the host team moves and there are no other tenants, no ticket surcharges would be collected to pay back the bondholders. The bondholders could then proceed against property tax collections or any other taxes for repayment.

goodwill—The difference between a company's book value and its market value. The difference is based on the fact that the company has value that is not reflected in its books, or if goodwill is on the books, it is an additional value based on various valuation techniques. The name *Coca-Cola*, for example, represents a tremendous asset (a name recognized worldwide) that is hard to place a value on.

gross profit margin—The income of a company before operating expenses, interest, and taxes are paid.

horizontal merger—A type of merger that occurs when two companies in the same line of business are joined.

hostile takeover—A takeover that occurs against the desires of the target company's management and board of directors.

illiquid—A company that does not have sufficient liquid assets such as stocks and marketable securities to cover short-term debt.

income—Any money received during a given time period by either an individual or a company. Income can be derived from such sources as salaries, investment returns, or asset sales.

income statement—A method of tracking a company's revenue and expenses over any given time period.

income tax—A levy imposed by the government on an individual's taxable income. The taxable income is calculated by deducting all allowable deductions (such as unreimbursed business expenses) from the gross income.

incremental budgeting—A budget based on slight changes from the preceding period's budget such as increasing the budget 10% over the prior year due to anticipated higher sales and expenses. In a **decrement budget**, the numbers are decreased.

independent audit—An external review of the finances by individuals who are not directly involved with the documents that are being reviewed.

inflation—An increase in the price level of products that could be due to increased demand. The increased demand for products can force prices to increase, which leads to a chain reaction of increasing wages and material costs.

informal liquidation—Selling some assets to avoid forced bankruptcy. Often undertaken when a company has more assets than debt and can sell some assets to avoid. Also called assignment.

informal reorganization—A plan undertaken by a company and creditors to try to keep a company going outside of the bankruptcy process.

initial public offering—A company's first attempt at issuing and hopefully selling stocks to the public.

intangible assets—An asset that lacks physical substance (while a tangible asset such as machinery or a building can be touched) and usually is hard to value such as goodwill or a trademark.

interest (*i*)—The amount a lender charges for loaning money to a borrower. **Interest rates** are normally expressed in relation to an annual period. Interest can also mean an equity ownership position with a company. Thus, a professional sports team could own a 10% interest in a broadcasting station, which means it owns 10% of the station.

interest rate—The cost of borrowing money expressed in percentage terms over the course of a year.

internal rate of return (IRR)—A calculation that is designed to provide an investor with the effective annual return from a given investment. The initial cash investment is analyzed in comparison with the present value of cash returns.

inventory—Raw material or goods in stock that have not yet been sold or manufactured.

junk bond—A high-yield bond with a low credit rating. Smaller or new companies without a significant financial track record of sales or earnings often issue these bonds.

leveraged buyout—The purchase of a business using the assets of the purchased company as collateral to secure financing.

liabilities—Any legal or financial obligations. Typical examples are long-term debt, retained earnings, shareholders' equity, and taxes owed. Liabilities are the opposite of **assets**.

limited liability corporation (LLC)—A form of business organization that allows pass-through for taxation and liability protection at a reduced cost compared to corporations.

line item budget—A budget that lists every expense and revenue source on a separate line to help administrators identify every single source of revenue or expenses.

line of credit—The maximum preapproved amount a company or individual can borrow without having to go to a different lending source.

liquid—A condition in which an individual or company has enough cash or liquid assets that can be sold quickly (CDs, Treasury bonds, high-quality corporate bonds, stocks) to meet current debt obligations. Inventories are traditionally not considered liquid because it can take time to sell inventory. Accounts receivable are similar in that it can take time to collect them. Factoring, which entails selling inventories or accounts receivable, is rapidly changing the nature of liquid assets because inventories and accounts receivable can be sold in a relatively short amount of time.

liquid asset—A type of asset that can be quickly converted to cash such, as stocks and bonds owned by a company.

liquidity—How quickly and easily an asset can be converted to cash.

loan—A transaction between a lender and a borrower in which the borrower contractually agrees to repay the principal amount and interest. By repaying the loan in a systematic manner, the borrower engages in loan.

long term—Longer than one year and possibly 5 years or 10 years.

managerial accounting—Type of accounting that focuses on the analysis and evaluation of accounting information as part of the managerial process of planning, decision making, and controlling.

marginal cost—The change in costs associated with the volume produced. If it costs $1 to produce each of 1,000 baseballs and $0.80 each to produce any additional balls, then the marginal cost of producing additional balls is $0.80.

marginal tax—The tax paid on the last dollar earned. It can be unwise to earn more money after a certain point because the higher earning level results in a higher tax liability.

margin (profit)—Profits after taxes divided by sale. This calculation shows whether a company made an acceptable percentage of profit based on total sales. A sport manufacturing company with millions in sales and minimal profits is possibly wasting money. In contrast, a company such as a sport services firm may have a lower income level but a higher profit margin. Also called **net profit margin**. *See also* **profit margin**.

marketable securities—Securities (such as stock) that are easy to sell on major markets such as the NYSE.

market index—A market gauge to help investors appreciate market trends. The most famous index is the Dow Jones Industrial Average (Dow). Other indexes include Barron's 50-Stock Average, Standard & Poor's 400 Industrials, and the Value Line Average.

market value—The true price in a competitive marketplace of a product, service, or investment vehicle. Supply and demand significantly affect the market value, which is why a ticket for the Super Bowl with a face value of $150 may be sold on the street for $2,000. The $2,000 price is the market value.

maturity—The time when a loan, bond, or other obligation becomes due and payable. Maturity value is the amount owed once the maturity date is reached.

merger—The combining of two or more businesses into one through a purchase, an acquisition, or a pooling of interests.

mortgage—A long-term loan (typically 15 or 30 years) secured by real property. If the mortgage loan value is less than the property's market value, the property owner may be able to take out another loan called a second mortgage.

municipal bonds—Bonds that are issued by government entities and have significant benefits such as the security of a government entity to repay the loan and tax deductibility of income from the bond. However, the interest rates are typically lower than for corporate-issued bonds. Municipal bonds are nicknamed *munis*.

mutual funds—A pool of investors' money used buy a diverse collection of investment securities. These funds are very attractive to investors since they do not require a significant investment, and the risk of loss is lower because the fund invests in numerous companies. Professional managers make the buy and sell decisions.

NASDAQ—The National Association of Securities Dealers Automated Quotations is a subsidiary of the National Association of Securities Dealers that uses electronic networking to facilitate buying and selling (trading) of the over-the-counter market's 5,000 most active stocks.

net income—Revenue less expenses.

net present value (NPV)—The difference between the **present value** of the future income and the required investment.

net profit margin—The net income of a company after interest and taxes are paid.

net working capital—The amount of money available to pay bills. It is calculated by subtracting current liabilities from current assets.

net worth—The difference between a company's total assets and total liabilities. The resulting number is the owners' or shareholders' equity in the company.

New York Stock Exchange (NYSE)—The largest and most respected securities exchange. Often called the big board.

noncompete contract—A contract clause that limits a person or organization from competing with others.

note (promissory)—A legally transferable debt instrument wherein the borrower agrees to pay a stated amount at a certain date, and the obligation is good no matter who eventually owns the note. Thus, after someone borrows money and signs a note to purchase something, the note can be sold to several subsequent companies without affecting the borrower's obligation to repay.

operational budget—A budget used to examine all revenues and expenses over a period of time (typically a month, a quarter, or a year), which a company uses to plan its operations.

opportunity cost—The cost of the next best alternative forgone. If a city invests in one thing, then the city might need to forgo another thing that would have been invested in but for the first thing. This is an additional cost associated with the first thing, over and beyond the actual construction cost. Also called implicit cost.

overcapitalization—Situation that occurs when an organization raises too much money through stocks and bonds, which is unhealthy if it has to pay down debt or pay dividends.

over-the-counter exchange—An informal trading environment used to trade unlisted securities. Unlike the New York Stock Exchange, which is a formal trading environment, the over-the-counter exchange is not one building or trading floor. Dealers use electronics and telecommunication through the NASDAQ network to make trades. The over-the-counter exchange does not have the capitalization requirements that the NYSE does.

owners' equity—The value remaining after liabilities are subtracted from assets. Stock and accumulated earnings are added together, then dividends are subtracted to calculate total owners' equity.

par value—An arbitrary value assigned to a share so that it can be sold when it is issued.

payback period—The amount of time necessary to recover an initial investment. The payback period can be calculated by dividing the initial investment by the annual cash flow.

payroll—The total amount of wages owed to all employees.

performance budget—A budget that is based on meeting certain predetermined goals such as number of tickets sold.

preemptive right (or preemption)—Agreement that allows a shareholder to purchase a percentage of any future shares issued by the company that matches the percentage of shares he currently owns. This allows an investor to maintain the same percentage control of a business before shares are sold to the general public, which can dilute his ownership interest.

preferred stock—A type of stock that has some features similar to those of a stock and some similar to those of a bond. Preferred stocks represent ownership equity and can generate dividend income, but they also have a guaranteed dividend and a superior claim right over other stocks. The superior claim rights allow preferred stock shareholders to sell assets or seize earnings if the company folds.

prepaid expenses—Expenses paid in advance such as insurance or fees that cover future services.

present value (PV)—The current value of a future amount of money. If you win the lottery, you might be able to take several million dollars now or 10 times that amount over a number of years. Such payouts are based on the fact that if you invest a certain sum now, it will be worth more in the future. Individuals can use a present value table to analyze the value of future income streams.

present value factor—A formula based on the concept of **time value of money**, which is the idea that an amount received today is worth more than if the same amount was received at a future date. Any amount received today can be invested to earn additional monies. Also called a **discount factor**.

price–earnings growth (PEG) ratio—An estimate of what the future quarterly earnings will be along with using the previous three trailing estimates. Otherwise similar to the traditional price–earnings (PE) ratio.

price–earnings (PE) ratio—A comparison between a stock's market value and the strength of a company's earnings. It can help determine a stock's market price. To calculate this, multiply the estimated earnings per share by the estimated price–earnings ratio.

principal—The amount invested in any given security.

profitability ratios—A class of financial metrics used to assess a business's ability to generate earnings relative to its associated expenses.

profit margin—Revenue in excess of expenses. *See also* **margin (profit)**.

pro forma—A document (such as a business plan) that utilizes assumed, forecasted, or informal data presented in advance of the actual or formal information to help project future results.

property, plant, and equipment (PPE)—Elements added to a stadium, arena, or other facility such as scoreboard, speakers, or chairs.

prospectus—A document from a company that highlights key financial data about the company and the proposed security but does not discuss when the security will be issued or the exact price.

proxy—A document signed by a shareholder who does not attend a shareholders' meeting, which allows a designated person to vote on company-related issues on their behalf.

public offering—Stock a company offers to the general public after filing the necessary registration with the **SEC**.

pure-play stock—The stock of a company that has only one line of business (e.g., only the bowling industry). An investor may want to play (invest in) one industry, and the company's exclusive position in that industry makes it a good investment prospect for that investor. Several mutual funds were started in the 1990s to invest in specific sport categories, such as auto racing or companies that own or sponsor professional sports teams.

quick ratio—An analysis of the ability of a company to liquidate current assets (excluding hard-to-sell items such as inventory) to pay off current liabilities. Cash is added to marketable securities and accounts receivable, and these liquid assets are divided by current liabilities. If the resulting number is less than 1, then the company does not have enough liquid assets to pay current liabilities. If the ratio is greater than 1, then the company has more than enough liquid assets to pay off current liabilities.

rate of return—The gain or loss that might result from an investment decision. Expressed as a percentage.

recession—A downturn in the business cycle in which various economic indicators such as the gross national product, employment rate, consumer spending, and other indicators decline.

refinance—Consolidating or reworking any and possibly all outstanding debts to make repayment easier or to avoid financial hardship such as bankruptcy.

reinvestment—Using the dividends, interest, or profits from an investment to buy more of that investment rather than receiving a cash payout.

relegation—The process of an English football club being sent down to a lower division (tier) if it has a very bad season.

replacement cost—The cost someone would incur if they needed to replace property. Capital equipment in sport, such as a new ice resurfacing machine or a new air-conditioning system, can be very expensive. Thus, companies have to plan for replacement costs either by setting aside money over a long period of time or by ensuring the potential to issue new securities or borrow necessary funds.

retained earnings—Earnings not paid out as dividends but instead reinvested in the core business or used to pay off debt.

return—Any value received from an investment. It can include dividend payments, interest rate, or appreciation in value over a period of time.

return on assets (ROA)—The calculated investment return obtained from assets purchased by a company. Any new assets purchased should be able to generate increased return over and beyond what could have been earned if the money was invested in a CD or other liquid investment option. To calculate ROA, net income is divided by total assets.

return on equity (ROE)—The degree to which an investment in an ownership position (equity) within a company produced a rate of return greater than what could have been earned if the money had been invested elsewhere, if any. ROE is calculated by dividing net income by shareholders' equity. Similar to **return on assets**.

revenue—Money coming into a business.

revenue bond—Government-issued bond whose interest and principal payments are repaid from specified revenue sources. A baseball stadium could be built using revenue bonds secured by hotel and rental-car tax revenues.

ripple effect—The reverberation of money through an economy after it is spent.

SEC—*See* **Securities and Exchange Commission (SEC)**.

secured bond—A bond secured by a specific item, or collateral, which can be sold if the bond is not repaid.

securities—Any financial instruments that provide an ownership interest in the issuing company. Typical examples include stocks and bonds.

Securities and Exchange Commission (SEC)—Independent regulatory agency established by the U.S. federal government in the 1930s to regulate securities markets. To protect investors, the SEC requires full financial disclosure for all securities and regulates issues such as insider trading.

serial bond—A bond that matures over regularly scheduled dates, in contrast to a bond that matures on only one given date.

share—A unit of ownership interest in either a company or a financial vehicle (e.g., a mutual fund).

shareholder—An individual who owns a share in a company.

short term—Within a one-year period.

short-term debt—Current liabilities that need to be repaid within one year, such as utility bills, payments for inventory, taxes owed, employee wages owed, and related liabilities.

simple rate of return—A method used to calculate the return that can be obtained on a given investment. To calculate the simple rate of return, we divide the investment's annual income by the initial investment.

sinking fund—Money set aside to invest in income-producing securities that are later cashed in to pay off a financial obligation. Without setting aside money in anticipation of repaying a loan, a company may be forced to issue additional securities to raise the necessary cash or may need to borrow the money.

special tax bond—A municipal bond paid for with revenue from excise taxes levied on such items as alcohol or tobacco sales. Such "sin taxes" have been used to fund stadium projects such as Jacobs Field in Cleveland.

statement of cash flows—A document that summarizes a firm's cash flows resulting from operations, financing activity, and investment activity.

static budget—A budget that anticipates future revenue and expenses and does not change over the budgetary period.

stock—Wealth people might have, such as cash or other investments. The owners of shares of stock in a company are called stockholders.

stock dividend—Additional stock issued to a company's shareholders if the company does not have enough cash to pay a dividend. If a stock dividend is issued, the shares outstanding for the company are increased, and this reduces the per share value of all shares.

stock exchange—A marketplace where stock and other securities are traded. Also called a **stock market**.

stockholders—Individuals, group, or organization that holds one or more shares in a company, and in whose name the share certificate is issued.

stockholders' equity—The amount of capital given to a business by its shareholders, plus donated capital and earnings generated by the operation of the business, less any dividends issued.

stock market—A marketplace where stock and other securities are traded. Also called a **stock exchange**.

subordinate debenture—An unsecured bond that would be paid only after senior bonds are paid.

sunk costs—Past costs incurred that might affect a subsequent decision. The cost of a purchased item or security is irrelevant for many decisions, but it would be relevant if you wished to sell and would sell only for a specified rate of return higher than the initial purchase price.

t—In a financial formula, the time frame for a given investment.

tangible assets—Assets that can be felt, seen, and held, such as concession items.

taxable income—Adjusted gross income less any allowed deductions or exemptions such as business expenses, capital losses, or charitable giving.

term loan—A loan that calls for regular periodic payments, usually for three years or more.

time value of money—The concept that money decreases in value over time. Because one dollar today is worth more than one dollar next year (assuming there will be inflation), investment decisions need to be made with a critical eye toward the future value of a dollar.

total asset turnover ratio—Ratio that shows how quickly a company uses its assets to make money. A low ratio means that assets are not being turned over quickly enough to generate additional revenue.

treasurer—A person who deals with banks, stockholders, institutional investors, bondholders, and other stakeholders or potential stakeholders to educate them about how a company is doing and what it might need for future growth.

Treasury bill (T-bill)—A short-term government obligation issued in a minimum denomination of $10,000 and scheduled to mature in three months, six months, or a year. T-bills are considered to be the safest investment vehicle because they are 100% backed by the U.S. government.

triple bottom line—A measure of corporate sustainability that examines social, environmental, and financial variables.

undercapitalization—Situation that occurs when a sport corporation raises some money but not enough to meet the anticipated needs.

upselling—Trying to increase the total amount of a transaction by adding additional elements or amounts to an initial order.

value (V)—The monetary worth of an item. Value can be expressed as what you could obtain on the market if you had to sell an item. The final value is determined through a valuation process.

variable costs—Costs that vary with each unit produced and include items such as raw materials. Semivariable costs vary somewhat with production such as machine maintenance. If a machine is not used, maintenance will decrease, while if it is used extensively maintenance costs would increase.

variance—The difference between the amount budgeted for a given expense and the actual expense incurred. It is sometimes called variance analysis.

vertical merger—A buyer expands operations forward toward the final consumer or backward in the direction of the source of raw materials.

Wall Street—A street in New York City in the heart of the financial district where the New

York Stock Exchange and the American Stock Exchange are located.

weighted average cost of capital (WACC)—An average representing the expected return on all of a company's sources of capital. Each source of capital, such as stocks, bonds, and other debt, is weighted in the calculation according to its importance in the company's capital structure.

working capital—The amount of money available to pay bills. To calculate working capital, current liabilities are subtracted from current assets. Sometimes refers to current assets only.

yield (rate of return)—The income earned by a given investment.

zero-based budgeting (ZBB)—Budget founded on the concept that organizations and their programs need to justify their existence. The resulting budget would distribute money to the programs that produce the greatest benefits, and the components that produce lower benefits would either be eliminated from the budget or receive fewer funds.

zero coupon bond—A bond that does not pay interest on a semiannual or annual basis; rather the semiannual interest payments are added to the principal, with the principal and interest being paid at maturity. These bonds are called zero coupon because the bondholder does not need to clip and redeem coupons in order to obtain the interest payments.

References

Chapter 1

Bomey, N. (2016, November 1). Performance Sports files for Ch. 11 bankruptcy. *USA Today*, p. 2B.

Bomey, N. (2017a, February 16). Another sporting goods chain files for bankruptcy. *USA Today*, p. 6B.

Bomey, N. (2017b, May 16). Dick's Sporting Goods' stock sinks as retail industry's woes deepen. *USA Today*, p. 2B.

Bomey, N. (2017c, March 6). For sports retailers, clock has run out. *USA Today*, pp. 1B-2B.

Bomey, N. (2017d, August 16). Investors unhappy as Dick's warns sales could fall. *USA Today*, p. 4B.

Bomey, N. (2017e, March 22). Titleist maker a bit teed off over Costco's cheaper golf balls. *USA Today*, p. 6B.

The bottom line. (2017, June 16). *The Week*, 17(826), 32.

Financial literacy. (2017, February). *Inc. Magazine*, 56-57.

Griffith, E. (2017, June 15). You'll laugh! Cry! (Maybe buy.). *Fortune*, 175(7), 94.

Jones, C. (2017a, March 23). Sears, Kmart may lack cash to stock shelves. *USA Today*, p. 1B.

Jones, C. (2017b, March 23). What's killing Sears and Kmart? *USA Today*, p. 2B.

Jones, S. (2016, October 31). *Performance Sports Group enters into "stalking horse" asset purchase agreement with investor group led by Sagard Capital and Fairfax Financial for U.S. $575 million* [Press release]. Performance Sports Group. Retrieved from https://cases.primeclerk.com/psg/Home-DownloadPDF?id1=NDg2NjI1&id2=0

Madhani, A. (2017, March 27). As Sears falters, shadow darkens over American malls. *USA Today*, p. 5B.

McCoy, K. (2017a, March 23). Sears' financial woes trigger pension concerns. *USA Today*, p. 1B.

McCoy, K. (2017b, February 16). Top scams targeting senior citizens. *USA Today*, p. 1B.

Murphy, M. (2017, May 15-21). Debrief. *Bloomberg Businessweek*, pp. 54-59.

Nicastro, S. (2017, May 18). 5 steps to digging out of business debt. *USA Today*, p. 6B.

Peltz, J. (2016, April 28). Sports Authority to liquidate. *The Hartford Courant*, p. A7.

Schrotenboer, B. (2017a, March 28). Abandoned cities woo other sports. *USA Today*, p. 6C.

Schrotenboer, B. (2017b, April 19). Gulf widens between NFL teams. *USA Today*, pp. 1C and 6C.

To build a ballpark, first you need to build support. (2017, May). *Athletic Business*, 41(4), 12.

Wahba, P. (2017, June 15). The death of retail is greatly exaggerated. *Fortune*, 175(7), 33.

Wallace, A. (2016a, May 11). Dick's could snare 80 to 180 stores from Sports Authority. *The Denver Post*, p. 8A.

Wallace, A. (2016b, February 11). Why Sports Authority is headed for bankruptcy. *The Denver Post*. Retrieved from www.denverpost.com/2016/02/11/why-sports-authority-is-headed-for-bankruptcy

Xu Klein, J., Church, S., & Coleman-Lochner, L. (2016, May 11). *The Denver Post*, p. 13A.

Chapter 2

90min. (2017, September 21). Man United posts record-breaking revenue figures in 2016-17. *Sports Illustrated*. Retrieved from www.si.com/soccer/2017/09/21/man-utd-post-record-breaking-revenue-figures-after-raking-nearly-ps600m-201617

Arlington Soccer Association. (2012, March). Guide for travel team treasurers. Retrieved from www.arlingtonsoccer.com/wp-content/uploads/2011/02/Guide-for-Travel-Team-Treasurers-updated-April-2012.pdf

Badenhausen, K. (2017, October 3). Esports leagues set to level up with permanent franchises. *Forbes*. Retrieved from www.forbes.com/sites/kurtbadenhausen/2017/10/03/esports-leagues-grow-up-with-permanent-franchises/#16d3988c21d6

Berkowitz, S., & Myerberg, P. (2017, July 7). State opens checkbook for Wyoming. *USA Today*, p. 4C.

Berkowitz, S., & Schnaars, C. (2017, July 7-9). Schools' money flows to athletes. *USA Today*, pp. 1A-2A.

Boksenbaum-Granier A., & Jefferson, R. (2017, October 16). Soccer star Neymar's next score: TV rights. *Bloomberg Businessweek*, pp. 19-20.

Dalgleish, M. (2017, February 27). Michigan athletic department $240M in debt. *The Score*. Retrieved from www.thescore.com/news/1241631

Entrepreneur. (2017). Curves. Retrieved from www.entrepreneur.com/franchises/curves/282265

Euorstat. (2017, February). Government expenditure on recreation, culture and religion. Retrieved from http://ec.europa.eu/eurostat/statistics-explained/index.php/Government_expenditure_on_recreation,_culture_and_religion

Evershed, N. (2016, May 3). Your tax dollars: How is the government spending your money in the 2016 federal budget? *The Guardian*. Retrieved from www.theguardian.com/australia-news/datablog/ng-interactive/2016/may/03/your-tax-dollars-how-is-the-government-spending-your-money

Franchise Help. (2017). Fitness industry analysis 2017—cost & trends. Retrieved from www.franchisehelp.com/industry-reports/fitness-industry-report

Gibson, R. (2011, August 22). Franchising—in search of more muscle: Why is the Curves franchise in such bad shape? *Wall Street Journal*. Retrieved from www.wsj.com/articles/SB100014240527023033658045764320620 58517684

Leader Board. (2016, August 23). The world's most valuable teams. *Forbes*, p. 28.

Murphy, D. (2014, October 23). Michigan drops 2015 ticket prices. *ESPN*. Retrieved from www.espn.com/college-football/story/_/id/11751719/michigan-wolverines-lower-prices-student-tickets-football-games-2015

Novy-Williams, E. (2017, August 14). Why European soccer is coming to America. *Bloomberg Businessweek*, pp. 15-16.

Pitino Pocketed 98% of UL's Adidas Proceeds. (2017, October 6). In Brief. *USA Today*. p. 7C.

Reuters. (2017, September 4). IPL television and broadcast rights sold for massive £1.97bn to Star India. Retrieved from www.theguardian.com/sport/2017/sep/04/ipl-rights-sold-star-india-cricket-twenty-20

Rhoda, B., Wrigley, B., & Habermas, E. (2010). How to increase revenue as industry evolves. *Sports Business Journal, 13*(27), 28.

Schrotenboer, B. (2014, February 5). NFL takes aim at $25 billion, but at what price? *USA Today Sports*. Retrieved from www.usatoday.com/story/sports/nfl/super/2014/01/30/super-bowl-nfl-revenue-denver-broncos-seattle-seahawks/5061197

Shell, A. (2017, September 5). Fitting high-priced elite sports into the family budget. *USA Today*, p. 1B.

Sherman, R. (2016, April 12). The NCAA's new March Madness TV deal will make them a billion dollars a year. *SB Nation*. Retrieved from www.sbnation.com/college-basketball/2016/4/12/11415764/ncaa-tournament-tv-broadcast-rights-money-payout-cbs-turner

Snider, M. (2017, September 27). NFL ratings take hit, but don't blame anthem dispute. *USA Today*, p. 1B.

Statista. (2017). Public sector expenditure on recreational and sporting services in the United Kingdom (UK) from 2011/2012 to 2016/2017 (in million GBP). Retrieved from www.statista.com/statistics/298898/united-kingdom-uk-public-sector-expenditure-recreational-and-sporting-services/

StatsDad. (2011). Youth baseball: Budget planning for a select season. Retrieved from www.statsdad.com/2011/11/youth-baseball-budget-planning-for.html

Strauss, K. (2014, May 27). Crash diet: After shedding thousands of locations, can

Curves get back in shape? *Forbes*. Retrieved from www.forbes.com/sites/karsten-strauss/2014/05/27/crash-diet-after-shedding-thousands-of-locations-can-curves-get-back-in-shape/#6e9f95361b3b

Chapter 3

Brigham, E., & Ehrhardt, M.C. (2014). *Financial management: Theory and practice* (14th ed.) New York: Dryden Press.

Griffin, M.P. (1991). *Intermediate finance for non-financial managers*. Toronto, ON: Amacom.

Patterson, C. (2017, May 2). Nick Saban gets big bonus, signs extension, locks in $1M contact for non-coordinator. cbssports.com. Retrieved from www.cbssports.com/college-football/news/nick-saban-gets-big-bonus-signs-extension-locks-in-1m-contract-for-non-coordinator

Chapter 4

Amir, T. (2014, May 31). Malcolm Glazer's legacy is Manchester United's debt burden. World Soccer Talk. Retrieved from www.world-soccertalk.com/2014/05/31/malcolm-glazers-legacy-is-manchester-uniteds-debt-burden

Conn, D. (2015, September 17). Manchester United to pay Malcolm Glazer's six children £15m every year. *The Guardian*. Retrieved from https://www.theguardian.com/football/2015/sep/17/manchester-united-malcolm-glazer-children-15m-year

Cummings, J. (1982, October 20). DeLorean, automobile executive, arrested in drug smuggling case. *The New York Times*. Retrieved from www.nytimes.com/1982/10/20/us/delorean-automobile-executive-arrested-in-drug-smuggling-case.html

Durso, J. (1986, September 26). Doubleday and president of Mets to buy ball club from publisher. *The New York Times*. Retrieved from www.nytimes.com/1986/09/26/sports/doubleday-and-president-of-mets-to-buy-ball-club-from-publisher.html

Gregorian, D. (2016, February 20). John Rigas, 91, who founded and looted cable company Adelphia and is dying, was released by Manhattan federal court judge. Retrieved from www.nydailynews.com/new-york/adelphi-founder-dying-released-prison-feds-article-1.2538110

Lamberti, C. (2012, June 6). The hustler: Bill Veeck and roster depreciation allowance. *White Sox Observer*. Retrieved from www.chicagonow.com/white-sox-observer/2012/06/the-hustler-bill-veeck-and-roster-depreciation-allowance

Roth, M. (1999, April 28). STAPLES Center's groundbreaking finance package is largest-ever for a sports arena. Staples Center. Retrieved from https://www.staplescenter.com/news/detail/staples-centers-groundbreaking-finance-package-is-largest-ever-for-a-sports-arena

UPI. (2003, January 13). Sabres file for bankruptcy. Retrieved from https://www.upi.com/Sabres-file-for-bankruptcy/84651042486198

Part I Case Study

Alkhalisi, Z. (2017). Qatar slashes budget for 2022 World Cup by at least 40%. CNN Money. Retrieved from http://money.cnn.com/2017/04/05/news/economy/qatar-2022-budget-soccer/index.html

Associated Press (AP). (2013). Deloitte: Qatar to spend $200 billion for World Cup. *USA Today*. Retrieved from www.usatoday.com/story/sports/soccer/2013/07/09/deloitte-qatar-to-spend-200-billion-world-cup/2501815

Associated Press (AP). (2014). How World Cup cash is paid to teams, players. *USA Today*. Retrieved from www.usatoday.com/story/sports/soccer/2014/07/11/how-world-cup-cash-is-paid-to-teams-players/12532323

Associated Press (AP). (2017). Russia increases 2018 World Cup budget by $325 million. *ESPN FC*. Retrieved from www.espnfc.com/fifa-world-cup/story/3055194/russia-increases-2018-world-cup-budget-by-$325-million

Borden, S., Schmidt, M., & Apuzzojune, M. (2015, June 2). Sepp Blatter decides to resign as FIFA President in about-face. *New York Times*. Retrieved from www.nytimes.com/2015/06/03/sports/soccer/sepp-blatter-to-resign-as-fifa-president.html?_r=0

Curtis, J. (2017, January 10). Start saving (or swapping)! FIFA votes to expand the World Cup to 48 teams—and the internet's main concern is how much it's going to cost to complete a Panini sticker album. *Daily Mail*. Retrieved from www.dailymail.co.uk/news/article-4105488/Start-saving-swapping-FIFA-votes-expand-World-Cup-48-teams-internet-s-main-concern-s-going-cost-complete-Panini-STICKER-ALBUM.html#ixzz4ZEycs1eA

Dave Richards sorry for comments about Fifa and Uefa. (2012, March 14). BBC Sport. Retrieved from www.bbc.com/sport/football/17374070

Davis, E. (2016, March 31). Women earn the glory while men earn the money in U.S. soccer. Five Thirty Eight. Retrieved from https://fivethirtyeight.com/features/women-earn-the-glory-while-men-earn-the-money-in-u-s-soccer

FIFA. (2014). *Regulations, 2014 FIFA World Cup Brazil*. Retrieved from www.fifa.com/mm/document/tournament/competition/01/47/38/17/regulationsfwcbrazil2014_update_e_neutral.pdf

Harris, N. (2105, April 25). Qatar paid £17.17billion to host the 2022 World Cup finals, and new research shows where all that money went. Mail Online. Retrieved from www.dailymail.co.uk/sport/football/article-3055550/Qatar-paid-17-17billion-host-2022-World-Cup-finals-new-research-shows-money-went.html#ixzz4mZdZSZNj

Pfeiffer, A. (2015, July 6). World Cup women players overpaid compared to male counterparts. *The Daily Caller*. Retrieved from http://dailycaller.com/2015/07/06/world-cup-women-players-overpaid-compared-to-male-counterparts/#ixzz4ZN6dyjyp

Soergel, A. (2014, June 17). What does it cost to win the World Cup? *US News & World Report*. Retrieved from www.usnews.com/news/blogs/data-mine/2014/06/17/what-does-it-cost-to-win-the-world-cup

U.S. Soccer Federation. (2016). *2016 annual general meeting*. Retrieved from http://media.philly.com/documents/2016+U.S.+Soccer+Annual+General+Meeting+Minutes.pdf

Zimbalist, A. (2011, summer). Brazil's long to-do list. *Americas Quarterly*. Retrieved from http://americasquarterly.org/zimbalist

Zimbalist, A. (2016). *Corruption and the bidding process for the Olympics and World Cup. Transparency International. Global corruption report: Sport.* New York, NY: Routledge.

Chapter 5

Appenzeller, H. (2011). *Ethical behavior in sport*. Durham, NC: Carolina Academic Press.

Badenhausen, K. (2016, January 28). Warriors, Chase Bank tie up ranks among biggest stadium naming rights deals ever. *Forbes*. Retrieved from www.forbes.com/sites/kurt-badenhausen/2016/01/28/warriors-chase-tie-up-joins-ranks-of-biggest-stadium-naming-rights-deals/#1f74764655c0

Berkowitz, S. (2017, August 29). This year's 'guarantee games' worth $150 million for college football programs. *USA Today*. Retrieved from www.usatoday.com/story/sports/ncaaf/2017/08/29/guarantee-games-worth-150-million-college-football-programs/608668001/

Brigham, E. F., & Ehrhardt, M. C. (2014). *Financial management: Theory and practice* (14th ed.). Cincinnati, OH: South-Western College Publishers.

Cabrera, C. (2017). How much are MLB ticket prices 2017: Highest–lowest. Barry's Tickets. Retrieved from www.barrystickets.com/blog/mlb-ticket-prices

Craig, R. (2016, November 17). Big time college sports: Spending student dollars on marketing and entertainment. *Forbes*. Retrieved from www.forbes.com/sites/ryancraig/2016/11/17/big-time-college-sports-spending-student-dollars-on-marketing-and-entertainment/#67af58c5607e

Form 10-K. (2017, February 23). Under Armour, Inc. Retrieved from http://files.shareholder.com/downloads/UARM/5643200105x0xS1336917-17-17/1336917/filing.pdf

Fulks, D. (2016, July). Revenues and expenses: Division I intercollegiate athletics programs report 2004-15. National Collegiate Athletic Association. Retrieved from www.ncaa

publications.com/productdownloads/D1REV-EXP2015.pdf

Gaines, C. (2014, September 10). Microsoft paid the NFL $400 million to use its tablets, but announcers are calling them iPads. *Business Insider*. Retrieved from www.businessinsider.com/microsoft-nfl-surface-ipads-2014-9

Gate receipts as percentage of total revenue in 2010 to 2016. (2017). Statista. Retrieved from www.statista.com/statistics/193364/percentage-of-ticketing-revenue-in-the-nfl-since-2006/

Halley, J. (2010, December 7). High schools get in logo game. *USA Today*, p. 1C.

How Rio Olympics 2016 total revenue to reach $4 billion. (2015, February 2015). Total Sportek. Retrieved from www.totalsportek.com/money/rio-olympics-2016-total-revenue-4-billion/

Howard, D. R., & Crompton, J. L. (2004). *Financing sport* (2rd ed.). Morgantown, WV: Fitness Information Technology.

Howard, D. R., & Crompton, J. L. (2013). *Financing sport* (3rd ed.). Morgantown, WV: Fitness Information Technology.

Kahn, A. (2017, August 25). Deep blue: An oral history of Appalachian State vs. Michigan. *The Michigan Insider*. Retrieved from https://247sports.com/college/michigan/Article/Deep-Blue-An-oral-history-of-Appalachian-State-vs-Michigan-106500832.

Kaplan, D. (2016, February 29). NFL halfway to $25B goal. *Street and Smith Sport Business Journal*. Retrieved from www.sportsbusinessdaily.com/Journal/Issues/2016/02/29/Leagues-and-Governing-Bodies/NFL-revenue.aspx

Kelleher, M. (2016, December 9). Manchester United announce record revenue of £515.3m for 2016. Sky Sports. Retrieved from www.skysports.com/football/news/11667/10575273/manchester-united-announce-record-revenue-of-515-3m-for-2016

Koba, M. (2012, January 30). Luxury suites rule in professional sports revenue. CNBC. Retrieved from www.cnbc.com/id/45960973

NBC's Notre Dame deal extended. (2013, April 8). ESPN. Retrieved from www.espn.com/college-football/story/_/id/9186897/nbc-extends-notre-dame-fighting-irish-football-deal-2025

Nightengale, B., & McCarthy, M. (2009). Empty spring seats spawn creative regular season deals. *USA Today*. Retrieved from www.usatoday.com/sports/baseball/2009-03-08-Ticket_deals_N.htm

Rogoway, M. (2016, October 8). Phil and Penny Knight's charitable contributions top $2 billion. *The Oregonian/OregonLive*. Retrieved from www.oregonlive.com/business/index.ssf/2016/10/phil_and_penny_knights_charita.html

Rovell, D. (2017, September 12). Warriors sign jersey-patch advertising deal with Rakuten. *ESPN*. Retrieved from www.espn.com/nba/story/_/id/20680169/golden-state-warriors-sign-jersey-patch-advertising-deal-rakuten

Seating map. (2017). The New England Patriots. Retrieved from www.gillettestadium.com/patriots-seating-chart

Sherman, R. (2016, April 12). The NCAA's new March Madness TV deal will make them a billion dollars a year. *SB Nation*. Retrieved from www.sbnation.com/college-basketball/2016/4/12/11415764/ncaa-tournament-tv-broadcast-rights-money-payout-cbs-turner

Smith, M. (2014, June 16). LRG purchase takes Learfield into licensing. *Street & Smith's SportsBusiness Journal*. Retrieved from www.sportsbusinessdaily.com/Journal/Issues/2014/06/16/Colleges/Learfield.aspx

Smith, M., & Ourand, J. (2017, September 19). Learfield, IMG College close to merger, reshaping college space. *Street & Smith's SportsBusiness Journal*. Retrieved from www.sportsbusinessdaily.com/Daily/Morning-Buzz/2017/09/19/Learfield.aspx

Solomon, J. (2016, January 19). SEC rakes in $527.4 million in first year of CFP and SEC Network. CBS Sports. Retrieved from www.cbssports.com/college-football/news/sec-rakes-in-5274-million-in-first-year-of-cfp-and-sec-network/

Thomas, A. (2014, July 28). The European soccer transfer market, explained. *SB Nation*. Retrieved from www.sbnation.com/

soccer/2014/7/28/5923187/transfer-window-soccer-europe-explained

Ticket sales as share of total Major League Baseball revenue from 2009 to 2016. (2017). Statista. Retrieved from www.statista.com/statistics/193408/percentage-of-ticketing-revenue-in-the-mlb-since-2006/

Total Sportek staff. (2017a, January 19). Top 10 biggest TV rights in sports (currently active). Retrieved from www.totalsportek.com/money/biggest-tv-deals-sports/

Total Sportek staff. (2017b, November 12). 50 most expensive football player transfers of all time. Retrieved from www.totalsportek.com/list/expensive-player-transfers-football-history

Under Armour Annual Report. (2016). Retrieved from http://investor.underarmour.com/static-files/170d67af-acda-45af-b032-3888434e6017

Which Professional Sports Leagues Make the Most Money. (2016, July 1). How Much. Retrieved from https://howmuch.net/articles/sports-leagues-by-revenue

Chapter 6

Appenzeller, H. (2011). *Ethical behavior in sport.* Durham, NC: Carolina Academic Press.

Bowman, J. (2017, June 18). Under Armour is blowing its chance with Steph Curry. The Motley Fool. Retrieved from www.fool.com/investing/2017/06/18/under-armour-is-blowing-its-chance-with-steph-curr.aspx

The Business of Baseball: Los Angeles Dodgers. (2017). *Forbes.* Retrieved from www.forbes.com/teams/los-angeles-dodgers

Chelsea players salaries 2017-2018 (Player contracts revealed). (2017, August 15). Total Sportek. Retrieved from www.totalsportek.com/football/chelsea-player-salaries

Competitive balance tax. (2017). Major League Baseball. Retrieved from http://m.mlb.com/glossary/transactions/competitive-balance-tax

Cronin, B. (2010, May 5). Sports legends revealed: How did the 'Larry Bird exception' to the NBA salary cap get its name? *Los Angeles Times.* Retrieved from http://latimesblogs.latimes.com/sports_blog/2010/05/sports-legends-revealed-how-did-the-larry-bird-exception-to-the-nba-salary-cap-get-its-name.html

Front office directory. (2017). Philadelphia 76ers. Retrieved from www.nba.com/sixers/front-office-directory

Fulks, D. (2016). *Revenues and expenses: Division I intercollegiate athletics programs report 2004-15.* National Collegiate Athletic Association. Retrieved from www.ncaapublications.com/productdownloads/D1REVEXP2015.pdf

Gaines, C. (2017, November 24). The 25 highest-paid coaches in college football. *Business Insider.* Retrieved from www.businessinsider.com/college-football-highest-paid-coaches-2017-10/#25-jim-mora-36-million-1

Kadet, A. (2011, June 12). Charity "cashathons": High-cost fundraising. Wall Street Journal Sunday. *Hartford Courant*, p. 4.

Lincoln Financial Field. (2017). NRG. Retrieved from www.nrg.com/renewables/projects/business/lincoln-financial-field

Martin, E. (2017, August 27). Here's how much the highest-paid NFL players make now, compared to their first year in the league. *CNBC.com.* Retrieved from www.cnbc.com/2017/08/25/how-much-highest-paid-nfl-players-make.html

NBA contracts summary. (2017). Basketball reference. Retrieved from www.basketball-reference.com/contracts

NCAA salaries. (2017). *USA Today.* Retrieved from http://sports.usatoday.com/ncaa/salaries/mens-basketball/coach

NFL team cash payroll tracker. (2017). Spotrac. Retrieved from www.spotrac.com/nfl/cash

Nightengale, B. (2017, November 13). Dodgers lead group of 6 MLB teams who must pay luxury tax for 2017 salaries. *USA Today.* Retrieved from www.usatoday.com/story/sports/mlb/2017/11/13/dodgers-mlb-luxury-tax-offenders-2017-top-payrolls/857918001

Perry, D. (2017, April 3). Here's every MLB team's opening day payroll for 2017: As you would expect the Dodgers lead the way. CBS Sports. Retrieved from www.cbssports.com/mlb/news/heres-every-mlb-teams-opening-day-payroll-for-2017

Shaikin, B. (2016, March 28). A look at how Major League Baseball salaries have grown more than 20,000% the last 50 years. *Los Angeles Times*. Retrieved from www.latimes.com/sports/mlb/la-sp-mlb-salaries-chart-20160329-story.html

Thompson, E. (2016, September 28). UF baseball coach Kevin O'Sullivan inks 10-year, $12.5 million deal. *Orlando Sentinel*. Retrieved from http://sports.usatoday.com/ncaa/salaries/mens-basketball/coach

Venook, J. (2017, May 17). The NBA's latest attempt to promote competition: $200 million contracts. *The Atlantic*. Retrieved from www.theatlantic.com/business/archive/2017/05/nba-super-max-contract/526935

Wagner, L. (2017, April 25). Here are the 2017 salaries for MLS players. *Deadspin*. Retrieved from https://deadspin.com/here-are-the-2017-salaries-for-mls-players-1794648467

Wilen, H. (2017, August 1). Under Armour posts quarterly losses, announces layoffs as part of restructuring. *Baltimore Business Journal*. Retrieved from www.bizjournals.com/baltimore/news/2017/08/01/under-armour-posts-quarterly-loss-announces.html

Chapter 7

Bowl no bonanza for UConn. (2011, March). *Business New Haven*, p. 7.

Brigham, E., & Gapenski, L. (1994). *Financial management: Theory and practice* (7th ed.). Fort Worth, TX: Thomson-South-Western Press.

Casagrande, M. (2017, February 4). How Alabama football makes its money. AL.com. Retrieved from www.al.com/alabamafootball/index.ssf/2017/02/how_alabama_football_makes_its.html

Elkins, L. (1996, June). Tips for preparing a business plan. *Nation's Business*, p. 58.

Hall, G. (2013, May 2). And down the track, it's a race to the profit line. *USA Today*, p. 6b.

Pounds, M. (1997, October 27). Finding the money to start up a business and how to write a business plan. *Houston Chronicle*, pp. 1D-2D.

Chapter 8

Brigham, E., & Gapenski, L. (1994). *Financial management: Theory and practice* (7th ed.). Fort Worth, TX: Thomson-South-Western Press.

Goldstein, P., & Alden, B. (2011, April/May). Pie vs. pie. Athletic Management, *23*(3), pp. 39-43.

Grover, R., & Lowry, T. (2001, September 3). Those smackdowns are taking their toll. Business Week, p. 40.

Koller, T., Goedhart, M., & Wessels, D. (2005). *Valuation: Measuring and managing the value of companies* (4th ed.). Hoboken, NJ: Wiley.

Pratt, P., & Niculita, A. (2007). *Valuing a business* (5th ed.). New York: McGraw Hill.

Ross, S.A., Westerfield, R.W., & Jaffe, J. (2008). Corporate finance (8th ed.). Boston, MA: McGraw-Hill Irwin.

Schmidgall, R., Singh, A.J., & Johnson, A. (2007, November/December). Current sales: Forecasting practices in the U.S. club industry. Club Management, 26-9, 46-7.

Steps for improving your firm's cash flow. (1998, November). Nation's Business, 12.

WWF fires COO, 39 employees to aid profits. (2001, November 10). Connecticut Post, p. B1.

Chapter 9

Ambrosini, D. (2002, February 10). Bankrolled by an 'Angel.' *Connecticut Post*, p. F1.

Battersby, M. (1999, July). Finance options. *Fitness Management*, 36-37.

Bogen, J. (1966). *Corporation finance*. New York, NY: Alexander Hamilton Institute.

Broome, T., Jr. (2001, September). A loan at last: Special small business loan programs.

Brigham, E., & Gapenski, L. (2017). *Financial management: Theory and practice (15th ed.)*. Boston, MA: Cengage Learning.

Caro, R. (2000, January). A financial look at the next millennium. *Fitness Management*, 56.

Club hopping: Bally Total Fitness off credit watch. (2004, December 13). Retrieved from www.FitnessBusinessPro.com

Cohen, A. (1999, July). Fit financing. *Athletic Business, 11*.

Company (2012). Retrieved from http://sandiego. padres.mlb.com/sd/team/exec_bios/moores. jsp

Detroit Empowerment Zone Transition Office. (n.d.). *Empowerment Zone projects* [Brochure]. Detroit, MI: City of Detroit.

Evanson, D.R. (1997, May). Capital pitches that succeed. *Nation's Business*, pp. 40-41.

Goldman, S. (2011, November 18). *LA Fitness acquires 171 Bally Total Fitness clubs*. Retrieved from http://clubindustry.com/forprofits/ lafitness-acquires-bally-total-fitness-20111118

Griffin, M.P. (1991). *Intermediate finance for nonfinancial managers*. Toronto, ON: Amacom.

Horine, L. (1999). *Administration of physical education and sport programs* (4th ed.). Boston: McGraw-Hill.

Hovey, J. (1998a, March). A little-known pathway to growth. *Nation's Business*, 40-42.

Hovey, J. (1998b, July). Cheap funding through bonds. *Nation's Business*, 50-51.

Hovey, J. (1998c, November). Using inventory for collateral. *Nation's Business*, 42-43.

Liberation Investments delivers letter to Bally Total Fitness Holding Corp. (2005, July 19). Retrieved from http://home.businesswire.com/portal/ site/google/index.jsp?ndmViewId=news_ views&news

Marullo, G.G. (1998, March). Rewards and risks in lending to your child. *Nation's Business*, 27-28.

Nelton, S. (1998a, June). Seeking funding? Get organized. *Nation's Business*, 40-42.

Nelton, S. (1998b, November). Sizing up the megabanks. *Nation's Business*, 14-21.

Paul Allen. (2002). Retrieved from www.thestandard .com/people/profile/0,1923,1302,00.html

Pounds, M. (1997, October 27). Finding the money to start up a business and how to write a business plan. *Houston Chronicle*, pp. 1D-2D.

Pro Football Hall of Fame. (2007). *Art Rooney*. Retrieved from www.profootballhof.com/hof/ member.jsp?player_id=183

Pryde, J. (1998, February). A lending niche helps small firms. *Nation's Business*, 52-53.

Reynes, R. (1998, October). Low-profile money sources. *Nation's Business*, 32-33.

SBA. (2002). Retrieved from www.sbaonline. sba.gov

SBIC Program Overview. (2018). Retrieved from www.sba.gov/sbic/general information/ program-overview

Sichelman, L. (1998, August 24). Trumping the credit bureau. *Houston Chronicle*, p. 1D.

Spiro, H. (1996). *Finance for the nonfinancial manager*. New York: Wiley.

Tan, K. (2000, January 31). Interactive technology boosts sports business. *Wall Street Journal*, p. B9.

U.S. Securities and Exchange Commission. (2008, February 28). *Bally Total Fitness settles financial fraud charges with SEC*. Litigation Release #20470. Retrieved from www.sec.gov/ litigation/litreleases/2008/lr20470.htm

Value of venture capital investment in the United States from 1995 to 2017 (in billion U.S. dollars. (2018). Statistica.com. Retrieved from www.statista.com/statistics/277501/venture- capital-amount-invested-in-the-united-states- since-1995

Chapter 10

Boise State sells stock to improve facilities. (2009, November 12). *USA Today*, p. 5C.

Brigham, E.F., & Gapenski, L. (2017). *Financial management: Theory and practice* (15th ed.) Boston, MA: Cengage Learning.

Flamm, M. (2010, June 21-27). LeBron-onomics. *Cains New York Business, 26*(25), 1.

Foust, D. (2008, May 26). The perils of going public. *Business Week/Golf Digest*, pp. 64-65.

Frey, L. (2011). How the smallest market in professional sports had the easiest financial journey: The renovation of Lambeau Field. *Sports Lawyers Journal, 18*(1), 259-282.

Greenberg, M., & Gray, J. (1996). *The stadium game*. Milwaukee, WI: National Sports Law Institute of Marquette University Law School.

Howard, D. R., & Crompton, J. L. (2013). *Financing sport* (3rd ed.). Morgantown, WV: Fitness Information Technology.

Howard, T. (2005, October 14). Investors can capitalize when companies score sport sponsorship. *USA Today*, p. 5B.

Investopedia staff. (2010, January 2). *Knowing your rights as a shareholder*. Retrieved from www.investopedia.com/articles/01/050201.asp

Kaplan, D. (1998, November 9-15). Slugger's bond plan striking out. *Street & Smith's Sports-Business Journal, 1*, 3.

Kaplan, D. (2001, March 12-18). Securitization era opens for athletes. *Street & Smith's Sports-Business Journal. 3*, 1, 43.

Kasler, D. (2015, September 14). Sacramento completes Kings arena financing with $272.9 million bond sale. *Sacramento Bee*. Retrieved from www.sacbee.com/news/local/city-arena/article36414231.html

Lascari, S. (1998, October-November). Sports facility issues, part two. Stock of sports franchise: A sound investment or scam? *For the Record* (Marquette University Law School), *9*(5), 3.

Lewis, A. (1999, June 8). Suits seek to halt Ascent sale: Prospective buyers wait as shareholders say $400 million bid by Lauries is too low. *Denver Rocky Mountain News*, p. 1B.

Morgan, M. (2010, October 2). It's a new financial ballgame for Memphis Redbirds. *Commercial Appeal*. Retrieved from www.commercialappeal.com/news/2010/oct/02/its-a-new-financial-ballgame-for-birds

Much, P., & Phillips, J. (1999). *Sports teams and the stock market* [marketing letters]. Chicago, IL: Houlihan Lokey Howard & Zukin.

Owner. (2002). Retrieved from www.nba.com/nuggets/news/kroenke_bio.html

Packers sell 185,000 stock shares in first two days. (2011, December 8). Yahoo Sports. Retrieved from http://sports.yahoo.com./nfl/news?slug=ap-packers-stocksale

Petchesky, B. (2013, November 14). Here's how Cobb County will pay for the Braves' ballpark. Retrieved from https://deadspin.com/heres-how-cobb-county-will-pay-for-the-braves-ballpar-1464404976

Polansky, R. (2009, July 9). First stadium bonds cost taxpayers more than $2.4 billion. *Miami Today News*. Retrieved from www.miamitodaynews.com/news/090709/story2.shtml

Roper, E. (2016, July 22). Taxes to pay for now-open U.S. Bank Stadium rebound, thanks to gamblers. *Minneapolis Star Tribune*. Retrieved from www.startribune.com/taxes-to-pay-for-u-s-bank-stadium-rebound/387999002

Snyder, M. (2017, January 24). The Braves want $14M more from Cobb County taxpayers for their new stadium. *CBS Sports*. Retrieved from www.cbssports.com/mlb/news/the-braves-want-14m-more-from-cobb-county-taxpayers-for-their-new-stadium

Thomas secures his future. (1998, July 13). *Sports Illustrated, 89*(2), 32.

Two Denver franchises sold. (1999, April 27). *Houston Chronicle*, p. 11B.

Wal-Mart heir buying Denver teams, arena. (2000, April 25). *Connecticut Post*, p. D4.

Part IV Case Study

Armon, R. (2015, June 28). University of Akron football attendance lowest in nation. Retrieved from www.ohio.com/akron/news/top-stories-news/university-of-akron-football-attendance-lowest-in-nation

delos Santos, J., & Weinstein, A. (2017, November 28). Unprecedented drop in attendance hits Cal football. *The Daily Californian*. Retrieved from www.dailycal.org/2017/11/28/unprecedented-drop-attendance-hits-cal-football

Frederickson, K. (2017, August 13). Colorado State, Colorado to seek athletics revenue through football stadium naming rights. *The Denver Post*. Retrieved from www.denverpost.com/2017/08/12/colorado-state-colorado-football-stadium-naming-rights

Knight Commission. (2013). Academic and athletic spending database for NCAA Division I. Retrieved from http://spendingdatabase.knightcommission.org/reports/c2a633ff

Lyell, K. (2017, March 20). Take a look inside CSU's new on-campus stadium. *Coloradoan*. Retrieved from www.coloradoan.com/story/

sports/csu/football/2017/03/20/csus--campus-stadium-coming-together/99416972

Maxcy, J., & Larson, D. (2014, January 20). Reversal of fortune or glaring misallocation: Is a new football stadium worth the cost to a university? Retrieved from https://ssrn.com/abstract=2382280 and http://dx.doi.org/10.2139/ssrn.2382280

Sirota, D., & Perez, A. (2016, January 11). College football: Public universities spend millions on stadiums, despite slim chance for payoff. *IB Times*. Retrieved from www.ibtimes.com/college-football-public-universities-spend-millions-stadiums-despite-slim-chance-2258669

Stephens, M. (2015, June 18). Colorado State on-campus stadium: By the numbers. Retrieved from www.coloradoan.com/story/sports/csu/football/2015/06/18/colorado-state-football-stadium/28932383

Chapter 11

Accounting Coach. (2018). What is the difference between vertical analysis and horizontal analysis? (n.d.). Retrieved from www.accountingcoach.com/blog/vertical-analysis-horizontal-analysis

Investopedia. (n.d.). Intangible assets. Retrieved from www.investopedia.com/terms/i/intangibleasset.asp#ixzz4oh8LOTlV

Chapter 12

Abrams, R. (2016, October 17). How small businesses can prevent a holiday cash-flow disaster. *USA Today*, p. 5B.

Bomey, N. (2017, February 1). Under Armour slumps as Curry's shoes fizzle. *USA Today*, p. 6B.

Brealey, R., Myers, S., and Marcus, A. (2008) Fundamentals of corporate finance, 6th edition. New York, NY: McGraw Hill.

Brigham, E. F., & Ehrhardt, M. C. (2011). *Financial management: Theory and practice* (13th ed.). New York, NY: Dryden Press.

Brook, T. V. (2014, December 15). Congress eliminates guard's ad budget for racing. *USA Today*, p. 5A.

Coyne, K., Coyne, S., & Coyne, E., Sr. (2010, May). When you've got to cut costs—now.

Harvard Business Review. Retrieved from https://hbr.org/2010/05/when-youve-got-to-cut-costs-now

Ernest, W. (2002, May). Seeing green. *Club Industry*, pp. 41-42.

Foster, T. (2016, February). Kevin Plank built Under Armour into a $4 billion behemoth. He's just spent almost $1 billion to get into an entirely new business. Can this decade's most unlikely tech startup beat Nike? *Inc. Magazine*, pp. 88-95.

Gluck, J. (2016, July 1). NASCAR deals with declines. *USA Today*, p. 1C.

Immoo, L., Lochhead, S., Ritter, R., & Zhao, Q. (1996). The costs of raising capital. *Journal of Financial Research*, *19*, 59-74.

Internal Revenue Service (2010). Form 535. www.irs.gov/forms-pubs/about-publication-535.

Lashinsky, A. (2015). Nike's master craftsman. *Fortune*, *172*(7), 94-102.

Monroe, R. (2016, July 4-10). Stomping grounds. *Bloomberg's Businessweek*, pp. 42-47.

Novy-Williams, E., & De Vynck, G. (2016, February 15-21). The loonie is driving NHL players crazy. *Bloomberg's Businessweek*, pp. 14-15.

Olson, P. (2015). The jocks versus the geeks. *Forbes*, *196*(5), 80-90.

Ross, S. A., Westerfield, R. W., & Jordan, B. D. (2008). *Fundamentals of corporate finance* (8th ed.). Boston, MA: McGraw Hill.

Snider, M. (2016, October 26). Under Armour shares dive as it lowers forecast. *USA Today*, p. 3B.

Statt, N. (2014, April 18). Exclusive: Nike fires majority of FuelBand team, will stop making wearable hardware. Retrieved from www.cnet.com/news/nike-fires-fuelband-engineers-will-stop-making-wearable-hardware

Townsend, M. (2017, February 6-12). Can sneaker makers come home again? *Bloomberg BusinessWeek*, pp. 17-19.

Chapter 13

Morningstar. (2015). Leverage ratios. Retrieved from http://news.morningstar.com/classroom

2/course.asp?docId=145093&page=5&CN=sample

Premier League. (2017). Discover the origins and history of the top tier of English football. Retrieved from www.premierleague.com/history

Chapter 14

Abrams, R. (2016, August 15). Join the crowd: Funding is now easier. *USA Today*, p. 2B.

Battersby, M. (2003). How much is your health club worth? *Fitness Management, 19*(7), 38-41.

Beech, J., Horsman, S., & Magraw, J. (2008). The circumstances in which English football clubs become insolvent. Coventry, England: Coventry University Centre for the International Business of Sport (CIBS).

The bottom line. (2017). *The Week—News at a Glance, 17*(848), 31.

Brigham, E. F. & Ehrhardt, M. C. (2011). *Financial management: Theory and practice* (13th ed.). New York, NY: Dryden Press.

Brigham, E., & Gapenski, L. (1994). *Financial management: Theory and practice* (7th ed.). Fort Worth, TX: Thomson-South-Western Press.

Broni, P. (1999, December). Take my loan . . . please. *Inc. Magazine*, p. 163.

Buchanan, L., & Marikar, S. (2017/2018). The first 90 days. *Inc. Magazine*, pp. 17-30.

Charlton standard catalogue of Canadian coins (44th ed.). (1990). Toronto, ON: Charlton Press.

Cheeseman, H. (2010). *Business law* (6th ed.). Upper Saddle River, NJ: Prentice Hall.

Footstar completes acquisition. (2000, March 8). *Wall Street Journal*, p. A4.

For the record. (1998, September 21-27). *Street & Smith's SportsBusiness Journal, 1*, 34.

Gandley, W., & Stanley, D. (1978). *Canada/B.N.A. postage stamp catalogue* (9th ed.). Paris, ON: Canadian Wholesale Supply.

Grant, L. (2005, March 23). Gnarly: Quicksilver buys ski company. *USA Today*, p. 5B.

King, B., & Brockington, L. (1998). Forces push both sides in Yanks' deal. *Street & Smith's Sports-Business Journal, 1*(1), 46.

King, B., & Lombardo, J. (2012). League-owned teams = headache. *Street and Smith's Sports-Business Journal, 14*(42), p. 1.

Lee, C. (1999, July). Managing the process. *ABA Journal*, p. 62.

Livingston, A. (1998, July). Avoiding pitfalls when selling a business. *Nation's Business*, pp. 25-26.

Livingstone, J.L. (Ed.). (1997). *The portable MBA in finance and accounting* (2nd ed.). New York, NY: Wiley.

Pells, E. (2006, May 26). Enterprising brothers converted NBA buyout of ABA team into multimillion-dollar windfall. Retrieved from www.seattlepi.com/news/article/Enterprising-brothers-converted-NBA-buyout-of-ABA-1204630.php

Peterson, A. (2016, June 30). Paying for dream has its limits. *The Hartford Courant*, p. C6.

Pratt, S., Reilly, R., & Schweihs, R. (2000). *Valuing a business: The analysis and appraisal of closely held companies* (4th ed.). New York, NY: McGraw-Hill.

Random shots: In memory: Richard "Dick" Cabela. (2014). *American Rifleman, 162*(5), 28.

Ross, S. A., Westerfield, R. W., & Jaffe, J. (2008). *Corporate finance* (8th ed.). Boston, MA: McGraw-Hill Irwin.

Ryman, R. (2016, April 15). Lambeau concession volunteers earned $1.16M. Packers News. Retrieved from www.packersnews.com/story/news/2016/04/15/lambeau-concession-volunteers-earned-116m/81936836/

Schaefer, S. (2017, February 28). Nature's bounty. *Forbes*, p. 34.

Shapiro, S. (1999). Valuation of law practices. *Law Firm Governance, 4*(2), 26-33.

Siegel, J., Shim, J., & Hartman, S. (1992). *Dictionary of personal finance*. New York, NY: Macmillan.

Smith, M., & Ourand, J. (2017, September 19). Learfield, IMG College close to merger, reshaping college sports business space. *Street & Smith's SportsBusiness Journal*. Retrieved from www.bizjournals.com/bizjournals/news/2017/09/19/learfield-img-college-close-to-merger-reshaping.html

Speedway Motorsports Annual Report. (2006). Available: http://phx.corporate-ir.net/phoenix.zhtml?c=99758&p=irol-reports. Retrieved January 4, 2007.

Stern, A. (2017). NASCAR teams trimming, and drivers feel the pinch. *Street and Smith's Sports Business Journal, 20*(31), pp. 1, 47.

Thornton, E. (2002, January 12). It sure is getting hostile. *Business Week*, pp. 28-30.

Wahba, P. (2017, October 1). Racing to build an endurance sports empire. *Fortune*, pp. 117-121.

Part V Case Study

Bonesteel, M. (2017, December 15). Disney-Fox deal benefits ESPN. *Hartford Chronicle*, p. A1.

Booton, J. (2017, December 11). NFL inks multi-year deal with Verizon to expand live streaming. SportTechie. Retrieved from www.sporttechie.com/nfl-inks-multi-year-live-streaming-deal-verizon/?utm_source=SportTechie+Updates&utm_campaign=c179bb0494-SportTechie_Weekly_News_12_17_2017&utm_medium=email&utm_term=0_5d2e0c085b-c179bb0494-294396349

Deitsch, R., & Wertheim, L. (2017). Year in sports 2017. *Sports Illustrated, 127*(19), 48-50.

Desser, E. (2017). Twelve ways sports networks will adapt to evolving marketplace. *SportsBusiness Journal, 20*(29), 23.

Fisher, M. (2015, April 5). Baseball is struggling to hook kids—and risks losing fans to other sports. *The Washington Post*. Retrieved from www.washingtonpost.com/sports/nationals/baseballs-trouble-with-the-youth-curve--and-what-that-means-for-the-game/2015/04/05/2da36dca-d7e8-11e4-8103-fa84725dbf9d_story.html?utm_term=.6fecea500649

Gillette, F. (2016, November 3). The NFL was a sure thing for TV networks. Until now. *Bloomberg Businessweek*. Retrieved from www.bloomberg.com/news/articles/2016-11-03/nfl-was-a-sure-thing-for-tv-networks-until-now

Kell, J. (2017). Is craft beer all froth? *Fortune, 175*(6), 15.

Lev-Ram, M. (2017). Can China save Hollywood? *Fortune, 175*(7), 9-10.

Liebman, B. (2010, June 6). Reasons for the decline of horse racing. *The Rail*. Retrieved from https://therail.blogs.nytimes.com/2010/06/06/reasons-for-the-decline-of-horse-racing/

London Times. (2017, January 20). Horse racing finishes second in British sporting attendance in '16. *Street & Smith's Sports Business Daily Global Journal*. Retrieved from www.sportsbusinessdaily.com/Global/Issues/2017/01/20/Leagues-and-Governing-Bodies/Racing.aspx

Minkel, E. (2015, June 4). The sport of kings is dying. Long live the Belmont Stakes! *New Republic*. Retrieved from https://newrepublic.com/article/121970/slow-decline-sport-kings

Neate, R. (2016, August 4). SeaWorld shares sink to record low as attendance keeps falling. *The Guardian*. Retrieved from www.theguardian.com/us-news/2016/aug/04/seaworld-shares-sink-record-low-attendance-falling

Puente, M. (2016, April 13). Are popular music fests pricing out everyday, middle class music fans? *USA Today*. Retrieved from www.usatoday.com/story/life/music/2016/04/12/popular-music-fests-pricing-out-everyday-middle-class-music-fans/82747404/

Shaw, L. (2017, February 8). America's music festivals could use a boost, with or without U2. *Bloomberg Businessweek*. Retrieved from www.bloomberg.com/news/articles/2017-02-08/u2-tapped-to-boost-bonnaroo-as-cracks-appear-in-festivals-market

Sisario, B. (2013, January 28). As music streaming grows, royalties slow to a trickle. *New York Times*. Retrieved from www.nytimes.com/2013/01/29/business/media/streaming-shakes-up-music-industrys-model-for-royalties.html?_r=0

Snider, M. (2017, August 3). Movie theaters getting pinched. *USA Today*, p. 3B.

Sports Law Center. (1992). *Sports attendance GNP*. San Francisco, CA: Sports Law Center.

Glossary

Siegel, J., Shim, J., & Hartman, S. (1992). *Dictionary of personal finance*. New York, NY: Macmillan.

Suggested Resources

Stocks

New York Stock Exchange

www.nyse.com

North American Securities Administrators Association

www.nasaa.org

NASDAQ Stock Market

www.nasdaq.com

U.S. Securities and Exchange Commission

www.sec.gov

U.S. Securities and Exchange Commission EDGAR Database of Filings by Public Companies

www.10kwizard.com

Business and Government Organizations and Associations

Business Consortium Fund

The Business Consortium Fund, Inc., is a nonprofit business development program of the National Minority Supplier Development Council.

www.bcfcapital.com

Certified Development Company

The National Association of Development Companies is the trade association of SBA-certified development companies and other lenders delivering SBA loans and financing for small businesses.

www.nadco.org

Federal Reserve Board

www.federalreserve.gov

National Association of Investment Companies

The National Association of Investment Companies is the largest network of diversely owned private equity firms and hedge funds.

www.naicpe.com

National Association of Women Business Owners

Founded in 1975, the National Association of Women Business Owners is the unified voice of over 10.1 million women-owned businesses in the United States.

www.nawbo.org

National Minority Business Council

www.nmbc.org

National Minority Supplier Development Council

The National Minority Supplier Development Council advances business opportunities for certified minority business enterprises and connects them to corporate members.

www.nmsdc.org

Service Corps of Retired Executives Association

The Service Corps of Retired Executives Association dubs itself the "Counselors to America's Small Business." It is a nonprofit association comprising 13,000-plus volunteer business counselors throughout the United States and its territories.

www.sba.gov/offices/headquarters/oed/resources/148091

United States Small Business Administration

The U.S. Small Business Administration (SBA) has delivered millions of loans, loan guarantees, contracts, counseling sessions, and other forms of assistance to small businesses.

www.usa.gov/federal-agencies/small-business-administration

Internet Resources

The American Finance Association

The American Finance Association touts itself as the premier academic organization devoted to the study and promotion of knowledge about financial economics.

http://afajof.org

American Institute of Certified Public Accountants

The American Institute of Certified Public Accountants represents the certified public accountant profession's nationally regarding rule making and standard setting and serves as an advocate before legislative bodies, public interest groups, and other professional organizations.

www.aicpa.org/content/aicpa

Financial Literacy & Education Commission

www.mymoney.gov

International Journal of Sport Finance Blog

http://ijsf.wordpress.com

Global Sports and Entertainment—Morgan Stanley

www.morganstanley.com/what-we-do/wealth-management/global-sports-entertainment

John Wall Street

This site offers a daily e-mail highlighting sport finance topics.

https://johnwallstreet.com

Knight Commission on Collegiate Athletics

www.knightcommission.org

Practical Money Skills for Life

Practical Money Skills offers interactive tools and educational resources to help individuals and communities build stronger financial futures.

www.practicalmoneyskills.com/games

It also has a financial football game with quiz questions.

www.practicalmoneyskills.com/play/financial_football

Professor Ian Giddy's Finance Resources on the Web

This site provides resources for instructors in finance.

http://pages.stern.nyu.edu/~igiddy

Yahoo Finance

http://finance.yahoo.com

Print Resources

Athletic Business
www.athleticbusiness.com

Athletic Management
www.momentummedia.com

Barron's
www.barrons.com

Business Week
www.businessweek.com

Dun & Bradstreet
www.dnb.com

Forbes
www.forbes.com

NCAA News
www.ncaa.org

SportsBusiness Daily
www.sportsbusinessdaily.com

Street & Smith's SportsBusiness Journal
www.sportsbusinessjournal.com

Wall Street Journal
www.wsj.com

Index

Note: Page references followed by an italicized *f* or *t* indicate information contained in figures or tables, respectively.

About the Authors

Gil Fried, JD, is a professor and the chair of the sport management department in the College of Business at the University of New Haven. He worked as a financial analyst with Paul Kagan Associates and analyzed numerous broadcasting contracts. He has written a significant number of books and articles, taught graduate and undergraduate courses in sport finance, and lectured on finance topics to various audiences. In addition to teaching and writing, Fried serves as an expert witness in various personal and financial injury matters related to the sports and entertainment industry.

Fried enjoys playing badminton and collecting stamps—particularly revenue and sport stamps to utilize in his teaching.

Tim DeSchriver, EdD, is an associate professor in the department of hospitality business management at the University of Delaware. DeSchriver has worked as a field economist for the U.S. Department of Labor and has taught undergraduate and graduate courses in sport finance and sport economics since 1998. He has authored and contributed to several books and sport finance–related publications in refereed journals.

In his spare time, DeSchriver enjoys road cycling, mountain biking, and hiking.

Michael Mondello, PhD, is a professor in the department of marketing and the associate director of the Vinik Sport and Entertainment Management program at the University of South Florida. He teaches finance and analytics, with research interests in financial and analytical issues related to sport organizations, including competitive balance, economic impact analysis, contingent valuation, ticket pricing, and stadium financing.

Mondello's work has been published in *International Journal of Sport Finance, Economic Development Quarterly, Sport Marketing Quarterly, International Journal of Sport Management, Journal of Sports Economics, Journal of Sport Management,* and *Management Decision.* He has also written a Harvard Business School case examining strategic philanthropy and the Tampa Bay Lightning. Mondello was recognized as a research fellow of the North American Society for Sport Management (NASSM) in 2007.